THE LAW AND PRACTICE OF EXPULSION
AND EXCLUSION FROM THE UNITED KINGDOM

Resort by the state to measures of exclusion and expulsion from the territory of the UK and/or from British citizenship have multiplied over the past decade, following the so-called 'War on Terror', increased globalisation, and the growing politicisation of national policies concerning immigration and citizenship.

This book, which focuses on the law and practice governing deportation, removal and exclusion from the UK, the denial of British citizenship, and deprivation of that citizenship, represents the first attempt by practitioners to provide a cohesive assessment of UK law and practice in these areas. The undertaking is a vital one because, whilst these areas of law and practice have long existed as the hard edge of immigration and nationality laws, in recent years the use of some powers in this area has greatly increased and such powers have arguably expanded beyond secondary existence as mere mechanisms of enforcement. The body of law, practice and policy created by this process is one which justifies treatment as a primary concern for public lawyers.

The book provides a comprehensive analysis of the law in these areas and its background. This involves a consideration of interlocking international and regional rights instruments, EU law and the domestic regime. It is a clear and comprehensive everyday guide for practitioners and offers an invaluable insight into likely developments in this dynamic area of public law.

The Law and Practice of Expulsion and Exclusion from the United Kingdom

Deportation, Removal, Exclusion and Deprivation of Citizenship

General Editor

Eric Fripp
MA (St Andrews) LLM MA LLM (London),
of Gray's Inn, Barrister

Deputy Editors

Rowena Moffatt
BA (Oxon) LLM (College of Europe), of the Inner Temple, Barrister
Ellis Wilford
MA (Cantab), of Gray's Inn, Barrister

Foreword by
The Rt Hon the Lord Hope of Craighead KT

·HART·
PUBLISHING
OXFORD AND PORTLAND, OREGON
2015

Published in the United Kingdom by Hart Publishing Ltd
16C Worcester Place, Oxford, OX1 2JW
Telephone: +44 (0)1865 517530
Fax: +44 (0)1865 510710
E-mail: mail@hartpub.co.uk
Website: http://www.hartpub.co.uk

Published in North America (US and Canada) by
Hart Publishing
c/o International Specialized Book Services
920 NE 58th Avenue, Suite 300
Portland, OR 97213-3786
USA
Tel: +1 503 287 3093 or toll-free: (1) 800 944 6190
Fax: +1 503 280 8832
E-mail: orders@isbs.com
Website: http://www.isbs.com

© The editors and contributors severally, 2015

The editors and contributors have asserted their right under the Copyright,
Designs and Patents Act 1988, to be identified as the authors of this work.

Hart Publishing is an imprint of Bloomsbury Publishing plc.

All rights reserved. No part of this publication may be reproduced, stored in a retrieval
system, or transmitted, in any form or by any means, without the prior permission of Hart
Publishing, or as expressly permitted by law or under the terms agreed with the appropriate
reprographic rights organisation. Enquiries concerning reproduction which may not be
covered by the above should be addressed to Hart Publishing Ltd at the address above.

British Library Cataloguing in Publication Data
Data Available

ISBN: 978-1-84946-589-2

Typeset by Compuscript Ltd, Shannon
Printed and bound in Great Britain by
CPI Group (UK) Ltd, Croydon CR0 4YY

Foreword

BY LORD HOPE OF CRAIGHEAD KT

Sixty years ago, the law on the aspects of immigration control and nationality law with which this book deals were so simple that it would hardly have been worth contemplating devoting an entire work to them. How things have changed. The world has become larger and more volatile. There is an ever-increasing need to exercise a strict control over the number of people who can be allowed to enter and remain in this country. The UK is simply not big enough to accommodate all those who, for a variety of reasons, would wish to live and work here. Because travelling to these islands no longer presents the problem that it once did, the volume of traffic that arrives here from all parts of the world has reached proportions that not so long ago would have been unimaginable. As a result, restricting the number of immigrants is high on the political agenda, and it is not just a matter of numbers. There is an increasingly pressing need to exclude those who present a threat to our security or come here simply in search of a better life than they can enjoy in their country of origin.

But the freedom of action that the state once enjoyed to expel or exclude anyone who has no right to live here has been increasingly circumscribed. The rights and freedoms that everyone enjoys under the European Convention on Human Rights and other international instruments to which this country is a party must be respected, and the courts are increasingly being called upon to ensure that this is so. Inevitably there is a tension between the inclination of the executive to impose ever more strict controls and the response of the judiciary to those who assert that their rights are being violated. More and more legislation, and more and more case law, is the result. As the law on the subject has become ever more complicated, there is a real need for a reliable book to which one can turn for guidance as to what the law is and where it can be found. A newcomer on the scene that takes a fresh approach to the subject is especially welcome.

The system that this book uses has been carefully designed to take the reader step by step through the different regimes that make up the framework of the law about expulsion and exclusion in all its various international and domestic aspects, before dealing with the practical matters of procedure and remedies. This is a neat approach to a complex problem. It recognises the importance of context, which in law is everything. A sound appreciation of the framework around which the law has been built and is still developing provides the key to its understanding. These are the principles which the reader is being asked to follow when being taken through the matters of law and practice that are identified and expanded upon in the following chapters. The result is a comprehensive volume on the subject which will be greatly valued by all those who use it. It deserves to be on the bookshelves of all those who seek to practise within this carefully defined area of immigration and nationality law.

The authors and contributors are to be congratulated on the work they have done to bring this volume to publication, and of course they are entitled to a well-earned rest.

But no book devoted to this area of the law can expect to survive for very long without being kept up to date. So I hope that this will be the first edition of many, as it earns for itself a permanent and welcome place on our bookshelves.

David Hope
July 2014

Preface

This book focuses upon the law and practice of expulsion and exclusion from the UK, and of denial or deprivation of British citizenship. Underlying the effort to create it has been the fact that these areas are cumulatively of such significance that it is necessary, and desirable, to consider them separately from the broader body of law and practice in the areas of immigration and nationality.

What are the special features that these areas of law and practice possess? The responsible Minister, the Secretary of State for the Home Department, or his or her officials or other agents, may variously expel or exclude an alien (or another person who has no right to enter and or to whom no right to remain has been given), or deny British citizenship or other status where this is sought, or take such status from someone who already possesses it. In broad terms such actions represent the sharp end of state authority exercised in the realm of immigration and/or nationality. Such decisions determine whether an individual has access to the advantages of being in the United Kingdom, and/or the still greater advantages which come from being a British citizen. In the mass, such decisions resolve who is able to be in the UK, and/or who is within the body of UK citizens.

Against this it remains true that sometimes an act of expulsion or exclusion simply follows from another primary decision: for instance, the foreign visitor or student whose leave to remain runs out and who remains in the UK in general becomes liable to removal. If a non-citizen commits an offence or otherwise comes within the ambit of the relevant powers, he or she may be deported. In such circumstances the existence and exercise of legal powers, and the practices surrounding these, are secondary to the primary factor of absence of leave to remain, or responsibility for a serious criminal act. In the realm of nationality an individual not considered to have a suitably good character may be refused naturalisation, or a minor, aged over 10, may be refused registration as a British citizen. Finally, under the current power a British citizen—even one whose citizenship comes through birth or descent—may be deprived of that citizenship if that appears to the Secretary of State for the Home Department conducive to the public good (subject to protection against imposition of statelessness by this means).

It might be asked why the examination of the law and practice surrounding such powers should be considered a worthwhile endeavour. Most of these powers are, after all, generally created by Parliament and exercised by the executive as instruments to enable the resolution of relatively unremarkable situations. Against this, however, the exercise of each of these powers is not always straightforwardly derivative of other relatively uncontroversial matters. The circumstances of exercise of a power will depend upon the scope of that power and upon the policy of the executive applied in each case. Where the power is a wide one, the judgment of the executive will have considerable latitude, free from the restraints imposed by the original legislator. And considered in aggregate, the Secretary of State's battery of powers to exclude or expel those without an unconditional right of abode within the UK are of considerable importance in terms of creating an important area of activity dominated by the executive.

Preface

It might have been said formerly that the extent of the Secretary of State's immigration powers, exercised under immigration law in relation to aliens or others without unconditional right of abode, was somewhat offset by the relative irrevocability of British citizenship or its predecessor statuses, to which an unconditional right to enter the UK and remain there attached. But if, as the present Secretary of State has repeatedly asserted, 'citizenship is a privilege, not a right',[1] then that proposition is true of everyone, not just of the young Britons fighting in Syria whose situation prompted this assertion. In other words, all British citizens enjoy that citizenship and the attached right of abode essentially as a matter of willed sufferance on the part of the executive. As Caroline Sawyer has observed, if British citizenship may be taken away with relative ease by the exercise of a broad executive power, that 'in turn, changes the nature of British citizenship itself'.[2] The removal of the right of abode which attends deprivation of nationality creates in principle the scope for a broad exclusion from the United Kingdom's territory and political community (that is, the community of British citizens).

The exercise of wide powers by the executive is a common feature across UK immigration and nationality laws. The extent of the relevant powers and the degree to which these are exercised are subject to secondary, softer sources of 'law' such as, in the case of immigration, the Immigration Rules HC 395 or, as regards both immigration and nationality, guidance published by the state. But does the existence and form of such powers justify particular examination? This work suggests that it does. Five justifications might be cited: (i) the constitutional significance of at least some law and practice in this area; (ii) the importance of decisions to those affected and, whether in the case of individual decisions or cumulatively, to the broader community; (iii) the desirability of understanding the administrative law characteristics of the relevant law and practice; (iv) the increased scope of such powers over recent years; and (v) the substantially increased exercise of such powers, again a relatively recent phenomenon.

The first of those reasons claims 'constitutional significance'. Can that claim be made good, or is it purely rhetorical? I would suggest that the nature and extent of the state's powers to expel and exclude individuals from the territory of the UK, or the denial or removal of British citizenship, lend to at least some of these a wider significance which might be characterised as constitutional in character. This is be particularly the case as regards powers concerning citizenship, but, as already noted, broad powers of deprivation of citizenship create a potential continuum between British citizens, with rights to enter and remain, and non-citizens exposed to the rigours of immigration control including the possibility of expulsion: under a legal regime showing such a continuum, the two may be inextricably linked. Further, decisions by the executive as to who shall become, or remain, a citizen have important democratic aspects apart from the important matter of conditional as opposed to unconditional access to the territory. Such decisions determine who is a potential political actor within the democratic structure, such as who is able to stand for election or to vote.

---

[1] A Ross, P Galey and N Morris, 'Exclusive: No Way Back for Britons Who Join the Syrian Fight, says Theresa May' *The Independent* (23 December 2013).
[2] Caroline Sawyer, '"Civis Britannicus Sum" No Longer? Deprivation of British Nationality' (2013) 27(1) *Journal of Immigration Asylum and Nationality Law* 23, 39.

Preface

There are substantial problems of definition, as to what characteristics warrant designation as 'constitutional.' As set out in chapter 7, individual liberty (subject to definition and to Parliamentary sovereignty) has been understood as one such right. Recently, in *Thoburn v Sunderland City Council* [2002] EWHC 195 (Admin), [2003] QB 151, Laws LJ identified the existence of a class of 'constitutional statutes' protected from implied repeal, including the Magna Carta of 1215 and other great instruments such as the Bill of Rights 1689, the Act of Union 1707, the Reform Acts of the nineteenth century reshaping the electoral franchise, the European Communities Act 1972, the Human Rights Act 1998, the Scotland Act 1998 and the Government of Wales Act 1998. Of the distinction drawn between these and ordinary statutes, he noted (at [62]) that:

> The two categories must be distinguished on a principled basis. In my opinion a constitutional statute is one which (a) conditions the legal relationship between citizen and State in some general, overarching manner, or (b) enlarges or diminishes the scope of what we would now regard as fundamental constitutional rights. (a) and (b) are of necessity closely related: it is difficult to think of an instance of (a) that is not also an instance of (b). The special status of constitutional statutes follows the special status of constitutional rights.

Those observations, with which Crane J agreed, have more recently received express support from the Supreme Court in *R (otao HS2 Action Alliance and others) v Secretary of State for Transport and another* [2014] UKSC 3; [2014] 1 WLR 324, at [207] per Lords Neuberger and Mance, with whom five other members of the Court agreed. Whether a matter possesses 'constitutional' status of course is not a constant: the designation of matters as 'constitutional' differs even among modern democratic states such as Canada, France, Germany or the USA. But at least on its face, the withholding or withdrawal of citizenship would appear to be a matter within the boundaries canvassed in the *Thoburn* case, and even if provisions for entry by non-citizens into the UK, or remaining in it, are not comparable, this subject matter will frequently intersect with rights defined by values such as liberty, dignity or private or family life. Writing extra-judicially on the subject of fundamental rights prior to the selective incorporation of rights under the European Convention on Human Rights and Fundamental Freedoms (ECHR) by the Human Rights Act 1998, Sir John Laws described rights embedded in Article 8 ECHR as being 'rights [which] have become an axiom, or series of axioms, about whose desirability there can be no serious argument … given the nature of the ideals enshrined in the [ECHR] … to deny it is by necessary implication to assert a totalitarian position in which individuals are subservient to the ends of the state'.[3] Sir John concluded that 'many of its Articles reflect what are nowadays no more than obvious norms in a developed democratic society', informing the development of the common law without express or implicit incorporation.[4] As discussed in detail at chapters 3 and 5, international and Council of Europe human rights regimes intersect frequently with the areas of law and practice particularly addressed by this work, whilst the Council of Europe regime, the ECHR, is in substantial part now incorporated into domestic law by the Human Rights Act 1998. In recent years the Supreme Court has shown a willingness to find immediate recourse to the ECHR unnecessary given parallel protection by the

---

[3] Sir John Laws, 'Is the High Court the Guardian of Fundamental Constitutional Rights?' [1993] *Public Law* 59, 60.
[4] ibid 63.

fundamental rights arising under the common law, whose content may be informed in turn by the ECHR or other international laws, for instance in *Osborn v Parole Board* [2013] UKSC 61, [2014] 1 All ER 369, [57]–[63], per Lord Reed.

The second reason cited above is that decisions in this area are, generally for those affected and often also for the state, important ones. Expulsion and exclusion prevent individuals from having access to the territory of the UK where they may have important interests, such as but not limited to various forms of private or family life. At another level, the denial or deprivation of British citizenship denies or removes a legal status, that of British citizen, which is the strongest if not the sole form of British nationality and is under UK immigration law effectively synonymous with possession of the right of abode in the UK. Expulsion or exclusion from the territory of the UK, or the denial or removal of the benefits of citizenship, therefore potentially bring far-reaching consequences for an affected individual in the form of the loss of the rights which are given by the law to non-citizens present on the territory, or the greater rights, including the right of entry and abode in the territory, given to citizens.

A third reason is that in general, expulsion or exclusion from the territory of the UK, or the denial or removal of citizenship and therefore of attached rights and benefits, represent fields in which the executive branch has been given broad powers. So long as the executive acts within these powers, it conforms to the primary meaning of the concept of the 'rule of law'[5], namely the principle of legality. But as Forsyth has noted, this does not license the freewheeling use of discretionary powers:

> That [acting within lawfully granted powers] is the principle of legality. But the rule of law demands something more, since otherwise it would be satisfied by giving the government unrestricted discretionary powers, so that everything that they did was within the law. *Quod principi placuit legis habet vigorem* (the sovereign's will has the force of law) is a perfectly legal principle, but it expresses rule by arbitrary power rather than rule according to ascertainable law. The secondary meaning of the rule of law, therefore, is that government should be conducted within a framework of recognized rules and principles which restrict discretionary power. Coke spoke in picturesque language of 'the golden and straight metwand' of law, as opposed to the 'uncertain and crooked cord of discretion'.[6]

Lord Bingham has made similar observations writing extra-judicially on the rule of law:

> The rule of law does not require that official or judicial decision-makers should be deprived of all discretion, but it does require that no discretion should be unconstrained so as to be potentially arbitrary. No discretion may be legally unfettered.[7]

It will be evident that to attempt an account of the law and practice focusing upon expulsion or exclusion from the territory of the UK, or the denial or removal of British citizenship, necessitates the isolation of certain legal powers from the broader law and practice of, respectively, immigration and nationality law. An individual acquires the right to be in the UK by the grant of leave to enter as a student or a worker, just as he

---

[5] Section 1 of the Constitutional Reform Act 2005 now recognises 'the existing constitutional principle of the rule of law'.

[6] Sir W Wade and C Forsyth, *Administrative Law* (10th edn, Oxford, Oxford University Press, 2009), 18 (the Coke reference is 4 Inst. 41).

[7] T Bingham, *The Rule of Law* (London, Allen Lane/Penguin, 2010) 54.

or she may be denied this by the application of measures for expulsion or exclusion under the Immigration Rules. And someone may be denied the benefits of citizenship by reason of failure to meet requirements of birth or descent, not just by a refusal of the Secretary of State to approve registration or naturalisation. The presence of broad discretionary powers is clearer in some areas—for instance, in relation to deportation and deprivation of British citizenship—than in others—such as administrative removal, or exclusion by refusal of leave to enter or remain, or the denial of British citizenship by refusal of registration (if a minor) or naturalisation (if an adult). But within the latter areas there may be occasions which represent a broader exercise than others—for example, an individual who seeks entry clearance or leave to enter the UK as a student may fail either for some reason specific to that category of application under the Immigration Rules, such as insufficient evidence of financial support or the lack of a valid certificate of sponsorship provided by the institution of proposed study, or by a much broader judgment under para 320(11) of the Immigration Rules HC 395, within the General Grounds for Refusal at Part 9 of those Rules, by which the application 'should normally be refused' if the applicant 'has previously contrived in a significant way to frustrate the intentions of these Rules'. This work does not seek to cover the first eventuality, even though at one level (refusal), the result is the same. The distinction which I and my colleagues have drawn is one based not on the presence of refusal, but on the broad character of the power in question. Accordingly, this work does not attempt to cover the wider immigration law matter of the rules relating to entry or remaining as a student, but does seek to consider closely the General Grounds for Refusal contained in the Immigration Rules. It acknowledges that even within those General Grounds, the provisions set out vary substantially in character: para 320(11) obviously affords considerable power to the deciding officer, whereas mandatory refusal under para 320(3) or (7) on the basis of, in the first case, failure to show 'a valid national passport or other document satisfactorily establishing ... identity and nationality' and, in the second case, the advice of the Medical Inspector that 'for medical reasons, it is undesirable to admit a person seeking leave to enter the United Kingdom' has a very different character. An adequate survey could not be complete without an account of the General Grounds for Refusal, but requires recognition of internal variations within these.

Finally, a fourth reason for examination of the law and practice in these areas is that whilst measurement of the use of relevant powers is surprisingly uncertain, there has clearly in recent years come to be greater (sometimes far greater) use of the powers in question. This will be obvious alike to practitioners, to those responsible for administration in these areas and to those who adjudicate the proceedings which arise in respect of some decisions. The greater use of powers validly provided by Parliament is not a matter to be deplored unreflectively, but it increases still further the significance of understanding the characteristics of the present law and practice in these areas.

This work has therefore been organised following the precept that whilst in principle wider matters within immigration and nationality laws and practice will affect an individual's possession of the right to be in the UK or of British citizenship, a core group of important matters may be identified determining a question of access either to lawful presence in the territory or to citizenship, of relatively general application, and typically apportion either broad discretion or a substantial area of judgment to the executive.

Preface

Within the work, chapter one, in Part A, sets out a short account of the antecedents to the current law, and chapters two to seven, in Part B, detail and examine the applicable legal framework, providing a background for the commentary in the following parts, which address specific practice areas. Part B includes an account of the legal framework including important and often neglected areas such as international law (chapter two), international human rights law (chapter three), hybrid regimes including international refugee and statelessness laws (chapter four), a detailed account of the cases interpreting relevant rights under the ECHR whilst identifying other relevant Council of Europe instruments (chapter five), and an account, intelligible to non-specialists, of the applicable EU law (chapter six), closing with a succinct account of the sources of the domestic law, which are dealt with in detail in subsequent parts (chapter seven).

The core of this work is provided in Parts C and D. Part C addresses in turn the three primary bases for expulsion or exclusion established under domestic law: deportation (chapter eight), administrative removal (chapter nine) and exclusion (chapter ten). In the case of deportation, addressed in chapter eight, a statutory structure is set out in the Immigration Act 1971 by which the primary grounds upon which an individual is 'liable to deportation' inter alia include, by section 3(5)(a) of the Immigration Act 1971, that of being a non-citizen in respect of whom 'the Secretary of State deems his deportation to be conducive to the public good'. By section 5(1) of the Immigration Act 1971, where a person is liable to deportation, 'the Secretary of State may make a deportation order'. The exercise of that broad power has over time been shaped by various provisions in the Immigration Rules, and guidance has come and gone. By the UK Borders Act 2007 (UKBA 2007), Parliament inserted within this framework a scheme by which, save where one of a list of tightly drawn exceptions arises (and sometimes, notwithstanding the arising of such an exception), the condition for liability to deportation at section 3(5)(a) Immigration Act 1971 is deemed to be met and the discretion at section 5(1) Immigration Act 1971 turned into a duty. Somewhat surprisingly, there continues to be no accurate record of the number of occasions on which this apparatus has been engaged, something that on its face can only impede the holding of informed public or parliamentary debate, but the numbers are substantial.[8] The enactment of the Human Rights Act 1998 brought into force, as potential restraints upon the operation of the deportation scheme, provisions in the ECHR, including Articles 3 and 8. Other restraints, which are applicable in cases concerning European Economic Area nationals or family members, apply under EU law. The ECHR and EU law restraints have come to have great importance in this context, in part because whilst they have remained stable in their application (even if the understanding of their scope has developed), effectively

---

[8] The Migration Observatory at the University of Oxford in its *Briefing: Deportations, Removals and Voluntary Departures from the UK*, 2nd revision, 23 June 2014, states (at 3) of the Home Office administrative data that: 'Deportations are included in data on enforced removal and voluntary departures, as they may be carried out by any of these methods. But they are not identified separately except in provisional information on deportation of foreign national prisoners from case management files, and so are discussed only briefly.' The same report shows numbers of 'foreign national offenders' removed during the years 2009–13 as being over 4,000 in each of those years and 4,667 in 2013. But 'foreign national offenders' is a subcategory of those who may face deportation, and the total number of individuals whose deportation has been deemed conducive to the public good or otherwise have otherwise been identified as liable to deportation, and the total number of decisions made under s 5 Immigration Act 1971, appears not to be recorded.

every source of domestic law guidance as to the exercise of this broad power has been removed.

Chapter nine sets out the Secretary of State's power to remove under the Immigration Act 1971. The justification for such powers, which are applied to individuals who have no legal basis for presence, or continued presence, in the territory, is clear in principle and practice. They are used by the Secretary of State on a considerable scale: the Migration Observatory in the University of Oxford states that in 2013, some 50,741 individuals were removed or departed under threat of removal, and that this represented an increase of 14.5 per cent over 2012 and was more than twice the equivalent figure for 2004.[9] That figure would on the face of it include deportation cases as a subgroup, but to a degree which remains unclear, given the absence of complete figures for the exercise of deportation powers.

Chapter ten considers the executive's powers to exclude an alien, or national without right of abode, and the variety of forms in which these are exercised in practice, from the refusal to grant entry clearance on an application made at an overseas post to a refusal of leave to enter at the frontier.

Part D addresses denial of nationality (chapter eleven), and deprivation of nationality (chapter twelve). As considered in chapter eleven, whilst the provisions of the British Nationality Act 1981 leave substantial areas of discretion to the Secretary of State in relation to registration and naturalisation, the way in which that discretion is exercised is extensively set out in published guidance. This provides a significant contrast to the law and practice of deprivation of nationality, in which the provision creating the power of deprivation at section 40(2) British Nationality Act 1981 (BNA 1981) has been repeatedly amended. An extremely wide power has been created by successive changes. By amendment to BNA 1981, made by section 4 Nationality Immigration and Asylum Act 2002, the Secretary of State was given the power to deprive an individual of any of a range of 'citizenship statuses' if 'satisfied ... [that a person had acted in a way which was] seriously prejudicial to the vital interests of the UK' or an overseas territory. The omission of an earlier limitation to deprivation of a nationality which had attached by registration or naturalisation extended this provision to British citizens by birth, descent or adoption, among others, greatly increasing its scope. Subsequently, section 56 Immigration Asylum and Nationality Act 2006 was amended, greatly weakening the threshold for deprivation at section 40(2) BNA 1981, which was now reset to enable denationalisation 'if the Secretary of State is satisfied that deprivation is conducive to the public good'. This power, and an equivalent power permitting the right of abode to be removed from non-British citizens given to it under statute, were embedded in law, notwithstanding the warning of the Parliamentary Joint Committee on Human Rights that both provisions were seriously flawed. As regards deprivation of citizenship, it concluded:

[T]hat the new test for deprivation of citizenship contains insufficient guarantees against arbitrariness in its exercise in light of (i) the significant reduction in the threshold, (ii) the lack of

---

[9] Migration Observatory (n 8) 4: 'In 2013, as Figure 1 shows, 50,741 people were removed from the UK or departed voluntarily after the initiation of removal. This is an increase of 14.5% from 2012, and more than double the number from 2004. This figure excludes individuals refused entry at port and subsequently removed.'

requirement of objectively reasonable grounds for the Secretary of State's belief, and (iii) the arbitrariness of the definition of the class affected, and that it therefore gives rise to a risk of incompatibility with a number of human rights standards.[10]

Finally, Part E addresses procedures and remedies. As at Part B, hitherto neglected topics, such as international remedies (chapter thirteen), are outlined and explained. The examination of international law remedies highlights the extent to which the UK, despite its history of participation in the creation of international law and the international and Council of Europe rights regimes, has been reticent to commit itself fully: this is particularly true of individual petitions under human rights instruments to which the UK is a party. A striking if perhaps overlooked fact is the failure of the UK to sign or ratify the Optional Protocol to the International Covenant on Civil and Political Rights 1966 (ICCPR), which would enable individuals subject to its jurisdiction, and claiming to be victims of a violation by a State Party of any of the ICCPR rights, to petition the United Nations Human Rights Committee for its judgment concerning the claim of violation, subject to the exhaustion of 'all available domestic remedies'. Indeed, the UK appears to be alone amongst the 47 members of the Council of Europe in not being one of the 115 State Parties to the Optional Protocol. This is of particular relevance given that Article 12(4) ICCPR contains an important right to protection from 'arbitrary deprivation' of 'the right to enter his own country' applicable to expulsion or exclusion, and in some circumstances to nationality decisions, and Article 13 ICCPR provides procedural rights applicable to the expulsion of lawfully present aliens.

This Part continues with a focused account of EU and Council of Europe remedies (chapters fourteen and fifteen respectively), before setting out the domestic law and practice surrounding remedies by appeal or judicial review (chapter sixteen).

The law in these areas has been and remains subject to constant change. We have sought to render the law, to the best of our ability, as at 1 October 2014.

Eric Fripp
Editor

Rowena Moffatt
Ellis Wilford
Deputy Editors

1 October 2014

---

[10] House of Lords and House of Commons Joint Committee on Human Rights, *Counter-Terrorism Policy and Human Rights: Terrorism Bill and Related Matters*, Third report of session 2005–06 (HL paper 75-I, HC 561-I), 7.

Acknowledgments

There are many people the deputy editors and I wish to thank. Over the years we have each benefited from much excellent teaching and instruction by others and from working with committed and insightful colleagues. Since the idea for this project came together, our contributors, all busy members of the Bar and members of our Chambers at Lamb Building, have exerted themselves considerably. Our Clerks in Chambers, in particular Gary Goodger, Senior Clerk, and Phil Silverman, team leader for immigration, asylum and nationality, have been laudably supportive, coping graciously with the sometimes spontaneous desire of several members of Chambers to set aside time for writing at short notice. Keelin McCarthy and Richard Mobbs of Lamb Building contributed to early work in relation to the project. We have had considerable help from others: Kenneth Campbell QC (Scotland), Richard Drabble QC, Dr Daniel Wilsher, and Mark Blundell each assisted us by reading and commenting upon parts of the draft text, and generous suggestions were made by Lord Hope of Craighead KT, who kindly acceded to our request for a Foreword. We remain grateful to Richard Hart for seeing promise in the project and to Hart Publishing for bringing the ensuing product to fruition. Any errors that remain are our own.

Eric Fripp
1 October 2014

Table of Contents

Foreword by Lord Hope of Craighead KT v
Preface vii
Acknowledgments xv
List of Contributors xix
List of Acronyms xxi
Table of Cases xxiii
Table of Legislation xlv

Part A: Background

1. Foundations of the System 3

Part B: Legal Framework

2. Public International Law (General) 13
3. International Human Rights Law 41
4. International Law: Hybrid Regimes 73
5. Council of Europe Instruments 115
6. EU Law 185
7. Domestic Law 211

Part C: Deportation, Removal and Exclusion

8. Deportation 229
9. Administrative Removal of Persons 293
10. Exclusion from the UK 323

Part D: Denial and Deprivation of Citizenship

11. Denial of British Citizenship 361
12. Deprivation of British Citizenship or Right of Abode 383

Part E: Procedure and Remedies

13. International Remedies 415
14. Remedies under EU Law 429
15. Council of Europe Remedies 443
16. Domestic Remedies 459

Select Bibliography 493
Index 497

List of Contributors

General Editor

Eric Fripp
MA (History) St Andrews, LLM London, MA (Medical Law/Ethics) London (King's College London), LLM London (London School of Economics)
Of Gray's Inn, Barrister
Lamb Building, Elm Court, Temple EC4Y 7AS

Deputy Editors

Rowena Moffatt
BA (English and Modern Languages) Oxon, LLM (College of Europe, Bruges)
Of the Inner Temple, Barrister
Lamb Building, Elm Court, Temple EC4Y 7AS

Ellis Wilford,
MA (History) Cantab
Of Gray's Inn, Barrister
Lamb Building, Elm Court, Temple EC4Y 7AS

Contributors

Sandra Akinbolu
LLB (Essex), LLM (Essex)
Of the Middle Temple, Barrister
Lamb Building, Elm Court, Temple EC4Y 7AS

Bojana Asanovic
BA (History) London
Of the Middle Temple, Barrister
Lamb Building, Elm Court, Temple EC4Y 7AS

Emma Daykin
LLB (Coventry)
Of the Inner Temple, Barrister
Lamb Building, Elm Court, Temple EC4Y 7AS

Jamil Dhanji
BA (Social and Political Sciences) Cantab
Of the Middle Temple, Barrister
Lamb Building, Elm Court, Temple EC4Y 7AS

Stephanie Motz
LLB (London, King's College London), BCL (Oxon)
Of Gray's Inn, Barrister
Lamb Building, Elm Court, Temple EC4Y 7AS (door tenant)
and Advokatur Kanonengasse, Militärstrasse 76, Postfach 8021 Zürich

David Sellwood
BSc (Politics and International Relations) (Southampton); LLB (College of Law); LLM (Nottingham)
Of the Inner Temple, Barrister
Lamb Building, Elm Court, Temple EC4Y 7AS

Additional Research

Raphael Jesurum
BSc (Psychology) (Reading); MSc (Research Methods in Psychology) (Reading)
Of Gray's Inn, Barrister
Lamb Building, Elm Court, Temple EC4Y 7AS

List of Acronyms

AA 1905	Aliens Act 1905
AIA 1993	Asylum and Immigration Act 1993
AITCA 2004	Asylum and Immigration (Treatment of Claimants etc) Act 2004
ARA 1914	Aliens Restriction Act 1914
ARSIWA	Articles on Responsibility of States for Internationally Wrongful Acts
BCIA 2009	Borders, Citizenship, and Immigration Act 2009
BNA 1948	British Nationality Act 1948
BNA 1981	British Nationality Act 1981
BNSAA 1914	British Nationality and Status of Aliens Act 1914
BNSAA 1918	British Nationality and Status of Aliens Act 1918
CAT	Convention against Torture and Other Cruel, Inhuman or Degrading Treatment or Punishment 1984
CATHB	Convention on Action against Trafficking in Human Beings 2005
CCA 1984	County Courts Act 1984
CCQRCNL	Convention on Certain Questions Relating to the Conflict of Nationality Laws 1930
CEDAW	Convention on the Elimination of All Forms of Discrimination against Women 1979
CERD	Convention on the Elimination of All Forms of Racial Discrimination 1969
CFREU	Charter of Fundamental Rights of the European Union
CIA 1962	Commonwealth Immigrants Act 1962
CIA 1968	Commonwealth Immigrants Act 1968
CJEU	Court of Justice of the European Union
CPED	Convention for the Protection of All Persons from Enforced Disappearance 2006
CRA 2005	Constitutional Reform Act 2005
CRC	Convention on the Rights of the Child 1989
CRPD	Convention on the Rights of Persons with Disabilities 2006
CRS	Convention on the Reduction of Statelessness 1961
CSR	Convention Relating to the Status of Refugees 1951
CSSP	Convention Relating to the Status of Stateless Persons 1954
CSTP	Convention for the Suppression of the Traffic in Persons and of the Exploitation of the Prostitution of Others 1950
CUKC	Citizen of the United Kingdom and the Commonwealth
DFT	detained fast track
ECA 1972	European Communities Act 1972
ECHR	European Convention on Human Rights and Fundamental Freedoms 1950
ECN	European Convention on Nationality 1997
ECO	Entry Clearance Officer

List of Acronyms

ECtHR	European Court of Human Rights
EEA	European Economic Area
EIG	Enforcement and Instructions and Guidance
FNO	Foreign National Offender
FRY	Former Republic of Yugoslavia
GRETA	Group of Experts on Action against Trafficking in Human Beings
HRA 1998	Human Rights Act 1998
IA 1971	Immigration Act 1971
IA 2014	Immigration Act 2014
IAA 1999	Immigration and Asylum Act 1999
IAC	Immigration and Asylum Chamber
IANA 2006	Immigration, Asylum and Nationality Act 2006
ICCPR	International Covenant on Civil and Political Rights
ICESCR	International Covenant on Economic, Social and Cultural Rights 1966
ICJ	International Court of Justice
ILHT	international law of human trafficking
ILPA	Immigration Law Practitioners' Association
IO	immigration officer
IRL	international refugee law
ISL	international statelessness law
LASPO 2012	Legal Aid, Sentencing and Punishment of Offenders Act 2012
MWC	Convention on the Protection of the Rights of All Migrant Workers and Members of Their Families 1990
NIAA 2002	Nationality, Immigration and Asylum Act 2002
NRM	National Referral Mechanism
PCIJ	Permanent Court of International Justice
PPSTP	Protocol to Prevent, Suppress and Punish Trafficking in Persons, Especially Women and Children 2000
SCA 1981	Senior Courts Act 1981
SSHD	Secretary of State for the Home Department
SIAC	Special Immigration Appeals Commission
TCEA	Tribunals, Courts and Enforcement Act 2007
TEU	Treaty on European Union
TFEU	Treaty on the Functioning of the European Union
UDHR	Universal Declaration of Human Rights 1948
UKBA 2007	UK Borders Act 2007
UN	United Nations
UNGA	United Nations General Assembly
UNHCR	United Nations High Commissioner for Refugees
UNHRC	United Nations Human Rights Committee
UNRWA	United Nations Relief and Works Agency
VCLT	Vienna Convention on the Law of Treaties 1969
VoT	victim of (human) trafficking

Table of Cases

A (Afghanistan) v SSHD [2009] EWCA Civ 825 .... 5.24, 5.128, 5.183
A v SSHD [2004] UKHL 56, [2005] 2 AC 68 .... 10.86, 10.88, 16.79
A v United Kingdom, app no 9773/82 (1982) 5 EHRR 296 .... 5.199
A v United Kingdom, app no 3455/05 [2009] ECHR 301, (2009)
 49 EHRR 29 .... 5.129, 5.224, 16.103
AA v ECO (Addis Ababa) [2013] UKSC 81; [2014] 1 All ER 774 .... 5.101
AA v Sweden, app no 14499/09 (28 June 2012) 5.44
AA v Switzerland, app no 58802/12 [2014] ECHR 3 .... 5.52
AA v United Kingdom, app no 8000/08 [2011] ECHR 1345 .... 5.103, 5.114, 5.121,
 5.134, 5.149, 5.155
AA (Nigeria) v SSHD [2010] EWCA Civ 773, [2011]
 1 WLR 564 .... 7.28, 7.33, 10.44–10.45, 12.42
AB (Jamaica) v SSHD [2008] EWCA Civ 784 .... 4.47
AB v SSHD [2012] EWHC 226, [2012] 4 All ER 276 .... 14.35
Abdilahi Abdulwahidi v The Netherlands, app no 21741/07 (12 November 2013) 15.54
Abdolkhani and Karimnia v Turkey, app no 30471/08 (22 September 2009) 5.211
Abdul Wahab Khan v United Kingdom, app no 11987/11
 (admissibility decision, 28 January 2014) 5.18, 5.25
Abdulaziz, Cabales and Balkandali v United Kingdom, app nos 9214/80;
 9473/81; 9474/81 [1985] ECHR 7; (1985) 7 EHRR 471 .... 1.13, 3.49, 5.15, 5.24,
 5.101, 5.130, 5.150, 5.178–5.179
Abdullahi v Bundesasylamt (C–394/12) [2014] 1 WLR 1895 .... 14.27
Aboubacar Diakité v Commissaire général aux réfugiés et aux apatrides (C–285/12) [2014] 1
 WLR 2477 .... 6.78
Abu Hamza v SSHD [2010] UKSIAC 23/2005 .... 12.56, 12.58, 12.60
Acosta, In re (1985) 19 I & N 211 .... 4.55
Adamally and Jaferi (s 47 Removal Decisions: Tribunal Procedures) [2012]
 UKUT 00414 (IAC) 9.33
Adams and Benn v United Kingdom, app nos 28979/95; 30343/96 (1997)
 88A D & R 137 .... 5.195
Aden Ahmed v Malta, app no 55352/12 [2013] ECHR 720 .... 5.45
Advic v United Kingdom, app no 25525/94 [1995] ECHR 57, (1995) 20 EHRR CD125 .... 5.108
AE and FE v SSHD [2003] EWCA Civ 1032, [2004] QB 531 .... 4.43
AF (Jamaica) v SSHD [2009] EWCA Civ 240 .... 8.73, 8.81
AG (Eritrea) v SSHD [2007] EWCA Civ 801, [2008] 2 All ER 28 .... 5.116, 8.89
Agee v United Kingdom (1976) 7 DR 164 .... 15.41
Aguas del Tunari v Bolivia (ICSID ARB/02/0311, Decision on Respondent's
 Objections to Jurisdiction, 21 October 2005) 2.13
AH Khan v United Kingdom, app no 6222/10 (2012) 55 EHRR 30 .... 5.163
AHK v SSHD [2012] EWHC 1117 (Admin) 11.42–11.43
AHK v SSHD [2013] EWHC 1426 (Admin) 5.187, 11.7, 11.12, 11.42–11.43,
 12.9, 12.15
Ahmad (Removal of Children over 18: Pakistan) [2012] UKUT 267 (IAC),
 [2013] Imm AR 1 .... 9.87

Table of Cases

Ahmadi (s 47 Decision: Validity; Sapkota) [2012] UKUT 00147 (IAC) 9.33
Ahmadou Sadio Diallo (Republic of Guinea v Democratic Republic of the Congo),
  Merits, Judgment (2010) ICJ Reports 639 ....2.51
Ahmed v Austria, app no 25964/94 (1997) 24 EHRR 278 ....5.60
Ahmed (General Grounds of Refusal—Material Non-disclosure) Pakistan
  [2011] UKUT 351 (IAC) 10.44, 10.46
Ahmed Abdi v Malta, app no 43985/13 ....5.229
Ahmed Mahad (formerly AM (Ethiopia)) v ECO [2009] UKSC 16, [2010] WLR 48...............7.32
Ahmut v The Netherlands (28 November 1996)..5.178
Ahorugeze v Sweden no 37075/09 (2012) 55 EHRR 2...5.91
Aklagaren v Fransson (C–617/10) [2013] 2 CMLR 46 ....6.7
Al-Adsani v United Kingdom, app no 35763/97 (2002) 34 EHRR 11.......................................2.14
Al Jedda v SSHD [2008] UKSIAC 66/2008; [2012] EWCA Civ 358;
  [2013] UKSC 62, [2014] 1 AC 253 ....12.58–12.59, 12.62–12.63
Al Jedda v United Kingdom, app no 27021/08 [2011] ECHR 1092,
  (2011) 53 EHRR 23 ....5.14
Al-Medawi v SSHD [1989] UKHL 7, [1990] 1 AC 876..8.119
Al-Moayad v Germany, app no 35865/03
  (admissibility decision, 20 February 2007) 5.87, 5.90, 5.94
Al-Nashif v Bulgaria, app no 50963/99 [2002] ECHR 502 ....5.104, 5.124
Alabama Claims of the United States of America against Great Britain,
  Reports of International Arbitral Awards (14 September 1872) 2.16
Alam and Khan v United Kingdom, app no 2991/66...5.204
Aleksanyan v Russia no 46468/06 [2008] ECHR 1745..15.54
Alif v The Netherlands, app no 60915/09 (24 May 2011)..15.54
Alim v Russia, app no 39417/07 [2011] ECHR 1453 ....5.146
Alokpa v Ministre du Travail, de l'Emploi et de l'Immigration (C–86/12)
  [2014] INLR 145...6.33
Al-Saadoon and Mufdhi v United Kingdom, app no 61498/08 [2010]
  ECHR 285, (2010) 51 EHRR 9 ....5.14, 5.21, 5.31, 5.33
Al-Sabah v IAT [1992] Imm AR 223 ....8.68
Al-Sirri v SSHD [2012] UKSC 54, [2013] 1 AC 745 ....4.73, 4.76
Al-Skeini v Secretary of State for Defence [2007] UKHL 26, [2008] 1 AC 153 ....5.203
Al-Skeini v United Kingdom, app no 55721/07 [2011] ECHR 1093, (2011)
  53 EHRR 18..5.9, 5.11, 5.14
AM (s 88(2): 'Immigration Document') Somalia [2009] UKAIT 00008 ....10.39
AM and AM (Armed Conflict: Risk Categories) Somalia CG [2008] UKAIT 00091..................4.32
AM and BM (Trafficked Women) Albania CG [2010] UKUT 80 (IAC)............................4.23, 4.61
AMM (Conflict; Humanitarian Crisis; Returnees; FGM) Somalia CG [2011]
  UKUT 00445 (IAC)...5.44
Amrollahi v Denmark, app no 56811/00 [2002] ECHR 585 ....5.151, 5.157
Amuur v France, app no 19776/92 [1996] ECHR 25, (1996) 22 EHRR 533 ....5.11
Anayo v Germany, app no 20578/07 [2010] ECHR 2083, (2012)
  55 EHRR 5...5.102, 5.107, 5.159
Andrejeva v Latvia, app no 55707/00 [2009] ECHR 297 ....5.218
Andric v Sweden, app no 45917/99 (1999) 28 EHRR CD218 ....5.228
Anisminic Ltd v Foreign Compensation Commission [1969] 2 AC 147 ....16.2
Antwi v Norway, app no 26940/10 [2012] ECHR 259 ....5.140, 5.144, 5.158
Anufrijeva v Southwark LBC [2003] EWCA Civ 1406, [2004] QB 1124 ....16.127
AP (Trinidad & Tobago) v SSHD [2011] EWCA Civ 551 ....8.117
Aponte v The Netherlands, app no 28770/05 [2011] ECHR 1850 ....5.145

Table of Cases

Aristimuño Mendizabal v France, app no 1431/99 [2006] ECHR 34 ....5.123, 5.126
Arusha and Demushi (Deprivation of Citizenship—Delay) Albania [2012]
    UKUT 80 (IAC) 12.40, 12.47
AS v Canada (68/80, 31 March 1981, CCPR/C/12/D/68/1980)..3.52
AS (Pakistan) [2008] EWCA Civ 1118..5.166
AS and DD (Libya) v SSHD [2008] EWCA Civ 289, [2008] HRLR 28 ....5.63
Assange v Swedish Prosecution Authority (Rev 1) [2012] UKSC 22, [2012] 2 AC 471 ....2.20
Aswat v United Kingdom, app no 17299/12 [2013] ECHR 322, (2014)
    58 EHRR 1 ....5.45–5.46, 5.50, 5.70
AT (Pakistan) v SSHD [2010] EWCA Civ 567, [2010] Imm AR 675 ....8.31
Attorney General v Guardian Newspapers Ltd (No 2) [1990] 1 AC 109 ....2.21
Attorney General of Canada v Cain and Gilhula [1906] AC 542 ....1.6, 2.40, 10.1, 10.3
Attorney General of Canada v Ward [1993] 2 SCR 689..4.17, 4.64
Auad v Bulgaria, app no 46390/10 (11 October 2011)...5.60
Aumeeruddy-Cziffra and 19 Other Mauritian Women v Mauritius
    (35/78, 9 April 1981, CCPR/C/12/D/35/1978) 3.53
AW Khan v United Kingdom, app no 47486/06 [2010] ECHR 27, (2010)
    50 EHRR 47 .... 5.103, 5.128, 5.134, 5.139,
                                                                                                                5.149, 5.163, 5.172
AXA General Insurance v HM Advocate [2011] UKSC 46, [2012] 1 AC 868............................7.16
Aydin v Turkey, app no 23178/94 [1997] ECHR 75, (1998) 25 EHRR 251..............................5.41
Azam v SSHD [1974] AC 18...1.17
B and L v United Kingdom, app no 36536/02 (2006) 42 EHRR 11 ....5.197
B v SSHD [2000] EWCA Civ 158, [2000] INLR 361 ....8.52
B2 v SSHD (Deportation—Preliminary Issue—Allowed) [2012]
    UKSIAC 114/2012...12.56
B2 v SSHD [2013] EWCA Civ 616 ....12.60
Babar Ahmad v United Kingdom, app nos 24027/07; 11949/08;
    36742/08 [2012] ECHR 609, (2013) 56 EHRR 1 ....5.38, 5.40, 5.46, 5.49–5.50
Bader and Kanbor v Sweden, app no 13284/04 [2005] ECHR 939, (2008)
    46 EHRR 13 ....5.21, 5.30, 5.90
Bagdanaviciene v SSHD [2003] EWCA Civ 1605, [2004] WLR 1207 ....4.39
Baghli v France, app no 34374/97 [1999] ECHR 135 ....5.139
Bah [2012] UKUT 196 (IAC)..9.63
Bah v United Kingdom, app no 56328/07 [2011] ECHR 1448, (2012) 54 EHRR 21 ....5.221
Bahaddar v The Netherlands, app no 25894/94 (1998) 26 EHRR 278...5.33
Balogun v United Kingdom, app no 60286/09 [2012] ECHR 614, (2013)
    56 EHRR 3 ....5.134, 5.148, 15.53
Baltaji v Bulgaria, app no 12919/04 (12 July 2011) 5.233, 5.237
Banković v Belgium, app no 52207/99 [2001] ECHR 890, (2007)
    44 EHRR SE5 ....2.14, 5.10–5.11, 5.13–5.14
Barberá, Messegué and Jabardo v Spain, app no 10590/83 [1988]
    ECHR 25, (1989) 11 EHRR 360 ....15.40
Barcelona Traction (Belgium v Spain (Second Phase)) (1970)
    ICJ Reports 3 ....2.24, 2.60, 4.17, 11.4
Batayav v SSHD [2003] EWCA Civ 1489..4.28
Bayatyan v Armenia, app no 3459/03 (27 October 2009)..5.192
Baysakov v Ukraine, app no 54131/08 [2010] ECHR 221 ....5.55
BE (Iran) v SSHD [2008] EWCA Civ 540, [2009] INLR 1..4.33
Behrami and Saramati v France, app nos 71412/01; 78166/01 (2007) 45 EHRR SE85................5.14
Beldjoudi v France, app no 12083/86 [1992] ECHR 42, (1992) 14 EHRR 801 ....5.151

Table of Cases

Benhebba v France, app no 53441/99 .... 5.168–5.169, 5.171
Bensaid v United Kingdom, app no 44599/98 [2001] ECHR 82, (2001)
  33 EHRR 205 .... 5.67, 5.70, 5.113
Berrehab v The Netherlands, app no 10730/84 [1988] ECHR 14, (1989)
  11 EHRR 322 .... 5.101, 5.129, 5.151
Bettati (C–341/95) [1998] ECR I–4355 .... 6.77
BH v The Lord Advocate (Scotland) [2012] UKSC 24, [2013] 1 AC 413 .... 8.86, 8.94
Biao v Denmark, app no 38590/10 [2014] ECHR 304 .... 5.180, 5.187, 5.222
Bibi v ECO [2007] EWCA Civ 740, [2008] INLR 683 .... 12.26, 12.28
Blagojevic v The Netherlands, app no 49032/07 (9 June 2009) 5.14
Bolat v Russia, app no 14139/03 (2008) 46 EHRR 18 .... 5.233, 5.235–5.236
Bond v The Netherlands (352/85) [1988] ECR 2085 .... 6.15
Bonsignore v Stadt Köln (67/74) [1975] ECR 297 .... 6.46–6.47, 10.101
Bouchelkia v France, app no 23078/93 [1997] ECHR 1, (1997)
  25 EHRR 686 .... 5.134, 5.139, 5.142
Boughanemi v France, app no 22070/93 [1996] ECHR 19, (1996) 22 EHRR 228 .... 5.101
Boujlifa v France, app no 25404/94 [1997] ECHR 83, (1997) 30 EHRR 419 .... 5.138–5.139
Boultif v Switzerland, app no 54273/00 [2001] ECHR 497, (2001)
  33 EHRR 50 .... 5.129, 5.131–5.132,
                                                                                                                        5.150, 5.157, 8.87
Bousarra v France, app no 25672/07 [2010] ECHR 1999 .... 5.102, 5.137
Boyle v United Kingdom, app no 16580/90 (9 February 1993) 5.106
Boyle and Rice v United Kingdom, app no 9659/82 [1988] ECHR 3, (1988)
  10 EHRR 425 .... 5.208
Brasserie du Pêcheur SA v Germany; R v Secretary of State
  for Transport ex p Factortame Ltd (C–46/93 and C–48/93) [1996] ECR I–1029 .... 14.28
British Oxygen Co Ltd v Board of Trade [1971] AC 610 .... 11.33
Bundesrepublik Deutschland v B and D (C–57/09 and C–101/09) [2010]
  ECR I–10979 .... 6.79
Bundesrepublik Deutschland v Y & Z (C–71/11) [2013] 1 CMLR 5 .... 5.191
Burden v United Kingdom, app no 13378/05 [2008] ECHR 357, (2008) 47 EHRR 38 .... 5.105
Burghartz v Switzerland, app no 16213/90 [1994] ECHR 2, (1994) 18 EHRR 101 .... 5.110
Butt v Norway, app no 47017/09 (4 December 2012) 5.106, 5.148, 5.154
Butt, Kiran, Siddique and Patel [2014] EWHC 264 (Admin) 16.168
Cakani v SSHD [2013] EWHC 16 (Admin) 10.73
Canepa v Canada (UNHRC, 558/93, 3 April 1997, CCPR/C/59/D/558/1993) 3.23
Carltona Ltd v Commissioner of Works [1943] 2 All ER 560 .... 8.123
Carpenter (C–60/00) [2002] ECR I–6279 .... 6.33, 6.49
Case of Proclamations (1611) 12 Co Rep 74 .... 7.26
Castro v SSHD (Removals: s 47 (as Amended)) Philippines [2014] UKUT 234 (IAC) 9.84
CB (United States of America) v Entry Clearance Officer (Los Angeles)
  [2008] EWCA Civ 1539 .... 10.68
CDS [2010] UKUT 305 (IAC), [2011] Imm AR 126 .... 5.111
Centros Ltd v Erhvervsog Selskabsstyrelsen (C–212/97) [1999] ECR I–01459 .... 10.111
Cetinkaya v Land Baden–Württemberg (C–467/02) [2004] ECR I–10898 .... 6.70
CG v Bulgaria, app no 1365/07 [2008] ECHR 349, (2008) 47 EHRR 51 .... 5.125
Chahal v United Kingdom, app no 22414/93 [1996] ECHR 54, (1996)
  23 EHRR 413 .... 5.36–5.37, 5.40, 5.61,
                                                                                                                        5.63, 5.210, 16.77
Chandra v The Netherlands, app no 53102/99 (admissibility decision, 13 May 2003) 5.146
Chen Shi Hai v Minister for Immigration and Multicultural Affairs (2000) 201 CLR 293 .... 4.50

Table of Cases

Chief Constable of North Wales Police v Evans [1982] 1 WLR 1155 .... 16.114
Chikwamba v SSHD [2008] UKHL 40, [2008] 1 WLR 1420 .... 8.92
Christodoulido v SSHD [1985] Imm AR 179 .... 1.18
CILFIT (283/81) [1982] ECR 3415 .... 14.44
Ciliz v The Netherlands, app no 29192/95 [2000] 2 FLR 469 .... 5.176
Cimade, Groupe d'information et de soutien des immigrés (GISTI) v
 Ministre de l'Intérieur, de l'Outre–mer, des Collectivités territoriales
 et de l'Immigration (C–179/11) [2013] 1 WLR 333 .... 6.19
Clift v United Kingdom, app no 7205/07 (13 July 2010) 5.221
CM v SSHD [1997] Imm AR 336 .... 8.52
CN and V v France, app no 67724/09 (11 October 2012) 5.78
CN v France, app no 4239/08 (2013) 56 EHRR 24 .... 5.78, 5.82
Čonka v Belgium, app no 51564/99 [2002] ECHR 14, (2002) 34 EHRR 54 .... 5.211, 5.228
Constance Ragan Salgado v United Kingdom (11/2006, 22 January 2007,
 CEDAW/C/37/D/11/2006) 13.48
Cooper v Attorney General [2010] EWCA Civ 464, [2011] QB 976 .... 14.33
Corfu Channel (1949) ICJ Reports 4 .... 2.14
Costa v ENEL (6/64) [1964] ECR I–585 .... 6.9
Council of Civil Service Unions v Minister for the Civil Service [1985] AC 374 .... 16.2, 16.119
Cox v Turkey, app no 2933/03 [2010] ECHR 700, (2012)
 55 EHRR 13 .... 5.193, 5.195, 10.86, 10.88
CR v United Kingdom, app no 20190/92 [1995] ECHR 51 .... 5.96
Criminal Proceedings against Calfa (C–348/96) [1999] ECR I–11 .... 6.15, 6.46
Cruz Varas v Sweden, app no 15576/89 [1991] ECHR 26, (1991) 14 EHRR 1 .... 5.20, 5.36
Csoszanski v Sweden, app no 22318/02 (admissibility decision, 27 June 2006) 5.86, 5.98
CT and KM v Sweden, Communication No 279/2005,
 UN Doc CAT/C/37/D/279/2005 (2007) 3.77–3.78
Cyprus v Turkey, app no 25781/94 [2001] ECHR 331; (2002) 35 EHRR 30 .... 5.14
D v Turkey, app no 24245/03 (22 June 2006) 5.41
D v United Kingdom, app no 30240/96 (1997) 24 EHRR 425 .... 5.33, 5.40, 5.66, 5.69
DA (Colombia) v SSHD [2009] EWCA Civ 682 .... 8.52
Dalea v France, app no 964/07 (admissibility decision, 2 February 2010) 5.15, 5.204
Dalia v France no 26102/95 [1998] ECHR 5 .... 5.139
Danian v SSHD [1999] EWCA Civ 3000, [1999] INLR 533 .... 4.26
Daytbegova v Austria, app no 6198/12 (admissibility decision, 4 June 2013) 5.75
De Souza Ribeiro v France, app no 22689/07 [2012] ECHR 2066 .... 5.122, 5.209, 16.57
DEB (C–279/09) [2011] CMLR 21 .... 14.14
Deliallisi (British Citizen: Deprivation Appeal: Scope) Albania [2013] UKUT 439 (IAC) 12.47
Dereci (C–256/11) [2011] ECR I–11315 .... 6.33
Dervish v SSHD [1972] Imm AR 48 .... 8.129
DH v Czech Republic, app no 57325/00 [2006] ECHR 113, (2006) 43 EHRR 41 .... 5.217, 5.219
Diallo v Czech Republic, app no 20493/07 [2011] ECHR 1015 .... 5.208, 15.42
Dickson v United Kingdom, app no 44362/04 [2007] ECHR 1050, (2008) 46 EHRR 41 .... 5.201
Dillenkofer v Germany (C–178/94 to C–179/94, C–188/94 to C–190/94)
 [1996] ECR I–4845 .... 14.28
DJ (Defective Notice of Decision) Iraq [2004] UKIAT 00194 .... 16.13
Djokaba Lambi Longa v The Netherlands, app no 33917/12 (9 October 2012) 5.14
DM (Zambia) v SSHD [2009] EWCA Civ 474 .... 5.174
DNM v Sweden, app no 28379/11 (27 June 2013) 5.62
Dorr and Unal v Sicherheitsdirektion für das Bundesland Kärnten (C–136/03)
 [2005] ECR I–04759 .... 6.70

Dorsch Consult (C–54/96) [1997] ECR I–4961 ....14.37
DP (United States of America) v SSHD [2012] EWCA Civ 365..7.27
Drozd and Janousek v France and Spain, app no 12747/87 [1992] ECHR 52,
 (1992) 14 EHRR 74...5.14, 5.88
Dudgeon v United Kingdom, app no 7525/76 [1981] ECHR 5, (1981) 4 EHRR 149 ....5.110
Dzhaksybergenov v Ukraine, app no 12343/10 [2011] ECHR 240 ....5.55
E (Iran) v SSHD [2003] UKIAT 00166 ....4.60
East African Asians v United Kingdom, app no 4403/70 [1973] ECHR 2, (1981)
 3 EHRR 76..5.17, 5.24, 5.41
EB (Ethiopia) v SSHD [2007] EWCA Civ 809, [2009] QB 1 ....4.15, 4.22
EB (Kosovo) v SSHD [2008] UKHL 41, [2009] 1 AC 1159 ..... 5.119–5.120, 5.135, 5.155, 8.93, 8.95
Einhorn v France, app no 71555/01 (admissibility decision, 16 October 2001) 5.90
El-Ali v SSHD [2002] EWCA Civ 1103, [2003] 1 WLR 1811 ....4.71
El Boujaïdi v France, app no 25613/94 [1997] ECHR 76, [2000] 30 EHRR 223 ....5.139, 5.149
Elettronica Sicula SpA (ELSI) (United States of America v Italy) (1989) ICJ Reports 15...........2.48
Elgafaji v Staatssecretaris van Justitie (C–465/07) [2009] ECR I–921...6.78
El–Masri v Former Yugoslav Republic of Macedonia, app no 39630/09 [2012] ECHR 2067,
 (2013) 57 EHRR 25..5.12
Elmi v Australia, Communication No 120/1998, UN Doc CAT/C/22/D/120/1998 (1999) 3.72
EM (Eritrea) v SSHD [2014] UKSC 12, [2014] 2 WLR 409 ....5.36, 5.75
EM (Lebanon) v SSHD [2008] UKHL 64, [2009] AC 1198...5.23, 5.148
Emre v Switzerland, app no 42034/04 (22 May 2008) 5.164, 5.174–5.175
Emre v Switzerland (No 2), app no 5056/10 (2014) 59 EHRR 11 ....5.172
EN (Serbia) v SSHD [2009] EWCA Civ 630, [2010] 1 QB 633 ....4.82, 6.84
EO (Deportation Appeals: Scope and Process) Turkey [2008] EWCA Civ 671,
 [2008] INLR 295 ....8.72
Equal Opportunities Commission v Secretary of State for Employment [1995] 1 AC 1........16.117
Ergat v Stadt Ulm (C–329/97) [2000] ECR I–1487..6.70
Eritrea Ethiopia Claims Commission, Partial Award: Civilians Claims—Eritrea's
 Claims 15, 16, 23 & 27–32, Permanent Court of International Arbitration,
 The Hague (17 December 2004) 2.49–2.50
ERT (C–260/89) [1991] ECR I–2925 ....6.5
Eskinazi and Chelouche v Turkey, app no 14600/05 (6 December 2005)................................15.53
European Commission v United Kingdom (Kadi (No 2)) (C–584/10 P, C–593/10 P and
 C–595/10 P) [2014] 1 CMLR 24 ....14.23
European Roma Rights Centre v Immigration Officer, Prague Airport *see* R
 (European Roma Rights Centre) v Immigration Officer at Prague Airport
Evans v United Kingdom, app no 6339/05 [2006] ECHR 200, (2006) 43 EHRR 21 ....5.110
Ezzouhdi v France, app no 47160/99 (13 February 2001) 5.108, 5.137, 5.168–5.169
F (para 320(8)—Type of Leave) USA [2013] UKUT 00309 (IAC) 10.67
F v Finland, app no 38885/02 (2006) 43 EHRR 12 ....5.52
F v Switzerland, app no 11329/85 [1987] ECHR 32, (1988) 10 EHRR 411 ....5.197
FA v United Kingdom, app no 20658/11 (admissibility decision, 10 September 2013)...5.83, 15.41
FA (Iraq) v SSHD [2011] UKSC 22, [2011] 3 CMLR 23 ....14.10
Farquharson (Removal—Proof of Conduct) [2013] UKUT 00146 (IAC) 9.63
Farrakhan (Human rights, Entry Clearance, Proportionality) USA [2005] UKIAT 00112 ......10.85
FH (Post–flight Spouses) Iran [2010] UKUT 275 (IAC)..5.24, 5.183
FK (Kenya) v SSHD [2008] EWCA Civ 119..4.47
Fornah v SSHD *see* SSHD v Fornah
Francovich and Bonifaci v Italy (C–6/90 and C–9/90) [1991]
 ECR I–5357 .... 14.28, 14.30, 14.32–14.33, 14.35

Table of Cases

Francovich v Italy (C–479/93) [1995] ECR I–3843..6.14
FV (Italy) v SSHD [2012] EWCA Civ 1199, [2013] 1 WLR 3339..6.54
G1 (Sudan) v SSHD [2012] EWCA Civ 867, [2013] QB 1008.....................6.27, 11.14, 11.25, 12.17
Gaforov v Russia, app no 25404/09 (2011) ECHR 365 ....5.55
Galic v The Netherlands, app no 22617/07 (9 June 2009) 5.14
Gashi and Nikshiqi v SSHD [1997] INLR 96 ....4.17
Gaskin v United Kingdom (1989) 12 EHRR 36 ....3.49
Gaygusuz v Austria, app no 17371/90 [1996] ECHR 36, (1997) 23 EHRR 364..............5.216, 5.218
Gebhard v Consignol dell Ordine degli Advocat AE Procuratori
   di Milano (C–55/94) [1995] ECR I–4165..6.12, 10.101
Gebremedhin v France, app no 25389/05 (2010) 50 EHRR 29 ....5.211
Genc v SSHD [1984] Imm AR 180...8.54
Genovese v Malta, app no 53124/09 [2011] ECHR 1590, (2014)
   58 EHRR 25 ....5.187, 5.220, 11.7, 11.12,
   12.9, 12.15
Gentilhomme v France, app nos 48205/99; 48207/99; 48209/99 [2002] ECHR 441...................5.14
Gezginci v Switzerland, app no 16327/05 (9 December 2010)..5.163
Ghaidan v Godin-Mendoza [2004] UKHL 30, [2004] 2 AC 557...3.50
Giry v Dominican Republic (193/1985, 20 July 1990, CCPR/C/39/D/193/1985) 3.44
Golak Nath v State of Punjab 1967 AIR 1643, 1967 SCR (2) 762...7.8
Gomez (Non-state Actors: Acero-Garces Disapproved) (Colombia) [2000]
   UKIAT 00007, [2001] WLR 549..4.64
Goodwin v United Kingdom, app no 28957/95 [2002] ECHR 588, (2002)
   35 EHRR 18..5.198
Goremsandhu v SSHD [1996] Imm AR 250 ....8.52
GR v The Netherlands, app no 22251/07 (10 January 2012)...................................5.212, 5.214
Green (Article 8—New Rules) Jamaica [2013] UKUT 254 (IAC)..8.101
Grzelczyk (C–184/99) [2001] ECR I–6193...6.58
Gül v Switzerland, app no 23218/94 [1996] ECHR 5...5.180
Gurguchiani v Spain, app no 16012/06 [2009] ECHR 2063 ....5.97
Gurung v SSHD [2012] EWCA Civ 62, [2012] INLR 401 ....8.81, 8.114–8.115
GW (EEA reg 21: 'fundamental interests') Netherlands [2009]
   UKAIT 00050 ....5.194, 10.108–10.109
H (Somalia) v ECO [2004] UKIAT 00027 ....5.24, 5.181
H and B v United Kingdom, app nos 70073/10 and 44539/11 (9 April 2013)...........................5.62
Hamid [2012] EWHC 3070 (Admin) 16.168
Hammel v Madagascar (155/1983, 3 April 1987, CCPR/C/OP/2, 179) 3.37–3.39
Hariri v SSHD [2003] EWCA Civ 807 ....4.28
Harkins and Edwards v United Kingdom, app nos 9146/07 and 32650/07
   [2012] ECHR 45, (2012) 55 EHRR 19...5.40, 5.51
Harrison (Jamaica) v SSHD [2012] EWCA Civ 1736, [2013] 2 CMLR 23 ....6.65
Harrow LBC v Ibrahim (C–310/08) [2010] ECR I–01065 ....6.33
Hasanbasic v Switzerland, app no 2166/09 [2013] ECHR 520 ....5.131, 5.143, 5.175
Haydin v Sweden [1998] CAT/C/21/D/101/1997..3.75, 3.79
Hedley Lomas (C–5/94) [1996] ECR I–2553 ....14.29
Hendriks v The Netherlands (201/85, 27 July 1988, CCPR/C/33/D/201/1985) 3.51
HH (Iran) v SSHD [2008] EWCA Civ 504 ....5.207
HH (Mogadishu: Armed Conflict: Risk) Somalia CG [2008] UKAIT 00022 ....4.32
HH Somalia [2010] EWCA Civ 426, [2010] Imm AR 563..6.78
HH v Deputy Prosecutor of the Italian Republic, Genoa [2012] UKSC 25,
   [2013] 1 AC 338 ....5.129, 8.86, 8.94

HID, BA v Refugee Applications Commissioner (C–175/11) [2013] 2 CMLR 31 .... 6.19, 14.25
Hilal v United Kingdom, app no 45276/99 [2001] ECHR 214, (2001)
    33 EHRR 2 .... 5.36, 5.42, 5.61
Hirsi Jamaa v Italy, app no 27765/09 [2012] ECHR 1845, (2012)
    55 EHRR 21 .... 5.13, 5.55, 5.212, 5.229
HJ (Iran) v SSHD; HT (Cameroon) v SSHD [2010] UKSC 31, [2011]
    1 AC 596 .... 4.19–4.20, 4.24, 4.59
HK (Turkey) v SSHD [2010] EWCA Civ 583 .... 5.137, 5.159
HLR v France, app no 24573/94 [1997] ECHR 23, [1998] 26 EHRR 29 .... 5.20, 5.59
HM (Iraq) v SSHD [2010] EWCA Civ 1322 .... 5.114
HMHI v Australia, Communication No 177/2001, CAT/C/28/D/177/2001 (2002) 3.72, 3.76
Hode and Abdi v United Kingdom, app no 22341/09 [2012] ECHR 1871,
    (2013) 56 EHRR 27 .... 5.183, 5.221
Hopu and Bessert v France (549/93, 29 July 1997, CCPR/C/60/D/549/1993/Rev.1) 3.51
Horvath v SSHD [1999] EWCA Civ 3026, [2000] INLR 15; [2000]
    UKHL 37, [2001] 1 AC 489 .... 4.19–4.20, 4.38, 5.59
Hoxha v SSHD [2005] UKHL 19, [2005] 1 WLR 1063 .... 4.61, 4.70
Huang v SSHD; Kashmiri v SSHD [2007] UKHL 11; [2007] 2 AC 167 .... 5.106, 5.117–5.118,
                                                                                                     8.90, 8.96, 8.117
Hussein v SSHD [2009] EWHC 2492 (Admin), [2010] Imm AR 320 .... 8.31
Husseini v Sweden, app no 10611/09 (13 October 2011) 5.62
Hysi v SSHD [2005] EWCA Civ 711, [2005] INLR 602 .... 4.47
I v Sweden, app no 61204/09 [2013] ECHR 813 .... 5.73
Ibrahim Mohammed v The Netherlands, app no 1872/04
    (10 March 2009, struck out of list) 5.123
ID v SSHD [2005] EWCA Civ 38, [2006] 1 All ER 183 .... 7.6
Idemugia v France, app no 4125/11 (admissibility decision, 27 March 2012) 5.82
IH (s.72; 'Particularly Serious Crime') Eritrea [2009] UKAIT 00012 .... 4.82
IK v Austria, app no 2964/12 [2013] ECHR 252 .... 5.73
Ilaşcu v Moldova and Russia, app no 48787/99 [2004] ECHR 318 (2005) 40 EHRR 46 .... 5.11
IM v France, app no 9152/09 (2 February 2012) 5.213
Indira Nehru Gandhi v Raj Narain AIR 1975 SC 2299, (1975) Supp SCC 1 .... 7.8
Inland Revenue Commissioners v National Federation of Self-Employed and
    Small Businesses Ltd [1982] AC 617 .... 16.135
Internationale Handelsgesellschaft v Einfuhr und Vorratsstelle für Getreide und
    Futtermittel (11/70) [1970] ECR 1125 .... 6.9
Inze v Austria, app no 8695/79 [1987] ECHR 28, (1988) 10 EHRR 394 .... 5.220
Ireland v United Kingdom, app no 5310/71 [1978] ECHR 1, [1978]
    2 EHRR 25 .... 5.39–5.40, 5.42
Islam v SSHD; R v SSHD ex p Shah [1999] UKHL 20, [1999]
    2 AC 629 .... 4.23, 4.48, 4.50, 4.54–4.55, 4.62
Ismail Derin v Landkreis Darmstadt-Dieburg (C–325/05) [2007] ECR I–06495 .... 6.70
Ismoilov v Russia, app no 2947/06 (2009) 49 EHRR 42 .... 5.65, 5.205
Issa v Turkey, app no 31821/96 [2004] ECHR 629; (2005) 41 EHRR 27 .... 5.14
Izuazu (Article 8—New Rules) Nigeria [2013] UKUT 45 (IAC),
    Imm AR 13 .... 8.96, 8.101–8.102, 8.107
JA (Ivory Coast) and ES (Tanzania) v SSHD [2009] EWCA Civ 1353,
    [2010] Imm AR 381 .... 5.174
Jabari v Turkey, app no 40035/98 [2000] ECHR 369, [2001] INLR 136 .... 5.209–5.210
Jackson v Attorney General [2005] UKHL 56, [2006] 1 AC 262 .... 7.14–7.18
Jain v SSHD [1999] EWCA Civ 3009, [2000] INLR 71 .... 4.59

Janjanin v SSHD [2004] EWCA Civ 448, [2004] Imm AR 264 ....5.111
Jankov v Germany, app no 35112/92 (13 January 2000).......................................5.168–5.169, 5.171
Januzi v SSHD; Hamid, Gaafar, and Mohammed v SSHD [2006]
  UKHL 5, [2006] 2 AC 426 ....4.44–4.47
JD (Congo) [2012] EWCA Civ 327, [2012] 1 WLR 3273...16.26
JH Rayner (Mincing Lane) Ltd v Department of Trade and Industry [1990] 2 AC 418.............2.21
Jin Tao He v SSHD [2002] EWCA Civ 1150, [2002] Imm AR 590..4.35
JM v Jamaica, Communication No 165/1984, UN Doc CCPR/C/OP/2 (1984) 3.19
Jong Kim Koe v MIMA [1997] 306 FCA 4.67
Joseph Grant v United Kingdom, app no 10606/07 [2009] ECHR 26 ....5.141, 5.153
JRC v Costa Rica (296/88, 30 March 1989, CCPR/C/35/D/296/1988)...3.44
JS v United Kingdom (38/2012, 27 November 2012, CEDAW/C/53/D/38/2012) 13.49
JT (Cameroon) v SSHD [2008] EWCA Civ 878, [2009] 1 WLR 1411 ....8.107, 9.102
K and T v Finland, app no 25702/94 [2009] ECHR 289, (2001) 31 EHRR 18 ....5.104
KAB v Sweden, app no 886/11 [2013] ECHR 814..5.58
Kadi (No 2) see European Commission v United Kingdom
Kaboulov v Ukraine, app no 41015/04 [2009] ECHR 1903...5.55
Kalashnikov v Russia, app no 47095/99 [2002] ECHR 596, (2002) 36 EHRR 587...................5.49
Kanagaratnam v Belgium, app no 15297/09 [2011] ECHR 2420, (2012) 55 EHRR 26 ....5.43
Kapri v The Lord Advocate (representing the Government of the
  Republic of Albania) (Scotland) [2013] UKSC 48; [2013] 1 WLR 2324 ....5.88
Karassev v Finland, app no 31414/96 (1999) 28 EHRR CD132 ....5.184
Karker v France (833/1998, 30 October 2000, CCPR/C/70/D/833/1998)..................................3.45
Kasonga, Re Judicial Review [2013] CSOH 152 ....11.38
Kasymakhunov v Russia, app no 29604/12 (14 November 2013) 5.65
Katrinak v SSHD [2001] EWCA Civ 832, [2001] INLR 499 ....4.25
Kaveh Yaragh Tala v Sweden, Communication No 43/1996,
  UN Doc CAT/C/17/D/43/1996 (1996) 3.78
Kawogo v United Kingdom, app no 56921/09 (strike out decision, 3 September 2013) 5.78
Kaya v Germany, app no 31753/02 [2007] 2 FCR 527 ....5.103, 5.136–5.138, 5.168
Kaya v Romania, app no 33970/05 (2010) 50 EHRR 14 ....5.233
KB (Trinidad and Tobago) v SSHD [2010] EWCA Civ 11, [2010] 1 WLR 1630 ....5.131
Keegan v Ireland (1994) 18 EHRR 342 ....3.49
Keenan v United Kingdom, app no 27229/95 [2001] ECHR 242, (2001) 33 EHRR 38 ....5.27
Keles v Germany, app no 32231/02 [2005] ECHR 950 ....5.137, 5.166, 5.168
Kenneth McAlpine v United Kingdom (6/2011, 13 November 2012,
  CRPD/C/8/D/6/2011)..13.50
Kesavananda v Kerala 1973 AIR 1461, (1973) 4 SCC 225 ....7.8
Khawaja v SHHD [1983] UKHL 8, [1984] AC 74..8.54, 9.47, 9.72, 12.34
Kinuthia v SSHD [2001] EWCA Civ 2100; [2002] INLR 133..4.30–4.31
KK (Nationality: North Korea) Korea CG [2011] UKUT 92 (IAC) 4.66
KK IH HE (Palestinians, Lebanon, Camps) Palestine CG [2004] UKIAT 00293 ....4.35
KK v France, app no 18913/11 (10 October 2013)..5.213
Klip and Krüger v The Netherlands, app no 33257/96 (1997) 91–A DR 66 ....5.200
Kobler (C–224/01) [2004] QB 848...14.33
Konstatinov v The Netherlands, app no 16351/03 [2007] ECHR 336 ....5.108
Koua Poirrez v France, app no 40892/98 [2003] ECHR 459, (2005) 40 EHRR 2 ....5.218
Kroon v The Netherlands (1994) 19 EHRR 263...3.49
Krotov v SSHD [2004] EWCA Civ 69, [2004] 1 WLR 1825..4.33
Kudła v Poland, app no 30210/96 [2000] ECHR 512, (2000) 35 EHRR 198 ....5.209
Kugathas v SSHD [2003] EWCA Civ 31, [2003] INLR 170 ....5.108

Kuric v Slovenia, app no 26828/06 [2012] ECHR 1083, (2013)
    56 EHRR 20 .... 5.125, 5.184, 5.186, 5.218
L v Federal Republic of Germany, app no 10564/83 (1986) 8 EHRR CD262 .... 5.227
L v Finland, app no 25651/94 [2000] ECHR 176 .... 5.106
L1 v SSHD [2013] EWCA Civ 906 .... 11.18, 12.54
Ladd v Marshall [1954] 1 WLR 1489 .... 8.74
Lamichhane v SSHD [2012] EWCA Civ 260, [2012] 1 WLR 3064 .... 16.74
Land Baden-Württemberg v Panagiotis Tsakouridis (C–145/09) [2010]
    ECR I–11979 .... 6.42, 6.48, 6.52, 6.55
Laskey, Jaggard and Brown v United Kingdom, app nos 21627/93, 21826/93,
    21974/93 [1997] ECHR 4, (1997) 24 EHRR 39 .... 5.110
Latif (s 120—Revocation of Deportation Order) Pakistan [2012] UKUT 78 (IAC) 8.133, 10.34
Lazarevic v SSHD [1997] EWCA Civ 1007, [1997] 1 WLR 1107 .... 4.22
LCB v United Kingdom, app no 23413/94 [1998] ECHR 49, (1999) 27 EHRR 212 .... 5.27
LD (Article 8—Best Interests of Child) Zimbabwe [2010] UKUT 278 (IAC) 5.162
Lebbink v The Netherlands app no 45582/99 [2004] ECHR 240,
    (2005) 40 EHRR 18, [2004] 2 FLR 463 .... 3.49, 5.104
Levez v TJ Jennings (Harlow Pools) Ltd (C–326/96) [1998] ECR I–7835,
    [1999] 2 CMLR 363 .... 14.8
LG (Italy) v SSHD [2008] EWCA Civ 190 .... 6.54
Liu and Liu v Russia, app no 42086/05 [2007] ECHR 1056, (2008) 47 EHRR 33 .... 5.124
LM v R [2010] EWCA Crim 2327, [2011] 1 Cr App R 12 .... 4.98
Loizidou v Turkey, app no 15318/89 [1995] ECHR 10; (1995) 20 EHRR 99 .... 2.14, 5.14
Lotus *see* SS Lotus
LR v United Kingdom, app no 49113/09 .... 5.22
Luberti v Italy, app no 9019/80 [1984] ECHR 3, (1984) 6 EHRR 440 .... 15.39
Lupsa v Romania, app no 10337/04 (8 June 2006) 5.124, 5.234
M v Bulgaria, app no 41416/08 (26 July 2011) 5.124
M v Croydon LBC [2012] EWCA Civ 595, [2012] 1 WLR 2607 .... 16.142
M v SSHD [2003] EWCA Civ 146, [2003] 1 WLR 1980 .... 8.52, 8.70, 8.74
M and S v Italy and United Kingdom, app no 2584/11
    (admissibility decision, 13 March 2012) 5.227
MA v Cyprus, app no 41872/10 [2013] ECHR 717 .... 5.21
MA (Ethiopia) v SSHD [2009] EWCA Civ 289, [2010] INLR 1 .... 4.15, 4.21–4.22
MA (Ethiopia—Mixed Ethnicity—Dual Nationality) Eritrea [2004] UKIAT 00324 .... 4.67
MA (Pakistan) v SSHD [2009] EWCA Civ 953, [2010] Imm AR 196 .... 8.92
MA (Palestinian Territories) v SSHD [2008] EWCA Civ 304 .... 4.22
Maaouia v France, app no 39652/98 [2000] ECHR 455, [2001] 33 EHRR 42 .... 5.204
MacCormick v Lord Advocate [1953] CSIH 2, 1953 SC 396 .... 7.12
Madafferi and Madafferi v Australia, CCPR/C/81/D/1011/2001 .... 3.21, 3.24
Madah v Bulgaria, app no 45237/08 [2012] ECHR 821 .... 5.125
Mahajna v Home Secretary (Deportation Hate Speech—Unacceptable Behaviour)
    [2012] UKUT B1 (IAC) 5.194, 10.70
Mamatkulov and Askarov v Turkey, app nos 46827/99 and 46951/99 [2005]
    ECHR 64, ECHR 2005 I 5.40, 5.88, 5.205, 15.52
Marbury v Madison 5 US 137 (1803), 1 Cranch 137 .... 7.8
Marckx v Belgium, app no 6833/74 [1979] ECHR 2, (1979) 2 EHRR 330 .... 5.106
Marguš v Croatia, app no 4455/10 [2014] ECHR 523 .... 5.99
Marleasing SA v La Commercial Internacional de Alimentación SA (C–106/89)
    [1990] ECR I–4135 .... 6.10
Maroufidou v Sweden (58/1979, 9 April 1981, CCPR/C/OP/1, 80 (1985)) 3.36, 3.41–3.43

Table of Cases

Masih (deportation—public interest—basic principles) Pakistan [2012]
UKUT 46 (IAC) 8.81
Maslov v Austria, app no 1638/03 [2008] ECHR 546, [2009]
INLR 47 .... 5.114, 5.132–5.135, 5.139, 5.143,
5.150, 5.160, 5.164–5.166, 5.169,
5.172, 8.87, 8.130
Matra Communication SAS v SSHD [1999] EWCA Civ 860, [1999] 1 WLR 1646 ....14.9
Mawaka v The Netherlands, app no 29031/04 [2010] ECHR 762 ....5.151
McCarthy (C–434/09) [2011] ECR I–3375 ....6.6
McCawley v The King [1920] AC 691 ....7.16
McFarlane v Ireland, app no 31333/06 [2010] ECHR 1272 ....15.41
Medvedyev v France, app no 3394/03 [2010] ECHR 384 ....5.14
Mengesha Kimfe v Switzerland; Agraw v Switzerland, app nos 24404/05;
3295/06 [2010] ECHR 1233 ....5.147
Metock v Minister for Justice (C–127/08) [2008] ECR I–6241 ....6.30
MF (Article 8—New Rules) Nigeria [2012] UKUT 393 (IAC) 8.101–8.102
MF (Nigeria) v SSHD [2013] EWCA Civ 1192, [2014]
1 WLR 544 .... 8.71, 8.97–8.98, 8.101–8.104, 8.107–8.108
MH v SSHD [2008] EWHC 2525 (Admin) 11.7, 11.18, 11.37, 12.9
MH (Iraq) v SSHD [2007] EWCA Civ 852 ....4.37
MI v SSHD [2014] EWCA Civ 826 ....4.21
MI (Fair Trial, Pre Trial Conditions) Pakistan CG [2002] UKIAT 02239 ....4.27
Miah v United Kingdom, app no 53080/07 [2010] ECHR 721 ...... 5.141, 5.160, 5.165, 5.172, 8.130
Micheletti (C–369/90) [1992] ECR I–4239 ....6.24
Mikuli v Croatia, app no 53176/99, ECHR 2002–I 5.131
Minister for Immigration and Multicultural Affairs v Ibrahim [2000]
HCA 55, (2000) 204 CLR 1 ....4.13
Minister for Immigration and Multicultural Affairs v Khawar [2002]
HCA 14, (2002) 210 CLR 1 ....4.13
Minister for Immigration and Multicultural Affairs v Sarrazola [2001] FCA 263 ....4.50
MK (Somalia) v ECO [2008] EWCA Civ 1453, [2009] 2 FLR 138 ....5.101
MM v Minister for Justice (C–277/11) (22 November 2012) 6.19
MM (Zimbabwe) [2012] EWCA Civ 279 ....5.175
MN (Ahmadis—Country Conditions—Risk) Pakistan CG [2012] UKUT 389 (IAC) 4.24
MN (Non-recognised Adoptions: Unlawful Discrimination)
India [2007] UKAIT 00015 ....5.101
Mohammed v Austria, app no 2283/12 (6 June 2013) 5.76
Mohammed Hussein v The Netherlands, app no 27725/10
(admissibility decision, 2 April 2013) 5.75
Mohamoud (Paras 352D and 309A—De Facto Adoption) Ethiopia
[2011] UKUT 378 (IAC) 5.101
Mokrani v France, app no 52206/99 (2005) 40 EHRR 5.............................. 5.131, 5.137, 5.155
Montoya v SSHD [2002] EWCA Civ 620, [2002] INLR 399 .... 4.24, 4.61
Moustaquim v Belgium, app no 12313/86 [1991] ECHR 3, (1991) 13 EHRR 802 .... 5.97, 5.101
MRAX v Belgian State (C–459/99) [2002] ECR I–659,
[2003] 1 WLR 1073 .... 6.35, 10.114
MS (Ivory Coast) v SSHD [2007] EWCA Civ 133, [2007] Imm AR 538 ....5.123
MS (Palestinian Territories) v SSHD [2010] UKSC 25, [2010] WLR 1639 ....9.26
MSS v Belgium and Greece, app no 30696/09 [2011] ECHR 108, (2011)
53 EHRR 2 .... 5.45, 5.55, 5.68–5.69, 5.71,
5.73–5.74, 5.211, 6.88

MT (Ahmadi—HJ (Iran)) Pakistan [2011] UKUT 277 (IAC) 4.24, 5.191
MT (Palestinian Territories) v SSHD [2008] EWCA Civ 1149, [2009] Imm AR 290 .... 4.22
MT (Zimbabwe) v SSHD [2007] EWCA Civ 455 .... 5.108
Mubilanzila Mayeka and Kaniki Mitunga v Belgium, app no 13178/03 [2006]
  ECHR 1170, (2008) 46 EHRR 23 .... 5.43–5.44
Muminov v Russia, app no 42502/06 (2011) 52 EHRR 23 .... 5.65, 5.92
Musgrove v Chun Teeong Toy (Victoria) [1891] AC 272 .... 1.6
Musiał v Poland, app no 28300/06 [1999] ECHR 15, (2001) 31 EHRR 29 .... 5.45, 5.50
Muskhadzhieyava v Belgium, app no 41442/07 (19 January 2010) 5.43
Mutombo v Switzerland, Communication No 13/1993, UN Doc A/49/44 .... 3.76
Mwanje v Belgium, app no 10486/10 (2013) 56 EHRR 35 .... 5.72
N v Finland no 38885/02 (2006) 43 EHRR 12 .... 5.47, 5.59
N v Sweden, app no 23505/09 [2011] Imm AR 38 .... 5.44, 5.47
N v United Kingdom, app no 26565/05 (2008) 47 EHRR 39 .... 5.67, 5.69, 5.72
N v United Kingdom, app no 16458/12 (pending) 5.207
N (Kenya) v SSHD [2004] EWCA Civ 1094, [2004] INLR 612 .... 8.52, 8.81, 10.68
N (Uganda) v SSHD [2007] EWCA Civ 802 .... 5.114
NA v United Kingdom, app no 25904/07 [2008] ECHR 616, (2009)
  48 EHRR 15 .... 5.33, 5.47, 5.56, 5.61
Nada v Switzerland, app no 10593/08 [2012] ECHR 1691, (2013) 56 EHRR 18 .... 5.16, 5.175
Naletilić v Croatia, app no 51891/99 (2000) 29 EHRR CD219 .... 5.99
Narenji Haghighi v The Netherlands, app no 38165/07 (2009) 49 EHRR SE8 .... 5.145
Nasri v France, app no 19465/92 [1995] ECHR 24, (1996) 21 EHRR 458 .... 5.149, 5.174
Nationality Decrees Issued in Tunis and Morocco, Advisory Opinion,
  1923 PCIJ (ser B) No 4 .... 2.32, 2.34
Nazli v Stadt Nürnberg (C–340/97) [2000] ECR I–957 .... 6.44, 6.46, 6.70, 8.68
Nekvedavcius v Germany, app no 46165/99 (admissibility decision, 19 June 2003) 5.102
Niemietz v Germany, app no 13710/88 [1992] ECHR 80, (1992) 16 EHRR 97 .... 5.109
NK v France, app no 7974/11 (19 December 2013) 5.213
Nnamdi Onuekwere v SSHD (C–378/12) (16 January 2014) 6.32, 6.56
Nnyanzi v United Kingdom, app no 21878/06 [2008] ECHR 282 .... 5.144
Nolan and K v Russia, app no 2512/04 (2011) 53 EHRR 29 .... 5.189–5.190, 10.186
Norris v Government of the United States of America (No 2) [2010]
  UKSC 9, [2010] 2 AC 487 .... 8.86
Nottebaum (Liechtenstein v Guatemala) (1955) ICJ Reports 4 .... 2.6, 2.35–2.37, 2.45, 2.60
Noune v SSHD [2000] EWCA Civ 306, [2001] INLR 526 .... 4.38
NS v SSHD (C–411/10 and C–493/10) [2011] ECR I–13905 .... 6.18–6.19, 6.88
NSF v UK (10/2005, 30 May 2007, CEDAW/C/38/D/10/2005) 13.47
Nsona v The Netherlands, app no 23366/94 [1996] ECHR 62, (2001) 32 EHRR 170 .... 5.43
Nunez v Norway, app no 55597/09 [2011] ECHR 1047, (2014)
  58 EHRR 17 .... 5.140, 5.144, 5.147, 5.155,
                                                                                                                5.161, 5.170, 15.53, 16.57
Nylund v Finland, app no 27110/95 (admissibility decision, 29 June 1999) 5.102
Nystrom v Australia (1557/2007, 1 September 2011, CCPR/C/102/
  D/1557/2007) 3.25–3.28, 3.32
O and B v Minister voor Immigratie, Integratie en Asiel (C–456/12) [2014]
  3 WLR 799 .... 6.33, 10.111
O and S v Maahanmuuttovirasto; Maahanmuuttovirasto v L (C–356/11
  and C–357/11) [2013] WLR 1093 .... 6.33
O'Donoghue v United Kingdom, app no 34848/07 [2010] ECHR 2022, (2011)
  53 EHRR 1 .... 5.200

Table of Cases

Öcalan v Turkey, app no 46221/99 [2005] ECHR 282, (2005) 41 EHRR 45..............5.14, 5.21, 5.28
Öcalan v Turkey (No 2), app nos 24069/03, 197/04, 6201/06, 10464/07 [2014]
 ECHR 286..5.96
Odelola v SSHD [2009] UKHL 25, [2009] 1 WLR 1230...7.30, 7.32, 7.34
Odièvre v France, app no 42326/98 [2003] ECHR 86, (2004) 38 EHRR 43..........................15.22
OFNATS v Ahmed (C–45/12) (13 June 2013)...6.33
Ogundimu (Article 8—New Rules) Nigeria [2013] UKUT 60 (IAC)....................................8.101
OH (Serbia) v SSHD [2008] EWCA Civ 694, [2009] INLR 109..............................8.52, 8.81, 8.114
Oladehinde v IAT [1990] UKHL 11, [1991] 1 AC 254..8.67, 8.123
Olazabal (C–100/01) [2002] ECR I–10981..6.42, 6.50
Omkarananda and the Divine Light Zentrum v Switzerland, app no 8118/77
 DR 25 (19 March 1981)...5.189
Omojudi v United Kingdom, app no 1820/08 [2009] ECHR 1942, (2010)
 51 EHRR 10...5.111, 5.114, 5.148,
 5.152, 5.158
Omoregie v Norway app no 265/07 [2008] ECHR 761, [2009] Imm AR 170.....................5.144
Omoruyi v SSHD [2000] EWCA Civ 258, [2001] Imm AR 175.......................................4.31, 4.52
Onur v United Kingdom, app no 29696/07 [2009] ECHR 289................5.103, 5.155, 5.175, 8.130
Orfanopoulos and Olivieri v Verwaltungsgericht Stuttgart
 (C–482/01 and C–493/01) [2004] ECR I–5257..............................6.41, 6.45–6.46, 6.56, 10.105
Oršuš v Croatia, app no 15766/03 [2010] ECHR 337, (2011) 52 EHRR 7..........................5.219
Oshlakov v Russia, app no 56662/09 (3 April 2014)..5.55
Osman v Denmark, app no 38058/09 (14 June 2011)...5.182
Osman v United Kingdom, app no 23452/94 [1998] ECHR 101, (2000) 29 EHRR 245.......5.32
Othman (Abu Qatada) v United Kingdom, app no 8139/09 [2012]
 ECHR 56, (2012) 55 EHRR 1...5.63–5.65, 5.84–5.85,
 5.89–5.90, 5.93
Ouanes v SSHD [1998] 1 WLR 218...4.62
Oulane v Minister voor Vreemdelingenzaken en Integratie (C–215/03)
 [2005] ECR I–01215..6.35, 10.114
Ozhogina and Tarasova (Deception within para 320(7B)—Nannies)
 Russia [2011] UKUT 00197 (IAC)..10.48
Paladi v Moldova, app no 39806/05 [2009] ECHR 450, (2008) 47 EHRR 15..................15.52
Palanci v Switzerland, app no 53080/07 [2014] ECHR 311...5.138
Palmisani v INPS (C–261/95) [1997] ECR I–4025...14.9
Panjeheighalehei v Denmark, app no 11230/07 (13 October 2009).................................5.205
Pasquerias de Bermeo SA and Naviera Laida SA v Commission
 (C–258/90 to C–259/90) [1992] ECR I–2901..14.29
Patel v SSHD [1993] Imm AR 392...8.38
Patel v SSHD [2013] UKSC 72, [2014] 1 All ER 1157....................................5.113, 5.118, 9.30
Peerbocus v SSHD [1987] Imm AR 331...8.64
Pensionsversicherungsanstalt v Brey (C–140/12) [2014] 1 WLR 1080............................6.58
Perry v Latvia, app no 30273/03 (8 November 2007)..5.190
PI v Oberbürgermeistern der Stadt Remscheid (C–348/09) [2012] QB 799............6.40–6.42, 6.53
Piermont v France, app nos 15773/89; 15774/89 [1995] ECHR 14, (1995)
 20 EHRR 301...5.195
Pini v Romania, app nos 78028/01, 78030/01 [2004] ECHR 275, (2005)
 40 EHRR 13..3.49, 5.101, 5.107
PK (Congo) v SSHD [2013] EWCA Civ 1500..8.81
PO (Trafficked Women) Nigeria CG [2009] UKAIT 00046...4.23
Polat (C–349/06) [2007] ECR I–08167...10.103

Table of Cases

Polidario v Switzerland, app no 33169/10 [2013] ECHR 766 .... 5.147, 5.153, 5.177
Popov v France, app nos 38472/07 and 38474/07 (19 January 2012) 5.43
PR (Sri Lanka), SS (Bangladesh) and TC (Zimbabwe) [2011]
  EWCA Civ 988, [2012] 1 WLR 73 .... 16.26
PRC, Re Judicial Review [2013] CSOH 128 .... 11.42–11.43
Preston (C–78/98) [2000] ECR I–3201 .... 14.9
Pretty v United Kingdom, app no 2346/02 [2002] ECHR 427,
  (2002) EHRR 1 .... 5.110, 5.113, 5.131
PS (para 320(11) Discretion: Care Needed) India [2010] UKUT 440 (IAC) 10.60
PS (Prison Conditions; Military Service) Ukraine CG [2006] UKAIT 00016 .... 5.49
QD (Iraq) v SSHD [2009] EWCA Civ 620, [2011] 1 WLR 689 .... 6.78
R (A) v Chief Constable of Kent Constabulary [2013] EWCA Civ 1706,
  [2014] BMLR 22 .... 16.120
R (Adan) v SSHD [1999] EWCA Civ 1948, [1999] 3 WLR 1274 .... 4.36
R (AHK) v SSHD [2009] EWCA Civ 287, [2009] 1 WLR 2049 .... 11.18, 11.37
R (Alapati) v SSHD [2009] EWHC 3712 (Admin) 9.72
R (Ali) v SSHD [2009] EWHC 2126 (Admin) 9.98
R (Al-Tamimi) v SSHD [2007] EWHC 1962 (Admin) 11.42
R (Alvi) v SSHD [2012] UKSC 33, [2012] 1 WLR 2208 .... 7.23, 7.27, 8.19, 8.36, 9.20,
                                                                        10.17, 10.72–10.73, 11.15, 12.18
R (Amirifard) v SSHD [2013] EWHC 279 (Admin) 11.42
R (Amirthanathan) v SSHD [2002] EWHC 2595, [2003] All ER (D) 29 (May) 7.38
R (Anufrijeva) v SSHD [2003] UKHL 36, [2004] AC 604 .... 8.119, 9.82
R (Ashraf) v SSHD [2013] EWHC 4028 (Admin) 16.148
R (Atamewan) v SSHD [2013] EWHC 2727 (Admin), [2014] 1 WLR 1959 .... 2.22, 5.242
R (Awuku) v SSHD [2012] EWHC 3298 (Admin) 16.168
R (B) v Secretary of State for the Foreign and Commonwealth Office [2004]
  EWCA Civ 1344, [2005] QB 643 .... 5.14, 5.22
R (B and J) [2012] EWHC 3770 (Admin) 16.168
R (BA (Nigeria)) v SSHD [2009] UKSC 7, [2010] 1 AC 444 .... 8.131
R (Bagdanavicius) v SSHD [2005] UKHL 38, [2005] 2 AC 668 .... 5.59
R (Bahta) v SSHD [2011] EWCA Civ 895, [2011] 5 Costs LR 857 .... 16.142
R (Baiai) v SSHD [2008] UKHL 5, [2009] AC 287 .... 5.200
R (Bancoult) v Secretary of State for Foreign and Commonwealth Affairs
  [2008] UKHL 61, [2009] AC 453 .... 1.18, 7.6, 7.9, 7.25
R (Beoku-Betts) v SSHD [2008] UKHL 390, [2009] 1 AC 115 .... 5.151, 8.91
R (Boxall) v The Mayor and Burgesses of Waltham Forest LBC (2000) 4 CCLR 258 .... 16.142
R (C) v SSHD [2008] EWHC 2448 (Admin) 6.83
R (Cahonyo) v Entry Clearance Officer [2013] EWHC 365 (Admin) 10.67
R (Cart) v Upper Tribunal [2011] UKSC 28, [2011] 2 WLR 36 .... 16.9
R (Corner House Research) v Director of the Serious Fraud Office [2008]
  EWHC 714 (Admin) 16.117
R (Countryside Alliance) v (1) Attorney General and (2) Secretary of State for
  Environment, Food and Rural Affairs [2006] EWCA Civ 817, [2007] QB 305 .... 6.13
R (DA (Iran)) v SSHD [2014] EWCA Civ 654 .... 11.39, 11.42–11.43
R (Daley-Murdoch) v SSHD [2011] EWCA Civ 161, [2011] WLR D 56 .... 9.31, 16.54
R (Delena Wells) v Secretary of State for Transport, Local Government and
  the Regions (C–201/02) [2004] ECR 1–723 .... 14.28
R (E) v SSHD [2012] EWHC 1927 (Admin) 9.17
R (EM (Eritrea)) v SSHD [2012] EWCA Civ 1336, [2013] 1 WLR 576 .... 6.19
R (Erdogan) v SSHD [2004] EWCA Civ 1087, [2004] All ER (D) 421 (Jul) 8.121

Table of Cases

R (Essa) v Upper Tribunal (Immigration and Asylum Chamber) [2012]
EWCA Civ 1718, [2012] WLR (D) 393 ....6.13
R (European Roma Rights Centre) v Immigration Officer at Prague
Airport [2004] UKHL 55, [2005] 2 AC 1 ....2.41, 4.13, 5.14
R (Farrakhan) v SSHD [2002] EWCA Civ 606, [2002] 3 WLR 481 ....5.19, 10.83–10.85, 10.109
R (Fawad Ahmadi) v SSHD [2005] EWCA Civ 1721, [2005]
All ER (D) 169 (Dec) 5.107
R (Fazal-E-Haq) v SSHD [2009] EWHC 357 (Admin) 9.72
R (Forrester) v SSHD [2008] EWHC 2307 (Admin) 8.67, 11.32
R (George) v SSHD [2014] UKSC 28, [2014] 1 WLR 1831 ....8.44, 8.134
R (Hashemi) v The Upper Tribunal (IAC) [2013] EWHC 2316 (Admin) 9.85
R (Hiri) v SSHD [2014] EWHC 254 (Admin) 11.42–11.43
R (HM (Malawi)) v SSHD [2010] EWHC 1407 (Admin) 8.129
R (HS2 Action Alliance) v Secretary of State for Transport [2014]
UKSC 3, [2014] 1 WLR 324 ....7.5, 7.19
R (Iran) v SSHD [2005] EWCA Civ 982, [2005] Imm AR 535..16.21
R (Ivlev) v Entry Clearance Officer New York [2013] EWHC 1162 (Admin) 10.69
R (Jasbir Singh) v SSHD [2013] EWHC 2873 (Admin) 16.158–16.159
R (Joseph) v SSHD [2002] EWHC 758 (Admin) 7.38
R (JS (Sri Lanka)) v SSHD [2010] UKSC 15, [2011] 1 AC 184 ....4.74
R (K) v Camden and Islington Health Authority [2001]
EWCA Civ 240, [2002] QB 198 ....5.203
R (Kaur) v SSHD (C–192/99) [2001] ECR I–1237 ....6.24, 11.25
R (Kaziu, Bakijasi and Hysaj) v SSHD [2014] EWHC 832 (Admin) 12.31–12.34
R (Krasniqi and Kadria) v SSHD [2010] EWHC 3405 (Admin); [2011]
EWCA Civ 696 ....12.29–12.31, 12.34
R (Kumar) v SSHD (Acknowledgement of Service; Tribunal Arrangements)
(IJR) [2014] UKUT 104 (IAC)..16.159
R (Lim) v SSHD [2006] EWHC 3004 (Admin), [2006] All ER (D) 410 (Nov);
[2007] EWCA Civ 773, [2008] INLR 60 ....9.66–9.67, 9.99
R (Lord Carlile of Berriew QC and others) v SSHD [2013] EWCA Civ 199 ....10.85
R (Lumba) v SSHD [2011] UKSC 12, [2012] 1 AC 245..8.79, 11.33
R (Mahmood) v SSHD [2000] EWCA Civ 315, [2001] 1 WLR 840..5.120
R (Medhanye) v SSHD [2011] EWHC 3012 (Admin)...6.19
R (Messaoudi) v SSHD [2003] EWHC 1834 (Admin) 11.42, 11.43
R (Mirza) v SSHD [2011] EWCA Civ 159, [2011] Imm AR 484..9.30
R (MK (Iran)) v SSHD [2010] EWCA Civ 115, [2010] 1 WLR 2059 ....5.97, 5.207
R (Munir) v SSHD [2012] UKSC 32, [2012] 1 WLR 2192 .... 7.23, 8.19, 8.36, 9.20, 10.17,
10.72–10.73, 11.15, 12.18
R (Nagre) v SSHD [2013] EWHC 720 (Admin) 8.71, 8.96–8.97, 8.101–8.102, 8.107
R (Naik) v SSHD [2011] EWCA Civ 1546, [2012] Imm AR 381............................5.23, 5.194, 10.69,
10.87–10.88
R (Negassi) v SSHD [2013] EWCA Civ 151, [2013] 2 CMLR 45 ....14.35
R (Poyraz) v SSHD [2014] UKUT 151 (IAC)..8.74
R (Quila) v SSHD [2011] UKSC 45, [2012] 1 AC 621 ....5.179, 5.197
R (Ramalingum) v SSHD [2009] EWHC 453 (Admin) 11.19, 11.35, 11.38
R (Rashid) v SSHD [2004] EWHC 2465 (Admin), All ER (D) 316 (Oct);
[2005] EWCA Civ 744, [2005] INLR 550 ....7.37–7.38
R (Razgar) v SSHD [2003] EWCA Civ 840, [2003] Imm AR 529;
[2004] UKHL 27, [2004] 2 AC 368 .... 5.19, 5.24, 5.109, 5.115–5.117,
8.88–8.90, 8.120, 16.53, 16.166

R (RK (Nepal)) v SSHD [2009] EWCA Civ 359, [2009] All ER (D) 226 (Apr) 9.99
R (S) v SSHD [2007] EWCA Civ 546, [2007] INLR 450 .... 7.38
R (Saleh) v SSHD [2008] EWHC 3196 (Admin), [2008] All ER (D) 15 (Dec) 9.99
R (Sepet) v SSHD [2001] EWCA Civ 681; [2003] UKHL 15, [2003]
    1 WLR 856 .... 4.12, 4.19–4.21, 4.33–4.34,
                                                                                                              4.50, 4.63, 5.192
R (Shaw) v SSHD [2013] EWHC 42 (Admin) 9.67
R (Sivakumaran) v SSHD [1987] UKHL 1, [1988] AC 958 .... 4.37, 4.81
R (Sivakumaran) v SSHD [2003] UKHL 14, [2003] 1 WLR 840 .... 4.49–4.50
R (ST (Eritrea)) v SSHD [2012] UKSC 12, [2012] 2 AC 135 .... 3.35, 4.78
R (Stellato) v SSHD [2007] UKHL 5, [2007] 2 AC 70 .... 7.29
R (Thamby) v SSHD [2011] EWHC 1763 (Admin) 11.42–11.43
R (Thapa) v SSHD [2014] EWHC 659 (Admin) 9.59
R (Tientchu) v IAT [2000] EWCA Civ 385 .... 4.27
R (Ullah) v Special Adjudicator [2004] UKHL 26, [2004] 2 AC 323 .... 4.20, 5.19, 5.191
R (V) v AIT [2009] EWHC 1902 (Admin) 8.55
R (V) v SSHD [2013] EWHC 765 (Admin) 8.55
R (Vagh) v SSHD [2012] EWHC 1841 (Admin) 11.38
R (Yameen) v SSHD [2011] EWHC 2250 (Admin) 4.24
R (Yussuf) v SSHD [2005] EWHC 2847 .... 5.181
R (Zahid) v SSHD [2013] EWHC 4290 (Admin) 9.67
R (Zhang) v SSHD [2013] EWHC 891 (Admin), [2014] 2 All ER 560 .... 8.92
R (Zhou) v SSHD [2003] EWCA Civ 51, [2003] INLR 211 .... 9.67
R v Asfaw [2008] UKHL 31, [2008] 1 AC 1061 .... 2.20
R v Bhagwan [1972] AC 60 .... 1.16, 7.9
R v Bouchereau (30/77) [1977] ECR 1999 .... 6.46, 10.103, 10.105
R v Bow Street Metropolitan Stipendiary Magistrate ex p Pinochet
    Ugarte (No 3) [1999] UKHL 17, [2000] 1 AC 147 .... 2.4
R v CIO Gatwick Airport ex p Singh (Harjendar) [1987] Imm AR 346 .... 8.38
R v Governor of Pentonville Prison ex p Cheng [1973] AC 931 .... 4.64
R v Home Secretary ex p Venables [1998] AC 407 .... 8.79
R v IAT ex p Ahmud Khan [1982] Imm AR 134 .... 8.54
R v IAT ex p Cheema, Ullah and Kawol [1982] Imm AR 124 .... 8.54
R v IAT ex p Florent [1985] Imm AR 141 .... 8.52
R v IAT ex p Ghazi Khan [1983] Imm AR 32 .... 8.54
R v IAT ex p Sunsara [1995] Imm AR 15 .... 8.38
R v IAT ex p Walteros-Castenada (CO/2383/99, 27th June; unreported) 4.62
R v Jones [2006] UKHL 16, [2007] 1 AC 136 .... 2.18
R v Kluxen [2010] EWCA Crim 1081, [2011] 1 WLR 218 .... 8.21, 8.39, 8.52, 8.68, 8.70, 8.81
R v Lyons [2002] UKHL 44, [2003] 1 AC 976 .... 2.21
R v Minister of Defence ex p Smith [1996] QB 517 .... 16.121
R v Nasir Ali [2001] EWCA Crim 2874, [2002] 2 Cr App R (S) 32 .... 9.48
R v Port of London Authority ex p Kynoch Ltd [1919] 1 KB 176 .... 11.33
R v Secretary of State for Foreign and Commonwealth Affairs ex p
    World Development Movement Ltd [1995] 1 WLR 386 .... 16.117
R v Secretary of State for Transport ex p Factortame (No 2) [1990]
    UKHL 13, [1991] 1 AC 603 .... 7.15, 7.18
R v Secretary of State for Transport ex p Factortame (No 5) [1998]
    1 CMLR 1353; [1999] UKHL 44, [2000] 1 AC 524 .... 14.31, 14.34
R v Secretary of State for Transport ex p Presvac Engineering Ltd (1992)
    Admin LR 121 .... 16.131

Table of Cases

R v SSHD ex p Abdulnasir Savas (C–37/98) [2000] ECR I–02927..6.71
R v SSHD ex p Adan [1998] UKHL 15, [1999] 1 AC 293 .... 4.15, 4.32, 4.65
R v SSHD ex p Adan; R v SSHD ex p Aitseguer [2000] UKHL 67, [2001] 2 AC 477 ....2.12
R v SSHD ex p Amankwah [1994] Imm AR 240...8.73, 8.81
R v SSHD ex p Bagga [1991] 1 QB 485...8.42
R v SSHD ex p Brind [1991] 1 AC 696 ....2.21
R v SS for Transport ex p Factortame (No 2) [1991] AC 603..6.9
R v SSHD ex p Fayed [1996] EWCA Civ 946, [1997] 1 All ER 228 .... 11.18, 11.36, 11.40, 16.2
R v SSHD ex p Fayed (No 2) [2000] EWCA Civ 523, [2001]
  Imm AR 134 .... 11.18, 11.40, 11.42–11.43
R v SSHD ex p Figueiredo [1993] Imm AR 606...8.52
R v SSHD ex p Hastrup [1996] EWCA Civ 1333, [1996] Imm AR 616 ....8.73, 8.81
R v SSHD ex p Hosenball [1977] 1 WLR 766, [1977] 3 All ER 452 ....8.51, 8.67
R v SSHD ex p Malhi [1991] 1 QB 194..8.67
R v SSHD ex p Montana [2001] 1 WLR 552 .... 11.7, 11.12, 11.38, 12.9, 12.15
R v SSHD ex p Naheed Ejaz [1994] QB 496, [1994] 2 All ER 436..............................12.26–12.28
R v SSHD ex p Obi [1991] Imm AR 420 ....9.46
R v SSHD ex p Parvaz Akhtar [1981] QB 46 .... 12.26–12.28, 12.31
R v SSHD ex p Rukshanda Begum [1990] COD 107...16.135
R v SSHD ex p Sanusi [1999] INLR 198 ....8.64
R v SSHD ex p Simms [1999] UKHL 33, [2000] 2 AC 115...7.8–7.9
R v SSHD ex p Sultan Mahmood [1981] QB 59 .... 12.26–12.28, 12.31
R v SSHD ex p Thakrar [1974] QB 684 ....2.55, 10.2
R v SSHD ex p Urmaza [1996] COD 479 ....8.73
R v SSHD ex p Venables and Thompson [1997] UKHL 25, [1998] AC 407......................2.22, 11.33
R v SSHD ex p Vladic [1998] Imm AR 542 ....8.64–8.65, 8.121
R v SSHD ex p Yasin [1995] Imm AR 118 ....8.81
R v International Stock Exchange ex p Else [1993] QB 534 ....14.44
Radovanovic v Austria, app no 42703/98 (2005) 41 EHRR 6.................... 5.137, 5.139, 5.165–5.166,
                                                                                                          5.168–5.169
Raghbir Singh v SSHD [1996] Imm AR 507 ....8.51
Rahimi v Greece, app no 8687/08 (5 April 2011)..5.43, 5.46
Rahman v SSHD [2014] EWCA Civ 11, [2014] 1 WLR 3574...9.86
Rajan v New Zealand (820/1998, 7 August 2003, CCPR/C/78/D/820/1998)....................3.57
Randhawa v Minister for Immigration, Local Government and
  Ethnic Affairs 124 ALR 265 ....4.41
Rantsev v Cyprus and Russia, app no 25965/04 [2010] ECHR 22,
  (2010) 51 EHRR 1... 5.32, 5.80–5.81, 15.26
Raymond van der Elst v Office des Migrations Internationales (C–43/93)
  [1994] ECR I–3803 ....6.34, 6.62
RB (Algeria) v SSHD [2009] UKHL 10, [2010] 2 AC 110 ....4.29–4.30
RC v Sweden, app no 41827/07 [2010] ECHR 307 ....5.48
Revenko v SSHD [2000] EWCA Civ 500, [2001] QB 601..4.15, 4.65
Rewe-Zentralfinanz eG and Rewe-Zentral AG v Landwirtschaftskammer
  für das Saarland (33/76) [1976] ECR 1989 ....14.11
RG (Colombia) v SSHD [2006] EWCA Civ 57, [2006] Imm AR 297 ....4.19
Rhimou Chakroun v Minister van Buitenlandse Zaken (C–578/08) [2010] 3 CMLR 5...........5.183
Richards v SSHD [2013] EWCA Civ 244..8.116
RJ (India) v SSHD [2012] EWCA Civ 1865, [2012] All ER (D) 48 (Dec)...................................9.89
RM (Kwok On Tong: HC395 para 320) India [2006] UKAIT 00039 ....10.54
RN (Returnees) Zimbabwe CG [2008] UKAIT 00083...4.35

Table of Cases

Robinson v SSHD and IAT [1997] EWCA Civ 3090, [1998] QB 929..........................4.41–4.42, 4.44
Rodrigues da Silva and Hoogkamer v The Netherlands, app no 50435/99
 [2006] ECHR 86, (2007) 44 EHRR 34 ....5.147, 5.178
Rondel v Worsley [1969] 1 AC 181 ....16.168
Rottmann (European Citizenship) (C–135/08) [2010] QB 761......... 6.24–6.27, 11.14, 11.25, 12.17
Roux (C–363/89) [1991] ECR I–00273 ....6.63
Royer (48/75) [1976] ECR 497 ....6.63
RT (Zimbabwe) v SSHD [2012] UKSC 38, [2013] 1 AC 152 .... 4.20, 4.24, 4.59, 4.64, 5.191
RU (Bangladesh) v SSHD [2011] EWCA Civ 651, [2011] Imm AR 662 ....8.81, 8.114
RU v Greece, app no 2237/08 (7 June 2011)..5.73
Ruiz Zambrano (C–34/09) [2011] ECR I–1177 .... 6.6, 6.33, 6.60, 6.65, 8.33
Rustamov v Russia, app no 11209/10 [2012] ECHR 1372..5.55
Rutili v Ministre de l'intérieur (41/74) [1975] ECR 1219 ....6.41, 6.44
S & G (C–457/12) [2014] 3 WLR 843 ....6.33
SA (Political Activist—Internal Location) Pakistan [2011] UKUT 30...4.47
SA v Sweden, app no 66523/10 (27 June 2013) 5.62
Saadi v Italy, app no 37201/06 [2008] ECHR 179, (2009)
 49 EHRR 30.. 5.38, 5.40, 5.54, 5.63, 13.37
Saddam Hussein v Albania, app no 23276/04 (2006) 42 EHRR SE16 ....5.14
Said v The Netherlands, app no 2345/02 [2005] ECHR 461, (2006) 43 EHRR 14......................5.33
Salah Sheekh v The Netherlands, app no 1948/04 [2007] ECHR 36....................... 5.53, 5.60–5.61
Sale, Acting Commissioner, Immigration and Naturalisation
 Service v Haitian Centers Council Inc 509 US 155 (1993) 4.13
Sampanis v Greece, app no 32526/05 (5 June 2008) 5.219
Samsonnikov v Estonia, app no 52178/10 [2012] ECHR 1373 ....5.108, 5.139, 5.164
Sanade (British Children—Zambrano—Dereci) [2012] UKUT 00048 (IAC).................6.65, 8.129
Sandralingham v SSHD [1995] EWCA Civ 16, [1996] Imm AR 97 ....4.12
Sapkota v SSHD [2011] EWCA Civ 1320, [2012] Imm AR 254 ....9.30
Saribal v SSHD [2002] EWHC 1542 (Admin), [2002] INLR 596 ....8.74
Savchenkov v SSHD [1995] EWCA Civ 47, [1996] Imm AR 28 ....4.61
SB (PSG—Protection Regulations—Reg 6) Moldova CG [2008] UKAIT 00002......................4.61
Schal and Kopf v Austria, app no 30141/04 (22 November 2010) 5.104, 5.198
Scoppola v Italy (No 2), app no 10249/03 [2009] ECHR 1297...5.96
SE (Zimbabwe) v SSHD [2014] EWCA Civ 256, [2014] Imm AR 855 ....8.81, 8.117
Sejdovic v Italy, app no 56581/00 [2006] ECHR 181 ....5.90
Selmouni v France, app no 25803/94 [1999] ECHR 66 ....5.40–5.41
Şen v The Netherlands, app no 31465/96 (2003) 36 EHRR 7.................... 5.101, 5.131, 5.156, 5.181
Sepet v SSHD *see* R (Sepet) v SSHD
Sezen v The Netherlands, app no 50252/99 (2006) 43 EHRR 30 ....5.156, 5.158
SF v Sweden, app no 52077/10 (15 May 2012) 5.52
SH v Austria, app no 57813/00 [2011] ECHR 1878 ....5.201
SH v United Kingdom, app no 19956/06 [2010] ECHR 2254, (2012) 54 EHRR 4 ....5.41
SH (Palestinian Territories) v SSHD [2008] EWCA Civ 1150, [2009] Imm AR 306.............4.22
Shala v Switzerland, app no 52873/09 [2012] ECHR 1931...5.138
Shamayev v Georgia and Russia, app no 36378/02 [2005] ECHR 233 ....5.73, 5.210
Sharipov v Russia, app no 18414/10 (11 October 2011)...5.55
SHH v United Kingdom, app no 60367/10 [2013] ECHR 102, (2013) 57 EHRR 18 ....5.71–5.72
Siliadin v France, app no 73316/01 [2005] ECHR 545, (2006) 43 EHRR 16......................5.77–5.79
Singh v Belgium, app no 33210/11 (2 October 2012)..5.210
Singh v ECO New Delhi [2004] EWCA Civ 1075, [2005] QB 608 ....3.49–3.50, 5.101
Singh v IAT [1986] UKHL 11, [1986] 1 WLR 910 ....8.80–8.81

Table of Cases

Singh v SSHD [2014] EWCA Civ 932 ....8.81
Siragusa (C–206/13) (6 March 2014)...6.5
Sisojeva v Latvia, app no 60654/00 [2007] ECHR 16, (2007) 45 EHRR 33 ....5.123, 5.185
SK (Albania) v SSHD [2003] UKIAT 00023 ....4.61
SL (Vietnam) v SSHD [2010] EWCA Civ 225, [2010] INLR 651.................................8.73, 8.81
Slivenko v Latvia, app no 48321/99 [2003] ECHR 498, (2004)
  39 EHRR 24..5.112, 5.184, 5.226
Smirnova v Russia, app nos 46133/99; 48183/99 [2003] ECHR 397, (2004)
  39 EHRR 22...5.184
Smith v Ministry of Defence [2013] UKSC 41, [2014] 1 AC 52...5.14
Soering v United Kingdom, app no 14038/88 [1989] ECHR 14, (1989)
  11 EHRR 439.. 5.11, 5.20–5.21, 5.23, 5.33,
                                                                                                          5.35–5.36, 5.88
Soldatenko v Ukraine, app no 2440/07 [2008] ECHR 1142 ....5.55
SS (India) v SSHD [2010] EWCA Civ 388 ....8.73, 8.81
SS (Nigeria) v SSHD [2013] EWCA Civ 550, [2014] 1 WLR 998 ....8.116–8.117
SS Lotus (1927) PCIJ Rep Series A No 10..5.13
SS v United Kingdom, app no 12096/10 (admissibility decision, 24 January 2012) 5.62, 5.204
SSHD v AF [2009] UKHL 28, [2010] 2 AC 269..16.103
SSHD v AF and AE [2010] EWHC 42 (Admin)...5.203
SSHD v AH [2007] UKHL 49, [2008] AC 678..4.46
SSHD v Ahmadi [2013] EWCA Civ 512, [2013] 4 All ER 442 ....9.33, 9.84–9.85
SSHD v Al Jedda *see* Al Jedda v SSHD
SSHD v CS (C–304/14)..8.33
SSHD v Fornah; K v SSHD [2006] UKHL 46, [2007]
  1 AC 412 .... 4.23, 4.25, 4.50, 4.56–4.58, 4.62, 6.77
SSHD v Hacene Akrich (C–109/01) [2003] ECR I–09607...10.111
SSHD v HH (Iraq) [2009] EWCA Civ 727, [2010] INLR 78 ....8.73
SSHD v Hicks (David) [2006] EWCA Civ 400, [2006] INLR 203 ....1.11, 12.50
SSHD v Iftikhar Ahmed [1999] EWCA Civ 3003, [2000] INLR 1..................................4.26
SSHD v Information Commissioner and Cobain (Information rights:
  Freedom of information—absolute exemptions) [2014] UKUT 306 (AAC).......12.53
SSHD v MG (Portugal) (C–400/12) [2014] 1 WLR 2441 ....6.55
SSHD v Muhammad Sazzadur Rahman (C–83/11) [2013] QB 249 ....6.31
SSHD v Nasseri [2009] UKHL 23, [2010] 1 AC 1 ....16.120
SSHD v Pankina [2010] EWCA Civ 719, [2011] 1 QB 376.............................5.113, 7.21, 7.26, 7.31
SSHD v Rehman [2001] UKHL 47, [2003] AC 153 ....8.51, 10.83, 10.86
SSHD v SK (Sri Lanka) [2012] EWCA Civ 16 ....11.42–11.43
SSHD v TB (Jamaica) [2008] EWCA Civ 977, [2009] INLR 221 ....4.82
ST v France, app no 20649/92 (Commission decision, 8 February 1993) 5.235
Stec v United Kingdom, app nos 65731/01; 65900/01, [2006] ECHR 1162.................5.217
Stewart v Canada, Communication No 538/1993,
  UN Doc CCPR/C/58/D/538/1993 (1996) 3.21–3.22, 3.26, 3.52
Stoichkov v Bulgaria, app no 9808/02 (24 March 2005)...5.85, 5.90
Suarez v SSHD [2002] EWCA Civ 722, [2002] 1 WLR 2663 ....4.50, 4.64
Sufi and Elmi v United Kingdom, app nos 8319/07; 11449/07
  [2011] ECHR 1045 (2012) 54 EHRR 9 .... 5.41–5.42, 5.57–5.58, 5.60, 5.62, 5.69, 5.71
Sukhjinder Kaur v SSHD [1998] Imm AR 1...10.47
Sun Myung Moon (Human Rights, Entry Clearance, Proportionality)
  USA [2005] UKIAT 00112..5.194, 10.85
Sürek v Turkey app no 26682/95 (1999) 7 BHRC 339 ....10.86

xli

Table of Cases

Surinder Singh (C–370/90) [1992] ECR I–4265 .... 6.33, 6.67
Svazas v SSHD [2002] EWCA Civ 74, [2002] WLR 1891 .... 4.21, 4.45
SW v United Kingdom, app no 20166/92 [1995] ECHR 52 .... 5.96
Szabo v Sweden, app no 28578/03 (admissibility decision, 27 June 2006) 5.86, 5.98
T v Immigration Officer [1996] UKHL 8, [1996] AC 762 .... 4.75
Tahzeem Akhtar v IAT [1991] Imm AR 326 .... 12.42
Takush v Greece, app no 2853/09 (17 January 2012) 5.234
Tarakhel v Switzerland, app no 29217/12 .... 5.75
Tariq v SSHD [2011] UKSC 35, [2012] 1 AC 452 .... 16.103
Taylor v New Zealand Poultry Board [1984] 1 NZLR 394 .... 7.12–7.13
Teixeira v Lambeth LBC and SSHD (C–480/08) [2010] ECR I–1107 .... 6.33
Thirunavukkarasu v Minister of Employment and Immigration (1993)
    109 DLR (4th) 682 .... 4.41
Thlimmenos v Greece, app no 34369/97 [2000] ECHR 162, (2001)
    31 EHRR 15 .... 5.192, 5.216–5.217
Thoburn v Sunderland City Council [2002] EWHC 195 (Admin), [2003] QB 151 .... 7.5–7.6
Thomas v Baptiste (Trinidad and Tobago) [1999] UKPC 13, [2000] 2 AC 1 .... 2.19
Thomas v Gonzales 409 F 3d 1177 (9th Cir, 2005) 4.50
TI v United Kingdom, app no 43844/98 [2000] ECHR 705 .... 5.73
TM and CM v Republic of Moldova, app no 26608/11 .... 5.44
Toala v New Zealand, Communication No 675/1995,
    UN Doc CCPR/C/70/D/675/1995 (2000) 3.18, 3.20
Tomasz Ziolkowski and Barbara Szeja v Land Berlin
    (C–424/10 and C–435/10) [2011] ECR I–14035 .... 6.61
Tomic v United Kingdom, app no 17837/03 (admissibility decision, 14 October 2003) 5.84
Toumi v Italy, app no 25716/09 (5 April 2011) 5.65
Treebhowan (Mauritius) v SSHD; Hayat (Pakistan) v SSHD [2012] EWCA Civ 1054 .... 8.92
Trojani v Centre public d'aide social de Bruxelles (C–456/02) [2004] ECR I–07573 .... 6.58
Tuquabo-Tekle v The Netherlands, app no 60665/00 [2005]
    ECHR 803, [2006] Fam Law 267 .... 5.131, 5.181
Udeh v Switzerland, app no 12020/09 [2013] ECHR 328 .... 5.153–5.154, 5.162
Udoh v SSHD [1972] Imm AR 89 .... 8.129
UE (Nigeria) [2010] EWCA Civ 975, [2012] 1 WLR 127 .... 5.111, 8.95
Ülke v Turkey, app no 39437/98 (2009) 48 EHRR 48 .... 5.192
Üner v The Netherlands, app no 46410/99 [2006] ECHR 873, (2007)
    45 EHRR 14 .... 5.111, 5.114, 5.131–5.133,
                                                                                                    5.135–5.136, 5.143, 5.150, 5.152,
                                                                                                    5.154, 5.156, 5.159, 5.163–5.164,
                                                                                                    5.167–5.169, 5.171, 8.87
Useinov v The Netherlands, app no 61292/00 (admissibility decision, 11 April 2006) 5.154
V v Minister for Immigration and Multicultural Affairs [1999] FCA 428 .... 4.64
Vallianatos v Greece, app nos 29381/09; 32684/09 (7 November 2013) 5.203
Van der Mussele v Belgium, app no 8919/80 [1983] ECHR 13, (1984) 6 EHRR 163 .... 5.79
Van Duyn v Home Office (No 2) (41/74) [1974] ECR 1337 .... 2.56, 6.44, 6.50, 10.2, 10.102
Van Gend en Loos v Netherlandse Administratie der Berlastingen (26/62)
    [1963] ECR 1 .... 6.9
VD (Albania) v SSHD [2004] UKIAT 00115 .... 4.61
VEBIC (C–439/08) [2011] 4 CMLR 12 .... 14.14
VF v France, app no 7196/10 (admissibility decision, 29 November 2011) 5.22, 5.81–5.82
Vilvarajah v United Kingdom, app nos 13163/87; 13164/87; 13165/87
    [1991] ECHR 47, (1991) 14 EHRR 248 .... 5.20, 5.36, 5.53

xlii

Table of Cases

Vinter v United Kingdom, app nos 66069/09; 130/10; 3896/10 [2013]
 ECHR 645, (2012) 55 EHRR 34 ....5.51
VL v Switzerland, Communication No 262/2005, UN Doc CAT/C/37/D/262/2005 (2007) 3.80
VM (FGM, Risks, Mungiki, Kikuyu/Gikuyu) Kenya CG [2008] UKAIT 00049 ....4.47
VMRB v Canada (236/1987, 18 July 1988, CCPR/C/33/D/236/1987) 3.44
VNIM v Canada, Communication No 119/1998, UN Doc CAT/C/29/D/119/1998 (2002) 3.76
Voulfovitch v Sweden, app no 19373/92 (Commission decision, 13 January 1993) 5.235
VW (Uganda) [2009] EWCA Civ 5, [2009] INLR 295 ....5.120
Warsame v Canada (1959/2010, 1 September 2011,
 CCPR/C/102/D/1959/2010) 3.25, 3.27–3.28, 3.32
Willcox and Hurford v United Kingdom, app nos 43759/10,
 43771/12 [2013] ECHR 292 ....5.85, 5.91
WM v Denmark, app no 17392/90 DR 73 ....5.14, 5.84
Women on Waves and others v Portugal, app no 31276/05 (3 February 2009) 5.196, 10.86
X v Belgium and the Netherlands (1975) 7 D&R 75 ....3.49
X v Federal Republic of Germany, app no 1611/62
 (Commission decision, 25 September 1965) 5.14
X v France (1982) 31 D&R 241 ....3.49
X v Germany, app no 7175/75; DR 6, 138 (admissibility decision, 12 July 1976) 5.199
X v United Kingdom, app no 7547/76 (Commission decision, 15 December 1977) 5.14
X and Y v The Netherlands, app no 7229/75 (Commission decision, 15 December 1977) 5.201
X and Y v Switzerland, app nos 7289/75; 7349/76 DR 9 ....5.14
X, Y and Z v United Kingdom (1997) 24 EHRR 143 ....3.49
Xhavara v Italy and Albania, app no 39473/98 (admissibility decision, 11 January 2001) 5.13
YB (Eritrea) v SSHD [2008] EWCA Civ 360 ....4.26
Yefimova v Russia, app no 39786/09 (19 February 2013) 5.55
Yildiz v Austria, app no 37295/97 (2003) 36 EHRR 32 ....5.137
Yilmaz v Germany, app no 52853/99, 17 April 2003 ....5.139, 5.166, 5.168–5.169
Yunying Jia v Migrationsverket (C–1/05) [2007] QB 545 ....10.111
Z and T v United Kingdom, app no 27034/05 (admissibility decision,
 28 February 2006) 5.191
ZB (Pakistan) v SSHD [2009] EWCA Civ 834, [2010] INLR 195 ....5.108
ZH (Tanzania) v SSHD [2011] UKSC 4, [2011] 2 AC 166 ....8.81, 8.94, 9.95
Zhu and Chen (C–200/02) [2004] ECR I–9925 ....6.33, 6.64, 6.67
ZT (Kosovo) v SSHD [2009] UKHL 6, [2009] 1 WLR 348 ....16.164, 16.167
ZZ (France) v SSHD (C–300/11) [2013] QB 1136 ....14.21–14.22, 16.103
ZZ (France) v SSHD [2014] EWCA Civ 7, [2014] QB 820 ....14.23, 16.103

Table of Legislation

National

United Kingdom

Statutes

Act of Union 1707 .... 1.3, 7.5, 7.11–7.12
Aliens Act 1793 .... 1.5
Aliens Act 1905 .... 1.6–1.7
Aliens Registration Act 1826 .... 1.5
Aliens Removal Act 1848 .... 1.5
Aliens Restriction Act 1914 .... 1.7
Asylum and Immigration Appeals Act 1993
    s 2 .... 2.20, 8.76
Asylum and Immigration (Treatment of Claimants etc) Act 2004
    s 8 .... 8.107, 9.102
    Sched 3 para 5(3)(a) 16.56
        para 10(3) 16.56
        para 15(3) 16.56
        para 19(b) 16.56
Anti-Terrorism, Crime and Security Act 2001 .... 16.75
    Pt 4 .... 16.79
Bill of Rights 1689 .... 7.5, 7.11
Borders, Citizenship and Immigration Act 2009 .... 11.20
    Pt 2 .... 7.43, 11.20
    s 54A(4) 9.94
    s 55 .... 9.47, 9.95
British Nationality Act 1948 .... 1.13, 13.48
    Pt II 1.13
    s 20 .... 1.14
British Nationality Act 1981 .... 1.19–1.21, 1.24, 7.39–7.43, 8.38,
                                        11.16–11.18, 11.22–11.23, 11.27–11.29,
                                        11.31, 11.35–11.36, 11.38, 13.48
    Pt 1 .... 11.17, 11.22
    s 1 .... 1.21, 7.40, 11.17, 11.28
    s 2 .... 1.21, 7.40, 11.17, 11.28
    s 3 .... 7.40, 11.28
        (1) 7.42, 11.29, 11.35, 11.38
    ss 3–5 .... 1.21, 7.40, 11.17
    s 4(2) 7.42
        (4) 7.42
    s 4A 7.42, 11.29
    s 4B 11.38

s 6 .... 1.21, 7.40, 11.17–11.18, 11.42
   (1) 7.42, 11.18, 11.28–11.29, 11.39
   (2) 7.42, 11.28–11.29
s 10 .... 7.40
s 12 .... 7.42, 11.29
s 13 .... 7.42, 11.29
   (1) 7.42, 11.29
   (3) 7.42, 11.29
s 40 .... 1.22, 12.2, 12.27, 12.67, 16.80
   (1) 12.19
   (2) 6.27, 12.20, 12.49–12.50, 12.53–12.54, 12.57, 12.60, 12.68–12.69
   (2)–(3) 12.36
   (3) 12.36, 12.38, 12.40, 12.42–12.43, 12.48
   (4) 12.36, 12.56–12.58, 12.60–12.61
   (4A) 12.21, 12.36, 12.61–12.62, 12.66
     (b) 12.61
     (c) 12.61–12.62
   (5) 12.19, 12.67, 16.33
     (b) 12.27
   (6) 12.19
s 40A 16.33, 16.80
   (1) 12.67
   (2) 12.67
   (3) 12.67
s 40B 12.21
   (5) 12.21
   (6) 12.21
s 41A 11.29, 11.39
s 44(1) 11.35
   (2) 11.36
Sched 1 .... 7.42, 11.17, 11.29, 11.39, 11.42
   para 1 .... 7.42, 11.29
   para 2 .... 11.28–11.29
Sched 2 .... 11.11
British Nationality and Status of Aliens Act 1914
   s 1 .... 1.8
   s 2 .... 1.8
   s 7(1) 1.9–1.10
     (2) 1.10
British Nationality and Status of Aliens Act 1918 .... 1.9–1.11, 1.14
   s 3 .... 1.11
British Overseas Territories Act 2002
   s 3 .... 1.21, 7.40
     (2) 1.21
Children Act 1989
   s 17 .... 9.31
Claim of Right Act 1689 .... 7.11
Commonwealth Immigrants Act 1962 .... 1.15
   s 2 .... 1.16
   s 3 .... 1.16
Commonwealth Immigrants Act 1968 .... 1.15

Table of Legislation

Constitutional Reform Act 2005
  s 1(23) 7.14
  Sched 2 Pt 1 ....16.146
County Courts Act 1984
  s 38(3) 16.128
Crime and Courts Act 2013
  s 22 ....16.146
Criminal Justice Act 2003
  s 22 ....10.52
Criminal Procedure (Insanity) Act 1964
  s 5 ....8.28
European Communities Act 1972 ....2.20, 7.5, 7.18
  s 2 ....6.2
    (1) 1.23, 7.16
    (4) 7.16
Human Rights Act 1998 ....2.21, 5.7, 5.29, 5.203, 5.231, 6.13, 7.5, 7.115,
                             8.47, 8.76, 8.81, 8.84, 8.107, 8.120, 9.95, 9.102,
                             14.14, 15.6, 16.120–16.121, 16.125–16.127
  s 3(1) 7.16
  s 4 ....7.20, 15.41, 16.147
  s 6 ....9.37, 16.43, 16.47, 16.52, 16.57
  s 7(1) 16.125
    (7) 16.125
  s 8(1) 16.126
    (2) 16.126
Hunting Act 2004 ....7.14
Immigration Act 1971 ....1.17, 1.19–1.21, 1.24, 2.20, 6.71, 7.22–7.29,
                                7.39, 8.1, 8.24, 9.21, 11.38, 16.79
  s 1 ....10.19, 10.73
    (1) 1.17, 7.25
    (3) 9.54
    (4) 7.22
    (9) 9.54
  s 2 ....1.17, 8.38, 10.1
    (1) 11.16, 12.1, 12.49
      (a) 1.20, 11.16
      (b) 1.20, 11.16, 12.2, 12.20
  s 2A 12.2, 12.20, 12.36, 12.50, 12.69, 16.35
  s 3 ....8.22, 8.36, 8.41, 8.44, 10.72–10.73
    (1) 1.21, 7.41, 10.18
      (a) 8.56, 8.100, 9.46
      (c) 9.65
    (2) 7.22–7.24, 7.26, 7.29, 7.32, 10.18, 10.73, 11.15, 12.18
    (5) 8.41, 8.52, 8.63, 16.31
      (a) 8.21, 8.37, 8.39–8.40, 8.43, 8.45–8.46,
                                      8.48, 8.50–8.56, 8.60–8.61, 8.67,
                                      8.70, 8.81, 8.111, 8.113,
                                      8.117, 9.37, 9.71, 11.32, 16.57
      (b) 8.37, 8.39, 8.69, 10.33
    (5)–(6) 8.20, 8.37, 8.41, 8.56, 12.35
    (6) 8.37, 8.39, 8.63, 8.70–8.82, 16.57

xlvii

(8)	8.42
(9)	9.46
s 3A(3)	9.60
s 3C	9.32, 9.61, 16.54, 16.84
(3)	9.61
s 3D	9.32, 16.84
s 4	9.81
s 5	8.22, 8.36, 8.40
(1)	8.22, 8.27, 8.31, 8.41, 8.44, 8.50, 8.56–8.108–8.109, 8.111, 8.113, 8.117–8.120, 8.133–8.134, 9.53, 10.34, 11.32, 16.35
(a)	8.52, 8.70, 8.124
(1)–(2)	12.35
(2)	8.44, 8.118, 8.124, 8.131, 16.35
(3)	8.22, 8.69
(3)–(4)	8.133, 10.34
(4)	8.22, 8.69
s 6	16.30
(1)	8.70
(2)	8.64
(6)	8.121
s 7	8.42, 8.49, 8.58
(2)	8.42
(5)	8.42
s 8	8.49, 8.58, 9.64
(1)	8.42, 9.28
(2)	8.42
(3)–(3A)	8.42
(4)	8.42
s 9(4)(b)	9.54–9.55
s 11(1)	3.35, 9.42
s 15	8.67
s 24(1)(a)	9.50
(b)	9.70
s 24A	9.48–9.49, 9.60, 9.71
s 26(1)(c)	9.47, 9.49
(d)	9.49
s 32(2)	8.123
s 33	9.47
(1)	9.22, 9.28, 9.41–9.43
s 40(2)	12.36
Sched 2	3.35, 8.33, 9.1, 9.22, 9.25–9.28, 9.39–9.59, 9.81, 9.95, 10.113
para 1(1)	8.23
(3)	7.32, 7.36, 10.72–10.73
para 8	9.26, 9.40
(1)(c)	9.26
(2)	9.40
paras 8–10	16.35
paras 8–15	9.25–9.28

para 9(1)	9.26
(2)	9.26
para 10	9.40
para 10A	16.35
para 12(2)	16.35
paras 12–15	9.28
Sched 3 para 2(1)–(3)	8.132
Sched 4 para 4	9.55
Sched 23 para 8	10.115
para 10	10.115
para 10A	10.115
para 11	10.115
paras 16–18	10.115
paras 21–24	10.115
Immigration Act 2014	7.43, 8.50, 8.53, 8.56, 8.120, 8.131, 9.1, 9.23, 9.96, 12.56, 16.5, 16.29, 16.45–16.69, 16.80, 16.83, 16.85
s 1	9.29, 9.80, 9.87
(1)	9.90
(2)	9.90
(3)	9.90
(4)	9.90
(5)	9.90
(6)	9.83
s 2	9.93
s 3	9.94
s 15	7.31, 12.69, 16.46–16.47, 16.49
(2)	12.69
(5)	16.55
s 16	16.68
s 17	16.56–16.57
(1)	16.57
(3)	16.57
s 18	16.86
s 66	12.21
(2)	12.21
(3)	12.21
Sched 9 para 53	16.47
Immigration and Asylum Act 1999	
s 9	9.61
s 10	9.1, 9.23, 9.29–9.31, 9.59–9.83, 9.95, 16.30
(1)	9.29, 9.80
(a)	9.37, 16.35
(b)	9.87, 16.35
(ba)	9.73
(c)	9.87, 9.89, 16.35
(2)–(6)	9.81
(7)–(9)	9.81
(10)	9.81
s 60(9)	10.83
s 108	10.62

Table of Legislation

Immigration, Asylum and Nationality Act 2006	12.55
s 7	16.32, 16.42
s 12	16.47
s 47	9.1, 9.23, 9.30, 9.32–9.34, 9.79, 9.84–9.86, 9.95, 9.97, 16.35
(1)	9.34
(2)	9.34
s 56(1)	12.50
Legal Aid, Sentencing and Punishment of Offenders Act 2012	
s 134	10.52
(3G)	10.53
s 140	8.53, 8.81
Limitation Act 1980	
s 2	14.34
Magna Carta 1215	7.5–7.6
National Assistance Act 1948	
s 21	9.31
Nationality, Immigration and Asylum Act 2002	3.42, 9.57, 13.48, 16.3–16.5, 16.11, 16.29–16.44, 16.46–16.58, 16.69–16.74, 16.80–16.90
Pt 5	8.50, 8.56, 8.65, 8.105–8.108, 8.112, 12.67, 16.3
Pt 5A	8.107, 8.120, 9.100–9.102
s 4	12.50
s 5(3)	16.90
s 10	16.35
s 72	4.75, 4.82, 6.84
(4)(a)	8.46
s 76	16.35
(3)	9.73, 9.79
s 78A	9.93
(4)(a)	9.93
s 82	10.91, 12.69, 16.13, 16.18, 16.29, 16.35–16.36, 16.39, 16.43, 16.46, 16.69, 16.80, 16.83
(1)	9.96, 10.81, 10.90, 16.55, 16.71
(a)	16.47, 16.52, 16.56
(b)	16.47, 16.52, 16.56
(c)	16.47, 16.52, 16.56
(2)	12.69, 16.39
(a)	16.35, 16.48
(b)	16.35, 16.48
(c)	16.35, 16.48
(d)	16.35
(e)	9.79, 9.98, 16.35
(f)	9.79, 16.35
(g)	16.35
(h)	9.26, 16.35
(ha)	9.86, 16.35
(i)	16.35
(ia)	16.35

l

Table of Legislation

(ib)	16.35
(j)	8.66, 8.120, 16.31, 16.35
(j)–(k)	8.118
(k)	8.131, 16.35
(3A)	8.118, 8.120
s 83	16.38–16.39, 16.44, 16.49, 16.83
(2)	16.80
(3)	16.44
(4)	16.44
s 83A	16.38, 16.40, 16.44, 16.49, 16.80, 16.83
s 84	8.120, 8.131, 16.29, 16.43, 16.55, 16.69, 16.83
(1)	7.30
(a)	16.43, 16.52
(b)	16.43, 16.52
(c)	16.43
(d)	16.43
(e)	8.120, 16.43
(f)	16.43
(g)	16.43
s 85	16.55
(6)	16.55
s 86(3)(a)	7.31
s 88	16.36
(2)(a)	16.36
(b)	16.36
(ba)	16.36
(c)	16.36
(d)	16.36
(d)	10.32
(4)	16.37
s 88A(1)	16.36
s 91	16.36
s 92	16.56
(1)	16.32
(2)	16.32
(a)	16.56
(b)	16.56
(3)(a)	16.56
(b)	16.56
(4)	16.47, 16.56
(a)	16.32
(b)	16.32
ss 92–98	16.32
s 94	8.129, 8.131, 16.32, 16.54, 16.164
(1)	16.56
(3)	16.164
(4)	16.164
(7)	16.56
s 94A	16.32

s 94B 8.120, 16.57
   (1) 16.57
   (2) 16.57
   (3) 16.57
s 96 .... 8.131, 16.32, 16.54
   (2) 16.73
s 97 .... 16.80, 16.83, 16.86
   (3) 16.85
   (4) 16.82
s 97A 16.32, 16.85
   (1) 16.86
   (3) 16.42
s 113 .... 16.47
s 117B 8.106, 9.101
   (1) 8.106
s 117C 8.106
   (1) 8.106
   (6) 8.108
s 120 .... 9.30, 16.55, 16.72–16.74
   (2)(c) 16.72
Naturalisation Act 1844 .... 1.3
Race Relations Act 1976
  s 1(1)(a) 11.35
  s 3(1) 11.19
  s 19(b) 16.43
  s 19B 11.35
   (1) 11.19
  s 19D(1) 11.35
Rehabilitation of Offenders Act 1974 .... 8.53, 8.81, 10.76
  s 4 .... 10.35
Scotland Act 1998 .... 7.15
Senior Courts Act 1981
  s 31(3) 16.116
Social Security Administration Act 1992
  s 105 .... 10.62
Special Immigration Appeals Commission Act 1997 .... 16.75
  s 1(3) 16.75
  s 2(1) 16.83
   (2)(e) 16.83
  s 2B 12.67, 16.3
  s 2E 16.86
   (3) 16.86
  s 5 .... 16.78
   (3) 16.90–16.91
  s 6 .... 16.91, 16.93
   (4) 16.95
  s 7 .... 16.112
  s 87 .... 12.67, 16.3
Tribunals, Courts and Enforcement Act 2007
  s 3 .... 16.6
  s 9 .... 16.22

s 11	16.21
(1)	16.21
s 18(6)	16.146
UK Borders Act 2007	6.71, 8.1, 8.21, 8.39–8.40, 8.81, 8.124, 12.35
Pt 5	8.35
s 32	8.24, 8.28, 8.30, 8.50, 8.62–8.66, 8.72, 8.109–8.120, 16.31
(1)	8.24, 8.31, 8.46, 8.48, 8.61, 8.100
(1)–(3)	8.40, 8.57, 8.109
(2)	8.46, 8.100
(4)	8.40, 8.43, 8.46–8.49, 8.58, 8.113–8.114, 8.116–8.117, 16.57
(5)	8.24–8.27, 8.57, 8.59–8.62, 8.64, 8.109, 8.113, 8.117–8.118, 8.120, 8.122, 16.31
(7)	8.48, 8.59
ss 32–33	8.46–8.49, 8.57–8.61
s 33	8.25, 8.30, 8.40, 8.48, 8.60–8.61, 8.109, 8.111
(1)	8.47, 8.59, 8.109, 8.117
(a)	8.61
(b)	8.49, 8.58
(2)–(6A)	8.47, 8.59
(7)	8.61, 8.116–8.117
(a)	8.60–8.61
(b)	8.40, 8.47, 8.61
s 34(1)	8.26, 8.57
(1)–(2)	8.110
(2)	8.26, 8.57, 8.122
(3)	8.26, 8.122
(4)	8.27
s 37	8.42
s 38(1)	8.28
(2)	8.29
(3)	8.28
(4)	8.30
s 56A	8.53, 8.55, 8.81
s 59	8.31
Sched 3	8.42

Secondary Legislation

Asylum and Immigration Tribunal (Fast Track Procedure) Rules 2005, SI 2005/506	16.10, 16.17–16.20
r 8(1)	16.18
(2)	16.18
r 10	16.18
r 14(2)(a)	16.20
r 17(2)(a)	16.20
r 18	16.20
r 28	16.19
(a)	16.19
(b)	16.19
(c)	16.19
(d)	16.19

r 30 .... 16.19
   (1)(a) 16.19
      (b) 16.19
      (c) 16.19
Asylum and Immigration Tribunal (Procedure) Rules 2005,
SI 2005/230 .... 16.10–16.16, 16.19
r 6(1) 16.11–16.12
r 7(1)(a) 16.11
      (b) 16.11
   (2)(a)(i) 16.12
      (ii) 16.12
r 10(5) 16.14
r 24(2) 16.16
   (3) 16.16
r 25(2) 16.16
r 55(5)(a) 16.13
      (b) 16.13
      (c) 16.13
r 57(1)(a) 16.13
      (b) 16.16
Channel Tunnel (International Arrangements) Order 1993, SI 1993/1813
Sched 4 .... 9.27
Civil Procedure Rules 1998, SI 1998/3132
r 3.1(2)(a) 16.132
PD 16 para 15 .... 16.130
Pt 23 .... 16.124
r 44.2 .... 16.140
r 44.3(4)–(5) 16.141
Pt 52 .... 16.112
r 52.13 .... 16.9
Pt 54 .... 16.116
r 54.1(2)(f) 16.118
r 54.5(1) 16.131
   (2) 16.132
r 54.6 .... 16.130
   (2) 16.130
r 54.7 .... 16.133
r 54.8(2)(a) 16.134
      (b) 16.134
r 54.9(1) 16.134
r 54.12(3) 16.136
   (7) 16.136
r 54.14 .... 16.137
r 54.17 .... 16.118
PD 54A 16.130
   para 5.9 .... 16.130
   para 8.5 .... 16.136
   para 15.1 .... 16.138
   para 15.2 .... 16.138
   para 17 .... 16.139
Pt 68 .... 14.47

Table of Legislation

First-tier Tribunal and Upper Tribunal (Chambers) (Amendment No 2) Order 2013,
　SI 2013/2068 ....16.149
Human Rights Act 1998 (Amendment) Order 2004, SI 2004/1574 ....5.29
Immigration Act 2014 (Commencement No 1, Transitory and Saving
　Provisions) Order 2014, SI 2014/1820 .... 8.105, 9.100, 12.21, 16.57
Immigration, Asylum and Nationality Act 2006 (Commencement No 8 and
　Transitional and Saving Provisions) Order 2008, SI 2008/310 ....16.36
Immigration (European Economic Area) Regulations 2006,
　SI 2006/1003 .... 6.67–6.68, 8.32–8.33, 8.70,
　　　　　　　　　　　　　　　　　　　　　　　　　　　　9.35–9.38, 10.21, 10.97,
　　　　　　　　　　　　　　　　　　　　　　　　　　　　16.50, 16.69–16.71
　Pt 4 ....9.24, 10.21
　reg 2 ....8.33, 10.114, 16.70
　reg 8 ....10.106
　reg 11 ....9.46
　reg 13 ....10.111
　reg 15 ....8.68
　reg 15A 6.67
　reg 15B 8.32
　reg 19 .... 6.67, 8.32, 8.77, 10.21, 10.106, 10.110
　　(1A) 8.33
　　(3) 9.35–9.36
　　　(a) 9.36, 9.95
　　　(b) 8.33, 8.68, 9.37
　　　(c) 9.95
　　(4) 9.36
　　(5) 8.68, 9.36
　　(6) 8.77
　reg 20A 8.33, 16.70
　reg 21 .... 8.33, 8.68, 8.77, 9.35–9.36,
　　　　　　　　　　　　　　　　　　　　　　　　　　　　　　　　　10.107, 10.109
　　(2) 8.33, 8.68
　　(3) 8.33, 8.68
　　(4) 8.68
　　(5) 10.101, 10.105
　　(7) 8.33
　reg 21A 8.33
　reg 21B 8.33, 10.110–10.111
　　(2) 9.35
　regs 22–24 ....8.33
　reg 24 ....10.113
　　(2)–(4) 9.37
　　(3) 8.33
　　(5) 9.37
　　(6) 9.37
　reg 24 ....10.112
　reg 24AA 9.37
　regs 25–30 ....16.3
　reg 26 ....10.114, 16.69
　　(5) 16.71
　reg 27(1)(aa) 10.114

lv

reg 28	16.80
(5)	16.82
reg 29AA	10.115
(3)	10.115
(6)	10.115

Immigration (Control of Entry through Republic of Ireland) Order 1972,
SI 1972/1610 ....9.54
- art 3(1)(a) 9.54
  - (b)(i) 9.54
    - (ii) 9.54
    - (iii) 9.54
    - (iv) 9.54

Immigration (Exemption from Control) Order 1972, SI 1972/1613 ....8.42

Immigration (Leave to Enter or Remain) Order 2000, SI 2000/1161 ....9.60
- art 8(3) 9.51
- art 9 ....9.51

Immigration (Notices) Regulations 2003, SI 2003/658
- reg 4 ....8.118
- reg 5 ....8.118
  - (1)(a) 9.97
- reg 7(2)–(3) 8.119

Special Immigration Appeals Commission (Procedure) Rules 2003,
SI 2003/103 ....16.78, 16.91–16.112
- r 2 ....16.99
- r 4 ....16.98
  - (3) 16.95
- r 7 ....16.104
- r 8 ....16.104
- r 9 ....16.105
- r 9A 16.106
- r 10 ....16.99
- r 10A(3) 16.99
- r 27 ....16.112
- r 32 ....16.95
- r 34 ....16.93
- r 35 ....16.94
- r 36(3) 16.97
  - (4) 16.96
  - (5) 16.96
- r 37 ....16.91, 16.100
  - (2) 16.92
- r 38 ....16.100
  - (4)(c) 16.100
- r 40 ....16.106
- r 47(3) 16.111

Supreme Court Rules 2009, SI 2009/1603 ....14.47
- r 42 ....14.47
- PD 11 ....14.47

Transfer of Functions of the Asylum and Immigration Tribunal Order 2010,
SI 2010/21 ....16.10

Tribunal Procedure (Amendment No 4) Rules 2013, SI 2013/2067 ....16.149

Table of Legislation

Tribunal Procedure (Upper Tribunal) Rules 2008, SI 2008/2698 .... 16.10, 16.23–16.24
   r 5(3)(a) 16.23
   r 21(2) 16.23
      (3)(aa)(i) 16.23
      (3A)(a) 16.23
      (6)(a) 16.23
   rr 27–33A 16.155
   r 28A(2)(b) 16.151
   r 30 .... 16.155
      (1)(a) 16.156
        (b) 16.156
      (3)(a) 16.157
      (4) 16.157
      (4A) 16.157
      (5) 16.157
UK Borders Act 2007 (Commencement No 3 and Transitional Provisions)
Order 2008, SI 2008/1818 .... 8.31
   para 2 .... 8.31
Upper Tribunal (Immigration and Asylum) (Judicial Review)
(England and Wales) Fees (Amendment) Order 2013, SI 2013/2069 .... 16.149

Germany
Reich Citizenship Law of 15 September 1935
   Art 2(1) 4.8

Trinidad and Tobago
Constitution
   s 4(a) 2.19

United States
Constitution
   Fourteenth Amendment 7.4, 7.8

European Union

Charters, Treaties
Charter of Fundamental Rights of the European Union 2000 .... 6.2, 6.5, 6.16–6.19,
                                                                                                                                                                                   6.28, 6.60, 14.3
   Titles I–III 6.18
   Titles V–VI 6.18
   Title VII 6.17
   Art 1 .... 6.19
   Art 4 .... 6.19, 6.88
   Art 7 .... 6.19, 8.84, 9.37
   Art 18 .... 6.19
   Art 21 .... 6.14
   Art 24 .... 9.37
   Arts 27–38 .... 6.18
   Art 41 .... 6.19, 6.86, 9.37
   Art 47 .... 6.19, 6.86, 9.37, 14.14, 14.21
      (1) 14.13

lvii

Art 48	6.19
Art 51(1)	6.7
(2)	6.17
Arts 51–54	6.17
Art 52(3)	6.19
Protocol 30	6.18
Art 1(1)	6.17
(2)	6.18
Treaty of Accession of Denmark, Ireland and United Kingdom 1972	
Final Act	6.24
Treaty of Amsterdam 1997	6.3, 14.39
Treaty on European Union 1992	6.2, 6.20
Art 4(3)	14.28
Art 6	6.17
(1)	6.16–6.17
(2)	6.16
(3)	6.16
Art 19	14.14, 14.37–14.38
(1)	14.12
(3)(b)	14.39
Treaty on the Functioning of the European Union 2008	6.2
Pt 3 Title V	14.50
Art 11	10.68
Art 18	6.14, 6.64
Art 19(1)	6.14
Art 20	6.20, 6.23, 6.25
Art 21	6.20, 6.30
Art 45	6.20, 6.31, 6.38, 6.62–6.63, 6.66
(3)	6.37, 10.98
Art 49	6.20, 6.31
Art 52	6.38, 6.62, 6.66
(1)	6.37
Art 56	6.20
Art 62	6.37–6.38, 6.62, 6.66
Arts 67–89	6.73
Art 77	6.73
Arts 77–80	6.73
Art 78	6.75–6.76
(1)	6.74
Art 79	6.75
(2)	6.75
(3)	6.75
Art 80	6.73
Art 83(1)	6.53
Art 263	14.1
Art 267	14.10, 14.37, 14.39–14.42
(4)	14.37
Art 268	14.51
Art 288	6.2, 14.24
Treaty of Lisbon 2007	6.16, 14.3, 14.39

Table of Legislation

Turkey–EEC Association Agreement 1963 .... 6.69–6.71, 8.68
   Dec 1/80 Arts 6–7 .... 6.69–6.70
      Art 14(1) 6.70
   Brussels Protocol 1970 .... 6.69

Secondary Legislation
Dir 64/221 (Public Policy) 6.63, 6.70
Dir 90/346 (Citizens) 6.64
Dir 96/71 (Posted Workers) 6.34
Dir 2003/9 (Reception) 6.19, 6.76
Dir 2003/86 (Family Reunification) 5.183
Dir 2003/109 (Long Term Residents) 6.38
Dir 2004/38 (Citizens) 6.30–6.68, 6.70, 9.36, 10.97,
                                                                                                                                                10.114, 14.15–14.22, 16.69
   Chap IV 6.37, 6.61
   Chap VI 8.17, 8.32, 9.18, 9.24,
                                                                                                                                                10.16, 10.21, 10.99
   Recital 16 .... 6.58, 8.32
   Recital 17 .... 6.32
   Recital 18 .... 6.32
   Recital 23 .... 6.61
   Art 1(c) 6.61
   Art 2 .... 6.31
      (2) 6.31
   Art 3 .... 6.31, 6.35, 10.106
      (2)(a) 6.31
   Art 5 .... 6.32
      (4) 6.35
   Art 6 .... 6.32, 10.111
   Art 7 .... 6.31–6.32
   Art 12 .... 6.32
   Art 13 .... 6.32
   Art 15(1) 6.59–6.60, 9.36
   Art 16 .... 6.32, 6.56
   Art 17 .... 6.32
   Art 24 .... 6.61
   Art 25(1) 6.35
   Art 27 .... 6.37, 6.47, 6.61–6.62,
                                                         6.64–6.65, 8.33, 10.99–10.100, 14.21
      (1) 14.16
      (2) 10.101, 10.105
      (3) 10.104
      (4) 10.104
   Arts 27–29 .... 6.46
   Art 28 .... 6.37, 6.39, 6.61–6.62, 6.64, 8.70, 10.111
      (1) 6.48, 9.36
      (2) 6.61
   Art 30 .... 6.59–6.60, 8.33, 9.36, 10.111,
                                                                                      14.16, 14.20–14.21
      (2) 14.21
   Arts 30–33 .... 6.70

lix

Table of Legislation

Art 31	6.59–6.60, 8.33, 9.36, 10.111, 14.17–14.18, 14.20–14.22
(3)	6.59, 9.36, 10.111, 14.18
(4)	9.37, 14.18
Art 32	9.96, 10.112, 14.19
Art 33	6.46
Art 35	10.111, 14.20
Dir 2004/81 (Residence Permit)	6.93
Dir 2004/83 (Qualification)	4.56, 4.59, 4.78, 5.207, 6.76–6.86, 6.93, 8.120, 16.110
Arts 5–12	6.77
Art 10(d)	4.56
Art 12(2)(b)	6.79
(c)	6.79
Art 15	6.77–6.78
Art 15C	6.78
Art 16	6.85
Art 17	6.83
(1)	6.80–6.81, 6.86
(d)	6.83
(2)	6.81
(3)	6.81
Art 24(2)	4.78
Dir 2005/85 (Procedures)	6.19, 6.76, 6.93, 14.15, 14.25
Art 23	14.25
Art 32(4)	5.207
Art 39(1)	14.25
(3)(a)	14.25
Dir 2008/115 (Returns)	
Art 11(2)	5.173
Dir 2011/36 (Trafficking)	6.90–6.93, 8.18, 9.19
Art 1	6.91
Art 2	6.92
Art 4	6.92
Art 11	6.92
Art 12	6.92
(3)	8.18, 9.19
Art 14	6.92
Dir 2011/93 (Sexual Abuse)	6.53
Reg 1612/68 (Freedom of Movement)	6.67
Art 12	6.33, 6.63
Reg 492/2011 (Freedom of Movement re–codified)	6.63
Art 10	6.33
Reg 604/2013 (Dublin III)	6.76, 6.87–6.89, 14.15, 14.26–14.27
Chap III	6.87
Art 18	6.87
Art 27	14.26–14.27

International

African Charter on Human and Peoples' Rights 1981
  Art 12(4) 2.51
  Art 18 .... 8.84
American Convention on Human Rights 1969
  Art 11 .... 8.84
  Art 17 .... 8.84
Articles on Responsibility for Internationally Wrongful Acts 2.16
  Art 4 .... 2.14
Convention on Action against Trafficking in Human Beings 2005 .... 2.22, 5.4, 5.242–5.247,
                                                                                                     9.16–9.17, 15.1–15.2,
                                                                                                     15.71–15.74
  Chap VII 15.71
  Art 10(2) 5.245, 8.16, 9.16, 10.14
  Art 13 .... 5.246, 8.16, 9.16
    (2) 5.246, 8.16, 9.16
  Art 14 .... 5.247, 8.16, 9.16
  Art 18 .... 5.245, 8.16, 9.16, 10.14
  Art 36 .... 15.71
Convention on Certain Questions relating to the Conflict
  of Nationality Law 1930 .... 2.33, 12.12
  Preamble 2.59
  Art 1 .... 2.33, 5.239, 11.4, 12.4
  Art 2 .... 2.33, 5.239
  Art 28 .... 2.33
Convention on the Elimination of All Forms of
  Discrimination against Women 1979 .... 3.30, 3.58, 3.63–3.66,
                                                                                                   13.34, 13.44
  Art 1 .... 3.63, 8.9, 9.8, 10.9, 11.9, 12.11
  Art 2 .... 3.64
  Art 3 .... 3.64
  Art 4 .... 3.64
  Art 6 .... 3.65
  Art 7 .... 3.65
  Art 9 .... 3.66
  Optional Protocol 13.44–13.45
Convention on the Elimination of All Forms of
  Racial Discrimination 1969 .... 3.30, 3.58–3.62, 13.34
  Art 1(1) 3.59
    (2) 3.60
    (3) 3.60
    (4) 3.60
  Art 2 .... 3.61
  Art 5 .... 3.62
    (d) 8.9, 9.8, 10.9
      (i)–(ii) 11.9, 12.11
      (iii) 11.9, 12.11
Convention for the Protection of All Persons from
  Enforced Disappearance 2006 .... 3.58, 3.88
  Art 16 .... 3.88
    (1) 5.20, 5.47

Table of Legislation

Convention on the Protection of the Rights of All Migrant Workers and
  Members of their Families 1990..3.58, 3.85
  Art 1...3.85
  Art 22...3.85
  Art 23...3.85
Convention on the Reduction of Statelessness 1961..................4.93, 11.24, 12.6–12.7, 12.13–12.14
  Art 1..4.93, 11.11
  Art 2..4.93, 11.11
  Art 3..4.93, 11.11
  Art 4...4.93, 11.11, 12.64
  Art 5...4.93
  Art 6...4.93
  Art 7...4.93
    (1)(d)...12.64
  Art 8...4.93, 12.14, 12.66
    (1)...12.45
    (2)(b)..12.45
    (3)...12.66
  Art 9..4.93, 12.14
  Art 34...4.85
  Art 43...4.85
Convention on the Rights of the Child 1989.......................2.22, 3.30, 3.58, 3.82–3.84, 4.63, 13.34
  Art 3...5.161, 8.81, 8.94, 9.37, 9.95, 11.24
    (1)..2.22, 8.9, 9.8, 10.9, 11.9, 12.11
  Arts 3–5...3.82
  Art 7...3.83
  Art 8...3.83
  Art 9..3.84, 8.9, 9.8, 9.37, 10.9, 11.9, 12.11
  Art 10...3.84
  Art 12...9.37
  Art 13...9.37
  Art 40(i)...2.22
Convention on the Rights of Persons with Disabilities 2006...........................3.30, 3.58, 3.86–3.87,
                                                                                                                                4.63, 13.34, 13.44
  Art 1...3.86
  Art 18..3.87, 11.9, 12.11
    (a)...12.11
    (d)...8.9, 9.8, 10.9
  Optional Protocol...13.44–13.45
Convention relating to the Status of Refugees 1933...4.7–4.8
  Art 3...4.7
Convention relating to the Status of Refugees 1951................2.20, 2.30, 3.70, 3.74, 4.4, 4.9,
                                                                                                                    4.11–4.86, 4.89, 6.74, 6.77, 6.79,
                                                                                                                    8.47, 8.59, 8.61, 8.81, 8.83, 8.117,
                                                                                                                    8.120, 9.95, 10.10–10.11, 10.76,
                                                                                                                    10.93, 12.12, 16.43–16.44,
                                                                                                                    16.48, 16.52, 16.110
  Art 1...4.88
  Art 1A...4.70, 4.89
    (2)...4.11, 4.15, 4.24, 4.37, 4.50–4.51, 4.55, 4.59, 4.64–4.65,
                                                                        4.70–4.71, 4.77, 4.81, 4.85, 8.10, 9.9, 10.10, 12.12

Table of Legislation

Art 1C 9.9, 10.10
   (1) 4.68
   (2) 4.69
   (3) 4.69
   (5) 4.70, 6.85
   (6) 4.70
Arts 1C–1F 4.68
Art 1D 4.71
Arts 1D–1E 9.9, 10.10
Arts 1D–1F 4.71
Art 1E 4.72
Art 1F 4.73, 11.42
   (a) 4.74
   (b) 4.75, 6.79, 6.83
   (c) 4.76, 6.79
Art 3 ....4.28
Art 32 ....3.35, 4.77–4.79, 4.81, 4.90, 5.37, 8.12, 9.11
   (1) 4.81, 8.10, 9.9
   (2) 8.10, 9.9
   (3) 8.10, 9.9
Art 33 ....4.16, 4.77, 4.80–4.81, 4.89, 5.37, 8.12, 9.11
   (1) 5.20, 8.11, 9.10
   (2) 3.74, 4.75, 4.82, 6.83, 8.11, 9.10
Art 34 ....4.83–4.84, 4.91–4.92, 11.10, 11.24
Art 43 ....4.84
Protocol relating to the Status of Refugees 1967 ....4.9, 6.74
Convention concerning the Status of Refugees coming from Germany 1938 ....4.8
Convention relating to the Status of Stateless Persons 1954 ....4.85–4.92, 10.11, 12.4
   Preamble 4.86
   Art 1 ....2.60, 4.88, 12.60
      (1) 2.31, 4.87, 12.12, 12.58
   Art 2 ....4.88
   Art 31 ....4.90
      (1) 8.12, 9.11
   Art 32 ....4.91–4.92, 11.10, 11.24
      (2) 8.12, 9.11
      (3) 8.12, 9.11
Convention for the Suppression of the Traffic in Persons and of the
Exploitation of the Prostitution of Others 1950 ....4.95
   Art 18 ....4.95
   Art 19 ....4.95
      (2) 4.95
Convention against Torture and Other Cruel, Inhuman or
Degrading Treatment or Punishment 1984 ....3.17, 3.58, 3.67–3.81, 8.7, 13.34
   Art 1 ....3.72
      (1) 3.67, 5.41, 5.47
   Art 2 ....3.68
      (2) 3.74
   Art 3 ....3.69, 3.72–3.76, 3.78–3.79, 3.81
      (1) 3.70, 5.20, 8.7, 9.6, 10.7
   Art 16 ....3.73

Table of Legislation

Convention on the Transfer of Sentenced Persons 1983..5.86, 5.98
   Additional Protocol 5.86, 5.98
European Convention on Human Rights and
   Fundamental Freedoms 1950..............................2.3, 2.20–2.21, 3.13, 5.4–5.238, 6.16, 7.15, 8.59,
                                                  8.61, 8.117, 10.12–10.15, 10.76, 10.84,
                                                  10.92–10.93, 12.45, 15.1–15.70, 16.32,
                                                  16.43, 16.47, 16.85, 16.110, 16.120
   Art 1 .... 2.14, 5.8–5.14, 5.19, 5.229
   Art 2 ....3.17, 4.46, 5.6, 5.21, 5.26–5.33, 5.81,
                                                     5.223, 6.78, 8.14, 9.14, 10.12
   Arts 2–12 ....5.7
   Art 3 ....3.17, 3.72, 3.74, 4.46, 5.6, 5.17, 5.20–5.21,
                                                    5.28, 5.30, 5.33–5.73, 5.81–5.82, 5.89,
                                                     5.93–5.94, 5.174, 5.191–5.192, 5.210,
                                                     5.223, 5.229, 6.78, 6.82, 6.88, 8.14, 8.33,
                                                     8.81, 8.113, 9.14, 9.95, 10.12, 16.57, 16.99
   Art 4 ....4.23, 5.22, 5.77–5.83, 5.223, 8.14, 9.14, 10.12
     (1) 5.77
     (3) 5.77, 5.79
   Art 5 ....5.84–5.87, 5.98, 5.224, 8.14, 9.14, 10.12, 16.127
     (1) 5.87, 5.224
   Art 6 .... 4.29–4.30, 5.85, 5.88–5.94, 5.204–5.205, 5.207,
                                                    5.214, 6.19, 6.86, 8.14, 9.14, 10.12, 14.14
   Art 7 .... 5.95–5.99, 5.223, 8.14, 9.14, 10.12
     (1) 5.95
     (2) 5.95, 5.99
   Art 8 ....3.49, 5.6, 5.15–5.16, 5.23–5.25, 5.100–5.121, 5.123, 5.127,
                                              5.129–5.132, 5.134–5.135, 5.147–5.151, 5.157, 5.159–5.160,
                                              5.172, 5.174–5.176, 5.178, 5.180, 5.182, 5.184–5.185, 5.187,
                                              5.199, 5.201, 5.209, 5.212, 5.222, 5.226, 5.234, 6.65, 8.14–8.15,
                                              8.52, 8.71–8.72, 8.76, 8.80–8.81, 8.83–8.105, 8.107–8.108,
                                              8.114, 8.116–8.117, 8.120, 8.126, 8.129–8.130, 9.14–9.15,
                                              9.37, 9.67, 9.95, 9.100–9.102, 10.12–10.13, 10.38, 10.67,
                                              10.85, 11.7, 11.12, 11.24, 11.38, 12.9, 12.15, 12.47,
                                              16.45, 16.53, 16.57
     (1) 5.106, 5.112, 5.116, 8.89
     (2) 5.116, 5.150, 8.89
   Arts 8–11 ....5.197
   Art 9 .... 5.188–5.192, 8.14, 9.14, 10.12, 10.86
   Arts 9–11 ....5.188–5.196
   Art 10 ....5.188, 5.193–5.196, 8.14, 9.14, 10.12, 10.86–10.88, 10.109
     (1) 5.193
     (2) 5.193
   Art 11 .... 8.14, 9.14, 10.12
   Art 12 ....5.197–5.201
   Art 13 ....5.21, 5.76, 5.125, 5.202–5.214, 5.229, 6.88, 15.6, 15.42
   Art 14 .... 5.7, 5.186–5.187, 5.192, 5.199–5.200,
                                                     5.215–5.222, 11.12, 11.24, 12.15
   Art 15 ....5.37, 5.223–5.224
     (1) 5.77
     (2) 5.95

Table of Legislation

Art 16	5.5
Arts 16–18	5.7
Art 19	15.3
Art 20	15.11
Art 22	15.11
Art 23	15.11
Art 24(1)	15.20
Art 25	15.12, 15.21
(e)	15.20
Art 26	15.13
(3)	15.14
Art 27(1)–(2)	15.14
(3)	15.14
Art 28	15.16
Art 29	15.17
Art 32	15.4
Art 33	15.4
Art 34	5.9, 15.4, 15.29, 15.36, 15.39, 15.59, 16.125
Art 35	15.30, 15.38–15.39
(2)	15.39
(3)	15.43
(a)	15.44
(b)	15.45–15.47
Art 36	15.27, 15.48
(1)(a)	15.49
(b)	15.49
(c)	15.49
(2)	15.28
Art 38(4)	15.22
Art 39(1)	15.26
Art 41	15.64–15.65
Art 43	15.68
Art 44(1)	15.68
(2)	15.68
Art 46	15.69
Art 47	15.4, 15.9
Art 56(1)	5.9
(4)	5.9
Protocol 1 Arts 1–3	5.7
Art 2	5.219
Protocol 4	5.238
Art 3	5.225–5.231
Art 4	5.6, 5.225–5.231
Protocol 6	5.21, 5.28
Protocol 7 Art 1	5.6, 5.206, 5.232–5.238
Protocol 13	5.21
Art 1	5.7, 5.29, 5.31
Protocol 14	15.7, 15.45
Protocol 15	15.8, 15.46
Protocol 16	15.9

Table of Legislation

European Convention on Nationality 1997	5.4, 5.239–5.241, 11.13, 12.13, 15.1
Art 1	5.239
Art 3	5.239
Art 4	5.240, 12.16
Art 5	5.240
Art 6	5.241, 11.13
Arts 6–9	5.241
Art 7	5.241
(1)	12.16
Art 8	5.241
Art 9	5.241
Art 10	5.241, 11.13
Art 11	5.241, 11.13
Art 12	5.241, 11.13
Art 13	5.241, 11.13
Art 23	5.241
ILO Forced Labour Convention No 29	
Art 2(2)	5.79
International Covenant on Civil and Political Rights 1966	3.13–3.58, 3.83, 4.17–4.19, 4.43, 13.34, 13.37
Art 2	3.30, 8.8, 9.7, 10.8
(1)	3.16, 11.8, 11.24, 12.10
Art 3	8.8, 9.7, 10.8, 11.8, 11.24, 12.10
Art 4(1)	3.15
Art 6	3.14–3.15, 3.17, 8.6, 9.5, 10.6
Art 7	3.14–3.15, 3.17, 3.72, 3.74, 5.47, 8.6, 9.5, 10.6
Art 8	4.23, 8.6, 9.5, 10.6
Art 9	3.29, 4.19, 8.6, 9.5, 10.6, 12.5
Art 12	13.45
(4)	2.60, 3.14, 3.18–3.32. 3.52, 4.22, 8.8–8.9, 9.7–9.8, 10.5, 10.8–10.9, 11.7, 11.24, 12.9
Art 13	2.51, 3.14, 3.22, 3.33–3.45, 8.8, 9.7, 13.45
Art 15	4.19
Art 17	3.14, 3.23, 3.29, 3.46–3.53, 3.57, 8.8, 8.84, 9.7, 10.8, 11.7, 11.24, 12.9
Art 23	3.14, 8.84
(1)	3.46–3.53, 3.57, 8.8, 9.7, 10.8, 11.7, 11.24, 12.9
Art 24	3.14, 3.54–3.57
(1)	3.57
(3)	3.55–3.56, 11.6, 12.9
International Covenant on Economic, Social and Cultural Rights 1966	3.13, 4.18, 4.43, 13.34
Statute of the International Court of Justice 1945	
Art 38(1)	2.7
(a)	2.8
(b)	2.8
(c)	2.8
(d)	2.8–2.10
Art 59	2.9
Treaty of London 1949	5.1–5.3
Art 1(a)	5.1
(b)	5.1

Table of Legislation

Art 3 ....5.2–5.3
Art 4 ....5.3
Treaty of Washington 1871
    Art 1 ....2.16
United Nations Charter 1945 .... 2.7, 2.29, 3.2, 13.4–13.5
United Nations Convention on the Law of the Sea 1982
    Art 92 ....5.13
United Nations Convention against Transnational Organised Crime 2000 ....4.96
    Art 4(a) 5.80
    Palermo Protocol to Prevent, Suppress and Punish Trafficking in Persons,
        Especially Women and Children 2000 .... 4.96–4.100, 8.13
        Art 2 ....4.97
        Art 3 .... 4.98, 8.13, 9.12
            (a) 5.80
        Art 7 ....4.99
        Art 8 ....4.100
            (2) 8.13, 9.12
            (6) 8.13, 9.13
Universal Declaration of Human Rights 1948 .... 2.3, 3.5–3.14, 3.55, 8.84
    Art 2 ....3.7
    Art 3 ....3.6
    Art 5 ....3.6
    Art 7 ....3.6
    Art 9 ....3.6, 3.8
    Art 12 ....3.6, 8.84
    Art 13 ....3.8, 10.5
        (2) 13.8
    Art 14 ....3.8–3.9
    Art 15 .... 2.50, 2.60, 3.10–3.11, 3.14,
                                                                                                       11.5–11.6, 12.8
        (2) 2.49
    Art 16(3) 8.84
    Art 29 ....3.12
    Art 30 ....3.12
Vienna Convention on the Law of Treaties 1969
    Art 18 ....11.13
    Art 27 ....2.16
    Art 31 ....2.11–2.12
    Art 32 ....2.11–2.12
    Art 46 ....2.16
    Art 53 ....2.4

Part A
Background

1
Foundations of the System

Contents

A. Introduction 1.1
B. Aliens and Subjects 1.2
C. Developments in the Late Nineteenth and Early Twentieth Centuries 1.6
D. Primary Developments from the Outbreak of the First World War
   to the End of the Second World War 1.7
E. Primary Post-war Developments 1.13
F. The Coming of European Law 1.23
G. Conclusion 1.24

A. Introduction

This chapter seeks to provide a short account of the background to the modern regimes of immigration and nationality law in the UK, so that the context of the provisions focused upon in chapters 8–12 may be understood. **1.1**

B. Aliens and Subjects

In his *Commentaries on the Law of England*, published in 1768, Blackstone noted the initial distinction of status among persons on the territory as being the separation of aliens from subjects: **1.2**

> THE first and most obvious division of the people is into aliens and natural-born subjects. Natural-born subjects are such as are born within the dominions of the crown of England, that is, within the ligeance, or, as it is generally called, the allegiance of the king; and aliens, such as are born out of it. Allegiance is the tie, or *ligamen*, which binds the subject to the king, in return for that protection which the king affords the subject … The thing itself, or a substantial part of it, is founded in reason and the nature of government.[1]

For centuries, the dominant form of status first in England and Wales and then throughout the United Kingdom was not citizenship but subjecthood. Those identified as 'natural-born' subjects possessed as a consequence of that status an extensive right of entrance to and residence in the territory. After the Act of Union 1707, subjects of the Crown both in England **1.3**

---

[1] Sir W Blackstone, *Commentaries on the Laws of England* (Oxford, Clarendon, 1768, 18th edn 1829, S Sweet, R Pheney, A Maxwell, Stevens and Sons), Book I, ch X, 366.

and Wales and in Scotland became British subjects. Naturalisation by an alien, giving status as a British subject, was possible only by means of a private Act of Parliament until the Naturalisation Act 1844 created the power to grant nationality administratively. Throughout this period, British subjects were recognised as having a broad common law right to enter and remain in the UK, with which the executive could interfere only when enabled to do this by statute. Holdsworth concluded in 1932 that: 'The Crown has never had a prerogative power to prevent its subjects from entering the United Kingdom, or to expel them from it.'[2]

1.4   Whilst the state retained broad powers to expel or exclude aliens, the executive's powers over immigration control, prior to the late nineteenth century, were obscure and rarely exercised. The common law was seen by Blackstone as providing a strong guarantee of individual liberty:

> Next to personal security, the law of England regards, asserts, and preserves, the personal liberty of individuals. This personal liberty consists in the power of locomotion, of changing situation, or removing one's person to whatsoever place one's own inclination may direct, without imprisonment or restraint, unless by due course of law.[3]

That right Blackstone saw as pre-existing, but as reaffirmed by Magna Carta, that 'great charter of liberties, which was obtained, sword in hand, from King John, and afterwards, with some alterations, confirmed in parliament by King Henry the Third, his son … [which was] for the most part declaratory of the principal grounds of the fundamental law of England'.[4] Whilst the right might be limited, as Blackstone noted, 'by due course of law', that is, by statute, in practice legal restraints upon entry and remaining by aliens were limited and administration even of such restraints as existed was not assiduously developed. Writing in 1978, Guy Goodwin-Gill could state confidently that: 'From shortly after the end of the Napoleonic Wars until 1905 no foreigners were excluded or expelled from Great Britain.'[5]

1.5   The imposition by statute of limitations upon entrance by aliens was not wholly unknown in the eighteenth and early nineteenth centuries, but was generally viewed as representing a temporary infringement of personal liberty justified by some particular perceived emergency and was therefore limited in duration and effect. The Aliens Act 1793, which was designed to address the threat from Revolutionary France, empowered the executive to prevent landing by aliens in the UK and allowed for the deportation of any alien who had been imprisoned. Although designed to expire within a year of entry into the statute book, it was described by Erskine May as 'equivalent to the suspension of Habeas Corpus'.[6] By the Aliens Registration Act 1826, the executive surrendered its statutory power to order the deportation of a domiciled alien even where the alien had committed no offence. The Aliens Removal Act 1848, another expressly temporary measure, owed its existence to a desire to insulate the UK from the consequences of the liberal revolutions then being attempted on the Continent.

---

[2] Sir W Holdsworth, *A History of English Law* (London, Methuen, 1932) vol X, 393.
[3] Blackstone (n 1) Book I, ch I, 133–35.
[4] ibid 127.
[5] G Goodwin-Gill, *International Law and the Movement of Persons between States* (Oxford, Clarendon, 1978) 97.
[6] Sir T Erskine May, Baron Farnborough, *The Constitutional History of England since the Accession of George III* (London, Longmans Green & Co, 1901) vol III, 51.

C. Developments in the Late Nineteenth and Early Twentieth Centuries

The relatively relaxed position which prevailed as regards immigration control in the mid-nineteenth century came to be modified towards the end of that century in the face of increased flows of migrants, most notably large numbers of people from Central and Eastern Europe departing to the rapidly developing Americas, often through ports in Western Europe, and Chinese nationals transshipped as labour to many parts of the British Empire and elsewhere. The Crown's power to legislate to exclude aliens was first positively identified by the Privy Council on appeal from the courts of the self-governing colony of Victoria in the case of *Musgrove v Chun Teeong Toy* (Victoria) [1891] AC 272, 282, the decisive judgment being that '[the plaintiff, seeking to maintain his action] can only do so if he can establish that an alien has a legal right, enforceable by action, to enter British territory. No authority exists for the proposition that an alien has any such right'. That judgment coincided with a prolonged period of public alarm in the UK and some of its colonial territories and Dominions at the perceived undesirability of large-scale Chinese labour migration. In *Attorney General of Canada v Cain and Gilhula* [1906] UKPC 55; [1906] AC 542, Lord Atkinson, delivering the judgment of the Privy Council, cited writings of the legal commentator Vattel (1714–67) as the sole authority for the proposition that: 'One of the rights possessed by the supreme power in every State is the right to refuse to permit an alien to enter that State, to annex what conditions it pleases to the permission ... and to expel or deport from the State, at pleasure, even a friendly alien.'[7] The power identified by the Privy Council was not reflected in UK statute until the passing of the Aliens Act 1905 (AA 1905) marked the opening of a new era of peacetime legislation intended to respond to the fear of migration aroused by the movement of impoverished aliens who were increasingly able to access international travel. AA 1905 aimed in particular to regulate the arrival of poor immigrants, applying to 'steerage passengers' arriving for disembarkation in the UK on 'immigrant ships', defined as ships bringing to the UK 20 or more alien steerage passengers.

1.6

D. Primary Developments from the Outbreak of the First World War to the End of the Second World War

Shortly after the outbreak of the First World War, AA 1905 was effectively superseded by the Aliens Restriction Act 1914 (ARA 1914), which introduced additional powers of

1.7

---

[7] The authority cited is Vattel, *Law of Nations*, Book I, section 231; book II, section 125. Online versions of Books I and II are accessible at www.constitution.org/vattel/vattel_01.htm and www.constitution.org/vattel/vattel_02.htm. The account given in the *Cain* case represents a markedly coloured account of the right of expulsion or control, which Vattel deliberately balanced with the right of a human person, derived from the law of nature or of God, 'to dwell somewhere on earth', derived 'from nature, or rather from its Author ... and the introduction of property cannot have impaired the right which every man has to the use of such things as are absolutely necessary—a right which he brings with him into the world at the moment of his birth': see Vattel, Book I, sections 229–31.

control. ARA 1914 permitted the entry of aliens only via approved ports and following the grant of leave by an immigration officer (unless they were crew members or in transit). As with the framework provided by AA 1905, the ARA 1914 regime granted immigration officers a very broad degree of discretion. Upon peace being restored, the primary focus of those charged with statutory power was generally the exclusion of aliens unable to maintain themselves.

1.8 The outbreak of war also brought developments in nationality law. Whilst subjects continued to have wide rights, section 1 British Nationality and Status of Aliens Act 1914 (BNSAA 1914), enacted in some haste three days after the UK declared war on Germany at the outbreak of the First World War, established statutory criteria for status as a 'natural-born' British subject. It also provided for naturalisation on a more substantial scale: section 2 BNSAA 1914 provided that the Secretary of State for the Home Department (SSHD) might grant naturalisation as a matter of absolute discretion to applicants meeting requirements of residence in the dominions or Crown service, good character, adequate knowledge of the English language and intention, if successful, to reside in the dominions or to remain in Crown service.

1.9 Whilst naturalisation therefore became far more accessible, BNSAA 1914 correspondingly provided for deprivation of British nationality obtained by naturalisation. By section 7(1) BNSAA 1914, SSHD was empowered to revoke by order any certificate of naturalisation 'where it appears to the Secretary of State that the certificate of naturalisation granted by him has been obtained by false representation or fraud'. Subsequently section 1 British Nationality and Status of Aliens Act 1918 (BNSAA 1918) substituted a new section 7 BNSAA 1914 imposing upon the Secretary of State a duty to revoke nationality in certain circumstances, including obtaining by 'false representation or fraud, or by concealment of material circumstances, or that the person to whom the certificate is granted has shown himself by act or speech to be disaffected or disloyal to His Majesty', or if '(in any case) the continuance of the certificate is not conducive to the public good' and one of several conditions is met. The conditions were, broadly: (i) involvement in trading with the enemy; (ii) being sentenced within His Majesty's dominions to imprisonment for twelve months or more, or penal servitude, or a fine of one hundred pounds or more; (iii) not having been of good character at the date of grant of the certificate; (iv) ordinary residence outside His Majesty's dominions of more than 7 years save as a representative of a British subject, firm, or company carrying on business, or an institution established, in His Majesty's dominions, or in the service of the Crown, without maintaining substantial connection with His Majesty's dominions; or (v) remaining, according to the law of a state at war with the United Kingdom, a subject of that State.

1.10 Accordingly, the law, from the coming into effect of BNSAA 1918, provided for, on the one hand, revocation where naturalisation had been obtained by the exercise of false representation or fraud, concealment of material circumstances, or where disaffection or disloyalty had been shown 'by act or speech' (at section 7(1) BNSAA 1914 as amended), and on the other hand, revocation if one or more of the conditions in section 7(2) BNSAA 1914 applied and continuance of naturalised citizenship was not conducive to the public good (section 7(2) BNSAA 1914, as amended).

1.11 Section 3 BNSAA 1918 further created a power in the Secretary of State to revoke the grant of a certificate of naturalisation in respect of a person who had previously been the subject of a country which at the date of the grant was at war with His Majesty and, subject to exceptions, also provided that, for a period of ten years after the termination of the war, no certificate of naturalisation should be granted to any subject of a country which at the time of the passing of the Act was at war with the UK. As Pill LJ was later to observe of the BNSAA 1918 regime in *SSHD v Hicks* [2006] EWCA Civ 400 [17]: 'The provisions of the Act demonstrate strong hostility towards the then enemies of His Majesty and those who traded with them.'

Whilst restrictions on aliens increased, British subjects continued to possess freedom of movement into the UK to a striking degree. Many individuals with a connection by birth in a British territory, naturalisation or other means were entitled to recognition as British subjects. Citizens of self-governing Commonwealth countries were held to be British subjects, as were citizens of trusts, colonies and protectorates where legislation passed in London determined the acquisition of subjecthood by reason of connection to that territory. British subjects continued to have an extensive right to enter and live in the UK. In 1948 one of the rights Jones considered as definitively attaching to status as a British subject was that of entry to and remaining in the UK.[8] The right was only gradually circumscribed in the first decades after the Second World War.

1.12

E. Primary Post-war Developments

The extensive right of entry to the UK then available to British subjects was bound to come under pressure as some units of the nineteenth-century empire gained an increasing degree of autonomy and sought to control immigration from elsewhere, sometimes including the UK. In the UK there was increased desire to limit access from overseas to the home territory as the war years passed into memory and decolonisation proceeded. The British Nationality Act 1948 (BNA 1948) reflected a final attempt at compromise between, on the one hand, the fragmentation of nationalities within the British Empire and Dominions, and, on the other hand, the maintenance of a single common status giving rights within the wider territory, including rights of entry to and residence in the UK. Part II of the BNA 1948 introduced the status of Citizen of the United Kingdom and the Commonwealth (CUKC), the core of a statutory nationality scheme whereby local citizenship in any qualifying territory would additionally give access to a broader composite status. This status gave a right of entry to the UK, but elsewhere in the Commonwealth attracted differing levels of respect, with most Commonwealth countries claiming the sovereign right to impose restrictions on entry by CUKCs from elsewhere, undermining the intended reciprocal nature of the scheme. In time, domestic reaction in the UK to migration from the Commonwealth, particularly the Caribbean, prompted a move towards restriction in the UK. It was noteworthy that the number of people entitled to enter and live in the UK was very large compared to the actual population of the territory. In *Abdulaziz, Cabales and Balkandali v UK* App Nos 9214/80; 9473/81; 9474/81 [1985] ECHR 7, (1985) 7 EHRR 471, it was noted at [38] that in mid-1962, approximately 600 million people had the right to enter and reside lawfully in the UK.

1.13

---

[8] J Mervyn Jones, 'The British Nationality Act 1948' 25 *British Yearbook of International Law* (1948) 158, 161.

1.14 Section 20 BNA 1948 replaced earlier duties in respect of deprivation of nationality with a power, exerciseable by the Secretary of State, to revoke nationality obtained through naturalisation (as an adult) or registration (as a minor). The conditions for exercise of the power broadly revisited the BNSAA 1918 conditions, save that ordinary residence outside His Majesty's dominions or being the subject of a state at war with the UK ceased to provide a basis for removal of British nationality.

1.15 In 1962, in a response to fears of large scale immigration expressed by some persons in the United Kingdom, the right of entry of CUKCs to the UK was attenuated by the Commonwealth Immigrants Act 1962 (CIA 1962) extending immigration control to citizens of Commonwealth countries. This was extended, and backed by criminal sanction, in the Commonwealth Immigrants Act 1968 (CIA 1968). In this period, CUKC status remained the primary basis for the right to enter and remain in the UK.

1.16 In the early decades after the end of the Second World War, residual aspects of the liberty of movement possessed by British subjects under the common law survived in the absence of systematic codification of laws for immigration control. In a criminal appeal decided in the dying years of the broad right of British subjects to enter the UK, *R v Bhagwan* [1972] AC 60, a British subject, as then defined, entered the UK clandestinely by landing on a deserted beach as a dramatic means by which to avoid presenting himself to an immigration officer for examination under section 3 CIA 1962, on the basis that an immigration officer afforded the opportunity to exercise the power of examination might take a decision to refuse admission to the applicant under power given by section 2 CIA 1962. There was at that time no provision in law which expressly limited the time or place at which a Commonwealth citizen and British subject might enter the UK, and it was held that the clandestine beach arrival, designed to avoid the risks of refusal of entry attached to examination, did not constitute an offence known to the law of England and Wales, despite the clear objective of thwarting the scheme created by the CIA 1962.

1.17 By the time that case was decided, the application of immigration control had been consolidated, with repeal of much of the earlier legislation, by the Immigration Act 1971 (IA 1971), the foundation stone of present British immigration law. The possibility of a British subject landing on a deserted beach by night, without the commission of any illegal act, was ended by section 1(1) IA 1971, by which freedom 'to live in, and to come and go into and from, the United Kingdom without let or hindrance except such as may be required under and in accordance with this Act to enable their right to be established or as may be otherwise lawfully imposed' was limited to those defined by section 2 IA 1971 as possessing the 'right of abode' in the UK, then defined as British 'patrials', a term adopted in essence to denote an inner subgroup of British subjects to whom right of abode was granted, distinguished from the broader group subjected to systematic immigration control. The fundamental change brought about by IA 1971 is illustrated in the decision of the House of Lords in *Azam & Ors v SSHD* [1973] UKHL 7; [1974] AC 18, in which earlier clandestine entrants unsuccessfully sought to rely, after the coming into effect of IA 1971, upon possession of a common law freedom of presence in the UK.

1.18 The right of abode has therefore come to hold particular importance as the key indicator of a right under domestic law to enter, leave or remain in the UK without being subject to immigration control. It has been held to be 'a creature of the law', but also an important source of liberty, so that general or ambiguous words in legislation 'will not readily be construed as removing it'.⁹ It is bestowed by statute. Executive action (including the issue of a passport or certificate of entitlement) cannot operate so as to confer the right of abode on any person who does not have it already by statute.¹⁰

The analogue of IA 1971 in the field of British nationality law is the British Nationality Act 1981 (BNA 1981). From 1 January 1983, BNA 1981 displaced CUKC status and created a citizenship specific to the UK, replacing patrial status as the link to possession of right of abode under IA 1971. The new citizenship was 'British citizenship', like its predecessor in essence a label denoting possession of the right of abode in the UK. The evolution of nationality law through IA 1971 and then BNA 1981 therefore reflects a restrictive redefinition of entitlement to enter and remain in the UK without subjection to immigration control. As Plender has stated with particular reference to BNA 1981: 'Whereas in other countries nationality law commonly forms the basis for the imposition of immigration control, in the United Kingdom the immigration law provided the inspiration for [BNA 1981].'¹¹

1.19

Under IA 1971, as amended by BNA 1981, there are in essence two potential routes to possession of the right of abode in the UK. The first is possession of British citizenship. Under section 2(1)(a) IA 1971, as amended with effect from 1 January 1983 by section 39(2) BNA 1981, any British citizen possesses the right of abode in the UK. A second basis of entitlement to the right of abode applies to certain persons resident in the UK as CUKCs upon the coming into force of IA 1971. Under section 2(1)(b) IA 1971, as amended by BNA 1981, entitlement to the right of abode extends to Commonwealth citizens who immediately before commencement of BNA 1981 on 1 January 1983 were Commonwealth citizens with the right of abode under section 2(1) IA 1971.

1.20

BNA 1981 further provided that individuals become entitled to citizenship by one of four routes: birth or adoption (section 1 BNA 1981), descent (section 2 BNA 1981), registration (sections 3-5 and 10 BNA 1981) or naturalisation (section 6 BNA 1981). Beyond this, the narrowing of entitlement to the right of abode in the UK has left a number of persons who possess some status as 'British' without British citizenship and the accompanying right of abode: (i) some British Overseas Territories Citizens who have not over time acquired British citizenship, in particular those linked to the UK Sovereign Base areas in Cyprus who were excluded from transition to British citizenship under section 3 British Overseas Territories Act 2002;¹² (ii) British Overseas Citizens; (iii) British Nationals (Overseas); (iv) British protected persons; or (v) British subjects. Like aliens, those persons who possess some other British 'citizenship status', but are denied a right of abode by IA 1971, are subject to immigration control. Section 3(1) IA 1971, as amended by section 39 of the British Nationality Act 1981 and paragraphs 43 and 44(1) of Schedule 14 to the Immigration and Asylum Act 1999, provides that a person who is not a British citizen shall not enter the UK unless given leave to do so in accordance with the provisions of or made under the Act that he may be given leave to enter or remain for a limited or for an indefinite period, and that if he is given leave to enter or to remain in the UK, it may be given subject to conditions restricting his employment or occupation or requiring him to register with the police.

1.21

---

⁹ *R (otao Bancoult) v SSHD* [2008] UKHL 61, [2009] AC 453, per Lord Bingham at [45].
¹⁰ *Christodoulidou v SSHD* [1985] Imm AR 179.
¹¹ R Plender, *International Migration Law* (Leiden, Martinus Nijhoff, 1988) 25.
¹² Section 3(2) British Overseas Territories Act 2002.

1.22 Section 40 BNA 1981 consolidated into the regime the power of the Secretary of State to revoke nationality obtained through naturalisation (as an adult) or registration (as a minor) if (i) that status was obtained by fraud, false representation or concealment of material fact, or (ii) that person had (a) shown himself by act or speech to be disloyal or disaffected towards Her Majesty, or (b) had, during any war in which Her Majesty was engaged, unlawfully traded or communicated with an enemy or been engaged in or associated with business to his knowledge carried on in such a manner as to assist an enemy in that war, or (c) had, within the period of five years from the relevant date, been sentenced in any country to imprisonment for a term of not less than 12 months, providing that in any of the last three cases deprivation of nationality was prohibited unless the Secretary of State was satisfied that it was conducive to the public good to proceed, and deprivation would not leave the subject of that action stateless.

F. The Coming of European Law

1.23 By virtue of section 2(1) European Communities Act 1972, a regime for the free movement of persons within the legal space of the European Community entered into the UK legal order on 1 January 1973 upon the UK's accession to the European Economic Community. Section 2(1) ECA 1972 provides that:

> 2(1) All such rights, powers, liabilities, obligations and restrictions from time to time created or arising by or under the Treaties, and all such remedies and procedures from time to time provided for by or under the Treaties, as in accordance with the Treaties are without further enactment to be given legal effect or used in the United Kingdom shall be recognised and available in law, and be enforced, allowed and followed accordingly.

By section 2(1) ECA 1972, all national authorities in the UK—including courts and tribunals—are required to ensure that EU law rights are made available and enforced domestically.

G. Conclusion

1.24 The core structure latterly represented by IA 1971 as regards immigration law and BNA 1981 in respect of nationality law has over time been modified significantly by further legislation, a process which continues. The primary current powers, and such limitations as exist thereupon, are identified at chapters 8–12 respectively.

Part B
Legal Framework

2

Public International Law (General)

Contents

A. Introduction 2.1
B. Terms 2.6
C. Content and Sources of International Law 2.7
D. Interpretation of Treaties 2.11
E. State Responsibility 2.14
F. Application of International Law to the UK 2.15
G. International Law within the UK 2.17
H. Protection 2.23
I. The Significance of Nationality in International Law 2.29
J. Attributing Nationality for the Purposes of International Law 2.31
K. Rights and Duties of States: (i) Expulsion and Exclusion of Aliens;
   and (ii) Admission of Nationals 2.38
   K1. Exclusion or Expulsion of Aliens 2.40
   K2. Standards Applicable in Expulsion Cases 2.45
   K3. Admission to State of Nationality 2.52
L. International Law and Denial or Deprivation of Nationality 2.58

A. Introduction

Public international law, referred to below simply as 'international law', has been concerned in its classical form primarily with the relations of states. Over time, international law has acquired a broader reach and subsidiary and hybrid legal regimes have come into existence. In the words of a leading general work in the field, *Oppenheim's International Law*: 2.1

> International law is the body of rules which are legally binding upon states in their intercourse with each other. These rules are primarily those which govern the relations of states, but states are not the only subjects of international law. International organisations and, to some extent, also individuals may be subjects of rights conferred and duties imposed by international law.[1]

This book can provide only a short summary of the international law bearing on its subject matter. A fuller account may be found in *Oppenheim's International Law* or in the best single-volume introduction to international law in English, *Brownlie's* 2.2

---

[1] R Jennings and A Watts (eds), *Oppenheim's International Law* (9th edn, vol 1 ('*Peace*'), Oxford, Oxford University Press, 1992) Part 1 4 §1.

Principles of Public International Law.[2] Other relevant works include Weis' *Nationality and Statelessness*,[3] Goodwin-Gill's *International Law and the Movement of Persons between States*,[4] Plender's *International Migration Law*[5] and, on the use of international law domestically in England and Wales, Shaheed Fatima's *Using International Law in Domestic Courts*.[6]

2.3   The immediate roots of modern international law lie in the late fifteenth and early sixteenth centuries, during which states became more centralised and powerful, and conflict increasingly pervasive and damaging.[7] The notion of international relations as involving sovereign states subject to a developed legal regime grew out of the work of a number of theorists and promoters, including the Dutch politician, diplomat and writer Hugo de Groot, or Grotius (1563–1645). But despite the development of a theoretical underpinning by scholars, a legal framework extending beyond the conduct of diplomacy and war was slow to develop until the settlements concluding the First World War and the foundation of the League of Nations as a result of the Paris Peace Conference. The League of Nations system failed prior to and during the Second World War, prompting very important wartime and postwar developments aimed at the establishment of a better grounded system for collective security, disarmament and the resolution of international disputes. Those developments included the foundation of the United Nations on 24 October 1945, the issuance of the Universal Declaration of Human Rights 1948 (UDHR),[8] the creation of the Council of Europe in 1949 and the subsequent signing of the European Convention on Human Rights and Fundamental Freedoms 1950 (ECHR).[9]

2.4   International law has a number of forms. In general, a division can be made between customary international law, which has arisen from the customs and practices observed by nations, and treaty law, which arises from particular agreements between states referred to variously as treaties, conventions, protocols, declarations and so on. Customary international law is held to bind all states, whilst treaty law binds states which have ratified the instrument in question once it has entered into force. There may, however, be a substantial overlap between customary and treaty law. First, treaty law may codify customary law so as to render its content more certain or to enable any extension or revision to be clearly set out. Second, where a treaty regime is subscribed to very widely, key features may over time inform customary international law. Within

---

[2] J Crawford (ed), *Brownlie's Principles of Public International Law* (8th edn, Oxford, Oxford University Press, 2012).

[3] P Weis, *Nationality and Statelessness* (Leiden, Brill, 1979).

[4] G Goodwin-Gill, *International Law and the Movement of Persons between States* (Oxford, Clarendon, 1978).

[5] R Plender, *International Migration Law* (Leiden, Martinus Nijhoff, 1988).

[6] S Fatima, *Using International Law in Domestic Courts* (Oxford, Hart Publishing, 2005) (a second edition as *International Law and Foreign Affairs in English Courts* is due in January 2015).

[7] The period saw conflict throughout England, Ireland and Scotland against a background of widespread violence globally, including the Thirty Years' War, in which a third of the population of Central Europe is thought to have died. The German verb 'magdeburgisieren' (to make a Magdeburg of somewhere) refers to the devastating humanitarian consequences of a 1631 assault by troops of the Holy Roman Emperor upon the eponymous city in southern Germany: G Parker, *Global Crisis: War, Climate Change, and Catastrophe in the Seventeenth Century* (New Haven, Yale University Press, 2013) 29 and 90.

[8] See further ch 3.

[9] See further ch 5.

the broader range of international law norms, an *ius cogens* norm of international law is one from which no state may derogate and which may be modified only by a subsequent norm of general international law having the same character.[10] In *R v Bow Street Metropolitan Stipendiary Magistrate ex p Pinochet Ugarte (No 3)* [1999] UKHL 17, [2000] 1 AC 147, 197–99, the House of Lords identified the international criminalisation of torture as an *ius cogens* norm. 'Particular' international law by contrast is that which binds only some states.[11]

It is convenient for present purposes to separate classical international law, which is considered in this chapter, from certain distinct regimes or sub-regimes within international law, such as international human rights law, hybrid international law regimes which may be partly focused on human rights but also possess other purposes, the laws associated with the Council of Europe, and EU law, much of which is incorporated into UK domestic law. These sub-regimes are tritely a part of international law, not something outside it. The purpose of delineating particular regimes is to identify the distinct origin and content of each regime and allow the process of development of international law to be recognised. In general, it can be said that all of the regimes or sub-regimes referred to have developed relatively recently, compared with 'classical' international law,[12] and that overall this took place after the end of the twentieth century. These regimes are examined elsewhere in Part B of this work.

2.5

B. Terms

Some terms employed in this chapter require definition. 'Nationality' is the term denoting attachment to a state for the purposes of international law and reflects a concept which has evolved from the earlier categorisation of any given individual as either a 'subject', identifying status as the subject of a sovereign power, generally a monarch in the pre-modern and early modern period, or as the converse of a national, namely an alien. Nationality is determined by the domestic law of a state, but international tribunals and other states will consider norms of international law in relation to any question of recognition under international law of a person's nationality status.[13] The possession

2.6

---

[10] Article 53 Vienna Convention on the Law of Treaties 1969. *Oppenheim's International Law* states that: 'General international law is that which is binding upon a great many states. General international law, such as provisions of certain treaties which are widely, but not universally, binding and which establish rules appropriate for universal application, has a tendency to become universal international law [binding upon all States].' Jennings and Watts (n 1) Part 1 4–5 §1.

[11] Jennings and Watts (n 1) Part 1 4–5 §1.

[12] By this term is meant the body of international law also known as the law of nations, which was well established prior to the First World War and has continued to exist and to develop since.

[13] In a decision focused upon the identification of the country of nationality entitled to exercise international protection of a national where two countries claimed that status under their national laws, the International Court of Justice stated that an international body may for the purposes of international law assess the relevance of nationality on the basis of whether there is a real and effective link: 'According to the practice of States, to arbitral and judicial decisions and to the opinions of writers, nationality is a legal bond having as its basis a social fact of attachment, a genuine connection of existence, interests, and sentiments, together with the existence of reciprocal rights and duties.' *Nottebohm case (Liechtenstein v Guatemala)* (1955) ICJ Reports 4, 23. See paras 2.35–2.37 below.

of nationality is most usually evidenced by possession and presentation of a passport. In common parlance in the UK, 'nationality' is often used synonymously with another familiar phrase, 'citizenship'. But the latter term is generally used to refer to status under national law. It may in the context of some other states be a functional synonym for nationality, because possession of one means possession of the other, but in the UK, it identifies a status created under domestic law common to some but not all of those who possess UK nationality. In UK practice, British citizens are treated as UK nationals, as are holders of certain other statuses linked to the UK.

C. Content and Sources of International Law

2.7 The content of international law has only been partly codified by international treaty-making or other means and some norms are identifiable only by reference to international custom or 'general principles of law recognised by civilised nations'. The sources of international law are now conventionally identified by reference to the matters admissible in dispute resolution before the International Court of Justice (ICJ), which is the principal judicial organ of the UN, established in June 1945 by the Charter of the United Nations. Article 38(1) of the ICJ Statute provides that:

1. The Court, whose function is to decide in accordance with international law such disputes as are submitted to it, shall apply:
    a. international conventions, whether general or particular, establishing rules expressly recognized by the contesting states;
    b. international custom, as evidence of a general practice accepted as law;
    c. the general principles of law recognized by civilized nations;
    d. subject to the provisions of Article 59, judicial decisions and the teachings of the most highly qualified publicists of the various nations, as subsidiary means for the determination of rules of law.
2. This provision shall not prejudice the power of the Court to decide a case *ex aequo et bono*, if the parties agree thereto.[14]

2.8 Article 38(1)(a) ICJ Statute refers to treaties, which represent an important source of obligation in international law. They have great importance in practice because of the relative clarity of their content and because of the direct evidence of agreement to be bound which ratification of a treaty by a state provides. The content of treaty law may overlap with and thereby codify that of customary international law. Article 38(1)(b) refers to customary international law not codified by treaty. 'Custom' in this context means a general practice which is recognised as answering legal obligation: the term of art 'usage', by contrast, means a general practice not reflecting legal obligation. The wording of the Statute at this point is not ideal: customary international law in principle has legal character prior to, but is supported by, evidence of practice 'accepted by law' rather than the converse. As to Article 38(1)(c), whilst the meaning of this provision is

---

[14] 'Ex aequo et bono' means something like 'from right and equity' and gives the Court the power to decide a matter on wider grounds in the light of agreement by the parties to an action before it. This approach has never been invoked by the ICJ.

not universally agreed, *Brownlie* here endorses the earlier view expressed in *Oppenheim's International Law*- '[t]he intention is to authorize the Court to apply the general principles of municipal jurisprudence, in particular of private law, insofar as ... applicable to relations of States'[15]—whilst clarifying the content of permissible borrowing as limited to 'modes of general legal reasoning as well as comparative law analogies in order to make a coherent body of rules ... the content of which has been influenced by domestic law but which is still its own creation'.[16] Finally, Article 38(1)(d) sets out 'subsidiary means' for the determination of international law including judicial decisions, reflecting the reality that decisions of international or even of domestic courts dealing with relevant subject matter, whilst not establishing international law, may be taken as evidence of its content. Some decisions in international arbitration proceedings, whilst not establishing law, may acquire recognition as expressing it, as may expressions of opinion by leading commentators.

That list notably omits specific mention of decisions of the ICJ itself. Article 59 ICJ Statute, referred to at Article 38(1)(d), provides that: 'The decision of the [ICJ] has no binding force except between the parties and in respect of that particular case.' Decisions of the ICJ do not have precedential force as would judicial decisions in a common law system such as that of England and Wales. In theory the ICJ applies the law and cannot make it. In practice, however, its views are given great weight by reason of its continuity, competence and wide jurisdiction.[17] The ICJ is not bound by its own decisions as legal precedent, but in practice has consistently sought to create and then to extend a body of decision-making possessing internal coherence. Decisions of other senior international or domestic courts may also be looked to where these provide evidence concerning the content of applicable international law norms. 2.9

In practice these sources of law may today frequently be supplemented by so-called 'soft law' sources—for instance, resolutions of the UN General Assembly, statements of treaty interpretation bodies and arbitration decisions—which in some cases fall within Article 38(1)(d) and, whilst not having binding force, may be important as indicative of evolving practice and the development of customary legal norms in the absence of full codification of international law. 2.10

D. Interpretation of Treaties

Treaties are particularly prominent as sources of norms because they tend to express standards more clearly than the more scattered and disparate material within which evidence has to be sought for customary norms. Much relevant international law is set out in treaties and related international instruments, and questions of interpretation may have great importance. Treaties fall to be interpreted in accordance with the Vienna Convention on the Law of Treaties 1969 (VCLT) and in particular with the 'General rule 2.11

---

[15] Crawford (n 2) 34–35; Jennings and Watts (n 1) Part 1 36–40 §12.
[16] Crawford (n 2) 35.
[17] Crawford (n 2) 40–41.

of interpretation' at Article 31 and supplementary means of interpretation at Article 32 therein:

Article 31

General rule of interpretation

1. A treaty shall be interpreted in good faith in accordance with the ordinary meaning to be given to the terms of the treaty in their context and in the light of its object and purpose.
2. The context for the purpose of the interpretation of a treaty shall comprise, in addition to the text, including its preamble and annexes:
   (a) any agreement relating to the treaty which was made between all the parties in connection with the conclusion of the treaty;
   (b) any instrument which was made by one or more parties in connection with the conclusion of the treaty and accepted by the other parties as an instrument related to the treaty.
3. There shall be taken into account, together with the context:
   (a) any subsequent agreement between the parties regarding the interpretation of the treaty or the application of its provisions;
   (b) any subsequent practice in the application of the treaty which establishes the agreement of the parties regarding its interpretation;
   (c) any relevant rules of international law applicable in the relations between the parties.
4. A special meaning shall be given to a term if it is established that the parties so intended.

Article 32

Supplementary means of interpretation

Recourse may be had to supplementary means of interpretation, including the preparatory work of the treaty and the circumstances of its conclusion, in order to confirm the meaning resulting from the application of article 31, or to determine the meaning when the interpretation according to article 31:
(a) leaves the meaning ambiguous or obscure; or
(b) leads to a result which is manifestly absurd or unreasonable.

2.12   In principle, any international instrument will have a single correct interpretation uncoloured by specifically domestic understandings: *R v SSHD ex p Adan, R v SSHD ex p Aitseguer* [2000] UKHL 67, [2001] 2 AC 477 at 516C–518C, per Lord Steyn (with whom Lords Slynn, Hobhouse and Scott agreed):

> It follows that, as in the case of other multilateral treaties, the Refugee Convention must be given an independent meaning derivable from the sources mentioned in articles 31 and 32 [VCLT] and without taking colour from distinctive features of the legal system of any individual contracting state. In principle therefore there can only be one true interpretation of a treaty ...

Domestically, the VCLT standards have frequently been affirmed as authoritative, as in *ex p Adan, ex p Aitseguer* per Lord Slynn:

> Just as the courts must seek to give a 'Community' meaning to words in the Treaty of Rome ('worker') so the Secretary of State and the courts must in the absence of a ruling by the International Court of Justice or uniform state practice arrive at their interpretation on the basis of the Convention as a whole read in the light of any relevant rules of international law, including [VCLT]. The Secretary of State and the courts of the United Kingdom have to decide what this phrase in this Treaty means. They cannot simply adopt a list of permissible or legitimate or possible or reasonable meanings and accept that any one of those when applied would be in compliance with the Convention.

Although the VCLT rules develop pre-existing currents in public international law practice, they do contrast with some earlier features of interpretation, as illustrated, for example, by the arbitral award in *Aguas del Tunari v Bolivia* (ICSID ARB/02/0311, Decision on Respondent's Objections to Jurisdiction, 21 October 2005, §91): 2.13

> [T]he Vienna Convention represents a move away from the canons of interpretation previously common in treaty interpretation and which erroneously persist in various international decisions today. For example, the Vienna Convention does not mention the canon that treaties are to be construed narrowly, a canon that presumes States cannot have intended to restrict their range of action ...

E. State Responsibility

Under the established principles of international law, a state (in the present context the UK) is in general considered responsible for acts by its ministers or officials or those acting under their direction. Under Article 4 of the International Law Commission's Articles on the Responsibility of States for Internationally Wrongful Acts, 'the conduct of any State organ shall be considered an act of that State under international law'. Attribution to a state in general is not eluded if it pleads that a decision taken by its official was in excess of authority or unlawful in domestic law: 'In international law there is a clear reason for disregarding a plea of unlawfulness under domestic law: the lack of express authority cannot be decisive as to the responsibility of the state.'[18] The state's responsibility is not limited to acts or omissions occurring within its home territory and in essence depends upon whether the relevant conduct can be attributed to that state applying established principles.[19] The state does not have to be the direct perpetrator of an unlawful act: for example, in the *Corfu Channel*[20] case, Albania was held liable to the UK for damage done to British ships by mines laid in Albanian waters by a third state, Yugoslavia, because the Albanian authorities were aware of the threat these posed and failed to warn of their presence. The principles relating to attribution of an international law wrong are relatively complex,[21] but in the immigration and nationality context, it is difficult to see how the UK could in anything but the most unusual circumstances disclaim responsibility for a decision taken by a minister or official, or an omission by him or her. The scope of law made by a treaty will be interpreted taking into account the content of international law more widely. Interpreting Article 1 ECHR, which sets out the scope of that instrument, the Grand Chamber of the European Court of Human Rights (ECtHR) in *Banković and others v Belgium and others*—app 52207/99, [2001] ECHR 890, (2007) 44 EHRR SE5, at [57], held that: 2.14

> [T]he principles underlying [ECHR] cannot be interpreted and applied in a vacuum. The Court must also take into account any relevant rules of international law when examining questions concerning its jurisdiction and, consequently, determine State responsibility in conformity with the governing principles of international law, although it must remain mindful

---

[18] Crawford (n 2) 549.
[19] Crawford (n 2) 542–55.
[20] *Corfu Channel case* (1949) ICJ Reports 4, judgment of 9 April 1949.
[21] Crawford (n 2) 542–55.

of the Convention's special character as a human rights treaty (the above-cited *Loizidou* judgment (*merits*), at §§ 43 and 52). The Convention should be interpreted as far as possible in harmony with other principles of international law of which it forms part (*Al-Adsani v UK* [GC], no. 35763, § 60, to be reported in ECHR 2001).

F. Application of International Law to the UK

2.15 Whilst this has changed considerably over time, the traditional position has been that international law applies only on the international level, between and amongst states and other international actors such as the UN or its agencies. Whilst this is no longer the case, it remains the case that most core norms of classical international law continue to operate exclusively, or primarily, between states.

2.16 The application of international law domestically is considered below. At an international level, however, it is well established that a state such as the UK cannot avoid liability for what is otherwise an international law wrong by reliance upon its own constitutional or other law, or some lacuna in this. The principle was established in the *Alabama Claims* case,[22] in which the US sought, and recovered, substantial damages from the UK for permitting the Confederate States to fit out vessels as raiders in British dockyards during the American Civil War, the absence of domestic laws prohibiting this being found irrelevant. More recently, Articles 27 and 46 VCLT have codified this as regards treaties, stating that 'A party may not invoke the provisions of its international law as justification for its failure to perform a treaty', Article 46 providing a limited exception if consent to be bound was given in breach of domestic law authority to do so, in a way which would be objectively evident to any state conducting itself in the matter in accordance with normal practice and in good faith, and 'a rule of its internal law of fundamental importance' is concerned. The International Law Commission in its Articles on Responsibility of States for Internationally Wrongful Acts (ARSIWA) provides that 'The characterization of an act of a State as internationally wrongful is governed by international law. Such characterization is not affected by the characterization of the same act as lawful by internal law.'

G. International Law within the UK

2.17 An important obstacle to reliance upon international law in the UK is that it is not directly enforceable in any UK jurisdiction, unless it has been incorporated into domestic law. This is so because of the shape of the domestic legal structure. In the legal systems of constituent parts of the UK, the conclusion and ratification of treaties is part of the prerogative of the Crown, and if such treaties (or customary international law) had direct effect, then the Crown prerogative could be used to conclude treaties, or legal standards could be invoked, which would affect the subject without any consent of

---

[22] Reports of International Arbitral Awards, *Alabama Claims of the United States of America against Great Britain*, award rendered on 14 September 1872 by the tribunal of arbitration established by Article I of the Treaty of Washington of 8 May 1871, vol XXIX, 125–34.

Parliament. The UK is therefore a 'dualist' rather than a 'monist' state, so that international law establishes domestic law only when, and to the extent that it is either incorporated into national law or otherwise engaged by the common law. In a 'monist' state, such as, for example, the Netherlands, international law is directly effective in domestic courts and tribunals without any requirement for incorporation.

2.18 Thereafter the position as regards customary international law and treaty law diverges. As to the former, a number of earlier authorities have suggested that customary international law is in its entirety 'part of the law of England' by implicit if not express incorporation. In *R v Jones* [2006] UKHL 16, [2007] 1 AC 136, [11], Lord Bingham observed that he would 'hesitate, at any rate without much fuller argument, to accept this proposition in quite the unqualified terms in which it has often been stated. There seems to be truth in [the contention] that international law is not a part, but is one of the sources, of English law'. The 'dominant principle' cited in *Brownlie* is that 'customary rules [of international law] are to be considered part of the law of the land and enforced as such, with the qualification that they are incorporated only insofar as is not inconsistent with Acts of Parliament or prior judicial decisions of final authority', though a rival interpretation also cited is that customary international law is incorporated into domestic law only where there has been express incorporation.[23]

2.19 By contrast, treaties are not subject to any general assumption of incorporation into domestic law. This longstanding principle was succinctly restated in the Privy Council in *Thomas and another v Baptiste (Trinidad and Tobago) and others* [1999] UKPC 13, [2000] 2 AC 1, in appeals from the rejection *inter alia* of a constitutional motion by two prisoners facing execution for murder in Trinidad and Tobago on the basis that they each had a constitutional right to have an outstanding application to the Inter-American Commission on Human Rights considered and determined before execution. Section 4(a) of the Constitution of Trinidad and Tobago affirmed *inter alia* the right to life, and not to be deprived thereof save 'by due process of law'. Lord Millett at [26]–[27] said the following:

26. Their Lordships recognise the constitutional importance of the principle that international conventions do not alter domestic law except to the extent that they are incorporated into domestic law by legislation. The making of a treaty, in Trinidad and Tobago as in England, is an act of the executive government, not of the legislature. It follows that the terms of a treaty cannot effect any alteration to domestic law or deprive the subject of existing legal rights unless and until enacted into domestic law by or under authority of the legislature. When so enacted, the Courts give effect to the domestic legislation, not to the terms of the treaty. The many authoritative statements to this effect are too well known to need citation. It is sometimes argued that human rights treaties form an exception to this principle. It is also sometimes argued that a principle which is intended to afford the subject constitutional protection against the exercise of executive power cannot be invoked by the executive itself to escape from obligations which it has entered into for his protection. Their Lordships mention these arguments for completeness. They do not find it necessary to examine them further in the present case.

27. In their Lordships' view, however, the appellants' claim does not infringe the principle which the Government invoke. The right for which they contend is not the particular right to petition the Commission or even to complete the particular process which they initiated when they lodged their petitions. It is the general right accorded to all litigants not to

---

[23] Crawford (n 2) 41.

Part B – Legal Framework

have the outcome of any pending appellate or other legal process pre-empted by executive action. This general right is not created by the Convention; it is accorded by the common law and affirmed by section 4(a) of the Constitution. The appellants are not seeking to enforce the terms of an unincorporated treaty, but a provision of the domestic law of Trinidad and Tobago contained in the Constitution. By ratifying a treaty which provides for individual access to an international body, the Government made that process for the time being part of the domestic criminal justice system and thereby temporarily at least extended the scope of the due process clause in the Constitution.

2.20   Some standards of international law are binding in the UK by virtue of their incorporation into domestic statutes, as with a core of EU law incorporated by the European Communities Act 1972, though EU law not incorporated so tritely remains unincorporated in international law: *Assange v The Swedish Prosecution Authority (Rev 1)* [2012] UKSC 22, [2012] 2 AC 471, per Lord Mance at [210]). Others are partly incorporated by statute, a significant example being the ECHR. Norms may be so similar as between domestic law and international law as to create real doubt as to whether there is formal incorporation. For example, in *R v Asfaw* [2008] UKHL 31, [2008] 1 AC 1061 [29], Lord Bingham dismissed earlier references in the House of Lords to 'incorporation' of the Convention relating to the Status of Refugees 1951:

> It is plain from these authorities that the British regime for handling applications for asylum has been closely assimilated to the Convention model. But it is also plain (as I think) that the Convention as a whole has never been formally incorporated or given effect in domestic law.

The same instrument may provide an example of partial incorporation for limited purposes, namely restraining the content of particular rules: section 2 Asylum and Immigration Act 1993 (AIA 1993) provides that: '[n]othing in the immigration rules (within the meaning of the 1971 Act) shall lay down any practice which would be contrary to the Convention.'

2.21   Thus, incorporated treaties have domestic legal effect to the extent that this is created given the particular context and extent of their incorporation. By contrast unincorporated treaties do not create directly enforceable rights in the UK and a breach of an unincorporated treaty by the UK is without domestic legal effect. However, that notwithstanding, international law may inform domestic law and/or practice and in some cases may be separately appealed to. Where a decision has to be made between two possible interpretations of a domestic statute, there is a 'presumption whereby the courts prefer that which avoids conflict between our domestic legislation and our international treaty obligations', but this is 'a mere canon of construction which involves no importation of international law into the domestic field': *R v SSHD ex p Brind* [1991] 1 AC 696, 748B–C, per Lord Bridge of Harwich. In *R v Lyons and others* [2002] UKHL 44, [2003] 1 AC 976, a challenge to convictions pre-dating the domestic incorporation of parts of ECHR by the Human Rights Act 1998, which could not be applied retrospectively, the appellants sought to rely upon ECHR directly, Lord Hoffmann (with whom Lord Hobhouse and Millett agreed) at [27] and [40] indicated that although the judiciary forms one of the three organs of the British state, this does not create legal competence in the judicial branch to apply an unincorporated treaty provision:

> In other words, the Convention is an international treaty and the ECtHR is an international court with jurisdiction under international law to interpret and apply it. But the question of whether the appellants' convictions were unsafe is a matter of English law. And it is firmly

established that international treaties do not form part of English law and that English courts have no jurisdiction to interpret or apply them: *JH Rayner (Mincing Lane) Ltd v Department of Trade and Industry* [1990] 2 AC 418. Parliament may pass a law which mirrors the terms of the treaty and in that sense incorporates the treaty into English law. But even then, the metaphor of incorporation may be misleading. It is not the treaty but the statute which forms part of English law. And English courts will not (unless the statute expressly so provides) be bound to give effect to interpretations of the treaty by an international court, even though the United Kingdom is bound by international law to do so. Of course there is a strong presumption in favour of interpreting English law (whether common law or statute) in a way which does not place the United Kingdom in breach of an international obligation. As Lord Goff of Chieveley said in *Attorney-General v Guardian Newspapers Ltd (No.2)* [1990] 1 AC 109, 283:

> I conceive it to be my duty, when I am free to do so, to interpret the law in accordance with the obligations of the Crown under [the Convention].

...

> The argument that the courts are an organ of State and therefore obliged to give effect to the State's international obligations is in my opinion a fallacy. If the proposition were true, it would completely undermine the principle that the courts apply domestic law and not international treaties. There would be no reason to confine it to secondary obligations arising from breaches of the treaty. The truth of the matter is that, in the present context, to describe the courts as an organ of the State is significant only in international law. International law does not normally take account of the internal distribution of powers within a State. It is the duty of the State to comply with international law, whatever may be the organs which have the power to do so. And likewise, a treaty may be infringed by the actions of the Crown, Parliament or the courts. From the point of view of international law, it ordinarily does not matter. In domestic law, however, the position is very different. The domestic constitution is based upon the separation of powers. In domestic law, the courts are obliged to give effect to the law as enacted by Parliament. This obligation is entirely unaffected by international law.

2.22 Therefore, unincorporated treaties, or customary international law, may shape domestic law through the strong common law presumption that legislation, and/or the common law itself, is presumed not to seek to breach international law obligations. Unincorporated treaties or customary international law may also inform the interpretation of the legitimate range or focus of an executive policy or of decision-making by a state body. So, for example, in *R v SSHD ex p. Venables and Thompson* [1997] UKHL 25, [1998] AC 407, a case concerning the setting of the penal tariff for two juvenile offenders, Lord Browne-Wilkinson referred to the Convention on the Rights of the Child 1989 (CRC: this instrument is addressed in more detail in chapter 3):

> The Convention has not been incorporated into English law. But it is legitimate in considering the nature of detention during Her Majesty's pleasure (as to which your Lordships are not in agreement) to assume that Parliament has not maintained on the statute book a power capable of being exercised in a manner inconsistent with the treaty obligations of this country. Article 3(i) requires that in the exercise of administrative, as well as court, powers the best interests of the child are a 'primary consideration'. Article 40(i) shows that the child offender is to be treated in a manner which takes into account 'the desirability of promoting the child's reintegration and the child's assuming a constructive role in society'. The Secretary of State contends that he is entitled to fix a tariff which will endure throughout the childhood of the offender and that neither in fixing that tariff nor in considering any revision of it will he have

any regard to the welfare of the child. Such a policy would infringe the treaty obligations of this country.

So too in *R (Atamewan) v SSHD* [2013] EWHC 2727 (Admin), [2014] 1 WLR 1959, a Divisional Court of Aikens LJ and Silber J quashed a decision found to have been based upon a policy which was disloyal to the Council of Europe Convention on Action against Trafficking in Human Beings 2005 by imposing upon it the concept of a 'historic' victim of trafficking not recognised as a victim entitled to recognition due to the passage of time.[24]

H. Protection

2.23 Under international law, a state has a right of protection of its nationals. An individual possessing the nationality of one state, and present on the territory of another, may be protected by the former state, whose sovereignty extends to its national, whilst subject to the territorial sovereignty of the latter. This right to protect its nationals is the means by which the state may enforce the duty of another state to treat non-nationals or aliens in accordance with defined international norms whilst they remain on its territory, and in the circumstances of intended removal from it.[25]

2.24 In relation to the treatment of an alien by a state, a breach of accepted standards may cause the alien's state of nationality to exercise its right to protect its national. But some fundamental norms are norms *erga omnes*, or obligations owed 'toward all'. In the *Barcelona Traction* case (*Belgium v Spain*) (*Second Phase*) (1970) ICJ Reports 3, the ICJ described the legal relationship created by entrance to the territory of a state by an alien. It held at [33]–[34] that at least certain core protections of individuals constituted *erga omnes* norms:

> 33. When a State admits into its territory foreign investments or foreign nationals, whether natural or juristic persons, it is bound to extend to them the protection of the law and assumes obligations concerning the treatment to be afforded them. These obligations, however, are neither absolute nor unqualified. In particular, an essential distinction should be drawn between the obligations of a State towards the international community as a whole, and those arising vis-a-vis another State in the field of diplomatic protection. By their very nature the former are the concern of all States. In view of the importance of the rights involved, all States can be held to have a legal interest in their protection; they are obligations *erga omnes*.
>
> 34. Such obligations derive, for example, in contemporary international law, from the outlawing of acts of aggression, and of genocide, as also from the principles and rules concerning the basic rights of the human person, including protection from slavery and racial discrimination. Some of the corresponding rights of protection have entered into the body of general international law (*Reservations to the Convention on the Prevention and Punishment of the Crime of Genocide, Advisory Opinion, I.C.J. Reports 1951*, p. 23); others are conferred by international instruments of a universal or quasi-universal character.

2.25 *Oppenheim's International Law* notes that whilst all states are subject to obligations as regards their treatment of aliens, 'those obligations (generally speaking) can only be

---

[24] For more detail, see the works of S Fatima (n 6).
[25] Jennings and Watts (n 1) Part 2 935–39 §411.

invoked by the state whose nationality the alien possesses'.[26] A breach of obligations by a state in the treatment of another state's national may be answerable by the second state exercising a recognised right of 'diplomatic protection' on behalf of the affected national. A breach of a recognised *erga omnes* norm, by contrast, is one in which all states have a recognised legal interest.

2.26 The existence of a state's right to exercise diplomatic protection in relation to nationals and certain other persons has always been recognised, and that right is plainly a part of international law. The Draft Articles on Diplomatic Protection submitted by the International Law Commission to the United Nations General Assembly in 2006[27] define this as 'the invocation by a State, through diplomatic action or other means of peaceful settlement, of the responsibility of another State for an injury caused by an internationally wrongful act of that State to a [national]'.[28] A general restraint is the requirement in international law that the individual or group who is the object of internationally wrongful treatment should have exhausted any remedies available in the state responsible. The Draft Articles, which seek to codify customary law, bar the exercise of diplomatic protection where local remedies have not been exhausted, save where, inter alia, there is no reasonable possibility of redress through local means, there is undue delay attributable to the state in pursuing such redress, the injured person is manifestly precluded from pursuing local remedies, or the state responsible for the act or acts in question has waived the requirement for exhaustion.

2.27 What constitute appropriate circumstances for the exercise of international protection is a contested question, complicated by the existence of a large body of international law material, much of which is focused upon a state's protection of economic interests. Brownlie concludes that the 'preponderant doctrine' supports the existence of a so-called 'international minimum standard', the boundaries of which are debated.[29] At the focus of that debate is the standard expressed by a US-Mexico Claims Commission addressing the killing of a US national in Mexico. The US alleged that the Mexican authorities were liable for failure to conduct adequate investigation into the death. The Commission stated the position in law to be that '... the treatment of an alien, in order to constitute an international delinquency, should amount to an outrage, to bad faith, to wilful neglect of duty, or to an insufficiency of governmental action so far short of international standards that every reasonable and impartial man would readily recognize its insufficiency'.

2.28 Although states are the main subjects of customary international law, individuals evidently are affected even where they are the objects rather than directly the subjects of international law (for instance, where a person is expelled from one state to another, the expulsion may breach a duty of the expelling state owed to the receiving state), and they may also be subject to rights and duties under it (the person expelled may have a right under international law not to be expelled). This has come to be generally accepted, particularly as the structure of human rights protection in international law has grown, something which is examined below.

---

[26] ibid, Part 1 5 §1.
[27] ILC, Draft Articles on Diplomatic Protection, 2006, Official Records of the General Assembly, 61st Session, Supp 10 (A/61/10).
[28] Or a stateless person or refugee recognised as such by the state seeking to exercise diplomatic protection, who is lawfully and habitually resident in that state at the date of injury (Draft Articles, article 8): hence a refugee of, say, Afghan or Somali nationality, lawfully and habitually resident in Germany and barred from entry or expelled from the UK, might on this measure seek German diplomatic protection in respect of a claimed international law wrong by the UK.
[29] Crawford (n 2) 610–26.

I. The Significance of Nationality in International Law

2.29   Nationality is important in international law as the principal link between the individual and the state to which he or she belongs. The term denotes membership of that state for purposes of international law.[30] Whilst international law is not restricted to questions between states, and many rules of international law (such as those created by human rights treaties, or hybrid treaties with a human rights element) plainly devolve rights or duties upon individuals, certain legal norms still emanate from the treatment of the individual as the subject of relations between states. As noted in *Oppenheim's International Law*:

> It is through the medium of their nationality that individuals can normally enjoy benefits from international law … Such individuals as do not possess any nationality enjoy, in general, only limited protection, since if they are aggrieved by a state there is no national state which is competent to take up their case. As far as international law is concerned, there is, apart from obligations (now quite extensive) expressly laid down by treaty—and in particular the general obligation, enshrined in the Charter of the United Nations, to respect human rights and fundamental freedoms—no restriction upon a state maltreating such stateless individuals. On the other hand, if individuals who possess nationality are wronged abroad, it is, as a rule, their home state exclusively which has a right to ask for redress, and these individuals themselves have no such right. It is for this reason that nationality is very important for international law.[31]

2.30   In international law individuals generally look to the state of their nationality for protection of their essential interests, which are in international law treated as potential or actual emanations of the national interest of the state. Individuals with no nationality, or no nationality effective for relevant purposes (such as refugees and stateless persons), may be protected in common with others by general human rights instruments or regional or domestic legal regimes, but have no state of nationality to which to look for protection. In some cases, as under CSR, an individual who cannot look to a state of nationality for protection may look to the international community.[32]

J. Attributing Nationality for the Purposes of International Law

2.31   Whether an individual is a national of a state for domestic law purposes depends upon the law of that state. For some purposes, international law deliberately looks to the domestic law and practice of a particular state, and not beyond this: for example, Article 1(1) of the Convention Relating to the Status of Stateless Persons 1954 (CSSP) defines 'stateless person' as a person 'not considered as a national by any State under the

---

[30] The definition from international law is distinct from the alternative definition of nationality as relating to membership of an ethnically or otherly defined 'nation', such as Celts or Slovenes. See, eg, Weis (n 3) 3: 'The term "nationality" … is a politico-legal term denoting membership of a State. It must be distinguished from nationality as a historico-biological term denoting membership of a nation. In the latter sense it means the subjective corporate sentiment of unity of members of a specific group forming a '"race" or "nation" which may, though not necessarily, be possessed of a territory.'
[31] Jennings and Watts (n 1) vol 1 849 §377.
[32] See further ch 4.

operation of its law'. The factual question is restricted to questions of domestic law and the state's operation of its own domestic law. This is entirely logical, even if the position of the state in question is deplored by the international community and may not be recognised under international law, because the object of the particular test is to determine what that state considers the position to be as regards a particular individual, so as to ascertain whether the individual is without the protection of that state.

In other circumstances it is necessary to consider the question of nationality more broadly, because the object is to determine, for example, whether a particular state possesses the right to protect an individual on the basis that he or she is its national. A tie of nationality between that individual and the state of nationality according to its domestic law may not be recognised by others. The classical position that the grant or withholding of nationality was an aspect of domestic sovereignty substantially protected from international law has over time been relaxed somewhat, at least as regards the recognition of a bond of nationality founded on domestic law by another state or by the international community. In its *Advisory Opinion* in the *Nationality Decrees Issued in Tunis and Morocco* case,[33] the PCIJ at [40]–[41] held that: 2.32

40. The question whether a certain matter is or is not solely within the jurisdiction of a State is an essentially relative question; it depends upon the development of international relations. Thus, in the present state of international law, questions of nationality are, in the opinion of the Court, in principle within this reserved domain.
41. For the purpose of the present opinion, it is enough to observe that it may well happen that, in a matter which, like that of nationality, is not, in principle, regulated by international law, the right of a State to use its discretion is nevertheless restricted by obligations which it may have undertaken towards other States. In such a case, jurisdiction which, in principle, belongs solely to the State, is limited by rules of international law.

The League of Nations Convention on Certain Questions Relating to the Conflict of Nationality Law 1930 (CCQRCNL) provides by articles 1 and 2 that: 2.33

Article 1

It is for each State to determine under its own law who are its nationals. This law shall be recognised by other States in so far as it is consistent with international conventions, international custom, and the principles of law generally recognised with regard to nationality.

Article 28

Any question as to whether a person possesses the nationality of a particular State shall be determined in accordance with the law of the State.

In this context the question of nationality for purposes of international (as contrasted with domestic) law is, in the language of the *Tunis and Morocco* opinion, 'an essentially relative question' depending upon 'the development of international relations' today.[34] Whether the nationality status indicated by domestic law is also attributed for purposes of international law depends upon the consistency of national conduct with international law. 2.34

---

[33] *Nationality Decrees Issued in Tunis and Morocco on 8 November 1921*, Advisory Opinion, 1923 PCIJ (ser B) No 4 (7 February 1923).
[34] ibid [40].

2.35 In the *Nottebohm* case *(Liechtenstein v Guatemala)* (1955) ICJ Reports 4, Mr Nottebohm was a German national long resident in Guatemala. Anticipating that he might be interned as an enemy alien in the event of war with Germany, he travelled to Liechtenstein shortly after the outbreak of the Second World War and obtained its nationality, as a result of which his German nationality was withdrawn automatically. He was naturalised as a Liechtenstein citizen after 11 days in that country, paying to obtain waiver of the normal three-year residency requirement. He then returned to Guatemala, where, upon that country declaring war on Germany, he was detained and transferred to a US military base for deportation. He sought the protection of Liechtenstein for the purpose of an international claim against Guatemala. However, the ICJ found that Liechtenstein was not entitled to protect him in that context because 'in order to be capable of being invoked against another State, nationality must correspond with the factual situation', and implicitly his did not:

> According to the practice of States, to arbitral and judicial decisions and to the opinions of writers, nationality is a legal bond having as its basis a social fact of attachment, a genuine connection of existence, interests and sentiments, together with the existence of reciprocal rights and duties. It may be said to constitute the juridical expression of the fact that the individual upon whom it is conferred, either directly by the law or as the result of an act of the authorities, is in fact more closely connected with the population of the State conferring nationality than with that of any other State. Conferred by a State, it only entitles that State to exercise protection vis-a-vis another State, if it constitutes a translation into juridical terms of the individual's connection with the State which has made him its national.[35]

2.36 The Court found that the facts revealed 'on the one hand, the absence of any bond of attachment between Mr Nottebohm and Liechtenstein and, on the other hand, the existence of a long-standing and close connection between him and Guatemala, a link which his naturalization in no way weakened'. It found that his Liechtenstein nationality, valid under the law of that country, did not give rise to a right of protection against Guatemala on the international plane:

> That naturalization was not based on any real prior connection with Liechtenstein, nor did it in any way alter the manner of life of the person upon whom it was conferred in exceptional circumstances of speed and accommodation. In both respects, it was lacking in the genuineness requisite to an act of such importance, if it is to be entitled to be respected by a State in the position of Guatemala. It was granted without regard to the concept of nationality adopted in international relations.[36]

2.37 The *Nottebohm* decision on the narrow interpretation of its outcome goes to whether a state may exert diplomatic protection in respect of an individual, finding that it cannot in the absence of a relevant link, perhaps particularly where the state against which protection is sought is one with which, as in the case, there was a strong historic link. However, it is strongly arguable that the principle expounded in the decision is broader in application to issues of validity of a claim to nationality considered under international law. On this construction, the presence of a bond of attachment is a precondition for attribution of nationality, notwithstanding that the domestic law of a state identifies

---

[35] *Nottebohm* case, 20.
[36] ibid.

that individual as such.[37] Yet the possession of such a bond alone is not constitutive of nationality in the absence of this arising under domestic law.

K. Rights and Duties of States: (i) Expulsion and Exclusion of Aliens; and (ii) Admission of Nationals

For the state of nationality, the possession by an individual of its nationality entails its own right to protect that individual abroad, as outlined at para 2.23 above. Equally, for the state in which that individual is present, if he or she is not its national, the ability to control the presence of an alien on its territory is a significant aspect of sovereignty. International law therefore involves substantial obligations as between a state of nationality and a state of sojourn wishing to expel the former state's national. There is a strong expectation in international law that a state will admit a national to its territory. *Oppenheim's International Law* observes that the nationality of an individual acquires importance both in relation to protection of nationals abroad and in the obligation of the state of nationality to accept the return of a national to its territory: 2.38

> The function of nationality becomes apparent with regards to individuals abroad ... especially on account of one particular right and one particular duty of every state towards all other states. The right is that of protection over its nationals abroad which every state holds, and occasionally vigorously exercise, as against other states ... The duty is that of receiving on its territory such of its nationals as are not allowed to remain on the territory of other states. Since no state is obliged by international law to allow foreigners to remain within its boundaries, it may, for many reasons, happen that certain individuals are expelled from all foreign countries. The state of nationality of expelled persons is bound to receive them on its territory ...[38]

In the present context, two matters are particularly important: the right of a state to exclude or expel aliens, on the one hand, and the duty of a state of nationality to admit its nationals on the other. The state of nationality in all or almost all circumstances must admit its nationals where this is required by an expelling state. But it is in general not bound to admit an alien and it may expel aliens with substantial but not absolute freedom. 2.39

K1. Exclusion or Expulsion of Aliens

The conventional view amongst jurists is that states have always possessed the power to exclude or expel aliens. In *Attorney-General of Canada v Cain and Gilhula* [1906] UKPC 55, [1906] AC 542, Lord Atkinson in the Privy Council observed at 546A–B that: 2.40

> One of the rights possessed by the supreme power in every State is the right to refuse to permit an alien to enter that State, to annex what conditions it pleases to the permission to enter it, and to expel or deport from the State, at pleasure, even a friendly alien, especially if it considers his presence in the State opposed to its peace, order, and good government, or to its social or material interests ...

---

[37] See Crawford (n 2), 513–18.
[38] See Jennings and Watts (n 1) Part 2 857–58 §379.

2.41 It has been said that this right of expulsion extended even to persons seeking asylum facing serious harm, though a state might choose not to exercise the right where considerations of humanity militated against doing so. In *R (otao European Roma Rights Centre and others) v Immigration Officer at Prague Airport and another* [2004] UKHL 55, [2005] 2 AC 1, Lord Bingham referred to the practice of states in classical international law:

> 12. It has been the humane practice of this and other states to admit aliens (or some of them) seeking refuge from persecution and oppression in their own countries. The generous treatment of French Protestants in this country is an early and obvious example ... and many later examples spring to mind. But even those fleeing from foreign persecution have had no right to be admitted and no right of asylum. There is a wealth of authority to this effect: ...
> 13. Over time there came to be recognised a right in sovereign states to give refuge to aliens fleeing from foreign persecution and to refuse to surrender such persons to the authorities of their home states ... But these rights were not matched by recognition in domestic law of any right in the alien to require admission to the receiving state or by any common law duty in the receiving state to give it.

2.42 In some part these expressions of the traditional position may not be fully supported by the earlier theorists and may invite questioning as to whether Lord Bingham's 'humane practice' remained a matter of pure discretion or whether it over some period became possessed of a legal character. However, the view that there was an absolute or near-absolute right to exclude or expel is well established, and the practical effect of it is now sufficiently mitigated by developments in human rights and other laws that enquiry into the earlier position may be academic.

2.43 *Oppenheim's International Law* expresses the right of expulsion in customary international law as being substantial but not wholly unfettered:

> The right of states to expel aliens is generally recognised. It matters not whether the alien is only on a temporary visit, or has settled down for professional business or other purposes on its territory, having established his domicile there.
>
> On the other hand, while a state has a broad discretion in exercising its rights to expel aliens, its discretion is not absolute. Thus, by customary international law it must not abuse its right by acting arbitrarily in taking its decision to expel an alien, and it must act reasonably in the manner in which it effects an expulsion.
>
> Beyond this, however, customary international law provides no detailed rules regarding expulsion, and everything accordingly depends upon the merits of the individual case. Theory and practice correctly make a distinction between expulsion in time of hostilities and in time of peace. A belligerent may consider it convenient to expel all hostile nationals residing, or temporarily staying, within its territory: although such a measure may be very hard on individual aliens, it is generally accepted that such expulsion is justifiable. As regards expulsion in time of peace, on the other hand, the opinions and practice of states differ substantially as to what may constitute a just cause for expulsion. While some causes (such as engaging in espionage activities) are universally accepted as justifying expulsion, other causes are more debatable: yet no state which expels an alien will admit not having had a just cause for doing so. The matter is scarcely susceptible of answer once and for all by the establishment of a body of rules. The borderline between discretion and arbitrariness, although elastic, is nevertheless a real one, and in case of doubt it is for an impartial organ to determine whether it has been overstepped.[39]

---

[39] Jennings and Watts (n 1) Part 2 940–41 §413.

The more recent account in *Brownlie* states that: 2.44

> In principle expulsion of aliens is also within the discretion of the state, but this discretion is not unlimited. In particular the power must be exercised in good faith and not for an ulterior motive. While the expelling state has a margin of appreciation in applying the concept of '*ordre public*', this concept is to be measured against human rights standards. The latter are applicable also to the *manner* of expulsion …[40]

This exclusive citation of human rights standards in *Brownlie* tends to obscure the continuing relevance of customary international law, not abolished by the parallel development of a body of treaty based human rights norms. In most circumstances the best modern position may be that the two are not mutually exclusive and may inform each other or be mutually reinforcing: the application of the customary international law principles in modern conditions may be informed by human rights law, and understanding of customary international law may be useful to the interpretation of human rights provisions.

K2. Standards Applicable in Expulsion Cases

As to measures of exclusion or expulsion, it is clear that notwithstanding the relative freedom that international law permits states as regards expulsion to its territory, that freedom is not absolute. In the *Nottebohm* case Judge Read in a dissenting opinion noted that: 2.45

> As a result of the admission of an alien, whether as a permanent settler or as a visitor, a whole series of legal relationships come into being. There are two States concerned, to which I shall refer as the receiving State and the protecting State. The receiving State becomes subject to a series of legal duties vis-a-vis the protecting State, particularly the duty of reasonable and fair treatment. It acquires rights vis-a-vis the protecting State and the individual, particularly the rights incident to local allegiance and the right of deportation to the protecting State. At the same time the protecting State acquires correlative rights and obligations vis-a-vis the receiving State, particularly a diminution of its rights as against the individual resulting from the local allegiance, the right to assert diplomatic protection and the obligation to receive the individual on deportation. This network of rights and obligations is fundamentally conventional in its origin—it begins with a voluntary act of the protecting State in permitting the individual to take up residence in the other country, and the voluntary act of admission by the receiving State. The scope and content of the rights are, however, largely defined by positive international law. Nevertheless, the receiving State has control at all stages because it can bring the situation to an end by deportation.[41]

The key early elaboration of principle regarding the ability of a state to expel an alien without a breach of the rights of the state of his or her nationality is that of the American lawyer Jackson H Ralston, acting as umpire in the *Boffolo* arbitration held under the Italian-Venezuelan Mixed Claims Commission. The case concerned the expulsion by Venezuela of an Italian national. Noting that there was a broad power of expulsion available to a state of residence, the umpire went on to observe that 'there may be a broad difference between the right to exercise a power and the rightful exercise of that power'.[42] In conclusion the umpire stated: 2.46

---

[40] Crawford (n 2) 609.
[41] *Nottebohm* case (n 34) 4 at 47.
[42] X Reports of International Arbitral Awards (1903) 528 at 532.

Part B – Legal Framework

Summing up the foregoing, we may (in part repeating) say:

1. A State possesses the general right of expulsion; but,
2. Expulsion should only be resorted to in extreme instances, and must be accomplished in the manner least injurious to the person affected.
3. The country exercising the power must, when occasion demands, state the reason of such expulsion before an international tribunal, and an inefficient reason or none being advanced, accepts the consequences.
4. In the present case the only reasons suggested to the Commission would be contrary to the Venezuelan constitution, and as this is a country not of despotic power, but of fixed laws, restraining, among other things, the acts of its officials, these reasons (whatever good ones may in point of fact have existed) cannot be accepted by the umpire as sufficient.[43]

2.47 In 1988, Plender, considering and digesting the work of earlier commentators, pointed to the increasing conditionality attached to the right of expulsion of non-nationals:

That a State has in general the right to expel aliens from its territory is not in doubt. The right has long been acknowledged; and has its corollary (if not its precise counterpart) in the duty of each State to readmit to its territory those of its nationals who have been lawfully expelled from other States. In recent years it has become increasingly apparent, however, that the right of expulsion is subject to significant restrictions imposed by public international law.uch restrictions apply both in the case of collective expulsion and in the case of the expulsion of individuals.[44]

Various illustrations have been provided in *Oppenheim*[45] and by Plender.[46]

2.40 An important requirement in relation to many norms is the avoidance of arbitrariness. The scope of that concept is described by the ICJ in the *Elettronica Sicula SpA (ELSI) (United States of America v Italy) Case* (1989) ICJ Reports 15. In that case the Mayor of Palermo had issued an order under Italian law requisitioning assets of an enterprise owned by a US enterprise. The ICJ declined to find that this was arbitrary:

Arbitrariness is not so much something opposed to a rule of law, as something opposed to the rule of law. This idea was expressed by the Court in the *Asylum* case, when it spoke of 'arbitrary action' being 'substituted for the rule of law'. It is a wilful disregard of due process of law, an act which shocks, or at least surprises, a sense of juridical propriety. Nothing in the decision of the Prefect, or in the judgment of the Court of Appeal of Palermo, conveys any indication that the requisition order of the Mayor was to be regarded in that light.[47]

It found that the order was not an arbitrary one because 'consciously made in the context of an operating system of law and of appropriate remedies of appeal'.[48]

2.49 In assessing whether actions were arbitrary in the context of the deprivation of nationality, the Eritrea Ethiopia Claims Commission, in its partial award announced on 17 December 2004, 'considered several factors, including whether the action had a basis in law whether it resulted in persons being rendered stateless; and whether there were legitimate reasons for it to be taken given the totality of the circumstances'.[49] Recognising that 'international

---

[43] ibid 537.
[44] Plender (n 5) 459.
[45] Jennings and Watts (n 1), Part 2 940–48 §413.
[46] Plender (n 5) 459–62.
[47] *Elettronica Sicula SpA (ELSI) (United States of America v Italy)* (1989) ICJ Reports 15, 76.
[48] ibid 76–77.
[49] *Eritrea Ethiopia Claims Commission, Partial Award: Civilians Claims—Eritrea's Claims 15, 16, 23 & 27–32*, Permanent Court of International Arbitration, The Hague, 17 December 2004 [60].

law limits States' power to deprive persons of their nationality', the Commission attached 'particular importance to the principle expressed in Article 15, paragraph 2, of the Universal Declaration of Human Rights, that "no one shall be arbitrarily deprived of his nationality"'.[50]

2.50 The decisions of the Commission in that case reveal an approach giving some attention to the pressures of war upon each state, but also show that the Commission did not accept that wartime conditions excused substantial wrongs. It stated that where Ethiopia had 'devised and implemented a system applying reasonable criteria to identify individual dual nationals thought to pose threats to its wartime security', deprivation of Ethiopian nationality had not been shown to be arbitrary.[51] But it also found that even allowing for the existence of armed conflict, Ethiopia had breached international law in its denaturalisation and expulsion of rural people of Eritrean background but possible Ethiopian or dual nationality, expelled summarily to Eritrea on or after the outbreak of war,[52] and family members caught up in wartime deportations of Eritreans without regard to their own nationality.[53] It held that Ethiopia had breached international law by 'erroneously depriving at least some Ethiopians who were not dual nationals of their Ethiopian nationality' and that where persons were permitted to remain but treated as aliens, with 'no process to identify individuals warranting special consideration and no apparent possibility of review or appeal', then:

> Considering that rights to such benefits as land ownership and business licenses, as well as passports and other travel documents were at stake, the Commission finds that this wide-scale deprivation of Ethiopian nationality of persons remaining in Ethiopia was under the circumstances arbitrary and contrary to international law.[54]

Those decisions, citing Article 15 of the UDHR, once again show that international human rights provisions may inform broader international standards.

2.51 More recently, the ICJ in the *Diallo* case[55] considered arbitrariness in the context of expulsion of a lawfully present alien, looking to Article 13 of the International Covenant on Civil and Political Rights (ICCPR) and the relevant protection under Article 12(4) of the African Charter on Human and Peoples' Rights, and found that the scope of 'arbitrariness' is not restricted to breach of domestic law and/or of specific human rights instruments:

> 65. It follows from the terms of the two provisions cited above that the expulsion of an alien lawfully in the territory of a State which is a party to these instruments can only be compatible with the international obligations of that State if it is decided in accordance with 'the law', in other words the domestic law applicable in that respect. Compliance with international law is to some extent dependent here on compliance with internal law. However, it is clear that while 'accordance with law' as thus defined is a necessary condition for compliance with the above-mentioned provisions, it is not the sufficient condition. First, the applicable domestic law must itself be compatible with the other requirements of the Covenant and the African Charter; second, an expulsion must not be arbitrary in nature, since protection against arbitrary treatment lies at the heart of the rights guaranteed by the international norms protecting human rights, in particular those set out in the two treaties applicable in this case.

---

[50] ibid [60].
[51] ibid [72].
[52] ibid [89].
[53] ibid [97].
[54] ibid [75].
[55] *Ahmadou Sadio Diallo (Republic of Guinea v Democratic Republic of the Congo)*, Merits, Judgment (2010) ICJ Reports 639, 663 [65].

K3. Admission to State of Nationality

2.52 There is a strong expectation in international law that a state will admit a national to its territory. Weis, writing in 1979, considered that: 'One of the elements inherent in the concept of nationality is the right to settle and to reside in the territory of nationality or, conversely, the duty of the State to grant and permit such residence to its nationals.'[56] Whilst he noted the question of 'the right of sojourn' between a national and his or her state as not being a question of international law:

> It may, however, become a question bearing on the relations between States. The expulsion of nationals forces other States to admit aliens, but, according to established principles of international law, the admission of aliens is in the discretion of each State—except where a State is bound by treaty to accord such admission. It is likewise an accepted rule of international law that States are not—unless bound by treaty obligations—under an obligation to grant aliens an unconditional and unlimited right of residence, though they may not expel them arbitrarily and without just cause. It follows that the expulsion of a national may only be carried out with the consent of the State to whose territory he is to be expelled, and that the State of nationality is under a duty towards other States to receive its nationals back on its territory ...[57]

2.53 In 1959 Van Panhuys, having surveyed the corpus of earlier international law learning, observed that 'A State's duty to admit its own nationals corresponds to the right of expulsion of the foreign State'[58] and of the duty further stated that:

> The duty to admit nationals is considered so important a consequence of nationality that it is almost equated with it ... This duty corresponds to the right of expulsion of the State of residence ... but cannot be explained as derived from it as Castrén seems to do ... Both rules are consequences of customary international law and are closely connected with the essence of nationality, that is, as long as the foreign national did not acquire the nationality of the State of residence, it is presumed that he belongs to the politico-legal community of his own State and consequently, the responsibility for him lies, according to international law, at the door of his State ...[59]

2.54 The duty in question was at that early stage understood as one owed between states, not one to which a state could be bound by an individual: 'According to international law the duty of admission only exists towards foreign States and not towards the national, though the custom, not to deny admission to nationals, is sometimes reflected in municipal law.'[60] Van Panhuys further stated that the position was varied in the case of a dual national. In such circumstances one country of nationality was not bound to grant admission to its national if faced with expulsion by another country of nationality:

> A State whose national also possesses other nationalities is not in duty bound to admit him unless the pertinent request comes from a non-national State.[61]

2.55 The principle was tested in 1972 by President Idi Amin's expulsion from Uganda of many persons of Asian origin. A large number of them were, under the nationality law

---

[56] Weis (n 3) 45.
[57] Weis (n 3) 50.
[58] HF Van Panhuys, *The Rôle of Nationality in International Law: An Outline* (Leiden, AW Sijthoff, 1959) 56.
[59] ibid.
[60] ibid.
[61] ibid.

then in force, British subjects. In the House of Lords, Lord Hailsham LC, on the day following the announcement that expulsion would be enforced by Uganda, stated that:

> [T]he Attorney General, acting in his capacity as the professional legal adviser to the Government ... advised us that in international law a State is under a duty as between other States to accept in its territories those of its nationals who have nowhere else to go. If a citizen of the United Kingdom is expelled, as I think illegally from Uganda, and is not accepted for settlement elsewhere, we could be required by any State where he then was to accept him. I think that is good law; I also think it is part of the international facts of life.[62]

This expression adds the important caveat that a national must have 'nowhere else to go' prior to the state of nationality being obliged to allow entry to its territory. The UK response to the crisis was not to admit all those affected, but to seek third countries prepared to accommodate some or all of the total.[63] In a subsequent appeal, *R v SSHD ex p Thakrar* [1974] QB 684 (CA), the Court of Appeal upheld the refusal of entry to a Ugandan Asian under new legislation, considering that the duty founded on nationality did not extend to a protected person without historic ties of allegiance to the UK. The Court held that even if the contrary was true, it was not for the courts of England and Wales to enforce the international law norm in the absence of domestic incorporation, and the rules of international law governed the relations between states only and could not be relied on by the applicant for his own benefit.

In the light of the views of commentators and other evidence of international law, it is unsurprising that in 1974 the European Court of Justice affirmed in *Van Duyn v Home Office (Workers)* [1974] EUECJ R-41/74, [1974] ECR 1337 that 'it is a principle of international law, which the EEC treaty cannot be assumed to disregard in the relations between member states, that a state is precluded from refusing its own nationals the right of entry or residence'. 2-56

Strong assertions of the duty to admit nationals appear to be echoed by all significant commentators. In 1988 Plender, considering and digesting the work of earlier commentators, pointed to a high degree of consistency on the obligation of a state to admit the return of its nationals: 2-57

> The principle that every State must admit its own nationals to its territory is accepted so widely that its existence as a rule of law is virtually beyond dispute. The principle is often implied by those who assert that each State has the right to deny admission to aliens. Among the more specialised writers, those who defend the existence of the principle include François, Weis, Goodwin-Gill, and Van Panhuys ...[64]

L. International Law and Denial or Deprivation of Nationality

In customary international law there are few restraints on the denial or deprivation of nationality: this has been viewed classically as an area of relatively strong, if not absolute, 2.58

---

[62] HL Deb 14 September 1972, vol 335, col 497.
[63] HL Deb 14 September 1972, vol 335, col 488: 'We are in particularly close touch with the Indian Government on this matter. Over a dozen other countries have responded favourably, and I mention with particular appreciation the generous offers by Canada, New Zealand and Sweden. Discussions have also been opened with the Inter-Governmental Committee for European Migration, which it is hoped may be able to assist by organising movement to Latin American countries.'
[64] Plender (n 5) 459.

control by states. However, the operation of the international system, based upon the attachment of individuals to states by nationality, is endangered by the existence and growth of exceptions to that system, in the form of individuals or groups without any or effective nationality. Despite disapproval by other members of the international community, instances in which states have contributed to this problem are historically numerous:

> During the present [twentieth] century the practice of withdrawing nationality from dissident individuals or groups has become increasingly widespread. In the 1920s, between one and two million people were deprived of their Soviet citizenship by the Bolsheviks. The German Reich followed a similar policy in respect of Jews in the 1930s. Measures of a comparable character (although on a smaller scale) were adopted during the same decade by the Italian and Turkish authorities. The Ugandan authorities under … Idi Amin Dada did not purport to withdraw Ugandan citizenship from the Asian community in 1972 but declared a policy of scrutinising the claim to Ugandan citizenship of each Asian resident and of imprisoning those residents whose claims to citizenship were found to be false. The effect on the departure of the Asian community was much the same as it would have been in the event of a candid act of denaturalization.[65]

2.59 The Preamble of CCQRCNL acknowledged the difficulties faced at a time when large-scale denationalisation by some states had created serious international problems, and many states required military service of citizens, took both statelessness and multiple nationality to be inimical to the functioning of the international system:

> Considering that it is of importance to settle by international agreement questions relating to the conflict of nationality laws;
>
> Being convinced that it is in the general interest of the international community to secure that all its members should recognise that every person should have a nationality and should have one nationality only;
>
> Recognising accordingly that the ideal towards which the efforts of humanity should be directed in this domain is the abolition of all cases both of statelessness and of double nationality;

Concerns regarding dual nationality are no longer widely expressed. However, as will be shown in chapters 3 and 5, international human rights law and Council of Europe instruments include some standards capable of extending to this area. And as chapter 4 demonstrates, the deprivation of national protection by the imposition of statelessness represented a significant motivator for the development of what are now distinct international refugee and statelessness law regimes.

2.60 It is possible that with the growth of human rights and other standards such as the Article 15 UDHR 'right to a nationality', subsequent provisions in the binding post-UDHR instruments and the prohibition upon arbitrary deprivation of return to an 'own country' under Article 12(4) ICCPR, an argument could now be made for the existence of an international law norm prohibiting arbitrary deprivation of nationality, particularly where this imposes statelessness. As further chapters, in particular chapters 3 and 5, will show, a series of non-discrimination norms have developed in human rights law. And as already noted at paragraph 2.24 above, the ICJ in the *Barcelona Traction* case recognised race discrimination amongst other obligations *erga omnes*.

---

[65] Plender (n 5) 144.

The UN Secretary General has suggested, essentially on this basis, that international law now contains a norm prohibiting arbitrary deprivation of nationality by states.[66] And applying *Nottebaum* principles, it appears possible that such a deprivation would not be recognised as binding other actors at the level of international law. As early as 1959, van Panhuys observed that: 'The considerations which have prompted a State to repudiate part of its population may be entirely detestable, but it is quite another question whether it is correct for the society of States to act as if the outcasts still belonged to the State in question.'[67] It is therefore plausible that international law contains at least some basis upon which a deprivation of nationality would be regarded as ineffective.[68]

However, *Oppenheim's International Law* notes that international practice shows a tendency to regard deprivation of nationality as effective,[69] and Plender equally acknowledges that modern state practice provides only 'some support' for the proposition that a decree depriving an individual of nationality may be ineffective to relieve the state of its duty of re-admission, although: 2.61

> [E]vidence suggests that in current international law a State cannot always release itself of its obligation to admit certain of its own nationals to its territory by promulgating a decree which deprives certain persons of their nationality ... A decree which discriminates on racial grounds, or is in any other sense 'arbitrary', need not be recognized by other States as effective to deprive of their nationality those to whom it purports to apply. Where the element of arbitrariness is absent, the denaturalization decree may nevertheless be ineffective to relieve the former State of nationality of its obligation to readmit the individual. This will be the case if the decree deprives of nationality a person who has already gained admission to another State, on the understanding that he will be readmitted to his country of origin, and who has not obtained any other national status. This conclusion may be defended on the traditional principle of good faith, coupled with the well-established rule that each State owes to each other State duty to refrain from frustrating the latter's right to expel aliens.[70]

The section above has considered questions concerning deprivation of nationality having a purely internal element, in that the deprivation takes place within the territory of the state which withdraws its nationality and no attempt at expulsion accompanies it. If expulsion is contemplated, then on the principles already established, it is only another state of nationality which can be obliged to accept the expellee. If no such state exists, and no other is prepared to admit an expellee on a discretionary basis, then the exclusion of an individual by withdrawal of his or her nationality, or an attempt to expel him or her after such withdrawal, then the external element of the process would raise serious issues under international law. An illustration is provided by exchanges in the House of Commons in June 1959, shortly before of the release of a nuclear scientist, Klaus Fuchs, 2.62

---

[66] *Human Rights and Arbitrary Deprivation of Nationality: Report of the Secretary-General*, 19 December 2013, A/HRC/25/28 [4].

[67] Van Panhuys (n 57) 163.

[68] It should be kept in mind that this is a different test from that incorporated in some contexts posited solely on the position of the state, for example, the definition of a 'stateless person' as 'a person who is not considered as a national by any State under the operation of its law' at Article 1 of the Convention on the Status of Stateless Persons (CSSP), examined in ch 4. So, a state may regard another as breaching international law in removing its nationality from an individual and may denounce the removal as invalid under international law, whilst also recognising the affected individual as stateless under the CSSP.

[69] Jennings and Watts (n 1), Part 1 879–80.

[70] Plender (n 5) 146–49.

who had been stripped of his British nationality and imprisoned following his disclosure of nuclear secrets to the Soviet Union. Mr Herbert Morrison asked Mr RAB Butler, the Secretary of State, whether deportation was planned upon release from custody. Mr Butler responded that: 'I have investigated the answer to that question also. In law, Fuchs could be deported but no other country can be required to accept a stateless deportee. Therefore, the power of deportation is not effectively available in this case.[71]

2.63 As Plender has noted, in relation to deprivation of nationality: 'A State's obligation to admit its own nationals to its territory could easily be circumvented if it were always open to the State to withdraw its nationality from those it wished to exclude.'[72] Weis has also pointed to the offence which deprivation of nationality may do on the international plane:

> When a national of one State is expelled to another State which has not consented to admit him, or when a State is prevented from returning a foreign national to the State of his nationality by the latter's refusal to receive him back, the foreign State may demand from the State of nationality that it should refrain from expulsion or, as the case may be, re-admit its national, on the ground of the duty of the State to grant towards its national the right to reside on its territory.[73]

2.64 Weis was of the view, subsequently supported by Plender,[74] that the denial of a right to enter or remain by a state responsible for deprivation of nationality might create a duty of re-admission owed to a state where that individual was left by deprivation of nationality and refusal of admission, or to any state to which the individual in question might, without the approval of that state and therefore in breach of its territorial supremacy, be expelled:

> The question [of re-admission] raises a far more practical and grave issue in the case of loss of nationality by unilateral action of the State, that is by deprivation of nationality. It seems fitting to call such deprivation of nationality by unilateral action denationalisation, as distinction from renunciation ... In the case of denationalisation, the doctrine of survival of the duty of readmission after the loss of nationality follows, in fact, from the principle of territorial supremacy: this supremacy might be infringed by such unilateral action in so far as that action would deprive other States of the possibility of enforcing their recognised right to expel aliens supposing that no third State, acting in pursuance of its legitimate discretion, was prepared to receive them.
>
> ... loss of nationality by denationalisation should therefore, by itself, not entail the loss of the right of sojourn; it should not relieve the State from the obligation to receive the former national back on its territory.[75]

2.65 Weis considered that an especially strong engagement with international law arose where an individual had entered the territory of a foreign state on showing evidence of his nationality, the nationality then being withdrawn whilst the individual remained on the territory:

> Since the question only becomes practical if the denationalised individual is forced to leave the country of his former nationality or if, being abroad, he is expelled by the State of residence

---

[71] HC Hansard 11 June 1959, vol 606, col 1176. Fuchs was ultimately offered entry to the German Democratic Republic (East Germany) and left the UK.
[72] Plender (n 5) 144.
[73] Weis (n 3) 46.
[74] Plender (n 5) 149.
[75] Weis (n 3) 54.

and refused readmission, two cases must be distinguished: denationalisation before leaving and denationalisation after leaving the State of nationality. In both cases it is generally considered that the duty to permit residence or to readmit the former national persists, but in the latter case an additional argument may be adduced: that the good faith of a State which has admitted an alien on the assumption that the State of his nationality is under an obligation to receive him back would be deceived if by subsequent denationalisation this duty were to be extinguished.[76]

2.66 In 1927, Sir John Fischer Williams, CBE KC, a former Assistant Legal Adviser to the Home Office, considered the 1921 decree by which the new Union of Soviet Socialist Republics withdrew nationality from a very large number of persons originating in Russia, but by the date of the decree outside its territory, which in most cases rendered those individuals stateless:

> Apart from this general argument, it may be said that when a state issues to one of its nationals a passport for foreign travel, it impliedly undertakes with any state whose officials admit the bearer to its territory on the faith of the passport, that it will receive back the bearer of the passport, should he be expelled. Country A cannot in fact, in the language of a British passport, 'request and require' country B to aid and assist X, whom it describes as its own national, and then without the assent of country B disclaim the implied undertaking.[77]

2.67 The UK in 1932 ratified the Special Protocol Concerning Statelessness 1930, which came into force in 2004 upon 10 countries having ratified or acceded to it.[78] Article 1 thereof provides that if a person loses his or her nationality whilst in another state, without acquiring an alternative nationality, the last state of nationality is bound to admit him if he becomes permanently indigent or has served a sentence of imprisonment of a month or more: 'In the first case the State whose nationality such person last possessed may refuse to receive him, if it undertakes to meet the cost of relief in the country where he is as from the thirtieth day from the date on which the request was made. In the second case the cost of sending him back shall be borne by the country making the request.' This long-neglected provision of binding a small number of states is not likely to be of positive use in determining the general content of international law.

2.68 Accordingly, although there appears to be no evidence for a general international law duty in all circumstances to repatriate former nationals, there is good ground to perceive a more nuanced but important duty or range of duties. In addition, some of the human rights instruments addressed in chapters 3 and 5 and the refugee law described in chapter 4 now provide significant protections.

2.69 International standards therefore arise, but in many cases are applicable either exclusively or mainly to the external dimension of deprivation of nationality: where an individual through the deprivation of nationality is refused return to the UK and left on the territory of another state. When the focus is put on the position of the individual, it is clear that in most cases, stronger standards, generally given primarily to the individual rather than to the states, are now set by human rights and hybrid instruments, which will be examined in chapters 3 and 4 respectively.

---

[76] ibid 54–55.
[77] JF Williams, 'Denationalization' (1927) 8 *British Yearbook of International Law* 45. The authors are grateful to Professor Guy Goodwin-Gill, Senior Research Fellow, All Souls College, University of Oxford for pointing to this item in the course of a seminar and discussion concerning these issues.
[78] A significant number of the early ratifications were of colonies, with membership thereafter increasing primarily by succession of states.

3

International Human Rights Law

Contents

A.	Introduction	3.1
B.	UDHR	3.5
C.	ICCPR	3.14
	C1. Scope of ICCPR	3.16
	C2. Articles 6 and 7 ICCPR	3.17
	C3. Article 12(4) ICCPR	3.18
	C4. Article 13 ICCPR	3.33
	C5. Articles 17 and 23(1) ICCPR	3.46
	C6. Article 24 ICCPR	3.54
D.	Post-ICCPR Instruments	3.58
	D1. CERD	3.59
	D2. CEDAW	3.63
	D3. CAT	3.67
	D4. CRC	3.82
	D5. MWC	3.85
	D6. CRPD	3.86
	D7. CPED	3.88

A. Introduction

Just as the development of international law as the law of nations was supported by a desire to create a restraining framework on international relations motivated by the extremities of conflict and abuse seen during the Thirty Years' War and the surrounding period, so the development after 1945 of a law of human rights was made possible by the events of the 1930s and the Second World War, including the conduct by the National Socialist regime in Germany of genocidal campaigns against persons of Jewish and Roma origin, and wholesale abuses against political opponents, prisoners of war, persons of non-approved sexual orientation, persons suffering mental or other disability and others. *Oppenheim's International Law* describes the Second World War as provoked by a state (Nazi Germany), which 'displayed a ruthless denial of fundamental human rights' later answered by the conviction that 'international recognition and protection of human rights was in accordance not only with an enlightened conception of the objects of international law but also with an essential requirement of international peace'.[1] The Preamble to the Declaration of the United Nations dated 1 January 1942 (the term 'United Nations' then referring to the UK, the US, the Soviet Union, the

3.1

---

[1] R Jennings and A Watts (eds), *Oppenheim's International Law* (9th edn, volume 1 (*Peace*), Oxford, Oxford University Press, 1992) 988.

Republic of China and their allies),[2] committing its signatories to participation in the conflict against Nazi Germany and its allies, stated the conviction:

> [T]hat complete victory over their enemies is essential to defend life, liberty, independence and religious freedom, and to preserve human rights and justice in their own lands as well as in other lands, and that they are now engaged in a common struggle against savage and brutal forces seeking to subjugate the world…

3.2 The Charter of the United Nations, signed on 26 June 1945, cited among the purposes of the organisation 'promoting and encouraging respect for human rights and for fundamental freedoms for all without distinction as to race, sex, language, or religion'. However, the Charter did not seek to define or enumerate those rights, something which was to be accomplished by a later instrument.

3.3 Initially under the ambit of the UN, and later also amongst regional groups of states, a body of human rights law has since developed. This growing body of international human rights law contrasts strongly in many respects with earlier principles concerning international law. Whilst some instruments still contain language that suggests a focus upon the duties of a state, others are plainly phrased as creating rights for individuals. The development of a body of international human rights law represents a clear and important development which has predominantly occurred since the founding of the UN and the end of the Second World War. *Oppenheim's International Law* states that:

> [I]t was formerly generally recognised that, apart from obligations undertaken by treaty, a state was entitled to treat both its own nationals and stateless persons at discretion and that the manner in which it treated them was not a matter with which international law, as a rule, concerned itself.

> However, the need for international rules to protect individuals from inhuman treatment by states, even if the state is that state is the state whose nationality the individual has or even if he is stateless, has been increasingly recognised. While the extent to which the rules which have grown up constitute customary international law is still open to question, the present scope of rules of international law which serve to protect the individual from treatment which denies the basic rights of a human being has involved a fundamental change in this area of international law.[3]

3.4 These human rights accrue, as the name suggests, from the status of being human, rather than from, for example, citizenship or nationality. 'Rights' is a term with different interpretations. For present purposes, the phrase 'human rights' here and below primarily denotes entitlements attaching to one person (person A) by reason of that person's humanity, which must be respected by another (person B) or by the state, or, perhaps, by 'the international community' legally expressed through the UN's various organs, so that person A is given some form of claim against person B, or against the state, or another authoritative body. This is the type of right identified as a 'claim-right' by the American jurist Wesley

---

[2] The original signatories were the 'Big Four' (the US, the UK, the USSR and China), eight Allied governments-in-exile, nine American allies in the Caribbean and Central America, the four British Dominions and British India. By the end of the war, other states had acceded to the Declaration, including the Philippines, France, every Latin American state except Argentina, and various independent states of the Middle East and Africa.

[3] Jennings and Watts (n 1) 849–50.

Newcomb Hohfeld in the leading typography of 'rights'.[4] This definition highlights the existence of the gap between aspiration and effective access in a state such as the UK in which international standards are enforceable only if incorporated domestically. Where there is no domestic remedy for the breach of a protected right, it is difficult to maintain that rights fully satisfy Hohfeld's definition. The access of individuals to certain rights is therefore marred by an absence of domestic incorporation even of some very important standards. This is examined further in relation to remedies in chapters thirteen to fifteen.

B. UDHR

The initial human rights instrument of the new era was the UDHR, promulgated as a resolution of the United Nations General Assembly (UNGA Resolution 217A) passed on 10 December 1948. It marks an important milestone for human rights generally, as well as for the application of human rights principles to the particular fields addressed in this work, traditionally seen as *loci* of deference to the prerogatives of individual states[5] and domestically often regarded as areas of executive discretion or prerogative.

3.5

Like subsequent human rights instruments, UDHR generally did not seek to impose any general limitation upon the expulsion or exclusion by states of non-nationals. Inter alia, it cited many more general rights potentially relevant in this context, notably rights to 'life, liberty and security of person' (Article 3), the prohibition of 'torture or cruel, inhuman or degrading treatment or punishment' (Article 5), the discriminatory denial of equal protection (Article 7), 'arbitrary arrest, detention or exile' (Article 9) and 'arbitrary interference with privacy, family, home or correspondence' against which 'Everyone has the right to the protection of the law' (Article 12).

3.6

An important aspect of almost every human rights regime is a prohibition of discrimination on enumerated grounds. Article 2 UDHR provides that:

3.7

> Everyone is entitled to all the rights and freedoms set forth in this Declaration, without distinction of any kind, such as race, colour, sex, language, religion, political or other opinion, national or social origin, property, birth or other status. Furthermore, no distinction shall be made on the basis of the political, jurisdictional or international status of the country or territory to which a person belongs, whether it be independent, trust, non-self-governing or under any other limitation of sovereignty.

As will become clear, the original categories, in respect of which discrimination is prohibited under international law, have been supplemented in more recent instruments.

Apart from the fleeting reference to exile, prohibited under Article 9 UDHR, which was not specifically echoed later in ICCPR, Articles 13 and 14 UDHR are the provisions bearing most directly upon immigration control. Article 13 provides that:

3.8

Article 13

...

(2) Everyone has the right to leave any country, including his own, and to return to his country.

---

[4] Se generally W Hohfeld, *Fundamental Legal Conceptions as Applied to Judicial Reasoning* (New Haven, Yale University Press, 1923).
[5] See further ch 2.

Article 13(2) UDHR set out an important right substantially developed in later instruments and decisions.

3.9 Article 14 UDHR provides that 'Everyone has the right to seek and to enjoy in other countries asylum from persecution', excepting 'prosecutions genuinely arising from non-political crimes or from acts contrary to the purposes and principles of the United Nations'. Whilst this was an important statement at that time, the development in intervening years of a distinct international refugee law regime has reduced the practical value of this provision.[6]

3.10 Article 15 UDHR provides that:

(1) Everyone has the right to a nationality.
(2) No one shall be arbitrarily deprived of his nationality nor denied the right to change his nationality.

These provisions reflected the recent historical phenomenon of large-scale deprivation of nationality by the Soviet Union and by Nazi Germany, as well as enhanced appreciation of the difficulty that statelessness on any scale presents both to the individuals concerned and to the international community. The provision is of great importance as affirming that nationality could be the subject of international protection of individual rights, not merely through rights and obligations between states as in classical international law. As Gunnar Schram explains: 'Until then [the human rights aspect of nationality] had never received this degree of recognition. Article 15 thus constitutes a remarkable development in international human rights law, providing a foundation upon which an elaborate legal structure has since been built.'[7]

3.11 The right to a nationality attested in Article 15 UDHR and in certain later instruments has been interpreted as meaning that in principle no one should be without a nationality, reflecting the importance of nationality given that, notwithstanding other protections for human rights, 'an individual's legal bond to a particular state through citizenship remains in practice an essential prerequisite to the enjoyment and protection of the full range of human rights'.[8] It does not, however, have the effect that any particular state is identified as subject to the duty to provide its nationality to a particular individual.

3.12 In contrast to later instruments in which limitations on rights are attached separately to individual rights, UDHR contained two limiting clauses of general application in Articles 29 and 30:

Article 29
(1) Everyone has duties to the community in which alone the free and full development of his personality is possible.
(2) In the exercise of his rights and freedoms, everyone shall be subject only to such limitations as are determined by law solely for the purpose of securing due recognition and

---

[6] See further ch 4.
[7] G Schram, in A Eide, G Alfredsson et al (eds), *The Universal Declaration of Human Rights: A Commentary* (Oslo, Scandinavian University Press, 1992) 229.
[8] M Adjami and J Harrington, 'The Scope and Content of Article 15 of the Universal Declaration of Human Rights' (2008) 27(3) *Refugee Survey Quarterly* 94.

respect for the rights and freedoms of others and of meeting the just requirements of morality, public order and the general welfare in a democratic society.

(3) These rights and freedoms may in no case be exercised contrary to the purposes and principles of the United Nations.

Article 30

Nothing in this Declaration may be interpreted as implying for any State, group or person any right to engage in any activity or to perform any act aimed at the destruction of any of the rights and freedoms set forth herein.

3.13 UDHR rights are not directly enforceable. It was anticipated that the UDHR would be followed both by regional instruments and by a binding international covenant. The first was accomplished soon thereafter in Europe by the ECHR. The second was ultimately accomplished by the ICCPR and the International Covenant on Economic, Social and Cultural Rights 1966 (ICESCR), the UN having decided to produce two instruments, whilst incorporating a lower level of impetus (progressive accomplishment) as regards goals identified in the latter. Both instruments entered into force in 1976. The UK has signed and ratified each of them.

C. ICCPR

3.14 The ICCPR is a significant pillar of international human rights law. Whilst the right to nationality in Article 15 UDHR has not been incorporated into the ICCPR, it provides protection of life in Article 6 ICCPR, prohibits torture or cruel inhuman or degrading treatment in Article 7 ICCPR, and, in the context of entry and remaining on the territory, provides a key provision in Article 12(4) ICCPR prohibiting arbitrary deprivation of the right to enter one's 'own country'. The ICCPR also provides procedural rights in relation to expulsion, including deportation and extradition, in Article 13, protection for family and home in Articles 17 and 23, and some rights for children relevant in the immigration and nationality context in Article 24.

3.15 Articles 6 and 7 are non-derogable, that is, they may not be suspended in any circumstances. The other provisions referred to are derogable, but only in certain closely defined circumstances. The derogation provision at Article 4(1) ICCPR provides that States Parties:

In time of public emergency which threatens the life of the nation and the existence of which is officially proclaimed ... may take measures derogating from their obligations under the present Covenant to the extent strictly required by the exigencies of the situation, provided that such measures are not inconsistent with their other obligations under international law and do not involve discrimination solely on the ground of race, colour, sex, language, religion or social origin.

C1. Scope of ICCPR

3.16 Article 2(1) ICCPR provides that:

Each State Party to the present Covenant undertakes to respect and to ensure to all individuals within its territory and subject to its jurisdiction the rights recognized in the present Covenant,

Part B – Legal Framework

without distinction of any kind, such as race, colour, sex, language, religion, political or other opinion, national or social origin, property, birth or other status.

The ICCPR rights therefore apply generally to all persons present in the territory or otherwise subject to the state's jurisdiction. Save where the contrary is specified, they apply regardless of nationality, citizenship or legality of presence based upon presence in territory. The United Nations Human Rights Committee (UNHRC) has emphasised this repeatedly: in its General Comment No 15 (The Position of Aliens Under the Covenant), it states expressly that:

1. Reports from States parties have often failed to take into account that each State party must ensure the rights in the Covenant to 'all individuals within its territory and subject to its jurisdiction' (art. 2, para. 1). In general, the rights set forth in the Covenant apply to everyone, irrespective of reciprocity, and irrespective of his or her nationality or statelessness.
2. Thus, the general rule is that each one of the rights of the Covenant must be guaranteed without discrimination between citizens and aliens. Aliens receive the benefit of the general requirement of non-discrimination in respect of the rights guaranteed in the Covenant, as provided for in article 2 thereof. This guarantee applies to aliens and citizens alike. Exceptionally, some of the rights recognized in the Covenant are expressly applicable only to citizens (art. 25), while article 13 applies only to aliens. However, the Committee's experience in examining reports shows that in a number of countries other rights that aliens should enjoy under the Covenant are denied to them or are subject to limitations that cannot always be justified under the Covenant.[9]

C2. Articles 6 and 7 ICCPR

3.17 Articles 6 and 7 ICCPR set out protections from arbitrary deprivation of life and from torture or cruel, inhuman or degrading treatment or punishment. Unlike the protections in the later Convention against Torture and Other Cruel, Inhuman or Degrading Treatment or Punishment (CAT) 1984, these are not restricted to circumstances in which the state is complicit. Whilst these international human rights are of lesser importance in the UK because of other applicable protections, including those provided by Articles 2 and 3 ECHR,[10] their protection by the ICCPR should be noted:

Article 6

1. Every human being has the inherent right to life. This right shall be protected by law. No one shall be arbitrarily deprived of his life.
2. In countries which have not abolished the death penalty, sentence of death may be imposed only for the most serious crimes in accordance with the law in force at the time of the commission of the crime and not contrary to the provisions of the present Covenant and to the Convention on the Prevention and Punishment of the Crime of Genocide. This penalty can only be carried out pursuant to a final judgement rendered by a competent court.
3. When deprivation of life constitutes the crime of genocide, it is understood that nothing in this article shall authorize any State Party to the present Covenant to derogate in any way

---

[9] United Nations Human Rights Committee, *CCPR General Comment No 15: The Position of Aliens under the Covenant*, 11 April 1986, HRI/GEN/1/Rev.9 (Vol I).
[10] See ch 5.

International Human Rights Law

from any obligation assumed under the provisions of the Convention on the Prevention and Punishment of the Crime of Genocide.

4. Anyone sentenced to death shall have the right to seek pardon or commutation of the sentence. Amnesty, pardon or commutation of the sentence of death may be granted in all cases.
5. Sentence of death shall not be imposed for crimes committed by persons below eighteen years of age and shall not be carried out on pregnant women.
6. Nothing in this article shall be invoked to delay or to prevent the abolition of capital punishment by any State Party to the present Covenant.

Article 7

No one shall be subjected to torture or to cruel, inhuman or degrading treatment or punishment. In particular, no one shall be subjected without his free consent to medical or scientific experimentation.

C3. Article 12(4) ICCPR

In the context of expulsion and deprivation of nationality, an important protection is provided by the prohibition on arbitrary deprivation of a right to enter under Article 12(4) ICCPR:

4. No one shall be arbitrarily deprived of the right to enter his own country.

The right of entry in Article 12(4) ICCPR necessarily implies the right to remain. The UNHRC has concluded that exile from one's 'own country' is barred by the ICCPR,[11] and in *Simalae Toala v New Zealand*, Communication No 675/1995, UN Doc CCPR/C/70/D/675/1995 (2000) treated deprivation of nationality as potentially within its remit because of the consequential loss of the right to enter. It has done this both in Concluding Observations on Reports by States[12] and in its General Comment 27, already referred to, which states that: 'A State party must not, by stripping a person of nationality or by expelling an individual to a third country, arbitrarily prevent this person from returning to his or her own country.'[13] In its General Comment 27, the UNHCR states that:

> 19. The right of a person to enter his or her own country recognizes the special relationship of a person to that country. The right has various facets. It implies the right to remain in one's own country. It includes not only the right to return after having left one's own country; it may also entitle a person to come to the country for the first time if he or she was born outside the country (for example, if that country is the person's State of nationality). The right to return is of the utmost importance for refugees seeking voluntary repatriation. It also implies prohibition of enforced population transfers or mass expulsions to other countries.

In the context of Article 12(4) ICCPR, the term 'his own country' contemplates the possibility of a relevant link not dependent upon the possession of nationality or citizenship. The UNHRC has found that it is incumbent upon an individual alleging a breach of

3.18

3.19

---

[11] UN Human Rights Committee, Concluding Observations on the Dominican Republic (1993) UN Doc CCPR/C/790/Add 18, at [6].
[12] ibid.
[13] Human Rights Committee, *General Comment 27, Freedom of Movement (Art 12)*, UN Doc CCPR/C/21/Rev.1/Add.9 (1999).

Article 12(4) ICCPR to prove that the state in question is 'his own country', though as, for instance, in *JM v Jamaica*, Communication No 165/1984, UN Doc CCPR/C/OP/2 at 17 (1984), the state may be expected to demonstrate that it has discharged any burden upon it to make enquiries in response to a claim of relevant linkage. Hannum, writing in 1987 before the UNHRC had begun to develop its current body of decision making on the point, considered the best interpretation, to be that it encompassed 'nationals, citizens, and permanent residents'.[14] Subsequently, however, the UNHRC has not included permanent residents per se within this ambit, and has followed a much more restrictive approach than Hannum predicted. In 1999 the UNHRC said in its General Comment 27[15] that the language:

> [E]mbraces, at the very least, an individual who, because of his or her special ties to or claims in relation to a given country, cannot be considered to be a mere alien. This would be the case, for example, of nationals of a country who have there been stripped of their nationality in violation of international law, and of individuals whose country of nationality has been incorporated in or transferred to another national entity, whose nationality is being denied them. The language ... permits a broader interpretation that might embrace other categories of long-term residents, including but not limited to stateless persons arbitrarily deprived of the right to acquire the nationality of the country of such residence...

3.20 Article 12(4) ICCPR is therefore potentially relevant to a denial of the right of entry, including a denial of entry which follows from an arbitrary deprivation of nationality. The guidance attaches particular emphasis to statelessness or effective statelessness on the part of the individual in question as favouring protection by a link to the territory, whilst not excluding the possibility of non-stateless long term residents showing a country to be their own. It appears likely that in most cases the possession of a state's nationality would make that state an individual's 'own country', but this will not always be the case. Exceptions to the application of Article 12(4) in such circumstances might arise, for example, where a state terminating nationality is held not to be an individual's 'own country' because the possession of nationality has been of a fleeting or purely technical nature: in the *Toala* case at [11.5], the UNHRC found that a particularly short-lived acquisition of nationality by operation of law, in the absence of other significant connection such as residence, did not make that country an individual's 'own country'.

3.21 The UNHRC in responding to petitions has generally followed a restrictive path as to the question of at what stage settled immigrants or those unlawfully present for a substantial time may treat the country of residence as their 'own'. In *Charles E Stewart v Canada*, Communication No 538/1993, UN Doc CCPR/C/58/D/538/1993 (1996), 12.5–9 and *Francesco Madafferi and Anna Maria Immacolata Madafferi v Australia*, CCPR/C/81/D/1011/2001, UN Human Rights Committee (HRC), 26 August 2004, 9.6, the UNHRC held that a person who enters as an immigrant cannot normally regard the state of residence as his or her 'own country' when that person has not acquired its nationality and continues to retain the nationality of a country of origin,

---

[14] H Hannum, *The Right to Leave and Return in International Law and Practice* (Dordrecht, Martinus Nijhoff, 1987) 59.

[15] Human Rights Committee, *General Comment 27, Freedom of Movement (Art 12)*, UN Doc CCPR/C/21/Rev.1/Add.9 (1999) [20].

though an exception might arise in limited circumstances, such as those created by arbitrary or unreasonable impediments on the acquisition of nationality.

In *Stewart v Canada*, the applicant to the UNHRC was a British citizen in his mid-thirties who had been resident in Canada since the age of seven. He had assumed himself to be a citizen, but was in fact a permanent resident and as such was susceptible to deportation, which he faced due to repeated minor offending. In considering his individual petition, the majority decision expressly recognised that the phrase 'his own country' denoted a concept wider than nationality, although this on the facts did not help Mr Stewart:

3.22

12.3 It must now be asked whether Canada qualifies as being Mr. Stewart's 'country'. In interpreting article 12, paragraph 4, it is important to note that the scope of the phrase 'his own country' is broader than the concept 'country of his nationality', which it embraces and which some regional human rights treaties use in guaranteeing the right to enter a country. Moreover, in seeking to understand the meaning of article 12, paragraph 4, account must also be had of the language of article 13 of the Covenant. That provision speaks of 'an alien lawfully in the territory of a State party' in limiting the rights of States to expel an individual categorized as an 'alien'. It would thus appear that 'his own country' as a concept applies to individuals who are nationals and to certain categories of individuals who, while not nationals in a formal sense, are also not 'aliens' within the meaning of article 13, although they may be considered as aliens for other purposes.

12.4 What is less clear is who, in addition to nationals, is protected by the provisions of article 12, paragraph 4. Since the concept 'his own country' is not limited to nationality in a formal sense, that is, nationality acquired on birth or by conferral, it embraces, at the very least, an individual who, because of his special ties to or claims in relation to a given country cannot there be considered to be a mere alien. This would be the case, for example, of nationals of a country who have there been stripped of their nationality in violation of international law and of individuals whose country of nationality has been incorporated into or transferred to another national entity whose nationality is being denied them. In short, while these individuals may not be nationals in the formal sense, neither are they aliens within the meaning of article 13. The language of article 12, paragraph 4, permits a broader interpretation, moreover, that might embrace other categories of long-term residents, particularly stateless persons arbitrarily deprived of the right to acquire the nationality of the country of such residence.

12.5 The question in the present case is whether a person who enters a given State under that State's immigration laws, and subject to the conditions of those laws, can regard that State as his own country when he has not acquired its nationality and continues to retain the nationality of his country of origin. The answer could possibly be positive were the country of immigration to place unreasonable impediments on the acquiring of nationality by new immigrants. But when, as in the present case, the country of immigration facilitates acquiring its nationality, and the immigrant refrains from doing so, either by choice or by committing acts that will disqualify him from acquiring that nationality, the country of immigration does not become 'his own country' within the meaning of article 12, paragraph 4, of the Covenant. In this regard it is to be noted that while in the drafting of article 12, paragraph 4, of the Covenant the term 'country of nationality' was rejected, so was the suggestion to refer to the country of one's permanent home.

12.6 Mr. Stewart is a British national both by birth and by virtue of the nationality of his parents. While he has lived in Canada for most of his life he never applied for Canadian nationality. It is true that his criminal record might have kept him from acquiring Canadian nationality by the time he was old enough to do so on his own. The fact is,

Part B – Legal Framework

> however, that he never attempted to acquire such nationality. Furthermore, even had he applied and been denied nationality because of his criminal record, this disability was of his own making. It cannot be said that Canada's immigration legislation is arbitrary or unreasonable in denying Canadian nationality to individuals who have criminal records.
>
> 12.7 This case would not raise the obvious human problems Mr. Stewart's deportation from Canada presents were it not for the fact that he was not deported much earlier...
>
> 12.8 Countries like Canada, which enable immigrants to become nationals after a reasonable period of residence, have a right to expect that such immigrants will in due course acquire all the rights and assume all the obligations that nationality entails. Individuals who do not take advantage of this opportunity and thus escape the obligations nationality imposes can be deemed to have opted to remain aliens in Canada. They have every right to do so, but must also bear the consequences. The fact that Mr. Stewart" criminal record disqualified him from becoming a Canadian national cannot confer on him greater rights than would be enjoyed by any other alien who, for whatever reasons, opted not to become a Canadian national. Individuals in these situations must be distinguished from the categories of persons described in paragraph 12.4 above.
>
> 12.9 The Committee concludes that as Canada cannot be regarded as 'Mr. Stewart's country', for the purposes of article 12, paragraph 4, of the Covenant, there could not have been a violation of that article by the State party.

There was a substantial dissent, with six members expressing a contrary view on the issue. In the majority decision a noteworthy feature is the reference at [12.5] to the possibility of a different answer were a country of immigration to place 'unreasonable impediments' in the way of acquisition of nationality by an immigrant. In the absence of any international norm creating a positive right to naturalisation in a country of residence for purposes of international law, 'unreasonable impediments' would be impediments which themselves breached international law norms, as arbitrary: for instance race discrimination or absence of fairness. Restriction per se is not contrary to any relevant norm. A state with a non-arbitrary policy that nevertheless imposed strong restrictions upon the giving of nationality, would not appear to breach any established international law standard.

3.23 Three years later, in 1997, the UNHRC in *Canepa v Canada* (UNHRC, 558/93, 3 April 1997, CCPR/C/59/D/558/1993) considered a case in which the Italian national applicant, then in his mid-thirties, had entered Canada aged five. There he had accumulated numerous convictions for narcotics offences, breaking and entering, and theft, and the UNHRC concluded both that Canada was not 'his own country' and that the deportation decision was not arbitrary given the procedural safeguards afforded the petitioner by Canada in relation to the decision. It noted that 'the separation of a person from his family by means of his expulsion could be regarded as an arbitrary interference with the family and as a violation of article 17 if in the circumstances ... the separation of the author from his family and its effects on him were disproportionate to the objectives of removal'.

3.24 The UNHRC more recently rejected a petition based upon Article 12(4) in *Madafferi v Australia* (1011/2001, 26 July 2004, CCPR/C/81/D/1011/2001), the petitioner being an Italian migrant to Australia, having arrived in that country as an adult, whose wife and four children were Australian citizens. By this time, the UNHCR had published guidance regarding Article 12(4) ICCPR in its General Comment No 27:

> 20. ... The scope of 'his own country' is broader than the concept 'country of his nationality'. It is not limited to nationality in a formal sense, that is, nationality acquired at birth

or by conferral; it embraces, at the very least, an individual who, because of his or her special ties to or claims in relation to a given country, cannot be considered to be a mere alien. This would be the case, for example, of nationals of a country who have there been stripped of their nationality in violation of international law, and of individuals whose country of nationality has been incorporated in or transferred to another national entity, whose nationality is being denied them. The language of article 12, paragraph 4, moreover, permits a broader interpretation that might embrace other categories of long-term residents, including but not limited to stateless persons arbitrarily deprived of the right to acquire the nationality of the country of such residence. Since other factors may in certain circumstances result in the establishment of close and enduring connections between a person and a country, States parties should include in their reports information on the rights of permanent residents to return to their country of residence.[16]

In *Madafferi* it was found, at [9.6], that Australia was not, as regards the petitioner, 'his own country'.

Since then, however, there have been two decisions of the UNHRC in deportation cases, published on the same day in 2011, which may show the beginnings of a more expansive approach to the concept of 'own country'. These are *Nystrom v Australia* (1557/2007, 1 September 2011, CCPR/C/102/D/1557/2007) and *Warsame v Canada* (1959/2010, 1 September 2011, CCPR/C/102/D/1959/2010). Both involved long term immigrants who were not stateless. 3.25

In *Nystrom v Australia* a majority of the UNHRC, at [7.4]–[7.6], found that Australia was the petitioner's 'own country' and that his deportation would be arbitrary: 3.26

7.4 On the first issue, the Committee recalls its General Comment No. 27 on freedom of movement where it has considered that the scope of 'his own country' is broader than the concept 'country of his nationality'. It is not limited to nationality in a formal sense, that is, nationality acquired at birth or by conferral; it embraces, at the very least, an individual who, because of his or her special ties to or claims in relation to a given country, cannot be considered to be a mere alien. In this regard, it finds that there are factors other than nationality which may establish close and enduring connections between a person and a country, connections which may be stronger than those of nationality. The words 'his own country' invite consideration of such matters as long standing residence, close personal and family ties and intentions to remain, as well as to the absence of such ties elsewhere.

7.5 In the present case, the author arrived in Australia when he was 27 days old, his nuclear family lives in Australia, he has no ties to Sweden and does not speak Swedish. On the other hand, his ties to the Australian community are so strong that he was considered to be an 'absorbed member of the Australian community' by the Australian Full Court in its judgement dated 30 June 2005; he bore many of the duties of a citizen and was treated like one, in several aspects related to his civil and political rights such as the right to vote in local elections or to serve in the army. Furthermore, the author alleges that he never acquired the Australian nationality because he thought he was an Australian citizen. The author argues that he was placed under the guardianship of the State since he was 13 years old and that the State party never initiated any citizenship process for all the period it acted on the author's behalf. The Committee observes that the State party has not refuted the latter argument. Given the particular circumstances of the case, the Committee considers that the author has established that Australia was his own country within the

---

[16] *CCPR, General Comment No 27: Article 12 (Freedom of Movement)*, 2 November 1999, CCPR/C/21/Rev.1/Add.9.

meaning of article 12, paragraph 4 of the Covenant, in the light of the strong ties connecting him to Australia, the presence of his family in Australia, the language he speaks, the duration of his stay in the country and the lack of any other ties than nationality with Sweden.

7.6 As to the alleged arbitrariness of the author's deportation, the Committee recalls its General Comment No. 27 on freedom of movement where it has stated that even interference provided for by law should be in accordance with the provisions, aims and objectives of the Covenant and should be, in any event, reasonable in the particular circumstances. The Committee considers that there are few, if any, circumstances in which deprivation of the right to enter one's own country could be reasonable. A State party must not, by stripping a person of nationality or by expelling an individual to a third country, arbitrarily prevent this person from returning to his or her own country. In the present case, the Minister's decision to deport him occurred almost 14 years after the conviction for rape and intentionally causing injury and over nine years after his release from prison on those charges, seven years after the armed robbery convictions and a number of years after his release from prison on the latter charges; and more importantly at a time where the author was in a process of rehabilitation. The Committee notes that the State party has provided no argument justifying the late character of the Minister's decision. In light of these considerations, the Committee considers that the author's deportation was arbitrary, thus violating article 12, paragraph 4 of the Covenant.

Five members recorded dissenting views, primarily because of their perception that the decision departed from the majority decision in *Stewart v Canada*, including the absence of statelessness, the importance to be given to absence of naturalisation where a reasonable system of naturalisation exists, and/or because the majority decision was viewed as taking General Comment No 27 to legitimise the extension of 'own country' beyond a country of nationality where this did not justify such a course.

3.27 The scope of the *Nystrom* decision might be said to turn on the fact that the petitioner had been in the care of the state as a minor without attention being given to his nationality position. But, as was stated by the dissenting members, this position is undermined by the decision of the UNHRC on another individual petition in the same session, *Warsame v Canada*. In that case, the petitioner was an adult born in Saudi Arabia of Somali descent. He never obtained Saudi Arabian citizenship and came to Canada aged four as a dependant of his mother, without being accorded refugee status. Subsequently he was convicted aged 20 of robbery, for which he was sentenced to nine months' imprisonment, and two years later he was convicted of possession of a scheduled substance for the purpose of trafficking, in respect of which he was sentenced to two years' imprisonment. Faced with deportation, he was unable to appeal, appeal against deportation being denied by Canadian law in cases where a custodial sentence of two years or more had been given. On a pre-removal risk assessment by the state, it was found in early 2007 that removal to Somalia posed a risk to life and a risk of cruel and unusual treatment or punishment. The case was referred to a Minister's Delegate, who in 2009 concluded that the petitioner did not face relevant personal risk if removed to Somalia and that he represented a danger to the Canadian public that outweighed humanitarian and compassionate hardships. The petitioner failed to challenge this, having been refused legal aid and lacking funds to pay for advice or representation in this respect.

A majority of the UNHRC's members, at [8.5], found that the petitioner's **3.28**
circumstances did render Canada 'his own country':

> 8.5 In the present case, the author arrived in Canada when he was four years old, his nuclear family lives in Canada, he has no ties to Somalia and has never lived there and has difficulties speaking the language. The Committee observes that it is not disputed that the author has lived almost all his conscious life in Canada, that he received his entire education in Canada and that before coming to Canada he lived in Saudi Arabia and not in Somalia…

This decision might be understood as turning narrowly on the acceptance of the UNHRC that the petitioner would face the risk of a violation of article 7 ICCPR if returned to Somalia, so that insofar as he continued to have an alternative Somali nationality, he could not return to the country of nationality without risk of serious human rights violations. Equally however it is not self-evident that the *Nystrom* and *Warsame* decisions represent a pair of narrow exceptional decisions rather than an indication of some opening out of the interpretation of 'own country' by the UNHRC.

Article 12(4) ICCPR invokes the concept of arbitrariness, common to other provisions in **3.29**
the ICCPR and elsewhere in international law, for example, prohibitions on arbitrary arrest or detention (Article 9) and arbitrary interference in private or family life (Article 17). Arbitrariness may denote a deprivation which defies national law or one which is in accordance with such law but is objectionable for some other reason, such as discrimination for some prohibited reason or absence of due process. The UNHRC in its General Comment 27 states that:

> The reference to the concept of arbitrariness in this context is intended to emphasize that it applies to all State action, legislative, administrative and judicial; it guarantees that even interference provided for by law should be in accordance with the provisions, aims and objectives of the Covenant and should be, in any event, reasonable in the particular circumstances. The Committee considers that there are few, if any, circumstances in which deprivation of the right to enter one's own country could be reasonable. A State party must not, by stripping a person of nationality or by expelling an individual to a third country, arbitrarily prevent this person from returning to his or her own country.[17]

A key circumstance in which an action will be considered arbitrary for the purposes of **3.30**
international law is where it is taken on the basis of prohibited discrimination. Article 2 ICCPR provides that other rights under that instrument are to be respected and ensured 'without distinction of any kind, such as race, colour, sex, language, religion, political or other opinion, national or social origin, property, birth or other status'. More specific protection against discrimination is provided for particular groups, such as members of racial minorities, women, children and the disabled, by other instruments, variously in the Convention on the Elimination of All Forms of Racial Discrimination 1969, the Convention on the Elimination of All Forms of Discrimination against Women 1979, the CRC, and the Convention on the Rights of Persons with Disabilities 2006, as examined below.

As to the definition of arbitrariness in this context, the General Comment states that: **3.31**

> 21. In no case may a person be arbitrarily deprived of the right to enter his or her own country. The reference to the concept of arbitrariness in this context is intended to emphasize that it

---

[17] UNHCR, *General Comment 27, Freedom of Movement (Art 12)*, UN Doc CCPR/C/21/Rev.1/Add.9 (1999), [21].

Part B – Legal Framework

applies to all State action, legislative, administrative and judicial; it guarantees that even interference provided for by law should be in accordance with the provisions, aims and objectives of the Covenant and should be, in any event, reasonable in the particular circumstances. The Committee considers that there are few, if any, circumstances in which deprivation of the right to enter one's own country could be reasonable. A State party must not, by stripping a person of nationality or by expelling an individual to a third country, arbitrarily prevent this person from returning to his or her own country.

3.32   In both *Nystrom v Australia* and *Warsame v Canada*, the majority held for the petitioner that deportation would be 'arbitrary'. In the latter case it reasoned (at [8.6]) that:

> 8.6 The Committee considers that there are few, if any, circumstances in which deprivation of the right to enter one's own country could be reasonable. A State party must not, by stripping a person of nationality or by expelling an individual to a third country, arbitrarily prevent this person from returning to his or her own country ... In the present case, a deportation of the author to Somalia would render his return to Canada *de facto* impossible due to Canadian immigration regulations. The Committee therefore considers that the author's deportation to Somalia impeding his return to his own country would be disproportionate to the legitimate aim of preventing the commission of further crimes and therefore arbitrary. The Committee concludes that, the author's deportation, if implemented would constitute a violation of article 12, paragraph 4, of the Covenant.

There was cogent dissent criticizing the reasons set out by the majority as insubstantial. In both *Nystrom* and *Warsame* there was dissent by a substantial minority.

C4. Article 13 ICCPR

3.33   Some other provisions of the ICCPR are relevant in the present context. Article 13 ICCPR provides procedural rights in relation to expulsion for aliens lawfully present in the state:

> Article 13
>
> An alien lawfully in the territory of a State Party to the present Covenant may be expelled therefrom only in pursuance of a decision reached in accordance with law and shall, except where compelling reasons of national security otherwise require, be allowed to submit the reasons against his expulsion and to have his case reviewed by, and be represented for the purpose before, the competent authority or a person or persons especially designated by the competent authority.

3.34   Expulsion of a lawfully present alien must comply with the state's own domestic laws, and the alien must be permitted to present arguments against expulsion and to seek review by competent authorities in the State, unless 'compelling reasons of national security' arise. General Comment No 15 at [9] provides that Article 13 'is applicable to all procedures aimed at the obligatory departure of an alien, whether described in national law as expulsion or otherwise'.

3.35   Article 13 ICCPR applies only if presence is lawful under domestic law, but General Comment No 15, at [9], indicates that if doubt exists as to the lawfulness of presence, Article 13 ICCPR should be considered to apply. 'Lawfully in the territory' generally means that a person is present in the territory with leave, or some other form of domestic law acknowledgement of a right to remain. Section 11(1) of the Immigration Act 1971 deems persons detained, or liable to detention but granted temporary admission under Schedule 2 to the Immigration Act 1971, as not having entered the UK, and the Supreme Court in *R (otao ST (Eritrea)) v SSHD* [2012] UKSC 12, [2012] 2 AC 135 held this to mean that a refugee granted only temporary admission was not lawfully present for the purposes of Article 32 of the Convention relating to the Status of Refugees 1951.[18] Whilst domestic law sets the standards that apply for the purposes of Article 13 ICCPR, these must be applied 'in good faith' and respecting certain norms.

The UNHCR in general has been reluctant to enter into the interpretation of domestic law or to criticise decisions of domestic courts, save in the presence of clear procedural defects. In *Maroufidou v Sweden*, (58/1979, 9 April 1981, CCPR/C/OP/1, 80 (1985), the complaint arose from Sweden's expulsion of a Greek citizen suspected of involvement in planning a terrorist operation in Sweden. The expulsion took place on the same day as the first instance confirmation of its lawfulness and prior to any further appeal or review. The UNHCR rejected the invitation to consider whether Swedish law had been correctly applied:

3.36

> 10.1 Anna Maroufidou claims that the decision to expel her was in violation of article 13 of the Covenant because it was not 'in accordance with law'. In her submission it was based on an incorrect interpretation of the Swedish Aliens Act. The Committee takes the view that the interpretation of domestic law is essentially a matter for the courts and authorities of the State party concerned. It is not within the powers or functions of the Committee to evaluate whether the competent authorities of the State party in question have interpreted and applied the domestic law correctly in the before it under the Optional Protocol, unless it is established that they have not interpreted and applied in good faith or that it is evident that there has been abuse of power.

By contrast, in *Hammel v Madagascar* (155/1983, 3 April 1987, CCPR/C/OP/2, 179), the UNHRC found a violation of Article 13 ICCPR. The petitioner, a French national, had been an *avocat* practising in Madagascar when he was expelled summarily by the authorities. The UNHRC set out the facts of the complaint at [2.4]:

3.37

> After 19 years as a member of the Madagascar bar, I was expelled from Madagascar as a French national by order of 11 February 1982, with 24 hours' notice. I was notified of the order on 11 February 1982 and there was a plane leaving at 8 p.m. I had two hours to pack my baggage at my home under surveillance by political police officers. I thus had no opportunity to avail myself of any of the remedies of appeal against the expulsion order that are provided for by law. When I later applied to the Administrative Chamber of the Supreme Court to have the expulsion order repealed, the proceedings ... were thwarted by the Government.

The UNHRC found (at [19.2]) that:

3.38

> 19.2 The Committee notes that in the circumstances of the present case, the author was not given an effective remedy to challenge his expulsion and that the State party has not shown that there were compelling reasons of national security to deprive him of that remedy. In formulating its views the Human Rights Committee also takes into account its general comment 15 (27) (see footnote 1), on the position of aliens under the Covenant, and in particular points out that

---

[18] See further ch 4.

Part B – Legal Framework

'an alien must be given full facilities for pursuing his remedy against expulsion so that this right will in all the circumstances of his case be an effective one'.

3.39 The UNHRC went on to express concern that 'based on the information provided by the State party ... the decision to expel Eric Hammel would appear to have been linked to the fact that he had represented persons before the Human Rights Committee', before condemning the link at [19.3]: 'it would be both untenable and incompatible with the spirit of [the ICCPR] and the Optional Protocol thereto, if States parties to these instruments were to take exception to anyone acting as legal counsel for persons placing their communications before the Committee for consideration under the Optional Protocol'.

3.40 Article 13 ICCPR was intended to exclude the possibility of arbitrary expulsion in individual cases. A parallel effect is to render unlawful, for the purposes of international law, mass expulsion, considered as expulsion without consideration of individual circumstances. The UNHRC's General Comment No 15 provides that:

> 10. Article 13 directly regulates only the procedure and not the substantive grounds for expulsion. However, by allowing only those carried out 'in pursuance of a decision reached in accordance with law', its purpose is clearly to prevent arbitrary expulsions. On the other hand, it entitles each alien to a decision in his own case and, hence, article 13 would not be satisfied with laws or decisions providing for collective or mass expulsions. This understanding, in the opinion of the Committee, is confirmed by further provisions concerning the right to submit reasons against expulsion and to have the decision reviewed by and to be represented before the competent authority or someone designated by it.

3.41 The right to be heard by a competent authority does not create any right to be heard by a judicial as opposed to an administrative body: in *Maroufidou v Sweden*, the process was administrative rather than judicial, this attracting no adverse finding by the UNHRC. However, that right must be 'effective': 'An alien must be given full facilities for pursuing his remedy against expulsion so that this right will in all the circumstances of his case be an effective one.' In *Maroufidou v Sweden*, a lawyer had been appointed to represent Ms Maroufidou in the domestic review application. In Concluding Observations in 1995 following consideration of the UK's periodic report to it, the UNHRC indicated the then absence of legal aid as amongst its principal concerns:

> The treatment of illegal immigrants, asylum-seekers and those ordered to be deported gives cause for concern. The Committee observes that the incarceration of persons ordered to be deported and particularly the length of their detention may not be necessary in every case and it is gravely concerned at incidences of the use of excessive force in the execution of deportation orders. The Committee also notes with concern that adequate legal representation is not available for asylum-seekers effectively to challenge administrative decisions.[19]

3.42 The UNHCR in subsequent Concluding Observations cited absence of legal aid for immigration bail applications amongst continuing concerns:

> The Committee remains concerned that the State party has continued its practice of detaining large numbers of asylum-seekers, including children. Furthermore, the Committee reiterates that it considers unacceptable any detention of asylum-seekers in prisons and is concerned that while most asylum-seekers are detained in immigration centres, a small minority of them

---

[19] UNHRC, *Concluding Observations on the United Kingdom*, 27 July 1995, CCPR/C/79/Add.55.

International Human Rights Law

continue to be held in prisons, allegedly for reasons of security and control. It is concerned that some asylum-seekers do not have early access to legal representation and are thus likely to be unaware of their right to make a bail application which is no longer automatic since the enactment of the Nationality, Immigration and Asylum Act 2002.[20]

In Concluding Observations following a report of Denmark to the UNHRC, the UNHRC said that: 3.43

> [A]sylum-seekers are entitled to have the assistance of legal counsel. The State Party should provide information as to the stages of the application procedures at which legal assistance may be had, and whether the assistance is free of charge at all stages for those who cannot afford it.[21]

A decision relating to a lawfully present alien must in any case be treated by 'a decision reached in accordance with law'. But other protections are inapplicable where 'compelling reasons of national security otherwise require'. In *VMRB v Canada* (236/1987, 18 July 1988, CCPR/C/33/D/236/1987) and *JRC v Costa Rica* (296/88, 30 March 1989, CCPR/C/35/D/296/1988), the UNHRC stated that 'It is not for the Committee to test a sovereign State's evaluation of an alien's security rating', though in those cases some explanation was provided by the respective state.[22] In *Giry v Dominican Republic* (193/1985, 20 July 1990, CCPR/C/39/D/193/1985), the petitioner was a French citizen detained by officials in the Dominican Republic and transported under guard to the US, where he was held and prosecuted for drug smuggling offences. The UNHRC implicitly went beyond finding the decision not in accordance with domestic law to reject the claim of the State Party that national security grounds arose: 3.44

> In spite of several invitations to do so, the State party has not furnished the text of the decision to remove the author from Dominican territory or shown that the decision to do so was reached 'in accordance with law' as required under article 13 of the Covenant. Furthermore, it is evident that the author was not afforded an opportunity, in the circumstances of the extradition, to submit the reasons against his expulsion or to have his case reviewed by the competent authority. While finding a violation of the provisions of article 13 in the specific circumstances ... the Committee stresses that States are fully entitled vigorously to protect their territory against the menace of drug dealing by entering into extradition treaties with other States. But practice under such treaties must comply with article 13 of the Covenant, as indeed would have been the case, had the relevant Dominican law been applied in the present case.

In *Karker v France* (833/1998, 30 October 2000, CCPR/C/70/D/833/1998) the petitioner, an Islamist politician from Tunisia lawfully resident in France and recognised as a refugee, was the subject of an exclusion order, which was not enforced because the petitioner could not be returned to Tunisia due to his refugee status. The UNHRC, at [9.3], found that there had been no violation of Article 13 ICCPR: 3.45

> The Committee notes that Mr. Karker's expulsion was decided by the Minister of the Interior for urgent reasons of public security, and that Mr. Karker was therefore not allowed to

---

[20] UNHRC, *Concluding Observations on the United Kingdom*, 30 July 2008, CCPR/C/GBR/CO/6, at [21].
[21] UNHRC, *Concluding Observations on Denmark*, 31 October 2000, CCPR/CO/70/DNK.
[22] *VMRB v Canada* (236/1987, 18 July 1988, CCPR/C/33/D/236/1987), at [6.3]; *JRC v Costa Rica* (296/88, 30 March 1989, CCPR/C/35/D/296/1988), at [8.4].

submit reasons against his expulsion before the order was issued. He did, however, have the opportunity to have his case reviewed by the Administrative Tribunal and the Council of State, and at both procedures he was represented by counsel. The Committee concludes that the facts before it do not show that article 13 has been violated in the present case.

C5. Articles 17 and 23(1) ICCPR

3.46 In expulsion cases two mutually reinforcing provisions relating to family and/or private life, Articles 17 and 23(1) ICCPR, have been treated as the provision of first recourse in cases concerning expulsion of settled migrants:

Article 17

1. No one shall be subjected to arbitrary or unlawful interference with his privacy, family, or correspondence, nor to unlawful attacks on his honour and reputation.
2. Everyone has the right to the protection of the law against such interference or attacks.

Article 23

The family is the natural and fundamental group unit of society and is entitled to protection by society and the State.

3.47 The UNHRC in its General Comment 16, at [3]–[4], has in this context said that:

3. The term 'unlawful' means that no interference can take place except in cases envisaged by the law. Interference authorized by States can only take place on the basis of law, which itself must comply with the provisions, aims and objectives of the Covenant.
4. The expression 'arbitrary interference' is also relevant to the protection of the right provided for in article 17. In the Committee's view the expression 'arbitrary interference' can also extend to interference provided for under the law. The introduction of the concept of arbitrariness is intended to guarantee that even interference provided for by law should be in accordance with the provisions, aims and objectives of the Covenant and should be, in any event, reasonable in the particular circumstances.[23]

3.48 The UNHRC in the same General Comment said, at [5], of the terms 'home' and 'family' that:

Regarding the term 'family', the objectives of the Covenant require that for purposes of article 17 this term be given a broad interpretation to include all those comprising the family as understood in the society of the State party concerned. The term 'home' in English, 'manzel' in Arabic, 'zhùzhái' in Chinese, 'domicile' in French, 'zhilische' in Russian and 'domicilio' in Spanish, as used in article 17 of the Covenant, is to be understood to indicate the place where a person resides or carries out his usual occupation. In this connection, the Committee invites States to indicate in their reports the meaning given in their society to the terms 'family' and 'home'.

This reference to the need to consider the local concept of 'family' is also reflected in General Comment No 19.[24]

---

[23] UNHRC, *General Comment 17, Article 17 (The Right to Respect of Privacy, Family, Home, Correspondence, and Protection of Honour and Reputation)*, HRI/GEN/1/Rev.9 (Vol. I) 191, [3]–[4].

[24] UNHRC, *General Comment 19, Article 23 (Protection of the Family, the Right to Marriage, and Equality of the Spouses)*, HRI/GEN/1/Rev.9 (Vol. I) 198, at [2].

In the UK it will therefore be appropriate to look to local definitions, for example, to the decision of the Court of Appeal in *Pawandeep Singh v ECO New Delhi* [2004] EWCA Civ 1075, [2005] QB 608 digesting and applying the jurisprudence of the ECtHR in *Lebbink v The Netherlands* [2004] 2 FLR 463: 'The existence or non-existence of "family life" for the purposes of article 8 [ECHR] is essentially a question of fact depending upon the real existence in practice of close personal ties.' In that decision Munby J observed at [58]–[59] the following: 3.49

58. Before turning to the central issue there are certain preliminary observations I wish to make. The first point is perhaps obvious but needs to be borne in mind. If one takes what until recently was the traditional or conventional form of family it can be seen that there are, in principle, four key relationships. First, there is the relationship between husband and wife. Secondly, there is the relationship between parent and child. Thirdly, there is the relationship between siblings. And, fourthly, there are relationships within the wider family: for example, the relationships between grandparent and grandchild, between nephew and uncle and between cousins. Each of these relationships can in principle give rise to family life within the meaning of Article 8…

59. It is also clear that 'family life' is not confined to relationships based on marriage or blood, nor indeed is family life confined to formal relationships recognised in law. Thus family life is not confined to married couples. A de facto relationship outside marriage can give rise to family life (*Abdulaziz, Cabales and Balkandali v United Kingdom* at [63]), even if the parties do not live together (*Kroon v The Netherlands* (1994) 19 EHRR 263 at [30]), and even if the couple consists of a woman and a female-to-male transsexual (*X, Y and Z v United Kingdom* (1997) 24 EHRR 143 at [37]). So there can be family life between father and child even where the parents are not married: *Keegan v Ireland* (1994) 18 EHRR 342 at [44]. Likewise there can be family life between a parent and a child even where there is no biological relationship: *X, Y and Z v United Kingdom* at [37] (family life existed as between the female-to-male transsexual partner of a woman and the child she had conceived by artificial insemination by an anonymous donor). A formal adoption creates family life between the adoptive parents and the child: *X v Belgium and the Netherlands* (1975) 7 D&R 75, *X v France* (1982) 31 D&R 241, *Pini v Roumania* (unreported—22 June 2004). Family life can exist between foster-parent and foster-child: *Gaskin v United Kingdom* (1989) 12 EHRR 36.

As to the need to appreciate changing family structures in relation to any definition of family life, powerful observations were made by Munby J at [61]–[65] of the *Singh* decision: 3.50

61. I have referred to the traditional or conventional form of family. That takes me on to my second point. Quite apart from the fact that the form the family has until recently tended to take in Protestant northern Europe differs in certain respects from what would until recently have been familiar in Catholic Mediterranean Europe, we need to remember, as Professor Lawrence Stone's great works have taught us, that what we currently view as the traditional or conventional form of family is itself a comparatively modern development. Moreover, and perhaps more to the point, we have to recognise that there have been very profound changes in family life in recent decades.
62. These changes have been driven by four major developments. First, there have been enormous changes in the social and religious life of our country. The fact is that we live in a secular and pluralistic society. But we also live in a multi-cultural community of many faiths … Secondly, there has been an increasing lack of interest in—in some instances a conscious rejection of—marriage as an institution. As Dr Stephen Cretney has noted (Cretney, *Family Law in the Twentieth Century: A History*, 2003, p 33), although there is no lack of interest in family life (or at least in intimate relationships), the figures demonstrate a striking decline

Part B – Legal Framework

in marriage. Thirdly, there has been a sea-change in society's attitudes towards same-sex unions… Fourthly, there have been enormous advances in medical, and in particular reproductive, science so that reproduction is no longer confined to 'natural' methods…

63. The result of all this is that in our multi-cultural and pluralistic society the family takes many forms. Indeed, in contemporary Britain the family takes an almost infinite variety of forms. Many marry according to the rites of non-Christian faiths. There may be one, two, three or even more generations living together under the same roof. Some people choose to live on their own. People live together as couples, married or not, and with partners who may not always be of the opposite sex. Children live in households where their parents may be married or unmarried. They may be the children of polygamous marriages. They may be brought up by a single parent. Their parents may or may not be their natural parents. Their siblings may be only half-siblings or step-siblings. Some children are brought up by two parents of the same sex. Some children are conceived by artificial donor insemination. Some are the result of surrogacy arrangements. The fact is that many adults and children, whether through choice or circumstance, live in families more or less removed from what until comparatively recently would have been recognised as the typical nuclear family. As Baroness Hale of Richmond observed in *Ghaidan v Godin-Mendoza* at [141]:

> [If a] couple are bringing up children together, it is unlikely to matter whether or not they are the biological children of both parties. Both married and unmarried couples, both homosexual and heterosexual, may bring up children together. One or both may have children from another relationship: this is not at all uncommon in lesbian relationships and the court may grant them a shared residence order so that they may share parental responsibility. A lesbian couple may have children by donor insemination who are brought up as the children of them both: it is not uncommon for each of them to bear a child in this way. A gay or lesbian couple may foster other people's children.

64. Many of these changes have given rise to profound misgivings in some quarters. We live in a society which on many social, ethical and religious topics no longer either thinks or speaks with one voice. These are topics on which men and woman of different faiths or no faith at all hold starkly differing views. All of those views are entitled to the greatest respect but it is not for a judge to choose between them. The days are past when the business of the judges was the enforcement of morals or religious belief. The Court of King's Bench, or its modern incarnation the Administrative Court, is no longer *custos morum* of the people. And a judge, although it may be that on occasions he can legitimately exercise the functions of an aedile, is no censor.

65. The law, as it seems to me, must adapt itself to these realities, not least in its approach to the proper ambit of Article 8…

3.51 The UNHRC has made clear that a state cannot frustrate the application of the ICCPR by imposing for this purpose a definition of 'family' or 'home' narrower than that which it would otherwise apply: *Hopu and Bessert v France* (549/93, 29 July 1997, CCPR/C/60/D/549/1993/Rev.1). It expressly rejected, in an individual petition relating to the Netherlands, the proposition that 'family' for the purposes of Article 23(1) ICCPR, referred only to a family unit during marriage, not extending to relationships between a divorced parent and the child of that marriage residing with the former spouse: *Hendriks v The Netherlands* (201/85, 27 July 1988, CCPR/C/33/D/201/1985).

3.52 In the immigration context, the UNHRC has found inadmissible, as revealing no breach of a protected right, a complaint directed at the refusal of the Canadian authorities to allow a permanent resident in Canada to be joined by her adopted daughter and grandson 17 years after the daughter returned from Canada to Poland, married and had a child: *AS v Canada* (68/80, 31 March 1981, CCPR/C/12/D/68/1980). In *Stewart v Canada*, referred to above in the discussion of Article 12(4) ICCPR, the UNHRC found that deportation under a legal process permitting representation and appeal, in which the deportation had not been found unlawful, could not be considered unlawful or arbitrary, so that there was no violation of Article 17 ICCPR.

Unequal treatment of immigrants or their spouses according to gender has been found to breach relevant standards: *Aumeeruddy-Cziffra and 19 Other Mauritian Women v Mauritius* (35/78, 9 April 1981, CCPR/C/12/D/35/1978). The UNHRC has treated the unification of the families of immigrants as an important priority, criticising Switzerland in an early report for its then regime of not permitting the spouses of foreign workers to enter for an initial period of 18 months: 'The Committee also notes that family reunification is not authorized immediately for foreign workers who settle in Switzerland, but only after 18 months, which, in the Committee's view, is too long a period for the foreign worker to be separated from his family.'[25]

3.53

C6. Article 24 ICCPR

Article 24 ICCPR sets out important provisions for the protection of children.

3.54

1. Every child shall have, without any discrimination as to race, colour, sex, language, religion, national or social origin, property or birth, the right to such measures of protection as are required by his status as a minor, on the part of his family, society and the State.
2. Every child shall be registered immediately after birth and shall have a name.
3. Every child has the right to acquire a nationality.

As will already be clear, the ICCPR does not duplicate the UDHR in asserting the existence of a general right to nationality. The provision most closely approaching an exception is Article 24(3) ICCPR, asserting the right to acquire nationality within a measure applicable only to children. Further, this does not compel a state to provide its nationality to a child on its territory, though in many cases, if not all cases, it may have that effect where a child would otherwise be stateless. The UNHRC in its General Comment 17 stated at [8] that:

3.55

> While the purpose of this provision is to prevent a child from being afforded less protection by society and the State because he is stateless, it does not necessarily make it an obligation for States to give their nationality to every child born in their territory. However, States are required to adopt every appropriate measure, both internally and in cooperation with other States, to ensure that every child has a nationality when he is born. In this connection, no discrimination with regard to the acquisition of nationality should be admissible under internal law as between legitimate children and children born out of wedlock or of stateless parents or based on the nationality status of one or both of the parents ...

This has been interpreted as obliging a State Party to confer its nationality on stateless children born or found within its territory, though an authoritative commentator has argued that the obligation upon a State Party in whose territory a stateless minor

3.56

---

[25] *Concluding Observations of the UNHRC: Switzerland*, 8 November 1996, CCPR/C/79/Add.70 [18].

is sojourning is secondary to the obligation which may attach to another State Party to which there is an arguably stronger binding tie, for example, through paternity or maternity.[26] The UNHCR has related the Article 24(3) ICCPR obligation, inter alia, to discriminatory practices impeding birth registration of children of undocumented refugees in Ecuador (which would support their identification as citizens by birth on the territory),[27] the failure by Colombia to confer its nationality on children born stateless on its territory[28] and Zimbabwean laws denying its citizenship to the children of Zimbabwean parents born abroad.[29]

3.57 In *Rajan v New Zealand* (820/1998, 7 August 2003, CCPR/C/78/D/820/1998), the parents of the child were Fijian nationals who had been admitted to New Zealand with their infant son on showing Australian residence permits whilst failing to disclose an ongoing investigation in Australia into whether those permits had been fraudulently obtained. One of the parents was subsequently granted New Zealand citizenship, still on the basis of omission to disclose relevant facts, and her Fijian citizenship was automatically annulled as a result. Their son was also granted New Zealand citizenship. Several months later, the authorities, having ascertained the true facts, took steps to revoke both grants of citizenship and to deport the family. Whilst the appeal was in progress, a daughter was born and acquired New Zealand citizenship by birth in the territory. The UNHRC found their claims of breaches of Articles 17, 23(1), and 24(1) to be unsubstantiated, observing that on the evidence, the parent deprived of New Zealand citizenship was held by the Fijian authorities thereafter to have a present status as a Fijian citizen and the son deprived of his New Zealand nationality retained Australian citizenship by birth and had not been rendered stateless.

D. Post-ICCPR Instruments

3.58 Since the ICCPR, there has been a string of instruments directed more specifically at human rights questions of particular types or affecting particular groups: for example, the Convention on the Elimination of All Forms of Racial Discrimination 1969 (CERD), the Convention on the Elimination of All Forms of Discrimination against Women 1979 (CEDAW), the Convention against Torture and Other Cruel, Inhuman or Degrading Treatment or Punishment 1984 (CAT), the CRC, the Convention on the Protection of the Rights of All Migrant Workers and Members of Their Families 1990 (MWC), the Convention on the Rights of Persons with Disabilities 2006 (CRPD) and the Convention for the Protection of All Persons from Enforced Disappearance 2006 (CPED). These are examined below in turn.

---

[26] M Nowak, *UN Covenant on Civil and Political Rights: CCPR Commentary* (Kehl am Rihen, NP Engel, 1993) 424–25.
[27] (1998) UN Doc CCPR/C/79/Add 92.
[28] (1997) UN Doc CCPR/C/79/Add 75.
[29] (1998) UN Doc CCPR/C/79/Add 89 [19].

D1. CERD

The fundamental purpose of the CERD, which has been signed and ratified by the UK, is to combat racial discrimination as inconsistent with principles of the dignity and equality of human beings. Racial discrimination is defined in Article 1(1) CERD: **3.59**

> In this Convention, the term 'racial discrimination' shall mean any distinction, exclusion, restriction or preference based on race, colour, descent, or national or ethnic origin which has the purpose or effect of nullifying or impairing the recognition, enjoyment or exercise, on an equal footing, of human rights and fundamental freedoms in the political, economic, social, cultural or any other field of public life.

Article 1(2) CERD disapplies the Convention's protections from situations in which distinction is drawn 'between citizens and non-citizens'. Article 1(3) CERD expressly protects from intrusion most domestic laws of nationality and citizenship, something which might be compared negatively with the greater readiness to address these areas in more recent treaties. Finally, under Article 1(4) CERD, special measures seeking to promote equality 'shall not be deemed racial discrimination, provided, however, that such measures do not, as a consequence, lead to the maintenance of separate rights for different racial groups and that they shall not be continued after the objectives for which they were taken have been achieved'. **3.60**

Article 2 CERD identifies the general obligation imposed by the instrument: **3.61**

> 1. States Parties condemn racial discrimination and undertake to pursue by all appropriate means and without delay a policy of eliminating racial discrimination in all its forms and promoting understanding among all races...
> 2. States Parties shall, when the circumstances so warrant, take, in the social, economic, cultural and other fields, special and concrete measures to ensure the adequate development and protection of certain racial groups or individuals belonging to them, for the purpose of guaranteeing them the full and equal enjoyment of human rights and fundamental freedoms. These measures shall in no case entail as a consequence the maintenance of unequal or separate rights for different racial groups after the objectives for which they were taken have been achieved.

Article 5 CERD provides inter alia for protection of individuals from discrimination in relation to certain nationality rights: **3.62**

> In compliance with the fundamental obligations laid down in article 2 of this Convention, States Parties undertake to prohibit and to eliminate racial discrimination in all its forms and to guarantee the right of everyone, without distinction as to race, colour, or national or ethnic origin, to equality before the law, notably in the enjoyment of the following rights:
>
> ...
>
> (d) Other civil rights, in particular:
>
> ...
>
> (ii) the right to leave any country, including one's own, and to return to one's country;
>
> (iii) the right to nationality.

D2. CEDAW

3.63 The CEDAW has also been signed and ratified by the UK. Under Article 1 CEDAW, 'discrimination against women' means:

> [A]ny distinction, exclusion or restriction made on the basis of sex which has the effect or purpose of impairing or nullifying the recognition, enjoyment or exercise by women, irrespective of their marital status, on a basis of equality of men and women, of human rights and fundamental freedoms in the political, economic, social, cultural, civil or any other field.

3.64 Under Article 2 CEDAW, States Parties condemn such discrimination 'in all its forms', agree to pursue by all appropriate means and without delay a policy of eliminating discrimination against women, to provide legislative protection for gender equality, and to ensure 'through law and other appropriate means, the practical realization of this principle'. Article 3 provides that States Parties shall take all appropriate measures in all fields to ensure the full development and advancement of women so as to guarantee the 'exercise and enjoyment of human rights and fundamental freedoms on a basis of equality with men'. Article 4 provides for positive discrimination without breach of the prohibition on discrimination in certain circumstances.

3.65 Article 6 CEDAW requires States Parties to take 'all appropriate measures' to suppress all forms of trafficking of women and/or exploitation of prostitution of women. Article 7 CEDAW requires States Parties to take all appropriate measures to eliminate discrimination against women in the political and public life of the country.

3.66 There is a specific protection as regards nationality in Article 9 CEDAW, which provides:

> 1. States Parties shall grant women equal rights with men to acquire, change or retain their nationality. They shall ensure in particular that neither marriage to an alien nor change of nationality by the husband during marriage shall automatically change the nationality of the wife, render her stateless or force upon her the nationality of the husband.
> 2. States Parties shall grant women equal rights with men with respect to the nationality of their children.

D3. CAT

3.67 The CAT has been signed and ratified by the UK. Article 1(1) defines torture as:

> [A]ny act by which severe pain or suffering, whether physical or mental, is intentionally inflicted on a person for such purposes as obtaining from him or a third person information or a confession, punishing him for an act he or a third person has committed or is suspected of having committed, or intimidating or coercing him or a third person, or for any reason based on discrimination of any kind, when such pain or suffering is inflicted by or at the instigation of or with the consent or acquiescence of a public official or other person acting in an official capacity. It does not include pain or suffering arising only from, inherent in or incidental to lawful sanctions.

3.68 Article 2 CAT confirms the absolute nature of the prohibition:

> 1. Each State Party shall take effective legislative, administrative, judicial or other measures to prevent acts of torture in any territory under its jurisdiction.

2. No exceptional circumstances whatsoever, whether a state of war or a threat of war, internal political instability or any other public emergency, may be invoked as a justification of torture.
3. An order from a superior officer or a public authority may not be invoked as a justification of torture.

In relation to expulsion and exclusion, Article 3 CAT is particularly important: **3.69**

1. No State Party shall expel, return (*refouler*) or extradite a person to another State where there are substantial grounds for believing that he would be in danger of being subjected to torture.
2. For the purpose of determining whether there are such grounds, the competent authorities shall take into account all relevant considerations including, where applicable, the existence in the State concerned of a consistent pattern of gross, flagrant or mass violations of human rights.

An important concept under Article 3(1) CAT common to a number of international law regimes is the prohibition of *refoulement* (return), a concept also important in the context of 1951 Convention Relating to the Status of Refugees (CSR), which is examined in the next chapter. **3.70**

Reliance in the CAT upon the principle of *non-refoulement* codifies a widening of the scope of *non-refoulement* to prevent return to torture or other relevant treatment, so that 'a State violates the absolute prohibition of torture not only if its own authorities subject a person to torture, but also if its authorities send a person to another state where there are substantial grounds for believing that the person would be in danger of being subjected to torture'.[30] **3.71**

Non-refoulement similarly arises in relation to the prohibition on cruel, inhuman and degrading treatment or punishment and torture, under both Article 3 ECHR and Article 7 ICCPR. In contrast to those treaties, the scope of *non-refoulement* under Article 3 CAT is a narrow one: it applies *only* to acts of torture, as defined under Article 1 CAT, that definition requiring 'infliction by or with the acquiescence of a public official or other person acting in an official capacity'. The Committee against Torture has adopted a relatively broad and non-literal interpretation of that formulation, however, expressly finding in *Elmi v Australia*, Communication No 120/1998, UN Doc CAT/C/22/D/120/1998 (1999), that proposed return to Somalia, where centralised authority had collapsed, might still breach the CAT because of the existence of de facto rule by local armed factions: **3.72**

> 6.5 [S]ome of the factions operating in Mogadishu have set up quasi-governmental institutions and are negotiating the establishment of a common administration. It follows then that, de facto, those factions exercise certain prerogatives that are comparable to those normally exercised by legitimate governments. Accordingly, the members of those factions can fall, for the purposes of the application of the Convention, within the phrase 'public officials or other persons acting in an official capacity' contained in article 1.

However, the Committee revisited the same question three years later in *HMHI v Australia*, Communication No 177/2001, CAT/C/28/D/177/2001 (2002). By that time, Somalia had a Transitional National Government. Whilst that administration was

---

[30] M Nowak et al, *The United Nations Convention against Torture: A Commentary* (Oxford, Oxford University Press, 2008) 127. This work remains the most authoritative commentary of the interpretation and implementation of the CAT.

Part B – Legal Framework

highly insecure, the Committee concluded that by reason of its existence, cases where the risk of torture arose from other entities, as in *Elmi*, no longer fell within the CAT.

3.73 Article 3 CAT does *not* apply to all acts that constitute cruel, inhuman or degrading treatment or punishment, a formula which encompasses a wider range of activity.[31] During the negotiation of the CAT, the original draft text included the more inclusive phrase,[32] but this was abandoned as the treaty was negotiated, to the disappointment of some participants.[33]

3.74 At first blush, the ambit of Article 3 CAT is a narrow one. However, as with Article 7 ICCPR and Article 3 ECHR, *non-refoulement* protection under the CAT is absolute, as is made clear by the wording of Article 2(2). There can be no lawful derogation under any circumstances. The protection against *refoulement* under the CSR is more exclusive: it only applies to refugees, and even then it does not apply where the individual constitutes a danger to the security or community of the host country, as per Article 33(2) CSR. Notwithstanding these differences, however, an overwhelming majority of cases before the Committee relating to Article 3 CAT show some overlap with the CSR.

3.75 In respect of the standard of proof, in order to secure protection under Article 3 CAT, an applicant must show there are substantial grounds for believing he or she would be in danger of being subjected to torture. The burden is on the applicant; the test is one of arguability, not high probability.[34] The applicant must show a risk that is foreseeable, real and personal, and beyond mere theory or suspicion.[35] When determining whether the applicant is *personally* at risk, consideration is to be given but is not limited to seven factors, as specified in the Committee's General Comment 1, at [8]:

(a) Is the State concerned [the one the applicant is being returned to] one in which there is evidence of a consistent pattern of gross, flagrant or mass violations of human rights (see article 3, para. 2 [CAT])?;

(b) Has the author been tortured or maltreated by or at the instigation of or with the consent or acquiescence of a public official or other person acting in an official capacity in the past? If so, was this the recent past?;

(c) Is there medical or other independent evidence to support a claim by the author that he/she has been tortured or maltreated in the past? Has the torture had aftereffects?;

(d) Has the situation referred to in (a) above changed? Has the internal situation in respect of human rights altered?;

(e) Has the author engaged in political or other activity within or outside the State concerned which would appear to make him/her particularly vulnerable to the risk of being placed in danger of torture were he/she to be expelled, returned or extradited to the State in question?;

(f) Is there any evidence as to the credibility of the author?;

(g) Are there factual inconsistencies in the claim of the author? If so, are they relevant?[36]

---

[31] The CAT does, however, prohibit cruel, inhuman and degrading treatment or punishment outside of *non-refoulement*, under Article 16.

[32] Draft Convention against Torture and Other Cruel, Inhuman and Degrading Treatment or Punishment, submitted to the Commission on Human Rights by Sweden (E/CN.4/1285).

[33] Report of the Working Group of the Commission on Human Rights (E/CN.4/1984/72) 4.

[34] UN Committee against Torture, General Comment 1, at paras 5 and 6.

[35] *Haydin v Sweden* [1998] CAT/C/21/D/101/1997.

[36] Committee against Torture, General Comment 1, Communications concerning the return of a person to a State where there may be grounds he would be subjected to torture (Article 3 in the context of Article 22), UN Doc A/53/44, annex IX at 52 (1998), at [8].

3.76 The fact the state to be returned to displays a consistent pattern of gross, flagrant or mass violations of human rights lends support to a finding that there are substantial grounds to believe the applicant would be tortured on return, as seen in *Mutombo v Switzerland*, Communication No 13/1993, UN Doc A/49/44 at 45 (1994). It is not, however, a prerequisite, and in one particular case—*VNIM v Canada*, Communication No 119/1998, UN Doc CAT/C/29/D/119/1998 (2002)—where there was no finding of a personal risk, the Committee did not even deem it necessary to consider the human rights situation in the country where the applicant was to be returned. Equally, such a finding does not make removal of an individual contrary to Article 3 CAT where there is an absence of personal risk. Indeed, in *HMHI v Australia*, Communication No 177/2001, CAT/C/28/D/177/2001 (2002), the Committee concluded that a consistent pattern of gross, flagrant or mass violations of human rights were to be found in Somalia, but that the applicant's removal there was not contrary to Article 3 CAT because there were no substantial grounds for believing that he personally would be at risk of torture.

3.77 Whether or not an individual has been tortured in the past is also relevant to the determination of future risk. For example, in *CT and KM v Sweden*, Communication No 279/2005, UN Doc CAT/C/37/D/279/2005 (2007), the Committee's finding that the first applicant was at risk of torture on return to Rwanda relied heavily on the fact she had been repeatedly raped whilst in detention there, prior to fleeing to Sweden. Whilst her account of being at risk of return was not deemed credible by the Swedish authorities, there was no dispute that she was a victim of torture; indeed, the rape was evidenced by the birth of a child shortly after the applicant arrived in Sweden.

3.78 The decision in *CT and KM v Sweden* is also relevant to subsection (c) of the General Comment, namely reliance on medical or other evidence to support a claim of past torture. The medical evidence featured heavily in the Committee's finding that removal to Rwanda would violate Article 3 CAT. Similarly, in *Kaveh Yaragh Tala v Sweden*, Communication No 43/1996, UN Doc CAT/C/17/D/43/1996 (1996), medical evidence confirming post-traumatic stress disorder and scars from burns was given weight by the Committee in finding that the applicant would be at risk on return to Iran. Such evidence, though desirable, may not be essential in every case.

3.79 Questions of credibility feature heavily in the Committee's jurisprudence. The Committee has repeatedly concluded that an applicant's account does not need to be accepted in full in order for Article 3 CAT to be engaged. In *Halil Haydin v Sweden*, Communication No 101/1997, UN Doc CAT/C/21/D/101/1997 (1998), the Turkish applicant's application for asylum in Sweden had been refused on credibility grounds. The Swedish government did not accept that if at risk of torture the applicant would have been released on a number of occasions by the Turkish authorities. Concluding that his removal would breach Article 3 CAT, the Committee stated, at [6.7], that:

> [C]omplete accuracy is seldom to be expected by victims of torture, especially when the victim suffers from post-traumatic stress syndrome; it also notes that the principle of strict accuracy does not necessarily apply when the inconsistencies are of a material nature. In the present case, the Committee considers that the presentation of facts by the author does not raise significant doubts as to the trustworthiness of the general veracity of his claims.

3.80 The Committee has also confirmed that late disclosure of sensitive details, for example, rape, should also be carefully considered before adverse credibility findings are made. In *VL v Switzerland*, Communication No 262/2005, UN Doc CAT/C/37/D/262/2005

(2007), the applicant had been raped on a number of occasions in Belarus, but only disclosed this during her appeal against the government's refusal to grant her asylum. The Committee's position on this was clear:

> 8.8 The State party has argued that the complainant is not credible because the allegations of sexual abuse and the medical report supporting these allegations were submitted late in the domestic proceedings. The Committee finds, to the contrary, that the complainant's allegations are credible. The complainant's explanation of the delay in mentioning the rapes to the national authorities is totally reasonable. It is well-known that the loss of privacy and prospect of humiliation based on revelation alone of the acts concerned may cause both women and men to withhold the fact that they have been subject to rape and/or other forms of sexual abuse until it appears absolutely necessary. Particularly for women, there is the additional fear of shaming and rejection by their partner or family members. Here the complainant's allegation that her husband reacted to the complainant's admission of rape by humiliating her and forbidding her to mention it in their asylum proceedings adds credibility to her claim. The Committee notes that as soon as her husband left her, the complainant who was then freed from his influence immediately mentioned the rapes to the national authorities in her request for revision of 11 October 2004. Further evidence of her psychological state or psychological 'obstacles', as called for by the State party, is unnecessary. The State party's assertion that the complainant should have raised and substantiated the issue of sexual abuse earlier in the revision proceedings is insufficient basis upon which to find that her allegations of sexual abuse lack credibility, particularly in view of the fact that she was not represented in the proceedings.

3.81 The Committee has also been clear that procedural safeguards at a domestic level are required. These include access to an asylum or other protective process that takes into account consistent patterns of gross human rights violations in the country of potential return, a suspensive appeals procedure,[37] adequate information and training on Article 3 CAT for public officials,[38] and the services of an interpreter where necessary, provided without charge. Crucially, individuals must be informed of their right to non-*refoulement* under Article 3 CAT.[39]

D4. CRC

3.82 The UK has signed and ratified the CRC, which contains provisions relevant to the protection of children's rights. Articles 3–5 CRC provide that:

Article 3

1. In all actions concerning children, whether undertaken by public or private social welfare institutions, courts of law, administrative authorities or legislative bodies, the best interests of the child shall be a primary consideration.
2. States Parties undertake to ensure the child such protection and care as is necessary for his or her well-being, taking into account the rights and duties of his or her parents, legal

---

[37] See, for example, the Committee's comments concerning the asylum process in France, during its 320th meeting on 14 September 1998: CAT/C/SR.320, at [23].

[38] See, for, example the Committee's questions put to the government of Bosnia and Herzegovina during its 667th meeting of 8 November 2005 CAT/C/SR.667, at [30].

[39] See, for example, the Committee's comments in relation to whether the Hong Kong government had advised Vietnamese nationals of Article 3 CAT 84: 234th meeting of 22 November 1995 CAT/C/SR.234, at [50].

guardians, or other individuals legally responsible for him or her, and, to this end, shall take all appropriate legislative and administrative measures.

3. States Parties shall ensure that the institutions, services and facilities responsible for the care or protection of children shall conform with the standards established by competent authorities, particularly in the areas of safety, health, in the number and suitability of their staff, as well as competent supervision.

Article 4

States Parties shall undertake all appropriate legislative, administrative, and other measures for the implementation of the rights recognized in the present Convention. With regard to economic, social and cultural rights, States Parties shall undertake such measures to the maximum extent of their available resources and, where needed, within the framework of international co-operation.

Article 5

States Parties shall respect the responsibilities, rights and duties of parents or, where applicable, the members of the extended family or community as provided for by local custom, legal guardians or other persons legally responsible for the child, to provide, in a manner consistent with the evolving capacities of the child, appropriate direction and guidance in the exercise by the child of the rights recognized in the present Convention.

Those duties of States Parties are general ones extending to all aspects of the conduct of State's parties dealings with matters concerning children.

3.83 Articles 7 and 8 CRC contain provisions relevant to the acquisition and retention of nationality by children:

Article 7

The child shall be registered immediately after birth and shall have the right from birth to a name, the right to acquire a nationality and, as far as possible, the right to know and be cared for by his or her parents.

2. States Parties shall ensure the implementation of these rights in accordance with their national law and their obligations under the relevant international instruments in this field, in particular where the child would otherwise be stateless.

Article 8

1. States Parties undertake to respect the right of the child to preserve his or her identity, including nationality, name and family relations as recognized by law without unlawful interference.
2. Where a child is illegally deprived of some or all of the elements of his or her identity, States Parties shall provide appropriate assistance and protection, with a view to re-establishing speedily his or her identity.

The rights of the child to acquire and preserve nationality generally overlap with the protection of the ICCPR where a state has ratified both instruments.

3.84 Articles 9 and 10 CRC set out standards regarding family unity:

Article 9

1. States Parties shall ensure that a child shall not be separated from his or her parents against their will, except when competent authorities subject to judicial review determine, in accordance with applicable law and procedures, that such separation is necessary for the best interests of the child. Such determination may be necessary in a particular case such

as one involving abuse or neglect of the child by the parents, or one where the parents are living separately and a decision must be made as to the child's place of residence.

2. In any proceedings pursuant to paragraph 1 of the present article, all interested parties shall be given an opportunity to participate in the proceedings and make their views known.
3. States Parties shall respect the right of the child who is separated from one or both parents to maintain personal relations and direct contact with both parents on a regular basis, except if it is contrary to the child's best interests.
4. Where such separation results from any action initiated by a State Party, such as the detention, imprisonment, exile, deportation or death (including death arising from any cause while the person is in the custody of the State) of one or both parents or of the child, that State Party shall, upon request, provide the parents, the child or, if appropriate, another member of the family with the essential information concerning the whereabouts of the absent member(s) of the family unless the provision of the information would be detrimental to the well-being of the child. States Parties shall further ensure that the submission of such a request shall of itself entail no adverse consequences for the person(s) concerned.

Article 10

1. In accordance with the obligation of States Parties under article 9, paragraph 1, applications by a child or his or her parents to enter or leave a State Party for the purpose of family reunification shall be dealt with by States Parties in a positive, humane and expeditious manner. States Parties shall further ensure that the submission of such a request shall entail no adverse consequences for the applicants and for the members of their family.
2. A child whose parents reside in different States shall have the right to maintain on a regular basis, save in exceptional circumstances personal relations and direct contacts with both parents. Towards that end and in accordance with the obligation of States Parties under article 9, paragraph 1, States Parties shall respect the right of the child and his or her parents to leave any country, including their own, and to enter their own country. The right to leave any country shall be subject only to such restrictions as are prescribed by law and which are necessary to protect the national security, public order (ordre public), public health or morals or the rights and freedoms of others and are consistent with the other rights recognized in the present Convention.

D5. MWC

3.85 The UK, in common with the US, Canada, Australia and New Zealand, and a large majority of Council of Europe members, has neither signed nor ratified MWC. The 47 States Parties are in general states of origin of migrant workers rather than states of sojourn. The existence of the instrument is therefore noted here for information purposes. Under Article 1, 'migrant worker' means 'a person who is to be engaged, is engaged or has been engaged in a remunerated activity in a State of which he or she is not a national'. The provisions of the treaty apply to migrant workers and their family members a number of safeguards. In particular, the treaty where applicable imposes certain procedural safeguards in respect of expulsion:

Article 22

1. Migrant workers and members of their families shall not be subject to measures of collective expulsion. Each case of expulsion shall be examined and decided individually.

2. Migrant workers and members of their families may be expelled from the territory of a State Party only in pursuance of a decision taken by the competent authority in accordance with law.
3. The decision shall be communicated to them in a language they understand. Upon their request where not otherwise mandatory, the decision shall be communicated to them in writing and, save in exceptional circumstances on account of national security, the reasons for the decision likewise stated. The persons concerned shall be informed of these rights before or at the latest at the time the decision is rendered.
4. Except where a final decision is pronounced by a judicial authority, the person concerned shall have the right to submit the reason he or she should not be expelled and to have his or her case reviewed by the competent authority, unless compelling reasons of national security require otherwise. Pending such review, the person concerned shall have the right to seek a stay of the decision of expulsion.
5. If a decision of expulsion that has already been executed is subsequently annulled, the person concerned shall have the right to seek compensation according to law and the earlier decision shall not be used to prevent him or her from re-entering the State concerned.
6. In case of expulsion, the person concerned shall have a reasonable opportunity before or after departure to settle any claims for wages and other entitlements due to him or her and any pending liabilities.
7. Without prejudice to the execution of a decision of expulsion, a migrant worker or a member of his or her family who is subject to such a decision may seek entry into a State other than his or her State of origin.
8. In case of expulsion of a migrant worker or a member of his or her family the costs of expulsion shall not be borne by him or her. The person concerned may be required to pay his or her own travel costs.
9. Expulsion from the State of employment shall not in itself prejudice any rights of a migrant worker or a member of his or her family acquired in accordance with the law of that State, including the right to receive wages and other entitlements due to him or her.

Article 23

Migrant workers and members of their families shall have the right to have recourse to the protection and assistance of the consular or diplomatic authorities of their State of origin or of a State representing the interests of that State whenever the rights recognized in the present Convention are impaired. In particular, in case of expulsion, the person concerned shall be informed of this right without delay and the authorities of the expelling State shall facilitate the exercise of such right.

D6. CRPD

The UK has signed and ratified the CRPD, the purpose of which is given in Article 1 as to 'promote, protect and ensure' the full and equal enjoyment of all human rights and fundamental freedoms by all persons with disabilities, and to promote respect for their inherent dignity. The subjects of the Convention, 'persons with disabilities', are given a non-exclusive definition in the second paragraph of Article 1 CRPD: **3.86**

> Persons with disabilities include those who have long-term physical, mental, intellectual or sensory impairments which in interaction with various barriers may hinder their full and effective participation in society on an equal basis with others.

3.87 Article 18 CRPD has provided reinforcement for broader standards, applying these expressly to the protection of persons suffering from disability:

Article 18 Liberty of movement and nationality

1. States Parties shall recognize the rights of persons with disabilities to liberty of movement, to freedom to choose their residence and to a nationality, on an equal basis with others, including by ensuring that persons with disabilities:
   a. Have the right to acquire and change a nationality and are not deprived of their nationality arbitrarily or on the basis of disability;
   b. Are not deprived, on the basis of disability, of their ability to obtain, possess and utilize documentation of their nationality or other documentation of identification, or to utilize relevant processes such as immigration proceedings, that may be needed to facilitate exercise of the right to liberty of movement;
   c. Are free to leave any country, including their own;
   d. Are not deprived, arbitrarily or on the basis of disability, of the right to enter their own country.
2. Children with disabilities shall be registered immediately after birth and shall have the right from birth to a name, the right to acquire a nationality and, as far as possible, the right to know and be cared for by their parents.

D7. CPED

3.88 The CPED entered into force in 2010, but has not yet been signed or ratified by the UK. In Parliament the responsible minister indicated in 2007 that the government 'need[s] to conduct a detailed analysis of the provisions of the treaty and their implications for implementation in order to determine the UK's position towards ratification, including whether we would need to make any reservations'.[40] Article 16 provides that:

1. No State Party shall expel, return (*'refouler'*), surrender or extradite a person to another State where there are substantial grounds for believing that he or she would be in danger of being subjected to enforced disappearance.
2. For the purpose of determining whether there are such grounds, the competent authorities shall take into account all relevant considerations including, where applicable, the existence in the State concerned of a consistent pattern of gross, flagrant or mass violations of human rights.

---

[40] Hansard HL Deb 26 June 2007, col 130W.

4

International Law: Hybrid Regimes

Contents

A. Introduction 4.1

B. International Refugee Law.. 4.5
    B1. Background 4.5
    B2. The Refugee Definition in the CSR.. 4.11
        'Alienage: A Refugee Must Be Outside His or Her Country of Nationality
        (or Country of Former Habitual Residence if Stateless)' 4.13
        'The Reason for Alienage Must Be "Fear"'... 4.14
        'The Fear Must Be Current, Not Historic'... 4.15
        'The Fear Must Be of "Being Persecuted"'... 4.16
        'The Fear Must Be "Well-Founded"' 4.37
        'That Persecution Must Be Persecution on the Basis of "Race,
        Religion, Nationality, Membership of a Particular Social Group or
        Political Opinion"'.. 4.48
        'The Refugee Must Be "Unable or, Owing to [Well-Founded Fear of
        Persecution] ... Unwilling" to Return to the Country of Nationality
        (or the Country of Former Habitual Residence if Stateless)'..................... 4.65
        'Where a Person Has More than One Nationality, He Must Have a Valid
        Reason Based on Well-Founded Fear for Failure to Avail Himself of the
        Protection of a Second or Further Country of Nationality'...................... 4.66
    B3. Cessation of Refugee Status.. 4.68
    B4. Exclusion of Refugee Status.. 4.71
    B5. Protection under CSR against Expulsion and/or *Refoulement*................... 4.77

C. International Statelessness Law 4.85
    C1. Background to the CSSP... 4.85
    C2. Protection in the CSSP against Expulsion; Absence of *Refoulement*
        Protection under the CSSP 4.89
    C3. The Convention on the Reduction of Statelessness 1961 .... 4.93

D. International Human Trafficking Law... 4.94
    D1. Historical Background 4.94
    D2. The Protocol to Prevent, Suppress and Punish Trafficking in Persons,
        Especially Women and Children 2000 .... 4.96

A. Introduction

The previous chapter set out international law instruments the dominant purpose of which is the protection of human rights, benefitting individuals directly by the creation of rights regimes designed to bind states.   **4.1**

This chapter in turn focuses upon international treaties with significance for the law of expulsion and exclusion, which are distinctive from the 'pure' human rights treaties in certain respects. Whilst the regimes examined here may create rights, and those rights   **4.2** may be very significant, they also have other international purposes, such as the sharing among states of perceived or actual burdens upon the international community.[1]

4.3 Three primary regimes are relevant here. The first two, international refugee law (IRL) and international statelessness law (ISL), emerged in their modern form after the Second World War and share common roots in the interwar regime for persons deemed to be lacking national protection. The third, the international law of human trafficking (ILHT), has some earlier antecedents and is somewhat fragmented in application, having different purposes—notably the criminalisation of trafficking related activities, the prevention of such activities, and the protection of victims—focused around a common subject area. Its emergence as a distinct legal regime is a very recent phenomenon.

4.4 There is an expansive secondary literature concerning these fields, most particularly IRL. The most comprehensive account is provided in *The 1951 Convention Relating to the Status of Refugees and its 1967 Protocol*, a detailed commentary on CSR by Zimmermann and other leading scholars. Other important works on IRL include those of Goodwin-Gill and McAdam in *The Refugee in International Law*[2] and James Hathaway in *The Law of Refugee Status*[3] and *The Rights of Refugees in International Law*.[4] An excellent work focusing upon the law and practice of asylum in the UK, including the law of refugees in the jurisdiction, is Symes and Jorro, *Asylum Law and Practice*.[5] Works concerning ISL and ILHT are cited in the Select Bibliography.

B. International Refugee Law

B1. Background

4.5 Although there has long been some degree of international or domestic practice concerning the seeking and giving of asylum at religious sites or by rulers of states, before the First World War there was no international regime for the protection of persons left without the protection of a state of nationality, whether through the absence of an effective nationality or through malignity on the part of that state. Immigration controls were generally limited, much of the world remained relatively open to migration, and persons suffering displacement or oppression were able to relocate with relative freedom. In the course of the First World War, however, many states imposed or

---

[1] Jane McAdam has noted this in relation to international refugee law: 'it is possible to discern various, and possibly conflicting, objects and purposes from the Preamble to [CSR]. This is borne out in the jurisprudence, where courts have sought to balance [the CSR's] humanitarian purpose, on the one hand, with the objective of facilitating burden-sharing among States of the refugee "problem", on the other'. J McAdam, in A Zimmermann (ed), *The 1951 Convention Relating to the Status of Refugees and its 1967 Protocol* (Oxford, Oxford University Press, 2011) 91–93.
[2] G Goodwin-Gill and J McAdam, *The Refugee in International Law* (3rd edn, Oxford, Oxford University Press, 2011).
[3] J Hathaway, *The Law of Refugee Status* (Toronto, Butterworths, 1992) and J Hathaway and M Foster, *The Law of Refugee Status* (2nd edn, Cambridge, Cambridge University Press, 2014).
[4] J Hathaway, *The Rights of Refugees in International Law* (Cambridge, Cambridge University Press, 2005).
[5] M Symes and P Jorro, *Asylum Law and Practice* (2nd edn, Hayward's Heath, Bloomsbury Professional, 2010).

strengthened controls on migration and these tended to remain largely in place after the conflict.

This created serious difficulties for individuals and for states. The war, the collapse of major powers and the creation of new states based on ethnic or language divisions had left very large numbers of persons alienated from their places of previous habitual residence or nationality, deprived of access to protection by a state as nationals. For instance, one to two million people had fled to Europe, China or elsewhere from the territory of the former Russian Empire in the years after 1918. The new Union of Soviet Socialist Republics, by a nationality decree of 15 December 1921, deprived many of these of nationality, leaving them stateless and without the ability to access documents for movement elsewhere or for legal registration in the states in which they were effectively stranded. Turkey and other countries followed similar policies, albeit on a smaller scale. By 1926, almost 10 million persons were estimated to be without national protection in Europe.⁶

In the face of this crisis, a body of international law incrementally developed. The first instruments addressed the problem as being absence of nationality, or statelessness, which had as its consequences the absence of diplomatic protection, mobility and access to employment. Their aim was in general to enable substitute documents to be provided to 'refugees' to allow them to migrate or seek to establish legal residence. In these early instruments 'refugees' were in general defined as persons of a particular ethnic or territorial background (Assyrian, Russian) identified as without the protection of the nationality of the state (Turkey, the USSR) ruling the territory from which they originated. The 1933 Convention Relating to the International Status of Refugees, the first attempt at a comprehensive treaty regarding refugees, did not develop a new refugee definition, but did contain the first provision in a legally binding modern treaty fettering the prerogative of a state to exclude or expel refugees, Article 3 providing that: 'Each of the Contracting Parties undertakes not to remove or keep from its territory by application of police measures, such as expulsions or non-admittance at the frontier (refoulement), refugees who have been authorised to reside there regularly, unless the said measures are dictated by reasons of national security or public order.' Eight countries including the UK had ratified the Convention by 1939, though many filed significant reservations.

Refugee law soon had to face new crises, of which the largest was the oppression and persecution of Jews and others in Nazi Germany from 1933 and elsewhere as Nazi domination spread. This was not initially a crisis of denationalisation like the preceding situations addressed by the earliest refugee instruments, but rather an attack on persons still regarded as nationals for the purposes of international law, but subject to persecution, including the formal or effective deprivation of citizenship rights, by their own state. Thus, whilst German Jews retained nationality in the early Nazi period, with the legal duties of loyalty to Germany this imposed, they were punitively excluded from the preferential status created for 'citizens of the Reich', Article 2(1) of the Reich Citizenship Law of 15 September 1935 providing that 'A citizen of the Reich is that subject only who is of German or kindred blood and who, through his conduct, shows that he is both desirous and fit to serve the German people and Reich faithfully.' Jews and other

---

⁶ A Zolberg, A Suhrke and A Aguayo, *Escape from Violence: Conflict and the Refugee Crisis in the Developing World* (New York, Oxford University Press, 1989) 18.

outsiders were politically disenfranchised, deprived of the protection of law and, by a series of legislative and administrative measures denuded of 'all rights usually attributed to nationals under municipal law ... [such that] [t]heir status was inferior to that of aliens'.[7] The 1938 Convention concerning the Status of Refugees coming from Germany, ultimately ratified only by Belgium and the UK, defined 'refugees' as 'Persons possessing or having possessed German nationality and not possessing any other nationality who are proved not to enjoy, in law or in fact, the protection of the German government', expressly extending status to those facing de facto absence of protection even where nationality had not been withdrawn. But the protection from refoulement provided by the Convention was much weaker than that envisioned by the 1933 Convention. In 1938 the international conference convened at Évian, following the Anschluss which caused many Jews and others to flee or be expelled from Nazi-dominated Austria, ran up against the disinclination of states to open their borders to refugees or accept additional restraints on exclusion or expulsion of aliens. A related phenomenon was the effective denial of documentation of citizenship to frustrate exercise of the right to return, directed at nationals abroad: the historian Timothy Snyder notes, with regard to the position of the many Jews possessing Polish citizenship resident in Germany and Austria that 'after the Anschluss, the Polish government demanded that all of its citizens living abroad register with embassies—and in October, right before the deadline, instructed its ambassador in Berlin not to stamp the passports of Jews. The Germans could see where this was headed, and responded by deporting about 17,000 Polish Jews to Poland in late October. Very often these were people whose entire lives had been spent in Germany'.[8] By the outbreak of the Second World War in 1939, the protection of refugees by international law had virtually collapsed.

4.9   After the Second World War, the international community confronted once more the problem of a European continent in which millions of persons were displaced and lacking either de facto or de jure national protection. The Office of the United Nations High Commissioner for Refugees (UNHCR) was set up on 1 January 1951 for an initial period of three years, in accordance with resolutions of the United Nations General Assembly. On 28 July 1951 CSR was concluded, entering into force on 22 April 1954. The regime was initially limited to persons displaced by events prior to 1 January 1951, and parties could declare that they recognised it subject to a geographical limitation to refugees created by events 'in Europe'. These limitations are generally disapplied by those states which have, in common with the United Kingdom, ratified the later Protocol relating to the Status of Refugees 1967, save that earlier declarations applying geographical limitations could be sustained. References to CSR below are to that instrument as currently applied by the UK, and the large majority of states which have ratified both CSR and its Protocol.

4.10   As will be seen, modern IRL does not extend to all persons without national protection, in general protecting only a subclass (albeit an important subclass) of the broader group.

---

[7] *Report on Nationality including Statelessness by Mr Manley O Hudson Special Rapporteur* (UN doc A/CN.4/50, 21 February 1952). In 1941 German Jews who had their ordinary residence abroad were stripped of German nationality.

[8] T Snyder, 'In the Cage, Trying to Get Out', *New York Review of Books* (24 October 2013) (www.nybooks.com/articles/archives/2013/oct/24/herschel-grynszpan-cage-trying-get-out).

B2. The Refugee Definition in the CSR

Under Article 1A(2) CSR, as modified in application by the 1967 Protocol, a refugee is defined inter alia as a person who: 4.11

> [O]wing to well-founded fear of being persecuted for reasons of race, religion, nationality, membership of a particular social group or political opinion, is outside the country of his nationality and is unable or, owing to such fear, is unwilling to avail himself of the protection of that country; or who, not having a nationality and being outside the country of his former habitual residence as a result of such events, is unable or, owing to such fear, is unwilling to return to it;
>
> In the case of a person who has more than one nationality, the term 'the country of his nationality' shall mean each of the countries of which he is a national, and a person shall not be deemed to be lacking the protection of the country of his nationality if, without any valid reason based on well-founded fear, he has not availed himself of the protection of one of the countries of which he is a national.

The ingredients of the refugee definition may be broken down as follows: 4.12

- i) Alienage: a refugee must be outside his or her country of nationality (or country of former habitual residence if stateless);
- ii) The reason for alienage must be 'fear';
- iii) The fear must be current, not historic;
- iv) The fear must be 'well-founded';
- v) That fear even where well-founded must be of 'being persecuted';
- vi) Such persecution must be on the basis of 'race, religion, nationality, membership of a particular social group or political opinion';
- vii) The refugee must be 'unable or, owing to [well-founded fear of persecution] ... unwilling' to return to the country of nationality (or the country of former habitual residence if stateless)';
- viii) Where a person has more than one nationality, he must have a valid reason based on well-founded fear for failure to avail himself of the protection of a second or further relevant country of nationality.

In *Sepet v SSHD* [2003] UKHL 15, [2003] 1 WLR 856, Lord Bingham at [7] observed that: 'Although it is no doubt true, as stated [by Simon Brown LJ in *Sandralingham v SSHD* [1995] EWCA Civ 16, [1996] Imm AR 97, 109] that the Convention definition raises a single composite question, analysis requires consideration of the constituent elements of the definition.' These elements are examined below, as are provisions for cessation of or exclusion from refugee status where the refugee definition otherwise has been or continues to be met.

'Alienage: A Refugee Must Be Outside His or Her Country of Nationality (or Country of Former Habitual Residence if Stateless)'

The purpose of CSR is to protect persons who are outside their states of origin and otherwise satisfy the refugee definition. It does not apply to persons who remain in their countries of origin, and the House of Lords held in *European Roma Rights Centre v Immigration Officer, Prague Airport* [2004] UKHL 55, [2005] 2 AC 1 that CSR did not prevent screening measures in home states by immigration officers seeking to detect   4.13

potential asylum seekers and avoid their transit to the UK. However, this should not be confused with the position of a person who has left his or her own country and is in transit, whether in the territory of a third state or on a ship or aircraft. Such people are refugees if they otherwise satisfy the requirements set out in CSR. Whether CSR binds states in their treatment of refugees who are not yet on their territory is controversial: the US Supreme Court in *Sale, Acting Comr, Immigration and Naturalisation Service v Haitian Centers Council Inc* 509 US 155 (1993) held that it did not, as has the High Court of Australia in *Minister for Immigration and Multicultural Affairs v Ibrahim* [2000] HCA 55, (2000) 204 CLR 1 and *Minister for Immigration and Multicultural Affairs v Khawar* [2002] HCA 14, (2002) 210 CLR 1 [42].

'The Reason for Alienage Must Be "Fear"'

4.14 This has been referred to as the requirement for a 'subjective fear' or 'subjective element', but the use of the word 'subjective' is unfortunate and should be avoided. The best interpretation is that a psychological state of trepidation is not necessary and that insistence upon this is incompatible with the CSR: were it otherwise, a baby or young child or person suffering from a mental disability preventing consciousness of reason for fear could not be a refugee, and the CSR would exclude the brave or rash individual able to cast off trepidation notwithstanding the presence of a relevant risk. A good account is that of Hathaway, who observes that:

> While the word 'fear' may imply a form of emotional response, it may also be used to signal an anticipatory appraisal of risk. That is, a person may fear a particular event in the sense that she apprehends that it may occur, yet she may or may not (depending on her emotional makeup) stand in trepidation of it actually taking place.[9]

He considered it clear from the drafting history that the term 'fear' identified the requirement for a forward-looking assessment of risk, not an interrogation concerning the emotional state of the subject. In the decision of the then Immigration Appeal Tribunal in *Asuming* (unreported; 11530; 11 November 1994), the Tribunal held that:

> [W]e understand 'fear' in the context of an asylum claim to be nothing more nor less than a belief in that which the appellant states is likely to happen if he returns to his country of origin ...

That conclusion has never been disapproved and the relative longevity of this authority in an area which has been heavily litigated seems to confirm the strength of the conclusion there expressed.

'The Fear Must Be Current, Not Historic'

4.15 A person becomes a refugee as soon as, and remains a refugee for as long as, he or she satisfies the requirements of Article 1A(2) CSR, including the requirement for well-founded fear. So long as there is a current fear, whether there was a fear at any particular

---

[9] Hathaway (n 3) 66. See also J Hathaway and W Hicks, 'Is There a Subjective Fear in the Refugee Convention's Requirement of "Well-Founded Fear?"' (2005) 26(2) *Michigan Journal of International Law* 505.

point in the past is in principle irrelevant. The provision does not require that the individual left his or her country because of a relevant fear, and circumstances may arise whilst an individual is outside that country creating a new entitlement under CSR, a refugee of this type being known as a refugee *sur place*. Equally, it is established that a historic fear does not satisfy the refugee definition. In *R v SSHD ex p. Adan* [1998] UKHL 15, [1999] 1 AC 293, the House of Lords rejected the submission that a past fear, coupled with current inability to return, satisfied Article 1A(2) the CSR. Per Lord Lloyd, at 308C, with whom Lords Goff, Slynn, Nolan and Hope concurred, 'it is the existence, or otherwise, of present fear which is determinative'. The Court of Appeal in *Revenko v SSHD* [2000] EWCA Civ 500, [2001] QB 601 held that this requirement for current well-founded fear applies where a claimant is stateless and cannot return to a place of former habitual residence, but does not have a current fear. In *MA (Ethiopia) v SSHD* [2009] EWCA Civ 289, [2010] INLR 1, the Court of Appeal examined a case based upon the claim by a woman from Ethiopia that she was subject to arbitrary exclusion by Ethiopia. The Court broadly reiterated the effect of the earlier decision in *EB (Ethiopia) v SSHD* [2007] EWCA Civ 809, [2009] QB 1, to the effect that arbitrary exclusion based upon the deprivation of citizenship and imposing effective statelessness could ground a valid claim under CSR, a current fear arising in such circumstances.

'The Fear Must Be of "Being Persecuted"'

CSR does not itself define the term 'persecution'. Paragraphs 51–53 of the Handbook published by the United Nations High Commissioner for Refugees[10] provide some guidance: 4.16

51. There is no universally accepted definition of 'persecution', and various attempts to formulate such a definition have met with little success. [From Article 33 CSR, it may be inferred that threat to life or freedom for relevant reason is always persecution.] Other serious violations of human rights—for the same reasons—would also constitute persecution.
52. Whether other prejudicial actions or threats would amount to persecution will depend on the circumstances of each case, including the subjective element to which reference has been made in the preceding paragraphs. The subjective character of fear of persecution requires an evaluation of the opinions and feelings of the person concerned. It is also in the light of such opinions and feelings that any actual or anticipated measures against him must necessarily be viewed. Due to variations in the psychological make-up of individuals and in the circumstances of each case, interpretations of what amounts to persecution are bound to vary.
53. In addition, an applicant may have been subjected to various measures not in themselves amounting to persecution (e.g. discrimination in different forms), in some cases combined with other adverse factors (e.g. general atmosphere of insecurity in the country of origin). In such situations, the various elements involved may, if taken together, produce an effect on the mind of the applicant that can reasonably justify a claim to well-founded fear of persecution on 'cumulative grounds'. Needless to say, it is not possible to lay down a general rule as to what cumulative reasons can give rise to a valid claim to refugee

---

[10] *Handbook on Procedures and Criteria for Determining Refugee Status under the 1951 Convention and the 1967 Protocol relating to the Status of Refugees*, HCR/IP/4/Eng/REV.1 Reedited, Geneva, January 1992, UNHCR 1979.

status. This will necessarily depend on all the circumstances, including the particular geographical, historical, and ethnological context.

4.17 In *Gashi and Nikshiqi v SSHD* [1997] INLR 96, the then Immigration Appeal Tribunal followed the Supreme Court of Canada in *Canada (Attorney General) v Ward* [1993] 2 SCR 689 in applying the analysis of persecution then recently set out by Hathaway in *The Law of Refugee Status*, to the effect that persecution 'may be defined as the sustained or systemic violation of basic human rights demonstrative of a failure of state protection'[11] or as 'the sustained or systemic failure of state protection in relation to one of the core entitlements which has been recognised by the international community'.[12] Hathaway was not alone in systematising a human rights-based approach: Goodwin-Gill had also identified basic human rights as providing a framework for the definition of persecution, focusing particularly upon rights identified by the ICJ as obligations *erga omnes* in the *Barcelona Traction* case[13] and developing this analysis further by reference to the ICCPR.[14] The reference by Hathaway to 'sustained or systematic' violation of relevant norms should not be taken over-literally: he and other commentators consistently agree that a very serious breach of core human values would plainly constitute persecution, even if this was not 'sustained' or 'systemic'.

4.18 Hathaway's approach delineates four categories of rights including: (i) first, provisions asserted in the UDHR then translated into the ICCPR and made non-derogable even in times of pressing national emergency, breach of which constitutes persecution in any circumstances; (ii) ICCPR rights which are derogable during an officially recognised and sufficiently serious public emergency, such as, inter alia, the right to be free from arbitrary arrest and detention and the right of freedom to expression, where the state cannot demonstrate any valid justification for temporary curtailment, violation of which will generally constitute persecution; (iii) rights under the ICESCR, where discriminatory discrimination or extreme deprivation amounts to persecution; and finally (iv) some rights under the UDHR not codified in the ICCPR or the ICESCR, violation of which will not ordinarily constitute persecution.[15]

4.19 Some criticism might be made of aspects of this scheme treated more rigidly than was likely intended: for instance, the building upon distinction between derogable and non-derogable ICCPR rights may not represent a firm basis for division between categories given a degree of arbitrariness in the original ICCPR categorisation.[16] And the domestic courts have noted the requirement that an apprehended violation be a serious one: *Horvath v SSHD* [1999] EWCA Civ 3026, [2000] INLR 15, per Ward LJ at [50]; *RG (Colombia) v SSHD* [2006] EWCA Civ 57, per Laws LJ at [19]; *Sepet v SSHD* [2003] UKHL 15, [2003] 1 WLR 856, 862, at [7], per Lord Bingham (referring to 'persecution as

---

[11] Hathaway (n 3) 104–05.
[12] ibid 112.
[13] International Court of Justice, *Barcelona Traction* case: *Belgium v Spain (Second Phase)* (1970) ICJ Rep 3, [33].
[14] G Goodwin-Gill, *The Refugee in International Law* (Oxford, Oxford University Press, 1983) 38–46.
[15] Hathaway (n 3) 108–12.
[16] Non-derogable rights under the ICCPR include the Article 15 ICCPR protection from retrospective declaration of a criminal offence, which is potentially applicable even where the effect is small, such as where, say, a historic parking offence is criminalised and a small fine is retrospectively imposed, whereas derogable ones include the intuitively more central right to 'liberty and security of person', protection against arbitrary arrest or detention under Article 9 ICCPR.

'a strong word' and linking this to dictionary definitions and to guidance by Hathaway, without suggestion of mutual incompatibility); and *HJ (Iran) v SSHD; HT (Cameroon) v SSHD* [2010] UKSC 31, [2011] 1 AC 596, at [12]–[16], per Lord Hope.

Overall, however, there has been very broad acceptance of internationally protected human rights in principle providing a key tool for interpretation of the requirement for 'persecution'. In particular Hathaway's interpretation has been repeatedly endorsed in the House of Lords and Supreme Court, for instance, in *Horvath v SSHD* [2000] UKHL 37, [2001] 1 AC 489, 495, per Lord Hope of Craighead (although Lords Lloyd and Clyde separately endorsed the use of a dictionary definition, without rejecting the Hathaway guidance); *Sepet v SSHD* [2003] UKHL 15, [2003] 1 WLR 856, 862, at [7], per Lord Bingham of Cornhill (in a speech concurred in by others, citing Lord Hope's reference in *Horvath* and referring to Hathaway as providing 'valuable guidance'); *R (Ullah) v Special Adjudicator* [2004] UKHL 26, [2004] 2 AC 323 at [32], per Lord Steyn, and in the Supreme Court, in *HJ (Iran) v SSHD* (Rev 1) [2010] UKSC 31, [2011] 1 AC 596 at [13], per Lord Hope and at [113], per Sir John Dyson SCJ; and *RT (Zimbabwe) and others v SSHD* [2012] UKSC 38, [2013] 1 AC 152, at [39], per Lord Dyson (with whom Lord Hope, Lady Hale, Lord Clarke, Lord Wilson and Lord Reed agreed). 4.20

In practice, whether a particular matter constitutes persecution for purposes of CSR may involve mixed questions of fact and law, the first looking at the circumstances and the second to the interpretation of CSR, as the Court of Appeal held in *MA (Ethiopia) v SSHD* [2009] EWCA Civ 289, [2010] INLR 1 as regards refusal of return where imperfect evidence of citizenship had been shown: see now also *MI & Anor v SSHD* [2014] EWCA Civ 826. Equally, if the conduct is of a character which has been held plainly within the definition, then the question may be treated as one of fact only. Some forms of conduct have been held always to meet the threshold for protection. In *Sepet v SSHD* [2001] EWCA Civ 681, [2001] INLR 33, Laws LJ indicated at [63] his conclusion that: 4.21

> There are some classes of case in which threatened conduct is of such a kind that it is universally condemned, by national or international law, and always constitutes persecution: torture, rape (though it is of course not necessarily persecution for a Convention reason). In those instances, the question whether or not there is persecution is straightforwardly a matter of fact. But it is not always so … There are other classes of case in which the threatened conduct is by no means necessarily unjustified at the bar of law or opinion: imprisonment is a plain instance (where its length is not disproportionate and its conditions are not barbarous). In such a case some further factor is required to turn the treatment in question into persecution. Torture is absolutely persecutory; imprisonment only conditionally so.

Some other forms of conduct may be more readily judged as persecution if representing a breach of duty by state agents. In *Svazas v SSHD* [2002] EWCA Civ 74, [2002] WLR 1891, at [38], Sedley LJ, with whom Simon Brown LJ concurred, rejected in terms the proposition that in some circumstances physical mistreatment by police officers might fall outside the scope of persecution because it was below a 'minimum level of severity':

> Mr Tam began his submissions by suggesting that the case is concluded by the adjudicator's finding (in paragraph 24) that 'the appellant's evidence does not show that that [police] brutality meets the minimum level of severity to amount to either persecution or torture'. Speaking for myself, I do not know what a minimum level of brutality is: brutality on the part of police officers is always unacceptable, and its repetition can amount to persecution. The IAT showed no inclination whatever to adopt this reason for their conclusion, and I am not surprised.

4.22　Given the nature and pre-history of the CSR regime, deprivation of nationality or exile may in significant respects provide paradigmatic examples of persecution. In *EB (Ethiopia) v SSHD* [2007] EWCA Civ 809, [2009] QB 1, the Court of Appeal accepted that arbitrary deprivation of nationality by a state of nationality, done for a relevant reason of ethnic or national background and with the consequence that the subject was left effectively stateless and was barred from return to his or her former home country, constituted persecution. By contrast, the situation of a draft evader excluded from return to his country by operation of law in *Lazarevic v SSHD* [1997] EWCA Civ 1007, [1997] 1 WLR 1107 was held not to be persecutory. Whilst the Court of Appeal in *MA (Ethiopia) v SSHD* [2009] EWCA Civ 289, [2010] INLR 1 expressed doubt that removal of nationality for a relevant reason per se constituted persecution, the Court in *EB (Ethiopia)* had expressly addressed a deprivation of nationality which was 'arbitrary' in international law terms, involving discriminatory breach of important international human rights norms including Article 12(4) ICCPR, and which imposed statelessness. The Court of Appeal has not to date accepted that the denial of return by a stateless person to a country of former habitual residence amounted to persecution, notwithstanding the extension of Article 12(4) ICCPR beyond the protection of nationals. In *MA (Palestinian Territories) v SSHD* [2008] EWCA Civ 304, Lord Justice Maurice Kay, with whom Lawrence Collins LJ and Sir William Aldous agreed, noted at [23] Canadian and New Zealand decisions which 'at their highest go no further than acceptance that, in some circumstances, to deny a stateless person re-entry *may* amount to persecution'. In other decisions of the same Court, such as *MT (Palestinian Territories) v SSHD* [2008] EWCA Civ 1149 and *SH (Palestinian Territories) v SSHD* [2008] EWCA Civ 1150, the Court has on the facts not found denial of return to be persecutory.

4.23　Conduct arising in the context of gender has been repeatedly recognised as persecution. Violence against women within the family, from which the state will not provide sufficient protection, creates a valid claim that persecution within the CSR is faced: in *Islam v SSHD; R v IAT, ex p Shah* [1999] UKHL 20, [1999] 2 AC 629, this had been accepted below, and the question considered by the House of Lords was whether the facts also showed a relevant reason for persecution, but the latter decision plainly endorses the proposition that the threshold for protection under CSR might be met in such a case. In *SSHD v Fornah; K v SSHD* [2006] UKHL 46, [2007] 1 AC 412, Lord Bingham at [16] recorded it as being 'common ground in this appeal that FGM constitutes treatment which would amount to persecution within the meaning of the Convention', while Baroness Hale at [87], referring to female genital mutilation (FGM) in one case and feared detention with the risk of sexual mistreatment and social stigma in the other, stated that: 'It was never in dispute that the harm which these two women feared was sufficiently serious to amount to persecution. Nor, eventually, was it disputed that their fears were well-founded. But it is worthwhile looking at the harm in a little more detail, because in each case it was either wholly or partly gender-specific.' In cases of human trafficking the Tribunal has treated acts not only of recrimination but also retrafficking as potentially constituting persecution, understandably given strong links with Article 8 ICCPR, Article 4 ECHR and the increasing development of other international and domestic laws concerning such trafficking: *PO (Trafficked Women) Nigeria CG* [2009] UKAIT 00046, at [162], which was implicitly followed in later decisions such as *AM and BM (Trafficked Women) Albania CG* [2010] UKUT 80 (IAC). In the latter decision the Tribunal accepted at [171] that 'where the victim of trafficking has a child, if it is considered that the family's sense of "honour" meant that a daughter could not live in the family home with an illegitimate child, that could lead to the family separating the child from the victim … [which] would amount to persecution'.

Credible threats of serious harm, aimed at coercion, have been found to ground a valid claim to protection: in *Montoya v SSHD* [2002] EWCA Civ 620, at [10], Schiemann LJ, delivering the judgment of the Court, indicated that: 'To make that threat [of deprivation of life or property] to Mr Montoya amounts to persecution and the contrary has not been argued.' In *HJ (Iran) v SSHD; HT (Cameroon) v SSHD* [2010] UKSC 31; [2011] AC 596 the Supreme Court held that an individual who would face persecution if he attempted to live openly revealing a protected characteristic which could otherwise be hidden (on the facts in the appeals, sexual orientation) would also qualify as a refugee under Article 1A(2) CSR where on the facts he would conceal that characteristic not from personal inhibition, but out of genuine fear of persecution, per Lord Hope at [35] and Lord Rodger at [82]. The Tribunal and the High Court have treated that proposition as applicable beyond sexual orientation cases in, for instance, *MT (Ahmadi—HJ (Iran)) Pakistan* [2011] UKUT 277 (IAC) and *R (otao Yameen) v SSHD* [2011] EWHC 2250 (Admin), and the Tribunal has sought to apply it in detail in *MN and others (Ahmadis—Country Conditions—Risk) Pakistan CG* [2012] UKUT 389 (IAC). In *RT (Zimbabwe) and others* [2012] UKSC 38, [2013] 1 AC 152, the Supreme Court found that enforcement by threats and violence of falsification of political loyalty created a well-founded fear of persecution (the root of persecution being the enforcement of protestations concerning political belief by threat of violence), even where the claimant had no strong feelings militating against this: see the judgment of Lord Dyson (effectively the judgment of the unanimous Supreme Court) at [25]–[45].   4.24

It is also well established that persecution may arise indirectly, as by the persecution of a close family member: per Schiemann LJ (as he then was) in *Katrinak v SSHD* [2001] EWCA Civ 832, [2001] INLR 499, at [23]: 'If I return with my wife to a country where there is a reasonable degree of likelihood that she will be subjected to further grave physical abuse for racial reasons, that puts me in a situation where there is a reasonable degree of risk that I will be persecuted. It is possible to persecute a husband or a member of a family by what you do to other members of his immediate family. The essential task for the decision taker in these sort of circumstances is to consider what is reasonably likely to happen to the wife and whether that is reasonably likely to affect the husband in such a way as to amount to persecution of him.' In *SSHD v Fornah; K v SSHD* [2006] UKHL 46, [2007] 1 AC 412, at [26], Lord Bingham, recording that 'claims based on fear of FGM have been recognised or upheld in courts all round the world', endorsed 'clearly expressed opinions of the UNHCR' that FGM, 'which causes severe pain as well as permanent physical harm, amounts to a violation of human rights, including the rights of the child, and can be regarded as persecution' so that 'a woman can be considered as a refugee if she or her daughters/dependants fear being compelled to undergo FGM against their will; or, she fears persecution for refusing to undergo or to allow her daughters to undergo the practice'.   4.25

It has been held that CSR applies to the brave, or rash, individual who would act on return in a way which would attract persecution, rather than suppressing this—for example, an Ahmadi Muslim intending to proselytise his faith if returned to Pakistan   4.26

in *SSHD v Iftikhar Ahmed* [1999] EWCA Civ 3003, [2000] INLR 1. Persecution may even be faced where an individual has, or may have, acted cynically in the UK so as to create risk for himself or herself on return, thereby erecting the basis for a claim under the CSR, although the Court of Appeal has said that such cases would call for careful examination: see *Danian v SSHD* [1999] EWCA Civ 3000, [1999] INLR 533, and reflections in *YB (Eritrea) v SSHD* [2008] EWCA Civ 360.

4.27 Prosecution is not assumed to constitute persecution. But neither is the fact of prosecution exclusive of the possibility of persecution: in *R (otao Tientchu) v IAT* [2000] EWCA Civ 385, at [19], Arden LJ, with whom Simon Brown and Rix LJJ concurred, observed that an adjudicator 'had to ascertain, in relation to detention or court proceedings, whether that was by way of persecution or prosecution, and the mere fact that the activity was unlawful did not resolve that question by that very fact'. An individual may be particularly targeted by the authorities of his or her state, using a politicised or unimpartial justice system. In *MI (Fair Trial, Pre Trial Conditions) Pakistan CG* [2002] UKIAT 02239, the Tribunal at [16] confirmed that:

> [A] refugee decision-maker will always need to be alive to issues of justice or injustice in the case of persons who fear persecution as a result of criminal charges brought against them. If in fact all a claimant faces is proper prosecution for an ordinary criminal offence, the Convention is not engaged at all. But if the legal process he will go through is one that would subject him to injustice, the harm he faces may well amount to persecution.

4.28 The Tribunal in that decision went on to set out guidance to be applied in the case-by-case assessment, conducted in light of international human rights standards, which would be necessary to determine whether prosecution amounted to persecution for the purposes of the CSR. This decision of the Tribunal has been referred to with approval in subsequent decisions of the Court of Appeal. In turn, this line of authority has distinguished cases in which an individual is targeted for reasons specific to him or her, and those in which the claim that ill treatment is faced rests on reference to a general pattern of ill treatment, the Court seeming to conclude that in the latter circumstances the requirement is to show 'a consistent pattern of gross and systematic violation of fundamental human rights by way of punishment for draft evasion or unauthorised departure from the country, before a case of persecution or Article 3 ill-treatment could be accepted': *Hariri v SSHD* [2003] EWCA Civ 807, at [8], per Laws LJ, with whom Mummery and Arden LJJ agreed. In *Batayav v SSHD* [2003] EWCA Civ 1489, at [37]–[39], Sedley LJ, with whom Mummery LJ and Munby J agreed, cautioned against the misuse of such terms as 'general' or 'systematic' or 'consistently happening' as obscuring focus upon the correct test:

> 38. Great care needs to be taken with such epithets. They are intended to elucidate the jurisprudential concept of real risk, not to replace it. If a type of car has a defect which causes one vehicle in ten to crash, most people would say that it presents a real risk to anyone who drives it, albeit crashes are not generally or consistently happening. The exegetic language in *Hariri* suggests a higher threshold than the IAT's more cautious phrase in *Iqbal*, 'a consistent pattern', which the court in *Hariri* sought to endorse.
> 39. There is a danger, if *Hariri* is taken too literally, of assimilating risk to probability. A real risk is in language and in law something distinctly less than a probability, and it cannot be elevated by lexicographic stages into something more than it is.

Some caution may be needed in this category of case to avoid convergence between CSR and Article 6 ECHR, in respect of which only an extreme violation of the right after removal would bar removal. Such considerations raise difficult questions of valuation: in *RB (Algeria) v SSHD* [2009] UKHL 10, [2010] 2 AC 110, Lord Phillips observed at [153] that: 4.29

> 136. This is neither an easy nor an adequate test of whether article 6 should bar the deportation of an alien. In the first place it is not easy to postulate what amounts to 'a complete denial or nullification of the right to a fair trial'. That phrase cannot require that every aspect of the trial process should be unfair. A trial that is fair in part may be no more acceptable than the curate's egg. What is required is that the deficiency or deficiencies in the trial process should be such as fundamentally to destroy the fairness of the prospective trial.

Persecution may also arise in circumstances auxiliary to prosecution, such as through potential treatment in detention. In *Kinuthia v SSHD* [2001] EWCA Civ 2100; [2002] INLR 133, the Court of Appeal found that the possibility of *ex post facto* assistance after severe mistreatment did not militate against a finding of persecution. The observation of Lord Phillips in *RB (Algeria) v SSHD* [2009] UKHL 10, [2010] 2 AC 110, at [137], plainly has relevance beyond the immediate context of challenge to expulsion relying upon Article 6 ECHR: 4.30

> 137. In the second place, the fact that the deportee may find himself subject in the receiving country to a legal process that is blatantly unfair cannot, of itself, justify placing an embargo on his deportation. The focus must be not simply on the unfairness of the trial process but on its potential consequences. An unfair trial is likely to lead to the violation of substantive human rights and the extent of that prospective violation must plainly be an important factor in deciding whether deportation is precluded.

The Court of Appeal has said that in considering whether persecution in the form of ill treatment is faced, the attitudes of a religious or other group to which a claimant wishes to adhere are in principle irrelevant: *Kinuthia*, at [9], per Pill LJ: 'In considering whether there is persecution on Convention grounds, it does not appear to me relevant in the present case to consider the attitude of the adopted religion to other religions or what the international community may think of it.' That said, unlawful behaviour by, for example, a cult leader or member might require consideration of whether what is feared is prosecution or persecution: *Omoruyi v SSHD* [2000] EWCA Civ 258, [2001] Imm AR 175. 4.31

In an early decision concerning CSR, in *R v SSHD ex p. Adan* [1998] UKHL 15, [1999] 1 AC 293, the House of Lords appears to have concluded that a differential test applied in 'civil war' cases so that some form of additional requirement beyond a well-founded fear of persecution for a relevant reason arose. The *Adan* decision has been almost universally criticised as mistaken, both by senior courts in other jurisdictions and by commentators, and the Tribunal in *HH and others (Mogadishu: Armed Conflict: Risk) Somalia CG* [2008] UKAIT 00022 and *AM & AM (Armed Conflict: Risk Categories) Somalia CG* [2008] UKAIT 00091 appears to have treated *Adan* as overtaken by EU asylum law. The best approach would appear to be that the requirement for 'differential risk' has, after a brief period of post-*Adan* adaptation, come to be interpreted as expressing the principle that not all victims of civil conflict are refugees per se, and thereafter as adding nothing 4.32

of substance beyond emphasis upon the invariable requirement of a well-founded fear of persecution for a relevant reason.[17]

4.33 The requirement to take part in military or equivalent state service may ground a claim that forced participation, or punishment for refusal, amounts to persecution. In *Sepet and another v SSHD* [2003] UKHL 15, [2003] 1 WLR 856, the House of Lords considered an appeal from *Sepet and another v SSHD* [2001] EWCA Civ 681, [2001] Imm AR 452, [2001] INLR 376, in which a majority (Laws and Jonathan Parker LJJ; Waller LJ dissented) had held that in principle, persecution did not arise in cases of punishment for refusal to do military service, or flight from such service, where an objection to that service was based upon a genuine political, religious or other relevant commitment. Lord Bingham, with whom Lords Steyn, Hoffmann, Hutton and Rodger agreed, first confirmed at [8] that:

> There is compelling support for the view that refugee status should be accorded to one who has refused to undertake compulsory military service on the grounds that such service would or might require him to commit atrocities or gross human rights abuses or participate in a conflict condemned by the international community, or where refusal to serve would earn grossly excessive or disproportionate punishment ...

In considering whether circumstances justify treating a military service evader or deserter as a refugee, the courts have been guided by international human rights law and also, in appropriate circumstances, by international humanitarian law, the law of war. In *Krotov v SSHD* [2004] EWCA Civ 69, [2004] 1 WLR 1825, the Court of Appeal found that a Russian claimant evading service in Chechnya could succeed in a claim under the Refugee Convention on the basis that his participation 'would or might require him ... to engage in activities contrary to the basic rules of human conduct, whereby punishment for desertion ... would itself be properly regarded as persecution'. In *BE (Iran) v SSHD* [2008] EWCA Civ 540, the claimant was an Iranian soldier who had deserted to avoid pressure to lay mines in areas where they would endanger Kurdish civilians. The Court of Appeal held that the Tribunal below had erred in applying international humanitarian law norms regarding minelaying because there was no present armed conflict and therefore no basis for the application of international humanitarian law, but that human rights norms as to the use of mines against a civilian population supported a parallel conclusion.

4.34 The question which arose on appeal in *Sepet and another* was whether the parameters of persecution extended to punishment or sanction in circumstances in which a coherent reason for abhorrence of military service based upon political, religious or other conviction arose, whether directed against military service per se or against particular military activities. Lord Bingham was moved by the absence of evidence of a human right of conscientious objection extending to this ground to conclude that sanction in such circumstances was not persecutory, observing at [21] that he felt 'genuine respect for the care and thoroughness with which Waller LJ has put forward his conclusions,

---

[17] E Fripp, 'Inclusion of Refugees from Armed Conflict: Combatants and Ex-combatants' in D Cantor and J-F Durieux (eds), *Refuge from Inhumanity? War Refugees and International Humanitarian Law* (Leiden, Brill/Nijhoff, 2014); 'International Humanitarian Law and the Interpretation of "Persecution" in Article 1A(2) CSR51' (2014) 26(3) *International Journal of Refugee Law* 382–403.

and … a measure of reluctance since they may well reflect the international consensus of tomorrow'.

Discrimination in socio-economic rights is more rarely accepted as persecution, but will amount to it in extreme circumstances. For instance, in *RN (Returnees) Zimbabwe CG* [2008] UKAIT 00083, the Tribunal accepted 'that discriminatory exclusion from access to food aid is capable itself of constituting persecution'. Denial of other socio-economic rights may also constitute persecution, depending upon the degree of the deprivation and/or its effect upon the subject. In *Jin Tao He v SSHD* [2002] EWCA Civ 1150, [2002] Imm AR 590, Schiemann LJ at [26] noted Counsel for the Secretary of State as accepting 'that where a Government makes it impossible for anyone of a particular social group to obtain employment then, at the least, it is necessary … to show reason why this is not persecution', and Buxton LJ at [38], with whom Carnwath LJ concurred, accepted that discriminatory denial of employment directed at members of a religious group potentially raised a human rights issue serious enough to engage CSR. In *KK IH HE (Palestinians, Lebanon, Camps) Palestine CG* [2004] UKIAT 00293, at [101]–[104], the Tribunal declined to treat serious discrimination in socio-economic entitlements between nationals and resident stateless persons as persecutory of the latter.

4.35

The fear may be of the state or its agents, but this is not an invariable requirement. It is well established that a relevant fear may, where the state is unwilling or unable to provide relevant protection, arise from non-state agents, as confirmed by the Court of Appeal in *R (otao Adan) v SSHD* [1999] EWCA Civ 1948, [1999] 3 WLR 1274, 1295–96, per Lord Woolf MR:

4.36

> [T]he issue we must decide is whether or not as a matter of law, the scope of article 1A(2) extends to persons who fear persecution by non-state agents in circumstances where the state is not complicit in the persecution, whether because it is unwilling or unable (including instances where no effective state authority exists) to afford protection. We entertain no doubt but that such persons, whose case is established on the facts, are entitled to the Convention's protection.

'The Fear Must Be "Well-Founded"'

The requirement of well-foundedness in Article 1A(2) CSR underlines the requirement for objective risk of a relevant consequence should a refugee be returned to his or her country. In *R (otao Sivakumaran) v SSHD* [1987] UKHL 1, [1988] AC 958, Lord Keith of Kinkel, with whom Lords Bridge, Griffiths and Goff agreed, concluded that:

4.37

> In my opinion the requirement that an applicant's fear of persecution should be well-founded means that there has to be demonstrated a reasonable degree of likelihood that he will be persecuted for a Convention reason if returned to his own country.

The relevant question, as expressed by Counsel for the Secretary of State and accepted by their Lordships' House, was not whether persecution was more likely than not, but:

> [W]hether in the light of those facts and circumstances there was a real and substantial risk that the applicant would be persecuted for a Convention reason if returned to the country of his nationality.

More recently, the Court of Appeal in *MH (Iraq) v SSHD* [2007] EWCA Civ 852, at [22], per Laws LJ, with whom Mummery LJ and Blackburne J agreed, reiterated that fear of events following from removal will be shown to be well-founded 'certainly in relation to future events, by showing that there is a real as opposed to a fanciful risk that they will happen'.

4.38 A fear will not be well founded if the claimed persecution originates from non-state agents and there is in the country in question a system of state protection which is sufficient to eliminate risk or to reduce the risk below the level at which a fear of persecution is well-founded. The House of Lords in *Horvath v SSHD* [2000] UKHL 37, [2001] 1 AC 489 rejected the proposition that entitlement would exist unless the home state was able to eliminate all risks of a relevant character, the need being for a 'sufficiency' or 'practical standard', taking account of the duty of states to their nationals. In *Noune v SSHD* [2000] EWCA Civ 306, [2001] INLR 526, the Court of Appeal (Schiemann and Tuckey LJJ and Sir Swinton Thomas) considered the effect of the standards established by their Lordships' House in *Horvath*:

> 28. However, there are a number of considerations in the present case which, giving it the most anxious scrutiny which the law requires, make us reluctant to affirm the decision of the Tribunal and agree that this appellant should be sent to Algeria without more ado.
> 1. ... It may be that the Tribunal ... considered that where the law enforcement agencies are doing their best and are not being either generally inefficient or incompetent (as that word is generally understood, implying lack of skill rather than lack of effectiveness) this was enough to disqualify a potential victim from being a refugee ... If that was the reading adopted by the Tribunal, we consider that it erred as a matter of law ...
> 3. The evidence before the Tribunal supported its view that there was not a total collapse of the state's protective machinery. What there was, was better than nothing. But this does not answer the question which the Tribunal had to answer, namely, whether there was a reasonable likelihood that the Appellant would be persecuted for a Convention reason. There seems to us to be a danger that the Tribunal considered the total collapse of the state's protective machinery to be a prerequisite for a successful claim to refugee status. If it did adopt that view, it was in error ...
> 5. It is important to examine whether this is a case, to use Lord Hope's words in *Horvath*, of 'isolated and random attacks' with which citizens in any state must expect to put up or whether, in the context of Algeria, there is a reasonable likelihood that an unwillingness by the appellant to aid the Islamists in their fight against the Government and indeed to wear the veil might very well be taken as an expression of political opinion and lead to persecution. It was relevant to consider whether the uncontentious material before the IAT showing the substantial death toll in Algeria inflicted by Islamists indicated that the law enforcement agencies were ineffective to prevent Islamists inflicting death and injury on those who were perceived by them to be opposed to their cause or whether the infliction of death or injury was in general because of a desire by the killers to obtain money or drugs or something of that kind.

4.39 The Court of Appeal subsequently confirmed that the level of protection provided had to be not simply sufficient in generic circumstances, but adequate as regards elevated risk in a particular case: *Bagdanaviciene v SSHD* [2003] EWCA Civ 1605, [2004] WLR 1207, at [55], per Lord Woolf LCJ, with whom Auld and Arden LJJ concurred:

> 55. ...
> 4) Sufficiency of state protection, whether from state agents or non-state actors, means a willingness *and* ability on the part of the receiving state to provide through its legal system

a reasonable level of protection from ill-treatment of which the claimant for asylum has a well-founded fear ...

5) The effectiveness of the system provided is to be judged normally by its systemic ability to deter and/or to prevent the form of persecution of which there is a risk, not just punishment of it after the event ...

6) Notwithstanding systemic sufficiency of state protection in the receiving state, a claimant may still have a well-founded fear of persecution if he can show that its authorities know or ought to know of circumstances particular to his case giving rise to his fear, but are unlikely to provide the additional protection his particular circumstances reasonably require.

4.40 Another matter pertaining to whether a claimed fear is in fact well founded may be internal relocation. This is not expressly stated in the CSR, but the concept is now well established in the jurisprudence and commentary. A fear of return is deemed not to be well founded where the risk in question is a localised one, and a reasonable alternative of internal relocation to an area of protection arises.

4.41 In *Robinson v SSHD and IAT* [1997] EWCA Civ 3090, [1998] QB 929, the Court (Lord Woolf MR Potter and Brooke LJJ) canvassed comparative authorities on the point:

17. It follows that if the home state can afford what has variously been described as 'a safe haven', 'relocation', 'internal protection', or 'an internal flight alternative' where the claimant would not have a well-founded fear of persecution for a Convention reason, then international protection is not necessary. But it must be reasonable for him to go to and stay in that safe haven. As the majority of the Federal Court of Australia observed in *Randhawa* [*Randhawa v Minister for Immigration, Local Government and Ethnic Affairs* 124 ALR 265]:

If it is not reasonable in the circumstances to expect a person who has a well-founded fear of persecution in relation to the part of a country from which he or she has fled to relocate to another part of the country of nationality it may be said that, in the relevant sense, the person's fear of persecution in relation to the country as a whole is well-founded.

See Black CJ at p 270 and Whitlam CJ at p 280.

18. In determining whether it would not be reasonable to expect the claimant to relocate internally, a decision-maker will have to consider all the circumstances of the case, against the backcloth that the issue is whether the claimant is entitled to the status of refugee. Various tests have been suggested. For example, (a) if as a practical matter (whether for financial, logistical or other good reason) the 'safe' part of the country is not reasonably accessible; (b) if the claimant is required to encounter great physical danger in travelling there or staying there; (c) if he or she is required to undergo undue hardship in travelling there or staying there; (d) if the quality of the internal protection fails to meet basic norms of civil, political and socio-economic human rights. So far as the last of these considerations is concerned, the preamble to the Convention shows that the contracting parties were concerned to uphold the principle that human beings should enjoy fundamental rights and freedoms without discrimination. In *Thirunavukkarasu* [*Thirunavukkarasu v Minister of Employment and Immigration* (1993) 109 DLR (4th) 682, 687], Linden JA, giving the judgment of the Federal Court of Canada, said at 687:

Stated another way for clarity, would it be unduly harsh to expect this person, who is being persecuted in one part of his country, to move to another less hostile part of the country before seeking refugee status abroad?

19. He went on to observe that while claimants should not be compelled to cross battle lines or hide out in an isolated region of their country, like a cave in the mountains, a desert or jungle,

Part B – Legal Framework

it will not be enough for them to say that they do not like the weather in a safe area, or that they have no friends or relatives there, or that they may not be able to find suitable work there.

4.42 At [29], the Court in conclusion went on to refer to an EU joint position and to commend the approach taken in the Canadian authority previously cited:

> 29. In our judgment, the Secretary of State and the appellate authorities would do well in future to adopt the approach which is so conveniently set out in paragraph 8 of the European Union's Joint Position. Where it appears that persecution is confined to a specific part of a country's territory the decision maker should ask: can the claimant find effective protection in another part of his own territory to which he or she may reasonably be expected to move? We have set out in paragraphs 18 and 19 of this judgment appropriate factors to be taken into account in deciding what is reasonable in this context. We consider the test suggested by Linden JA—would it be unduly harsh to expect this person to move to another less hostile part of the country?—to be a particularly helpful one. The use of the words 'unduly harsh' fairly reflects that what is in issue is whether a person claiming asylum can reasonably be expected to move to a particular part of the country.

4.43 The appeal in *AE and FE v SSHD* [2003] EWCA Civ 1032, [2004] QB 531 turned on whether a claimant's mental illness would be exacerbated by return to internal relocation, the Court of Appeal (Lord Phillips MR, Simon Brown and Ward LJJ) rejecting the proposition that a comparison between conditions in the UK and conditions in the contemplated place of internal relocation was relevant to reasonableness:

> 23. Relocation in a safe haven will not provide an alternative to seeking refuge outside the country of nationality if, albeit that there is no risk of persecution in the safe haven, other factors exist which make it unreasonable to expect the person fearing persecution to take refuge there. Living conditions in the safe haven may be attendant with dangers or vicissitudes which pose a threat which is as great or greater than the risk of persecution in the place of habitual residence. One cannot reasonably expect a city dweller to go to live in a desert in order to escape the risk of persecution. Where the safe haven is not a viable or realistic alternative to the place where persecution is feared, one can properly say that a refugee who has fled to another country is 'outside the country of his nationality by reason of a well-founded fear of persecution'.
>
> 24. If this approach is adopted to the possibility of internal relocation, the nature of the test of whether an asylum seeker could reasonably have been expected to have moved to a safe haven is clear. It involves a comparison between the conditions prevailing in the place of habitual residence and those which prevail in the safe haven, having regard to the impact that they will have on a person with the characteristics of the asylum seeker. What the test will not involve is a comparison between the conditions prevailing in the safe haven and those prevailing in the country in which asylum is sought.

In that appeal the Court of Appeal in judging the correct approach to reasonableness and undue harshness did not follow the approach of considering distinctly whether there was a shortfall between the human rights respected in practice at the place of proposed internal relocation, and those provided by significant international instruments such as the ICCPR and the ICESCR set out.

4.44 In *Robinson*, the Court had at [19] cited internal protection failing to meet 'basic norms of civil, political and socio-economic human rights', and the question of what relevance was to be given to such rights was eventually determined by the House of

Lords in *Januzi v SSHD; Hamid, Gaafar, and Mohammed v SSHD* [2006] UKHL 5, [2006] 2 AC 426 by Lord Bingham of Cornhill:

> 20. I would accordingly reject the appellants' challenge to the authority of [*AE and FE*] and dismiss all four appeals so far as they rest on that ground. It is, however, important, given the immense significance of the decisions they have to make, that decision-makers should have some guidance on the approach to reasonableness and undue harshness in this context. Valuable guidance is found in the UNHCR Guidelines on International Protection of 23 July 2003. In paragraph 7 II(a) the reasonableness analysis is approached by asking 'Can the claimant, in the context of the country concerned, lead a relatively normal life without facing undue hardship?' and the comment is made: 'If not, it would not be reasonable to expect the person to move there.' In development of this analysis the guidelines address respect for human rights in paragraph 28:
>
>> Respect for human rights
>>
>> Where respect for basic human rights standards, including in particular non-derogable rights, is clearly problematic, the proposed area cannot be considered a reasonable alternative. This does not mean that the deprivation of any civil, political or socio-economic human right in the proposed area will disqualify it from being an internal flight or relocation alternative. Rather, it requires, from a practical perspective, an assessment of whether the rights that will not be respected or protected are fundamental to the individual, such that the deprivation of those rights would be sufficiently harmful to render the area an unreasonable alternative.
>
> They then address economic survival in paragraphs 29–30:
>
>> Economic survival
>> The socio-economic conditions in the proposed area will be relevant in this part of the analysis. If the situation is such that the claimant will be unable to earn a living or to access accommodation, or where medical care cannot be provided or is clearly inadequate, the area may not be a reasonable alternative. It would be unreasonable, including from a human rights perspective, to expect a person to relocate to face economic destitution or existence below at least an adequate level of subsistence. At the other end of the spectrum, a simple lowering of living standards or worsening of economic status may not be sufficient to reject a proposed area as unreasonable. Conditions in the area must be such that a relatively normal life can be led in the context of the country concerned. If, for instance, an individual would be without family links and unable to benefit from an informal social safety net, relocation may not be reasonable, unless the person would otherwise be able to sustain a relatively normal life at more than just a minimum subsistence level.
>> If the person would be denied access to land, resources and protection in the proposed area because he or she does not belong to the dominant clan, tribe, ethnic, religious and/or cultural group, relocation there would not be reasonable. For example, in many parts of Africa, Asia and elsewhere, common ethnic, tribal, religious and/or cultural factors enable access to land, resources and protection. In such situations, it would not be reasonable to expect someone who does not belong to the dominant group, to take up residence there. A person should also not be required to relocate to areas, such as the slums of an urban area, where they would be required to live in conditions of severe hardship.
>
> These guidelines are, I think, helpful, concentrating attention as they do on the standards prevailing generally in the country of nationality. Helpful also is a passage on socio-economic factors in Storey, op cit, p 516 (footnotes omitted):
>
>> Bearing in mind the frequency with which decision-makers suspect certain asylum seekers to be simply economic migrants, it is useful to examine the relevance to IFA claims of

socio-economic factors. Again, terminology differs widely, but there seems to be broad agreement that if life for the individual claimant in an IFA would involve economic annihilation, utter destitution or existence below a bare subsistence level (Existenzminimum) or deny 'decent means of subsistence' that would be unreasonable. On the other end of the spectrum a simple lowering of living standards or worsening of economic status would not. What must be shown to be lacking is the real possibility to survive economically, given the particular circumstances of the individual concerned (language, knowledge, education, skills, previous stay or employment there, local ties, sex, civil status, age and life experience, family responsibilities, health; available or realisable assets, and so forth). Moreover, in the context of return, the possibility of avoidance of destitution by means of financial assistance from abroad, whether from relatives, friends or even governmental or non-governmental sources, cannot be excluded.

4.45 In *Januzi*, Lord Bingham at [21] rejected the proposition that internal relocation could not arise in any case concerned with state persecution, finding the question of whether relocation arose for consideration to be substantially factual:

> 21. ... There can ... be no absolute rule and it is ... preferable to avoid the language of presumption. The decision-maker, taking account of all relevant circumstances pertaining to the claimant and his country of origin, must decide whether it is reasonable to expect the claimant to relocate or whether it would be unduly harsh to expect him to do so. The source of the persecution giving rise to the claimant's well-founded fear in his place of ordinary domicile may be agents of the state authorised or directed by the state to persecute; or they may be agents of the state whose persecution is connived at or tolerated by the state, or not restrained by the state; or the persecution may be by those who are not agents of the state, but whom the state does not or cannot control. These sources of persecution may, of course, overlap, and it may on the facts be hard to identify the source of the persecution complained of or feared. There is, as Simon Brown LJ aptly observed in *Svazas v SSHD* [2002] EWCA Civ 74; [2002] 1 WLR 1891, para 55, a spectrum of cases. The decision-maker must do his best to decide, on such material as is available, where on the spectrum the particular case falls. The more closely the persecution in question is linked to the state, and the greater the control of the state over those acting or purporting to act on its behalf, the more likely (other things being equal) that a victim of persecution in one place will be similarly vulnerable in another place within the state. The converse may also be true. All must depend on a fair assessment of the relevant facts.

The 'relatively normal life' measure appeared to be reiterated in the speech of Lord Hope at [47], the satisfaction of the test being dependent upon the ability to lead 'a relatively normal life without facing undue hardship'.

4.46 Relatively unusually, overlapping issues of internal relocation returned once more to the House of Lords shortly afterwards. In *SSHD v AH and others* [2007] UKHL 49, [2008] AC 678, the refugee claimants were members of tribes from Darfur in Sudan, accepted as possessing a well-founded fear in their home area(s). Referring to [21] of the decision in *Januzi*, Lord Bingham observed at [4]:

> It is not easy to see how the rule could be more simply or clearly expressed. It is, or should be, evident that the enquiry must be directed to the situation of the particular applicant, whose age, gender, experience, health, skills and family ties may all be very relevant. There is no warrant for excluding, or giving priority to, consideration of the applicant's way of life in the place of persecution. There is no warrant for excluding, or giving priority to, consideration of conditions generally prevailing in the home country. I do not underestimate the difficulty of

making decisions in some cases. But the difficulty lies in applying the test, not in expressing it. The humanitarian object of the Refugee Convention is to secure a reasonable measure of protection for those with a well-founded fear of persecution in their home country or some part of it; it is not to procure a general levelling-up of living standards around the world, desirable though of course that is.

Their Lordships' House confirmed that there continued to be a test of unreasonableness or undue harshness, which could not be agglomerated with the separate question as to whether a risk of treatment contrary to Article 2 or 3 ECHR would be faced there. As per Lord Bingham (with whom all of their Lordships, and Baroness Hale of Richmond, agreed) at [9]: 'If the AIT considered that conditions in the place of intended relocation could not be unreasonable or unduly harsh unless they were liable to infringe an applicant's rights under article 3 or its equivalent, it was plainly wrong.' At [12]–[13], Lord Bingham rejected over-reliance upon comparisons, whether between the place of origin and the contemplated place of relocation or the national average and the contemplated place of relocation was required, each consideration being relevant but neither dominant. Baroness Hale of Richmond added to this analysis. Her comments were expressly supported only by Lord Brown of Eaton-under-Heywood, though were not disapproved by any member of their Lordships' House:

> We are all agreed that the correct approach to the question of internal relocation under the Refugee Convention is that set out so clearly by my noble and learned friend, Lord Bingham of Cornhill, in *Januzi and others v Secretary of State for the Home Department* [2006] UKHL 5, [2006] 2 AC 426, at para 21:
>> The decision-maker, taking account of all relevant circumstances pertaining to the claimant and his country of origin, must decide whether it is reasonable to expect the claimant to relocate or whether it would be unduly harsh to expect him to do so.
>
> As the UNHCR put it in their very helpful intervention in this case,
>> [T]he correct approach when considering the reasonableness of IRA [internal relocation alternative] is to assess all the circumstances of the individual's case holistically and with specific reference to the individual's personal circumstances (including past persecution or fear thereof, psychological and health condition, family and social situation, and survival capacities). This assessment is to be made in the context of the conditions in the place of relocation (including basic human rights, security conditions, socio-economic conditions, accommodation, access to health care facilities), in order to determine the impact on that individual of settling in the proposed place of relocation and whether the individual could live a relatively normal life without undue hardship.
>
> I do not understand there to be any difference between this approach and that commended by Lord Bingham in paragraph 5 of his opinion. Very little, apart from the conditions in the country to which the claimant has fled, is ruled out.

It follows that questions of internal relocation are highly factual, though some underlying principles may be detected. The Court of Appeal in *Hysi v SSHD* [2005] EWCA 711, [2005] INLR 602 per Judge LJ, at [26] and [33]–[37], deplored the expectation of the Tribunal that an individual should be expected to adopt and maintain a false identity to assure his safety in a place of internal relocation. In *AB (Jamaica) v SSHD* [2008] EWCA Civ 784 [31], Lloyd LJ (with whom Sedley and Carnwath LJJ concurred) noted that: 'It is plain that paragraph 20 of *Januzi* does not set out a model or prescribe how

4.47

a decision maker should proceed. It is not wrong to take as a first topic the question of lack of social welfare if that is one of the factors of importance on the facts of the case.' An applicant's traumatised state may be very relevant at this point: in *FK (Kenya) v SSHD* [2008] EWCA Civ 119 at [29], Sedley LJ, with whom Rix and Arden LJJ agreed, observed that: 'There may be cases where the tribunal is satisfied that, objectively, the appellant can be safe on relocation, but the appellant is so traumatised by past events that she remains in genuine terror of being returned there. The Home Secretary, by her counsel, accepts that cogent evidence to such effect may be relevant to whether internal relocation is unduly harsh.' In *VM (FGM, Risks, Mungiki, Kikuyu/Gikuyu) Kenya CG* [2008] UKAIT 00049, another Kenyan case, the appellant was a Kikuyu/Gikuyu woman seeking to escape the influence of the Mungiki sect. The Tribunal considered relevant whether in a place of contemplated relocation she risked encountering persons who would be able to force her to have FGM or to enforce this on her child, or inform the Mungiki of her whereabouts, and 'the religious and cultural context, the position of women within Kenyan society and the need for kinship links in the place of relocation in order to sustain such movement successfully'. In *SA (Political Activist—Internal Location) Pakistan* [2011] UKUT 30, the Tribunal found at [14]–[15] that the appellant should not be forced into relocation if the effect was to prevent the continuation of his political involvement or the pursuit of justice for the murder of his brother by political opponents.

'That Persecution Must Be Persecution on the Basis of "Race, Religion, Nationality, Membership of a Particular Social Group or Political Opinion"'

4.48   Victimisation or discriminatory treatment on the basis of an improper reason is central to the CSR. As Lord Hoffmann put it in *Islam v SSHD and Another, R v SSHD ex p Shah* [1999] UKHL 20, [1999] 2 AC 629, 650–51:

> In my opinion, the concept of discrimination in matters affecting fundamental rights and freedoms is central to an understanding of the Convention. It is concerned not with all cases of persecution, even if they involve denials of human rights, but with persecution which is based on discrimination. And in the context of a human rights instrument, discrimination means making distinctions which principles of fundamental human rights regard as inconsistent with the right of every human being to equal treatment and respect …

4.49   One context in which difficult issues arise is that of conduct by the authorities undertaken in the course of, if not to further, the investigation of terrorism or other crime. The House of Lords considered such a case in *R (otao Sivakumar) v SSHD* [2003] UKHL 14, [2003] 1 WLR 840, endorsing the judgment of Dyson LJ below, which had attached considerable weight to the use of torture against the claimant by the Sri Lankan authorities. Lord Hutton (with whom Lord Bingham concurred) identified at [29] the importance of the conduct of the interrogators for the inferences which could be drawn as to causation:

> Adopting this approach I consider that in the present case the proper conclusion to draw is that the acts of torture inflicted in such a sub-human way on the applicant were not inflicted solely for the reason of obtaining information to combat Tamil terrorism but were inflicted, at any rate in part, by reason of the torturers' deep antagonism towards him because he was a Tamil, and the torture was therefore inflicted for reasons of race or membership of a particular social group or political opinion.

In *SSHD v Fornah; K v SSHD* [2006] UKHL 46, [2007] 1 AC 412, at [17]–[18], Lord **4.50**
Bingham stated that:

> 17. The text of article 1A(2) of the Convention makes plain that a person is entitled to claim recognition as a refugee only where the persecutory treatment of which the claimant has a well-founded fear is causally linked with the Convention ground on which the claimant relies. The ground on which the claimant relies need not be the only or even the primary reason for the apprehended persecution. It is enough that the ground relied on is an effective reason. The persecutory treatment need not be motivated by enmity, malignity or animus on the part of the persecutor, whose professed or apparent motives may or may not be the real reason for the persecution. What matters is the real reason. In deciding whether the causal link is established, a simple 'but for' test of causation is inappropriate: the Convention calls for a more sophisticated approach, appropriate to the context and taking account of all the facts and circumstances relevant to the particular case.
>
> I do not understand these propositions to be contentious. They are in my opinion well-attested by authorities such as *Shah and Islam*, above, pp 653–655; *R (Sivakumar) v Secretary of State for the Home Department* [2003] UKHL 14, [2003] 1 WLR 840, paras 41–42; *Sepet v Secretary of State for the Home Department* [2003] UKHL 15, [2003] 1 WLR 856, paras 21–23; *Suarez v Secretary of State for the Home Department* [2002] EWCA Civ 722, [2002] 1 WLR 2663, para 29; *Chen Shi Hai v Minister for Immigration and Multicultural Affairs* (2000) 201 CLR 293, paras 32–33, 67–71; *Minister for Immigration and Multicultural Affairs v Sarrazola* [2001] FCA 263, para 52; and *Thomas v Gonzales* 409 F 3d 1177 (9th Cir, 2005). They are also reflected in the *Michigan Guidelines on Nexus to a Convention Ground*, published following a colloquium in March 2001. Whatever the difficulty of applying it in a particular case, I do not think that the test of causation is problematical in principle.

Race

Certain of the Convention reasons have attracted little interpretative jurisprudence **4.51**
because, in practice, they have not been controversial. The general meaning of 'race' in Article 1A(2) CSR appears never to have been litigated in a superior court in the UK, or even in any recorded Tribunal decision. The UNHCR Handbook has stated at para 68 that:

> Race, in the present connexion, has to be understood in its widest sense to include all kinds of ethnic groups that are referred to as 'races' in common usage. Frequently it will also entail membership of a specific social group of common descent forming a minority within a larger population. Discrimination for reasons of race has found world-wide condemnation as one of the most striking violations of human rights. Racial discrimination, therefore, represents an important element in determining the existence of persecution.

Religion

Whilst there are numerous cases involving persecution in which religion is invoked, the **4.52**
meaning of 'religion' for the purposes of the CSR has rarely had to be explored. A rare example is *Omoruyi v SSHD* [2000] EWCA Civ 258, [2001] Imm AR 175, in which the appellant had sought the protection of CSR on the basis of a claimed fear of a Nigerian cult, the Ogboni, extensively involved in criminal activities. Simon Brown LJ, with whom Waller LJ and Forbes J concurred, observed that:

> Let me at this stage deal with Mr Blake's argument that the Ogboni mafia itself is properly to be considered a religion for these purposes. There are, he suggests, clear religious elements to their

practices which merit such a characterisation: the worship of idols, sacrifice of animals and the like. This argument I would utterly reject. The notion that a 'devil cult' practising pagan rituals of the sort here described is in any true sense a religion I find deeply offensive. Assume opposition to such practices on the part of a secular state; is that to be regarded as a religious difference? I hardly think so. It seems to me rather that these rites and rituals of the Ogboni are merely the trappings of what can only realistically be recognised as an intrinsically criminal organisation—akin perhaps to the voodoo element of the Ton-Ton Macoutes in Papa Doc Duvalier's Haiti.

Nationality

4.53   CSR does not identify 'nationality' solely in the sense of 'citizenship' or nationality for the purposes of international law. In the face of the two definitions of 'nationality' identified by Weis, it at least is capable of accommodating the latter definition, looking to 'historico-biological' assessment of national identity.[18] In important respects, this assists the operation of CSR by eliding the scope for extensive, material argument about the meaning of 'race': to take an example, Czechs or Slovaks or Scots might not be a 'race' in the sense that 'Slavs' or 'Han Chinese' constitute a race, but either of them readily constitutes a nation or 'national group'. The UNHCR Handbook at para 74 states that:

> The term 'nationality' in this context is not to be understood only as 'citizenship'. It refers also to membership of an ethnic or linguistic group and may occasionally overlap with the term 'race'. Persecution for reasons of nationality may consist of adverse attitudes and measures directed against a national (ethnic, linguistic) minority and in certain circumstances the fact of belonging to such a minority may in itself give rise to well-founded fear of persecution.

Membership of a Particular Social Group

4.54   No 'Convention reason' has been more tested in litigation than membership of a 'particular social group'. It is important not only as a Convention reason in itself, but as a supplement to the list of more closed Convention reasons which by its presence encourages a flexible and balanced interpretation of entitlement under the CSR, rather than dispute over a set of relatively closed and rigidly defined concepts. In *Islam v SSHD and another; R v SSHD ex p Shah* [1999] UKHL 20; [1999] 2 AC 629, 651, which concerned the critical question (given the global phenomenon of gender-based discrimination, often to a persecutory degree) of whether women, or women in certain situations, might qualify, Lord Hoffmann related the definition of 'social group' to a central underlying purpose of the CSR—the protection of individuals from discriminatory oppression—noting that 'race, religion, nationality and political opinion' would have been the obvious bases of historically observed discrimination at the time of the CSR's negotiation:

> But the inclusion of 'particular social group' recognised that there might be different criteria for discrimination, *in pari materiae* with discrimination on the other grounds, which would be

---

[18] 'The term "nationality" ... is a politico-legal term denoting membership of a State. It must be distinguished from nationality as a historico-biological term denoting membership of a nation. In the latter sense it means the subjective corporate sentiment of unity of members of a specific group forming a '"race" or "nation" which may, though not necessarily, be possessed of a territory': P Weis, *Nationality and Statelessness in International Law* (London, Stevens and Sons Ltd, 1956) 3.

equally offensive to principles of human rights. It is plausibly suggested that the delegates may have had in mind persecutions in Communist countries of people who were stigmatised as members of the bourgeoisie. But the concept of a social group is a general one and its meaning cannot be confined to those social groups which the framers of the Convention may have had in mind. In choosing to use the general term 'particular social group' rather than an enumeration of specific social groups, the framers of the Convention were in my opinion intending to include whatever groups might be regarded as coming within the anti-discriminatory objectives of the Convention.

In *Islam; Shah* the members of their Lordships' House cited with approval a decision of the US Board of Immigration Appeals in *In re Acosta* (1985) 19 I & N 211, in which the Board rejected the claim of Salvadoran taxi drivers alleging feared persecution from the members of a competing taxi syndicate. Lord Steyn cited the key parts of the *Acosta* decision, which was approved: **4.55**

> We find the well-established doctrine of ejusdem generis, meaning literally, 'of the same kind', to be most helpful in construing the phrase 'membership in a particular social group'. That doctrine holds that general words used in an enumeration with specific words should be construed in a manner consistent with the specific words ... Each of [the other CSR reasons] describes persecution aimed at an immutable characteristic: a characteristic that either is beyond the power of an individual to change or is so fundamental to individual identity or conscience that it ought not be required to be changed ...
>
> Applying the doctrine of *ejusdem generis*, we interpret the phrase 'persecution on account of membership in a particular social group' to mean persecution that is directed toward an individual who is a member of a group of persons all of whom share a common, immutable characteristic. The shared characteristic might be an innate one such as sex, colour, or kinship ties, or in some circumstances it might be a shared past experience such as former military leadership or land ownership. The particular kind of group characteristic that will qualify under this construction remains to be determined on a case-by-case basis ... By construing 'persecution on account of membership in a particular social group' in this manner, we preserve the concept that refuge is restricted to individuals who are either unable by their own actions, or as a matter of conscience should not be required, to avoid persecution.

The decision established that membership of a 'social group' for purposes of Article 1A(2) CSR did not require that the group be a cohesive or organised one, but reinforced the conclusion in previous decisions that the group could not be established by the fact of persecution against its membership alone in the absence of relevant characteristic(s).

Subsequently, in *SSHD v Fornah; K v SSHD* [2006] UKHL 46, [2007] 1 AC 412, Lord Bingham at [16] referred to the EU Council Directive 2004/83/EC of 29 April 2004, effective as of 10 October 2006, which in Article 10(d) states that a group shall be considered to form a particular social group where 'in particular ... members of that group share an innate characteristic, or a common background that cannot be changed, or share a characteristic or belief that is so fundamental to identity or conscience that a person should not be forced to renounce it, and ... that group has a distinct identity in the relevant country, because it is perceived as being different by the surrounding society'. Lord Bingham concluded that this passage was not inconsistent with the CSR, but, endorsing criticism of that formula by the UNHCR, that it should not be read in its literal meaning as requiring both innate characteristic and distinct identity. Lord Brown echoed this at [118]. **4.56**

4.57   The *Fornah* appeal demonstrates the potential for complexity in practice of the 'particular social group' definition. The members of their Lordships' House divided as regards their preferred social group, Lord Hope, Lord Rodger and Lord Brown (at [56], [74] and [119] respectively) preferring a 'narrower' definition ('uninitiated indigenous females in Sierra Leone'), whilst Lord Bingham and Baroness Hale accepted the narrower definition whilst believing that the evidence and interpretation of the CSR justified favouring a 'wider' group of women in Sierra Leone or Sierra Leonean women belonging to ethnic groups following a practice of imposing FGM ([31] and [114] respectively). Lord Brown expressly accepted as viable, if not preferable, the wider view ([119]), so that a majority supported each approach as viable. In practice, the difference between approaches was on the facts of the appeal immaterial and there is nothing incoherent in interpretation producing viable alternative social groups.

4.58   In *K*, the appeal heard with *Fornah*, the House of Lords also recognised (per Lord Bingham at [21] and [24], Lord Hope at [51], Lord Rodger at [62]–[67], Baroness Hale at [106], Lord Brown at [117]) that the family as formed by kinship or marriage was a social group and that an individual persecuted by reason of membership in a family could seek protection, even if the persecution of family members was further to some original dispute not for any Convention reason.

4.59   The question of whether, in any given case, membership in a particular social group arises is one which will frequently fall to be analysed contextually on a case-by-case basis. However, some of the cases provide useful yardsticks. In *Jain v SSHD* [1999] EWCA Civ 3009, [2000] INLR 71, gay men were found to constitute a relevant group in the context of India, and minority groups defined by sexual orientation have been accepted as 'particular social groups' for the purposes of Article 1A(2) CSR in EU Council Directive 2004/83/EC and in many decisions since *Jain*, most conspicuously in *HJ (Iran) and HT (Cameroon) v SSHD* [2010] UKSC 31, [2011] 1 AC 596, an important decision identifying the scope for protection of a core personal identity, suppression of which will, if motivated by relevant fear, itself place the individual into a situation in which he or she might make good a claim to protection under CSR, since applied (in the context of political opinion) in *RT (Zimbabwe) and ors* [2012] UKSC 38, [2013] 1 AC 152. The recognition that groups defined by sexual orientation will often represent a 'particular social group' members of which are entitled to protection under CSR where required, is now widespread, at least in developed countries.

4.60   By contrast with sexual orientation cases, fear of punishment for sexual conduct breaching local mores by an individual not belonging to a group discriminated against by reason of sexual orientation has been held not to create membership in a particular social group, as in the case of an Iranian adulterer fleeing punishment in *E (Iran) v SSHD* [2003] UKIAT 00166.

4.61   One area of potential difficulty in establishing the precise limits of protection under CSR relates to cases in which a CSR reason of particular social group is raised in the context of criminal activity by alleged persecutors. In *Savchenkov v SSHD* [1995] EWCA Civ 47, [1996] Imm AR 28, persons declining to be informers for the Russian mafia were held not to be a social group. In *Montoya v SSHD* [2002] EWCA Civ 620, the Court of Appeal appears to have been ready to find that wealthy landowners could constitute a particular social group, but upheld a finding on the facts by the Tribunal that the reason for the actions feared was criminal extortion. By contrast, victims or former victims of human trafficking have been held to constitute a social group in some societies: *SK (Albania) v SSHD* [2003] UKIAT 00023; *VD (Albania) v SSHD* [2004] UKIAT 00115; *SB (PSG—Protection Regulations—Reg 6) Moldova CG* [2008] UKAIT 00002; *AM and BM (Trafficked Women) Albania CG* [2010] UKUT 80 (IAC). Cases in which there is relevant social discrimination should be positively distinguished. In *Hoxha and another v SSHD* [2005] UKHL 19, [2005] 1 WLR 1063, Baroness Hale stated inter alia that 'women who have been victims of sexual violence in the past are linked by an immutable characteristic which is at once independent of and the cause of their current ill-treatment. They are certainly capable of constituting a particular social group under the Convention', and this was endorsed by Lords Nicholls, Steyn and Hope.

In *Ouanes v SSHD* [1998] 1 WLR 218, 'a common employment' was said by the Court of Appeal in general not to create a particular social group for relevant purposes; however, the claimant in that case was an Algerian midwife seeking protection against recrimination by Islamists who targeted her because midwives were required to provide contraceptive advice. Were similar facts to be considered today following the decisions in *Islam; Shah* and *Fornah*, it may be thought likely that on the same facts, at least one relevant Convention reason chosen from attributed or actual religious belief or political opinion and/or relevant social group could be identified. This tends to highlight the difficulty of 'employment' cases and the real risk of failing to give weight to a politicised local context; possible current examples might be, for example, polio vaccination workers in Nigeria or Pakistan, or anti-terrorist policemen or policewomen in certain states and circumstances. In *R v IAT ex p Walteros-Castenada* (CO/2383/99, 27th June 2000; unreported), it was argued vigorously for the Secretary of State that involvement in a Colombian union targeted by paramilitaries 'was in reality little more than an adjunct to common employment'. This was rejected in strong terms by Munby J:

4.62

> That observation, which I suspect many would find slightly surprising, even in the context of trade unionism in Western Europe in the comparatively recent past, seems to me to give significantly too narrow and restricted a view of the purpose, objectives and activities of trade unions and members of trade unions, struggling, either on their own or in conjunction with other groups or individuals, for what they conceived to be social and economic justice in second and third world countries characterised by societies and regimes which they perceive as socially and economically oppressive and unjust.

Although that claim succeeded on the basis that a Convention reason of 'political opinion' arose, it is likely that an alternative Convention reason of membership in a particular social group would if necessary have been available.

Just as the appreciation of persecution on the basis of gender and/or sexual orientation has greatly developed in recent years, broader understanding of CSR continues to develop as human rights norms develop. The categories of causation represent an important area in which understanding of the scope of CSR continues to develop. In *R otao Sepet and another v SSHD* [2003] UKHL 15, [2003] 1 WLR 856, Lord Bingham at [6] endorsed separate earlier conclusions of two other notable judges to the effect that the application of the CSR is dynamic, reacting to changing rather than static circumstances:

4.63

> It is plain that the Convention has a single autonomous meaning, to which effect should be given in and by all member states, regardless of where a decision falls to be made ... It is also,

I think, plain that the Convention must be seen as a living instrument in the sense that while its meaning does not change over time its application will …

In this, the development of international human rights law, which as already seen has been assigned an important role in interpreting the scope of persecution, may have an ancillary role as identifying prohibited bases of discrimination. For instance, in Pakistan persons (including children) afflicted by mental illness may be considered victims of possession by evil spirits or 'djinns' and be subjected to harm in the course of alleged 'exorcism' or closed away from contact with others, a phenomenon which might plainly support a claim under CSR supported by reference to norms in the Convention on the Rights of the Child 1988 and the Convention on the Rights of Persons with Disabilities 2006.

Political Opinion

4.64 CSR protects from persecution by reason of political opinion. The term is a broad one, not limiting its scope to views within a party political system or dictatorship, or to persecution from the state. It includes protection from having to parrot false political views as a condition for safety: *RT (Zimbabwe) and others v SSHD* [2012] UKSC 38, [2013] 1 AC 152. The Tribunal, examining the relevant principles in *Gomez (Non-state Actors: Acero-Garces Disapproved) (Colombia)* [2000] UKIAT 00007, [2001] WLR 549, later treated as correct by the Court of Appeal in *Suarez v SSHD* [2002] EWCA Civ 722, [2002] 1 WLR 2663, set out the applicable understanding of 'political' by reference to dictionary definitions and jurisprudence:

> 27. The term 'political' within the phrase 'political opinion' has to be given a broad meaning but not one that is entirely undifferentiated. In conventional political science and political theory, the term 'political' is confined to matters pertaining to government or governmental policy. This is reflected in some of the dictionary definitions, e.g. the Oxford English Dictionary defines political as:
>
> [O]f, belonging, or pertaining to the state or body of citizens, the government and policy, esp. in civil and secular affairs; public; civil; or pertaining to the science or art of politics.
>
> 28. It is clearly this classical definition which Lord Diplock wished to affirm in *R v Governor of Pentonville Prison ex parte Cheng* [1973] AC 931:
> Politics are about government. 'Political' as descriptive of an objective to be achieved must, in my view, be confined to the object of overthrowing or changing the government of a state or inducing it to change its policy or escape from its territory the better so to do. No doubt any act done with any of these objects would be a 'political act'.
>
> 29. However, as noted by Hill, J in a recent Australian Federal Court judgment, *V v Minister for Immigration and Multicultural Affairs* [1999] FCA 428 on the term 'political' within Art 1A(2):
> It clearly is not limited to party politics in the sense that expression is understood in a parliamentary democracy. It is probably narrower than the usage of the word in connection with the science of politics, where it may extend to almost every aspect of society. It suffices here to say that the holding of an opinion inconsistent with that held by the government of a country explicitly by reference to views contained in a political platform or implicitly by reference to acts (which where corruption is involved, either demonstrate that the government

itself is corrupt or condones corruption) reflective of an unstated political agenda, will be the holding of a political opinion.

30. The need for the 'political opinion' ground to be construed broadly arises in part from the role of the Refugee Convention in the protection of fundamental human rights, which prominently include the rights to freedom of thought and conscience, of opinion and expression and of assembly and association … This entails that even in contexts where the persecutor may be simply another private individual, if his persecutory actions against a claimant are motivated by an intention to stifle his or her beliefs, the opinion being imputed can be seen as political, at least where the state authorities are unable to afford effective protection against such actions.

31. A broad construction is also required by the fact that the ground has to operate to protect a person against harm from non-state agents as well as state agents of persecution. Reference to 'non-state *agents*' is not, in our view, always helpful since it can wrongly imply that such entities have agency in the context of state responsibility. This Tribunal prefers to talk of 'non-state actors' In the context of state agents of persecution, it is difficult to quarrel with the formulation given by Hathaway, *Law of Refugee Status*, 154:
Essentially any action which is perceived to be a challenge to governmental authority is therefore appropriately considered to be the expression of a political opinion.

Where however the claim is of persecution at the hands of non-state actors, a definition of political which was confined to the machinery of government or to governmental authority in any narrow sense would have the effect in many cases of rendering the political opinion ground inoperative. In the context of non-state actors the need for a more inclusive, multi-sided definition of political was made very evident in the case of *Canada (Attorney-General) v Ward* (1993) 2 SCR 689, 746. In concluding that the term went wider than a simple question of party allegiance the Supreme Court held:
Political opinion as a basis for a well-founded fear of persecution has been defined quite simply as persecution of persons on the ground 'that they are alleged or *known* to hold opinions that are contrary to or critical of the policies of the government or ruling party' … The persecution stems from the desire to put down any dissent viewed as a threat to the persecutors. Grahl-Madsen's definition assumes that the persecutor from whom the claimant is fleeing is always the government or ruling party, or at least some party having parallel interests to those of the government. As noted earlier, however, international refugee protection extends to situations where the state is not an accomplice to the persecution, but is unable to protect the claimant. In such cases, it is possible that a claimant may be seen as a threat by a group unrelated, and even opposed, to the government because of his or her political viewpoint, perceived or real. The more general interpretation of political opinion suggested by Goodwin-Gill … i.e., 'any opinion on any matter in which the machinery of the state, government, and policy may be engaged' reflects more care in embracing situations of this kind.

'The Refugee Must Be "Unable or, Owing to [Well-Founded Fear of Persecution] … Unwilling" to Return to the Country of Nationality (or the Country of Former Habitual Residence if Stateless)'

It is sufficient to be either 'unable' or 'unwilling' to return: these are alternatives, not cumulative requirements. But the inability or unwillingness must be current, not just historic, and because Article 1A(2) must be read as a whole, the requirement for a current well-founded

4.65

fear for a relevant reason or reasons is not dispensed with where an individual is 'unable' rather than 'unwilling' to return, as per *R v SSHD ex p Adan* [1998] UKHL 15, [1999] 1 AC 293 and *Revenko v SSHD* [2000] EWCA Civ 500, as cited at para 4.15 above.

'Where a Person Has More than One Nationality, He Must Have a Valid Reason Based on Well-Founded Fear for Failure to Avail Himself of the Protection of a Second or Further Country of Nationality'

4.66   An individual who would otherwise qualify as a refugee by reference to his or her country of nationality may still be disbarred from refugee status if there is a second country to which that individual could look for protection, in relation to which no relevant fear of persecution arises. Some problems of interpretation arise in practice concerning the linked concepts of 'nationality' and 'protection': in effect, whether refugee status is barred by possession of a second nationality, but that nationality is in some sense not 'effective', whether because it is not recognised by the country of nationality or because that state will not permit its national to enter and remain on its territory. In *KK and others (Nationality: North Korea) Korea CG* [2011] UKUT 92 (IAC), the Tribunal at [37] endorsed an opinion of Professor Guy Goodwin-Gill to the effect that interpretation did 'not permit an interpretation which would require the asylum seeker to take steps to obtain a possible second nationality. On the other hand, an asylum seeker who is recognised as possessing another nationality is obliged, in the absence of a well-founded fear of persecution in that other country, to take steps to avail himself or herself of its protection'.

4.67   As to the required content of 'protection' constitutes in this context, in *MA and others (Ethiopia—Mixed Ethnicity—Dual Nationality) Eritrea* [2004] UKIAT 00324, the Tribunal at [46] accepted that 'the protection offered by a state of second nationality must be "effective" as envisaged in the UNHCR Handbook [at paras 106–07] and in [an earlier Australian decision in *Jong Kim Koe v MIMA* [1997] 306 FCA]'. That would require not only a right of entrance, rather than merely consular protection abroad, but also the guaranteeing of a number of substantive human rights. In the later case of *KK and others*, the matter did not arise directly for decision and the Tribunal did not refer to the previous decision cited on this subject, noting at [67] that any finding 'is likely to require us to go further than was merited by the submissions before us', stating the key question to be not 'effectiveness', but the content of 'protection', which is not defined. It would therefore appear that the position presently recognised in the UK is not fully settled, though in practice different approaches may produce similar outcomes.

B3. Cessation of Refugee Status

4.68   A number of separate provisions in Articles 1C–1F provide for cessation or exclusion from entitlement. These may be seen in the copy of the CSR at Appendix A. For purposes of Article 1C(1) CSR, the application to a country of origin for a passport or residence document would risk interpretation as a re-availment of the protection of that country. There is little useful authority, though domestically the Secretary of State has a policy under which cessation of refugee status (and of any leave to remain in the UK reflective of that status) may be considered if a refugee chooses to return to his or her own country and/or to obtain or use a passport issued by that country.[19] Paragraph 121 of the UNHCR Handbook states that 'if a refugee applies for and obtains a national passport or its renewal, it will, in the absence of proof to the contrary, be presumed that he intends to avail himself of the protection of his country of nationality' and UK practice is alert to this. The guidance does state that: 'Obtaining a national passport or an extension of its validity, and then using it for travel, should not automatically lead to termination of refugee status.'[20] It indicates that consideration will focus upon whether there was some urgent reason for return, such as the acquisition of legal papers, whether a request for approval of travel was made to the Secretary of State prior to departure and whether the length of the visit is consistent with the urgent purpose for it. Another relevant factor may be whether the individual had been issued with, or was awaiting, a CSR travel document, so that use of a national passport appears more elective than would otherwise be the case.

4.69 Article 1C(2) CSR is again covered by the Secretary of State's policy, by which, where a refugee has lost or been deprived of his or her nationality, he or she subsequently resumes that nationality voluntarily: 'The re-acquisition of nationality must be voluntary. The granting of nationality by operation of law or by decree does not imply voluntary re-acquisition, unless the nationality has been expressly or impliedly accepted.'[21] Article 1C(3) CSR applies in the parallel position of a refugee taking the nationality of a third country and thereby acquiring the protection of that nationality, so that surrogate protection under the CSR is no longer necessary. The Secretary of State's guidance concedes that a 'short visit to the country in question is not likely to constitute "re-establishment"' if undertaken for exceptional reasons approved by the Secretary of State, such as for a family funeral or to visit a sick relative. Where approval has not been sought prior to travel, the guidance states that the case should be considered on its own merits, taking into account factors such as the length and nature of the visit, and any pattern of previous visits.[22] A pattern of visits to a country neighbouring the refugee's country of origin may create suspicion if circumstances suggest that the refugee may be travelling indirectly but is re-established in the country of origin.

4.70 Article 1C(5) CSR applies where 'the circumstances in connection with which the refugee was recognised have ceased to exist, and he can no longer continue to refuse to avail himself of the protection of his country of nationality'. The policy of the Secretary of State records that 'Significant' and 'non-temporary' equates to changes which are 'fundamental' and 'nontransitory'.[23] Article 1C(6) is the analogue for Article 1C(5) applicable to stateless persons where the conditions which led to their identification as entitled to protection under Article 1A(2) CSR have ceased. The policy provides that cessation will operate only if in fact the individual would be permitted to return to the former country of habitual residence.[24] However, each of these two provisions contains a limiting provision by which the clause 'shall not apply to a refugee falling under

---

[19] Home Office, *Policy, Guidance & Casework Instruction: Cancellation, Cessation and Revocation of Refugee Status v3.0*, December 2008.
[20] ibid 4.4.
[21] ibid 4.2.2.
[22] ibid 4.2.3.
[23] ibid 4.2.5.
[24] ibid 4.2.6.

[Article 1A(1) CSR] who is able to invoke compelling reasons arising out of previous persecution for refusing to avail himself of the country of nationality/former habitual residence'. Article 1A(1) CSR is the provision for extension of protection under CSR to persons who had been recognised under certain other named refugee instruments predating CSR, and the House of Lords in *Hoxha and another v SSHD* [2005] UKHL 19, [2005] 1 WLR 1063 confirmed that the limiting provision only covers such pre-1951 cases. Accordingly, the limiting provisions attached to Articles 1C(5) and (6) have almost certainly ceased to be of practical significance.

B4. Exclusion of Refugee Status

4.71 Articles 1D–F CSR set out the conditions in which notwithstanding an individual satisfying Article 1A(2) CSR, the benefits of the instrument do not apply. Article 1D CSR, cited by the UNHCR Handbook at para 142 as related to 'Persons already receiving UN protection or assistance', applies only to persons who at the date of signature of the CSR on 28 July 1951 were receiving relevant protection or assistance, and the only possible UN agency providing this at the relevant time would have been the United Nations Relief and Works Agency (UNRWA). In *El-Ali v SSHD* [2002] EWCA Civ 1103, [2003] 1 WLR 1811, the Court of Appeal held that the exclusion was limited to those receiving UNRWA protection or assistance on 28 July 1951 and that cessation referred to cessation by some official decision of or concerning the UNRWA, but that in the event of this occurring, the relevant individuals did not have to satisfy Article 1A(2). It is therefore a provision approaching obsolescence as time moves on.

4.72 Article 1E CSR, which is little used, is related by the UNHCR Handbook at para 144 to 'Persons not considered to be in need of international protection' and applies in a limited range of circumstances in which an individual is resident in a third country and is recognised by the authorities in that country as having rights and obligations consistent with citizenship, 'but not formal citizenship'. A footnote to para 144 of the UNHCR Handbook suggests that the intention behind the provision was the specific one of excluding persons of German ethnic background displaced from their own states of original nationality, but granted status and rights in the Federal Republic of Germany.

4.73 Lastly, Article 1F CSR, according to the heading in the UNHCR Handbook above para 146, applies to: 'Persons considered not to be deserving of international protection.' In each case there must be 'serious reasons for considering that' the relevant condition for application is met. In *Al- Sirri v SSHD* [2012] UKSC 54, [2013] 1 AC 745, at [75], Lady Hale and Lord Dyson, in a judgment with which other members of the Court concurred, agreed with the UNHCR that the exclusion clauses in the CSR 'must be restrictively interpreted and cautiously applied'. The Court endorsed the following propositions in this connection:

> 75. (1) 'Serious reasons' is stronger than 'reasonable grounds'.
> (2) The evidence from which those reasons are derived must be 'clear and credible' or 'strong'.
> (3) 'Considering' is stronger than 'suspecting'. In our view it is also stronger than 'believing'. It requires the considered judgment of the decision-maker.
> (4) The decision-maker need not be satisfied beyond reasonable doubt or to the standard required in criminal law.

(5) It is unnecessary to import our domestic standards of proof into the question. The circumstances of refugee claims, and the nature of the evidence available, are so variable. However, if the decision-maker is satisfied that it is more likely than not that the applicant has *not* committed the crimes in question or has *not* been guilty of acts contrary to the purposes and principles of the United Nations, it is difficult to see how there could be serious reasons for considering that he had done so. The reality is that there are unlikely to be sufficiently serious reasons for considering the applicant to be guilty unless the decision-maker can be satisfied on the balance of probabilities that he is. But the task of the decision-maker is to apply the words of the Convention (and the Directive) in the particular case.

In Article 1F(a) CSR, a 'crime against peace, a war crime, or a crime against humanity, as defined in the international instruments drawn up to make provision in respect of such crimes' refers to the instruments at para 150 and annexes V and VI of the UNHCR Handbook. In *R (JS (Sri Lanka)) v SSHD* [2010] UKSC 15, [2011] 1 AC 184, Lord Brown at [2] noted the importance of narrow interpretation because of the serious consequences of exclusion from the benefits of the CSR. He went on, in a judgment with which the other members of the panel agreed, to outline the circumstances in which complicity in such acts would ground exclusion ([33]–[40]). 4.74

Article 1F(b) CSR applies where there is serious reason to believe that a significant non-political crime has been committed prior to admission to the UK as a refugee. Minor offences do not engage the clause even if repeated, and the UNHCR has suggested that capital crimes or other grave punishable acts were envisaged as the trigger for application. In relation to another point in the CSR at which criminal conduct may be relevant, Article 33(2) CSR, the UK has by a domestic deeming provision under section 72 of the Nationality Immigration and Asylum Act 2002 prescribed an approach at odds with most readings of the CSR, but the statutory deeming does not extend to interpretation of Article 1F(b) CSR and, in the absence of such extension, attempts to apply a similar deeming by analogy but unsupported by statute would be weak. In *T v Immigration Officer* [1996] UKHL 8, [1996] AC 762, the House of Lords reviewed the question of whether an offence is 'political', concluding that acts to be covered by the phrase had to be committed for a political purpose and there had to be a sufficiently close and direct link between the crime and the alleged political purpose, so that, for instance, an act of terrorism directed against civilians was not relevantly 'political'. 4.75

In Article 1F(c) CSR, 'acts contrary to the purposes and principles of the United Nations' are delineated by reference to the UN Charter at [10]–[11] in the decision of the Supreme Court jointly prepared by Lady Hale and Lord Dyson, with which other members of the Court agreed, in *Al- Sirri v SSHD* [2012] UKSC 54, [2013] 1 AC 745. The Court set out a 'general approach' to be followed, agreeing at [16] with the submission that the exclusion provision fell to be interpreted restrictively. 4.76

B5. Protection under CSR against Expulsion and/or *Refoulement*

Even for those who satisfy the refugee definition in Article 1A(2) CSR, that instrument does not provide a general right to territorial asylum, that is, to protection from removal from the state in which a claim is made. It does, however, provide a series of rights. Of particular importance for present purposes are Articles 32 and 33 CSR, which provide 4.77

protection respectively against expulsion from the receiving state (for a lawfully present refugee) and against *refoulement*, or expulsion or return to a place where a refugee would face a relevant threat.

4.78   Article 32 (Expulsion) provides:

1. The Contracting States shall not expel a refugee lawfully in their territory save on grounds of national security or public order.
2. The expulsion of such a refugee shall be only in pursuance of a decision reached in accordance with due process of law. Except where compelling reasons of national security otherwise require, the refugee shall be allowed to submit evidence to clear himself, and to appeal to and be represented for the purpose before competent authority or a person or persons specially designated by the competent authority.
3. The Contacting States shall allow such a refugee a reasonable period within which to seek legal admission into another country. The Contracting States reserve the right to apply during that period such internal measures as they may deem necessary.

As seen above in relation to Article 32 CSR, the structure of entitlement to the rights under the CSR depends in each case upon the possession of some degree of attachment to the asylum state. Protection from expulsion under Article 32 CSR requires at least lawful presence. The lawfulness of an individual's presence is generally assessed by reference to domestic standards in the host country, though a minimal level of international law content may be necessary for the purposes of the CSR. In *R (otao ST (Eritrea)) v SSHD* [2012] UKSC 12, [2012] 2 AC 135, the Supreme Court, declining to adopt the view advanced by Hathaway,[25] held per Lord Hope at [29]–[40] and Lord Dyson at [54]–[66] that lawful presence was not created by the grant of temporary admission to an asylum seeker or refugee after substantial presence in the country and a finding by the responsible tribunal that she was a refugee. However, as the Supreme Court recognised, the requirement of 'lawful presence' in the CSR may be of diminished importance since the transposition into domestic law of Council Directive 2004/83/EC of 29 April 2004 on minimum standards for the qualification and status of third country nationals or stateless persons as refugees or as persons who otherwise need international protection (the Qualification Directive). This is because the content of the protection granted goes further in some respects than the Refugee Convention. For example, Article 24(2) of the Qualification Directive requires a residence permit to be issued as soon as possible where an applicant qualifies as a refugee.

4.79   Further, whilst containing a general prohibition against the expulsion of lawfully present refugees, Article 32 CSR provides for expulsion in certain limited circumstances, namely on the basis of national security or public order.

4.80   The core protection contained in the CSR is the protection against expulsion or return of a refugee to a place where a threat to life of freedom arises. Article 33 CSR (Prohibition of expulsion or return ('*refoulement*')) provides:

1. No Contracting State shall expel or return ('*refouler*') a refugee in any manner whatsoever to the frontiers of territories where his life or freedom would be threatened on account of his race, religion, nationality, membership of a particular social group or political opinion.

---

[25] Hathaway (n 4) sections 3.1.3 and 4.2.3.

2. The benefit of the present provision may not, however, be claimed by a refugee whom there are reasonable grounds for regarding as a danger to the security of the country in which he is, or who, having been convicted by a final judgment of a particularly serious crime, constitutes a danger to the community of that country.

Protection from *refoulement*, which denotes return or expulsion to a state where 'life or freedom' would be threatened, is based upon the simple application of the state's territorial or other jurisdiction; unlike protection from expulsion under Article 32 CSR, where applicable, Article 33 is engaged by presence alone. The Article 32(1) requirement for threat to life or freedom has been interpreted by the House of Lords as not creating a different test from the citation of 'persecution' at Article 1A(2) CSR, so that any refugee facing persecution is potentially protected from *refoulement* by Article 33 CSR: *R v SSHD ex p Sivakumaran* [1987] UKHL 1, [1988] AC 958, per Lord Goff, with whom Lords Keith, Bridge and Griffiths concurred. **4.81**

The UK has by a domestic deeming provision under section 72 of the Nationality Immigration and Asylum Act 2002 prescribed an approach at odds with most readings of the CSR, in essence presuming any conviction followed by a custodial sentence of two years or more to constitute conviction of a 'particularly serious crime and to constitute [that person as] a danger to the community of the UK'. In *SSHD v TB (Jamaica)* [2008] EWCA Civ 977, [2009] INLR 221, Stanley Burnton LJ, with whom Thorpe and Rix LJJ concurred, observed at [38] that there were two disjunctive requirements 'reasonable grounds for regarding as a danger to the security of the [UK]' and being 'convicted by a final judgment of a particularly serious crime constitutes a danger to the community of [the UK]: 'in the latter case, the refugee must in fact have been convicted of a particularly serious crime and must in fact constitute a danger to the community. It was therefore insufficient for the purposes of Article 33.2 for the Secretary of State to consider only that there were reasonable grounds for regarding TB to be a danger to the community'. Subsequently, in *EN (Serbia) v SSHD and another* [2009] EWCA Civ 630, [2010] 1 QB 633, Stanley Burnton LJ, with whom Hooper and Laws LJJ concurred, largely supported the earlier decision of the Tribunal in *IH (s.72; 'Particularly Serious Crime') Eritrea* [2009] UKAIT 00012, finding that the statutory presumptions in section 72 of the Nationality Immigration and Asylum Act 2002 fell to be read as rebuttable. **4.82**

Article 34 CSR ('Naturalization') anticipates the assimilation of refugees into the citizenship of the state of refuge. It provides: **4.83**

The Contracting States shall as far as possible facilitate the assimilation and naturalization of refugees. They shall in particular make every effort to expedite naturalization proceedings and to reduce as far as possible the charges and costs of such proceedings.

This provision does not compel states to permit naturalisation of refugees, or to create conditions for naturalisation of refugees more liberal than those available to other aliens, though it has been said to import an obligation upon states to decide any naturalisation application by a refugee 'in good faith'.[26] Hathaway cites as examples of breaches of Article 34 CSR the domestic law of Zambia excluding refugees from naturalisation even where they could satisfy the standards demanded of ordinary resident aliens and a reported Australian policy of denying naturalisation to refugees who passed through another state en route **4.84**

---

[26] R Marx, in Zimmermann (n 1) 1451–52; Hathaway (n 4) 979–90, in particular 988–89.

to Australia.[27] So, a measure concerning naturalisation imposing particular disadvantage upon refugees or a subclass of refugees may breach Article 34 CRS. The second sentence of Article 43 CRS creates somewhat stronger duties in relation to naturalisation proceedings where naturalisation provisions accessible to refugees do exist, but also leaves very substantial ground for judgment by the authorities of individual states.

C. International Statelessness Law

C1. Background to the CSSP

4.85   Having dealt, by way of the CSR, with the position of the persons defined therein as refugees, the international community returned to the position of the broader group. The instrument in which the position of members of that group was addressed was the CSSP. In significant respects this follows the outline of the CSR, some provisions being identical. The most significant distinctions include the absence of the concept of persecution at Article 1A(2) CSR (which founds the existence of two separate regimes: one for refugees as defined in the CSR and one for stateless persons) and the absence from the CSSP of any equivalent to the CSR as a provision restricting removal where presence is not lawful.

4.86   The Preamble to the CSSP points to the 'profound concern' of the UN for stateless persons not already protected by the CSR and for their 'widest possible' exercise of fundamental rights and freedoms. As with the CSR, a substantial proportion of the provisions of the CSSP guarantee particular rights to those identified as beneficiaries: Articles 3–32.

4.87   Article 1(1) CSSP defines the class covered:

> For the purpose of this Convention, the term 'stateless person' means a person who is not considered as a national by any State under the operation of its law.

In chapter two it was noted that, whilst nationality is in principle dependent upon national laws, norms of international law might affect the attribution of nationality (or the absence of this) for the purposes of international law. Article 1(1) CSSP expressly defines statelessness by reference to whether an individual is 'not considered as a national by any State under the operation of its law': that is to say, it asks exclusively what the state considers the nationality status of an individual to be. So Article 1(1) CSSP would exclude from the scope of 'stateless person' someone who is 'considered as a national under the operation of its law' by state X, even if on the level of international law other states or organisations do not recognise as valid the domestically valid grant of nationality by state X. The term would include someone who has been denationalised in a way that is valid in domestic law but invalid (most likely as arbitrary) for purposes of international law. In either case the definition looks to the stance of the state in question excluding considerations of validity of its stance under international law. The sense of this is that CSSP is concerned primarily with whether individuals have or do not have national protection, not with the international law legitimacy of a domestically valid grant or withdrawal of nationality. It should be noted that Article 1(1) CSSP refers to state

---

[27] Hathaway (n 4) 989.

conduct 'under the operation of its law', not simply to 'its law'. This would seem to support the proposition that an individual is stateless for purposes of Article 1(1) CSSP if he or she appears entitled to nationality under national law, but the authorities in that state arbitrarily or otherwise unlawfully deny this.

Equally, as in Article 1 CSR, the CSSP then sets out various circumstances in which it does not apply, even if an individual is stateless in the sense of Article 1. Thus, Article 2 provides: **4.88**

This Convention shall not apply:

(i) To persons who are at present receiving from organs or agencies of the United Nations other than the United Nations High Commissioner for Refugees protection or assistance so long as they are receiving such protection or assistance;
(ii) To persons who are recognized by the competent authorities of the country in which they have taken residence as having the rights and obligations which are attached to the possession of the nationality of that country;
(iii) To persons with respect to whom there are serious reasons for considering that:
  (a) They have committed a crime against peace, a war crime, or a crime against humanity, as defined in the international instruments drawn up to make provisions in respect of such crimes;
  (b) They have committed a serious non-political crime outside the country of their residence prior to their admission to that country;
  (c) They have been guilty of acts contrary to the purposes and principles of the United Nations.

C2. Protection in the CSSP against Expulsion; Absence of *Refoulement* Protection under the CSSP

As already seen, a critical element of the CSR is the *non-refoulement* obligation under Article 33 CSR. Article 33 CSR is applicable to any refugee, save where there are reasonable grounds for regarding that individual as a danger to the security of his or her country of sojourn, or who constitutes a danger to the community of that country following conviction by a final judgment of a particularly serious crime. This reflects the emphasis on well-founded fear in the country of origin as the reason for a refugee's unwillingness or inability to return. The CSSP contains no equivalent provision, and *refoulement* protection is available only where an individual who is stateless as defined by the CSSP is also a refugee as defined at Article 1A CSR. **4.89**

The CSSP does at Article 31 contain a provision equivalent to Article 32 CSR concerning expulsion. But like Article 32 CSR, Article 31 CSSP depends upon the individual seeking protection from expulsion being 'lawfully in' the territory. As a consequence, the provision is effective whilst an individual possesses (in UK terms) lawful presence in the form of leave to remain, but does not apply to unlawful entrants or overstayers. Article 31 CSSP provides: **4.90**

1. The Contracting States shall not expel a stateless person lawfully in their territory save on grounds of national security or public order.
2. The expulsion of such a stateless person shall be only in pursuance of a decision reached in accordance with due process of law. Except where compelling reasons of national security

otherwise require, the stateless person shall be allowed to submit evidence to clear himself, and to appeal to and be represented for the purpose before competent authority or a person or persons specially designated by the competent authority.

3. The Contracting States shall allow such a stateless person a reasonable period within which to seek legal admission into another country. The Contracting States reserve the right to apply during that period such internal measures as they may deem necessary.

4.91 Article 32 CSSP, concerning access to naturalisation, mirrors Article 34 CSR, save for the substitution of 'stateless persons' for 'refugees' as the beneficiary class. It provides:

> The Contracting States shall as far as possible facilitate the assimilation and naturalization of stateless persons. They shall in particular make every effort to expedite naturalization proceedings and to reduce as far as possible the charges and costs of such proceedings.

4.92 Applying the same principles to Article 32 CSSP as have been applied to Article 34 CSR, no duty is created to permit naturalisation, but rather a 'good faith' obligation may arise, as a result of which the unjustified imposition of disadvantage vis-a-vis aliens may breach Article 32 CSSP.

C3. The Convention on the Reduction of Statelessness 1961

4.93 In 1961, a further instrument, the Convention on the Reduction of Statelessness (CRS), attempted to reduce the scope for perpetuation of statelessness. Most relevantly for the present purposes, Article 1 CRS requires a State Party to grant its nationality to a person born in its territory who would otherwise be stateless in specified circumstances (the full text can be found at Appendix A). Article 2 CRS provides that 'A foundling found in the territory of a Contracting State shall, in the absence of proof to the contrary, be considered to have been born within that territory of parents possessing the nationality of that State' and this is extended to births on ships or aircraft by Article 3 CRS. By Article 4 CRS, the grant of nationality to someone 'not born in the territory of a Contracting State, who would otherwise be stateless, if the nationality of one of his parents at the time of the person's birth was that of that State' is required. Article 5 CRS provides that where domestic law entails loss of nationality as a consequence of any change in the personal status of a person, such as marriage, termination of marriage, legitimation, recognition or adoption, this will only occur if the individual is not thereby rendered stateless. Provisions of particular importance in the avoidance of statelessness are the following:

Article 6

If the law of a Contracting State provides for loss of its nationality by a person's spouse or children as a consequence of that person losing or being deprived of that nationality, such loss shall be conditional upon their possession or acquisition of another nationality.

Article 7

1. (*a*) If the law of a Contracting State permits renunciation of nationality, such renunciation shall not result in loss of nationality unless the person concerned possesses or acquires another nationality.

(b) The provisions of subparagraph (a) of this paragraph shall not apply where their application would be inconsistent with the principles stated in articles 13 and 14 of the Universal Declaration of Human Rights approved on 10 December 1948 by the General Assembly of the United Nations.
2. A national of a Contracting State who seeks naturalization in a foreign country shall not lose his nationality unless he acquires or has been accorded assurance of acquiring the nationality of that foreign country.
3. Subject to the provisions of paragraphs 4 and 5 of this article, a national of a Contracting State shall not lose his nationality, so as to become stateless, on the ground of departure, residence abroad, failure to register or on any similar ground.
4. A naturalized person may lose his nationality on account of residence abroad for a period, not less than seven consecutive years, specified by the law of the Contracting State concerned if he fails to declare to the appropriate authority his intention to retain his nationality.
5. In the case of a national of a Contracting State, born outside its territory, the law of that State may make the retention of its nationality after the expiry of one year from his attaining his majority conditional upon residence at that time in the territory of the State or registration with the appropriate authority.
6. Except in the circumstances mentioned in this article, a person shall not lose the nationality of a Contracting State, if such loss would render him stateless, notwithstanding that such loss is not expressly prohibited by any other provision of this Convention.

Article 8

1. A Contracting State shall not deprive a person of its nationality if such deprivation would render him stateless.
2. Notwithstanding the provisions of paragraph I of this article, a person may be deprived of the nationality of a Contracting State:
   (a) in the circumstances in which, under paragraphs 4 and 5 of article 7, it is permissible that a person should lose his nationality;
   (b) where the nationality has been obtained by misrepresentation or fraud.
3. Notwithstanding the provisions of paragraph 1 of this article, a Contracting State may retain the right to deprive a person of his nationality, if at the time of signature, ratification or accession it specifies its retention of such right on one or more of the following grounds, being grounds existing in its national law at that time:
   (a) that, inconsistently with his duty of loyalty to the Contracting State, the person
      (i) has, in disregard of an express prohibition by the Contracting State rendered or continued to render services to, or received or continued to receive emoluments from, another State,
      or
      (ii) has conducted himself in a manner seriously prejudicial to the vital interests of the State;
   (b) that the person has taken an oath, or made a formal declaration, of allegiance to another State, or given definite evidence of his determination to repudiate his allegiance to the Contracting State.
4. A Contracting State shall not exercise a power of deprivation permitted by paragraph 2 or 3 of this article except in accordance with law, which shall provide for the person concerned the right to a fair hearing by a court or other independent body.

Article 9

A Contracting State may not deprive any person or group of persons of their nationality on racial, ethnic, religious or political grounds.

D. International Human Trafficking Law

D1. Historical Background

4.94 A recent but rapidly developing area of law is that of international human trafficking law, in relation to which there are now both international and regional instruments.

4.95 An early instrument was the Convention for the Suppression of the Traffic in Persons and of the Exploitation of the Prostitution of Others 1950 (CSTP). This was not signed by the UK and was primarily aimed at the detection and punishment of criminal activities related to trafficking. As seen below, Articles 18 and 19 looked towards 'eventual repatriation' of 'aliens who are prostitutes'. They are set out at Appendix A to show the shape of the law before a modern law of international human trafficking began to develop. Given the freedom of states at the time, it is perhaps worth noting the presence of at least one restriction on repatriation, namely Article 19(2) CSTP, which provides that: 'Repatriation shall take place only after agreement is reached with the State of destination as to identity and nationality as well as to the place and date of arrival at frontiers.' Article 19(2) also requires States Parties to permit access to their territories for the transit of 'aliens who are prostitutes'.

D2. The Protocol to Prevent, Suppress and Punish Trafficking in Persons, Especially Women and Children 2000

4.96 CSTP remained the only international instrument specifically focused upon (some forms of) human trafficking and prostitution until the adoption in 2000 of the Protocol to Prevent, Suppress and Punish Trafficking in Persons, Especially Women and Children 2000 (PPSTP),[28] which supplemented the United Nations Convention against Transnational Organised Crime 2000 (CTOC). PPSTP was signed by the UK on 14 December 2000 and was ratified on 9 February 2006.

4.97 PPSTP seeks to define, address and prevent the crime of trafficking in persons, especially women and children, at an international level. The purposes of PPSTP are set out in the Preamble:

[T]hat effective action to prevent and combat trafficking in persons, especially women and children, requires a comprehensive international approach in the countries of origin, transit and destination that includes measures to prevent such trafficking, to punish the traffickers

---

[28] This is better known as one of the three 'Palermo Protocols' to the CTOC or, in human trafficking law, as 'the Palermo Protocol'.

and to protect the victims of such trafficking, including by protecting their internationally recognized human rights,

And Article 2 (Statement of purpose), which states:

The purposes of this Protocol are:

(a) To prevent and combat trafficking in persons, paying particular attention to women and children;
(b) To protect and assist the victims of such trafficking, with full respect for their human rights; and
(c) To promote cooperation among States Parties in order to meet those objectives.

4.98 The application of the PPSTP in the UK has now been considered on a number of occasions, including in *LM and others v R* [2010] EWCA Crim 2327, [2011] 1 Cr App R 12, the point in the case concerning the failure to protect victims from criminal charges. Key terms 'trafficking in persons' is defined in Article 3:

For the purposes of this Protocol:

(a) 'Trafficking in persons' shall mean the recruitment, transportation, transfer, harbouring or receipt of persons, by means of the threat or use of force or other forms of coercion, of abduction, of fraud, of deception, of the abuse of power or of a position of vulnerability or of the giving or receiving of payments or benefits to achieve the consent of a person having control over another person, for the purpose of exploitation. Exploitation shall include, at a minimum, the exploitation of the prostitution of others or other forms of sexual exploitation, forced labour or services, slavery or practices similar to slavery, servitude or the removal of organs;
(b) The consent of a victim of trafficking in persons to the intended exploitation set forth in subparagraph (a) of this article shall be irrelevant where any of the means set forth in subparagraph (a) have been used;
(c) The recruitment, transportation, transfer, harbouring or receipt of a child for the purpose of exploitation shall be considered 'trafficking in persons' even if this does not involve any of the means set forth in subparagraph (a) of this article;
(d) 'Child' shall mean any person under eighteen years of age.

4.99 Article 7 PPSTP deals with the status of victims of trafficking in receiving states and provides as follows:

1. … each State Party shall consider adopting legislative or other appropriate measures that permit victims of trafficking in persons to remain in its territory, temporarily or permanently, in appropriate cases.
2. In implementing the provision contained in paragraph 1 of this article, each State Party shall give appropriate consideration to humanitarian and compassionate factors.

4.100 Article 8 PPSTP covers the repatriation of victims of trafficking in persons in the following terms:

1. The State Party of which a victim of trafficking in persons is a national or in which the person had the right of permanent residence at the time of entry into the territory of the receiving State Party shall facilitate and accept, with due regard for the safety of that person, the return of that person without undue or unreasonable delay.
2. When a State Party returns a victim of trafficking in persons to a State Party of which that person is a national or in which he or she had, at the time of entry into the territory of the

receiving State Party, the right of permanent residence, such return shall be with due regard for the safety of that person and for the status of any legal proceedings related to the fact that the person is a victim of trafficking and shall preferably be voluntary.

3. At the request of a receiving State Party, a requested State Party shall, without undue or unreasonable delay, verify whether a person who is a victim of trafficking in persons is its national or had the right of permanent residence in its territory at the time of entry into the territory of the receiving State Party.

4. In order to facilitate the return of a victim of trafficking in persons who is without proper documentation, the State Party of which that person is a national or in which he or she had the right of permanent residence at the time of entry into the territory of the receiving State Party shall agree to issue, at the request of the receiving State Party, such travel documents or other authorization as may be necessary to enable the person to travel to and re-enter its territory.

5. This article shall be without prejudice to any right afforded to victims of trafficking in persons by any domestic law of the receiving State Party.

6. This article shall be without prejudice to any applicable bilateral or multilateral agreement or arrangement that governs, in whole or in part, the return of victims of trafficking in persons.

5
Council of Europe Instruments

Contents

A. Introduction 5.1
    A1.   The Council of Europe 5.1

B. The ECHR 5.5
    B1.   The ECHR and Immigration and Nationality Law and Practice 5.5
    B2.   Extent of Application of the ECHR 5.8
            The Geographical and Other Extent of the ECHR under
            Article 1 ECHR 5.8
    B3.   Jurisdiction and Immigration Applications or Migration 5.15
    B4.   Application of the ECHR: Foreign and Domestic Cases 5.19
    B5.   Article 2 ECHR 5.26
    B6.   Article 3 ECHR 5.34
            Nature of the Rights Protected 5.34
            Flexibility of the Standard 5.42
            Burden and Standard of Evidence 5.47
            Prison and Detention Conditions 5.49
            Grossly Disproportionate Sentences 5.51
            Sur Place Activities 5.52
            Membership of a Group Subject to Systematic Ill-Treatment and
            Situations of General Violence 5.53
            Non-state Persecution and Sufficiency of Protection 5.59
            Internal Relocation Alternative 5.61
            Diplomatic Assurances 5.63
            'Treatment' or Naturally Occurring Event or Illness
            and Living Conditions 5.66
            Expulsion to a Contracting Party and 'Dublin' Cases 5.73
    B7.   Article 4 ECHR 5.77
    B8.   Article 5 ECHR 5.84
    B9.   Article 6 ECHR 5.88
    B10. Article 7 ECHR 5.95
    B11. Article 8 ECHR 5.100
            Meaning of Private and Family Life 5.101
            Leading Authorities in the UK 5.115
    B12. Time of Assessment 5.121
    B13. Interference, in Accordance with the Law and Legitimate Aim 5.122
            Proportionality: Relevant Factors 5.130
            The Nature and Seriousness of the Offence and Time Elapsed Since its
            Commission 5.136
            The Length of the Applicant's Stay in the Country from which He
            or She is to Be Expelled 5.143
            The Time Elapsed Since the Offence was Committed and
            the Applicant's Conduct During that Period 5.149
            The Nationalities of the Various Persons Concerned 5.150
            The Applicant's Family Situation, Such as the Length of the Marriage,
            and Other Factors Expressing the Effectiveness of a Couple's
            Family Life 5.151
            Whether the Spouse Knew About the Offence at the Time When He
            or She Entered into a Family Relationship 5.154
            Whether There are Children of the Marriage, and if so their Age 5.156

The Seriousness of the Difficulties Which the Spouse is Likely to
Encounter in the Country to Which the Applicant is to Be Expelled ... 5.157
The Best Interests and Well-being of the Children, in Particular
the Seriousness of the Difficulties Which Any Children of the Applicant
are Likely to Encounter in the Country to Which the Applicant is
to be Expelled.. 5.159
The Solidity of Social, Cultural and Family Ties with the Host Country
and with the Country of Destination... 5.163
Duration of Exclusion 5.166
Relevant Health Issues.. 5.174
Pending Family Proceedings... 5.176
Family Reunion.. 5.178
Deprivation of Nationality and Residence... 5.184
- B14. Articles 9–11 ECHR.. 5.188
- B15. Article 12 ECHR 5.197
- B16. Article 13 ECHR 5.202
- B17. Article 14 ECHR 5.215
- B18. Article 15 ECHR 5.223
- B19. Articles 3 and 4 of Protocol 4 to the ECHR.. 5.225
- B20. Article 1 of Protocol 7 to the ECHR 5.232

C. The ECN 5.239

D. The CATHB 5.242

A. Introduction

A1. The Council of Europe

5.1 The Council of Europe was founded on 5 May 1949 by the agreement of its initiating statute, also known as the Treaty of London. This was ratified by the UK in July 1949. Under Article 1(a) of Chapter 1 of the Treaty of London, the aim of the Council of Europe is 'to achieve a greater unity between its members for the purpose of safeguarding and realising the ideals and principles which are their common heritage and facilitating their economic and social progress'. This aim is pursued in Article 1(b):

> [T]hrough the organs of the Council by discussion of questions of common concern and by agreements and common action in economic, social, cultural, scientific, legal and administrative matters and in the maintenance and further realisation of human rights and fundamental freedoms.

5.2 Article 3 of the Treaty of London provides that:

> Every member of the Council of Europe must accept the principles of the rule of law and of the enjoyment by all persons within its jurisdiction of human rights and fundamental freedoms, and collaborate sincerely and effectively in the realisation of the aim of the Council as specified in Chapter I.

5.3 In Article 4, any European state deemed to be able and willing to fulfil the provisions of Article 3 may be invited to become a member of the Council of Europe by the Committee of Ministers and shall then become a member by deposit of an instrument of accession. States' commitments extend to the whole of their territories, and the territory of Council of Europe Member States stretches to the eastern boundary of the Russian Federation.

The Council of Europe presently has 47 members. For present purposes, three instruments made under its aegis are particularly relevant: first, the European Convention for the Protection of Human Rights and Fundamental Freedoms 1950 (ECHR), to which the UK is a party and to which 16 Protocols have to date been created—accession to the Council of Europe requires ratification of the ECHR, to be completed within one year;[1] second, the European Convention on Nationality 1997 (ECN), which has been ratified by 20 members of the Council, but not by the UK; and, third, the Council of Europe Convention on Action against Trafficking in Human Beings 2005 (CATHB), which has been ratified by 41 members of the Council, including the UK.

B. The ECHR

B1. The ECHR and Immigration and Nationality Law and Practice

Save for Article 16 ECHR, which provides for a derogation in respect of the political activity of aliens as regards freedom of speech, association and the prohibition on discrimination, the ECHR was drafted without direct regard to questions of immigration or nationality, reflecting the contemporary view that this was in general an area in which considerations of national sovereignty militated against the imposition of binding standards. Notwithstanding this, broader standards set in the ECHR possess substantial importance in relation to deportation, removal or exclusion, and may have indirect relevance to nationality questions.

There are no ECHR provisions binding on the UK which expressly regulate the expulsion and exclusion of aliens. Expulsion of aliens is alluded to in Article 4 of Protocol 4 to the ECHR (prohibition on collective expulsion of aliens) and Article 1 of Protocol 7 to the ECHR (procedural guarantee in respect of expulsion for lawfully resident migrants). Exclusion of aliens is not specifically referred to. The UK has signed Protocol 4 but has not ratified it, and has neither signed nor ratified Protocol 7. The protection against expulsion and exclusion from the UK afforded to aliens by the ECHR in any other case rests upon the application of broad protections under general articles. The most significant in this context will generally be Articles 2 and 3 ECHR (respectively the right to life and freedom from torture or inhuman or degrading treatment or punishment) and Article 8 ECHR (the right to private and family life, home and correspondence).

The UK has by the Human Rights Act (HRA) 1998 incorporated a substantial number of ECHR protections, including Articles 2–12, 14, 16–18, Articles 1–3 of Protocol 1 and Article 1 of Protocol 13.

---

[1] Council of Europe Parliamentary Assembly Resolution 1031 (1994).

B2. Extent of Application of the ECHR

The Geographical and Other Extent of the ECHR under Article 1 ECHR

5.8 Article 1 provides that the 'High Contracting Parties shall secure to everyone within their jurisdiction the rights and freedoms defined in Section I of this Convention'. The jurisdiction of the ECHR is therefore constituted by reference to Contracting Parties' jurisdiction over persons and is not limited to nationals of Contracting Parties or to the national territory.

5.9 Article 56(1) ECHR further permits any of the Contracting Parties to declare by notification to the Council of Europe to what extent the ECHR extends 'to all or any of the territories for whose international relations it is responsible'. Article 56(4) ECHR permits Contracting Parties to 'declare on behalf of one or more of the territories to which the declaration relates that it accepts' the right of individual petition arising under Article 34 of the Convention. The UK has extended the application of the Convention and the right of individual petition to the following territories for whose international relations it is responsible: Anguilla, Bermuda, the British Virgin Islands, the Cayman Islands, the Falkland Islands, Gibraltar, the Bailiwick of Guernsey, the Isle of Man, the Bailiwick of Jersey, Montserrat, St Helena, Ascension and Tristan da Cunha, South Georgia and the South Sandwich Islands, the Sovereign Base Areas in Cyprus, and the Turks and Caicos Islands.[2] Such extension of the application of the Convention under Article 56 is separate and distinct from the question, considered below, whether a state has 'effective control' over an area outside its national territory: *Al-Skeini and others v UK* [GC] no 55721/07; [2011] ECHR 1093, (2011) 53 EHRR 18 [140].

5.10 The term 'jurisdiction' in the ECHR is given an autonomous meaning independent from its meaning in public international law, although the latter may be relevant to the interpretation of jurisdiction within the ECHR. State practice in the application of the ECHR and the fact that the ECHR is a living instrument are pertinent to the interpretation of 'jurisdiction' under Article 1 ECHR: *Banković and others v Belgium and others* [GC] no 52207/99; [2001] ECHR 890, (2007) 44 EHRR SE5 [59]–[64].

5.11 Jurisdiction under Article 1 ECHR is primarily territorial: *Soering v UK* no 14038/88, [1989] ECHR 14, [1989] 11 EHRR 439 [86]; *Banković*, at [61] and [67]; *Al-Skeini and others v UK* [GC] no 55721/07, [2011] ECHR 1093, (2011) 53 EHRR 18 [131]. Jurisdiction is presumed to be exercised throughout the state's territory (*Ilaşcu and others v Moldova and Russia* [GC] no 48787/99, [2004] ECHR 318 (2005) 40 EHRR 46 [312]) and includes the international transit zone at an international airport (*Amuur v France* no 19776/92, [1996] ECHR 25, (1996) 22 EHRR 533 [52].

5.12 Where foreign officials perform acts within the Contracting Party's territorial jurisdiction and with the acquiescence or connivance of a Contracting Party's authorities, the Contracting Party is responsible for these acts. In *El-Masri v Former Yugoslav Republic of Macedonia* [GC] no 39630/09, [2012] ECHR 2067, (2013) 57 EHRR 25, agents of the US renditions team were operating at Skopje Airport in the presence of

---

[2] See Council of Europe Treaty Office, List of declarations made with respect to the European Convention on Human Rights: http://conventions.coe.int/Treaty/Commun/ListeDeclarations.asp?NT=005&CM=8&DF=&CL=ENG&VL=1.

Macedonian officials and within Macedonia's territorial jurisdiction. The European Court of Human Rights held at [206] that the acts of the American agents fell within the jurisdiction of Macedonia.

Jurisdiction also pertains in accordance with customary international law and treaty law on board an aircraft or vessel, flying the flag of that state.³ In *Hirsi Jamaa and others v Italy* [GC] no 27765/09, [2012] ECHR 1845, (2012) 55 EHRR 21 [77], the ECtHR held that Italy's push-back of asylum-seekers in the Mediterranean fell within the jurisdiction: see also *Xhavara and others v Italy and Albania* no 39473/98 (admissibility decision, 11 January 2001); *Banković and others v Belgium and others* [GC] no 52207/99, [2001] ECHR 890, (2007) 44 EHRR SE5 [73].

5.13

Jurisdiction is not necessarily limited to territorial presence, but may apply extraterritorially in exceptional circumstances, including the following cases:

5.14

i. *Consular officials:* recognised instances of the extra-territorial exercise of jurisdiction by a state include cases involving the activities of its diplomatic or consular agents abroad and on board craft and vessels registered in, or flying the flag of, that state. In these specific situations, customary international law and treaty provisions have recognised the extra-territorial exercise of jurisdiction by the relevant state: *Banković and Ors v Belgium and Ors* [GC] no 52207/99; [2001] ECHR 890; (2007) 44 EHRR SE5, at [69], *Al-Skeini and Ors v United Kingdom* [GC] no 55721/07; [2011] ECHR 1093; (2011) 53 EHRR 18 [133];

ii. *Effective control over an area:* a Contracting Party exercises jurisdiction within the meaning of Article 1 ECHR, where it exercises 'effective control' over an area outside its national territory, lawfully or unlawfully through military action, whether it exercises such control directly through its armed forces or through a subordinate local administration: *Loizidou v Turkey (Preliminary Objections)* [GC] no 15318/89—[1995] ECHR 10; (1995) 20 EHRR 99, at [62] applied at [64]; *Cyprus v Turkey* [GC] no 25781/94; [2001] ECHR 331; (2002) 35 EHRR 30, at [76]; *Issa and Ors v Turkey* no 31821/96; [2004] ECHR 629; (2005) 41 EHRR 27, at [69]. In *Banković*, at [75], the Court held that overall control rather than detailed control over the policies and actions in that area might be sufficient to engage jurisdiction, but an instantaneous extra-territorial act, such as the bombing of Belgrade by NATO, did not involve the exercise of 'effective control'. This is likely no longer good law. In *Al-Skeini and Ors v United Kingdom* [GC] no 55721/07; [2011] ECHR 1093; (2011) 53 EHRR 18; [136]–[137] the Grand Chamber pointing to earlier cases observed at [136] that 'The Court does not consider that jurisdiction in the above cases arose solely from the control exercised by the contracting state over the buildings, aircraft or ship in which the individuals were held. What is decisive in such cases is the exercise of physical power and control over the person in question' and at [137] that:

> It is clear that, whenever the state through its agents exercises control and authority over an individual, and thus jurisdiction, the state is under an obligation under Article 1 to secure to that individual the rights and freedoms under section 1 of the Convention that are relevant to the situation of that individual. In this sense, therefore, the Convention rights can be 'divided and tailored'.

In *Smith and others v Ministry of Defence* [2013] UKSC 41; [2014] 1 AC 52 the Supreme Court applied this, concluding at [38] that the *al-Skeini* decision marked a rejection of the holding in *Banković* that the ECHR rights were indivisible in application so that, for

---

³ So-called flag state jurisdiction as defined in Article 92 of the UN Convention on the Law of the Sea; see also ICJ, *SS Lotus* (1927) PCIJ Rep Series A No 10.

example, the application of articles 2 or 3 could not arise in the context of armed action by a state affecting residents of a territory not under its control.

iii. *State agent authority and control:* a second instance in which the ECHR applies extraterritorially is when the acts of the Contracting Party's authority produce effects outside its territory: *Drozd and Janousek v France and Spain* no 12747/87; [1992] ECHR 52; (1992) 14 EHRR 74, at [91]. Three separate instances of this principle have been recognised in the Court's case law. First, acts of diplomatic or consular agents, who are present on foreign territory in accordance with international law, may amount to an exercise of jurisdiction when these agents exercise 'control and authority' over an individual or its possessions: *Bankovi*, at [73]; *Al-Skeini*, at [134]; *X v Federal Republic of Germany* no 1611/62 (Commission decision, 25 September 1965); *X v United Kingdom* no 7547/76 (Commission decision, 15 December 1977). The principle of 'control and authority' was found applicable to consular agents in *WM v Denmark* no 17392/90; DR 73, p. 193 (Commission decision, 14 October 1992), which concerned 17 nationals of the then German Democratic Republic who had sought refuge in the Danish embassy in East Berlin. The Commission accepted that the summoning of GDR police officers by Danish diplomatic staff engaged Denmark for purposes of Article 1 ECHR. In *R (otao 'B' and others) v Secretary of State for the Foreign and Commonwealth Office* [2004] EWCA Civ 1344; [2005] QB 643, the Court of Appeal, at [58], assumed jurisdiction to arise where applicants had sought asylum on the premises of a British consulate in Australia and had remained there for some time whilst enquiries were made. However, the requirement of 'control and authority' in such a situation does imply a requirement for engagement at a minimal level. In *R (otao European Roma Rights Centre v Immigration Officer at Prague Airport & Anor* [2004] UKHL 55; [2005] 2 AC 1, Lord Bingham at [21] expressed doubt that the functions performed by United Kingdom immigration officers at Prague airport involved the exercise of jurisdiction within Article 1 ECHR. Secondly, where a Contracting Party 'through the consent, invitation or acquiescence' of the government of a territory 'exercises all or some of the public powers normally to be exercised' by that government, and thereby, in accordance with custom, treaty or other agreement, authorities of the Contracting State carry out executive or judicial functions on that territory of another State, the Contracting Party is exercising jurisdiction: *Banković*, at [71]; *Al-Skeini and Ors v United Kingdom* [GC] no 55721/07; [2011] ECHR 1093; (2011) 53 EHRR 18, at [135]; *Gentilhomme and Others v France* nos 48205/99; 48207/99; 48209/99; [2002] ECHR 441 at [20]; *X and Y v Switzerland* nos 7289/75; 7349/76; DR 9, p 5 (Commission decision, 14 July 1977); [57]. Thirdly, and finally, Article 1 ECHR may apply by reason of the 'use of force by a State's agents operating outside its territory' over an individual thereby brought under the control of the State's authorities: *Al-Skeini and Ors v United Kingdom* [GC] no 55721/07; [2011] ECHR 1093; (2011) 53 EHRR 18, at [136]. The full and effective control principle also applies to vessels flying the flag of a third state where a Contracting Party is exercising *de facto* continued and uninterrupted control over the vessel and its crew: *Medvedyev and Ors v France* no 3394/03; [2010] ECHR 384, at [66]–[67]. This approach has been applied in a number of cases where the applicant was taken into the custody of State agents abroad, including handing an applicant over to Turkish officials abroad (*Öcalan v Turkey* [GC] no 46221/99; [2005] ECHR 282; (2005) 41 EHRR 45, at [91]), the detention of applicants in British-controlled military prisons until the moment they were handed over to the Iraqi authorities (*Al-Saadoon and Mufdhi v United Kingdom* no 61498/08; [2010] ECHR 285; [2010] 51 EHRR 9, and the detention of an applicant in the British-controlled detention facility in Basra (*Al-Jedda v United Kingdom* no 27021/08; [2011] ECHR 1092; (2011) 53 EHRR 23; [80]–[85]. However, Article 1 ECHR has been held not to apply to armed presence under United Nations auspices: *Behrami and Saramati v France and Ors* [GC] nos 71412/01; 78166/01; (2007) 45 EHRR SE85, (admissibility decision, 9 June 1999), para. 51. This principle has been held to apply to acts of the

International Criminal Tribunal for the former Yugoslavia in two admissibility decisions: *Galic v The Netherlands* (no 22617/07, 9 June 2009) and *Blagojevic v The Netherlands* (no 49032/07, 9 June 2009) and to a witness detained on International Criminal Court premises who applied for asylum in the Netherlands (*Djokaba Lambi Longa v The Netherlands* no 33917/12, 9 October 2012). Similarly it has been held that the arrest, detention and handover of Saddam Hussein to the Iraqi authorities involved no Contracting Party to an extent giving jurisdiction over these acts: *Saddam Hussein v Albania and Ors* no 23276/04 (admissibility decision, 14 March 2006);

iv. *Convention legal space:* The ECtHR had held in cases concerning Northern Cyprus that there must not be a 'vacuum' of protection in cases where the territory of one Convention State is occupied by the armed forces of another. In *Al-Skeini v United Kingdom* no 55721/07; [2011] ECHR 1093; (2011) 53 EHRR 18, at [142] the Court held that 'the importance of establishing the occupying State's jurisdiction in such cases does not imply, *a contrario*, that jurisdiction under Article 1 of the Convention can never exist outside the territory covered by the Council of Europe Member States.'

B3. Jurisdiction and Immigration Applications or Migration

5.15 In *Abdulaziz, Cabales and Balkandali v UK* nos 9214/80; 9473/81; 9474/81, [1985] ECHR 7, (1985) 7 EHRR 471, the UK did not attempt to argue that applications by family members outside the territory for permission to enter the UK to exercise family life with spouses there was outside the UK's jurisdiction, and immigration applications may fall within this. In *Dalea v France* no 964/07 (admissibility decision, 2 February 2010), a Romanian national living in Romania who had business relations with France and German companies and had travelled there previously on several occasions complained by reference to Article 8 ECHR regarding the refusal by France to issue a Schengen visa. No issue was raised in relation to jurisdiction, but the Court declared the application manifestly ill-founded on the basis of France's considerable margin of appreciation in relation to the regulation of entry and stay of non-nationals.

5.16 Similarly, in *Nada v Switzerland* [GC] no 10593/08, [2012] ECHR 1691, (2013) 56 EHRR 18, no issue of jurisdiction was raised regarding the applicant's residence outside Switzerland's territory. The Egyptian-Italian applicant was living in an Italian enclave surrounded by Switzerland and had been unable to remove his name from the Swiss Federal Taliban Ordinance, notwithstanding that suspicions of links with terrorists had been found to be unsubstantiated. The ECtHR at [189] and [191] held that the entry and travel ban violated the applicant's right to private life under Article 8 ECHR as it had 'prevented the applicant not only from entering Switzerland but also from leaving the enclave in which he lived to travel to any other part of Italy, the country of which he was a national' or from obtaining medical treatment in Italy.

5.17 In *East African Asians v UK* no 4403/70, [1973] ECHR 2, (1981) 3 EHRR 76, it was accepted that the UK had jurisdiction over British passport holders from East Africa, whose right of entry and stay in the UK they sought to restrict. The applicants were effectively refugees in orbit, since the continued residence of Asians in East Africa had also become illegal through the policies of Africanisation pursued by local states. The Commission at [207] and [212] found that the denial of entry and stay to nationals of the UK on discriminatory grounds, namely their colour or race, was so humiliating that it violated Article 3 ECHR, but at [214] no violation of Article 3 was found regarding

Part B – Legal Framework

applicants who were not British nationals but only British protected persons, although they similarly appeared to be within the UK's jurisdiction.

5.18 In the context of temporary residence permits, such as a student visa, no jurisdiction has been found to arise where an applicant was excluded on the grounds of suspected terrorist activity whilst abroad: *Abdul Wahab Khan v UK* no 11987/11 (admissibility decision, 28 January 2014) [25]. The mere institution of judicial proceedings in the territory of a Contracting Party was insufficient to bring that person within the jurisdiction of the Contracting Party: *Abdul Wahab Khan*, at [28].

B4. Application of the ECHR: Foreign and Domestic Cases

5.19 A distinction arises between what have been categorised respectively as 'foreign' and 'domestic' ECHR cases. A distinction has been drawn between, on the one hand, cases in which a violation of rights takes place on the territory of a state or otherwise within the relevant jurisdiction and, on the other hand, cases in which a violation of rights would be or has been perpetrated on the territory of another state—for example, following expulsion by the Member State. The distinction and terminology is that adopted by the House of Lords in *R (Ullah) v Special Adjudicator* [2004] UKHL 26, [2004] 2 AC 323 and *R (otao Razgar) v SSHD* [2004] UKHL 27, [2004] 2 AC 368. The distinction is based on the territorial scope of the ECHR, which under Article 1 imposes obligations on Contracting Parties in relation to persons within their respective jurisdictions only.

5.20 In relation to foreign cases, the ECHR contains no express prohibition on *refoulement*, or return to proscribed treatment, of the type provided in other instruments: most notably, at Article 33(1) CSR, Article 3(1) CAT or Article 16(1) CPED. However, in *Soering v UK* no 14038/88, [1989] ECHR 14, [1989] 11 EHRR 439, the ECtHR found the prohibition of *refoulement* to be inherent in the absolute and non-derogable prohibition on torture and inhuman and degrading treatment in Article 3 ECHR. This principle has been extended from extradition in *Soering* to asylum-seekers facing removal and deportation cases involving a real risk of treatment contrary to Article 3 ECHR: *Cruz Varas and others v Sweden* no 15576/89, [1991] ECHR 26, (1991) 14 EHRR 1 [69]–[70]; *Vilvarajah v UK* nos 13163/87; 13164/87; 13165/87, [1991] ECHR 47, (1991) 14 EHRR 248 [103] (concerning asylum); *HLR v France* [GC] no 24573/94, [1997] ECHR 23 [1998] 26 EHRR 29 (the first case involving fear of harm inflicted by non-state actors).

5.21 As regards the extraterritorial application of the right to life under Article 2 ECHR, Protocol 6 concerning the abolition of the death penalty in peacetime, and Protocol 13 concerning its abolition also in times of war, the ECtHR was in its early years very guarded in its decisions. However, given the 'considerable evolution since the *Soering* case was decided' and recognising that all of the Contracting Parties had by then signed Protocol 6 on the abolition of the death penalty in times of peace, the ECtHR in *Öcalan v Turkey* [GC] no 46221/99, [2005] ECHR 282, (2005) 41 EHRR 45 [163]–[166] found that the imposition of the death penalty following an unfair trial is prohibited under Article 2 ECHR. In *Bader and Kanbor v Sweden* no 13284/04, [2005] ECHR 939, (2008) 46 EHRR 13 [47]–[48], the Court further clarified that the expulsion to a state where there is a real risk that the death penalty would be imposed following an unfair trial constitutes a violation of Article 2 in addition to Article 3 ECHR, and in *MA v Cyprus* no 41872/10, [2013] ECHR 717 [119], the ECtHR found arguable a complaint addressed to the proposed expulsion of a Syrian Kurdish opposition activist under Article 2 ECHR, read with Article 13 ECHR. In a further step, the Court recognised in *Al-Saadoon and Mufdhi v UK* no 61498/08, [2010] ECHR 285, [2010] 51 EHRR 9 [123] that Article 2 ECHR and Protocol No 13 on the abolition of the death penalty under all circumstances, including in times of war, generally prohibit expulsion to a state where substantial grounds have been shown for believing that the individual would face a real risk of being subjected to the death penalty.

In relation to Article 4 ECHR, which prohibits slavery, servitude and forced or compulsory labour, the Court in *VF v France* no 7196/10 (admissibility decision, 29 November 2011) [14] did not exclude the possible extraterritorial applicability of Article 4 ECHR, given the absolute and non-derogable nature of that provision.[4]

5.22

Further, the ECtHR has found a prohibition on *refoulement* to be implicit in other ECHR articles, even if they are qualified or derogable provisions, where a violation by the country of origin following expulsion would amount to a 'flagrant denial' or 'gross violation' of the right(s) in question (*Soering v UK* no 14038/88 [1989] ECHR 14, [1989] 11 EHRR 439 [113]), with the exception of Article 10 ECHR: see *R (otao Naik) v SSHD* [2011] EWCA Civ 1546 [31]. The 'flagrant breach' standard applied in foreign cases is higher than the standard required for a breach in relation to domestic cases. It was met in the case of *EM (Lebanon) v SSHD* [2008] UKHL 64, [2009] AC 1198 as regards Article 8 ECHR. The case involved the threat of destruction of family life between a mother and her child in the country of origin following removal because under Sharia law, custody rights would automatically go to the father in highly adverse circumstances.

5.23

Article 8 ECHR has been recognised as imposing positive obligations on the Contracting Parties to enable family life on their territory in certain circumstances: *Abdulaziz, Cabales and Balkandali v UK* nos 9214/80; 9473/81; 9474/81, [1985] ECHR 7, (1985) 7 EHRR 471; *FH (Post-flight Spouses) Iran* [2010] UKUT 275 (IAC) [23]. Cases of family reunion or reunification concern the right to family life of the person present on the territory, and within the jurisdiction, of the UK. They are therefore properly considered as domestic rather than foreign cases and do not require the meeting of the higher threshold of foreign cases: *R (otao Razgar) v SSHD* [2004] UKHL 27, [2004] 2 AC 368 [51]–[53] (Baroness Hale); *A (Afghanistan) v SSHD* [2009] EWCA Civ 825; *H (Somalia)* UKIAT 00027; *East African Asians v UK* no 4403/70 [1973] ECHR 2; (1981) 3 EHRR 76 [230] (concerning some of the excluded persons whose wives lived in the UK).

5.24

Where the exclusion of a non-national with family members in the UK interferes with family life, it is considered a 'domestic case' and falls within the UK's jurisdiction, thus involving positive obligations under Article 8 ECHR. In *Abdul Wahab Khan v UK* no 11987/11 (admissibility decision, 28 January 2014), the ECtHR, in the context of a private life claim by a student with less than three years' residence in the UK prior to leaving voluntarily and who remained outside the UK on the date of application, the Court at [27] denied such positive obligations: the interference was held at [32] to be proportionate in any event given the applicant's suspected terrorist links.

5.25

---

[4] The Court communicated two cases relating to *refoulement* protection under Article 4 ECHR, but the applications were ultimately struck out of the list after the applicants were permitted to remain in the UK: *OGO v UK* no 13950/12 (strike out decision; 18 February 2012); *LR v UK* no 49113/09 (EctHR, strike out decision; 14 June 2011); see also *'B' and others, R (otao) v Secretary of State for the Foreign and Commonwealth Office* [2004] EWCA Civ 1344, [2005] QB 643; [58].

B5. Article 2 ECHR

5.26 Article 2 ECHR provides that, save for proportionate use of force in defence against unlawful violence, to effect a lawful arrest or prevent escape, or in lawful action to quell riot or insurrection: 'Everyone's right to life shall be protected by law. No one shall be deprived of his life intentionally save in the execution of a sentence of a court following his conviction of a crime for which this penalty is provided by law.'

5.27 In relation to the first sentence, the ECtHR has found, in a case concerned with failure by the British government to safeguard British servicemen exposed to nuclear weapons tests, that the state is required 'not only to refrain from the intentional and unlawful taking of life, but also to take appropriate steps to safeguard the lives of those within its jurisdiction': *LCB v UK* no 23413/94 [1998] ECHR 49, (1999) 27 EHRR 212, [36]. The duty is expressly extended to persons in custody: *Keenan v UK* no 27229/95 [2001] ECHR 242, (2001) 33 EHRR 38 [89]–[91].

5.28 As to the second sentence, it will be clear from the text that Article 2 ECHR did not give rise to any prohibition on the death penalty where imposed as a lawful sentence. Protocol 6 to the ECHR abolished the death penalty except in times of war. In *Öcalan v Turkey* [GC] no 46221/99 [2003] ECHR 125, (2003) 37 EHRR 10 [196]–[198] [204], the Court held that it 'could not be excluded' that capital punishment in peacetime had come to be regarded as an unacceptable, if not inhuman, form of punishment which was no longer permissible under Article 2 ECHR. However, it did not have to reach a final conclusion on the point because it found that the applicant had had an unfair trial and that execution following such a trial would breach both Article 2 and also (by the fear of wrongful execution attending such a proceeding) Article 3 ECHR.

5.29 Article 1 of Protocol 13 now provides that 'the death penalty shall be abolished' and that 'no-one shall be condemned to such penalty or executed', creating an absolute prohibition of the death penalty. Following the UK's ratification of Protocol 13, this provision has been incorporated into the list of protected rights under the HRA 1998[5] so that where there is a real risk that a person will be executed if expelled from the UK, such expulsion will violate Article 2 and Article 1 of Protocol 13 to the ECHR.

5.30 In *Bader and Kanbor v Sweden* no 13284/04, [2005] ECHR 939, (2008) 46 EHRR 13, the applicants were Syrian asylum-seekers resisting expulsion from Sweden to Syria, where one faced a capital sentence. The ECtHR found at [42] that 'an issue may arise under Articles 2 and 3 [ECHR] if a Contracting State deports an alien who has suffered or risks suffering a flagrant denial of a fair trial in the receiving State, the outcome of which was or is likely to be the death penalty' and at [48] that:

> [T]here are substantial grounds for believing that the first applicant would be exposed to a real risk of being executed and subjected to treatment contrary to Articles 2 and 3 if deported to his home country. Accordingly, the Court finds that the deportation of the applicants to Syria, if implemented, would give rise to violations of Articles 2 and 3 of the Convention.

5.31 In the case of *Al-Saadoon and Mufdhi v UK* no 61498/08, [2010] ECHR 285, (2009) 51 EHRR 9, the ECtHR concluded at [119]–[123] that the death penalty, except in times of war, had become an unacceptable form of punishment, so that Article 2 ECHR with

---

[5] By the Human Rights Act 1998 (Amendment) Order 2004, SI 2004/1574, with effect from 22 June 2004.

Article 1 of Protocol 13 to the ECHR prohibited the extradition or deportation of an individual to another state if substantial grounds have been shown 'for believing that he or she would face a real risk of being subjected to the death penalty there'.

Article 2 ECHR may extend to require a state to take measures to protect an individual at risk from criminal acts of others by doing 'all that could be reasonably expected of them to avoid a real and immediate risk to life of which they have or ought to have knowledge: *Osman v UK* [GC]no 23452/94 [1998] ECHR 101, (2000) 29 EHRR 245 [115]–[116]. In *Rantsev v Cyprus and Russia* no 25965/04 [2010] ECHR 22, (2010) 51 EHRR 1, the Court found that on the facts, there had been no violation of the Cypriot authorities' positive obligation to protect a trafficked woman who died in Cyprus in mysterious circumstances, but that there had been a breach of the procedural obligation to carry out an effective investigation: [218]–[223], [232]–[247]. 5.32

Article 2 ECHR is generally argued in addition to Article 3 ECHR rather than on a stand-alone basis. No expulsion case has succeeded solely on the basis of Article 2. In *Soering v UK* no 14038/88 [1989] ECHR 14, [1989] 11 EHRR 439, for example, the applicant succeeded on the basis of the 'death row phenomenon' rather than the prospect of execution itself. In the context of expulsion cases alleging a real risk of ill-treatment or death in the receiving state, the ECtHR generally prefers to examine the issue under Article 3 rather than Article 2 ECHR: *NA v UK* no 25904/07 [2008] ECHR 616, (2009) 48 EHRR 15 [95]; *D v UK* no 30240/96, (1997) 24 EHRR 425; *Said v The Netherlands* no 2345/02, [2005] ECHR 461, (2006) 43 EHRR 14 [37]; *Bahaddar v The Netherlands* no 25894/94 (1998) 26 EHRR 278 (Commission decision, 22 May 1995). In *Al-Saadoon and Mufdhi v UK* no 61498/08 [2010] ECHR 285, (2009) 51 EHRR 9 [142]–[144], the Court found that the transfer of arrested and detained Iraqi nationals from the physical custody of the British armed forces to the Iraqi authorities, where they faced a real risk of the death penalty and as a result a fear of execution by the Iraqi authorities, had constituted inhuman and degrading treatment in breach of Article 3 ECHR. 5.33

B6. Article 3 ECHR

Nature of the Rights Protected

Article 3 ECHR provides a non-derogable prohibition addressed to certain particularly abhorrent treatment: 5.34

No one shall be subjected to torture or to inhuman or degrading treatment or punishment.

In *Soering v UK* no 14038/88, [1989] ECHR 14, [1989] 11 EHRR 439, the ECtHR found an implied prohibition of *refoulement* in Article 3 ECHR by reference to the 'death row phenomenon', involving prolonged detention prior to execution. It was held that there was an absolute prohibition against removing the applicant given the prospect of a breach of Article 3 ECHR. 5.35

Since *Soering*, the Strasbourg Court has found that Article 3 ECHR may be engaged by expulsion, including deportation on national security grounds: *Cruz Varas and others v Sweden* no 15576/89 [1991] ECHR 26, (1991) 14 EHRR 1; *Vilvarajah v UK* no 13163/87; 13164/87; 13165/87 [1991] ECHR 47, (1991) 14 EHRR 248; *Chahal v UK* no 22414/93 [1996] ECHR 54, (1996) 23 EHRR 413; *Hilal v UK* no 45276/99 [2001] 5.36

ECHR 214, (2001) 33 EHRR 2. It has also been applied to risks attending the removal of asylum seekers or refugees to other signatories under common framework agreements for the distribution of responsibility for asylum claims. See, in the domestic context, *EM (Eritrea) v SSHD* [2014] UKSC 12, per Lord Kerr, with whom the four other members of the Court agreed, at [3] and [58]. See further chapter 7.

5.37 In *Chahal v UK* [GC] no 22414/93 [1996] ECHR 54, (1996) 23 EHRR 413, the ECtHR further stressed the absolute nature of the prohibition on *refoulement* and, contrary to the UK government's submission, denied that a balancing of interests was appropriate. The case concerned the proposed removal to India of a national of that country accused of support for Sikh separatist terrorism. The ECtHR held at [79]–[80] that:

> Article 3 enshrines one of the most fundamental values of democratic society. The Court is well aware of the immense difficulties faced by States in modern times in protecting their communities from terrorist violence. However, even in these circumstances, the Convention prohibits in absolute terms torture or inhuman or degrading treatment or punishment, irrespective of the victim's conduct. Unlike most of the substantive clauses of the Convention ... Article 3 makes no provision for exceptions and no derogation from it is permissible under Article 15 even in the event of a public emergency threatening the life of the nation.
>
> The prohibition provided by Article 3 against ill-treatment is equally absolute in expulsion cases ... In these circumstances, the activities of the individual in question, however undesirable or dangerous, cannot be a material consideration. The protection afforded by Article 3 is thus wider than that provided by Articles 32 and 33 of the United Nations 1951 Convention on the Status of Refugees.

5.38 The approach was again confirmed in *Saadi v Italy* [GC] no 37201/06 [2008] ECHR 179; (2009) 49 EHRR 30 [138]–[139]. In *Saadi,* which concerned Italy's attempt to deport a Tunisian national on national security grounds, the Grand Chamber of the ECtHR rejected the proposition that the risk of return could be counterbalanced by undesirable or dangerous conduct of the person to be returned, considering the argument of the UK government in favour of the contrary position to be misconceived. These principles were reaffirmed recently in *Babar Ahmad v UK* nos 24027/07; 11949/08; 36742/08 [2012] ECHR 609, (2013) 56 EHRR 1 [172]: 'The Court finds that the same approach must be taken to the assessment of whether the minimum level of severity has been met for the purposes of Article 3: this too can only be assessed independently of the reasons for removal or extradition.'

5.39 Despite the importance of the prohibition on torture in the ECHR scheme, the ECHR does not define torture or specify the elements which render treatment inhuman or degrading. In *Ireland v UK* no 5310/71 [1978] ECHR 1, [1978] 2 EHRR 25, the European Commission concluded that interrogations by the Special Branch in Northern Ireland employing 'disorientation' or 'sensory deprivation' techniques, including forced standing in stress positions, hooding, subjection to loud noise, deprivation of sleep, and deprivation of food and drink, did not amount to torture, but that they did amount to inhuman or degrading treatment. In order to amount to 'inhuman or degrading treatment', ill-treatment must reach a 'minimum level of severity', which at [162]:

> [D]epends on all the circumstances of the case, such as the duration of the treatment, its physical or mental effects and, in some cases, the sex, age and state of health of the victim, etc.

5.40 The ECtHR generally does not find it necessary to specify the nature of the Article 3 violation in expulsion cases. In *Harkins and Edwards v UK* nos 9146/07 and 32650/07 [2012] ECHR 45, (2012) 55 EHRR 19, the ECtHR held that in the extraterritorial context where a prospective assessment of ill-treatment is required, it is not always possible to distinguish between torture and inhuman and degrading treatment. The ECtHR therefore 'normally refrained from considering' how the ill-treatment in question should be characterised (at [122]–[123]); see also *Babar Ahmad and others v UK* nos 24027/07; 11949/08; 36742/08; 66911/09; and 67354/09 [2012] ECHR 609, (2013) 56 EHRR 1 [170]–[171]:

> 170. It is correct that the Court has always distinguished between torture on the one hand and inhuman or degrading punishment on the other (see, for instance, *Ireland v. the United Kingdom*, 18 January 1978, BAILII: [1978] ECHR 1, § 167, Series A no. 25; *Selmouni v. France* [GC], no. 25803/94, BAILII: [1999] ECHR 66, §§ 95-106, ECHR 1999 V). However, the Court considers that this distinction is more easily drawn in the domestic context where, in examining complaints made under Article 3, the Court is called upon to evaluate or characterise acts which have already taken place. Where, as in the extraterritorial context, a prospective assessment is required, it is not always possible to determine whether the ill-treatment which may ensue in the receiving State will be sufficiently severe as to qualify as torture. Moreover, the distinction between torture and other forms of ill-treatment can be more easily drawn in cases where the risk of the ill-treatment stems from factors which do not engage either directly or indirectly the responsibility of the public authorities of the receiving State (see, for example, *D. v. the United Kingdom*, 2 May 1997, BAILII: [1997] ECHR 25, *Reports of Judgments and Decisions* 1997 III, where the Court found that the proposed removal of a terminally ill man to St Kitts would be inhuman treatment and thus in violation of Article 3).
>
> 171. For this reason, whenever the Court has found that a proposed removal would be in violation of Article 3 because of a real risk of ill-treatment which would be intentionally inflicted in the receiving State, it has normally refrained from considering whether the ill-treatment in question should be characterised as torture or inhuman or degrading treatment or punishment. For example, in *Chahal* the Court did not distinguish between the various forms of ill-treatment proscribed by Article 3: at paragraph 79 of its judgment the Court stated that the 'Convention prohibits in absolute terms torture or inhuman or degrading treatment or punishment'. In paragraph 80 the Court went on to state that:
>
> > The prohibition provided by Article 3 against ill-treatment is equally absolute in expulsion cases. Thus, whenever substantial grounds have been shown for believing that an individual would face a real risk of being subjected to treatment contrary to Article 3 if removed to another State, the responsibility of the Contracting State to safeguard him or her against such treatment is engaged in the event of expulsion.
>
> Similar passages can be found, for example, in *Mamatkulov and Askarov v. Turkey* [GC], nos. 46827/99 and 46951/99 [2005] ECHR 64, § 67, ECHR 2005 I and *Saadi v. Italy* [GC], no. 37201/06 [2008] ECHR 179, § 125, ECHR 2008 ... where, in reaffirming this test, no distinction was made between torture and other forms of ill-treatment.

In *Aydin v Turkey* [GC] no 23178/94 [1997] ECHR 75, (1998) 25 EHRR 251, the Court found (at [86]) that abuse of a young female detainee by security agents in Turkey, including rape, amounted to torture. In *Selmouni v France* [GC] no 25803/94 [1999] ECHR 66; (1999) 29 EHRR 403, it was held at [102]–[103] that mental violence, such as urinating on the victim, threatening him or her with a syringe and blowtorch, accompanied by physical violence, amounted to torture. The definition of torture in Article 1(1) CAT, set out at para 3.66 in chapter 3, has been frequently cited, but the requirement of state involvement found in the CAT is not a part of Article 3 ECHR.

5.41

Part B – Legal Framework

In *Sufi and Elmi v UK* nos 8319/07; 11449/07 [2011] ECHR 1045, (2012) 54 EHRR 9, the Court at [276] found punishments under Sharia law, including amputation, flogging and corporal punishments to attain the minimal level of ill-treatment necessary to engage Article 3 ECHR, and in *D and others v Turkey* no 24245/03 (22 June 2006), it held at [46]–[53] that 100 lashes for fornication was inhuman treatment contrary to Article 3. In *East African Asians v UK* no 4403/70 [1973] ECHR 2, [1981] 3 EHRR 76 [207], the Commission, a precursor to the ECtHR, found that race discrimination could amount to degrading treatment. Finally, in *SH v UK* no 19956/06 [2010] ECHR 2254, (2012) 54 EHRR 4 [70], the Court held that where there were 'acts motivated by racial discrimination', this would be an 'aggravating factor' in deciding whether treatment reached the threshold under Article 3 ECHR.

Flexibility of the Standard

5.42 The assessment of ill-treatment pursuant to Article 3 ECHR must be 'relative, depending on all the circumstances of the case' (*Sufi and Elmi v UK* nos 8319/07; 11449/07 [2011] ECHR 1045, (2012) 54 EHRR 9 [213]; *Hilal v UK* no 45276/99; [2001] ECHR 214, (2001) 33 EHRR 2 [60]) and must take account of the 'mental effects' on the applicant: *Ireland v UK* no 5310/71 [1978] ECHR 1, [1978] 2 EHRR 25 [162]. The ECtHR has expressly accepted the vulnerability of an applicant as pertinent to the assessment under Article 3 ECHR. It has been established that treatment or punishment not amounting to inhuman or degrading treatment in relation to other individuals may amount to a violation of Article 3 ECHR in the case of a particularly vulnerable person.

5.43 One group given particular consideration in this context is children, who are considered to be particularly vulnerable, with unaccompanied migrant children being 'extremely vulnerable': *Mubilanzila Mayeka and Kaniki Mitunga v Belgium* no 13178/03 [2006] ECHR 1170, (2008) 46 EHRR 23 [55]. In a number of cases the ECtHR has found a violation of Article 3 in relation to the detention of accompanied children, but not the parent exposed to the same conditions: *Muskhadzhieyava and others v Belgium* no 41442/07 (19 January 2010) [43] [59]–[62]; *Popov v France* nos 38472/07 and 38474/07 (19 January 2012) [102]–[105]; *Kanagaratnam and others v Belgium* no 15297/09 [2011] ECHR 2420, (2012) 55 EHRR 26 [67]–[72]. The Contracting Parties to the ECHR owe vulnerable persons specific positive obligations to take requisite measures and precautions in order to prevent a violation of Article 3 ECHR. The removal of an unaccompanied minor without prior arrangements for her care and custody upon arrival was according to the Court 'bound to cause her extreme anxiety and demonstrated such a total lack of humanity towards someone of her age and in her situation as an unaccompanied minor as to amount to inhuman treatment': *Mubilanza Mayeka*, at [55] and [69]; contrast *Nsona v The Netherlands* no 23366/94 [1996] ECHR 62, (2001) 32 EHRR 170 [99]. The release of a 15-year-old child from detention without any assistance with finding accommodation, family tracing or any other support for his basic survival was also found to be in breach of Article 3 ECHR: *Rahimi v Greece* no 8687/08 (5 April 2011) [91]–[94].

5.44 In certain circumstances women may also be treated as vulnerable. In *N v Sweden* no 23505/09 (20 July 2010) [55]–[57], the ECtHR identified the oppression of women in some societies ('women are at particular risk of ill-treatment ... if perceived as not conforming to the gender roles ascribed to them by society, tradition and even the legal system') and evidence concerning their position in Afghanistan as relevant to the question of whether a real risk of ill-treatment contrary to Article 3 ECHR arose, ultimately accepting at [62] that this was so in the case of an Afghan woman who feared ill-treatment at the hands of her former husband, his family and society in general. However, in *AA and others v Sweden* no 14499/09 (28 June 2012), as regards a female Yemeni applicant facing domestic violence from her husband, the Court at [81]–[85] found no violation of Article 3 on the basis that she could avail herself of the support of shelters and non-governmental organsiations (NGOs) as well as the support of family members, such as her adult sons, and had proven to be independent by filing divorce proceedings in Yemen. In the context of domestic cases, the Court has recognised the subjective fear of a former victim of domestic violence as relevant to the threshold under Article 3 ECHR: *TM and CM v Republic of Moldova* no 26608/11 [41]. A mother may suffer 'deep distress and anxiety' as a result of her child's detention, qualifying her as a 'victim' under the Convention, particularly where mother and child have been separated in detention, so that the child's detention also amounts to a violation of Article 3 for the mother (*Mubilanzila Mayeka and Kaniki Mitunga v Belgium* no 13178/03 [2006] ECHR 1170, (2008) 46 EHRR 23 [104]–[105]), a theme picked up in the domestic treatment of Article 3—for instance, in *AMM and others (Conflict; Humanitarian Crisis; Returnees; FGM) Somalia CG* [2011] UKUT 00445 (IAC).

Other groups acknowledged as particularly vulnerable have included mentally ill persons dependent upon medical care, as in *Musiał v Poland* no 28300/06 [1999] ECHR 15, (2001) 31 EHRR 29 [87]; and *Aswat v UK* no 17299/12 [2013] ECHR 322, (2014) 58 EHRR 1, and asylum-seekers in Greece: *MSS v Belgium and Greece* [GC] no 30696/09 [2011] ECHR 108, (2011) 53 EHRR 2 [259] and [263]. *Aden Ahmed v Malta* no 55352/12 [2013] ECHR 720 concerned a young woman asylum seeker detained in Malta who was found to have endured degrading treatment there: 5.45

> 97. Although not acknowledged by the domestic authorities in the AWAS procedure, the Court considers that the applicant was in a vulnerable position, not only because of the fact that she was an irregular immigrant and because of her specific past and her personal emotional circumstances (see also *MSS*, cited above, § 232), but also because of her fragile health. The medical documents submitted by the applicant showed that she suffered from, *inter alia*, insomnia, recurrent physical pain and episodes of depression. The Government also confirmed at least fourteen medical visits during her detention. Accordingly, in addition to adequate surroundings, an appropriate and varied diet was also crucially important for the applicant in view of her state of health. However, the Government put forward no evidence that the food provided was adequate at the material time, as their submissions in this respect are limited to irrelevant points.
>
> 98. The Court observes that this situation and the aforementioned conditions persisted for a continuous period of fourteen and a half months. Moreover, the detention was imposed in the context of immigration and was therefore a measure which is applicable not to those who have committed criminal offences but to aliens who, often fearing for their lives, have fled from their own country.

Some decisions directly illustrate the differential treatment of 'vulnerable' individuals and others. The ECtHR has also found detention conditions in breach of Article 3 ECHR for a mentally ill applicant, who would not receive appropriate medical care, but not for healthy applicants: see *Aswat v UK* no 17299/12 [2013] ECHR 322, (2014) 58 EHRR 1 concerning the effect of prospective detention in a US 'supermax' prison upon 5.46

a mentally ill person and *Babar Ahmad v UK* nos 24027/07; 11949/08; 36742/08 [2012] ECHR 609, (2013) 56 EHRR 1 concerning the same regime as regards healthy prisoners. Even detention in adverse conditions of a short duration of two days can amount to degrading treatment taking account of the extremely vulnerable situation of a minor: *Rahimi v Greece* no 8687/08 (5 April 2011) [86].

Burden and Standard of Evidence

5.47 Article 3 ECHR, like other *refoulement* relevant provisions, such as Article 7 ICCPR, Article 1(1) CAT and Article 16(1) CPED (on all of which see chapter 3), requires a rigorous and independent scrutiny of any *refoulement* claim. The Court has held that the burden of proof only initially rests on the applicant to adduce evidence 'capable of proving that there are substantial grounds for believing that, if the measure complained of were to be implemented, he would be exposed to a real risk of being subjected to treatment contrary to Article 3': *N v Finland* no 38885/02 (2006) 43 EHRR 12 [167]; *NA v UK* no 25904/07 [2008] ECHR 616, (2009) 48 EHRR 15 [111]. Where such evidence is adduced, it is for the government 'to dispel any doubts about it': *N v Sweden* no 23505/09 (20 July 2010) [55].

5.48 In the Court's view, this duty of rigorous scrutiny under Article 3 imposes positive obligations on the Contracting Parties. In *RC v Sweden* no 41827/07 [2010] ECHR 307, the Court found that a medical report written by a general doctor, who was not an expert for scarring reports, had given a 'rather strong indication to the authorities that the applicant's scars and injuries may have been caused by ill-treatment or torture'. The ECtHR at [53] found that based on this report, the applicant had made out a prima facie case and the Swedish authorities were thus under a 'duty to ascertain all relevant facts' and 'ought to have directed that an expert opinion be obtained' as to the probable cause of the applicant's scars.

Prison and Detention Conditions

5.49 Prison conditions can also amount to degrading treatment where 'the suffering and humiliation involved must in any event go beyond that inevitable element of suffering or humiliation connected with a given form of legitimate treatment or punishment': *Kalashnikov v Russia* no 47095/99; [2002] ECHR 596, (2002) 36 EHRR 587 [95]. Where a prisoner is held in solitary confinement indefinitely, this amounts to a violation of Article 3 ECHR, even if this entails only 'relative isolation': *Babar Ahmad v UK* nos 24027/07; 11949/08; 36742/08; [2012] ECHR 609, (2013) 56 EHRR 1 [223]. However, in *Babar Ahmad* the ECtHR found that the applicants who faced extradition to the US as suspected Al-Qaeda terrorists where they would be detained in a 'supermax' prison in Florida did not risk ill-treatment contrary to Article 3 ECHR. This has translated into domestic case law, of which an example is *PS (Prison Conditions; Military Service) Ukraine CG* [2006] UKAIT 00016, which found a pattern of gross and systematic human rights violations.

5.50 Where a person is ill, particularly in case of mental illness, and there is a lack of appropriate medical care in detention, detention or imprisonment will on that basis amount to inhuman and degrading treatment contrary to Article 3 ECHR. The person's vulnerability and his or her inability 'to complain coherently or at all about how they are being affected by any particular treatment' will be pertinent to the assessment under Article 3: *Musiał v Poland* no 28300/06; [1999] ECHR 15, (2001) 31 EHRR 29 [87]. In *Aswat v UK* no 17299/12 [2013] ECHR 322, (2014) 58 EHRR 1, which was originally linked to other cases in *Babar Ahmad v UK* nos 24027/07; 11949/08; 36742/08; [2012] ECHR 609, (2013) 56 EHRR 1, but was later separated, the Court held at [50] that the 'feeling of inferiority and powerlessness which is typical of persons who suffer from a mental disorder calls for increased vigilance'. The Court at [51] took into account that the applicant's paranoid schizophrenia had led the British authorities to conclude that detention in hospital, rather than prison, was necessary to the prevention of relapse. The Court at [57] distinguished *Aswat* from the *Babar Ahmad* circumstances because in the former, there was a 'real risk that the applicant's extradition ... would result in a significant deterioration in his mental and physical health and that such deterioration would be capable of reaching the Article 3 threshold'.

Grossly Disproportionate Sentences

The imposition of a 'grossly disproportionate sentence in the receiving State' may also amount to ill-treatment contrary to Article 3 ECHR, but the Court has stressed that 'it will only be in very exceptional cases that an applicant will be able to demonstrate' a prospective violation of Article 3 based on sentencing: *Harkins and Edwards v UK* nos 9146/07 and 32650/07 [2012] ECHR 45, (2012) 55 EHRR 19 [134]. What is 'grossly disproportionate' depends on factors such as de jure and de facto availability of parole—including by pardon—the severity of the offence charged and mitigating circumstances. Based on these factors, the Court in *Harkins and Edwards* concluded at [139]–[140] that the risk in the US of the imposition of a mandatory life sentence without parole for murder charges was not grossly disproportionate so as to violate Article 3. The decision contrasts with decisions on the same issue in a domestic context. In *Vinter and others v UK* [GC] nos 66069/09; 130/10; 3896/10 [2013] ECHR 645, (2012) 55 EHRR 34, the Court at [119] found a violation of Article 3 ECHR on the basis of a mandatory life sentence without parole or review mechanism within 25 years of its imposition.

5.51

Sur Place *Activities*

The Court has developed specific principles in relation to *sur place* activities founding a *non-refoulement* claim, particularly in the context of government's disputing the genuineness of such activities. In *SF and others v Sweden* no 52077/10 (15 May 2012) [66]–[67], the Court considered it pertinent that the Iranian applicant had already been politically active in Iran, which supported the genuineness of his political activities in Sweden. In *F v Finland* no 38885/02 (26 July 2005) [165], the Court placed weight on the fact that the applicant had not played an active role in making his asylum case known to the public. In *AA v Switzerland* no 58802/12 [2014] ECHR 3 [41], it was material that the Sudanese applicant had joined the Sudanese opposition movement SLM-Unity in Switzerland several years before he had launched the equivalent of a fresh claim.

5.52

Membership of a Group Subject to Systematic Ill-Treatment and Situations of General Violence

5.53 The ECtHR generally requires that there are personal factors putting an applicant at a real risk of ill-treatment over and above the situation of the generality of persons in that country: *Vilvarajah v UK* nos 13163/87; 13164/87; 13165/87 [1991] ECHR 47, (1991) 14 EHRR 248 [111]. In a line of cases the ECtHR has, however, accepted that an applicant's membership of a group is in itself sufficient for an Article 3 breach to arise. In the first such case, *Salah Sheekh v The Netherlands* no 1948/04 [2007] ECHR 36, the ECtHR held at [148] that the applicant who was a Somali national of the Ashraf minority clan from a 'relatively unsafe area' of Somalia could not be 'required to establish the existence of further special distinguishing features concerning him personally', given that it was foreseeable that on his return, the applicant would be exposed to treatment in breach of Article 3.

5.54 In order to demonstrate membership of a 'group systematically exposed to a practice of ill-treatment', the applicant needs to establish 'that there are serious reasons to believe in the existence of the practice in question and his or her membership of the group concerned': *Saadi v Italy* [GC] no 37201/06 [2008] ECHR 179, (2009) 49 EHRR 30 [132]. The ECtHR found this standard was met in *Saadi* concerning the expulsion of a suspected Islamist terrorist to Tunisia under the regime of Ben Ali prior to the Arab Spring.

5.55 The ECtHR in *Soldatenko v Ukraine* no 2440/07 [2008] ECHR 1142 [72] has found criminal suspects facing extradition to Turkmenistan to be members of a group systematically exposed to torture or inhuman and degrading treatment, and for some time took the same position as regards extradition to Kazakhstan in *Kaboulov v Ukraine* no 41015/04 [2009] ECHR 1903 [112] and *Baysakov and others v Ukraine* no 54131/08 [2010] ECHR 221, in contrast to the position in *Dzhaksybergenov v Ukraine* no 12343/10 [2011] ECHR 240 [37].[6] Members of Hizb ut-Tahrir facing extradition to Uzbekistan and Tajikistan also belong to a group systematically exposed to ill-treatment: see, eg, *Gaforov v Russia* no 25404/09 (2011) ECHR 365 (Tajikistan); *Rustamov v Russia* no 11209/10 [2012] ECHR 1372 (Uzbekistan). A collective approach was also applied to the group of Somali and Eritrean migrants returned to Libya (*Hirsi Jamaa and others v Italy* [GC] no 27765/09 [2012] ECHR 1845, (2012) 55 EHRR 21) and asylum-seekers facing return to Greece (*MSS v Belgium and Greece* [GC] no 30696/09 [2011] ECHR 108, (2011) 53 EHRR 2).

5.56 The principle that in certain circumstances no personal distinguishing factors are required under Article 3 was extended to 'general situations of violence' which are 'of a sufficient level of intensity' to breach Article 3 in *NA v UK* no 25904/07 [2008] ECHR 616, (2009) 48 EHRR 15 [115]. The ECtHR, however, added the caveat that this test would only be met 'in the most extreme cases of general violence, where there was a real risk of ill-treatment simply by virtue of an individual being exposed to such violence on return'.

5.57 The first, and so far only, case in which the test of a general situation of violence of a sufficient level of intensity has been met is *Sufi and Elmi v UK* nos 8319/07; 11449/07

---

[6] See also *Sharipov v Russia* no 18414/10 (11 October 2011), at [36]; *Yefimova v Russia* no 39786/09 (19 February 2013); [200]–[201]; *Oshlakov v Russia* no 56662/09 (3 April 2014), at [84]–[85].

[2011] ECHR 1045, (2012) 54 EHRR 9, in which case the ECtHR found at [248]–[250] that, based on the 'large quantity of objective information ... the level of violence in Mogadishu is of sufficient intensity to pose a real risk of treatment reaching the Article 3 threshold to anyone in the capital', except for exceptionally well-connected powerful actors. The ECtHR at [241] set out a non-exhaustive list of factors to consider in such cases:

> [F]irst, whether the parties to the conflict were either employing methods and tactics of warfare which increased the risk of civilian casualties or directly targeting civilians; secondly, whether the use of such methods and/or tactics was widespread among the parties to the conflict; thirdly, whether the fighting was localised or widespread; and finally, the number of civilians killed, injured and displaced as a result of the fighting.

5.58 The factual assessment of the situation has been reconsidered in *KAB v Sweden* no 886/11 [2013] ECHR 814 [91], in which the Court found that the 'country information does not indicate that the situation is at present, of such a nature as to place everyone who is present in the city' at real risk of a breach of Article 3. The ECtHR did not, however, critically assess the quality of country information it relied on as normally required by the ECtHR as regards 'its independence, reliability and objectivity ... the authority and reputation of the author, the seriousness of the investigations by means of which they were compiled, the consistency of their conclusions and their corroboration by other sources': *Sufi and Elmi v UK* nos 8319/07, 11449/07 [2011] ECHR 1045, (2012) 54 EHRR 9 [230]. Instead, the ECtHR in *KAB* relied chiefly on the report of the Danish-Norwegian fact-finding mission which was based on anonymous sources and the ECtHR was satisfied with the evidence 'suggesting', 'appearing to agree' and 'indicating' that the situation in Mogadishu had improved (at [87]–[90]).[7]

Non-state Persecution and Sufficiency of Protection

5.59 The test for sufficiency of protection is outlined in *HLR v France* [GC] no 24573/94 [1997] ECHR 23 [40], the ECtHR finding that the positive obligations under Article 3 ECHR apply extraterritorially to non-state agent ill-treatment 'where the danger emanates from persons or groups of persons who are not public officials', provided it is 'shown that the risk is real and that the authorities of the receiving State are not able to obviate the risk by providing appropriate protection'. This equally applies where the authorities of the receiving state are 'not willing' to protect against the risks: *N v Finland* no 38885/02 (26 July 2005) [163]–[164]. In *R otao Bagdanavicius and another v SSHD* [2005] UKHL 38, [2005] 2 AC 668, the House of Lords held that whilst there were some differences between the *Horvath v SSHD* [2000] UKHL 37, [2001] 1 AC 489 formulation of the standard of protection required by the Refugee Convention (see chapter 4) and the Strasbourg formulation in *HLR*, the tests were the same in practice.

5.60 However, the ECtHR has rarely found violations of Article 3 ECHR in the context of expulsion where the fear expressed is one of harm inflicted at the hands of non-state actors. In *Ahmed v Austria* no 25964/94 (1997) 24 EHRR 278 concerning the withdrawal of asylum in the case of a convicted Somali national, the ECtHR held that even though

---

[7] See also the powerful dissenting opinions of Judges Power-Forde and Ziemele in *KAB v Sweden*.

the 'State authority had ceased to exist in Somalia', it was 'sufficient that those who hold substantial power within the State, even though they are not the Government, threaten the life and security of the applicant' (at [68]); see also two cases concerning contemplated return to Somalia, *Salah Sheekh v The Netherlands* no 1948/04 [2007] ECHR 36 (11 January 2007) and *Sufi and Elmi v UK* nos 8319/07, 11449/07 [2011] ECHR 1045, (2012) 54 EHRR 9. In *Auad v Bulgaria* no 46390/10 (11 October 2011) concerning a Palestinian stateless person to be returned to a refugee camp in Lebanon, the ECtHR found that the refugee camp Ain al-Hilweh in Lebanon was in fact controlled by Palestinian armed factions and had been described as a safe haven from the authority of the Lebanese state, leading the ECtHR to find a real risk from private Palestinian armed factions (at [103]).

Internal Relocation Alternative

5.61   The ECtHR has found that for an internal relocation alternative to exist, 'the person to be expelled must be able to travel to the area concerned, to gain admittance and be able to settle there, failing which an issue under Article 3 may arise': *Salah Sheekh v The Netherlands* no 1948/04 [2007] ECHR 36 [141]. Where the risk also emanates from the state authorities, no internal relocation alternative exists in the entire country, provided the government controls the entire country, or alternatively in government-controlled areas: *NA v UK* no 25904/07 [2008] ECHR 616, (2009) 48 EHRR 15 [98]; *Hilal v UK* no 45276/99 [2001] ECHR 214, (2001) 33 EHRR 2; *Chahal v UK* no 22414/93 [1996] ECHR 54, (1996) 23 EHRR 413.

5.62   In *Sufi and Elmi v UK* nos 8319/07, 11449/07 [2011] ECHR 1045, (2012) 54 EHRR 9, the ECtHR considered whether an internal relocation alternative existed for the applicants in other parts of Somalia. Apart from problems with safe access, the ECtHR further held that the living conditions in refugee camps in Somalia (and, oddly, Kenya, which is not an 'internal' relocation alternative) would amount to a violation of Article 3 ECHR because of the 'dire humanitarian conditions' in the camps (at [301]–[304] and [309]–[312]). The ECtHR placed weight on the importance of the traditional clan structure in Somalia, rendering 'close family connections' in an area for internal relocation crucial (at [294]). In its case law, the ECtHR has also referred to the 'reasonableness' of an internal relocation alternative: eg *SA v Sweden* no 66523/10 (27 June 2013) [56]; *DNM v Sweden* no 28379/11 (27 June 2013) [42]. However, precarious living conditions, as they appertain in Kabul or Mazar-i-Sharif, have been found not to result in a risk of ill-treatment reaching the Article 3 threshold: *Husseini v Sweden* no 10611/09 (13 October 2011) [95]–[98]; *SS v UK* no 12096/10 (admissibility decision, 24 January 2012); *H and B v UK* nos 70073/10 and 44539/11 (9 April 2013) [114].

Diplomatic Assurances

5.63   Notwithstanding the ECtHR's consistent reaffirmation of the absolute nature of *non-refoulement*, the non-derogable nature of the principle has been eroded by the development of a corpus of jurisprudence on diplomatic assurances. In *Othman (Abu Qatada) v UK* no 8139/09 [2012] ECHR 56, (2012) 55 EHRR 1, the ECtHR accepted that assurances against ill-treatment contrary to Article 3 ECHR may have the effect of rendering expulsion compatible with that Article even in relation to states in which torture is systematically employed. In earlier cases, the ECtHR was more circumspect as to the effect of assurances: *Chahal v UK* [GC] no 22414/93 [1996] ECHR 54, (1996) 23 EHHR 413 [105]; *Saadi v Italy* [GC] no 37201/06 [2008] ECHR 179, (2009) 49 EHRR 30 [147]–[148]. In *Chahal* the ECtHR at [105] refused to rely on assurances it acknowledged were given in good faith as human rights violations by the security services were recognised to be 'a recalcitrant and enduring problem'. In *Saadi v Italy* the ECtHR at [147]–[148] held that the relevant question was 'whether such assurances provided, in their practical application, a sufficient guarantee that the applicant would be protected against the risk of treatment prohibited by the Convention.' Domestic case law on assurances appears to adopt the assessment of the practical application of assurances in *Saadi*. In *AS and DD (Libya) v SSHD* [2008] EWCA Civ 289, the Court of Appeal upheld a conclusion by the Special Immigration Appeals Commission (SIAC) in relation to Libya under Gaddafi that despite assurances having been given in good faith, the risk of ill-treatment was too high.

In *Othman* at [188], the ECtHR summarised the general principles arising from its existing case law on diplomatic assurances, noting that a preliminary question was to ask 'whether the general human-rights situation in the receiving State excludes accepting any assurances whatsoever'. It then at [189] identified the following 11 factors relevant to the sufficiency of assurances: 5.64

- (i) whether the terms of the assurances have been sufficiently disclosed;
- (ii) whether these are specific or general in nature;
- (iii) the capacity of the author to bind the receiving State;
- (iv) if the assurances have been issued by the central government of the receiving State, whether local authorities or others can be restrained from any violation;
- (v) whether the assurances concern treatment which is legal or illegal in the receiving State;
- (vi) whether they have been given by a Contracting State;
- (vii) the length and strength of bilateral relations between the sending and receiving States, including the receiving State's record in abiding by similar assurances;
- (viii) whether compliance with the assurances can be objectively verified through diplomatic or other monitoring mechanisms, including providing unfettered access to the applicant's lawyers;
- (ix) whether there is an effective system of protection against the feared treatment in the receiving State, including whether it is willing to cooperate with international monitoring mechanisms (including international human rights NGOs), and whether it is willing to investigate allegations of torture and to punish those responsible;
- (x) whether the applicant has previously been ill-treated in the receiving State; and
- (xi) whether the reliability of the assurances has been examined by the domestic courts of the sending/Contracting State.

In the *Othman* case, the ECtHR found that torture was systemic in the proposed destination state, but concluded that the assurances were sufficient and eliminated any relevant risk of mistreatment on return. In particular, the assurances provided by the Ministry of Justice were more detailed, specific and significant, and thus more reliable, than assurances proffered in earlier cases. The ECtHR has, however, since cautioned against the reliance on diplomatic assurances from 'States where torture is endemic or persistent' in the case of Uzbek diplomatic assurances, which were 'couched in general stereotyped terms and did not provide for any monitoring mechanism': *Kasymakhunov v Russia* no 29604/12 (14 November 2013) [126]–[127]; see also the earlier cases of *Ismoilov v* 5.65

Russia no 2947/06 (24 April 2008) [31]–[32]; *Muminov v Russia* (merits) no 42502/06 (11 December 2008) [97]; see, in relation to Tunisia and the lack of monitoring prior to the Arab Spring, *Toumi v Italy* no 25716/09 (5 April 2011).

'Treatment' or Naturally Occurring Event or Illness and Living Conditions

5.66 In its case law, the ECtHR has developed a distinction based on the source of the risk of inhuman and degrading treatment. The ECtHR may, in principle, examine a future breach of Article 3 in health cases, where the 'source of the risk of proscribed treatment in the receiving country stems from factors which cannot engage either directly or indirectly the responsibility of the public authorities of that country, or which, taken alone, do not in themselves infringe the standards' of Article 3 ECHR. In *D v UK* no 30240/96 [1997] ECHR 25, (1997) 24 EHRR 425, the ECtHR at [51]–[53] found that the proposed deportation to St Kitts of an AIDS sufferer in an advanced state of the disease engaged Article 3 ECHR given the absence of moral or social support or of access to palliative or other medical care, but at [54] emphasised the exceptionality of the situation in that case:

> Against this background the Court emphasises that aliens who have served their prison sentences and are subject to expulsion cannot in principle claim any entitlement to remain in the territory of a Contracting State in order to continue to benefit from medical, social or other forms of assistance provided by the expelling State during their stay in prison. However, in the very exceptional circumstances of this case and given the compelling humanitarian considerations at stake, it must be concluded that the implementation of the decision to remove the applicant would be a violation of Article 3.

5.67 That decision has remained an isolated success. In *N v UK* [GC] no 26565/05 (2008) 47 EHRR 39, the ECtHR Grand Chamber elucidated a test of exceptionality by which it would only be 'in a very exceptional case, where the humanitarian grounds against removal are compelling' that expulsion would breach Article 3 ECHR and a significant reduction in life expectancy was insufficient to meet this threshold (at [42]). The threshold in mental health cases is equally exigent: *Bensaid v UK* no 44599/98 [2001] ECHR 82, (2001) 33 EHRR 205.

5.68 In *MSS v Belgium and Greece* [GC] no 30696/09 [2011] ECHR 108, (2011) 53 EHRR 2, the ECtHR held that Belgium's expulsion of the applicant to Greece under the Dublin II Regulation had violated Article 3 ECHR. For the first time, the ECtHR found that living conditions could amount to inhuman and degrading treatment. The ECtHR at [253] stressed that it had never excluded the applicability of Article 3 'where an applicant, who was wholly dependent on the State, found herself faced with official indifference in a situation of serious deprivation or want incompatible with human dignity'. It held at [263] that:

> [T]he Greek authorities have not had due regard to the applicant's vulnerability as an asylum seeker and must be held responsible, because of their inaction, for the situation in which he has found himself for several months, living in the street, with no resources or access to sanitary facilities, and without any means of providing for his essential needs. The ECtHR considers that the applicant has been the victim of humiliating treatment showing a lack of respect for his dignity and that this situation has, without doubt, aroused in him feelings of fear, anguish or inferiority capable of inducing desperation. It considers that such living conditions, combined

with the prolonged uncertainty in which he has remained and the total lack of any prospects of his situation improving, have attained the level of severity required to fall within the scope of Article 3 of the Convention.

5.69 The ECtHR explained in *Sufi and Elmi v UK* nos 8319/07, 11449/07 [2011] ECHR 1045, (2012) 54 EHRR 9 that a distinction arises between cases where the future harm would 'emanate not from the intentional acts or omission of public authorities or non-State bodies but from a naturally occurring illness and the lack of sufficient resources'—such as *D* and *N*—and cases where the future harm is 'predominantly due to the direct and indirect actions of the parties' to a conflict: *Sufi and Elmi*, at [282]–[283]. In the latter case, where the cause of future harm is 'solely or predominantly' related to state or non-state agent action, the exceptionality test in *N* does not apply, but the ECtHR instead applies the test set out in *MSS v Belgium and Greece* [GC] no 30696/09 [2011] ECHR 108, (2011) 53 EHRR 2 [254], 'which requires it to have regard to an applicant's ability to cater for his most basic needs, such as food, hygiene and shelter, his vulnerability to ill-treatment and the prospect of his situation improving within a reasonable time-frame'.

5.70 The ECtHR in *Aswat v UK* no 17299/12 [2013] ECHR 322, (2014) 58 EHRR 1 [57] distinguished the situation of the mentally ill applicant facing detention in a 'supermax' prison in the US from *Bensaid v UK* no 44599/98 [2001] ECHR 82; (2001) 33 EHRR 10 on the basis that the former case involved not expulsion to the home country, but extradition to a country where he had no ties, where he would be detained and where he would have no access to support from family and friends.

5.71 However, in *SHH v UK* no 60367/10 [2013] ECHR 102, (2013) 57 EHRR 18, the ECtHR decided by four votes to three that the *N* exceptionality test, rather than the standard set out in *MSS*, applied to an Afghan applicant who had been left seriously injured with one leg amputated during a rocket launch in Afghanistan (at [89]). The majority based its decision on the fact that future harm would emanate from lack of resources rather than intentional acts or omissions of state or non-state actors, and that the country conditions could not be compared to those that appertained in Mogadishu at the time of the decision in *Sufi and Elmi*. Somewhat surprisingly, the ECtHR at [89]–[91] further cited as relevant that Afghanistan was not a Contracting Party and was, unlike Greece in *MSS*, not bound by European legislation.

5.72 In *SHH* and subsequently, the ECtHR has appeared divided on the appropriate standard in Article 3 ECHR medical cases. In *Mwanje v Belgium* no 10486/10 (2013) 56 EHRR 35, the ECtHR held that the detention of an HIV-positive applicant in Belgium, where access to necessary treatment was unduly delayed by the authorities, violated Article 3 ECHR, but prospective expulsion to Cameroon (where on the evidence 98 per cent of HIV patients did not have access to treatment) would not create a new breach. Six out of the seven judges wrote a partly concurring opinion in which they expressed their dissatisfaction with the exceptionality test in *N* and expressed hope that the ECtHR would revisit this test, although for reasons of legal certainty, they also applied it to the facts of the case.

Expulsion to a Contracting Party and 'Dublin' Cases

5.73 The mere fact that the receiving state is a Contracting Party of the ECHR does not preclude the applicability of the *non-refoulement* obligation inherent in Article 3 ECHR:

TI v UK no 43844/98 [2000] ECHR 705. The ECtHR has found Article 3 breaches in cases involving expulsion to various states including Greece (*MSS v Belgium and Greece* [GC] no 30696/09 [2011] ECHR 108, (2011) 53 EHRR 2); Russia (*IK v Austria* no 2964/12 [2013] ECHR 252 and *I v Sweden* no 61204/09 [2013] ECHR 813); Georgia (*Shamayev and others v Georgia and Russia* no 36378/02 [2005] ECHR 233); and Turkey (*RU v Greece* no 2237/08 (7 June 2011)).

5.74 In *MSS* the ECtHR stressed that the Article 3 duty to examine a case rigorously also applies in the context of expulsions to the territory of a Contracting Party, provided 'substantial grounds have been shown for believing that the person concerned faces a real risk of being subjected to torture or inhuman or degrading treatment or punishment in the receiving country' (at [365]–[366]). Where the evidence on country conditions is such that 'the general situation was known to the [expelling] authorities ... the applicant should not be expected to bear the entire burden of proof' (at [352]). In *MSS* the ECtHR found at [359] that:

> [I]t was in fact up to the Belgian authorities, faced with the situation described above, not merely to assume that the applicant would be treated in conformity with the Convention standards but, on the contrary, to first verify how the Greek authorities applied their legislation on asylum in practice.

5.75 However, subsequent cases considering Dublin Regulation returns to Italy appear to have introduced a threshold requirement for demonstration of systemic flaws in the receiving state: *Mohammed Hussein v The Netherlands* no 27725/10 (admissibility decision, 2 April 2013) and *Daytbegova and another v Austria* no 6198/12 (admissibility decision, 4 June 2013). The ECtHR will have a renewed opportunity to clarify this test in the pending case of *Tarakhel v Switzerland* no 29217/12 concerning Dublin transfers to Italy, in which the Second Section of the ECtHR has relinquished jurisdiction to the Grand Chamber. Domestically, however, the Supreme Court in *EM (Eritrea) v SSHD* [2014] UKSC 12 has denied the lawfulness of such a threshold.

5.76 In *Mohammed v Austria* no 2283/12 (6 June 2013), the ECtHR considered the situation as regards Dublin returns to Hungary and found no breach of Article 3 ECHR. However, the ECtHR at [76] held that the applicant's fresh asylum claim had raised arguable issues under Article 3 ECHR based on 'recent alarming information concerning the situation of asylum-seekers in Hungary and the Austrian Asylum Court's own practice in autumn 2011 of staying transfers to Hungary and seeking updated information', so that the failure of the Austrian authorities to issue a fresh decision on this claim had deprived the applicant of an effective remedy in breach of Article 13 ECHR (at [80]–[83]).

B7. Article 4 ECHR

5.77 Article 4 ECHR prohibits 'slavery or servitude', or 'forced or compulsory labour' excluding work required in the ordinary course of lawful detention or conditional release therefrom, military service or other service substituted therefore, and service exacted 'in case of an emergency or calamity threatening the life or wellbeing of the community' (Article 4(3) ECHR). Article 4 ECHR therefore enshrines 'one of the fundamental values of democratic societies': *Siliadin v France* no 73316/01 [2005] ECHR 545, (2006) 43 EHRR 16

[112]. The prohibition on slavery or servitude under Article 4(1) ECHR is, pursuant to Article 15(2) ECHR, absolute and non-derogable, whereas the prohibition on forced or compulsory labour is subject to the exceptions listed in Article 4(3) ECHR and can be derogated from pursuant to Article 15(1) ECHR.

The difference between the various types of prohibited treatment under Article 4 ECHR is one of degree, with slavery being at the most extreme end of the scale and servitude being an 'aggravated' form of 'forced or compulsory labour': *CN and v France* no 67724/09 (11 October 2012) [91]. In *Siliadin v France* the ECtHR at [122] adopted for the purposes of the ECHR the pre-existing definition of 'slavery' as 'the status or condition of a person over whom any or all of the powers attaching to the right of ownership are exercised' holding that the treatment meted out to the Togolese applicant, who had come to France as a minor and had been forced to work as a domestic worker for the parents of her former employers, her passport having been confiscated, did not amount to slavery, as those responsible did not purport to exercise a 'genuine right of legal ownership over her'. However, the ECtHR found that she had been held in servitude in addition to having been subjected to forced and compulsory labour.[8] At [123]–[124], it defined 'servitude' as follows:

5.78

123. With regard to the concept of 'servitude', what is prohibited is a 'particularly serious form of denial of freedom' ... It includes, 'in addition to the obligation to perform certain services for others ... the obligation for the 'serf' to live on another person's property and the impossibility of altering his condition' ...
124. It follows in the light of the case-law on this issue that for Convention purposes 'servitude' means an obligation to provide one's services that is imposed by the use of coercion, and is to be linked with the concept of 'slavery' described above.

As regards 'forced or compulsory labour', the ECtHR has found relevant International Labour Organization (ILO) materials useful in the interpretation of Article 4 ECHR, given the 'striking similarity, which is not accidental, between' Article 4(3) ECHR and Article 2(2) of the ILO Forced Labour Convention No 29: *Van der Mussele v Belgium* no 8919/80 [1983] ECHR 13, (1984) 6 EHRR 163 [32]; *Siliadin*, at [115]–[116]. The ECtHR found 'forced or compulsory labour' to involve 'some physical or mental constraint', with work being exacted 'under the menace of any penalty' as well as 'performed against the person's will': *Van der Mussele*, at [34]; *Siliadin*, at [117].

5.79

The ECtHR has also found that trafficking of human beings falls within the scope of Article 4 ECHR. In *Rantsev v Cyprus and Russia* no 25965/04 [2010] ECHR 22, (2010) 51 EHRR 1, the ECtHR confirmed this, emphasising the close relationship between the international instruments concerned with human trafficking, including the CATHB, and Article 4 ECHR. Noting that 'trafficking in human beings as a global phenomenon has increased significantly in recent years' and 'the increasing recognition at international level of ... the need for measures to combat it' (at [277]), the ECtHR held (at [282]) that:

5.80

---

[8] For further cases involving domestic workers and the obligation to enact criminal law provisions directed at slavery and servitude, see also *CN v UK* no 4239/08 (2013) 56 EHRR 24 (holding that Article 4 required the UK to enact criminal law provisions dealing with offences of slavery, servitude and forced or compulsory labour); and *Kawogo v UK* no 56921/09 (strike out decision, 3 September 2013, after various declarations were made by the UK); *CN and V v France* no 67724/09 (11 October 2012) (holding in accordance with earlier findings in *Siliadin* that the failure to criminalise slavery and servitude violated Article 4).

Part B – Legal Framework

There can be no doubt that trafficking threatens the human dignity and fundamental freedoms of its victims and cannot be considered compatible with a democratic society and the values expounded in the Convention ... [T]he Court considers it unnecessary to identify whether the treatment about which the applicant complains constitutes 'slavery', 'servitude' or 'forced and compulsory labour'. Instead, the Court concludes that trafficking itself, within the meaning of Article 3(a) of the Palermo Protocol and Article 4(a) of the Anti-Trafficking Convention, falls within the scope of Article 4 of the Convention.

5.81 In the context of expulsion cases, a real risk of re-trafficking upon return may raise issues under Article 4 in addition to Articles 2 and 3 ECHR. While the ECtHR has not yet found a violation of Article 4 ECHR in an expulsion case, the ECtHR has expressly left open the possibility of an extraterritorial application of the absolute and non-derogable Article 4 ECHR: *VF v France* no 7196/10 (admissibility decision, 29 November 2011). Another issue in expulsion cases involving a risk of re-trafficking relates to the circumstances in which positive obligations under Article 4 ECHR can be imposed on the expelling state. The ECtHR held in *Rantsev* at [286] that 'positive obligations to take operational measures' arise where it has been 'demonstrated that the State authorities were aware, or ought to have been aware, of circumstances giving rise to a credible suspicion' that the applicant was at a real risk of being exploited or trafficked.

5.82 In the context of the duties upon states, issues may arise as to whether the authorities ought to have been aware of circumstances giving rise to such a suspicion. *VF v France* concerned a Nigerian prostitute who stated that she feared re-trafficking in the event of return to Nigeria. The ECtHR held that it could not be said that the French authorities were aware, or ought to have been aware, of a re-trafficking risk under Article 4 or a risk of inhuman and degrading treatment under Article 3 on return. The ECtHR at [13]–[15] held it material that the applicant had failed to self-identify as a victim of trafficking in her initial asylum claim and had made only 'extremely vague' claims on appeal.[9] However, self-identification as a victim is not essential; where 'the matter has come to the attention of the authorities they must act of their own motion': *CN v UK* no 4239/08 [2012] ECHR 1911, (2013) 56 EHRR 24 [69]. The ECtHR at [69] in that decision made it clear that Article 4 ECHR, like the preceding two ECHR articles, entails a procedural obligation to investigate independently where there is a credible suspicion that an individual's rights have been violated and such suspicion 'does not depend on a complaint from the victim or next-of-kin'.

5.83 The ECtHR has held that applicants raising a fear of ill-treatment or re-trafficking on return to their country of origin have to exhaust domestic asylum appeal remedies: *FA v UK* no 20658/11 (admissibility decision, 10 September 2013).

B8. Article 5 ECHR

5.84 Article 5 ECHR regulates deprivation of liberty, specifying admissible exceptions to the general right to liberty and security of the person. The ECtHR has not yet found a violation

---

[9] Late self-identification may also adversely affect credibility; see *Idemugia v France* no 4125/11 (admissibility decision, 27 March 2012), concerning a claim under Article 3 ECHR of a Nigerian who had been trafficked to Spain as a minor and forced into prostitution and to act as a drug mule, resulting in her arrest in France. Her late asylum claim, made only after almost three years in custody and being placed in immigration detention in France, adversely affected her credibility.

of the right to liberty and security in an expulsion case involving the extraterritorial application of Article 5 ECHR. The former uncertainty[10] as to the extraterritorial applicability of Article 5 was, however, resolved in *Othman (Abu Qatada) v UK* no 8139/09 [2012] ECHR 56, (2012) 55 EHRR 1 concerning an extradition request from Jordan for a suspected terrorist. The ECtHR confirmed that Article 5 ECHR applied in expulsion cases and that the host state would commit a violation of the Convention if it expelled a migrant to a state where he or she would be at a real risk of a flagrant denial of his or her Article 5 rights.

Issues concerning a flagrant violation of the right to liberty under Article 5 often stand in close connection with a flagrant denial of justice contrary to Article 6 ECHR. Where a conviction is the result of proceedings which constituted a flagrant denial of justice, the resulting deprivation of liberty would not be justified under Article 5 ECHR: *Willcox and Hurford v UK* nos 43759/10, 43771/12 [2013] ECHR 292 (admissibility decision, 8 January 2013) [95].[11] However, according to the ECtHR in *Othman*, the requisite flagrancy standard for an extraterritorial breach of Article 5 would only be met if the applicant on return to the receiving state faced arbitrary detention for a 'substantial period' after a flagrantly unfair trial that cannot be reopened, or without any trial whatsoever (at [231]–[233]). The ECtHR emphasised the very high threshold applicable in Article 5 foreign cases. On the facts of *Othman*, under Jordanian law, Mr Othman would have to be brought to trial within 50 days of his initial detention. In the view of the EctHR, this fell 'far short of the length of detention required for a flagrant breach of Article 5' (at [235]).   5.85

In *Szabo v Sweden* no 28578/03 (admissibility decision, 27 June 2006), which concerned the transfer of a sentenced Hungarian national from Sweden to Hungary under the Council of Europe Convention on the Transfer of Sentenced Persons 1983 and its Additional Protocol, the ECtHR at [1] did 'not exclude the possibility that a flagrantly longer de facto term of imprisonment in the administering State could give rise to an issue under Article 5', but considered that, provided this was foreseeable, an increase from having to serve six years and eight months until early release to serving eight years was 'not so disproportionate' that it would engage Sweden's responsibility under Article 5 ECHR: see also *Csoszanski v Sweden* no 22318/02 (admissibility decision, 27 June 2006).   5.86

In *Al-Moayad v Germany* no 35865/03 (admissibility decision, 20 February 2007), the ECtHR further held that 'extra-territorial measures of a respondent State resulting in the applicant's detention which entailed clear violations of international law, for instance in the case of forcing an applicant against his will to enter the respondent State in a manner that is inconsistent with the sovereignty of his host State' would raise issues as to the 'lawfulness' and the arbitrariness of such deprivation of liberty under Article 5(1) ECHR (at [81]).   5.87

---

[10] In *Tomic v UK* no 17837/03 (admissibility decision, 14 October 2003), the Court doubted the extraterritorial applicability of Article 5 ECHR (at [3]), but in *WM v Denmark* no 17392 DR 73, 193 (admissibility decision, 14 October 1992), the Commission held that Article 5 may exceptionally be engaged where an applicant risks suffering a flagrant denial of his ECHR rights (at [1]).

[11] See also *Stoichkov v Bulgaria* no 9808/02 (24 March 2005), which did not concern an extraterritorial violation of Article 5, but made the link between a 'flagrant denial of justice' and the resulting conviction and detention in violation of Article 5 ECHR (at [51]).

B9. Article 6 ECHR

5.88 Article 6 ECHR provides for the right to a fair trial. In *Soering v UK* no 14038/88 [1989] ECHR 14, [1989] 11 EHRR 439, the ECtHR did not exclude that an 'issue might exceptionally be raised under Article 6' extraterritorially where an applicant risks suffering a 'flagrant denial of a fair trial' (at [113]); see also *Mamatkulov and Askarov v Turkey* nos 46827/99, 46951/99 [2005] ECHR 64, (2005) 41 EHRR 25 [90]–[91].[12] In *Drozd and Janousek v France and Spain* no 12747/87 [1992] ECHR 52, (1992) 14 EHRR 74, the ECtHR at [110] explained the rationale behind the flagrancy standard as being that while Contracting Parties are not to impose the ECHR standard on third states, 'they are obliged to refuse co-operation if it emerges that a conviction is a result of a flagrant denial of justice'.

5.89 *Othman (Abu Qatada) v UK* no 8139/09 [2012] ECHR 56, 55 EHRR 1 was the first case in which the ECtHR found such a flagrant violation of Article 6. The ECtHR stressed, however, that the test would be a stringent one, stating at [260] that it required a 'breach of the principles of fair trial guaranteed by Article 6 which is so fundamental as to amount to a nullification, or destruction of the very essence, of the right'. The question before the ECtHR was whether the admission of evidence obtained by torture would constitute a flagrant denial of justice.[13] The ECtHR concluded at [267] that it would:

> [T]he admission of torture evidence is manifestly contrary, not just to the provisions of Article 6, but to the most basic international standards of a fair trial. It would make the whole trial not only immoral and illegal, but also entirely unreliable in its outcome. It would, therefore, be a flagrant denial of justice if such evidence were admitted in a criminal trial.

The ECtHR held at [281] that on the findings made previously by the SIAC, it followed that the test of flagrant breach was met.

5.90 The ECtHR has on other occasions identified situations in which a flagrant denial of justice might arise, listed in *Othman* at [259] as pertinent to expulsion cases, including the following:

i. Conviction *in absentia* with no possibility subsequently to obtain a fresh determination of the merits of the charge, without indication that the accused has waived his or her right to be present during the trial: *Stoichkov v Bulgaria* no 9808/02 (24 March 2005) [56], *Einhorn v France*, no 71555/01 (admissibility decision, 16 October 2001) [33]; *Sejdovic v Italy* [GC] no 56581/00 [2006] ECHR 181 [84];

ii. Trial which is summary in nature and conducted with a total disregard for the rights of the defence, such as where it transpires that 'no oral evidence was taken at the hearing, that all the evidence examined was submitted by the prosecutor and that neither the accused nor even his defence lawyer was present at the hearing': *Bader and Kanbor v Sweden* no 13284/04 [2005] ECHR 939; (2008) 46 EHRR 13 [47]–[48];

---

[12] For a domestic case where allegations of systemic judicial corruption in Albania were in the view of the Supreme Court sufficiently serious for them to be necessary' to examine whether a flagrant denial of justice would occur in the event of extradition, see *Kapri v The Lord Advocate (representing the Government of the Republic of Albania) (Scotland)* [2013] UKSC 48; [2013] 1 WLR 2324 (10 July 2013).

[13] The Court gave no indication as to whether ill-treatment not amounting to torture but constituting a violation of Article 3 would have the same effect.

iii. Detention 'because of suspicions that he has been planning or has committed a criminal offence without having any access to an independent and impartial tribunal to have the legality of his or her detention reviewed and, if the suspicions do not prove to be well-founded, to obtain release': *Al-Moayad v Germany* no 35865/03 (admissibility decision, 20 February 2007) [101];
iv. Deliberate and systematic refusal of access to a lawyer, especially for an individual detained in a foreign country (*Al-Moayad*, [101]).

Mere differences in legal systems or minor practical inadequacies do not rise to the level of flagrancy required under Article 6 ECHR. The ECtHR found the standard not to be met in *Ahorugeze v Sweden* no 37075/09 (2012) 55 EHRR 2 concerning the extradition of a Rwandan national of Hutu origin to Rwanda to stand trial on charges including genocide and crimes against humanity. In *Willcox and Hurford v UK* nos 43759/10, 43771/12 (admissibility decision, 8 January 2013), the ECtHR held that an irrebuttable presumption in Thai law that drugs of a certain quantity were always for distribution, not personal use, did not amount to a flagrant denial of justice, although the British High Court had found that there was a 'reasonably arguable case' that the drugs had been for the applicant's own use (at [93]–[98]). The ECtHR at [97] identified 'a material factor' as being that the applicant had not adverted to this injustice during his trial in Thailand or his request for a transfer to the UK.

5.91

The principles developed in relation to the extraterritorial application of Article 6 ECHR in extradition cases in principle also apply to expulsion decisions: *Muminov v Russia* no 42502/06 (11 December 2008) [130].

5.92

Many of the general principles applicable in Article 3 ECHR expulsion and extradition cases similarly apply in relation to Article 6 ECHR. The ECtHR stated in *Othman (Abu Qatada) v UK* no 8139/09 [2012] ECHR 56, 55 EHRR 1 that the standard of proof required in such cases would be that of a 'real risk', invoking the standard and burden of proof established as regards Article 3 expulsion cases. It is therefore for the applicant to adduce 'evidence capable of proving that there are substantial grounds for believing that, if he is removed from a Contracting State, he would be exposed to a real risk of being subjected to a flagrant denial of justice'.

5.93

As in Article 3 cases, diplomatic assurances may, in certain circumstances, obviate any risk of a flagrant denial of justice. In *Al-Moayad v Germany* no 35865/03 (admissibility decision, 20 February 2007), the applicant was subject to an extradition request from the US on suspicion of terrorist activities for Al-Qaeda and the extremist branch of Hamas. The US provided diplomatic assurances that the applicant would not be prosecuted by a military tribunal and would not be sentenced to death. In the ECtHR's view, set out at [67]–[69] and [104]–[105], the diplomatic assurances allayed any risk of a breach of Article 3 or 6 ECHR.

5.94

B10. Article 7 ECHR

Article 7 ECHR prohibits 'punishment without law' (Article 7(1)) excepting 'trial and punishment' for acts or omissions which at the time of commission were 'criminal according to the general principles of law recognised by civilised nations' (Article 7(2)). Article 7 lies at the core of the rule of law and constitutes an absolute and non-derogable guarantee pursuant to Article 15(2) ECHR.

5.95

5.96 The ECtHR's case law confirms that the guarantee enshrined in Article 7, 'an essential element of the rule of law, occupies a prominent place in the Convention system of protection, as is underlined by the fact' that it is non-derogable. In the ECtHR's view, Article 7 should be construed 'in such a way as to provide effective safeguards against arbitrary prosecution, conviction and punishment': *Öcalan v Turkey (No 2)* nos 24069/03, 197/04, 6201/06, 10464/07 [2014] ECHR 286 [171]; *Scoppola v Italy (No 2)* [GC] no 10249/03 [2009] ECHR 1297 [92]; *SW v UK* no 20166/92 [1995] ECHR 52 [34]; *CR v UK* no 20190/92 [1995] ECHR 51 [32].

5.97 The ECtHR has generally held that deportation is not a 'penalty' within the meaning of Article 7 where it is taken in pursuance of 'the law on aliens' rather than criminal law (*Moustaquim v Belgium* no 12313/86 [1991] ECHR 3, (1991) 13 EHRR 802).[14] However, the prohibition on punishment without a law under Article 7 ECHR provides certain safeguards in the context of expulsion measures. In *Gurguchiani v Spain* no 16012/06 [2009] ECHR 2063, the ECtHR found that the replacement of an 18-month custodial sentence, which the applicant was still serving, with an expulsion measure together with a 10-year re-entry ban amounted to a 'penalty' in the sense of Article 7 ECHR (at [40]). The retrospective change of the penalty based on a new legal provision was thus in breach of Article 7 (at [43]–[44]).

5.98 The extraterritorial applicability of Article 7 was accepted by the ECtHR in *Szabo v Sweden* no 28578/03 (admissibility decision, 27 June 2006) and *Csoszanski v Sweden* no 22318/02 (admissibility decision, 27 June 2006), in which the ECtHR raised Article 7 ECHR of its own motion. Both cases concerned the transfer of sentenced Hungarian nationals from Sweden to Hungary under the Council of Europe Convention on the Transfer of Sentenced Persons 1983 and its Additional Protocol. The ECtHR considered whether a later release date upon transfer to Hungary would amount to the retrospective imposition of a heavier penalty contrary to Article 7 ECHR, not imposing a flagrancy threshold in the context of Article 7—while applying a flagrancy threshold to the Article 5 ECHR argument. The application was rejected on the basis that the transfer of the applicant to Hungary was not 'penal' in character and the transfer decisions did not amount to a 'penalty' within the meaning of Article 7 ECHR.

5.99 The ECtHR has also pronounced in a number of cases that war crimes and crimes against humanity are 'punishable according to the general principles of law recognised by civilised nations' and thus fall within the exception in Article 7(2) ECHR. In *Naletilić v Croatia* no 51891/99 (admissibility decision, 4 May 2000), it so held in the context of the transfer of a Croatian national from Croatia to the International Criminal Tribunal for the former Yugoslavia on charges of crimes against humanity and war crimes for which the maximum term of imprisonment was life imprisonment, rather than the applicable 20 years in Croatia for the murder and kidnapping charges he had faced there. Similarly, in *Marguš v Croatia* [GC] no 4455/10 [2014] ECHR 523, the ECtHR held that the conviction, in 2007, of a former commander of the Croatian army on account of war crimes committed against the civilian population in 1991 did not breach Article 7 ECHR, notwithstanding the applicant's ability to point to an amnesty. The ECtHR relied on a growing tendency in international law to see the granting of amnesties in respect of grave breaches of human rights as unacceptable.

---

[14] See also *R (otao MK (Iran)) v SSHD* [2010] EWCA Civ 115, [2010] 1 WLR 2059.

B11. Article 8 ECHR

A critical protection under the ECHR is the right to respect for private and family life under Article 8, which provides that: 5.100

1. Everyone has the right to respect for his private and family life, his home and his correspondence.
2. There shall be no interference by a public authority with the exercise of this right except such as is in accordance with the law and is necessary in a democratic society in the interests of national security, public safety or the economic well-being of the country, for the prevention of disorder or crime, for the protection of health or morals, or for the protection of the rights and freedoms of others.

Meaning of Private and Family Life

In the present context, the ECtHR tends to look primarily to private and/or family life, giving broad definitions to each of these. The ECtHR's case law distinguishes between family life which arises out of formal legal relations and de facto relationships. De jure family life includes the relationship between a married couple: *Abdulaziz, Cabales and Balkandali v UK* nos 9214/80, 9473/81, 9474/81 [1985] ECHR 7, (1985) 7 EHRR 471 [62]. The relationship between parents and their children born of a marriage constitutes family life from the moment, and by the very fact of, birth and only ceases in exceptional circumstances: *Boughanemi v France* no 22070/93 [1996] ECHR 19, (1996) 22 EHRR 228; *Berrehab v The Netherlands* no 10730/84 [1988] ECHR 14, (1989) 11 EHRR 322 [21]. This is and remains so irrespective of difficulties in the parent-child relationship and periods of non-cohabitation (*Moustaquim v Belgium* no 12313/86 [1991] ECHR 3, (1991) 13 EHRR 802 [36]) and includes relationships that have been separated voluntarily (*Sen v The Netherlands* no 31465/96 [2001] ECHR 888 [28]). A lawful and genuine adoption gives rise to family life: *Pini and others v Romania* nos 78028/01, 78030/01 [2004] ECHR 275, (2005) 40 EHRR 13 [148].[15] 5.101

Biological fathers and their children born out of wedlock enjoy de facto family life, where close personal ties exist based on the nature of the relationship between the natural parents and a demonstrable interest in and commitment by the father to the child both before and after the birth: *Nylund v Finland* no 27110/95 (admissibility decision, 29 June 1999); *Nekvedavcius v Germany* no 46165/99 (admissibility decision, 19 June 2003). Where a father has never met his child, the relationship between him and his child may fall within the meaning of private life, which includes the determination of paternity: *Anayo v Germany* no 20578/07 [2010] ECHR 2083, (2012) 55 EHRR 5 [58]–[59]. 5.102

Family life may continue where children reach majority, but still live with their parents: *Bousarra v France* no 25672/07 [2010] ECHR 1999 [38]–[39] (concerning a 5.103

---

[15] For domestic case law on de facto and formal adoption, see: *Mohamoud (Paras 352D and 309A—De Facto Adoption) Ethiopia* [2011] UKUT 378 (IAC); *MK (Somalia) and others v ECO* [2008] EWCA Civ 1453; *MN (Non-recognised Adoptions: Unlawful Discrimination?) India* [2007] UKAIT 00015; *AA v ECO (Addis Ababa)* [2013] UKSC 81; [2014] 1 All ER 774. Family life may exist between a child and a de facto parent where there has been a genuine transfer or parental responsibility and this requires an assessment of the factual situation (*Singh v ECO, Delhi* [2004] EWCA Civ 1075).

24-year-old applicant); *Kaya v Germany* no 31753/02 [2007] 2 FCR 527 [58] (concerning a 23-year-old imprisoned applicant); *AA v UK* no 8000/08 [2011] ECHR 1345 [46]–[50]. It normally ceases to exist where the child has founded a family of his or her own, even if he or she continues to live with parents: *Onur v UK* no 29696/07 [2009] ECHR 289 [43]–[45]; *AW Khan v UK* no 47486/06 [2010] ECHR 27, (2010) 50 EHRR 47 [32].

5.104 Article 8 also protects de facto family life between unmarried couples, the existence of which is a question of fact 'depending upon the real existence in practice of close personal ties': *K and T v Finland* no 25702/94 [2009] ECHR 289, (2001) 31 EHRR 18 [150]. Cohabitation is a pertinent but not necessary factor to demonstrate de facto family life: *Lebbink v The Netherlands* no 45582/99 [2004] ECHR 240, 40 EHRR 18 [36]. Additional relevant factors include the length of the relationship and whether the couple have demonstrated their commitment to each other by having children together or by other means: *Al-Nashif v Bulgaria* no 50963/99 [2002] ECHR 502 [112]. The relationship of a same-sex couple living in a stable de facto relationship now falls within the notion of family rather than private life: *Schalk and Kopf v Austria* no 30141/04 (24 June 2010) [93]–[94]:

> 93. The Court notes that since 2001, when the decision in *Mata Estevez* was given, a rapid evolution of social attitudes towards same-sex couples has taken place in many member States. Since then a considerable number of member States have afforded legal recognition to same-sex couples (see above, paragraphs 27–30). Certain provisions of EU law also reflect a growing tendency to include same-sex couples in the notion of 'family' (see paragraph 26 above).
>
> 94. In view of this evolution the Court considers it artificial to maintain the view that, in contrast to a different-sex couple, a same-sex couple cannot enjoy 'family life' for the purposes of Article 8. Consequently the relationship of the applicants, a cohabiting same-sex couple living in a stable de facto partnership, falls within the notion of 'family life', just as the relationship of a different-sex couple in the same situation would.

5.105 Whilst legal recognition of the relationship through registration of a civil partnership is not necessary for the existence of family life, civil partners may, like married couples, be treated differently from merely cohabiting couples: *Burden v UK* [GC] no 13378/05 [2008] ECHR 357, (2008) 47 EHRR 38 [65]:

> As with marriage, the Grand Chamber considers that the legal consequences of civil partnership under the 2004 Act, which couples expressly and deliberately decide to incur, set these types of relationship apart from other forms of co-habitation. Rather than the length or the supportive nature of the relationship, what is determinative is the existence of a public undertaking, carrying with it a body of rights and obligations of a contractual nature. Just as there can be no analogy between married and Civil Partnership Act couples, on one hand, and heterosexual or homosexual couples who choose to live together but not to become husband and wife or civil partners, on the other hand (see *Shackell*, cited above), the absence of such a legally binding agreement between the applicants renders their relationship of co-habitation, despite its long duration, fundamentally different to that of a married or civil partnership couple.

5.106 Family members who are not part of the 'core' family may also have family life within the meaning of Article 8(1). Family life 'includes at least the ties between near relatives, for instance those between grandparents and grandchildren, since such relatives may play a considerable part in family life': *Marckx v Belgium* no 6833/74 [1979] ECHR 2, (1979) 2 EHRR 330 [45]. The ECtHR has stressed that 'the mutual enjoyment ... by grandparent and child, of each other's company constitutes a fundamental element of family life': *L v Finland* no 25651/94 [2000] ECHR 176 [101]. Family life has further been found to exist between uncle and nephew where the father had died (*Boyle v UK* no 16580/90 (9 February 1993) [45]) and where the children had lived with their uncle and aunt for years (*Butt v Norway* no 47017/09 (4 December 2012) [76]).[16]

Intended family life may fall within the ambit of Article 8, particularly where the present lack of family life is not attributable to the applicant: *Pini and others v Romania* nos 78028/01, 78030/01 [2004] ECHR 275, (2005) 40 EHRR 13 [143]–[146].[17] **5.107**

Other relationships between adults, such as between adult siblings, normally require further elements of dependency involving 'more than the normal emotional ties': *Ezzouhdi v France* no 47160/99 (13 February 2001) [34]; *Konstatinov v The Netherlands* no 16351/03 [2007] ECHR 336 (26 April 2007) [52]; *Advic v UK* no 25525/94 [1995] ECHR 57, (1995) 20 EHRR CD125 (06 September 1995); *Samsonnikov v Estonia* no 52178/10 [2012] ECHR 1373 (3 July 2012) [81].[18] Close relationships 'short of "family life" would generally fall within the scope of "private life"': *Anayo v Germany* no 20578/07 [2010] ECHR 2083, (2012) 55 EHRR 5 [58] (concerning the relationship between an applicant father and his two children born out of wedlock with whom he had never had any contact). **5.108**

In relation to private life, the ECtHR has provided an equally inclusive assessment.[19] In *Niemietz v Germany* no 13710/88 [1992] ECHR 80, (1992) 16 EHRR 97, the ECtHR held that it would be too restrictive to limit 'private life' to an inner circle finding that it instead comprises 'the right to establish and develop relationships with other human beings' (at [29]). **5.109**

Private life within the meaning of Article 8 ECHR includes the right to self-determination (*Pretty v UK* no 2346/02 [2002] ECHR 427, (2002) EHRR 1 [61]), elements of one's identity, such as names (*Burghartz v Switzerland* no 16213/90 [1994] ECHR 2, (1994) 18 EHRR 101 [24]) gender identification, sexual orientation and sexual life (*Dudgeon v UK* no 7525/76 [1981] ECHR 5, (1981) 4 EHRR 149 [41]; *Laskey, Jaggard and Brown v UK* nos 21627/93, 21826/93, 21974/93 [1997] ECHR 4, (1997) 24 EHRR 39 [36]) and the right to respect equally for decisions to have or not to have a child (*Evans v UK* [GC] no 6339/05 [2006] ECHR 200, (2006) 43 EHRR 21 [71]). **5.110**

---

[16] The House of Lords summarised this in *Huang v SSHD* [2007] UKHL 11; [2007] 2 AC 167 [18]: 'Human beings are social animals. They depend on others. Their family, or extended family, is the group on which many people most heavily depend, socially, emotionally and often financially ... Matters such as the age, health and vulnerability of the applicant, the closeness and previous history of the family, the applicant's dependence on the financial and emotional support of the family, the prevailing cultural tradition and conditions in the country of origin and many other factors may all be relevant.'

[17] In the domestic context, see *R (Fawad Ahmadi) v SSHD* [2005] EWCA Civ 1721, [2005] All ER (D) 169 (Dec).

[18] See also the domestic cases of *Kugathas v SSHD* [2003] EWCA Civ 31; *ZB (Pakistan) v SSHD* [2009] EWCA Civ 834, [42], finding dependency in the case of 'an insulin dependent diabetic who needs to be cared for and who is either wholly or largely financially dependent on her family in the UK'; *MT (Zimbabwe) v SSHD* [2007] EWCA Civ 455, [paras 12]–[-13], finding family life between adult cousins given the 'length of Ms M T's ties with her cousin, dating back to when she became an orphan at the age of 14; the long integration in his family from an early and vulnerable age; the cultural norm in the society that she came from for young adult females to remain in the family home; and, on any view, the shared experiences in Zimbabwe'.

[19] See also *Razgar* [2004] UKHL 27; [2004] 2 AC 368; [9]: 'It is plain that "private life" is a broad term, and the Court has wisely eschewed any attempt to define it comprehensively.'

Part B – Legal Framework

5.111　A large majority of migrants facing expulsion or exclusion will likely have established a private life for the purposes of Article 8 ECHR. The Grand Chamber in *Üner v The Netherlands* [GC] no 46410/99 [2006] ECHR 873, (2007) 45 EHRR 14 [59] held that: 'Regardless of the existence or otherwise of a "family life" ... the expulsion of a settled migrant constitutes interference with his or her right to respect for private life.' Private life was found to encompass the 'totality of social ties between settled migrants and the community in which they are living': *Üner v The Netherlands*, at [59]; *Omojudi v UK* no 1820/08 [2009] ECHR 1942, (2010) 51 EHRR 10 [36].[20]

5.112　Eviction from one's home in the context of removal may also constitute an interference with another matter protected by Article 8(1) ECHR, namely his or her 'home': *Slivenko v Latvia* [GC] no 48321/99 [2003] ECHR 498, (2004) 39 EHRR 24 [96].

5.113　The ECtHR has accepted that health and a person's physical and moral integrity also form part of private life. In *Bensaid v UK* no 44599/98 [2001] ECHR 82, (2001) 33 EHRR 10 [47], the Court held that: 'Mental health must also be regarded as a crucial part of private life associated with the aspect of moral integrity. Article 8 protects a right to identity and personal development, and the right to establish and develop relationships with other human beings and the outside world.' The ECtHR in *Pretty v UK* no 2346/02 [2002] ECHR 427, (2002) EHRR 1 [61] confirmed this approach by holding that private life extended to 'the physical and psychological integrity of a person'. However, in *Patel and others v SSHD* [2013] UKSC 72, [2014] 1 All ER 1157, Lord Carnwath, with whom Lords Kerr, Reed and Hughes agreed, observed at [57] that Article 8 ECHR did not encompass a right to presence in the UK for the purpose of education, distinct from private or family life:

> It is important to remember that Article 8 is not a general dispensing power. It is to be distinguished from the Secretary of State's discretion to allow leave to remain outside the rules, which may be unrelated to any protected human right. The merits of a decision not to depart from the rules are not reviewable on appeal: section 86(6). One may sympathise with Sedley LJ's call in [*Secretary of State for the Home Department v Pankina* [2010] EWCA Civ 719, [2011] 1 QB 376] for 'common sense' in the application of the rules to graduates who have been studying in the UK for some years (see para 47 above). However, such considerations do not by themselves provide grounds of appeal under Article 8, which is concerned with private or family life, not education as such. The opportunity for a promising student to complete his course in this country, however desirable in general terms, is not in itself a right protected under Article 8.

5.114　The factors to be examined in order to assess the proportionality of the deportation measure are the same regardless of whether family or private life is engaged: *Üner v The Netherlands* [GC] no 46410/99 [2006] ECHR 873, (2007) 45 EHRR 14 [59].[21] The ECtHR therefore sometimes refrains from classifying relationships as family or private life: *AA v UK* no 8000/08 [2011] ECHR 1345 [49]; *Omojudi v UK* no 1820/08 [2009] ECHR 1942, (2010) 51 EHRR 10 [36] and [45] (refraining from classifying the applicant's

---

[20] In the domestic context, education (*CDS* [2010] UKUT 305 (IAC); [2011] Imm AR 126), employment (*Janjanin v SSHD* [2004] EWCA Civ 448; [2004] Imm AR 264) and contributions to the community beyond employment (*UE (Nigeria)* [2010] EWCA Civ 975; [2012] 1 WLR 127) have been recognised as constituting private life.

[21] In the domestic context, it has also been held that the same analysis of Article 8 ECHR applies in cases involving private life as applies in cases involving family life: *JN (Uganda) v SSHD* [2007] EWCA Civ 802; *HM (Iraq) v SSHD* [2010] EWCA Civ 1322, requiring a detailed balancing exercise in a private life case.

relationship to his adult son and granddaughter, but taking it into account as relevant factor as regards proportionality); *Maslov v Austria* [GC] no 1638/03 [2008] ECHR 546, [2009] INLR 47 [63].

Leading Authorities in the UK

5.115 A substantial body of authority has now come into being in the UK concerning the way in which Article 8 ECHR cases should be handled. In *R (Razgar) v SSHD* [2004] UKHL 27, [2004] 2 AC 368, Lord Bingham at [17] identified five questions to be addressed in Article 8 ECHR case:

> In considering whether a challenge to the Secretary of State's decision to remove a person must clearly fail, the reviewing court must, as it seems to me, consider how an appeal would be likely to fare before an adjudicator, as the tribunal responsible for deciding the appeal if there were an appeal. This means that the reviewing court must ask itself essentially the questions which would have to be answered by an adjudicator. In a case where removal is resisted in reliance on Article 8, these questions are likely to be:
>
> (1) Will the proposed removal be an interference by a public authority with the exercise of the applicant's right to respect for his private or (as the case may be) family life?
> (2) If so, will such interference have consequences of such gravity as potentially to engage the operation of Article 8?
> (3) If so, is such interference in accordance with the law?
> (4) If so, is such interference necessary in a democratic society in the interests of national security, public safety or the economic well-being of the country, for the prevention of disorder or crime, for the protection of health or morals, or for the protection of the rights and freedoms of others?
> (5) If so, is such interference proportionate to the legitimate public end sought to be achieved?

5.116 As to the second question, in *AG (Eritrea) v SSHD* [2007] EWCA Civ 801, [2008] 2 All ER 28 [28], Sedley LJ, delivering the judgment of the court (the other members of the panel being Maurice Kay and Lawrence Collins LJJ), confirmed as regards the second question raised by Lord Bingham in *Razgar* that:

> It follows, in our judgment, that while an interference with private or family life must be real if it is to engage art. 8(1), the threshold of engagement (the 'minimum level') is not a specially high one. Once the Article is engaged, the focus moves, as Lord Bingham's remaining questions indicate, to the process of justification under art. 8(2). It is this which, in all cases which engage Article 8(1), will determine whether there has been a breach of the article.

5.117 In *Huang v SSHD; Kashmiri v SSHD* [2007] UKHL 11, [2007] 2 AC 167, the House revisited the issue. At [16]–[17], the Committee, *per* Lord Bingham, rejected the proposition that it should give deference to the view taken of the facts by the Secretray of State. At [20], it concluded that:

> In an Article 8 case where this question is reached, the ultimate question for the appellate immigration authority is whether the refusal of leave to enter or remain, in circumstances where the life of the family cannot reasonably be expected to be enjoyed elsewhere, taking full account of all considerations weighing in favour of the refusal, prejudices the family life of the applicant in a manner sufficiently serious to amount to a breach of the fundamental right protected by Article 8. If the answer to this question is affirmative, the refusal is unlawful and the authority must so decide. It is not necessary that the appellate immigration authority, directing itself

Part B – Legal Framework

along the lines indicated in this opinion, need ask in addition whether the case meets a test of exceptionality. The suggestion that it should is based on an observation of Lord Bingham in *Razgar* above, para 20. He was there expressing an expectation, shared with the Immigration Appeal Tribunal, that the number of claimants not covered by the Rules and supplementary directions but entitled to succeed under Article 8 would be a very small minority. That is still his expectation. But he was not purporting to lay down a legal test.

5.118 In *Patel and others v SSHD* [2013] UKSC 72, [2014] 1 All ER 1157, Lord Carnwath, with whom Lords Kerr, Reed and Hughes agreed, referred at [54] to the treatment in *Huang* of the failure to satisfy the Immigration Rules:

> The most authoritative guidance on the correct approach of the tribunal to Article 8 remains that of Lord Bingham in *Huang*. In the passage cited by Burnton LJ Lord Bingham observed that the rules are designed to identify those to whom 'on grounds such as kinship and family relationship and dependence' leave to enter should be granted, and that such rules 'to be administratively workable, require that a line be drawn somewhere'. But that was no more than the starting point for the consideration of Article 8. Thus in Mrs Huang's own case, the most relevant rule (rule 317) was not satisfied, since she was not, when the decision was made, aged 65 or over and she was not a widow. He commented at para 6:
>
> > Such a rule, which does not lack a rational basis, is not to be stigmatised as arbitrary or objectionable. But an applicant's failure to qualify under the rules is for present purposes the point at which to begin, not end, consideration of the claim under Article 8. The terms of the rules are relevant to that consideration, but they are not determinative.

At [56], he rejected the submission that that approach could 'be equated with a formalised 'near-miss' or 'sliding scale' principle', as:

> [U]nsupported by Strasbourg authority, or by a proper reading of Lord Bingham's words. Mrs Huang's case for favourable treatment outside the rules did not turn on how close she had come to compliance with rule 317, but on the application of the family values which underlie that rule and are at the heart also of Article 8. Conversely, a near-miss under the rules cannot provide substance to a human rights case which is otherwise lacking in merit.

5.119 In *EB (Kosovo)* [2008] UKHL 41, [2009] 1 AC 1159, Lord Bingham at [12] observed that (emphasis added):

> [T]he appellate immigration authority must make its own judgment and that judgment will be strongly influenced by the particular facts and circumstances of the particular case. The authority will, of course, take note of factors which have, or have not, weighed with the Strasbourg court. *It will, for example, recognise that it will rarely be proportionate to uphold an order for removal of a spouse if there is a close and genuine bond with the other spouse and that spouse cannot reasonably be expected to follow the removed spouse to the country of removal, or if the effect of the order is to sever a genuine and subsisting relationship between parent and child. But cases will not ordinarily raise such stark choices, and there is in general no alternative to making a careful and informed evaluation of the facts of the particular case. The search for a hard-edged or bright-line rule to be applied to the generality of cases is incompatible with the difficult evaluative exercise which Article 8 requires.*

5.120 Finally, in *VW (Uganda)* [2009] EWCA Civ 5, [2009] INLR 295, the Court of Appeal, elucidating the meaning of the speeches given in their Lordships' House on appeal in *EB (Kosovo)*, concluded that the treatment of Lord Phillips' earlier reference to 'insurmountable obstacle' in deciding *R (Mahmood) v SSHD* [2000] EWCA 315, [2001]

1 WLR 840 did not identify a concrete test a concrete test. Sedley LJ, delivering the judgment of the Court, said:

> 24. *EB (Kosovo)* now confirms that the material question in gauging the proportionality of a removal or deportation which will or may break up a family unless the family itself decamps is not whether there is an insuperable obstacle to this happening but whether it is reasonable to expect the family to leave with the appellant.

B12. Time of Assessment

In Article 8 ECHR, cases it used to be the ECtHR's approach to take the date of the decision as the relevant date of assessment. However, the ECtHR recognised in *AA v UK* no 8000/08 [2011] ECHR 1345 [67] the need to assess an expulsion order under Article 8 by reference to the facts known to the ECtHR at the time of the proceedings before it but postdating domestic proceedings, provided the applicant has not yet been expelled. Where expulsion has already taken place, the case will be assessed by reference to the facts which were known or ought to have been known to the authorities on the date of removal.

5.121

B13. Interference, in Accordance with the Law and Legitimate Aim

The question whether an interference has taken place is not affected by ex post facto developments. Where an immigrant was initially removed but later granted a residence permit, an interference had still taken place: *De Souza Ribeiro v France* no 22689/07 [2012] ECHR 2066 [91]–[99].

5.122

The failure to provide a lawfully present applicant with a residence permit constitutes an interference with the person's rights under Article 8 ECHR, where the lack of a permit has ramifications for the applicant's employment and social situation and his or her ability to rent a flat: *Aristimuño Mendizabal v France* no 1431/99 [2006] ECHR 34 [70]–[72]. Article 8 does not, however, guarantee the right to a particular residence permit where domestic legislation provides for different possible types of permit, provided regularisation removes any real and imminent risk of deportation: *Sisojeva v Latvia* [GC] no 60654/00 [2007] ECHR 16, (2007) 45 EHRR 33 [91], [98]–[100]; *Ibrahim Mohammed v The Netherlands* no 1872/04 (10 March 2009, struck out of list).[22]

5.123

In assessing whether an interference is 'in accordance with the law', the ECtHR draws on the general principles developed in relation to 'lawfulness' under the Convention. Not only does this require a basis in domestic law, it also implies certain requirements as to the quality of the law, including its foreseeability and accessibility. Where the relevant law, procedures and practice do not offer even a minimum degree of protection against arbitrariness, they do not meet the requisite standard of 'the law': *Al-Nashif v Bulgaria* no 50963/99 [2002] ECHR 502; *M and others v Bulgaria* no 41416/08 (26 July 2011) [96]; *Lupsa v Romania* no 10337/04 (8 June 2006) [32]–[34]. Thus, unfettered discretion

5.124

---

[22] An undertaking not to remove someone is insufficient: *MS (Ivory Coast) v SSHD* [2007] EWCA Civ 133.

or discretion without effective judicial control is not in accordance with the law: *Liu and Liu v Russia* no 42086/05 [2007] ECHR 1056, (2008) 47 EHRR 33 [56], [60]–[61].

5.125 In a number of Bulgarian cases, the ECtHR found the requirement of 'lawfulness' not to be met, because of an excessively deferential approach in national security cases: *CG and others v Bulgaria* no 1365/07 [2008] ECHR 349, (2008) 47 EHRR 51 [42]–[47]; *Madah and others v Bulgaria* no 45237/08 [2012] ECHR 821 [28]–[29] (the ECtHR also found a violation of Article 13 ECHR). Similarly, the ECtHR found that Slovenian legislation and administrative practice underlying a deprivation of the right of residence was lacking the requisite standards of foreseeability and accessibility on account of the failure to give the applicants an opportunity to challenge the automatic erasure and provide reasons for it: *Kurić and others v Slovenia* [GC] no 26828/06 [2012] ECHR 1083, (2013) 56 EHRR 20 [343]–[348]. The ECtHR attached considerable weight to the prior finding of the domestic Constitutional Court that the deprivation of residence rights was incompatible with domestic law.

5.126 The requirement for an interference to be 'in accordance with the law' includes an assessment as to whether the interference is in accordance with the applicant's rights under EU law: *Aristimuño Mendizabal v France* no 1431/99 [2006] ECHR 34 [79].

5.127 The state must not interfere with the exercise of Article 8 rights except in accordance with an exhaustive list of legitimate aims, namely: 'in the interests of national security, public safety or the economic well-being of the country, for the prevention of disorder or crime, for the protection of health or morals, or for the protection of the rights and freedoms of others'.

5.128 In expulsion cases, where a person is unlawfully present or no longer satisfies the requirements of the Immigration Rules, the legitimate aim will usually be 'the interests of … the economic well-being of the country' through maintaining a system of effective immigration control. It will otherwise be 'in the interests of … national security', 'for the prevention of disorder or crime' or for the 'protection of health and morals': see *AW Khan v UK* no 47486/06 [2010] ECHR 27, (2010) 50 EHRR 47 [38]. Where removal is in pursuance of a lawful immigration policy, generally the question of the existence of a legitimate aim will be answered in the affirmative.[23]

5.129 The balancing of the fundamental rights to family and private life against the public interest in favour of expulsion possesses is in many cases an inherent difficulty due to the difference in nature between these. Proportionality under Article 8 ECHR may require the weighing against each other of important incommensurable interests.[24] The ECtHR has recognised that Contracting Parties enjoy a certain margin of appreciation in assessing whether an expulsion measure would be disproportionate: *Berrehab v The Netherlands* no 10730/84 [1988] ECHR 14, (1989) 11 EHRR 322 [28]. Nevertheless, it is the ECtHR's task to assess whether the domestic courts have struck a fair balance between the competing interests at stake: *Boultif v Switzerland* no 54273/00 [2001] ECHR 497, (2001) 33 EHRR 50 [47]. The doctrine of margin of appreciation only

---

[23] For an example of a case which succeeded on the basis of legitimate aim, see *A (Afghanistan) v SSHD* [2009] EWCA Civ 825.

[24] See, eg, the observations of Lord Mance in *HH, PH and F-K HH v Deputy Prosecutor of the Italian Republic, Genoa; HP v Same; F-K v Polish Judicial Authority* [2012] UKSC 25; [2013] 1 AC 338; [103]: 'The difficulty is not just that the considerations on each side are powerful and conflicting, but that they are entirely different in nature. Balancing them against each other is inherently problematic.'

relates to the interplay between the ECtHR and the domestic courts, not to relations between different domestic state organs: *A and others v UK* [GC] no 3455/05 [2009] ECHR 301, (2009) 49 EHRR 29 [184].

Proportionality: Relevant Factors

The ECtHR's case law has developed significantly since the seminal judgment in *Abdulaziz, Cabales and Balkandali v UK* nos 9214/80; 9473/81; 9474/81 [1985] ECHR 7, (1985) 7 EHRR 471, which held that measures of immigration control must be compatible with Article 8 ECHR. **5.130**

The leading cases on expulsion following substantial residence in the host state are *Boultif v Switzerland* no 54273/00 [2001] ECHR 497, (2001) 33 EHRR 50 and *Üner v The Netherlands* [GC] no 46410/99 [2006] ECHR 873, (2007) 45 EHRR 14 [57]–[59].[25] Whilst *Boultif* and *Üner* were both deportation cases, many of the factors apply equally (with necessary adaptation) in non-deportation cases: *Hasanbasic v Switzerland* no 2166/09 [2013] ECHR 520 [55]. The following 10 factors have been given express recognition in *Üner* (at [57]–[59]) as relevant to the assessment of weight attached to a person's private or family life in a proportionality assessment: **5.131**

> 57. ... In the case of *Boultif* the Court elaborated the relevant criteria which it would use in order to assess whether an expulsion measure was necessary in a democratic society and proportionate to the legitimate aim pursued. These criteria, as reproduced in paragraph 40 of the Chamber judgment in the present case, are the following:
>
> — the nature and seriousness of the offence committed by the applicant;
> — the length of the applicant's stay in the country from which he or she is to be expelled;
> — the time elapsed since the offence was committed and the applicant's conduct during that period;
> — the nationalities of the various persons concerned;
> — the applicant's family situation, such as the length of the marriage, and other factors expressing the effectiveness of a couple's family life;
> — whether the spouse knew about the offence at the time when he or she entered into a family relationship;
> — whether there are children of the marriage, and if so, their age; and
> — the seriousness of the difficulties which the spouse is likely to encounter in the country to which the applicant is to be expelled.
>
> 58. The Court would wish to make explicit two criteria which may already be implicit in those identified in the *Boultif* judgment:
>
> — the best interests and well-being of the children, in particular the seriousness of the difficulties which any children of the applicant are likely to encounter in the country to which the applicant is to be expelled; and
> — the solidity of social, cultural and family ties with the host country and with the country of destination.

---

[25] The *Üner* criteria have been approved by the domestic courts; see, eg, *KB (Trinidad and Tobago) v SSHD* [2010] EWCA Civ 11, [2010] 1 WLR 1630 (Richards LJ).

As to the first point, the Court notes that this is already reflected in its existing case law (see, for example, *en v. The Netherlands*, no. 31465/96, § 40, 21 December 2001, *Tuquabo-Tekle and Others v. The Netherlands*, no. 60665/00, § 47, 1 December 2005) and is in line with the Committee of Ministers' Recommendation Rec(2002)4 on the legal status of persons admitted for family reunification (see paragraph 38 above).

As to the second point, it is to be noted that, although the applicant in the case of *Boultif* was already an adult when he entered Switzerland, the Court has held the '*Boultif* criteria' to apply all the more so (*à plus forte raison*) to cases concerning applicants who were born in the host country or who moved there at an early age (see *Mokrani v. France*, no. 52206/99, § 31, 15 July 2003). Indeed, the rationale behind making the duration of a person's stay in the host country one of the elements to be taken into account lies in the assumption that the longer a person has been residing in a particular country the stronger his or her ties with that country and the weaker the ties with the country of his or her nationality will be. Seen against that background, it is self-evident that the Court will have regard to the special situation of aliens who have spent most, if not all, their childhood in the host country, were brought up there and received their education there.

59. The Court considered itself called upon to establish 'guiding principles' in the *Boultif* case because it had 'only a limited number of decided cases where the main obstacle to expulsion was that it would entail difficulties for the spouses to stay together and, in particular, for one of them and/or the children to live in the other's country of origin' (op. cit., § 48). It is to be noted, however, that the first three guiding principles do not, as such, relate to family life. This leads the Court to consider whether the '*Boultif* criteria' are sufficiently comprehensive to render them suitable for application in all cases concerning the expulsion and/or exclusion of settled migrants following a criminal conviction. It observes in this context that not all such migrants, no matter how long they have been residing in the country from which they are to be expelled, necessarily enjoy 'family life' there within the meaning of Article 8. However, as Article 8 also protects the right to establish and develop relationships with other human beings and the outside world (see *Pretty v. United Kingdom*, no. 2346/02, § 61, ECHR 2002-III) and can sometimes embrace aspects of an individual's social identity (see *Mikulić v. Croatia*, no. 53176/99, §53, ECHR 2002-I), it must be accepted that the totality of social ties between settled migrants and the community in which they are living constitute part of the concept of 'private life' within the meaning of Article 8. Regardless of the existence or otherwise of a 'family life', therefore, the Court considers that the expulsion of a settled migrant constitutes interference with his or her right to respect for private life. It will depend on the circumstances of the particular case whether it is appropriate for the Court to focus on the 'family life' rather than the 'private life' aspect.

5.132 In *Maslov v Austria* [GC] no 1638/03 [2008] ECHR 546, [2009] INLR 47 [63], the ECtHR indicated that in cases involving minors and young adults who have not founded a family of their own, a reduced range of the *Boultif/Üner* criteria will apply, consistently with the differences between the situation of a minor or young adult, on the one hand, and that of an older adult, possibly with a family of his or her own, on the other. The applicant in *Maslov* had entered Austria lawfully at the age of six. Although he had committed a large number of offences when he was 14 and 15 years of age and had been sentenced to a total of two years and nine months' imprisonment, it was held at [100] that his deportation to Bulgaria, his country of nationality, represented a violation of Article 8 ECHR:

100. Having regard to the foregoing considerations, in particular the—with one exception— non-violent nature of the offences committed when a minor and the State's duty to facilitate his reintegration into society, the length of the applicant's lawful residence in Austria, his family,

social and linguistic ties with Austria and the lack of proven ties with his country of origin, the Court finds that the imposition of an exclusion order, even of a limited duration, was disproportionate to the legitimate aim pursued, 'the prevention of disorder or crime'. It was therefore not 'necessary in a democratic society'.

In examining the proportionality of exclusion, the ECtHR at [71] identified four factors (the first through third in the *Üner* list and the final factor in the extended list, namely solidity of social, cultural and family ties with each relevant country) as particularly relevant in such cases. It went on to underline the importance of the applicant's age in the analysis, including the age at which the offending occurred and the age at which the applicant came to the host country: 'when assessing the nature and seriousness of the offences committed by an applicant, it has to be taken into account whether he or she committed them as a juvenile or as an adult' (at [72]). Similarly, when assessing the solidity of the social, cultural and family ties with the host country, 'it evidently makes a difference whether the person concerned had already come to the country during his or her childhood or youth, or was even born there, or whether he or she only came as an adult' (at [73]). According to the Court, 'the special situation of aliens who have spent most, if not all, their childhood in the host country, were brought up there and received their education there' must be given particular weight (at [74]).

5.133

In a case to which *Maslov* principles apply, it is therefore established that the youth of the individual who has not yet formed his or her own family unit does not support the treatment of his or her private or family life as having less weight than in another case. On the contrary, in the range of cases covered by the ECtHR's guidance in *Maslov*, it is firmly established that in the case of a settled migrant or so-called 'second-generation immigrant' who has spent all or the majority of his or her childhood in the host country, 'very serious reasons are required to justify expulsion': *Maslov v Austria* [GC] no 1638/03; ECHR 2008, [2009] INLR 47 [75]; *Balogun v UK* no 60286/09 [2012] ECHR 614, (2013) 56 EHRR 3 [46]; *AW Khan v UK* no 47486/06 [2010] ECHR 27, (2010) 50 EHRR 47 [37]. The standard of very serious reasons to justify deportation in cases involving second-generation immigrants is thus a high one. Rape committed as a 17 year old was capable of justifying deportation due to the seriousness of the offence, notwithstanding the age of the criminal: *Bouchelkia v France* no 23078/93 [1997] ECHR 1, (1997) 25 EHRR 686 [51]. By contrast, the Court found that deportation was not justified by the seriousness of the offence in the case of a youth who had come to the UK aged 13 and committed rape at the age of 15: *AA v UK* no 8000/08 [2011] ECHR 1345. In *AA* the low risk of reoffending (at [63]) together with the applicant's 'exemplary conduct' and his 'commendable efforts to rehabilitate himself and to reintegrate into society over a period of seven years' (at [68]) led the Court to conclude that deportation would be disproportionate and contrary to Article 8 ECHR. Similarly, in the case of a conviction for importation of a significant quantity of heroin resulting in a seven-year custodial sentence, the lack of the applicant's ties to the home country and the applicant's good conduct since the offence was material to the Court's finding that the deportation of the applicant who had come to the UK aged three would be disproportionate: *AW Khan v UK* no 47486/06 [2010] ECHR 27, (2010) 50 EHRR 47 [50].

5.134

The factors identified variously in *Üner* and *Maslov* are not exhaustive of potential relevancies and represent an identification of the factors most commonly encountered and therefore recognised in decisions. Their identification, however, should be seen

5.135

Part B – Legal Framework

as an aid to a broadly based assessment of the relevant facts, of the type identified as necessary by Lord Bingham in *EB (Kosovo)* [2008] UKHL 41, [2009] 1 AC 1159 at [12]:

> [C]ases will not ordinarily raise such stark choices, and there is in general no alternative to making a careful and informed evaluation of the facts of the particular case. The search for a hard-edged or bright-line rule to be applied to the generality of cases is incompatible with the difficult evaluative exercise which Article 8 requires.

Some factors not expressly cited in the earlier guidance cases, or not cited in the lists set out in those decisions, have been recognised as relevant to proportionality. One is the medical position of the subject or of affected family members. Another is the duration, legal character and overall form of an exclusion order preventing return. Those factors are addressed below, after an examination of the factors cited in *Üner*.

The Nature and Seriousness of the Offence and Time Elapsed Since its Commission

5.136 The ECtHR assesses the gravity of the offending behaviour, where possible assessing the reasons for a sentence given by the criminal court: *Üner v The Netherlands* [GC] no 46410/99 [2006] ECHR 873, (2007) 45 EHRR 14 [63] ('As to the criminal conviction which led to the impugned measures, the Court is of the view that the offences of manslaughter and assault committed by the applicant were of a very serious nature'); *Kaya v Germany* no 31753/02 [2007] ECHR 538, [2007] Imm AR 802 at [62]:

> With regard to the nature and gravity of the offences committed by the applicant, the Court notes that these were very serious, including two attempts of aggravated trafficking in human beings, of procuration and of several counts of battery. The domestic courts put special emphasis on the exceptional brutality with which the applicant had abused his victims, one of which having been his former partner. They further found that the applicant's offences demonstrated that he had not been willing to respect the rights and dignity of his fellow human beings. Insofar as the applicant, in his written submissions before the Court, attempted to shift responsibility for the jointly committed offences towards the co-defendant, the Court notes that the District Court, in its judgment, had identified the applicant himself as the driving force behind the actions. Although the applicant was twenty years of age when committing those criminal offences and did not have a previous criminal record, their nature and gravity exclude the possibility to regard them as mere examples of juvenile delinquency. Accordingly, the District Court did not find any reason to apply juvenile law to the applicant's deeds. The relatively moderate prison sentence of three years and four months was, according to the District Court, only owed to the fact that the applicant had confessed his crimes during the main hearing.

5.137 As the example from *Kaya* illustrates, in assessing the gravity of the offence, the ECtHR takes into account the domestic criminal court's assessment of the offending behaviour and the sentence imposed: *Ezzouhdi v France* no 47160/99 (13 February 2001) [34]; *Yildiz v Austria* no 37295/97 (2003) 36 EHRR 32 [45]; *Mokrani v France* no 52206/99 (2005) 40 EHRR 5 [32]; *Bousarra v France* no 25672/07 [45]. A lenient sentence imposed by the domestic criminal court is pertinent to counter the government's submission as to the gravity of the offence: *Keles v Germany* no 32231/02 [2005] ECHR 950 [59] (concerning a road traffic offence).[26] The Court also pays attention to suspension of a significant part

---

[26] See *HK (Turkey) v SSHD* [2010] EWCA Civ 583; [28] (Sedley LJ).

of the custodial sentence where this is not automatic: *Radovanovic v Austria* no 42703/98 (2005) 41 EHRR 6 [34]: 'In the present case, despite the shorter duration of the applicant's stay in Austria the Court attaches considerable weight to the fact that although the applicant was convicted of aggravated robbery, he was only sentenced to a six-month unconditional term of imprisonment, whereas twenty-four months were suspended on probation.'

The Court places particular weight on the gravity of certain categories of offending. Violent offending is one of these (*Boujlifa v France* no 25404/94 [1997] ECHR 83, (1997) 30 EHRR 419 [44]; *Kaya v Germany* no 31753/02 [2007] ECHR 538, [2007] Imm AR 802 [62]), and even within this category it views certain forms of violent offending, such as serious instances of domestic violence, as of additionally heightened concern: *Shala v Switzerland* no 52873/09 [2012] ECHR 1931 [51]; *Palanci v Switzerland* no 53080/07 [2014] ECHR 311 [57].

5.138

Another area of heightened sensitivity is that of offending related to the import and/or distribution of drugs. In this area the Court has also held that 'it understands why the authorities show great firmness' regarding such offences and their commission weighs heavily against an applicant: *El Boujaïdi v France* no 25613/94 [1997] ECHR 76, [2000] 30 EHRR 223 [40]; *Baghli v France* no 34374/97 [1999] ECHR 135 [48]; *Dalia v France* no 26102/95 [1998] ECHR 5 [54]; however, see *AW Khan v UK* no 47486/06 [2010] ECHR 27, (2010) 50 EHRR 47 [40]; *Samsonnikov v Estonia* no 52178/10 [2012] ECHR 1373 (3 July 2012) [89]. The fact of offending within a category of particular concern is relevant even in a 'second-generation immigrant' case to which *Maslov* applies. *Radovanovic v Austria* no 42703/98 (2005) 41 EHRR 6 [34] was a case in which the ECtHR expanded on the seriousness attaching to drugs offences as a category, but found expulsion disproportionate on the particular facts, including the relatively short sentence, with a substantial part thereof suspended:

5.139

> The Court considers the present case needs to be distinguished from a number of cases concerning the expulsion of second generation immigrants, in which the Court found no violation of Article 8 of the Convention (see *Boujlifa v. France*, judgment of 21 October 1997, *Reports* 1997-VI, p. 2264, §42; *Bouchelkia v. France*, judgment of 29 January 1997, *Reports* 1997-I, p. 65, §§50–51; *El Boujaïdi v. France*, judgment of 26 September 1997, *Reports* 1997-I, p. 63, §§40–41; and *Dalia*, cited above, p. 92, §§53–54). These cases all involved second generation immigrants who arrived in the host country at an early age and were convicted of serious offences with lengthy terms of unconditional imprisonment. Furthermore, they concerned drug offences, the kind of offence, for which the Court has shown understanding of domestic authorities' firmness with regard to those who actively contribute to its spread (see *C. v. Belgium*, 7 August 1996, *Reports* 1996-III, p. 924, §35; *Dalia*, cited above, p. 92, §54, *Baghli v. France*, no. 34374/97, 30 November 1999, §48 *in fine*, ECHR 1999-VIII; and *Yilmaz v. Germany*, no. 52853/99, §46, 17 April 2003).

The frequency and duration of the offending behaviour is also pertinent. Where a series of offences has been committed over a significant period of time, even if they are non-violent offences such as aggravated immigration offences, this may weigh heavily against an applicant (*Antwi v Norway* no 26940/10 [2012] ECHR 259 [90]) and the ECtHR has accepted the legitimacy of enforcement action taken through immigration law rather than by criminal proceedings: see *Nunez v Norway* no 55597/09 [2011] ECHR 1047, (2014) 58 EHRR 17 [71]–[73].

5.140

While the Court recognises drug addiction as a mitigating factor in relation to acquisitive crime (*Miah v UK* no 53080/07 (admissibility decision, 27 April 2010; [25]), it has been reluctant to find deportation disproportionate where the drug-related offending

5.141

has continued over a long period of time and little time has elapsed since the most recent offence: *Joseph Grant v UK* no 10606/07 [2009] ECHR 26 [39]–[40].

5.142　Where deportation is based on the commission of a single offence, that offence may need to be particularly serious in order to justify deportation, but this may more readily be shown in relation to violence and serious drugs offences: *Bouchelkia v France* no 23078/93 [1997] ECHR 1, (1997) 25 EHRR 686 [51].

The Length of the Applicant's Stay in the Country from which He or She is to Be Expelled

5.143　The length of an applicant's stay in the territory of the Contracting Party is a particularly pertinent factor: for instance, see *Üner v The Netherlands* [GC] no 46410/99 [2006] ECHR 873, (2007) 45 EHRR 14 [57]; *Maslov v Austria* [GC] no 1638/03 [2008] ECHR 546, [2009] INLR 47 [71]. In the case of a lawful stay of 23 and 40 years of the applicants, the Court held that it was for the state to 'convincingly establish relevant and sufficient reasons' for the claim to a pressing social need for the continued exclusion of the applicants, who wished to return to Switzerland after failure to resettle successfully in the country of origin: *Hasanbasic v Switzerland* no 2166/09 [2013] ECHR 520 [57].

5.144　Different considerations, however, attach to unlawful presence. Applicants who have only remained in the territory of a Contracting Party illegally or entered as tourists and then overstayed cannot normally rely on the length of their illegal stay. The removal of an applicant who had lived in the UK for 10 years without any leave to remain was thus justified under Article 8 ECHR in *Nnyanzi v UK* no 21878/06 [2008] ECHR 282: see also *Nunez v Norway* no 55597/09 [2011] ECHR 1047, (2014) 58 EHRR 17 [67] and [72]; *Antwi v Norway* no 26940/10 [2012] ECHR 259 [89]. Similarly, a refused asylum-seeker who has never after the refusal of his or her asylum claim had lawful status cannot rely on the ties formed during his stay to the extent which would be possible had the stay been lawful: *Omoregie v Norway* no 265/07 [2008] ECHR 761, [2009] Imm AR 170.

5.145　An intermediate status attaches to presence which is not unlawful, but which does not reflect the official recognition of a right to stay or reside. Temporary admission or 'tolerated' status falls into this category. In *Aponte v The Netherlands* no 28770/05 [2011] ECHR 1850, the ECtHR at [59] said of 'tolerated' presence that:

> It therefore appears that her presence in the Netherlands as from that date was tolerated while she awaited the outcome of the administrative appeal proceedings taken by her. This cannot, however, be equated with lawful stay where the authorities explicitly grant an alien permission to settle in their country (see *Useinov*, cited above; and *Narenji Haghighi v. the Netherlands* (dec.), no. 38165/07, 14 April 2009). Accordingly, the total length of her stay in the Netherlands cannot be given the weight attributed to it by the applicant.

5.146　Leave which lapses does not legitimate periods of overstaying for relevant purposes, so that overstayers of tourist visas may not be permitted to rely on the weight of ties they form during their illegal stay: *Chandra v The Netherlands* no 53102/99 (admissibility decision, 13 May 2003). Non-compliance with residence regulations may weigh against a claimant, though the administration of those regulations is capable of providing a countervailing factor: *Alim v Russia* no 39417/07 [2011] ECHR 1453 [89]–[98].

5.147　However, a case in which unlawful or purely 'tolerated' stay has played a part may also involve positive obligations under Article 8 which are imposed on a Contracting Party to enable family life within its territory. In such cases the ties formed during an illegal stay are taken into account. In *Rodrigues da Silva and Hoogkamer v The Netherlands* no 50435/99 [2006] ECHR 86, (2007) 44 EHRR 34, the ECtHR found a violation of Article 8 rights of the applicant mother who had lived illegally in the Netherlands for 10 years, during which she regularly looked after her daughter, who was in the custody of the father. The Court took into account the ties between mother and daughter that had been formed during the mother's illegal stay, with the father playing a less prominent role during that time (at [42]), leading to a finding of a violation of Article 8 (at [43]–[44]). In *Nunez v Norway* no 55597/09 [2011] ECHR 1047, (2014) 58 EHRR 17, the Court similarly took into account the ties formed between the applicant mother and her children who resided with their father in Norway, even though the mother had fraudulently obtained residence permits and committed aggravated immigration offences, never having had lawful residence in Norway (see [67]; [72] and [84]); see also *Polidario v Switzerland* no 33169/10 [2013] ECHR 766. The Court has also accepted Article 8 rights arising in the context of illegally staying refused asylum-seekers who could not be removed and were prevented from living together due to federal legislation: *Mengesha Kimfe v Switzerland; Agraw v Switzerland* nos 24404/05; 3295/06 [2010] ECHR 1233.

5.148 Where some of the Article 8 ties were developed during an unlawful stay, but the applicant made several attempts to regularise his or her stay and was eventually granted leave to remain, the entirety of the ties and the length of the applicant's stay fell to be taken into full account under Article 8 ECHR: *Omojudi v UK* no 1820/08 [2009] ECHR 1942, (2010) 51 EHRR 10 [45]–[46]. In *Balogun v UK* no 60286/09 [2012] ECHR 614, (2013) 56 EHRR 3 [50], the ECtHR also concluded that an applicant brought to the UK illegally as a child, and granted leave to remain later, was not when faced with deportation to be penalised for his guardian's failure to regularise his stay earlier by exclusion from the benefit of the *Maslov* approach. In relation to the illegal stay of children, the Court has held that applicants could not be brought to bear the adverse consequences of the behaviour of their mother who had been deported years previously: *Butt v Norway* no 47017/09 (4 December 2012) [86]. The applicants had been granted a residence permit based on humanitarian considerations and then, based on false information, a settlement permit was issued to them. Although most of their residence in Norway had been unlawful, the applicants, who had been children, had not been aware of this for a substantial time. Although the removal of applicants whose ties had been formed almost exclusively during an illegal stay would only be disproportionate in exceptional circumstances, the Court found this to be the case given the applicants' very strong ties to Norway: *Butt v Norway* [79]; [88]–[89].[27]

The Time Elapsed Since the Offence was Committed and the Applicant's Conduct During that Period

5.149 The ECtHR in almost every case will look at the time which has elapsed since the index offence was committed and how an applicant has behaved during that period. In *El Boujaïdi v France* no 25613/94 [1997] ECHR 76, [2000] 30 EHRR 223 [40], the ECtHR observed of the applicant, already an offender, that: 'Once he was released, and at a time when he was unlawfully

---

[27] See also Baroness Hale in *EM (Lebanon) v SSHD* [2008] UKHL 64, [2009] AC 1198 [49]: 'In particular, a child is not to be held responsible for the moral failures of either of his parents.'

present in France, he continued to lead a life of crime and committed an attempted robbery.' The ECtHR will examine the time that has elapsed since its commission and the applicant's behaviour during this time, even where the offence was very serious: for instance, in *Nasri v France* no 19465/92 [1995] ECHR 24, (1996) 21 EHRR 458 [42] (involvement in a gang rape). In the case of a youth who had come to the UK aged 13 and committed rape at the age of 15 resulting in a four-year custodial sentence, the absence of a risk of reoffending together with the applicant's 'exemplary conduct' and his 'commendable efforts to rehabilitate himself and to reintegrate into society over a period of seven years' were given particular weight. The seriousness of the offence was not, in itself, sufficient to justify deportation in *AA v UK* no 8000/08 [2011] ECHR 1345 [63] and [68], and the ECtHR concluded that deportation would be disproportionate and contrary to Article 8 ECHR. See also *AW Khan v UK* no 47486/06 [2010] ECHR 27, (2010) 50 EHRR 47 [50] (discussed at 5.134 above).

The Nationalities of the Various Persons Concerned

5.150 The ECtHR has attached relatively little weight to the citizenship rights of family members, stressing rather in the seminal case of *Abdulaziz, Cabales and Balkandali v UK* nos 9214/80; 9473/81; 9474/81 [1985] ECHR 7, (1985) 7 EHRR 471 that Article 8 does not permit couples to choose their country of residence. Since that decision, however, the ECtHR has recognised in the deportation context that the 'nationalities of the various persons concerned' are relevant to the proportionality balancing exercise under Article 8(2) ECHR. But it is simply one factor amongst many: *Boultif v Switzerland* no 54273/00 [2001] ECHR 497, (2001) 33 EHRR 50 [40]; *Üner v The Netherlands* [GC] no 46410/99 [2006] ECHR 873, (2007) 45 EHRR 14 [57]; *Maslov v Austria* [GC] no 1638/03 [2008] ECHR 546, [2009] INLR 47 [71]. Whilst the ECtHR in *Üner* recognised the significance of the nationality of those concerned as a factor, the Dutch children of the applicant were also found to be of an adaptable age and to be able to follow the applicant to Turkey. However, on the facts, it was due to the seriousness of the offences (manslaughter and assault), the short duration of family life and the applicant's ties to Turkey that the Court found that the family's interests were outweighed by these factors (at [64]).

The Applicant's Family Situation, Such as the Length of the Marriage, and Other Factors Expressing the Effectiveness of a Couple's Family Life

5.151 The ECtHR considers the impact of an interference with the Article 8 rights of the family unit as a whole.[28] Thus, the rights of family members are important: *Berrehab v The Netherlands* no 10730/84 [1988] ECHR 14, (1989) 11 EHRR 322; *Beldjoudi v France* no 12083/86 [1992] ECHR 42, (1992) 14 EHRR 801; *Amrollahi v Denmark* no 56811/00 [2002] ECHR 585 [39]–[43]. In general, as a prerequisite for pertinence, it must be established that the family members are residing lawfully in the territory of the Contracting Party 'or, exceptionally, if there is a valid reason why it could not be expected' that the family member should follow the applicant to the country of origin: *Mawaka v The Netherlands* no 29031/04 [2010] ECHR 762 [61].

---

[28] See also *R (Beoku-Betts) v SSHD* [2008] UKHL 390, [2009] 1 AC 115.

Several of the *Üner/Boultif* criteria, particularly criteria iv, v, vii–ix, are pertinent to the weight to be attributed to an applicant's family life and the ECtHR often considers these cumulatively. Where family life is effective, the Court will give considerable weight to the situation of family members: *Omojudi v UK* no 1820/08 (2010) 51 EHRR 10 [46]:

5.152

> The Court attaches considerable weight to the solidity of the applicant's family ties in the United Kingdom and the difficulties that his family would face were they to return to Nigeria. The Court accepts that the applicant's wife was also an adult when she left Nigeria and it is therefore likely that she would be able to re-adjust to life there if she were to return to live with the applicant. She has, however, lived in the United Kingdom for twenty-six years and her ties to the United Kingdom are strong. Her two youngest children were born in the United Kingdom and have lived there their whole lives. They are not of an adaptable age and would likely encounter significant difficulties if they were to relocate to Nigeria. It would be virtually impossible for the oldest child to relocate to Nigeria as he has a young daughter who was born in the United Kingdom. Consequently, the applicant's wife has chosen to remain in the United Kingdom with her children and granddaughter. The applicant's family can, of course, continue to contact him by letter or telephone, and they may also visit him in Nigeria from time to time, but the disruption to their family life should not be underestimated. Although the Immigration Rules do not set a specific period after which revocation would be appropriate, it would appear that the latest the applicant would be able to apply to have the deportation order revoked would be ten years after his deportation.

Where particularly serious offending is concerned, the Court may consider a separation of family members proportionate, particularly where they have never cohabited. In *Joseph Grant v UK* no 10606/07 [2009] ECHR 26 [39]–[40], the ECtHR held that the applicant, who had lived in the UK for 34 years and was a heroin addict with 52 convictions, including violent offences, could maintain contact by telephone and email with his daughter, with whom he had never cohabited. However, in *Udeh v Switzerland* no 12020/09 [2013] ECHR 328, the ECtHR at [53] stressed in the context of a Nigerian drug offender that the contact which the applicant would maintain with his daughters of a previous marriage by visiting them in Switzerland could 'by no means be regarded as replacing the applicants' right to enjoy their right to live together, which constitutes one of the fundamental aspects of the right to respect for family life', the ECtHR finding a violation despite the applicant's commission of several drug-related offences leading to two custodial sentences; see also *Polidario v Switzerland* no 33169/10 [2013] ECHR 766 [73] (finding that limitation to telephone contact had deprived the applicant of an effective right to family life with her child).

5.153

Whether the Spouse Knew About the Offence at the Time When He or She Entered into a Family Relationship

Generally only family and social ties that have been formed prior to the time when it was brought to the applicant's attention that the persistence of those ties would be precarious are pertinent under Article 8 ECHR: *Üner v The Netherlands* [GC] no 46410/99 [2006] ECHR 873, (2007) 45 EHRR 14 [57]; *Butt v Norway* no 47017/09 (4 December 2012) [82]; *Udeh v Switzerland* no 12020/09 [2013] ECHR 328 [50]. This also applies

5.154

where the applicant sought to regularise his or her stay but this eventually failed, unless given 'assurances that he would be granted a right of residence by the competent ... authorities': *Useinov v The Netherlands* no 61292/00 (admissibility decision, 11 April 2006).

5.155 However, where the formation of stronger family ties after knowledge of the intention to remove an applicant is also due to a delay in immigration proceedings or a failure to take removal steps, these ties are taken into account.[29] The Court has done so in the context of delay in ordering an applicant's expulsion (*Nunez v Norway* no 55597/09 [2011] ECHR 1047, (2014) 58 EHRR 17 [82]), delay in taking steps in relation to an applicant's deportation after the applicant's exhaustion of appeal rights (*AA v UK* no 8000/08 [2011] ECHR 1345 [61]; [66], but contrast *Onur v UK* no 29696/07 [2009] ECHR 289 [56]) and unduly extended appeal proceedings over almost four years (*Mokrani v France* no 52206/99 [2003] ECHR 362, (2005) 40 EHRR 5 [34]–[35]).

Whether There are Children of the Marriage, and if so their Age

5.156 Where children are involved, their best interests must be a primary consideration. One of the factors the Court considers pertinent is whether the children are of an 'adaptable age' (*Üner*, at [64]). It is necessary to examine the cultural and linguistic environment in which they have grown up and the level of schooling received, as well as the ties they have to their parents' country of origin: *Şen v The Netherlands* no 31465/96 (21 December 2001) [40]; *Sezen v The Netherlands* no 50252/99 (2006) 43 EHRR 30 [47].

The Seriousness of the Difficulties Which the Spouse is Likely to Encounter in the Country to Which the Applicant is to Be Expelled

5.157 As a further factor which is essential to the assessment of the situation of an applicant's spouse, the ECtHR considers whether the spouse is likely to encounter difficulties by resettling in the country to which the applicant is to be expelled. Where the spouse does not have the same nationality as the applicant, the spouse cannot be expected to follow the applicant if this would cause 'obvious and serious difficulties' to the spouse who does not speak the language, has a different religion and has never been to the applicant's country of origin: *Amrollahi*, at [41]. In *Boultif v Switzerland* no 54273/00 [2001] ECHR 497, (2001) 33 EHRR 50, the Swiss spouse of the Algerian applicant had never lived in Algeria and spoke French, but not Arabic. The Court found at [53] that under these circumstances, she could not be expected to resettle in Algeria:

> The Court has considered, first, whether the applicant and his wife could live together in Algeria. The applicant's wife is a Swiss national. It is true that she can speak French and has had contact by telephone with her mother-in-law in Algeria. However, the applicant's wife has never lived in Algeria, she has no other ties with that country, and indeed does not speak Arabic. In these circumstances she cannot, in the Court's opinion, be expected to follow her husband, the applicant, to Algeria.

---

[29] The relevance of delay on the part of the removing authorities has also been recognised domestically; see *EB (Kosovo) v SSHD* [2008] UKHL 41, [2009] 1 AC 1159.

The Court concluded at [55] that it would be 'practically impossible' for the applicant to live his family life abroad. Although the applicant had in addition to less serious offences committed a robbery in a 'brutal manner', the ECtHR found him to be a 'comparatively limited danger to the public order' given his conduct since release and held that there had been a breach of Article 8 ECHR.

Where the spouses are of the same nationality, it is necessary to examine the spouse's ties to the state from which the applicant is to be expelled: *Antwi v Norway* no 26940/10 [2012] ECHR 259 [93]. Where the spouse has formed significant ties in the territory of the Contracting Party and has lived there for a significant period of time, this will weigh heavily against expulsion: *Omojudi v UK* no 1820/08 (2010) 51 EHRR 10 [46]; *Sezen v The Netherlands* no 50252/99 [2006] ECHR 87, (2006) 43 EHRR 30 [47].

5.158

The Best Interests and Well-being of the Children, in Particular the Seriousness of the Difficulties Which Any Children of the Applicant are Likely to Encounter in the Country to Which the Applicant is to be Expelled

The best interests and well-being of the children and the seriousness of any difficulties they would likely encounter in the destination state must be given due weight: *Üner v The Netherlands* [GC] no 46410/99 [2006] ECHR 873, (2007) 45 EHRR 14 [58]. Even where an individual has reached the age of 18, it remains arguable that there is no automatic cut-off point at 18 for an Article 8 assessment.[30] The best interests of the child must also be a primary consideration where the relationship with the children only falls within the scope of the applicant's private life: *Anayo v Germany* no 20578/07 [2010] ECHR 2083, (2012) 55 EHRR 5 [71].

5.159

The ECtHR in *Maslov v Austria* [GC] no 1638/03 [2008] ECHR 546, [2009] INLR 47 considered the best interests of minors in the juvenile justice system and recognised the state's duty to facilitate the reintegration into society of a minor who committed an offence as pertinent under Article 8 (at [100]). This duty does not carry the same weight in the case of young offenders who have reached majority: *Miah v UK* no 53080/07 (admissibility decision, 27 April 2010) [24].

5.160

Given that the best interests of the child must be a primary consideration under Article 3 CRC (see Chapter 3), 'sufficient weight' must also be attached to these in the context of deportation proceedings. In *Nunez v Norway* no 55597/09 [2011] ECHR 1047, (2014) 58 EHRR 17, a mother with 'long lasting and close bonds' with her lawfully resident children had lost custody of her children partly because of expulsion proceedings. The Court at [84] held that the children's best interests outweighed the mother's illegal stay in Norway, her commission of various immigration offences and her lack of strong ties to Norway.

5.161

Even where parents have separated, the Court recognises that it is in the child's best interests to 'grow up with both parents' with regular contact to the parent who does

5.162

---

[30] *HK (Turkey)* [2010] EWCA Civ 583; see also ch 3.

not have custody, which may mean permitting a separated parent to stay in the host country: *Udeh v Switzerland* no 12020/09 [2013] ECHR 328 [53].[31]

The Solidity of Social, Cultural and Family Ties with the Host Country and with the Country of Destination

5.163 The Court assesses the solidity of an applicant's ties both to his destination country and to his host country: *Üner v The Netherlands* [GC] no 46410/99 [2006] ECHR 873, (2007) 45 EHRR 14 [58]. The Court takes into account whether an applicant has made visits to his country of origin since coming to the host country (*AH Khan v UK* no 6222/10 (2012) 55 EHRR 30 [41]; contrast his brother's case: *AW Khan v UK* no 47486/06 [2010] ECHR 27, (2010) 50 EHRR 47 [42]). It also gives weight to a pattern of living intermittently in the country of origin: *Gezginci v Switzerland* no 16327/05 (9 December 2010) [69]–[70].

5.164 Both educational and linguistic ties are pertinent to the assessment of the solidity of ties to both countries. Where an applicant left his country of origin at a young age and does not speak the language, this will weigh heavily against deportation: *Maslov v Austria* [GC] no 1638/03 [2009] INLR 47 [96]–[97]; [100]. However, the Court undertakes its own assessment of the linguistic ties to the country and does not necessarily follow an applicant's implausible description of his language skills: *Üner*, at [62]; *Emre v Switzerland* no 42034/04 (22 May 2008) [55]; [80]. In *Samsonnikov v Estonia* no 52178/10 [2012] ECHR 1373 (3 July 2012) [88], the Estonia-based applicant's Russian naturalisation at the age of 20 and his attendance at a Russian school were evidence of his close links to Russia.

5.165 The place of residence not only of the core family but also of other relatives, such as parents, adult siblings or grandparents, may be pertinent to the assessment of the solidity of ties: *Miah v UK* no 53080/07 (admissibility decision, 27 April 2010) [25]; *Maslov*, at [96]; *Radovanovic v Austria* no 42703/98 [2004] ECHR 689, (2005) 41 EHRR 6 [36].

Duration of Exclusion

5.166 If exclusion from the UK is the consequence of expulsion, the duration of an exclusion measure is to be considered relevant: *Maslov v Austria* [GC] no 1638/03 [2008] ECHR 546, [2009] INLR 47.[32] The ECtHR has found in a number of cases that while expulsion was justified, the imposition of an indefinite exclusion order or re-entry ban was disproportionate: *Yilmaz v Germany* no 52853/99 [2003] ECHR 187, (2004) 38 EHRR 23 [48]–[49]; *Radovanovic v Austria* no 42703/98 [2004] ECHR 689, (2005) 41 EHRR 6 [37]; *Keles v Germany* no 32231/02 [2005] ECHR 950 [66].

5.167 In its decisions setting out guidance in this area, the ECtHR has recognised that the duration and legal character of a re-entry ban is relevant to the proportionality

---

[31] *LD (Article 8—Best Interests of Child) Zimbabwe* [2010] UKUT 278 (IAC); [26]–[28], requiring 'very weighty reasons' to justify separating a parent from a child.
[32] See also *AS (Pakistan)* [2008] EWCA Civ 1118; [27].

of exclusion. In *Üner v The Netherlands* [GC] 46410/99 [2006] ECHR 873, (2007) 45 EHRR 14, the Grand Chamber observed that:

> 65. The Court appreciates that the exclusion order imposed on the applicant has even more far-reaching consequences than the withdrawal of his permanent residence permit, as it renders even short visits to the Netherlands impossible for as long as the order is in place. However, having regard to the nature and the seriousness of the offences committed by the applicant, and bearing in mind that the exclusion order is limited to ten years, the Court cannot find that the respondent State assigned too much weight to its own interests when it decided to impose that measure…

In *Kaya v Germany* no 31753/02 [2007] ECHR 538, [2007] Imm AR 802, the ECtHR at [68]–[69] enlarged upon the potential significance of an unlimited or uncertain period of exclusion: 5.168

> 68. As to the proportionality of the impugned measure, the Court finally notes that the expulsion order issued against the applicant was not, from the outset, subject to a time-limit. In this context, the Court observes that in a number of cases it found a residence prohibition disproportionate on account of its unlimited duration (see, for instance, *Ezzouhdi v. France*, no. 47160/99, §35, 13 February 2001; *Yilmaz*, cited above, §§48–49, 17 April 2003; *Radovanovic v. Austria*, no. 42703/98, §37, 22 April 2004; and *Keles v. Germany*, no. 32231/02, §66, 27 October 2005) while, in other cases, it has considered the limited duration of a residence prohibition as a factor speaking in favour of its proportionality (see *Benhebba v. France*, no. 53441/99, §37; *Jankov v. Germany* (dec.), no. 35112/92, 13 January 2000; and *Üner*, cited above, §65).
>
> 69. Turning to the present case, the Court notes that domestic law provided that the exclusion from German territory could, as a rule, be limited in time upon separate request (see paragraph 33 above). There is nothing to indicate in the instant case that this possibility was merely theoretical. The Court further takes note of the Government's submissions that the applicant has in the meantime fulfilled the conditions attached to the time-limit and is no longer barred from entering German territory. Thus, it cannot be said that the applicant in this specific case was left without any perspective of returning to Germany.

In an otherwise borderline case, or a case to which the *Maslov* approach applies, even a finite period of exclusion (in that case 10 years) may render exclusion disproportionate. In *Maslov* at [98]–[99], the Grand Chamber found that the state interest was outweighed notwithstanding the limited duration of exclusion: 5.169

> 98. Lastly, when assessing the proportionality of the interference the Court has regard to the duration of an exclusion order. The Chamber, referring to the Court's case-law, has rightly pointed out that the duration of an exclusion measure is to be considered as one factor among others (see, as cases in which the unlimited duration of a residence prohibition was considered as a factor supporting the conclusion that it was disproportionate, *Ezzouhdi*, cited above, §35; *Yilmaz v. Germany*, no. 52853/99, §§48–49, 17 April 2003; and *Radovanovic*, cited above, §37; see, as cases in which the limited duration of a residence prohibition was considered as a factor in favour of its proportionality, *Benhebba*, cited above, §37; *Jankov v. Germany* (dec.), no. 35112/92, 13 January 2000; and *Üner*, cited above, §65).
>
> 99. The Grand Chamber agrees with the Chamber that the limited duration of the exclusion order is not decisive in the present case. Having regard to the applicant's young age, a ten-year exclusion order banned him from living in Austria for almost as much time as he had spent there and for a decisive period of his life.

Part B – Legal Framework

5.170 A relatively short administrative exclusion such as two years might still be disproportionate where this has potentially serious effects upon settled children: *Nunez v Norway* no 55597/09 [2011] ECHR 1047, (2014) 58 EHRR 17 [82]–[85].

5.171 While the fact that an exclusion order operates for a limited time span only may thus militate in favour of the proportionality of the measure (*Benhebba v France* no 53441/99 [2003] ECHR 342 [37]; *Jankov v Germany* no 35112/97 (admissibility decision, 13 January 2000); *Üner v The Netherlands* [GC] no 46410/99 [2006] ECHR 873, (2007) 45 EHRR 14 [65], the ECtHR nevertheless examines whether its length is proportionate in the circumstances of the individual case.

5.172 Thus, in *AW Khan v UK* no 47486/06 [2010] ECHR 27, (2010) 50 EHRR 47, which concerned a 10-year ban, the ECtHR found a violation of Article 8 were the applicant to be deported (at [98]). In *Maslov v Austria* [GC] no 1638/03 [2008] ECHR 546, [2009] INLR 47, the Court considered it as pertinent that the proposed exclusion order would have excluded the applicant for almost as many years as he had spent in Austria, namely 10 years, which constituted a 'decisive period of his life' (at [99]); however, see *Miah v UK* no 53080/07 (admissibility decision, 27 April 2010) [25]. The reduction of an indefinite re-entry ban to 10 years was found to be in breach of Article 8 ECHR in *Emre v Switzerland (No 2)* no 5056/10 (11 October 2011), where the Court held that the applicant should have been permitted to return to Switzerland immediately (at [68]).

5.173 It is noteworthy that the maximum duration of an entry ban under Article 11(2) EU Returns Directive[33] (which the UK has not adopted) is normally five years, with longer entry bans becoming possible only if the individual presents 'a serious threat to public policy, public security or national security'.

Relevant Health Issues

5.174 In its case law, the ECtHR has also recognised that medical issues (*Emre v Switzerland* no 42034/04 (22 May 2008) [71]; [81]–[83]), including the fact that an applicant is disabled (*Nasri v France* no 19465/92 [1995] ECHR 24, (1996) 21 EHRR 458 [43]) are relevant to the assessment of the proportionality of expulsion.[34] However, the standard remains an exigent one. In *N v UK* [GC] no 26565/05 (2008) 47 EHRR 39, the ECtHR Grand Chamber at [42], having elucidated a test of exceptionality by which it would only be 'in a very exceptional case, where the humanitarian grounds against removal are compelling' that expulsion would breach Article 3 ECHR and a significant reduction in life expectancy was insufficient to meet this threshold, found no reason to give detailed consideration to Article 8 ECHR thereafter ([52] *et seq*).

5.175 Where deportation will have a destabilising or otherwise adverse effect on an applicant's health, this is a further factor to be taken into account in the proportionality assessment: *Nada v Switzerland* [GC] no 10593/08 [2012] ECHR 1691, (2013) 56

---

[33] Directive 2008/115/EC of the European Parliament and of the Council of 16 December 2008 on common standards and procedures in Member States for returning illegally staying third-country nationals.

[34] This has also been recognised in the domestic context: *DM (Zambia) v SSHD* [2009] EWCA Civ 474; [20] (in the context of an AIDS sufferer); *JA (Ivory Coast) and ES (Tanzania) v SSHD* [2009] EWCA Civ 1353 [16]–[17].

EHRR 18 [191]; *Hasanbasic v Switzerland* no 2166/09 [2013] ECHR 520 [64]. In *Emre v Switzerland* the Court gave weight to the psychological problems of the then 23-year-old applicant, diagnosed with a borderline personality disorder after growing up in a violent family environment. The ECtHR found that although the psychological issues of the applicant may not have been sufficient in themselves to found a right to stay based on Article 8 with adequate medical services being available in Turkey, this was an additional pertinent factor rendering the applicant's return to his home country more difficult ([83]); contrast *Onur v UK* no 29696/07 [2009] ECHR 289 [60]. More recently in *MM (Zimbabwe)* [2012] EWCA Civ 279, Moses LJ observed at [5] that:

> The only cases I can foresee where the absence of adequate medical treatment in the country to which a person is to be deported will be relevant to Article 8, is where it is an additional factor to be weighed in the balance, with other factors which by themselves engage Article 8. Suppose, in this case, the appellant had established firm family ties in this country, then the availability of continuing medical treatment here, coupled with his dependence on the family here for support, together establish 'private life' under Article 8. That conclusion would not involve a comparison between medical facilities here and those in Zimbabwe. Such a finding would not offend the principle expressed above that the United Kingdom is under no Convention obligation to provide medical treatment here when it is not available in the country to which the appellant is to be deported.

Pending Family Proceedings

5.176 In the context of children and family proceedings, Article 8 ECHR also imposes positive obligations on the Contracting Parties to enable an applicant to stay in the country, while such proceedings are ongoing. Where deportation denies an applicant the possibility of 'any meaningful further involvement' in ongoing family proceedings, thus prejudging the outcome of such proceedings, deportation breaches Article 8 ECHR: *Ciliz v The Netherlands* no 29192/95 (11 July 2000) [71].

5.177 Such positive obligations further extend to measures that are necessary to institute custody proceedings, including the right to enter a country in order to obtain custody of one's child, and the positive obligations on states require that such measures be taken rapidly: see also *Polidario v Switzerland* no 33169/10 [2013] ECHR 766 [65]–[66], [76]–[77].

Family Reunion

5.178 Family reunion cases involve the positive obligations on Contracting Parties to admit into their territory family members of persons who are already lawfully present. Article 8 ECHR does not entail a general obligation on Contracting Parties to respect immigrants' choice of the country of their residence and to grant family reunion as a result. In its early case law, the ECtHR held that family life is not engaged by a refusal to permit family reunion: *Abdulaziz, Cabales and Balkandali v UK* nos 9214/80; 9473/81; 9474/81 [1985] ECHR 7, (1985) 7 EHRR 471. In its more recent case law on positive obligations under Article 8, the ECtHR has moved to a more sophisticated analysis, which considers whether the failure to permit family reunion or to issue a residence permit amounts to a breach of Article 8 ECHR in the circumstances of the particular case: *Rodrigues da Silva and Hoogkamer v The Netherlands* no 50435/99 [2006] ECHR 86, (2007) 44 EHRR 34 [38]:

> Next, it observes that the present case concerns the refusal of the domestic authorities to allow the first applicant to reside in the Netherlands; although she has been living in that country since 1994, her stay there has at no time been lawful. Therefore, the impugned decision did not constitute an interference with the applicants' exercise of the right to respect for their family life in that a resident status, entitling the first applicant to remain in the Netherlands, was withdrawn. The question to be examined in the present case is rather whether the Netherlands authorities were under a duty to allow the first applicant to reside in the Netherlands, thus enabling the applicants to maintain and develop family life in their territory. For this reason the Court agrees with the parties that this case is to be seen as one involving an allegation of failure on the part of the respondent State to comply with a positive obligation (see *Ahmut v. the Netherlands*, judgment of 28 November 1996, *Reports of Judgments and Decisions* 1996-VI, p. 2031, §63).

5.179 In the domestic context, the Supreme Court in *R (Quila and another) v SSHD* [2011] UKSC 45, [2012] 1 AC 621, per Lord Wilson at [43] declined to follow *Abdulaziz*.

5.180 The applicable principles in cases involving positive and negative obligations under Article 8 are similar: *Gül v Switzerland* no 23218/94 [1996] ECHR 5 [38]. The factors for the assessment of proportionality in the context of family reunion cases are the same as those in removal cases: *Biao v Denmark* no 38590/10; [2014] ECHR 304.

5.181 The Court has recognised that 'parents who leave children behind while they settle abroad cannot be assumed to have irrevocably decided that those children are to remain in the country of origin permanently and to have abandoned any idea of a future family reunion': *Şen v The Netherlands* no 31465/96 (21 December 2001) [40]; *Tuquabo-Tekle v The Netherlands* no 60665/00 [2005] ECHR 803, [2006] Fam Law 267 [45].[35]

5.182 In *Osman v Denmark* no 38058/09 (14 June 2011), the Court found that the refusal of entry clearance to a Somali girl who had grown up in Denmark but had been sent back by her father to a refugee camp in Kenya in order to look after her grandmother violated Article 8. Although it had been the father's decision to send her back, which fell within his parental rights, the authorities were not permitted to ignore the child's best interests, which outweighed the public interest in effective immigration control (at [73]–[76]).

5.183 In the context of a lack of family reunion rights for post-flight spouses of refugees as opposed to pre-flight spouses of refugees, the ECtHR decided in *Hode and Abdi v UK* no 22341/09 [2012] ECHR 1871, (2013) 56 EHRR 27 [48] and [52] that this constituted unjustifiable discrimination on the basis of their 'other status' as a refugee and his post-flight spouse.[36]

Deprivation of Nationality and Residence

5.184 While Article 8 ECHR does not guarantee a right to acquire a particular nationality or citizenship, an arbitrary denial of nationality raises an issue under Article 8 ECHR:

---

[35] This has been confirmed in domestic law in *H (Somalia) v ECO* [2004] UKIAT 00027; [14], as approved by the High Court in *R (Yussuf) v SSHD* [2005] EWHC 2847; [10] (Bean J).

[36] See also the domestic cases of *A (Afghanistan) v SSHD* [2009] EWCA Civ 825 and *FH (Post-flight Spouses) Iran* [2010] UKUT 275 (IAC); and the CJEU decision in C-578/08 *Rhimou Chakroun v Minister van Buitenlandse Zaken* (1 May 20010), which found no justification for the different treatment of post-flight and pre-flight spouses in relation to the reliance on public funds under the Family Reunification Directive 2003/86/EC (not adopted by the UK).

Karassev v Finland no 31414/96 (admissibility decision, 12 January 1999); *Slivenko v Latvia* [GC] no 48321/99 [2003] ECHR 498, (2004) 39 EHRR 24 [77]. The erasure from a residents' register leaving the applicant with no right of residence also constitutes an interference with Article 8 ECHR: *Slivenko*, at [96]; *Kurić and others v Slovenia* [GC] no 26828/06 [2012] ECHR 1083, (2013) 56 EHRR 20 [339]. Further, the confiscation of identity documents may constitute an interference with Article 8 where lack of documentation leads to various 'everyday inconveniences', including denial of access to employment and medical care: *Smirnova v Russia* no 46133/99; 48183/99 [2003] ECHR 397, (2004) 39 EHRR 22 [97].

Several cases concerning alleged denial or deprivation of nationality cases have arisen in a context where the applicants were deprived of a right of residence by reason of the absence of nationality. In *Sisojeva v Latvia* [GC] no 60654/00 [2007] ECHR 16, (2007) 45 EHRR 33, the applicants had in the late 1960s moved to Latvia as Soviet nationals. Upon Latvia gaining, or reasserting, its independence in 1991, they became stateless and in 1996 their residence permits were revoked and their names taken off the residents' register based on breaches of immigration law, although no active steps were taken to remove them. The ECtHR recognised that the removal of their names from the register of residents had resulted in a period of insecurity and legal uncertainty interfering with their rights under Article 8 ECHR. However, in its view, Latvia's ultimate proposal to regularise their stay by granting them residence permits, even if temporary, enabled 'the applicants to remain in Latvia and to exercise freely in that country their right to respect for their private and family life' and was thus 'adequate and sufficient to remedy their complaint', leading to the case being struck off the Court's list (at [98]–[99]; [102]).

5.185

The Court revisited the issue of deprivation of nationality in the context of statelessness and lack of a right to residence in *Kurić and others v Slovenia* [GC] no 26828/06 [2012] ECHR 1083, (2013) 56 EHRR 20. The applicants had been nationals of the Former Republic of Yugoslavia (FRY) and other constituent republics who had acquired permanent residence in Slovenia. Following the independence of Slovenia, they had failed to apply for Slovenian citizenship or their application had been refused. Their names were automatically deleted from the register of permanent residents in 1992, leaving them without a residence permit. The applicants had not been notified of this decision and only learnt about it much later. This had serious and enduring negative consequences, including detention and deportation of some, statelessness, eviction from their homes, inability to work or travel, loss of personal possessions and a life in shelters and parks. The ECtHR at [339] confirmed that the erasure from the register and its impact on the applicant's lives interfered with their private and family life and found this continuing interference not to have been in accordance with the law, although this was not strictly necessary, the ECtHR continued to examine the proportionality of the measure. The ECtHR at [353] confirmed the legitimate aim of national security, but at [359]–[360] denied proportionality on the basis that a restriction of Slovenian citizens could be justified but not the denial of permanent residence. The ECtHR further found a violation of Article 14 ECHR on the basis that non-nationals who were not nationals of the FRY had been able to retain permanent residence under Slovenian law, but nationals of the FRY had not (at [390]–[392]). Substantial just satisfaction was subsequently awarded to compensate for the loss of past income, making awards in respect of social allowances and child benefits: *Kurić and others v Slovenia* [GC] no 26828/06 [2012] ECHR 1083, (2013) 56 EHRR 20.

5.186

5.187   The denial of citizenship was found to fall within Article 8 ECHR in *Genovese v Malta* no 53124/09 [2011] ECHR 1590, (2014) 58 EHRR 25 concerning an applicant who had been born out of wedlock to a British mother and a Maltese father. Despite judicial determination of paternity, the applicant's father had refused to acknowledge his son on the birth certificate, leading to the Maltese authorities' refusal to grant the applicant Maltese citizenship. The applicant claimed that he had been discriminated against contrary to Article 14 taken with Article 8 ECHR. The ECtHR rejected the applicant's claim that the denial of citizenship had interfered with his family life with his father resident in Malta given the father's lack of interest in a relationship with his son. It found, however, an interference with the applicant's private life based on the denial of citizenship ruling that 'its impact on the applicant's social identity was such as to bring it within' Article 8 ECHR (at [33]). The applicant had been treated differently on the basis that he had been born out of wedlock and the ECtHR held that no reasonable or objective grounds had been adduced for this (at [45]–[49]).[37]

B14. Articles 9–11 ECHR

5.188   Important protections set out in other articles include the right to freedom of thought, conscience and religion (Article 9 ECHR), the right to freedom of expression (Article 10 ECHR) and the right to freedom of assembly and association (Article 11 ECHR).

5.189   The right to freedom of thought, conscience and religion in Article 9 ECHR applies to deportation cases in a domestic context, where a deportation or exclusion measure is 'designed to repress the exercise' of such rights or 'stifle the spreading of the religion or philosophy of the followers': *Omkarananda and the Divine Light Zentrum v Switzerland* no 8118/77 DR 25, 118 (Commission decision, 19 March 1981) [5]; *Nolan and K v Russia* no 2512/04 (12 February 2009) [62].

5.190   These principles have been found to apply in the following two cases. In *Perry v Latvia* no 30273/03 (8 November 2007), the Court held that the substitution of a residence permit for religious activities of a minister of a religious cult with a permit that did not allow such activities, based on national security considerations, breached that applicant's right to freedom of religion (at [10]; [56] and [65]). In *Nolan and K v Russia* no 2512/04 [2009] ECHR 262, (2011) 53 EHRR 29, the Court held that an entry ban on a former resident of Russia, whose previous permits had been granted based on the invitation from the Unification church and whose activities in Russia were 'primarily of a religious nature', violated Article 9 ECHR (at [63]; [66] and [70]–[75]).

5.191   There has not yet been a decision finding an extraterritorial violation of Article 9.[38] The Court considered the issue in *Z and T v UK* no 27034/05 (admissibility decision, 28 February 2006), finding that 'a real risk of a flagrant denial' of the right would need

---

[37] This was cited by Ouseley J in *AHK and others v SSHD* [2013] EWHC 1426 (Admin), who found an element of arbitrariness or discrimination necessary for Article 8 to be engaged (see ch 11); for differential treatment based on the number of years someone had been a national, see also *Biao v Denmark* no 38590/10 (25 March 2014, not yet final).

[38] But see the decision of the CJEU in *Bundesrepublik Deutschland v Y & Z* [2012] EUECJ C-71/11 regarding the right to freedom of religion, and the domestic case law concerning freedom of political expression in *RT (Zimbabwe) and others v SSHD* [2012] UKSC 38, [2012] Imm AR 1067, and freedom of religion in *MT (Ahmadi—HJ (Iran)) Pakistan* [2011] UKUT 277 (IAC).

to be demonstrated.[39] The Court, however, denied such a risk in the case of Pakistani Christians and stressed that a case reaching the threshold of such a flagrant denial would likely also involve a breach of Article 3 ECHR.

Issues regarding an extraterritorial application of Article 9 may also arise in the context of conscientious objection to miliary service. While Article 9 does not guarantee a right to conscientious objection, repeated criminal convictions for failure to perform military service have been found to amount to a breach of Article 3 ECHR: *Ülke v Turkey* no 39437/98 (24 January 2006); *Thlimmenos v Greece* [GC] no 34369/97 [2000] ECHR 162, (2001) 31 EHRR 15 (finding a breach of Article 14 taken with Article 9 in a domestic case concerning the refusal to wear a military uniform); *Bayatyan v Armenia* [GC] no 3459/03 (27 October 2009).[40]

5.192

Article 10 ECHR also finds application in the context of exclusion or deportation measures. Cases involving the exclusion of a third country national from the territory of a Contracting Party, where that person applies for entry clearance in order to give a political or religious speech or participate in a political or religious assembly or association, are generally considered under Article 10 ECHR. This is because the right to freedom of expression under Article 10(1) expressly includes the 'freedom to hold opinions and to receive and impart information and ideas ... *regardless of frontiers*' (emphasis added). The Court stressed this in *Cox v Turkey* no 2933/03 (2012) 55 EHRR 13 (at [31]):

5.193

> The Court considers that the ban on the applicant's re-entry is materially related to her right to freedom of expression because it disregards the fact that Article 10 rights are enshrined 'regardless of frontiers' and that no distinction can be drawn between the protected freedom of expression of nationals and that of foreigners. This principle implies that the Contracting States may only restrict information received from abroad within the confines of the justifications set out in Article 10 §2.

The test which applies in such cases was summarised in *R (Naik) v SSHD* [2011] EWCA Civ 1546 [48] (*per* Carnwath LJ):[41]

5.194

> However, where rights under Article 10 are engaged, given the special importance of the right to free speech, it is for the Court, looking at the interference complained of 'in the light of the case as a whole', to determine whether the reasons given to justify the interference were 'relevant and sufficient'. This will involve a judgment whether the measure taken was proportionate to the legitimate aims pursued, based on 'an acceptable assessment of the relevant facts', and in conformity with the principles embodied in Article 10 ... A range of factors may be relevant, including whether the speaker occupies 'a position of influence in society of a sort likely to amplify the impact of his words' ... The supervision must be 'strict', because of the importance of the rights in question, and the necessity for restricting them must be 'convincingly established'.

---

[39] This corresponds to the situation in domestic law; see *R (Ullah) v Special Adjudicator* [2004] UKHL 26, [2004] 2 AC 323.

[40] See also the domestic case of *R (Sepet and another) v SSHD* [2003] UKHL 15, [2003] 3 All ER 304; see also Article 10(2) of the European Charter on the right to conscientious objection.

[41] See also the domestic cases of *Mahajna v Home Secretary (Deportation Hate Speech—Unacceptable Hehaviour)* [2012] UKUT B1 (IAC); *GW (EEA reg 21: 'fundamental interests') Netherlands* [2009] UKAIT 00050; *Farrakhan, R (on the Application of) v SSHD* [2002] EWCA Civ 606, [2002] 3 WLR 481; and *Sun Myung Moon (Human Rights, Entry Clearance, Proportionality) USA* [2005] UKIAT 00112.

5.195   The applicant in *Cox v Turkey* was a university lecturer who had been banned from re-entering Turkey on account of the contents of her previous conversations with students and colleagues on controversial Kurdish and Armenian issues. The Court found that Turkey had failed to advance 'relevant and sufficient' reasons for the re-entry ban, leading to a breach of Article 10 ECHR (at [31]; [44]). Similiarly, in *Piermont v France* nos 15773/89; 15774/89 [1995] ECHR 14, (1995) 20 EHRR 301 (27 April 1995), the Court held that the French Polynesian expulsion and entry ban imposed on a German national based on his statements attacking French policies was in breach of Article 10 ECHR. However, national security concerns were accepted as relevant and sufficient reasons for the interference with Article 10 in *Adams and Benn v UK* nos 28979/95; 30343/96 (1997) 88A D & R 137. The UK had issued an exclusion order against Gerry Adams, the President of Sinn Féin who resided in Northern Ireland, preventing him from speaking in the House of Commons upon the invitation of Tony Benn. While in the Commission's view, both Adams' and Benn's Article 10 rights had been interfered with, the exclusion was justified, taking into account the volatile situation in Northern Ireland, despite ongoing efforts to establish a peace process acceptable to the various communities and the lifting of the exclusion order following the announcement of a ceasefire by the IRA.

5.196   Pertinently for exclusion cases, the Court has recognised that the method and place of communication of information and ideas can go to the essence of the right protected under Article 10 ECHR. In *Women on Waves and others v Portugal* no 31276/05 (3 February 2009), the Court found that the ban from territorial waters of reproductive rights protesters on boats, based on national security and public health reasons, was in breach of the right to impart information under Article 10 (at [28]; [30]). This was found notwithstanding the fact that they were able to inform about their campaign on mainland Portugal (at [39]; [41]).

B15. Article 12 ECHR

5.197   Article 12 ECHR guarantees the right of 'Men and women of marriageable age ... to marry and to found a family, according to the national laws governing the exercise of this right'. Article 12 is a fundamental right which, unlike Articles 8–11 ECHR, is not subject to limitations. While Contracting Parties enjoy a certain margin of appreciation in the light of the express reference to national laws in Article 12, the Court has stressed that national laws must not restrict or reduce the right in such a way or to such an extent that the very essence of the right is impaired: *B and L v UK* no 36536/02 (13 September 2005) [34]. States may thus regulate matters such as the minimum marriageable age, capacity, consent and prohibited degrees of consanguinity: *F v Switzerland* no 11329/85 [1987] ECHR 32, (1988) 10 EHRR 411 [32].[42]

5.198   While the wording of Article 12 restricts it to opposite-sex marriages, the scope of Article 12 may today extend to same-sex couples where 'national laws' so provide: *Schalk and Kopf v Austria* no 30141/04 (22 November 2010) [61]. Article 12 further guarantees the right of a post-operative transsexual to marry someone of the other sex than the newly assigned sex: *Goodwin v UK* [GC] no 28957/95 [2002] ECHR 588, (2002) 35 EHRR 18.

---

[42] In the domestic context, see *Quila and another, R (on the Application of) v SSHD* [2011] UKSC 45; [2012] 1 AC 621, finding no violation regarding a minimum age for marriage in order to prevent forced marriages.

Immigration measures such as a refusal of a residence permit to an applicant who wishes to get married may amount to a violation of Article 12, but only where the applicant is unable to get married abroad: *X v Germany* no 7175/75; DR 6, 138 (admissibility decision, 12 July 1976).[43] Article 12 does not confer a right to marry in any particular country and national law may impose restrictions, such as where an applicant applies for entry clearance for his fiancée in order to get married to her, whom he has never met and who would rely on social assistance: *no 9773/82 v UK* (1982) 5 EHRR 296.

5.199

Article 12 permits the imposition of restrictions in order to prevent marriages of convenience: *Klip and Krüger v The Netherlands* no 33257/96 (1997) 91-A DR 66 (3 December 1997). However, the right to marry in Article 12 has been found to prohibit the blanket ban of marriages for non-Anglican illegal residents in *O'Donoghue and others v UK* no 34848/07 [2010] ECHR 2022, (2011) 53 EHRR 1.[44] In the Court's view, set out at [87], any conditions relating to the right to marry would have to focus on the genuineness of the marriage. The Court found that the British Certificate of Approval scheme had prevented the applicants from getting married, thus impairing 'the very essence' of their right to marry (at [91]). The scheme was further found to be in breach of the prohibition on discrimination under Article 14 ECHR, as no reasons capable of providing an objective and reasonable justification for the discrimination based on religion had been adduced (at [102]).

5.200

Article 12 further guarantees the right to found a family, which overlaps considerably with Article 8 ECHR. Artificial insemination and other methods of medically assisted procreation fall within the scope of Article 8 ECHR: *Dickson and another v UK* [GC] no 44362/04 [2007] ECHR 1050, (2008) 46 EHRR 41; *SH and others v Austria* [GC] no 57813/00 [2011] ECHR 1878. This may include adoption in accordance with national law, but only extends to a right to adopt or integrate into a family a child which is the natural child of the couple: *X and Y v The Netherlands* no 7229/75 (Commission decision, 15 December 1977).

5.201

B16. Article 13 ECHR

Article 13 ECHR guarantees the 'right to an effective remedy before a national authority' where a person's rights guaranteed under the Convention have been violated, 'notwithstanding that the violation has been committed by persons acting in an official capacity'.

5.202

While Article 13 has not been incorporated into domestic law, domestic courts have stressed that applicants may not be left without an effective remedy under the Human Rights Act 1998. Applicants must, under the Human Rights Act or the common law, have effective remedies available to them for any breaches of the substantive guarantees under the ECHR: *Al-Skeini and others v Secretary of State for Defence* [2007] UKHL 26 [56]–[57] (per Lord Bingham); [147]–[148] (per Lord Brown); *R(K) v Camden*

5.203

---

[43] On the domestic case concerning a gay couple's inability to have their registered partnership recognised in India, see the unreported case of IA277272011 and IA277702011 [2013] UKAITUR IA277272011 (30 August 2013). See also *Vallianatos v Greece* [GC] no 29381/09; 32684/09 (07 November 2013), finding a violation of Article 14 taken with Article 8 on the basis of Greece's failure to extend registered partnerships from different-sex couples to same-sex couples.

[44] See also *R (Baiai) v SSHD* [2008] UKHL 5; [2009] AC 287.

and Islington Health Authority [2002] QB 198 [54] (per Sedley LJ); *SSHD v AF and AE* [2010] EWHC 42 (Admin) [73]–[76] (per Silber J).

5.204 In the context of expulsion and extradition proceedings, Article 13 ECHR is of particular significance because the right to a fair trial pursuant to Article 6 ECHR has been found to be inapplicable. The ECtHR so held in *Maaouia v France* [GC] no 39652/98 [2000] ECHR 455, [2001] 33 EHRR 42 [40], concerning deportation of an immigrant on account of various criminal offences.[45] The Court found that decisions regarding the entry, stay and deportation of non-nationals concern the determination of neither civil rights and obligations nor a criminal charge within the meaning of Article 6 ECHR; see also *SS v UK* no 12096/10 (admissibility decision, 24 January 2012) [85]. For the same reason, the Court decided in *Dalea v France* no 964/07 (admissibility decision, 2 February 2010) that Article 6 ECHR is not applicable to proceedings imposing a Schengen re-entry ban.

5.205 Generally, extradition proceedings also do not fall within the ambit of Article 6 ECHR: *Mamatkulov and Askarov v Turkey* nos 46827/99; 46951/99 [2005] ECHR 64, (2005) 41 EHRR 25 [82]. However, where extradition proceedings have a 'close link, in legislation, practice or fact, between the impugned statements made in the context of the extradition proceedings and the criminal proceedings pending against the applicants', Article 6 is applicable: *Ismoilov v Russia* no 2947/06 (24 April 2008) [163]; contrast *Panjeheighalehei v Denmark* no 11230/07 (13 October 2009).

5.206 Certain fair hearing guarantees have now been enshrined in Article 1 of Protocol 7 on the procedural safeguards relating to the expulsion of aliens, which the UK has neither signed nor ratified.

5.207 In the light of the procedural guarantees under the Common European Asylum System, particularly the Qualification Directive granting a right to refugee status provided that the refugee definition within the meaning of the CSR 50 is met as well as then granting a number of consequent rights in domestic law, including the right to work, access to medical and other state services and the right to an effective remedy under Article 47 of the EU Charter, it has been argued—so far unsuccessfully—that the scope of Article 6 ECHR should now encompass under its 'civil rights and obligations' limb the right to asylum: *R (otao MK (Iran) v SSHD* [2010] EWCA Civ 115; *HH (Iran) v SSHD* [2008] EWCA Civ 504. In a case currently pending before the EctHR, it is being argued that Article 6 ECHR applies to a fresh asylum claim because the right to have a fresh claim meeting the requirements of Article 32(4) of the Procedures Directive considered, taken with the right to an effective remedy under Article 47 of the EU Charter, constitutes a 'civil right': *N and others v UK* no 16458/12 (pending).

5.208 Article 13 ECHR guarantees the right to an effective remedy where a Convention right has been violated. The accessory nature of Article 13 does not require that an applicant demonstrate a violation of his rights. It is sufficient for an applicant to show that a violation is 'arguable', which must be determined 'in light of the particular facts and the nature of the legal issue or issues raised': *Boyle and Rice v UK* no 9659/82 [1988] ECHR 3, (1988) 10 EHRR 425 [53]–[55]. An arguable *refoulement* claim 'does not entail certainty'; it is sufficient that the fear of ill-treatment is 'subjectively well-founded and

---

[45] The ECtHR had, however, left open the possibility of the applicability of Article 6 in relation to an immigration case involving Article 8 ECHR in *Alam and Khan v UK* (2991/66) Eur Commission HR.

genuinely perceived as such' based on the available information on the human rights situation in that country and the personal circumstances of an applicant: *Diallo v Czech Republic* no 20493/07 [2011] ECHR 1015 [70].

Article 13 requires that there be a remedy to deal with the substance of an arguable complaint and to grant appropriate relief. The remedy must be effective in practice and in law: *Kudła v Poland* [GC] no 30210/96 [2000] ECHR 512, (2000) 35 EHRR 198, [157]–[158]. Article 13 does not require a specific procedure or one effective procedure; it is sufficient if the legal system as a whole provides for an effective remedy and Contracting States enjoy some discretion in this regard: *Jabari v Turkey* no 40035/98 [2000] ECHR 369, [2001] INLR 136; [48]. The guarantees required depend on the substantive Article that is being invoked: *De Souza Ribeiro v France* no 22689/07 [2012] ECHR 2066 [82]–[83] (in relation to a deportation case under Article 13 and Article 8 ECHR).

5.209

Given the importance of the guarantees provided in Article 3 ECHR, the margin of appreciation in cases involving Article 13 taken with Article 3 ECHR is limited: *Chahal v UK* [GC] no 22414/93 [1996] ECHR 54, (1996) 23 EHRR 413; [150]; *Shamayev and others v Georgia and Russia* no 36378/02 [2005] ECHR 233 [448]. In the asylum context, Article 13 guarantees an 'independent and rigorous scrutiny' of any claim involving a risk of treatment contrary to Article 3: *Jabari v Turkey*, at [50]. In *Singh and others v Belgium* no 33210/11 (2 October 2012) concerning Afghan Sikh asylum seekers who had been recognised as refugees by the UNHCR in India, the Court held that by failing to verify with the UNHCR the refugee status grant in India, the Belgian authorities had failed to comply with the requirements of Article 13 taken with Article 3 ECHR (at [104]–[105]).

5.210

Article 13 further includes the requirement that an asylum claim has automatic suspensive effect where a claim is arguable: *Gebremedhin [Gaberamadhien] v France* no 25389/05 (26 April 2007) [66]; *MSS*, at [293]; *Abdolkhani and Karimnia v Turkey* no 30471/08 (22 September 2009) [58]; *Čonka v Belgium* no 51564/99 [2002] ECHR 14, (2002) 34 EHRR 54 [75]; [83]. No exception is made for procedures under the Dublin Regulations: *MSS*, at [315].

5.211

One of the most fundamental requirements under Article 13 in the context of asylum proceedings is access to the asylum procedure. In *Hirsi Jamaa and others v Italy* [GC] no 27765/09, [2012] ECHR 1845, (2012) 55 EHRR 21, the Court found the failure to provide the Somali and Eritrean migrants with an opportunity to make an asylum claim, the failure to provide them with information about the Italian asylum system and the lack of interpreters and legal advisers to be in violation of Article 13 ECHR: *Hirsi Jamaa*, at [202]–[205]. But, in addition, the imposition of fees for applications for family reunion has been found to be in breach of Article 13 taken with Article 8 ECHR: *GR v The Netherlands* no 22251/07 (10 January 2012) [55].

5.212

Accelerated asylum procedures are not as such prohibited under Article 13, especially in manifestly ill-founded cases or substantially delayed asylum claims: *IM v France* no 9152/09 (2 February 2012) [142]; *KK v France* no 18913/11 (10 October 2013) [69]–[70] (delay in claiming asylum of two years after arrival); see also *NK v France* no 7974/11 (19 December 2013) [49]. However, the Court has criticised the use of accelerated asylum procedures for a first asylum procedure in *IM*. Short time limits, such as a time limit of five rather than 21 days to make an asylum claim, and the time limit for an appeal of 48 hours rather than two months had led to a non-effective procedure for the applicant

5.213

(at [143]–[144]). The procedure had failed to provide the applicant with access to interpreters and left him with very limited legal assistance, materially limiting his ability to adduce evidence to substantiate his claim (at [145]–[146]).

5.214 The protection afforded under Article 13 increasingly approaches that offered by Article 6 ECHR. The principles developed under Article 6 ECHR were found to be material to the interpretation of Article 13 ECHR in the context of the levying of fees, even though the requirements provided by Article 13 are less stringent than those developed under Article 6: *GR v The Netherlands* no 22251/07 (10 January 2012) [48]–[50].

B17. Article 14 ECHR

5.215 Article 14 ECHR prohibits discrimination on particular grounds when invoked in conjunction with other ECHR rights:

> The enjoyment of the rights and freedoms set forth in this Convention shall be secured without discrimination on any ground such as sex, race, colour, language, religion, political or other opinion, national or social origin, association with a national minority, property, birth or other status.

5.216 Article 14 ECHR only provides for an accessory prohibition on discrimination, which must fall within the ambit of one of the substantive Convention rights. This does not presuppose, however, that a substantive right has been violated; it is sufficient if the facts fall 'within the ambit' of such a right: *Gaygusuz v Austria* no 17371/90 [1996] ECHR 36, (1997) 23 EHRR 364 [36]; *Thlimmenos v Greece* [GC] no 34369/97 [2000] ECHR 162, (2001) 31 EHRR 15 [40].

5.217 The Court has defined 'discrimination' as the differential treatment of persons in similar situations on one of the prohibited grounds, without an objective and reasonable justification. An objective and reasonable justification must follow a 'legitimate aim' and there must be a 'reasonable relationship of proportionality between the means employed and the aim sought to be realised': *DH and others v Czech Republic* [GC] no 57325/00 [2006] ECHR 113, (2006) 43 EHRR 41 [175]; [196]. In certain circumstances, a failure to take positive action in order to correct an inequality through differential treatment also gives rise to a breach of Article 14: *Thlimmenos v Greece*, at [44]; *Stec and others v UK* [GC] nos 65731/01; 65900/01, [2006] ECHR 1162 [51].

5.218 Many of the prohibited grounds of differential treatment can arise in expulsion and exclusion cases, but the grounds relating to race, colour, language, national origin, birth and other status are likely to assume particular importance. Where differential treatment is based exclusively on national or ethnic origin, the Court requires 'very weighty reasons' as justification for such difference in treatment: *Gaygusuz v Austria*, at [42]; *Koua Poirrez v France* no 40892/98 [2003] ECHR 459, (2005) 40 EHRR 2 [46]. Such difference in treatment based on nationality was found to be in violation of Article 14 ECHR in *Andrejeva v Latvia* [GC] no 55707/00 [2009] ECHR 297 [88]–[89], which concerned the failure to pay a state pension to a permanent resident non-national which was available to Latvian nationals; on discrimination based on national origin, see also *Kurić and others v Slovenia* [GC] no 26828/06 [2012] ECHR 1083, (2013) 56 EHRR 20.

5.219 Further, in cases concerned with differential treatment based on race, colour or ethnic origin, the Court has held that any 'objective and reasonable justification' must be interpreted 'as strictly as possible': *Sampanis and others v Greece* no 32526/05 (5 June 2008) [69]; *Oršuš and others v Croatia* [GC] no 15766/03 [2010] ECHR 337, (2011) 52 EHRR 7 [156]. For instance, the Court held in *DH v Czech Republic* [GC] no 57325/00 [2007] ECHR 922, (2008) 47 EHRR 3 that separate schooling of Roma children in schools for children with special needs amounted to discrimination in violation of Article 14 taken with the right to education pursuant to Article 2 of Protocol 1.

Difference in treatment between persons born in and out of wedlock, including differences in nationality entitlements, are based on the prohibited ground of 'birth' (*Inze v Austria* no 8695/79 [1987] ECHR 28, (1988) 10 EHRR 394 [39]) and have been found to be in breach of Article 14: *Genovese v Malta* no 53124/09 [2011] ECHR 1590, (2014) 58 EHRR 25 [44]. 5.220

The terms 'other status' refer to a personal characteristic of the applicant, but the characteristic does not have to be 'innate or inherent': *Clift v UK* no 7205/07 (13 July 2010) [59]. Pertinently, the Court has found this to include the applicant's immigration status (*Hode and Abdi v UK* no 22341/09 [2012] ECHR 1871, (2013) 56 EHRR 27 [48]), as well as the immigration status of an applicant's son (*Bah v the UK* no 56328/07 [2011] ECHR 1448, (2012) 54 EHRR 21 [44]–[46]). 5.221

However, in *Biao v Denmark* no 38590/10 [2014] ECHR 304, the ECtHR did not find a violation of Article 14 taken with Article 8 ECHR in relation to a precondition for family reunion applications that the person making the application had held Danish nationality for at least 28 years prior to making the application for family reunion. Exceptions included persons born and raised in Denmark and persons with lawful residence of more than 28 years. The ECtHR accepted that there was differential treatment based on the number of years that the person had held Danish nationality, amounting to 'other status' (at [90]–[91]). However, in a judgment of a 4:3 majority, it found this difference to be objectively and reasonably justified in the particular circumstances of the case, in which it had found that no particularly close ties to Denmark existed. The ECtHR did, however, leave open the possibility that this rule may breach Article 14 in conjunction with Article 8 on different facts (at [103]–[106]). 5.222

B18. Article 15 ECHR

Article 15 ECHR provides that a State Party may (save that no derogation at all is permitted in relation to Articles 2 (barring deaths from lawful acts of war)), 3, 4, and 7: 5.223

> [I]n time of war or other public emergency threatening the life of the nation … take measures derogating from its obligations under this Convention to the extent strictly required by the exigencies of the situation, provided that such measures are not inconsistent with its other obligations under international law.

The Article requires that:

> Any High Contracting Party availing itself of this right of derogation shall keep the Secretary General of the Council of Europe fully informed of the measures which it has taken and the reasons therefor. It shall also inform the Secretary General of the Council of Europe when such measures have ceased to operate and the provisions of the Convention are again being fully executed.

5.224 In the case of *A and others v UK* no 3455/05 [2009] ECHR 301, (2009) 49 EHRR 29, the ECtHR found that the derogation entered in relation to Article 5(1) ECHR for the detention of suspected non-national terrorists was not 'strictly required' by the exigencies of a public emergency threatening the life of the nation. The ECtHR accepted the executive's and Parliament's assessment that there was, on the basis of a threat of serious terrorist attacks planned against the UK, a public emergency threatening the life of the nation. The ECtHR held that the derogation from Article 5 ECHR was not strictly required. It did not find it justified that indefinite detention without charge was required for non-nationals, but not nationals. The choice of an immigration measure to address the security problem was found to not adequately address the problem.

B19. Articles 3 and 4 of Protocol 4 to the ECHR

5.225 Protocol 4 to the ECHR entered into force on 2 May 1968. The UK has signed but not ratified it. Articles 3 and 4 provide as follows:

Article 3—Prohibition of expulsion of nationals

1. No one shall be expelled, by means either of an individual or of a collective measure, from the territory of the State of which he is a national.
2. No one shall be deprived of the right to enter the territory of the state of which he is a national.

Article 4—Prohibition of collective expulsion of aliens

Collective expulsion of aliens is prohibited.

5.226 Article 3 of Protocol 4 provides an absolute and unconditional prohibition on the expulsion of nationals. The question of whether an applicant is a national is 'determined, in principle, by reference to national law': *Slivenko v Latvia* [GC] no 48321/99 (admissibility decision, 23 January 2002) [77]. While the ECtHR has held that an arbitrary denial of nationality may amount to an interference with Article 8 ECHR, it has not yet decided whether Article 3 of Protocol 4 prohibits the arbitrary withdrawal or revocation of nationality.

5.227 The prohibition of expulsion of nationals also includes the right to return to one's own country: *L v Federal Republic of Germany* no 10564/83 (Commission decision, 10 December 1984); *M and S v Italy and UK* no 2584/11 (admissibility decision, 13 March 2012) [73]. However, the right of nationals to non-expulsion does not extend to extradition requests.

5.228 Article 4 of Protocol 4 provides for the absolute and unconditional prohibition on collective expulsions. The words 'collective expulsion' were defined by the Court in the admissibility decision in *Andric v Sweden* no 45917/99 (1999) 28 EHRR, in which the Court held that it referred to 'any measure compelling aliens, as a group, to leave a country, except where such a measure is taken on the basis of a reasonable and objective examination of the particular case of each individual alien of the group' (at [1]). The Court further confirmed that the collective expulsion provision does not apply where there are individual decisions taken in identical terms: 'the fact that a number of aliens receive similar decisions does not lead to the conclusion that there is a collective expulsion when each person concerned has been given the opportunity to put arguments against his expulsion to the competent authorities on an individual basis' (at [1]). In *Čonka v Belgium* no 51564/99 [2002] ECHR 14, (2002) 34 EHRR 54, the Court applied this to find at [63] a violation of Article 4 of Protocol 4 where the expulsion procedure did not provide 'sufficient guarantees demonstrating that the personal circumstances of each of those concerned had been genuinely and individually taken into account'.

In *Hirsi Jamaa and others v Italy* [GC] no 27765/09 [2012] ECHR 1845, (2012) 55 EHRR 21, the Court held that where the applicants were found to be within the jurisdiction of the Convention under Article 1 ECHR, there was a breach of Article 4 of Protocol 4 where a Contracting State prevented the entry of a group of migrants to its territory. On the facts of *Hirsi*, the Italian authorities had intercepted vessels containing Somali and Eritrean migrants coming from Libya and bound for Italy. The migrants were transferred onto Italian military ships and returned to Libya, where they were handed over to the Libyan authorities. The Court found a breach of Articles 3 and 13 ECHR, and Article 4 of Protocol 4.[46]

5.229

The judgment considerably extends the ambit of the prohibition on collective expulsions in light of the increasing use by Contracting States of policies to prevent asylum seekers from reaching their borders.[47] It further confirms the purpose of Article 4 of Protocol 4 as preventing the expulsion of aliens without the relevant authority undertaking an examination of their personal circumstances and enabling the individuals to lodge complaints (at [183]–[186]).

5.230

As noted above, Article 4 of Protocol 4 has not been ratified by the UK and has not been incorporated by the Human Rights Act 1998. Accordingly, the UK is not bound at an international level and Protocol 4 is not justiciable before domestic courts.

5.231

B20. Article 1 of Protocol 7 to the ECHR

Protocol 7 to the ECHR entered into force on 1 November 1988. The UK has neither ratified nor signed it. It provides inter alia for the attachment of procedural safeguards to the expulsion of aliens:

5.232

Protocol 7

Article 1—Procedural safeguards relating to expulsion of aliens

1. An alien lawfully resident in the territory of a State shall not be expelled therefrom except in pursuance of a decision reached in accordance with law and shall be allowed:
   a. to submit reasons against his expulsion,
   b. to have his case reviewed, and
   c. to be represented for these purposes before the competent authority or a person or persons designated by that authority.
2. An alien may be expelled before the exercise of his rights under paragraph 1.a, b and c of this Article, when such expulsion is necessary in the interests of public order or is grounded on reasons of national security.

---

[46] A currently pending case challenges the Maltese government's plans to send migrants arrived by boat back to Lybia: *Ahmed Abdi v Malta* no 43985/13, including claims under Articles 3, 13 and 4 of Protocol 4.

[47] Through, for example, interception at sea and bilateral agreements with third countries. See 'Case Comment, Immigration and Asylum: Refusal of Political Asylum Requests by Slovakian Nationals' (2002) 5 *European Human Rights Law Review* 351, 356; and Sheona York, 'Case Comment: Jamaa v Italy' [2012] *Journal of Immigration Asylum and Nationality Law* 283.

5.233 Article 1 of Protocol 7 provides for a series of procedural rights for aliens, namely that a decision on expulsion must be reached 'in accordance with the law' and aliens must be permitted to submit reasons against expulsion, have their case reviewed and be represented before the relevant authority. The issuing of a decision is a *conditio sine qua non* for compliance with Article 1 of Protocol 7 (*Bolat v Russia* no 14139/03 (5 October 2006) [82]) and the applicant must be provided with adequate notice of the decision, if necessary by way of adjournment (*Kaya v Romania* no 33970/05 (12 October 2006) [59]). Further it is a prerequisite that the factual basis for the expulsion decision be provided to the applicant: *Baltaji v Bulgaria* no 12919/04 (12 July 2011) [38]; [56]–[58] (also finding a violation of the lawfulness requirement under Article 8 ECHR); *Kaya v Romania*, at [59].

5.234 The requirement of 'lawfulness' of the decision further imports requirements of accessibility, foreseeability and protection against arbitrary interferences, similar to other ECHR articles: *Lupsa v Romania* no 10337/04 (8 June 2006) [55] (also finding a violation of the lawfulness requirement under Article 8 ECHR). Domestic legal provisions may thus nevertheless be found 'unlawful' based on arbitrariness. The expulsion prior to the expiry of the time limit to apply for suspensive effect, permitted under domestic law, was considered arbitrary and thus did not meet the requirements of 'lawfulness': *Takush v Greece* no 2853/09 (17 January 2012) [61]–[63].

5.235 The efficacy of the right is, however, limited. In particular, it only applies to aliens who are 'lawfully resident' in a Contracting State. The concept of 'lawful residence' is not autonomously defined, but is determined by reference to municipal law. It has been found to exclude decisions refusing asylum to asylum seekers (*ST v France* no 20649/92 (Commission decision, 8 February 1993)) and overstayers (*Voulfovitch and another v Sweden* no 19373/92 (Commission decision, 13 January 1993)). Further, it excludes aliens at the border and migrants whose status is or has become irregular, including those who have a new application for a residence permit pending. However, 'lawful residence' includes decisions revoking a residence permit against which a remedy has been taken (*Bolat v Russia* no 14139/03 (5 October 2006) [78]).

5.236 Expulsion is given an autonomous meaning under the ECHR. In the context of Article 1 of Protocol 7, it includes any measure 'compelling the alien's departure from the territory where he was lawfully resident' except for extradition: *Bolat v Russia*, at [79].

5.237 While review of the case is to be undertaken by a 'competent' authority, there is no requirement that it be judicial. However, the right of appeal to a person or body that is not independent, such as the minister of the department which issued the initial decision, does not meet the requirements of Article 1 of Protocol 7 'to have his case reviewed': *Baltaji v Bulgaria* no 12919/04 (12 July 2011) [58]. There is a general derogation where expulsion is necessary on the grounds of public order or national security.

5.238 As noted above, Protocol 7 has not been signed or ratified by the UK. As with Protocol 4, it may not therefore be relied upon internationally or domestically.

C. The ECN

5.239 By Article 1 ECN, the object of the treaty is to establish principles and rules relating to the nationality of natural persons and rules regulating military obligations in cases of multiple nationality. Article 3 ECN reproduces articles 1 and 2 of the League of Nations Convention on Certain Questions Relating to the Conflict of Nationality Law 1930 (CCQRCNL), which has already been set out at para 2.33 in Chapter 2:

Article 3—Competence of the State

1. Each State shall determine under its own law who are its nationals.
2. This law shall be accepted by other States in so far as it is consistent with applicable international conventions, customary international law and the principles of law generally recognised with regard to nationality.

5.240 Chapter II, consisting in Articles 4 and 5, sets out 'general principles' designed to guide nationality practice by states:

Article 4—Principles

The rules on nationality of each State Party shall be based on the following principles:

a. everyone has the right to a nationality;
b. statelessness shall be avoided;
c. no one shall be arbitrarily deprived of his or her nationality;
d. neither marriage nor the dissolution of a marriage between a national of a State Party and an alien, nor the change of nationality by one of the spouses during marriage, shall automatically affect the nationality of the other spouse.

Article 5—Non-discrimination
1. The rules of a State Party on nationality shall not contain distinctions or include any practice which amount to discrimination on the grounds of sex, religion, race, colour or national or ethnic origin.
2. Each State Party shall be guided by the principle of non-discrimination between its nationals, whether they are nationals by birth or have acquired its nationality subsequently.

5.241 Chapter III, consisting of Articles 6–9 inclusive, sets out 'rules' relating to nationality, including its acquisition (Article 6 ECN), its loss by operation of law or otherwise at the initiative of a state (Article 7 ECN), or a national (Article 8 ECN), and its recovery under conditions provided by municipal law by former nationals lawfully and habitually resident on its territory (Article 9 ECN). Amongst other provisions contained in the ECN are requirements at Chapter IV regarding procedural standards, by which states must ensure that decisions on applications related to its nationality are taken in a reasonable time (Article 10 ECN), that reasons in writing are given with decisions (Article 11 ECN), that decisions be susceptible to 'administrative or judicial review' under municipal law (Article 12 ECN) and that fees for nationality-related applications be reasonable and not raise an obstacle to application (Article 13 ECN). The ECN also contains provision for dealings by states with multiple nationality (Chapter V), with nationality where a new state comes into being ('state succession') (Chapter VI) and with military service (Chapter VII). Article 23 provides for cooperation between States Parties:

Article 23—Co-operation between the States Parties

1. With a view to facilitating co-operation between the States Parties, their competent authorities shall:
   a. provide the Secretary General of the Council of Europe with information about their internal law relating to nationality, including instances of statelessness and multiple nationality, and about developments concerning the application of the Convention;

b. provide each other upon request with information about their internal law relating to nationality and about developments concerning the application of the Convention.
2. States Parties shall co-operate amongst themselves and with other member States of the Council of Europe within the framework of the appropriate intergovernmental body of the Council of Europe in order to deal with all relevant problems and to promote the progressive development of legal principles and practice concerning nationality and related matters.

D. The CATHB

5.242   On 17 December 2008, the UK ratified the CATHB, which came into force in the UK on 1 April 2009. This relevantly provides as follows:

Chapter I—Purposes, scope, non-discrimination principle and definitions

Article 1—Purposes of the Convention

(a) to prevent and combat trafficking in human beings while guaranteeing gender equality;
(b) to protect the human rights of the victims of trafficking, design a comprehensive framework for the protection and assistance of victims and witnesses, while guaranteeing gender equality, as well as to ensure effective investigation and prosecution;
(c) to promote international cooperation on action against trafficking in human beings.

Article 2—Scope

This Convention shall apply to all forms of trafficking in human beings, whether national or transnational, whether or not connected with organised crime.

Article 3—Non-discrimination principle

The implementation of the provisions of this Convention by Parties, in particular the enjoyment of measures to protect and promote the rights of victims, shall be secured without discrimination on any ground such as sex, race, colour, language, religion, political or other opinion, national or social origin, association with a national minority, property, birth or other status.

Article 4—Definitions

For the purposes of this Convention:

a. 'Trafficking in human beings' shall mean the recruitment, transportation, transfer, harbouring or receipt of persons, by means of the threat or use of force or other forms of coercion, of abduction, of fraud, of deception, of the abuse of power or of a position of vulnerability or of the giving or receiving of payments or benefits to achieve the consent of a person having control over another person, for the purpose of exploitation. Exploitation shall include, at a minimum, the exploitation of the prostitution of others or other forms of sexual exploitation, forced labour or services, slavery or practices similar to slavery, servitude or the removal of organs;
b. The consent of a victim of 'trafficking in human beings' to the intended exploitation set forth in subparagraph (a) of this Article shall be irrelevant where any of the means set forth in subparagraph (a) have been used;
c. The recruitment, transportation, transfer, harbouring or receipt of a child for the purpose of exploitation shall be considered 'trafficking in human beings' even if this does not involve any of the means set forth in subparagraph (a) of this article;

d. 'Child' shall mean any person under eighteen years of age;
e. 'Victim' shall mean any natural person who is subject to trafficking in human beings as defined in this article.

In *R (Atamewan) v SSHD* [2013] EWHC 2727 (Admin), [2014] 1 WLR 1959, a Divisional Court of Aikens LJ and Silber J rejected the proposition that 'victim of trafficking' meant that only a victim subject to trafficking at that moment or that the passage of time or absence of perceived need for assistance removed qualification as a victim for purposes of the CATHB.

An Explanatory Report to the Trafficking Convention was published by the Council of Europe. This distinguishes 'human trafficking', as addressed by the Convention, from 'people smuggling': 5.243

> 7. The [Protocol to Prevent, Suppress and Punish Trafficking in Persons, Especially Women and Children, supplementing the United Nations Convention against Transnational Organized Crime (hereinafter 'the Palermo Protocol')] contains the first agreed, internationally binding definition (taken over into the Council of Europe convention) of the term 'Trafficking in persons' ... It is important to stress at this point that trafficking in human beings is to be distinguished from smuggling of migrants. The latter is the subject of a separate protocol to the United Nations Convention against Transnational Organized Crime ... While the aim of smuggling of migrants is the unlawful cross-border transport in order to obtain, directly or indirectly, a financial or other material benefit, the purpose of trafficking in human beings is exploitation. Furthermore, trafficking in human beings does not necessarily involve a transnational element; it can exist at [a] national level.

The Explanatory Report further provides relevantly that: 5.244

> 76. For there to be trafficking in human beings ingredients from each of the three categories (action, means, purpose) must be present together. There is, however, an exception regarding children: under Article 4(c) recruitment, transportation, transfer, harbouring or receipt of a child for the purpose of exploitation is to be regarded as trafficking in human beings even if it does not involve any of the means listed in Article 4(a). Under Article 4(d) the word 'child' means any person under 18 years of age.
> 77. Thus trafficking means much more than mere organised movement of persons for profit. The critical additional factors that distinguish trafficking from migrant smuggling are use of one of the means listed (force, deception, abuse of a situation of vulnerability and so on) throughout or at some stage in the process, and use of that means for the purpose of exploitation.

Under Article 10(2) CATHB, a state whose competent authorities have reasonable grounds to believe that a person has been the victim of trafficking in human beings shall not remove that person from its territory until the identification process as a victim of an offence provided for in Article 18 CATHB has been completed. 5.245

Article 13 CATHB provides that each State Party 'shall provide in its internal law a recovery and reflection period of at least 30 days, when there are reasonable grounds to believe that the person concerned is a victim' (in practice, the UK has provided a standardised period at 45 days in these circumstances). Under Article 13(2) CATHB, 'it shall not be possible to enforce any expulsion order against him or her' during this period. 5.246

Finally, under Article 14 CATHB, a State Party is required to issue a renewable residence permit to victims where the victim's stay is 'necessary owing to his or her personal situation; and/or for the purpose of cooperation with the competent authorities in investigation or criminal proceedings relating to trafficking'. 5.247

6
EU Law

Contents

A. Introduction 6.1
B. Regulating Principles of EU Law 6.4
   B1. Scope of EU Law 6.5
   B2. Supremacy and Direct and Indirect Effect 6.9
   B3. General Principles of EU Law 6.11
C. EU Fundamental Rights 6.16
D. The Free Movement Rights of EU Citizens and their Family Members 6.20
   D1. Denial or Deprivation of Nationality 6.23
   D2. Expulsion and Exclusion in EU Law 6.28
       Introduction 6.28
       Expulsion and Exclusion of EU Citizens Exercising Rights under the
       Treaties and the Citizens' Directive 6.37
       Expulsion and Exclusion of EU Citizens Not Exercising Rights under the
       Citizens' Directive 6.58
E. Turkish Nationals 6.69
F. International Protection in EU Law 6.72
   F1. The Qualification Directive 6.77
   F2. The Dublin III Regulation 6.87
G. The EU Law of Human Trafficking 6.90

A. Introduction

This chapter examines the law of the EU relevant to expulsion and/or exclusion from the territory of the UK and denial or deprivation of British and, consequentially, of EU citizenship. It does not expand upon the domestic statutory instruments transposing EU legislation or domestic case law, which are severally addressed in chapters 8 to 12. **6.1**

The UK acceded to the European Community, the precursor of the EU, on 1 January 1973. A substantial body of EU law is made directly applicable in the UK by virtue of section 2 European Communities Act 1972. The principal sources of EU law are the Treaties: the Treaty on European Union (TEU) and the Treaty on the Functioning of the European Union (TFEU), secondary legislation (including regulations, directives and decisions);[1] agreements with third countries;[2] case law of the Court of Justice of the **6.2**

---

[1] Article 288 TFEU (ex 249 EC).
[2] See, in the context of the subject matter of this work, eg, the EEC Turkey Association Agreement 1963 at section E.

Part B – Legal Framework

European Union (CJEU) and the General Court; the general principles of EU law; and the Charter of Fundamental Rights of the European Union (CFREU).

6.3 This chapter will cover first the overarching principles of EU law that may be of relevance to cases within the subject matter of this book. It will then consider expulsion, exclusion, denial or deprivation of nationality within the various EU regimes applicable in the UK.[3]

B. Regulating Principles of EU Law

6.4 There are a number of principles that determine and guide the application of EU law. It is beyond the scope of this work to cover them in detail; however, since they affect the ability of Member States to exclude individuals within the scope of EU law from rights protected by EU law, they may be relevant in challenging domestic measures of expulsion and/or exclusion and denial or deprivation of nationality.

B1. Scope of EU Law

6.5 The first important point is that EU law is only engaged where the act, omission or measure of a Member State authority falls within the scope of EU law. In general terms, the overall regulating principle is the existence of a sufficiently strong connection with the EU Treaties or secondary legislation.[4] The test has been framed in a number of ways in the case law of the CJEU. These include whether the national act, omission or measure implements or derogates from EU law (see Case C-260/89 *ERT* [1991] ECR I-2925) and whether it has its ultimate authority in EU law (see Case C-206/13 *Siragusa*, judgment of 6 March 2014). Where national action (etc) does not fall within the scope of EU law, the situation is purely internal and consequently EU norms, including the general principles and the CFREU, are not applicable. The principle has proved difficult to implement in practice and the CJEU has adopted a case-by-case consideration of the question of scope, which has led to a complicated jurisprudence.[5]

6.6 In the context of EU citizenship and free movement (examined in more detail below), in order to engage EU law, it is necessary to demonstrate the presence of a cross-border element or, more rarely, that Member State action would force the individual to leave the territory of the EU (Case C-34/09 *Ruiz Zambrano* [2011] ECR I-1177). Thus, simply holding EU citizenship on the basis of being a British national is insufficient to bring an individual within the scope of EU law.[6]

---

[3] Since the Treaty of Amsterdam, the UK has opted not to participate in various EU measures in asylum and immigration.

[4] But not the general principles or the CFREU, which apply only once it has been established that a case falls within the scope of EU law: see section B1.

[5] See, for a more detailed exploration of the scope of EU law, R Gordon QC and R Moffatt, *EU Law in Judicial Review* (2nd edn, Oxford, Oxford University Press, 2014).

[6] Equally, merely holding citizenship of both the UK and another Member State will not bring an individual within the scope of EU law without an element of free movement: Case C-434/09 *McCarthy* [2011] ECR I-3375.

Article 51(1) CFREU governs the application of the Charter to domestic law. It provides that the CFREU is binding on Member States 'only when they are implementing Union law'. The CJEU in Case C-617/10 *Akerberg Fransson* confirmed that 'implementing' under Article 51(1) CFREU had the same meaning as the previous case law on the scope of EU law (see para 6.5 above).

6.7

Once it is established that EU law is engaged, certain other regulating principles of EU law apply. Some of these which are relevant to the subject matter of this work are considered below.

6.8

B2. Supremacy and Direct and Indirect Effect

The foundational principles of the EU legal order, established by the CJEU in the 1960s, are those of supremacy and direct effect (see Case C-26/62 *Van Gend Loos v Netherlandse Administratie der Berlastingen* [1963] ECR 1; Case C-6/64 *Costa v ENEL* [1964] ECR I-585). In practice, supremacy requires an obligation on Member State authorities (including national courts and tribunals) to disapply any national provision which contradicts EU law: Case C-11/70 *Internationale Handelsgesellschaft v Einfuhr und Vorratsstelle fur Getreide und Futtermittel* [1970] ECR 1125; *R v SS for Transport exp Factortame (No 2)* [1991] AC 603. Direct effect permits the reliance before national courts on provisions of EU law (including the jurisprudence of the CJEU) that are sufficiently clear, precise and unconditional. The ability to rely on directly effective provisions of EU law is of particular importance in relation to directives where domestic transposition may be flawed or may not take account of recent case law developments.

6.9

Further, even in the absence of direct effect, Member States must interpret national law so as to be in conformity with applicable EU law as far as it is possible to do so: Case C-106/89 *Marleasing SA v La Commercial Internacional de Alimentacion SA* [1990] ECR I-4135.

6.10

B3. General Principles of EU Law

The CJEU has also identified and developed a number of 'general principles' of EU law. These constitute an important source of EU law in addition to the Treaties and secondary instruments. They apply only within the scope of EU law[7] and constitute important norms by which the lawfulness of EU legislation and national measures within the scope of EU law is assessed.

6.11

The general principle of proportionality is important in application to the subject area of this work. In very broad terms, proportionality under EU law requires Member States' acts, omissions or measures to be necessary in the public interest to attain the purpose in question: see, eg, Case C-55/94 *Gebhard v Consignol dell Ordine degli Advocat AE Procuratori di Milano* [1995] ECR I-4165.

6.12

It has been found domestically that EU proportionality demands more than proportionality in an HRA context: *R (Countryside Alliance) v (1) Attorney General and*

6.13

---

[7] See section B1 above.

(2) Secretary of State for Environment, Food and Rural Affairs [2006] EWCA Civ 817, [2007] QB 305. In essence, opinion is divided on whether the test of necessity in EU law is stricter such that the existence of less onerous means to achieve a legitimate aim would render other measures disproportionate. In the context of the proportionality of the deportation of an EU citizen, the failure to consider the EU dimension of an appeal has been held to constitute an error of law: *R (Essa) v Upper Tribunal (Immigration and Asylum Chamber) and another* [2012] EWCA Civ 1718, [2012] WLR (D) 393.

6.14 The general principle of non-discrimination is of unique importance in EU law as all free movement rights are founded upon it. In essence, the principle requires that 'similar situations should not be treated differently and that different situations should not be treated identically unless such differentiation is objectively justified': Case C-479/93 *Francovich v Italy* [1995] ECR I-3843 [43]. Various manifestations of the principle are found in the Treaties. Article 18 TFEU outlaws discrimination on grounds of nationality. This principle is expanded by virtue of Article 19(1) TFEU, which enables the EU institutions to 'take appropriate action to combat discrimination based on sex, racial or ethnic origin, religion or belief, disability, age or sexual orientation'. Within the scope of EU law, there is also protection against discrimination in Article 21 CFREU.

6.15 Of further relevance in the context of the subject matter of this book is the principle established in the case law that derogations from EU rights must be interpreted narrowly (Case C-348/96 *Criminal Proceedings against Calfa* [1999] ECR I-11) and may not be used for purely economic purposes: see, eg, Case 352/85 *Bond v The Netherlands* [1988] ECR 2085.

C. EU Fundamental Rights

6.16 The protection of fundamental rights under EU law has developed incrementally through the general principles since the 1970s. Following the entry into force of the Treaty of Lisbon on 1 December 2009, the CFREU became legally binding and of the same legal value as the Treaties: Article 6(1) TEU. The status of fundamental rights as general principles of law was also confirmed: Article 6(3) TEU. The Lisbon Treaty also provides for the accession of the EU to the ECHR: Article 6(2) TEU. Even once the EU has acceded to the ECHR, however, there will remain two separate but interlocking human rights regimes in the European legal space, in particular since the fundamental rights protected by EU law may be broader in application and greater in intensity (see para 6.19 below).[8]

6.17 As with the general principles, the CFREU operates only within the scope of EU law.[9] The application of the CFREU is set out in the 'General Provisions' in Title VII (Articles 51–54 CFREU)[10] and Article 6 TEU. Article 51(2) CFEEU provides that: 'The Charter does not extend the field of application of Union law beyond the powers of the Union

---

[8] For a detailed examination of the ECHR, see ch 5. For the domestic application of fundamental rights under the ECHR and the CFREU, see generally chs 8–12.
[9] For which see section B3 above.
[10] The third sentence of Article 6(1) TEU obliges the CFREU to be interpreted in accordance with its general provisions.

or establish any power or task for the Union, or modify powers and tasks as defined by the Treaties.' Similarly, Article 6(1) provides (relevantly) that: 'The provisions of the Charter shall not extend in any way the competences of the Union as defined in the Treaties.' Further, Article 1(1) of Protocol (No 30) on the Application of the Charter of Fundamental Rights of the European Union to Poland and to the UK provides:

> The Charter does not extend the ability of the Court of Justice of the European Union, or any court or tribunal of Poland or of the United Kingdom, to find that the laws, regulations or administrative provisions, practices or action of Poland or of the United Kingdom are inconsistent with the fundamental rights, freedoms and principles that it reaffirms.

The CJEU in Joined Cases C-411/10 and C-493/10 *NS v SSHD* [2011] ECR I-13905 has clarified that (at least) in respect of Titles I–III and V–VI of the CFREU,[11] Protocol (No 30) does not constitute an opt-out from or further limitation on the application of the CFREU. Accordingly, it does not 'exempt the ... United Kingdom from the obligation to comply with the provisions of the Charter or to prevent a court of one of those Member States from ensuring compliance with those provisions' (at [120]).   6.18

Many of the CFREU rights relevant to the subject matter of book have counterparts in the ECHR: most importantly, Article 4 CFREU prohibits torture and inhuman and degrading treatment, and Article 7 provides for respect for family and private life. Pursuant to Article 52(3) CFREU, Charter rights with counterparts in the ECHR should be interpreted in accordance with the meaning and scope of their corresponding ECHR rights as per the Strasbourg jurisprudence, although the EU may provide for greater protection. Importantly, there are some rights protected by the CFREU which have a broader scope than their Strasbourg counterparts. Most significantly for the purposes of this work, Article 47 CFREU (right to a fair trial) applies, unlike Article 6 ECHR, to immigration and asylum, while some rights protected by the CFREU do not have counterparts in Strasbourg: of particular relevance may be Article 41 (the right to good administration).[12] While the right to dignity (Article 1 CFREU) has not been seen by domestic courts as affording protection different from that expressly provided for in EU law,[13] the CJEU's interpretation of the Reception and Procedures Directives[14] clearly establishes Article 1 CFREU as having independent application. The application of the right to dignity extends not only to conditions encountered in the process of claiming international protection, but also other physical conditions and possibly international protection medical cases.   6.19

---

[11] The CJEU did not find it necessary to rule on the effectiveness of Article 1(2) of the Protocol, namely in relation to the CFREU's 'solidarity rights' (Articles 27–38).

[12] See, eg, Case C-175/11 *HID, BA v Refugee Applications Commissioner*, Refugee Appeals Tribunal, Minister for Justice, Equality and Law Reform, Ireland, judgment of 31 January 2013, [80]–[83] on Article 47 CFREU; and Case C-277/11 *MM v Minister for Justice*, Equality and Law Reform, Ireland, Attorney General, judgment of 22 November 2012, [81]–[94] on Articles 41, 47 and 48 CFREU.

[13] *Medhanye, R (on the Application of) v SSHD* [2011] EWHC 3012 (Admin) Hickinbottom [45]. In the Court of Appeal (*R (on the Application of EM (Eritrea)) v SSHD* [2012] EWCA Civ 1336, [2013] 1 WLR 576) the issue was not addressed but permission was granted on the issue to the Supreme Court, where it appears the issues were re-defined in the context of the Secretary of State's new position.

[14] Case C-179/11 *Cimade, Groupe d'information et de soutien des immigrés (GISTI) v Ministre de l'Intérieur, de l'Outre-mer, des Collectivités territoriales et de l'Immigration*, judgment of 27 September 2012, [42] and [56]; in relation to the Reception Directive; Joined Cases C-411/10 and C-493/10 *NS v SSHD* [2011] ECR I-13905, [2013] QB 102 [147]: Articles 1, 18 and 47 of the Charter do not lead to a different answer.

D. The Free Movement Rights of EU Citizens and their Family Members

6.20 The free movement of persons within the territory of the EU is one of the fundamental economic freedoms provided for in the TFEU. In particular, Article 45 provides for the free movement of workers, Article 49 governs the right to the freedom of establishment and Article 56 governs the freedom to provide cross-border services. Since the Treaty of Maastricht created EU citizenship in 1993, EU rights have been held to derive from EU citizenship. What is now Article 20 TFEU establishes citizenship of the EU and Article 21 TFEU provides for the right of EU citizens to move and reside freely within the territory of the EU.

6.21 Free movement rights are enjoyed by nationals of states belonging to European Economic Area (27 EU Member States and three parties to EEA Agreement: Iceland, Liechtenstein and Norway). The nationals of Switzerland have similar rights through the EC-Switzerland Agreement on the Free Movement of Persons.[15]

6.22 EU free movement rights should be distinguished from traditional domestic systems of immigration control based on state sovereignty and discretion over the entry, residence and expulsion of aliens. Accordingly, Member State authorities must apply a different set of principles to those individuals whose cases fall within the scope of EU law[16] and, as discussed below, there are specific rules applicable to the expulsion and/or exclusion of EU citizens and their family members. EU law may also impact upon administrative decisions on the denial or deprivation of citizenship. This is examined immediately below and also in chapters 11 and 12.

D1. Denial or Deprivation of Nationality

6.23 EU citizenship is not free-standing, but rather follows from possession of the nationality of a Member State. Article 20 TFEU reads (relevantly):

1. Citizenship of the Union is hereby established. Every person holding the nationality of a Member State shall be a citizen of the Union. Citizenship of the Union shall be additional to and not replace national citizenship.
2. Citizens of the Union shall enjoy the rights and be subject to the duties provided for in the Treaties. They shall have, inter alia:
   (a) the right to move and reside freely within the territory of the Member States;
   …

These rights shall be exercised in accordance with the conditions and limits defined by the Treaties and by the measures adopted thereunder.

6.24 It is therefore for each Member State, 'having due regard to Community law, to lay down the conditions for the acquisition and loss of nationality': Case C-369/90 *Micheletti and*

---

[15] Although following a referendum on 9 February 2014 in which the Swiss voted to impose quotas on immigration to the EU, the future of the extension of EU free movement to Switzerland is in question.
[16] See section B1 above.

others [1992] ECR I-4239 [10].[17] In Case C-192/99 *R (Kaur) v SSHD* [2001] ECR I-1237, the CJEU reaffirmed this in ruling that national legislation on nationality determined the scope of the Treaty *ratione personae*. Thus, in *Kaur* it was found that EU rights never arose in respect of persons not satisfying the national conditions for acquisition of nationality, but markedly this was in the context of examination of the Declarations defining who was a British national[18] and the finding that 'adoption of that declaration did not have the effect of depriving any person who did not satisfy the definition of a national of the United Kingdom of rights to which that person might be entitled under Community law'.[19] It is important to note that all the case law of the CJEU postdating *Micheletti* reiterated the fundamental principle that Member States must have regard to EU law in the context of both acquisition and denial of citizenship. The scope of this principle remains largely untested, especially in the context of the commitment to respect of fundamental rights.

The loss of the nationality of a Member State may be subject to procedural guarantees of EU law: Case C-135/08 *Rottmann* [2010] ECR I-1449. *Rottmann* concerned the application of EU law to a situation in which a Member State (Germany) sought to withdraw retroactively the grant of German nationality to a former Austrian national who had lost his Austrian nationality by operation of Austrian law upon the acquisition of German nationality. Noting that the acquisition and loss of nationality are matters of domestic competence, the Court observed that 'the fact that a matter falls within the competence of the member states does not alter the fact that, in situations covered by European Union law, the national rules concerned must have due regard to the latter' (at [41]). Thus, the fact that the withdrawal of the second nationality placed Rottmann in a position of losing the status and rights conferred by what is now Article 20 TFEU brought the matter within the ambit of EU law (at [42]).[20] As a result, the withdrawal of nationality had to observe the EU general principle of proportionality (at [55]).[21] The CJEU (at [56]) then identified relevant factors to be taken into account when assessing the proportionality of such a decision as being:

6.25

> [T]he consequences that the decision entails for the person concerned and, if relevant, for the members of his family with regard to the loss of the rights enjoyed by every citizen of the Union … whether that loss is justified in relation to the gravity of the offence committed by that person, to the lapse of time between the naturalisation decision and the withdrawal decision and to whether it is possible for that person to recover his original nationality.

---

[17] In this case the CJEU ruled that one Member State was not entitled to restrict the effects of the attribution of the nationality of another Member State by imposing an additional condition on recognition of that nationality for the purpose of exercising EU fundamental freedoms.

[18] Declaration by the Government of the United Kingdom of Great Britain and Northern Ireland on the definition of the term 'nationals', annexed to the Final Act of the Treaty concerning the Accession of the Kingdom of Denmark, Ireland and the United Kingdom of Great Britain and Northern Ireland to the European Communities [1972] OJ L73, 196; Declaration by the Government of the United Kingdom of Great Britain and Northern Ireland on the definition of the term 'nationals' [1983] OJ C23, 1), and of Declaration No 2 on Nationality of a Member State, annexed to the Final Act of the Treaty on European Union [1992] OJ C191, 98.

[19] Compare the deprivation of nationality in *Rottmann* (para 6.25 below).

[20] See section B1 above for further treatment of the scope of EU law.

[21] See section B3 above.

6.26　In policy terms, the Commission has 'stress[ed] the importance of acquiring nationality and civic citizenship as a means of facilitating positive integration' given the rights and responsibilities that citizenship brings in relation to legally resident third-country nationals.[22] Following *Rottmann*, the Commission announced that it will 'encourage initiatives and projects aimed at acquiring and sharing knowledge and exchanging experience on conditions and procedures for forfeiting Member States' nationality and, consequently, EU Citizenship, to disseminate good practices and, where necessary, facilitating coordination, without encroaching on national competences'.[23] Nevertheless, there is no instrument that has codified common practices or set common standards on the denial or withdrawal of citizenship.

6.27　The application of *Rottmann* in the domestic context is examined in more detail in chapters 11 and 12. It suffices to note here that it is less than clear whether domestic judicial rejection of the its application in *G1 (Sudan) v SSHD* [2012] EWCA Civ 867, [2013] QB 1008 is consistent with the approach taken by the CJEU, in particular when combined with the increasing focus on fundamental rights in EU law. In *G1 (Sudan)* the claimant, who had been deprived of his British nationality under section 40(2) British Nationality Act 1981 on account of G's alleged involvement in terrorist-related activities, sought to argue that following *Rottmann*, his case was within the scope of EU law and therefore substantive EU fundamental rights protections and proportionality should be applied. The Court of Appeal disagreed and found that the EU was not engaged at all.

D2. Expulsion and Exclusion in EU Law

Introduction

6.28　In general terms, EU citizens and their family members exercising free movement rights may only be expelled or excluded from the UK on the grounds of public policy, public security and public health, and on the principles set out below. EU citizens who are not exercising Treaty rights may be expelled on grounds other than public policy, security and health; however, expulsion must respect EU general principles of law and, in particular, the principle of proportionality and EU fundamental rights, including those protected by the CFREU.

6.29　It is beyond the scope of this work to cover in detail the conditions for attaining a right of entry or residence in EU law, but since the existence of an EU right of entry and/or residence is relevant to the type of expulsion or exclusion measures that a host state may employ, a summary of the central principles is provided below.[24]

6.30　Article 21 TFEU provides that: 'Every citizen of the Union shall have the right to move and reside freely within the territory of the Member States, subject to the

---

[22] Communication from the Commission to the Council, the European Parliament, the European Economic and Social Committee and the Committee of the Regions on immigration, integration and employment COM(2003) 336.
[23] Communication from the Commission to the Council, the European Parliament, the European Economic and Social Committee, under Article 25 TFEU, on progress towards effective EU Citizenship 2007–2010 COM(2010) 603.
[24] See further N Rogers, R Scannell and J Walsh, *Free Movement of Persons in the Enlarged European Union* (2nd edn, London, Sweet & Maxwell, 2012).

limitations and conditions laid down in the Treaties and by the measures adopted to give them effect.' It also enables secondary legislation in the area. Directive 2004/38/EC[25] (hereinafter 'the Citizens' Directive') is the most comprehensive piece of secondary legislation on the free movement rights of EU citizens and their family members.[26] The provisions of the Citizens' Directive 'cannot be interpreted restrictively, and must not in any event be deprived of their effectiveness': Case C-127/08 *Metock v Minister for Justice* [2008] ECR I-6241 [84].

6.31 The Citizens' Directive thus sets out the principles for the right of entry, residence and standards for expulsion (see later) of those entitled to exercise free movement rights (the core categories are workers, self-employed persons, students and self-sufficient persons)[27] and their family members as defined. There are two categories of family members with somewhat different status. Family members coming under Article 2 of the Citizens' Directive[28] enjoy automatic rights of entry and residence. On the other hand, 'the host Member State shall, in accordance with its national legislation, facilitate entry and residence' for family members coming under Article 3, which applies to unmarried partners in a durable relationship as well as certain dependent relatives not falling within Article 2,[29] thus making their rights of residence subject to a Member State's procedures.

6.32 Any EU citizen as well as his or her family members have a right to enter and reside in another Member State for an initial period of three months: Articles 5 and 6 Citizens' Directive. Beyond the initial three months, those individuals falling under the substantive free movement categories (generally, workers, self-employed persons, students and self-sufficient persons) have a right of residence. However, that continued right of residence is usually dependent on maintaining status as a worker, self-employed person etc.[30] Under certain circumstances, on the death, departure or divorce from the EU

---

[25] Directive 2004/38 of the European Parliament and of the Council of 29 April 2004 on the right of citizens of the Union and their family members to move and reside freely within the territory of the Member States amending Regulation (EEC) No 1612/68 and repealing Directives 64/221/EEC, 68/360/EEC, 72/194/EEC, 73/148/EEC, 75/34/EEC, 75/35/EEC, 90/364/EEC, 90/365/EEC and 93/96/EEC [2004] OJ L229/35 and as to its application Communication from the Commission to the European Parliament and the Council on guidance for better transposition and application of Directive 2004/38/EC on the right of citizens of the Union and their family members to move and reside freely within the territory of the Member States COM (2009)313.

[26] By virtue of the EEA Agreement and the EC-Switzerland Agreement on the Free Movement of Persons, the provisions of the Directive also apply to the EEA States and Switzerland, but see n 15 above.

[27] Article 7 Citizens' Directive lists these categories. See also Articles 45 (workers) and 49 (self-employed) TFEU. These categories have autonomous EU meanings that are not examined here. Regard should be had to general EU textbooks for a full account.

[28] Article 2(2): (a) the spouse; (b) the partner with whom the EU citizen has contracted a registered partnership, on the basis of the legislation of a Member State, if the legislation of the host Member State treats registered partnerships as equivalent to marriage and in accordance with the conditions laid down in the relevant legislation of the host Member State; (c) the direct descendants who are under the age of 21 or are dependants and those of the spouse or partner as defined in point (b); (d) the dependent direct relatives in the ascending line and those of the spouse or partner as defined in point (b).

[29] Article 3(2)(a): 'who, in the country from which they have come, are dependents or members of the household of the Union citizen having the primary right of residence, or where serious health grounds strictly require the personal care of the family member by the Union citizen.' On the question of who qualifies as a dependant relative, see Case C-83/11 *SSHD v Muhammad Sazzadur Rahman and others*, judgment of 5 September 2012.

[30] See Citizens' Directive, Article 7.

citizen, their family members can retain the right of residence.[31] The Citizens' Directive introduced a permanent right of residence for those who have settled on a long-term basis in a Member State as a vehicle to 'strengthen the feeling of Union citizenship and is a key element in promoting social cohesion, which is one of the fundamental objectives of the Union'.[32] A permanent right of residence is not subject to any conditions and is normally attained after five years of substantive compliance with the requirements of the Citizens' Directive.[33] Acquiring permanent residence has consequences for the ability of Member States to expel EU citizens and their family members.[34]

6.33 Distinct from rights acquired by family members of EU citizens under the Citizens' Directive, third-country nationals may derive a right to enter or reside from the EU citizenship of a relative in certain circumstances. To date, the case law has established the following derived rights of residence:

i. self-sufficient EU citizen children resident in a Member State other than that of their nationality may in certain circumstances confer a right to reside on their third-country national parents or primary carers: Case 200/02 *Zhu and Chen* [2004] ECR I-9925; Case C-86/12 *Alokpa v Ministre du Travail, de l'Emploi et de l'Immigration*, judgment of 10 October 2013 [27]–[30];

ii. the children of former workers who are in education and their carer(s) may have a right of residence following a broad interpretation of Article 12 of Regulation 1612/68 or the present Article 10 of Regulation 492/2011:[35] Case C-480/08 *Teixeira v London Borough of Lambeth and SSHD* [2010] ECR I-1107; Case C-310/08 *London Borough of Harrow v Ibrahim* [2010] ECR I-01065; Case C-45/12 *OFNATS v Ahmed*, judgment of 13 June 2013;

iii. EU citizens resident in their home Member State may confer a right of residence on their third country national family members if the EU citizen has some work link with another Member State and he or she would be discouraged from effectively exercising the right to work in another Member State if he or she could not live with the third country family members in the home Member State: Case C-60/00 *Carpenter* [2002] ECR I-6279; Case C-457/12 *S & G*, judgment of 12 March 2014;

iv. EU citizens who have moved to another Member State exercise a right of residence for more than three months and may confer a right of residence on their third country national family members once they have moved back to their home

---

[31] See Citizens' Directive, Articles 12 and 13.
[32] Citizens' Directive, preamble, recital 17. See also recital 18.
[33] Citizens' Directive, Articles 12, 13, 16 and 17. Note that certain categories obtain permanent residence for a period less than five years. The period of five years must be legal residence and cannot include periods of imprisonment, nor can the periods before and after imprisonment be aggregated to amount to five years: Case C-378/12 *Nnamdi Onuekwere v SSHD*, judgment of 16 January 2014. It is as yet undecided whether a period of inactivity may in fact permit aggregation of periods before and after so as to amount to five years.
[34] See para 6.37 *et seq*.
[35] Regulation (EEC) No 1612/68 of the Council of 15 October 1968 on freedom of movement for workers within the Community, as amended by Council Regulation (EEC) No 2434/92 of 27 July 1992 Regulation 492/2011 of the European Parliament and Council of 5 April 2011 on freedom of movement for workers within the Union re-codified the provisions of the Regulation 1612/68 and repealed the same, but preserved the provision in issue in the present case (Article 12 of Regulation 1612/68) in identical form in Article 10 of Regulation 492/2011.

Member State: Case C-370/90 *Surinder Singh* [1992] ECR I-4265; Case C-456/12 *O and B*, judgment of 12 March 2014;

v. EU citizen children who are present in the Member State of their nationality may confer a right to reside on their third country national family members where otherwise the EU citizen would be forced to leave the territory of the EU (Case C-34/09 *Ruiz Zambrano* [2011] ECR I-1177; Case 256/11 *Dereci* [2011] ECR I-11315) or where their decisions refusing residence permits at issue in the main proceedings are liable to undermine the effectiveness of the EU citizenship (Joined Cases C-356/11 and C-357/11 *O and S v Maahanmuuttovirasto; Maahanmuuttovirasto v L* [2013] WLR 1093 [53]; Case C-86/12 Alokpa, judgment of 10 October 2013).[36]

Also distinct from rights under the Citizens' Directive are the rights of third country nationals who are posted in a host Member State by a commercial undertaking based in another Member State. The CJEU in Case C-43/93 *Raymond vander Elst v Office des Migrations Internationales* [1994] ECR I-3803 held that where an undertaking established in one Member State is providing services in a host Member State, any of its non-EU national employees who are posted to the host Member State in relation to that service provision will not be subject to a requirement for work permits or to pay any attendant costs for as long as is necessary to carry out the work, provided that they are lawfully and habitually employed by the sending undertaking in the first Member State. Directive 96/71/EC (the Posted Workers Directive) regulates the employment conditions of *Vander Elst* posted workers.   6.34

It is not necessary for the EU citizens and their family members to obtain residence documents in order to enjoy the right of residence (Article 25(1) Citizens' Directive) and non-compliance with administrative formalities including non-production of identity documents cannot on its own justify expulsion or refusal of entry (Article 5(4) Citizens' Directive).[37] The situation is somewhat different for the family members falling under Article 3 Citizens' Directive where the Member States are required to facilitate their entry according to the national rules. In practice, it is generally advisable for the third country national family members of EU citizens to obtain documentation to facilitate their entry and exit from the UK. Without documentation, their right to seek and retain employment will be difficult to enforce.   6.35

As noted earlier, the principles that apply to expulsion and exclusion depend on whether or not an EU citizen is exercising Treaty rights. The two scenarios are examined in the following sections.   6.36

Expulsion and Exclusion of EU Citizens Exercising Rights under the Treaties and the Citizens' Directive

It is plain that expulsion and/or exclusion of those falling within the scope of the Citizens' Directive is only permissible on the terms specified in Chapter IV of the Directive. In general terms, expulsion and/or exclusion of these individuals is permissible   6.37

---

[36] The *Ruiz Zambrano* rights of residence are in a different category from the remaining 'derived' rights; as they concern a right more fundamental than the right to free movement, similar considerations must apply to them.

[37] See also Case C-459/99 *MRAX v Belgian State* [2002] ECR I-659 [62]; and Case C-215/03 *Oulane v Minister voor Vreemdelingenzaken en Integratie* [2005] ECR I-01215 [20]–[24].

only on the grounds of public policy, public security or public health. The key provisions are contained in Articles 27 and 28 of the Citizens' Directive[38] and are reproduced in full below:

Article 27 General principles

1. Subject to the provisions of this Chapter, Member States may restrict the freedom of movement and residence of Union citizens and their family members, irrespective of nationality, on grounds of public policy, public security or public health. These grounds shall not be invoked to serve economic ends.
2. Measures taken on grounds of public policy or public security shall comply with the principle of proportionality and shall be based exclusively on the personal conduct of the individual concerned. Previous criminal convictions shall not in themselves constitute grounds for taking such measures. The personal conduct of the individual concerned must represent a genuine, present and sufficiently serious threat affecting one of the fundamental interests of society. Justifications that are isolated from the particulars of the case or that rely on considerations of general prevention shall not be accepted.
3. In order to ascertain whether the person concerned represents a danger for public policy or public security, when issuing the registration certificate or, in the absence of a registration system, not later than three months from the date of arrival of the person concerned on its territory or from the date of reporting his/her presence within the territory, as provided for in Article 5(5), or when issuing the residence card, the host Member State may, should it consider this essential, request the Member State of origin and, if need be, other Member States to provide information concerning any previous police record the person concerned may have. Such enquiries shall not be made as a matter of routine. The Member State consulted shall give its reply within two months.
4. The Member State which issued the passport or identity card shall allow the holder of the document who has been expelled on grounds of public policy, public security, or public health from another Member State to re-enter its territory without any formality even if the document is no longer valid or the nationality of the holder is in dispute.

Article 28 Protection against expulsion

1. Before taking an expulsion decision on grounds of public policy or public security, the host Member State shall take account of considerations such as how long the individual concerned has resided on its territory, his/her age, state of health, family and economic situation, social and cultural integration into the host Member State and the extent of his/her links with the country of origin.
2. The host Member State may not take an expulsion decision against Union citizens or their family members, irrespective of nationality, who have the right of permanent residence on its territory, except on serious grounds of public policy or public security.
3. An expulsion decision may not be taken against Union citizens, except if the decision is based on imperative grounds of public security, as defined by Member States, if they:
   (a) have resided in the host Member State for the previous 10 years; or
   (b) are a minor, except if the expulsion is necessary for the best interests of the child, as provided for in the United Nations Convention on the Rights of the Child of 20 November 1989.

---

[38] See also Articles 45(3), 52(1) and 62 TFEU, which provide for derogations on the grounds of public policy, public security and public health from the rights to free movement of workers, self-employed and service providers, respectively.

Equally, the TFEU provides that those exercising Treaty rights as workers, self-employed persons or service providers may have limitations placed on their rights (including expulsion and/or exclusion) only on the grounds of public policy, security or health (Articles 45, 52 and 62 TFEU).[39]

6.38

The Citizens' Directive creates three tiers of protection for persons within its scope: i) EU citizens exercising Treaty rights against whom measures can be taken on grounds of public policy security and health; ii) permanent residents against whom measures can be taken on the basis of serious grounds of public policy security and health; and iii) those who have accrued 10 years' continuous residence against whom measures can be taken on imperative grounds of the same. Thus, in general terms, the degree of protection against expulsion and exclusion depends on the degree of integration.

6.39

There are autonomous EU definitions of 'public policy', 'public security' and 'public health'. Whilst there is scope for Member States to 'essentially retain the freedom to determine the requirements of public policy and public security in accordance with their national needs', it should be noted that 'those requirements must nevertheless be interpreted strictly, so that their scope cannot be determined unilaterally by each Member State without any control by the institutions of the European Union': Case C-348/09 *PI v Oberbürgermeisterin der Stadt Remscheid*, judgment of 22 May 2012 [23].

6.40

Measures taken on account of public policy are substantively different from those taken on account of public security and they must be identified correctly by the Member States. Invoking expulsion and/or exclusion on the basis of public policy is interpreted as preventing a genuine and sufficiently serious threat to a fundamental interest of society: Case 41/74 *Rutili v Minister de l'interieur* [1975] ECR 1219, [27]; Cases C-482/01 and C-493/01 *Orfanopoulos and Olivieri v Verwaltungsgericht Stuttgart* [2004] ECR I-5257, [77]–[82] and [66]. In cases involving public policy considerations, Member States should be able to demonstrate that the measure proposed against the EU citizen is a public policy matter by demonstrating the existence of special measures taken against its own nationals in similar circumstances: Case C-348/09 *PI v Oberbürgermeisterin der Stadt Remscheid*, judgment of 22 May 2012 [37].

6.41

The definition of public security was set out by the CJEU in Case C-145/09 *Land Baden-Württemberg v Panagiotis Tsakouridis* [2010] ECR I-11979 as including:

6.42

[A] threat to the functioning of the institutions and essential public services and the survival of the population, as well as the risk of a serious disturbance to foreign relations or to peaceful coexistence of nations, or a risk to military interests.

On the facts of *Tsakouridis*, the CJEU held that the fight against organised crime in drugs could fall within the concept of public security, but it would need to be of such intensity as to 'directly threaten the calm and physical security of the population as a whole or

---

[39] It is worth bearing in mind that in the field of immigration, there are a number of secondary instruments to which the UK is not a party. In matters relevant to this publication, it is worth mentioning the Long Term Residents' Directive (Council Directive 2003/109/EC of 25 November 2003 concerning the status of third country nationals who are long-term residents [2004] OJ L16/44) which prohibits expulsion of the long-term third country national residents who come within the scope of the Directive unless they constitute an actual and sufficiently serious threat to public policy or public security; where expulsion measures cannot be based on economic considerations and before taking a decision to expel, Member States must have regard to the duration of residence in their territory, the age of the person concerned, the consequences for the person concerned and family members and links with the country of residence or the absence of links with the country of origin.

a large part of it' (at [44], [45] and [47]). Case C-348/09 *PI v Oberbürgermeisterin der Stadt Remscheid*, judgment of 22 May 2012, a case involving very serious sexual offences against a child, proceeded on the basis that such offending was of a sufficiently serious nature to constitute a threat to public security. Public security entails both internal and external security and internal terrorist action may be considered as a matter of public security: Case C-100/01 *Olazabal* [2002] ECR I-10981.

6.43 In public health cases, the time for action by the state is limited to three months since arrival and in relation to strictly limited matters with epidemic potential as defined by the relevant instruments of the World Health Organization and where a person can only be required to submit themselves to medical examination only where there are 'serious indications' that this is necessary.

6.44 The case law of the CJEU establishes a number of principles that apply to the expulsion and exclusion of EU citizens on the basis of public policy or public security. First, the decision must be 'based exclusively on the personal conduct of the individual concerned': Case C 41/74 *Van Duyn v Home Office* [1974] ECR 1337; Case 41/74; *Rutili v Minister de l'interieur* [1975] ECR 1219. In *Van Duyn*, a case involving the expulsion from the UK of a Dutch Scientologist, the CJEU held that personal conduct did not necessarily have to be contrary to the criminal laws of the host Member State to constitute a ground for expulsion on the basis of public policy, provided that it was 'socially harmful'. The CJEU further held in *Van Duyn* that current membership of an organisation could constitute 'personal conduct' since membership indicated identification by the member with the aims and activities of the organisation. The requirement to establish 'personal conduct' means that general preventative measures to combat crime or deter other aliens cannot be justified on the basis of public policy, public security and public health: Case C-340/97 *Nazli v Stadt Nurnburg* [2000] ECR I-957 [61]. Further, an expulsion measure cannot serve economic ends and cannot be an automatic consequence of reliance on social assistance.[40]

6.45 Second, at the time of taking an expulsion measure or review by courts, a person must be a 'present threat': see Joined Cases C-482/01 and C-493/01 *Orfanopoulos and Olivieri v Verwaltungsgericht Stuttgart* [2004] ECR I-5257 [77]–[82], and *BF (Portugal) v SSHD* [2009] EWCA Civ 923. This is of particular significance where there has been a passage of time since the commission of an offence.

6.46 Third, and relatedly, previous convictions may be relevant, but may not in and of themselves justify expulsion in grounds of public policy or public security: Case C-30/77 *Bouchereau* [1977] ECR 1999. In *Bouchereau*, a case involving the UK's attempt to expel a French national convicted of a drugs offence, the CJEU said that the conviction was relevant only 'in so far as the circumstances which gave rise to that conviction are evidence of personal conduct constituting a present threat to the requirements of public policy' (see para 6.44 above). In other words, convictions may constitute an indication that they may be repeated (see also Cases C-482/01 and 493/01 *Orfanopoulos and Oliveri* [82] and [100]; and Case C-67/74 *Bonsignor v Stadt Koln* [1975] ECR 297, in which the CJEU talked of a 'propensity to act in the same way in the future'). Case C-348/96 *Criminal Proceedings against Calfa* [1999] ECR I-11 and Case C-340/97 *Nazli v Stadt Nurnburg* [2000] ECR I-957 demonstrate the fact that even in the case of serious drugs offences, personal conduct (as opposed to automatic exclusion) is the only permissible ground for exclusion or

---

[40] See further para 6.58.

expulsion. Article 33 permits automatic expulsion as a penalty or legal consequence of a custodial penalty, but only when this is compliant with Articles 27–29 and where it is subject to review in case of non-enforcement after two years following the decision.

Fourth, the threat in question must be sufficiently serious: Case C-30/77 *Bouchereau* [1977] ECR 1999. In *Bouchereau* the CJEU said: 6.47

> Recourse by a national authority to the concept of public policy presupposes, in any event, the existence, in addition to the perturbation of the social order which any infringement of the law involves, of a genuine and sufficiently serious threat to the requirements of public policy affecting one of the fundamental interests of society.

Fifth, of fundamental importance is the proportionality assessment integral to Article 27 Citizens' Directive. Once the criteria in Article 27 have substantively been met, the decision must balance the expulsion and/or exclusion measure against the personal factors enumerated in Article 28(1), namely the age, state of health of the person, his or her family and economic situation, length of residence in the Member State, social and cultural integration, and the extent of links with the country of origin. In all cases, including those involving the highest level of protection, to be weighed against lawful grounds for expulsion is the risk of 'compromising the social rehabilitation of the Union citizen in the state in which he has become genuinely integrated, which ... is not only in his interests but also in that of the European Union in general': Case C-145/09 *Land Baden-Württemberg v Panagiotis Tsakouridis* [2010] ECR I-11979 [50]. 6.48

Finally, within the scope of EU law,[41] Member State decisions on expulsion and exclusion to which the specific EU expulsion provisions do not apply must comply with the other general principles of EU law, including fundamental rights protected by the CFREU.[42] In Case C-60/00 *Carpenter* [2002] ECR I-6279, which pre-dated the Citizens' Directive, the CJEU found that since the expulsion of a third country national spouse interfered with her husband's ability to provide effective services across the EU, EU law was engaged and the interference with free movement had to be justified in the public interest and to comply with the principle of proportionality and fundamental rights. 6.49

In terrorism cases, two matters are of note. First, the CJEU has applied the same principles as in other criminal cases: Case C-100/01 *Olazabal* [2002] ECR I-10981. Second, as noted above, present membership of an organisation may be taken into account where the individual concerned participates in the activities of the organisation and identifies with its aims or designs, while past associations cannot, in general, constitute a present threat: Case C 41/74 *Van Duyn* [1974] ECR 1337 [17]. 6.50

As noted earlier, the Citizens' Directive introduces higher levels of protection for those deemed to be integrated in the host Member State to a greater extent. Thus, serious grounds for measures on account of public policy or public security are required for those who have permanent residence. 6.51

Those who had resided in a Member State for at least 10 years are considered to be most integrated and therefore deserving of a higher level of protection. Accordingly, measures against them can be taken on imperative grounds only. The same applies to minors. The CJEU in Case C-145/09 *Land Baden-Württemberg v Panagiotis Tsakouridis* [2010] 6.52

---

[41] See section B1 above.
[42] Equally, expulsion on grounds of public policy, security or health must be proportionate and compliant with fundamental rights.

ECR I-11979 referred to 'exceptional circumstances' for measures taken on imperative reasons grounds, which require the threat to public security to be 'of a particularly high degree of seriousness' and mentioned 'the exceptional seriousness of the threat': *Tsakouridis*, at [40] and [49].

6.53 In Case C-348/09 *PI v Oberbürgermeisterin der Stadt Remscheid*, judgment of 22 May 2012, the Grand Chamber found serious child abuse over a period of years (PI was sentenced to seven-and-a-half years' imprisonment for sexual assault, sexual coercion and rape of a minor over a number of years) as being capable of amounting to imperative grounds for expulsion (at [23]–[29]) 'as long as the manner in which such offences were committed disclose[d] particularly serious characteristics' (at [90]). It is of note that in *PI*, the CJEU noted that the EU had already legislated on minimum punishment for the type of offences in issue in Directive 2011/93[43] under Article 83(1) TFEU, which provides that the sexual exploitation of children is one of the areas of particularly serious crime with a cross-border dimension in which the EU legislature may intervene.

6.54 The English Court of Appeal has referred to a 'very high threshold' for imperative grounds: *LG (Italy) v SSHD* [2008] EWCA Civ 190 [32]. Such a threshold was not reached in a case of *FV (Italy) v SSHD* [2012] EWCA Civ 1199, [2013] 1 WLR 3339 concerning deportation following a conviction for a particularly violent manslaughter committed when intoxicated (indicted as murder, but provocation having been found by jury and attracting a sentence of eight years' imprisonment where there were previous drink-related offences).

6.55 The period of 10 years is calculated looking back from the date of decision ordering expulsion and must in principle be continuous: Case C-400/12 *SSHD v MG*, judgment of 16 January 2014.[44] To determine the period of 10 years in view of possible absences, all relevant factors must be taken into account, in particular, as the CJEU held in Case C-145/09 *Land Baden-Württemberg v Panagiotis Tsakouridis* [2010] ECR I-11979 [38]:

[T]he duration of each period of absence from the host Member State, the cumulative duration and the frequency of those absences, and the reasons why the person concerned left the host Member State, which may establish whether those absences involve the transfer to another Member State of the centre of the personal, family or occupational interests of the person concerned.

6.56 As regards periods of imprisonment, the CJEU has found that imprisonment interrupts the continuity of residence for the purposes of acquisition of permanent residence: Case C-378/12 *Nnamdi Onuekwere v SSHD*, judgment of 16 January 2014. *Onuekwere* did not consider the impact of previous case law in relation to maintaining worker status as it dealt with family members.[45]

---

[43] Directive 2011/93/EU of the European Parliament and of the Council of 13 December 2011 on combating the sexual abuse and sexual exploitation of children and child pornography, and replacing Council Framework Decision 2004/68/JHA [2011] OJ L335/1.

[44] The way in which the CJEU expressed this principle involves a careful examination of circumstances. It found that a period of imprisonment 'may—together with the other factors ... —be taken into account ... as part of the overall assessment required for determining whether the integrating links previously forged with the host Member State have been broken, and thus for determining whether the enhanced protection provided for in that provision will be granted' ([36]). The Court concluded that if there is previous residence of 10 years prior to imprisonment, that may be relevant to assessing the level of integration. In practice, this leaves the assessment of what level of protection a person is deserving of focused on individual circumstances.

[45] *Orfanopoulos and Olivieri v Verwaltungsgericht Stuttgart* [2004] ECR I-5257 [50]: 'Moreover, in respect more particularly of prisoners who were employed before their imprisonment, the fact that the person concerned was not available on the employment market during such imprisonment does not mean, as a general

The Citizens' Directive also provides for a number of procedural guarantees in relation to expulsion and exclusion. These are considered in chapter 14.

6.57

Expulsion and Exclusion of EU Citizens Not Exercising Rights under the Citizens' Directive

However, the restriction on the ability of Member States to expel and exclude EU citizens and their family members on the grounds of public policy, public security and public health may not apply to every EU citizen. EU citizens (and their family members) who have become inactive and an unreasonable burden on the social assistance system may be subject to an expulsion measure provided that the decision is proportionate[46] and respects fundamental rights as well as being subject to specific considerations enumerated in recital 16 of the preamble to the Citizens' Directive, whereby the Member State should examine 'whether it is a case of temporary difficulties and take into account the duration of residence, the personal circumstances and the amount of aid granted in order to consider whether the beneficiary has become an unreasonable burden on its social assistance system'. It is useful to note that these are similar considerations to those in benefits cases linked to whether there was lawful residence by recipients of benefits (Case C-140/12 *Pensionsversicherungsanstalt v Brey*, judgment of 19 September 2013; Case C-184/99 *Grzelczyk* [2001] ECR I-6193).

6.58

By way of Article 15(1) Citizens' Directive, the procedures provided for by Articles 30 and 31 Citizens' Directive 'shall apply by analogy to all decisions restricting freedom of movement of Union citizens and their family members on grounds other than public policy, security or public health'. Thus, Article 15(1) expressly imports procedural safeguards including proportionality contained in Article 31 Citizens' Directive. Since Article 31(3) directly refers to the need for proportionality of decisions in terms of Article 28 Citizens' Directive,[47] decisions to remove the non-active persons who are an unreasonable burden on social assistance arguably must be compliant with detailed considerations on proportionality under Article 28.

6.59

The expulsion and/or exclusion of those third country nationals with so-called derived rights of residence under EU law[48] will at the very least also need to be proportionate and comply with the fundamental rights protected in the CFREU. It is also argued that they are subject to the procedural guarantees of Articles 30 and 31 on the normal construction of Article 15(1) Citizens' Directive (see above). While the *Ruiz Zambrano* rights of residence are in a different category from the remaining 'derived' rights, as they concern a right more fundamental than the right to free movement, similar considerations must apply to them.

6.60

Thus, a careful reading of the Citizens' Directive may suggest that all expulsion decisions where EU citizens have some form of free movement rights should be subject to

6.61

---

rule, that he did not continue to be duly registered as belonging to the labour force of the host Member State during that period, provided that he actually finds another job within a reasonable time after his release.'

[46] The decision to remove a person is subject to limitations of EU law and principle of proportionality (Case C-456/02 *Trojani v Centre public d'aide social de Bruxelles* [2004] ECR I-07573).

[47] 'The redress procedures shall allow for an examination of the legality of the decision, as well as of the facts and circumstances on which the proposed measure is based. They shall ensure that the decision is not disproportionate, particularly in view of the requirements laid down in Article 28.'

[48] See further paras 6.61 *et seq.*

the protection of Articles 27 and 28. Article 27 refers to EU citizens and their family members as opposed to, for example, Article 24—the non-discrimination provision—which refers only to those EU citizens and their family members 'residing in a Member State on the basis of this Directive'. The only direct reference in Chapter IV to rights of residence defined by the Directive is to permanent residence in Article 28(2), which is a new status introduced by the Directive. It should also be noted that Article 28(2) in relation to imperative grounds does not refer to 'lawful residence', which is interpreted as reference to residence under the Citizens' Directive,[49] but merely to 'residence'. In that context, arguably the scope of the Citizens' Directive as per Article 1(c) ought to be interpreted in the light of recital (23), which states that 'Expulsion of Union citizens and their family members on grounds of public policy or public security is a measure that can seriously harm persons who, having availed themselves of the rights and freedoms conferred on them by the Treaty, have become genuinely integrated into the host Member State'—clearly referring to the freedoms guaranteed by the Treaty, not merely the Citizens' Directive. This interpretation is consistent with the function of expulsion and exclusion which applies to all persons, irrespective of their present or historic right to reside, where conditions of Chapter IV of the Citizens' Directive are met. Conversely, removal of those who are an unreasonable burden on public funds is a different matter and can be defeated as and when a person comes within the scope of the Citizens' Directive (eg, by getting a job).

6.62 However, even if the suggestion that Articles 27 and 28 Citizens' Directive are applicable to EU citizens, exercising some form of free movement right is in doubt, given that, as seen above, the free movement provisions in Articles 45, 52 and 62 TFEU clearly limit expulsion and/or exclusion to grounds of public policy, public security or public health, a consistent interpretation of standards for measures of exclusion and expulsion would require the same limitations to apply to the expulsion and/or exclusion of those with derived rights under EU law. These considerations also apply to posted workers under the *Van der Elst* rules (see para 6.34 above).

6.63 In relation to the line of cases establishing a right of residence for the carer and children in education of a former worker (see 6.33 above), since the right is derived from a broad interpretation of Article 12 of Regulation 1612/68 (now Regulation 492/2011), which, in turn, is made under the powers of Article 45 TFEU,[50] the same principles for expulsion and/or exclusion as under Article 45 TFEU should be applicable to those rights of residence.

6.64 Similarly, in *Chen* (see para 6.33 above), given that the source of rights to reside is derived from both Article 18 TFEU and the then Directive 90/346 (the precursor to the Citizens' Directive, to which standards of protection on the grounds of public policy security and health were applicable, as defined in the then Directive 64/221/EEC), this must render the protection from expulsion at least at the level envisaged by Citizens' Directive in order to give substance to the rights of EU citizens. Further, in cases where the free movement of a self-sufficient child had taken place and as a result it is plain that

---

[49] Cases C-424/10 and C-435/10 *Tomasz Ziolkowski and Barbara Szeja and others v Land Berlin* [2011] ECR I-14035.

[50] Which was at the time designed to go hand in hand with the predecessor provisions to the Citizens' Directive, including Directive 64/221/EEC establishing exclusion of grounds of public policy security and health. See, eg, Case 48/75 *Royer* [1976] ECR 497; Case C-363/89 *Roux* [1991] ECR I-00273.

he or she would have protection from expulsion under Articles 27 and 28, equivalent protection should be in any event afforded to the parent.

In *Ruiz Zambrano*, the domestic ruling tackling this issue at the Upper Tribunal level in *Sanade and others (British Children—Zambrano—Dereci)* [2012] UKUT 00048 (IAC) [82]–[84] suggested that the level of protection that a *Ruiz Zambrano* parent would be at least on the level provided in Article 27 of the Citizens' Directive or even in excess of that. However, when that case came to the Court of Appeal, the position advanced by both parties as recorded in the judgment was that in addition to protection afforded by Article 8 ECHR, the material difference in approach in *Ruiz Zambrano* cases of expulsion was that of an EU law proportionality assessment, although notably, this is not on the basis of any legal argument.[51] Nevertheless, in view of the fundamental status of EU citizenship, a proportionality assessment on those issues may result in the same result as that suggested in *Sanade*.

6.65

Given that the rights to reside in the derived category are to give effect to free movement rights, it would be inconsistent with the EU approach to expulsion of those in scope in a variety of instruments[52] to subject expulsion and exclusion measures to the grounds of public policy, security and health, and to afford lesser protection to those persons.

6.66

Despite these arguments to the contrary, the Immigration (European Economic Area) Regulations 2006, which transpose the Citizens' Directive into domestic law, afford an inferior level of protection from expulsion and/or exclusion to those who are defined in regulation 15A as having 'derivative rights' (namely, rights under Regulation 1612/68, *Ruiz Zambrano*, and *Chen* principles). This is arguably incorrect as a matter of EU law for the reasons set out above. The *Surinder Singh* cases (defined in regulation 9) are in a different category from the 'derivative' rights defined in Regulation 15A. This is because the Immigration (European Economic Area) Regulations 2006 treat the *Surinder Singh* cases as simply an exception to British citizens' exclusion from their scope, so the family members of returning UK citizens will attract the same level of protection against expulsion and/or exclusion as the family members of EU migrants.

6.67

Amendments to the Immigration (European Economic Area) Regulations 2006, which entered into force on 1 January 2014, have sought to create further opportunities for the authorities to expel and exclude EU citizens from the UK. These measures are considered in chapters 8–10. It suffices to note here that in some instances their compliance with EU law is questionable.

6.68

E. Turkish Nationals

Turkish nationals have rights under EU law by virtue of the Turkey EEC Association Agreement 1963, supplemented by the Brussels Protocol 1970 (collectively referred to as 'the Ankara Agreement'). The Association Council created under the Ankara Agreement

6.69

---

[51] *Harrison (Jamaica) v SSHD* [2012] EWCA Civ 1736, [2013] 2 CMLR 23 [2].
[52] Which includes measures under Articles 45, 52 and 62 TFEU; Citizens' Directive and predecessors; long-term residents, trafficked persons and beneficiaries of Turkish Association agreements.

provided for the creation of a Council of Association. This Council has adopted various decisions, amongst the most important being Decision 1/80, which provides for certain directly effective rights with a concomitant right of residence relating to employment for Turkish nationals and their family members (Articles 6–7). The standstill clause introduced by the Brussels Protocol permits Turkish self-employed persons to enter and reside under the Immigration Rules applicable in 1970 (the date on which the Protocol entered into force) or, where as is the case of the UK, a Member State acceded to the after 1970, the date of access of that Member State (1 January 1973 in the case of the UK). In practice, this makes the Immigration Rules in HC509 and HC510 applicable to the admission of self-employed Turkish nationals and their family members. The standstill clause in relation to workers applies from 20 December 1976 and the applicable rules in general would have been HC81 and HC82 (there is no material difference between those and HC509 and HC510).

6.70 The rights of Turkish nationals and their family members under Decision 1/80 are subject to limitations based on public policy, public security or public health: Article 14(1) of Decision 1/80. The CJEU had interpreted the scope of protection from expulsion to be wider than the simple wording of the Decision and included the existence of a genuine and sufficiently serious threat to public policy, circumstances of conviction amounting to present threat and prohibition against expulsion on general preventative grounds which at that time was contained in Directive 64/221/EEC. The CJEU's reasoning was based on the principle that the public policy exception must be interpreted consistently and thus by reference to the same principles in the area of freedom of movement (Case C-340/97 *Nazli v Stadt Nurnberg* [2000] ECR I-957 [56]). Accordingly, these are the same as those applicable to EU citizens under the Treaties and Citizens' Directive. As with any limitations on rights deriving from EU law, they must be construed restrictively: Case C-340/97 *Nazli v Stadt Nurnberg* [2000] ECR I-957 [63]; Case C-467/02 *Cetinkaya v Land Baden-Württemberg* [2004] ECR I-10898 [47]; C-329/97 *Ergat v Stadt Ulm* [2000] ECR I-1487 [56]. The same guarantees apply to family members.[53] It seems apparent from the above that the procedural guarantees of Articles 30–33 apply to Turkish workers and that the CJEU had ruled that the procedural guarantees under Directive 64/221, which was repealed and replaced by the Citizens' Directive, apply to Turkish nationals whose legal status is defined by Article 6 or Article 7 of Decision No 1/80 (Case C-136/03 *Dorr and Unal v Sicherheitsdirektion für das Bundesland Kärnten* [2005] ECR I-04759).

6.71 The situation for self-employed Turkish nationals whose position in the UK is regulated by the standstill clause is not entirely clear. At the very least, the law applicable to these individuals is that extant in 1973. As such, self-employed Turkish nationals who fulfil the conditions of residence in the immigration rules of 1973 may be expelled on conducive grounds under the Immigration Act 1971 (see further chapter 8). Other grounds of expulsion, such as automatic deportation under the UK Borders Act 2007 (see further chapter 8), do not apply since they postdate the relevant date in the standstill clause. It is strongly arguable that the reasoning in Case C-37/98 *R v SSHD ex parte Abdulnasir Savas* [2000] ECR I-02927, which demonstrates that the principles governing the rights of residence to Turkish workers are applicable to the self-employed (see [59]–[63]), leads to the conclusion that similar protection in relation to expulsion and/

---

[53] Case C-325/05 *Ismail Derin v Landkreis Darmstadt-Dieburg* [2007] ECR I-06495 [54].

or exclusion as that which attaches to the rights of residence of Turkish workers should be afforded to the self-employed, especially if viewed in the context of the approximation of rights under the Treaty with those under the Association Agreement and a purposive interpretation of the Association Agreement.

F. International Protection in EU Law

6.72 Apart from regulating the expulsion and exclusion of EU citizens and their family members and specific groups under association agreements, EU law provides for specific principles regulating the expulsion and exclusion of certain third country nationals who fall with the provisions of secondary legislation adopted under the Area of Freedom, Security and Justice. The following section first provides an overview of the competence of the EU in this area before examining the specific provisions relevant to expulsion and/or exclusion.

6.73 Articles 67–89 TFEU create the Area of Freedom, Security and Justice. Articles 77–80 TFEU set out the requirement for common policies for border checks, asylum and immigration which are 'governed by the principle of solidarity and fair sharing of responsibility, including its financial implications, between the Member States' (Article 80). This envisages common policies on the control of external borders, and the aim of a gradual introduction of an integrated management system of internal borders are in Article 77.

6.74 Article 78(1) TFEU provides for the common policy on asylum, subsidiary and temporary protection which must comply with the Geneva Convention of 28 July 1951 and the Protocol of 31 January 1967 relating to the status of refugees. Further, it enables the institutions to take legislative measures to establish a common European asylum system comprising: a uniform status of asylum and subsidiary protection; common procedures for the granting and withdrawal of asylum or subsidiary protection status; criteria and mechanisms for determining which Member State is responsible for considering an application for asylum or subsidiary protection; criteria and mechanisms regarding conditions for the reception of applicants for asylum or subsidiary protection; and partnership and cooperation with third countries for the purpose of managing inflows of people applying for asylum or subsidiary or temporary protection.

6.75 Article 79 TFEU is concerned with the common policy on immigration and Article 79(2) enables the EU to legislate in the areas of conditions of entry and residence and standards on the issue by Member States of long-term visas and residence permits, including those for the purpose of family reunification, illegal immigration and combatting trafficking in persons. Article 79(3) TFEU also enables the EU to conclude readmission agreements with third countries in respect of third country nationals present in the EU who no longer fulfil the conditions of residence. The secondary legislation adopted under Articles 78 and 79 TFEU does not bind the UK automatically, but it may decide to opt into specific measures. Whilst the UK has decided not to opt into any measures on immigration, it has opted into a number of norms regulating asylum. These are examined below.

6.76   Under the legal basis of Article 78 TFEU, there are four significant instruments that the UK has opted into, namely, the Qualification Directive,[54] the Procedures Directive,[55] the Reception Directive[56] and the Dublin Regulations, currently Dublin III.[57] The Qualification Directive and the Dublin III Regulation contain provisions relevant to the subject matter of this book and are discussed below. The Procedures Directive is examined in relation to EU remedies in chapter 14. The provisions of Reception Directive do not cover expulsion or exclusion and so are not examined in the following section.

F1. The Qualification Directive

6.77   The Qualification Directive is intended to guide the national bodies in the application of the Refugee Convention.[58] This is explored in more detail in chapter 4. It codifies the standards in relation to who qualifies as a beneficiary of international protection and the content of protection granted (see Articles 5–12). Subsidiary protection is available where there are substantial grounds for believing that there is a real risk of serious harm defined in Article 15.

6.78   The definition of serious harm in Article 15 of the Qualification Directive includes, in addition to death penalty and torture and inhuman and degrading treatment (broadly corresponding to Articles 2 and 3 ECHR), by subsection (c), 'serious and individual threat to a civilian's life or person by reason of indiscriminate violence in situations of international or internal armed conflict'. The CJEU in Case C-465/07 *Elgafaji and another v Staatssecretaris van Justitie* [2009] ECR I-921 confirmed the wider scope and the general nature of risk in Article 15C, but noted the high threshold of the level of indiscriminate violence, which would be exceptional and would result in a civilian being exposed to risk of serious threat by mere presence in the country or region (at [28]–[35]). The CJEU clarified that for the purposes of Article 15C, while there is no need to demonstrate individual targeting, in the context where this is the case, 'the more the applicant is able to show that he is specifically affected by reason of factors particular to his personal circumstances, the lower the level of indiscriminate violence required for him to be eligible for subsidiary protection' (at [39]). In the domestic context, in *HH Somalia* [2010] EWCA Civ 426, the Court of Appeal held that the collateral damage from discriminate violence is included in the victims for the purpose of Article 15C. In *QD (Iraq) v SSHD* [2009] EWCA Civ 620, [2011] 1 WLR 689, the Court of Appeal followed

---

[54] Council Directive 2004/83/EC of 29 April 2004 on minimum standards for the qualification and status of third country nationals or stateless persons as refugees or as persons who otherwise need international protection and the content of the protection granted [2004] OJ L304/12.

[55] Council Directive 2005/85/EC of 1 December 2005 on minimum standards on procedures in Member States for granting and withdrawing refugee status [2005] OJ L326/13.

[56] Council Directive 2003/9/EC laying down minimum standards for the reception of asylum seekers [2003] OJ L31/18.

[57] Regulation 604/2013.

[58] Where from the wording of the Qualification Directive there appears to be a divergence from the Refugee Convention principles, the interpretation of the Qualification Directive should be consistent with the Refugee Convention principles: *Fornah v SSHD* [2006] UKHL46, [2007] 1 AC 412 [118]. This is consistent with the principle that European legislation must insofar as possible be interpreted in a way consistent with international law in particular when it is intended to give effect to international instruments or treaties adopted by the EU: Case C-341/95 *Bettati* [1998] ECR I-4355 [20].

the principles in *Elgafaji* and excluded the possibility that exceptionality referred to any substantive test, but was in effect reflective of the intensity of indiscriminate violence. The CJEU has ruled that the notion of armed conflict is an autonomous concept in EU law and does not directly draw on the definition in international humanitarian law:

> [I]nternal armed conflict exists ... if a State's armed forces confront one or more armed groups or if two or more armed groups confront each other. It is not necessary for that conflict to be categorised as 'armed conflict not of an international character' under international humanitarian law; nor is it necessary to carry out, in addition to an appraisal of the level of violence present in the territory concerned, a separate assessment of the intensity of the armed confrontations, the level of organisation of the armed forces involved or the duration of the conflict.[59]

6.79 As with the Refugee Convention (see chapter 4), individuals may be excluded from protection under the Qualification Directive in a number of circumstances.[60] The CJEU interpreted terms of exclusion from the refugee status consistently with the Refugee Convention in Joined Cases C-57/09 and C-101/09 *Bundesrepublik Deutschland v B and D* [2010] ECR I-10979, which considered the interpretation of Article 12(2)(b) and (c). It concluded that membership of an organisation on the list forming the Annex to Common Position 2001/931 does not constitute 'a serious non-political crime' or 'acts contrary to the purposes and principles of the United Nations', even in the presence of active support of struggle, but must be determined on the basis of individual assessment of responsibility on the facts. It ruled that:

> [U]nder points (b) and (c) of Article 12(2) of Directive 2004/83, which are analogous to points (b) and (c) of Article 1F of the 1951 Geneva Convention, a third country national is excluded from refugee status where there are serious reasons for considering that 'he ... has committed' a serious non-political crime outside the country of refuge 'prior to his ... admission as a refugee' or that he 'has been guilty' of acts contrary to the purposes and principles of the United Nations.

Accordingly, it held that there is no requirement under the Qualification Directive for a person to constitute a present threat (*B and D*, at [102]–[105]) nor for a decision to be subject to a proportionality test (*B and D*, at [106]–[111]). The Court also ruled that exclusion from the protection of the Directive does not preclude the grant of a different protection status under national law.

6.80 Article 17(1) provides for exclusion of those eligible for subsidiary protection where 'there are serious reasons for considering' that:

(a) he or she committed a crime against peace, a war crime, or a crime against humanity, as defined in the international instruments drawn up to make provision in respect of such crimes;
(b) he or she has committed a serious crime;
(c) he or she has been guilty of acts contrary to the purposes and principles of the United Nations as set out in the Preamble and Articles 1 and 2 of the Charter of the United Nations;
(d) he or she constitutes a danger to the community or to the security of the Member State in which he or she is present.

---

[59] Case C-285/12 *Aboubacar Diakité v Commissaire général aux réfugiés et aux apatrides*, judgment of 30 January 2014.
[60] See further ch 4.

6.81 Those instigating or participating in matters defined in Article 17(1) are also excluded (Article 17(2)). Member States may exclude those persons who prior to their admission to the Member State have committed one or more crimes, outside the scope of para 1, which would be punishable by imprisonment, had they been committed in the Member State concerned, and if he or she left his or her country of origin solely in order to avoid sanctions resulting from these crimes (Article 17(3)).

6.82 In practice, exclusion from subsidiary protection would not necessarily mean departure from the territory, but exclusion from the status of subsidiary protection. This is because Article 3 ECHR would operate so as to exclude *refoulement*: see further chapter 5.

6.83 Exclusion under Article 17 Qualification Directive seems somewhat broader from that under the Refugee Convention in that it appears not to distinguish the significance of time when a crime relevant to expulsion under subpara (1)(b) may have been committed or the nature of the crime (unlike Refugee Convention Article 1F(b)) and that under Article 17(1)(d), there is no requirement for a conviction to have taken place for a person to constitute a danger to the community or the security (unlike Article 33(2) Refugee Convention). Article 17 is reflected in para 339D of the Immigration Rules.[61]

6.84 The domestic Court of Appeal in *EN (Serbia) v SSHD and another* [2009] EWCA Civ 630, [2010] 1 QB 633 ruled that an irrebuttable presumption of a serious crime which is the one attracting a sentence of two years created by section 72 of the Nationality, Immigration and Asylum Act 2002 would be inconsistent with the Qualification Directive, interpreting the relevant provision as raising only a rebuttable presumption.

6.85 Article 16 of the Qualification Directive provides for the cessation of status in circumstances reflective of those in Article 1C(5) of the Refugee Convention. Although there is no mention of the person being excluded by virtue of availing himself or herself of the protection of the country of nationality, it may be that such an act is relevant to establishing whether there had been a change of circumstances and whether the protection may no longer be required.

6.86 The determination of refugee status and subsidiary protection (including exclusion under Article 17(1) of the Qualification Directive) brings the matter within the scope of EU law and thus the procedural guarantees of Articles 41 and 47 CFREU apply to those claims, thereby effectively importing the standards of Article 6 ECHR to the determination of such matters. However, expulsion of failed asylum-seekers following the determination of refugee status/subsidiary protection extends beyond the remit of the Qualification Directive and therefore is unlikely to be found to be within the scope of EU law such that EU fundamental rights protections and proportionality standards apply.

F2. The Dublin III Regulation

6.87 On 1 January 2014, the Dublin III Regulation came into force. The Dublin III Regulation and its predecessors are concerned with the allocation of responsibility for refugee status determination between Member States. It sets down a hierarchy of criteria for

---

[61] In *R(C) v SSHD* [2008] EWHC 2448 (Admin) [26], it was held that, notwithstanding the word 'and' in sub-para (iii): 'danger to the community or to the security', the categories in para 339D are not cumulative requirements so that the word 'and' should be read as 'or'.

identifying the Member State responsible for the assessment of an asylum claim in the EU (see Chapter III of the Dublin III Regulation). Responsibility under Dublin III is assigned primarily on the grounds of the existence of family links, followed by a geographical mechanism on the basis of the Member State through which the asylum-seeker first entered the EU, Norway, Iceland and Switzerland. The central principle is one of mutual recognition: Dublin III aims to ensure that only one EU Member State should be responsible for the examination of an asylum claim and to deter multiple asylum claims. When it has been established that another Member State should have responsibility under Dublin III for the assessment of an asylum claim, the asylum seeker may be transferred to that Member State for refugee status determination to take place. In the Dublin III Regulation, the transfer is framed in terms of a duty on the receiving state to 'take charge' of and 'take back' an relevant asylum seeker (regulation 18).

However, there have been a number of challenges to the effectiveness of the Dublin scheme. These challenges have been based on the inadequacy of reception conditions in some Member States as well as the risk of *refoulement* that asylum seekers may face if they are transferred to certain Member States. Notably, in *MSS v Belgium and Greece* (2011) EHRR 2, the Grand Chamber of the ECtHR found a violation of Articles 3 and 13 ECHR on the part of Belgium by transferring asylum seekers back to Greece under the Dublin regime. A similar conclusion was reached by the CJEU in Case C-411/10 *NS* [2011] ECR I-13905, which held that Member States have an obligation as a matter of EU law not to transfer asylum seekers to Member States where they would face inhuman or degrading treatment contrary to Article 4 CFREU and Article 3 ECHR. In the UK, the Supreme Court has ruled that returns to Italy may violate Article 3 ECHR. It stated that the relevant question was whether there was a real risk of treatment sufficiently grave to breach Article 3 ECHR. It further clarified that it was not necessary to prove 'systemic deficiencies' in the asylum procedure and reception conditions, a test that had been thought may exist since the judgment of the CJEU in *NS*.

6.88

Accordingly, transfer under Dublin III must respect fundamental rights protected by the general principles and the CFREU as well as (it is to be presumed) the general principle of proportionality. Thus, it is clear that the hierarchy of criteria cannot act as an irrebuttable presumption and Dublin III must be applied in a way that is compliant with fundamental rights (and the general principle of proportionality) and are expressly subject to a full merits review (see chapter 14).

6.89

G. The EU Law of Human Trafficking

On 6 April 2013, EU Directive 2011/36/EU (the Trafficking Directive)[62] entered into force. The UK initially opted out of this Directive, but later reversed that position.

6.90

This Directive reflects the commitment of the EU to the prevention and combatting of trafficking, and imposes obligations on protecting the victims of trafficking.

6.91

---

[62] EU Directive 2011/36/EU of the European Parliament and of the Council of 5 April 2011 on preventing and combating trafficking in human beings and protecting its victims, and replacing Council Framework Decision 2002/629/JHA [2011] OJ L101/1.

Its subject matter, which is defined in Article 1, is that it 'establishes minimum rules concerning the definition of criminal offences and sanctions in the area of trafficking in human beings'.

6.92 There is a wide definition of punishable acts in Article 2 and minimum penalties are stipulated for specific acts in Article 4. An obligation to provide support and assistance to victims of trafficking where there are reasonable grounds to believe that a person is a victim of trafficking and a somewhat stronger duty to identify and support child victims are contained in Articles 11 and 14. Article 12 includes obligations on Member States to protect victims of trafficking in the criminal proceedings against their traffickers as well as to enable them to obtain compensation and have legal advice and assistance.

6.93 The Trafficking Directive does not regulate conditions of rights of residence of victims of trafficking and thus is silent on their protection from expulsion or exclusion. However, in the context of its endorsements of obligations from other international instruments, it can be read as reinforcing rights of residence provided for elsewhere.[63] For example, Directive 2004/81/EC[64] defines the rights of residence as well as the level of protection against non-renewal and withdrawal of residence to victims of trafficking on the basis of public policy and to the protection of national security; however, importantly, the UK is not a party to this Directive.

---

[63] See preamble, recital 10, where other instruments and the Council of Europe Convention on Action against Trafficking in Human Beings are said to be 'crucial steps in the process of enhancing international cooperation against trafficking in human beings'. In addition, the duty to protect and support victims of trafficking includes providing them with information which 'shall cover, where relevant, information on a reflection and recovery period pursuant to Directive 2004/81/EC, and information on the possibility of granting international protection pursuant to Council Directive 2004/83/EC of 29 April 2004 on minimum standards for the qualification and status of third country nationals or stateless persons as refugees or as persons who otherwise need international protection and the content of the protection granted and Council Directive 2005/85/EC of 1 December 2005 on minimum standards on procedures in Member States for granting and withdrawing refugee status or pursuant to other international instruments or other similar national rules'.

[64] Council Directive 2004/81/EC of 29 April 2004 on the residence permit issued to third country nationals who are victims of trafficking in human beings or who have been the subject of an action to facilitate illegal immigration, who cooperate with the competent authorities [2004] OJ L261.

7
Domestic Law

Contents

A.	Introduction	7.1
B.	The Constitution	7.2
	B1. Content of the UK Constitution	7.2
	B2. Fundamental Rights	7.6
	B3. Parliamentary Sovereignty	7.11
	B4. EU Law and Parliamentary Sovereignty	7.18
	B5. Other Restrictions on Parliamentary Sovereignty	7.20
C.	Prerogative Powers	7.21
	C1. Definition	7.21
	C2. Prerogative Powers in UK Immigration Law	7.22
	C3. Prerogative Powers in UK Nationality Law	7.24
D.	Sources of Domestic Immigration Law	7.25
	D1. Statute: IA 1971	7.25
	D2. The Immigration Rules	7.26
	D3. Guidance	7.35
	D4. Discretion Outside the Immigration Rules	7.37
E.	Sources of Domestic Nationality Law	7.39
	E1. Statute: BNA 1981	7.39
F.	Control by the Court	7.44

A. Introduction

This chapter sets out the various sources of domestic law in the United Kingdom, with particular attention to those important in the fields of immigration and nationality. The emphasis is upon sources of law and the characteristics of each, rather than upon a list of applicable provisions. The sheer volume of relevant material and the pace of change mean that a work possibly running to several volumes would be filled rapidly by an attempt to set out all of the applicable domestic law, and furthermore would rapidly become obsolete. The approach adopted here enables a focus on the characteristics and interrelationship of various sources of law which would not otherwise be possible. Accordingly the legal provisions relevant to the subject matter of each chapter in Parts D and E of the book are cited in those chapters, and not set out separately in this one.

7.1

Part B – Legal Framework

B. The Constitution

B1. Content of the UK Constitution

7.2 It is often asserted that the UK does not possess a codified constitution. What this means is that it does not have a constitution contained in a single document, or a readily identifiable set of documents. In 2001 the House of Lords created a Select Committee on the Constitution, which has adopted a loose practical definition of the constitution as:

> [T]he set of laws, rules and practices that create the basic institutions of the state, and its component and related parts, and stipulate the powers of those institutions and the relationship between the different institutions and between those institutions and the individual.[1]

7.3 This formula focuses upon the constitution as encompassing several spheres of activity: first, the existence and interrelation of the basic institutions of the state; and, second, the relationship between state institutions and the individual.

7.4 Whilst this encompasses questions concerning the powers which the state exercises over individuals, it does not identify specific areas as 'constitutional' in the way that, for example, the first paragraph of the Fourteenth Amendment to the US Constitution delineates its subject matter:

> All persons born or naturalized in the United States, and subject to the jurisdiction thereof, are citizens of the United States and of the State wherein they reside. No State shall make or enforce any law which shall abridge the privileges or immunities of citizens of the United States; nor shall any State deprive any person of life, liberty, or property, without due process of law; nor deny to any person within its jurisdiction the equal protection of the laws.

In the absence of a codified constitution in the UK, it is less easy to identify a particular subject as constitutional or otherwise. If every interaction of the state with an individual had constitutional status, then the definition might appear overly expansive. The House of Lords Select Committee in the report referred to above noted that various commentators tended to define a wide range of matters as of constitutional significance, not always agreeing with each other. It identified the following as being among the subjects commonly thought of as constitutional: (i) the role of the judiciary and judicial review; (ii) citizenship; (iii) personal freedoms, liberties and free speech; and (iv) the EU.

7.5 Most law in the United Kingdom either is, or depends upon powers created by, statute. The former category includes EU law incorporated by ECA 1972 and the ECHR provisions incorporated by HRA 1998 as well as most aspects of the law concerning acquisition or removal of British citizenship. The latter includes the substantial regulation of immigration by means of the Immigration Rules. In *Thoburn v Sunderland City Council* [2002] EWHC 195 (Admin), [2003] QB 151, Laws LJ pointed to the existence of a class of 'constitutional statutes' which as such were not liable to implied repeal by ordinary legislation. His list commenced with the Magna Carta of 1215, the Bill of Rights 1689 and the Act of Union 1707, and included ECA 1972, the HRA 1998 and the devolution instruments for Scotland and Wales. His conclusion that 'a constitutional

---

[1] House of Lords Select Committee on the Constitution, *Reviewing the Constitution: Terms of Reference and Method of Working*, First Report of 2001–2, para 11.

statute is one which (a) conditions the legal relationship between citizen and State in some general, overarching manner, or (b) enlarges or diminishes the scope of what we would now regard as fundamental constitutional rights' found support in the Supreme Court in *R (otao HS2 Action Alliance and others) v Secretary of State for Transport and another* [2014] UKSC 3, [2014] 1 WLR 324, per Lords Neuberger and Mance at [207].

B2. Fundamental Rights

In *Thoburn*, Laws LJ referred to the existence of 'fundamental constitutional rights'. He concluded that whether a statute enlarges or reduces the application of a fundamental constitutional right is important to the determination as to whether a statute is in turn itself constitutional. Such rights might arise from constitutional statutes, such as Magna Carta 1215, or directly from the common law without mention in any statute. Modern theorists have all defined a core area of protected common law rights outside statute, whilst in some examples pointing to statutes as reiterating pre-existing common law rights. As seen in chapter one, Blackstone considered there to be an absolute right of personal liberty[2] and Dicey also recognised a right to personal freedom.[3] *De Smith's Judicial Review* cites with approval[4] the observation of Brooke LJ (with whom Thomas and Jacob LJJ agreed), emphasising the importance of constitutional rights, in *ID and others v Home Office* [2005] EWCA Civ 38, [2006] 1 All ER 183 [129]:

7.6

> The transition from a world where decisions affecting personal liberty are made by officials of the executive who operate according to unpublished criteria ... to a world where the relevant criteria have to be published and where those officials are obliged to ensure that their decisions are proportionate and to justify them accordingly, is bound to be an uneasy one in the early years, and mistakes are bound to be made. But so long as detention, which may cause significant suffering, can be directed by executive decision and an order of a court (or court-like body) is not required, the language and the philosophy of human rights law, and the common law's emphatic reassertion in recent years of the importance of constitutional rights, drive inexorably, in my judgment, to the conclusion I have reached.

De Smith sets out a short list of constitutional rights identified in recent years, including access to judicial remedy, the right to life, 'the liberty of the person', the doing of justice in public, the right to a fair hearing, rights of access to legal advice and to confidential communication with a legal adviser, and freedom of movement within the UK.[5] Also on the list is the proposition that 'a British citizen has a fundamental right to live in, or return to, that part of the Queen's territory of which he is a citizen' (see further *R (otao Bancoult) v Secretary of State for Foreign and Commonwealth Affairs* [2008] UKHL 61, [2009] 1 AC 453).

What does it mean to identify a certain right or protection as a fundamental common law right? In *Thoburn*, Laws LJ identified 'constitutional' statutes as having protection

7.7

---

[2] Sir W Blackstone, *Commentaries on the Laws of England*, (Oxford, Clarendon, 1768; 18th edn 1829, S Sweet, R Pheney, A Maxwell, Stevens and Sons) Book I, ch I, 133–35.

[3] AV Dicey, *Introduction to the Study of the Law of the Constitution* (9th edn, London, Macmillan, 1939) ch 5.

[4] Lord Woolf, Professor Sir J Jowell, Professor Andrew le Sueur, C Donnelly and I Hare, *De Smith's Judicial Review* (7th edn, London, Sweet & Maxwell, 2013) para 5-042, p 264.

[5] ibid para 5-042, p 264.

Part B – Legal Framework

from implied repeal. That statement acknowledges that provisions in 'constitutional' statutes, as well as fundamental rights not codified by statute, remain liable to be set aside by express statutory provision.

7.8 Fundamental statutory or common law rights are not generally held to be embedded in the UK in the way which is true, for example, of the Fourteenth Amendment to the US Constitution, by which, for example, any person born in the US is a US citizen, and neither Congress nor the President may prevent this in the absence of constitutional amendment. In the US, the Supreme Court established in *Marbury v Madison* 5 US 137 (1803), 1 Cranch 137 that legislation incompatible with the Constitution was not law. A different form of embedding is that which the Indian Supreme Court has employed, for instance, in *Golak Nath v State of Punjab* 1967 AIR 1643, 1967 SCR (2) 762; *Kesavananda v Kerala* 1973 AIR 1461, (1973) 4 SCC 225, and *Indira Nehru Gandhi v Raj Narain* AIR 1975 SC 2299, (1975) Supp SCC 1, in response to attempts by the Indian legislature to amend the Constitution of India in respects which would weaken or do away with core political liberties or fundamental rights.[6] By contrast, the established position in England and Wales is held to be that Parliament will be presumed not to legislate contrary to the most fundamental rights (the so called 'principle of legality' first expressed in *R v Secretary of State for the Home Department ex p Simms* [1999] UKHL 33, [2000] 2 AC 115) unless it does so expressly and thereby confronts the political odium which may ensue.

7.9 This can be illustrated by reference to the common law right of abode (see para 7.06 above). In *R (otao Bancoult)*, Lord Hoffmann observed that clear statute trumped the right:

> 42. Sir Sydney's proposition that the Crown does not have power to remove an islander's right of abode in the territory is in my opinion also too extreme. He advanced two reasons. The first was that a right of abode was a fundamental constitutional right. He cited the 29th chapter of Magna Carta: 'No freeman shall be taken, or imprisoned... or exiled, or any otherwise destroyed... but by the lawful judgment of his peers, or by the law of the land.
>
> 43. 'But... by the law of the land' are in this context the significant words. Likewise Blackstone (*Commentaries on the Laws of England*,15th ed (1809), vol I, p 137): 'But no power on earth, except the authority of Parliament, can send any subject of England out of the land against his will; no, not even a criminal.'
>
> 44. That remains the law of England today. The Crown has no authority to transport anyone beyond the seas except by statutory authority. At common law, any subject of the Crown has the right to enter and remain in the United Kingdom whenever and for as long as he pleases: see *R v Bhagwan* [1972] AC 60. The Crown cannot remove this right by an exercise of the prerogative. That is because since the 17th century the prerogative has not empowered the Crown to change English common or statute law. In a ceded colony, however, the Crown has plenary legislative authority. It can make or unmake the law of the land.
>
> 45. What these citations show is that the right of abode is a creature of the law. The law gives it and the law may take it away. In this context I do not think that it assists the argument to call it a constitutional right. The constitution of [the British Indian Ocean Territory] denies the existence of such a right. I quite accept that the right of abode, the right not to be expelled from one's country or even one's home, is an important right. General or ambiguous words in legislation will not readily be construed as intended to remove such a right: see [*R v Secretary of State for the Home Department ex p Simms* [1999] UKHL 33, [2000] 2 AC 115 [131]–[132]]. But no such question arises in this case. The language of

---

[6] MP Jain, *Indian Constitutional Law* (5th edn, New Delhi, Wadhwa and Company, 2003,) chs XX and XLI.

section 9 of the Constitution Order could hardly be clearer. The importance of the right to the individual is also something which must be taken into account by the Crown in exercising its legislative powers a point to which I shall in due course return. But there seems to me no basis for saying that the right of abode is in its nature so fundamental that the legislative powers of the Crown simply cannot touch it.

The facts of the case illustrate a major weakness in the assumption that fundamental rights are protected by the risk of public odium in the event of express departure from them. Whilst potentially effective in the event of an attack on majority rights, effective political response may be relatively less likely in the case of breach of the fundamental rights of a small group of islanders far from the UK claimed to be justified by security or international relations considerations. Equally, a risk arises that a majority may not be offended by, and might even favour, breaches of the fundamental rights of certain groups, such as members of minority racial, political, religious or ethical groups, asylum-seekers or refugees, prisoners or the unemployed or undereducated.

In summary, therefore, fundamental constitutional rights are in the UK held to be protected from implied repeal (in the case of statutory rights). As regards fundamental rights outwith statute, their protection is by the 'principle of legality', which is in essence a principle of statutory interpretation: 'general or ambiguous words in legislation will not readily be construed as intended to remove such a right'. Such rights are held to give way before Parliamentary sovereignty (subject, at least in the view of some, to the rule of law: see paragraphs 7.11–17 below). 7.10

B3. Parliamentary Sovereignty

Parliamentary sovereignty is the principle of constitutional doctrine by which the Queen in Parliament is the highest legal authority in the UK. In broad terms it reflects the passing of primacy from the monarch to Parliament in England and Wales by the Bill of Rights 1689, and in Scotland the effect of the Claim of Right Act 1689 and later the Act of Union 1707. The effect of this is to produce a different overt balance from other European constitutional democracies, which in general describe 'the people' as sovereign. Parliamentary sovereignty has been described in the following way: 7.11

> What the doctrine establishes is the legal supremacy of *statute*. It means that there is no source of law higher than—ie more authoritative than—an Act of Parliament. Parliament may by statute make or unmake any law, including a law that is violative of international law or that alters a principle of the common law. And the courts are obliged to uphold and enforce it.[7]

As to Scotland, it has been suggested that some provisions of the Acts of Union of 1707 are so fundamental that they lie beyond amendment or nullification by ordinary statute. In the Inner House of the Court of Session, the Lord President, Lord Cooper, in *MacCormick v Lord Advocate* [1953] ScotCS CSIH 2, 1953 SC 396 at 411–12 reserved his opinion on the question of whether provisions in Article XIX of the Treaty of Union, preserving the Court of Session and the established laws relating to private right administered in Scotland, were 7.12

---

[7] European Scrutiny Committee, *The EU Bill and Parliamentary Sovereignty*, Written Evidence ordered by the House of Commons to be printed 6 December 2010, Written Evidence from Professor Adam Tomkins, John Millar Professor of Public Law, University of Glasgow.

not susceptible to amendment or nullification by ordinary statute. In England and Wales, there has as yet been no case in which the courts have refused to acknowledge as valid a statutory provision considered to violate a common law fundamental right. It is clear that this could occur only in an extreme case. In *Taylor v New Zealand Poultry Board* [1984] 1 NZLR 394 at 398, the President of the New Zealand Court of Appeal observed that some 'common law rights presumably lie so deep that even Parliament could not override them'.[8] Writing extra-judicially, Sir John Laws has observed that as a matter of constitutionality:

> [T]he fundamental sinews of the constitution, the cornerstones of democracy and of inalienable rights, ought not by law to be in the keeping of the government, because the only means by which these principles may be enshrined in the state is their possessing a status which no government has the right to destroy.[9]

7.13 Of the parliamentary sovereignty doctrine, Sir John concluded that: 'The thrust of this reasoning is that the doctrine of Parliamentary sovereignty cannot be vouched by Parliamentary legislation; a higher-order law confers it, and must of necessity limit it.'[10] Lord Woolf has also written that:

> [I]f Parliament did the unthinkable [by acting against the rule of law], then I would say that the courts would also be required to act in a manner which would be without precedent. Some judges might choose to do so by saying that it was an unrebuttable presumption that Parliament could never intend such a result. I myself would consider that there were advantages in making clear that ultimately there are even limits on the sovereignty of Parliament which it is the courts' inalienable responsibility to identify and uphold.[11]

7.14 The question of whether inherent limitations do protect fundamental rights, or some of these, or the rule of law—itself a concept whose scope is not firmly established—[12] remains unresolved. It was raised before the House of Lords in *Jackson v Attorney General* [2005] UKHL 56, [2006] 1 AC 262, in which the question was the validity of the Hunting Act 2004, passed without the consent of the House of Lords by means of the Parliament Acts and said to be incompatible with the fundamental rights of huntsmen and women. Technically, various comments made in *Jackson* about the sovereignty of Parliament were obiter and the context was not legislation passed by both Houses. The case represents the most significant recent source of judicial reflection upon the principle of parliamentary sovereignty. Lord Bingham at [9] stated that:

> 9. The bedrock of the British constitution is, and in 1911 was, the supremacy of the Crown in Parliament. It is, as Maurice Kay LJ observed in para 3 of his judgment, unnecessary for present purposes to touch on the difference, if any, made by our membership of the European Union. Then, as now, the Crown in Parliament was unconstrained by any entrenched or codified constitution. It could make or unmake any law it wished. Statutes, formally enacted as Acts of

---

[8] See also Sir R Cooke 'Fundamentals' [1988] *New Zealand Law Journal* 158.
[9] Sir J Laws, 'Law and Democracy' [1995] PL 72, 85. See also Sir J Laws, 'The Constitution: Morals and Rights' [1996] PL 622; and Lord Irvine, 'Response to Sir John Laws' [1996] PL 636.
[10] ibid.
[11] H Woolf, 'Droit Public—English Style' [1995] PL 57, 68–69.
[12] As the House of Lords Select Committee on the Constitution observed at para 23, section 1 Constitutional Reform Act 2005: 'This Act does not adversely affect (a) the existing constitutional principle of the rule of law, or (b) the Lord Chancellor's existing constitutional role in relation to that principle'. This provision begs several questions, the first of which is what the 'rule of law' actually means: Select Committee on the Constitution Sixth Report of 2006–2007, *Relations between the Executive, the Judiciary, and Parliament*, 11 July 2007, and *Appendix 5: Paper by Professor Paul Craig: The Rule of Law*.

Parliament, properly interpreted, enjoyed the highest legal authority. But such Acts required the consent of both Houses, Lords and Commons.

In the *Jackson* decision at [102], Lord Steyn indicated that parliamentary sovereignty was a general constitutional principle, but not an invariable one: 7.15

> 102. We do not in the United Kingdom have an uncontrolled constitution... In the European context the second *Factortame* decision made that clear: [1991] 1 AC 603. The settlement contained in the Scotland Act 1998 also points to a divided sovereignty. Moreover, the European Convention on Human Rights as incorporated into our law by the Human Rights Act 1998 created a new legal order... The classic account given by Dicey of the doctrine of the supremacy of Parliament, pure and absolute as it was, can now be seen to be out of place in the modern United Kingdom. Nevertheless, the supremacy of Parliament is still the general principle of our constitution. The judges created this principle. If that is so, it is not unthinkable that circumstances could arise where the courts may have to qualify a principle established on a different hypothesis of constitutionalism. In exceptional circumstances involving an attempt to abolish judicial review or the ordinary role of the courts, the Appellate Committee of the House of Lords or a new Supreme Court may have to consider whether this is a constitutional fundamental which even a sovereign Parliament acting at the behest of a complaisant House of Commons cannot abolish. It is not necessary to explore the ramifications of this question in this opinion. No such issues arise on the present appeal.

In the same decision, Lord Hope stated that parliamentary sovereignty was itself ultimately subject to the rule of law. 7.16

> 104. I start where my learned friend Lord Steyn has just ended. Our constitution is dominated by the sovereignty of Parliament. But Parliamentary sovereignty is no longer, if it ever was, absolute. It is not uncontrolled in the sense referred to by Lord Birkenhead LC in *McCawley v The King* [1920] AC 691, 720. It is no longer right to say that its freedom to legislate admits of no qualification whatever. Step by step, gradually but surely, the English principle of the absolute legislative sovereignty of Parliament which Dicey derived from Coke and Blackstone is being qualified.
>
> 105. For the most part these qualifications are themselves the product of measures enacted by Parliament. Part I of the European Communities Act 1972 is perhaps the prime example. Although Parliament was careful not to say in terms that it could not enact legislation which was in conflict with Community law, that in practice is the effect of section 2(1) when read with section 2(4) of that Act. The direction in section 2(1) that Community law is to be recognised and available in law and is to be given legal effect without further enactment, which is the method by which the Community Treaties have been implemented, concedes the last word in this matter to the courts. The doctrine of the supremacy of Community law restricts the absolute authority of Parliament to legislate as it wants in this area. This plainly is how the matter would be viewed in Luxembourg... Section 3(1) of the Human Rights Act 1998 has introduced a further qualification, as it directs the courts to read and give effect to legislation in a way that is compatible with the Convention rights. So long as it is possible to do so, the interpretative obligation enables the courts to give a meaning to legislation which is compatible even if this appears to differ from what Parliament had in mind when enacting it.[13]

Accordingly, it is clear that whilst the courts will seek to protect fundamental rights by declining to apply implicit repeal of important statutory provisions acknowledged as constitutional 7.17

---

[13] In a subsequent decision, *AXA General Insurance v HM Advocate and others* [2011] UKSC 46, [2012] 1 AC 868, Lord Hope at [50] observed that 'the question whether the principle of the sovereignty of the United Kingdom Parliament is absolute or may be subject to limitation in exceptional circumstances is still under discussion'.

and by interpreting legislation (whether legislation seeks to operate by mandating outcomes or by delegation of powers or duties) to avoid or minimise interference with fundamental common law rights, the question of whether parliamentary sovereignty is an immutable principle preventing a court from concluding that an Act of Parliament is invalid has not been conclusively resolved. It is plain, however, that the courts are likely in practice to contemplate such a course only in circumstances of substantial constitutional urgency.

B4. EU Law and Parliamentary Sovereignty

7.18 In some of the speeches made in *Jackson*, as set out above, EU law was cited as an area of incursion into the strong form of parliamentary sovereignty recognised by the classical writers, in particular by Dicey.[14] The ECA 1972 provided for the supremacy of EU law under the treaties, as was confirmed by the House of Lords in *R v Secretary of State for Transport ex p Factortame (No 2)* [1990] UKHL 13, [1991] 1 AC 603. Their Lordships' House acknowledged that the obligation to comply with a principle of EU law as affirmed by the European Court of Justice required it to deny effect to the terms of an Act of Parliament. In the course of his speech, Lord Bridge at [4] made the following observations:

> 4. Some public comments on the decision of the European Court of Justice, affirming the jurisdiction of the courts of Member States to override national legislation if necessary to enable interim relief to be granted in protection of rights under Community law, have suggested that this was a novel and dangerous invasion by a Community institution of the sovereignty of the United Kingdom Parliament. But such comments are based on a misconception. If the supremacy within the European Community of Community law over the national law of Member States was not always inherent in the E.E.C. Treaty it was certainly well established in the jurisprudence of the European Court of Justice long before the United Kingdom joined the Community. Thus, whatever limitation of its sovereignty Parliament accepted when it enacted the European Communities Act 1972 was entirely voluntary. Under the terms of the Act of 1972 it has always been clear that it was the duty of a United Kingdom court, when delivering final judgment, to override any rule of national law found to be in conflict with any directly enforceable rule of Community law ... Thus there is nothing in any way novel in according supremacy to rules of Community law in those areas to which they apply.

7.19 In the respect identified, the incursion into parliamentary sovereignty resulted from voluntary restriction accepted by Parliament through its passing of the ECA 1972 (see further, *R (otao HS2 Action Alliance and others) v Secretary of State for Transport and another* [2014] UKSC 3, [2014] 1 WLR 324). Clearly, the principles governing the supremacy of EU law apply only within the scope of EU law (see further chapter 6).

B5. Other Restrictions on Parliamentary Sovereignty

7.20 Parliament has itself enacted instruments which in effect delegate sovereignty or restrict its exercise. Leading examples include, for example, HRA 1998 (in which the interpretative provision at section 4 HRA 1998 is indicative of the desire to avoid direct collision

---

[14] Dicey (n 3) Part I.

with parliamentary sovereignty, and the declaration of incompatibility procedure in section 4 provides a procedure by which a court identifies a statutory provision as incompatible with a protected right, without being empowered under this provision to declare it invalid) and the devolution legislation for Wales and Scotland.

C. Prerogative Powers

C1. Definition

7.21 The Crown, by which is meant the monarch acting in a constitutional public capacity and not as a private individual, during the early modern period exercised very extensive powers over subjects by exercise of the royal prerogative, held to be a part of the common law. In the fifteenth and sixteenth centuries, the Crown had power to imprison people as an exercise of discretion under the prerogative. In the course of more recent history, the Crown's powers have been greatly reduced by judicial decision and legislation. The use of such powers as subsist in general terms falls to the Crown, according to the direction of the executive branch.[15] Examples of remaining powers under the prerogative include the declaration of war (though constitutional conventions may be developing which will etiolate even this power).

C2. Prerogative Powers in UK Immigration Law

7.22 IA 1971 provides at section 3(2) that:

> The Secretary of State shall from time to time (and as soon as may be) lay before Parliament statements of the rules, or of any changes in the rules, laid down by him as to the practice to be followed in the administration of this Act for regulating the entry into and stay in the United Kingdom of persons required by this Act to have leave to enter, including any rules as to the period for which leave is to be given and the conditions to be attached in different circumstances.

By a second paragraph in section 3(2) IA 1971, it is provided that if a statement of rules is disapproved by a resolution of that House passed within 40 days of being laid:

> [T]he Secretary of State shall as soon as may be make such changes or further changes in the rules as appear to him to be required in the circumstances, so that the statement of those changes be laid before Parliament at latest by the end of the period of forty days beginning with the date of the resolution (but exclusive as aforesaid).

Section 1(4) IA 1971 mandates that the rules referred to 'shall include provision for admitting...persons coming for the purpose of taking employment, or for purposes of study, or as visitors, or as dependants of persons lawfully in or entering the United Kingdom'.

---

[15] *Secretary of State for the Home Department v Pankina* [2010] EWCA Civ 719, [2011] 1 QB 376, per Sedley LJ at [19] closing an examination of the role of prerogative: 'The exercise of the Monarch's prerogative has passed since 1689—or perhaps more precisely, as Anson suggests, since 1714—to ministers of the Crown.'

7.23   IA 1971 has now been held to have comprehensively displaced the prerogative in the areas to which section 3(2) of the IA 1971 extends: *R (Munir) v SSHD* [2012] UKSC 32, [2012] 1 WLR 2192 and *R (Alvi) v SSHD* [2012] UKSC 33, [2012] 1 WLR 2208. Whilst the formula 'entry into and stay in the United Kingdom of persons required by this Act to have leave to enter, including any rules as to the period for which leave is to be given and the conditions to be attached in different circumstances' does not expressly cite deportation, removal or exclusion, it would seem on a reasonable interpretation that these are almost certainly encompassed. Accordingly, it is likely that the power of the Secretary of State across virtually the whole of immigration law, including deportation, removal and exclusion, now rests upon statute alone, the exercise of the prerogative having been excluded.

C3. Prerogative Powers in UK Nationality Law

7.24   An important distinction between the nationality and immigration laws of the UK is that IA 1971 does not treat nationality as being within the span of the rules required by section 3(2) IA 1971, providing only that 'account may be taken of citizenship or nationality' (implicitly that of applicants within the sphere of IA 1971). BNA 1981, the cornerstone of UK nationality law, does not on its face set down any requirement parallel to that applied in the immigration context by section 3(2) IA 1971. Accordingly, the prerogative cannot be positively identified as excluded by statute, although the primary powers exercised by the Secretary of State in relation to nationality are statutory ones and the prerogative is not expressly relied upon by the Secretary of State in this context. This may be an area in which the ability to exercise prerogative power has atrophied to the point of extinction, but no statute or decision exists to confirm it.

D. Sources of Domestic Immigration Law

D1. Statute: IA 1971

7.25   Whilst there has been extensive subsequent statute developing or otherwise amending the overall regime, IA 1971 is the foundation point for the current immigration control regime. Under section 1(1) IA 1971, those expressed to have a right of abode are held to be:

> [F]ree to live in, and to come and go into and from, the United Kingdom without let or hindrance except such as may be required under and in accordance with this Act to enable their right to be established or as may be otherwise lawfully imposed on any person.

The concept of 'right of abode' therefore has particular importance as the key indicator of a right under statute to enter, leave or remain in the UK without being subject to immigration control. The right of abode has been held to be 'a creature of the law', but also an important source of liberty, such that general or ambiguous words in legislation will not readily be construed as removing it (*R (otao Bancoult) v SSHD* [2008] UKHL 61, [2009] AC 453, per Lord Hoffmann at [45]).

D2. The Immigration Rules

Section 3(2) of the IA 1971 as already set out provides that the Secretary of State shall lay before Parliament statements of the rules, or of any changes in the rules, laid down by him or her as to the practice to be followed in the administration of immigration control. As the executive cannot make law without Parliament's authority (*Case of Proclamations* (1611) 12 Co Rep 74, cited in *SSHD v Pankina* [2010] EWCA Civ 719, [2011] 1 QB 376, [18]), IA 1971 requires the Immigration Rules, or changes thereto, to be subject to the negative resolution procedure before Parliament and the rules may not refer to external sources that have not themselves been laid before Parliament (*SSHD v Pankina*, above). **7.26**

In practice, the Secretary of State has long maintained a single 'master' version of the rules. The present version is set out in the Immigration Rules HC 395. Amendments to this are set out in Statements of Changes to the Immigration Rules. In recent years, this has occurred with considerable frequency. In *R (Alvi) v SSHD* [2012] UKSC 33, [2012] 1 WLR 2208, Lord Hope observed, at [11], that: **7.27**

> The system which the Secretary of State operates today in the administration of the 1971 Act is far removed from that which was contemplated at the time when the Bill that became that Act was being discussed in Parliament. The first versions of the rules were 17 and 20 pages long. The 1994 Statement of Changes in Immigration Rules (HC 395) extended to 80 pages. There have been over 90 statements of change since then, and HC 395 has become increasingly complex. The current consolidated version which is available on line from the UKBA website extends to 488 pages. Extensive use is now made of the internet, a system for the dissemination of information to the public that was, of course, unknown 40 years ago. 19 statements of changes in the Immigration Rules have been published on the website since February 2010. There have been four this year, the last of which was in June 2012. The ease with which information on a website can be removed, added to or amended encourages resort to these techniques to a degree that would have been wholly impracticable in the days of the mechanical typewriter. In *DP (United States of America) v Secretary of State for the Home Department* [2012] EWCA Civ 365, para 14 Longmore LJ lamented, with good reason, the absolute whirlwind which litigants and judges now feel themselves in due to the speed with which the law, practice and policy change in this field of law.

A short time earlier, in *AA (Nigeria) v SSHD* [2010] EWCA Civ 773, [2011] 1 WLR 564, Longmore LJ had observed, at [87], that: **7.28**

> I am left perplexed and concerned how any individual whom the Rules affect (especially perhaps a student, like Mr A, who is seeking a variation of his leave to remain in the United Kingdom) can discover what the policy of the Secretary of State actually is at any particular time if it necessitates a trawl through Hansard or formal Home Office correspondence as well as through the comparatively complex Rules themselves. It seems that it is only with expensive legal assistance, funded by the taxpayer, that justice can be done.

The Immigration Rules are by definition not legislation; they are neither statute nor statutory instrument. Whilst the rules are anticipated by section 3(2) of the IA 1971, they do not derive from it and are not delegated legislation (and therefore are not susceptible to challenge on pure ultra vires grounds). They are instruments stating the policy of the executive. The negative resolution procedure applied to them accords a relatively weak degree of democratic legitimacy, which is not comparable with that possessed by legislation: *R (Stellato) v SSHD* [2007] UKHL 5, [2007] 2 AC 70, per Lord Hope at [12]. **7.29**

7.30 Accordingly the Immigration Rules have been held to have a unique or *sui generis* legal status. In *Odelola v SSHD* [2009] UKHL 25, [2009] 3 All ER 1061, Lord Hoffmann at [6]–[7] observed that:

> 6. The status of the immigration rules is rather unusual. They are not subordinate legislation but detailed statements by a minister of the Crown as how the Crown proposes to exercises its executive power to control immigration. But they create legal rights: under section 84(1) of the Nationality, Immigration and Asylum Act 2002, one may appeal against an immigration decision on the ground that it is not in accordance with the immigration rules. So there is no conceptual reason why they should not create rights which subsequent rules should not, in the absence of express language, be construed as removing. The question is whether, on a fair reading, that is what they do.
> 7. In my opinion, if one looks at the function of the rules, they should not be so construed. They are, as I have said, a statement by the Secretary of State as to how she will exercise powers of control over immigration.

In the same decision, Lord Brown confirmed at [35] that the Rules are 'statements of administrative policy: an indication of how at any particular time the Secretary of State will exercise her discretion with regard to the grant of leave to enter or remain', and Lord Neuberger observed at [50] that: 'The rules contain a mixture of substantive and procedural provisions, and guidance to the legislation and practice, and they have to be laid before Parliament. However, they are not legislation.'

7.31 It is clear that the Secretary of State may depart from the Immigration Rules, or authorise officials to do so, if faced with compelling grounds for waiver of a relevant requirement. The rules however do not exist as mere statements of policy which may not be relied upon where the Secretary of State acts incompatibly with them. Under the NIAA 2002 appeals regime as presently in place,[16] since the Tribunal must allow an appeal against an immigration decision if it is not made in accordance with the immigration rules (section 86(3)(a) NIAA 2002). The rules consequently, as described in *SSHD v Pankina* [2010] EWCA Civ 719, [2011] 1 QB 376 constitute 'a code to be followed and a source of legal rights'.

7.32 The general approach to interpretation of the Rules has been frequently considered, most recently and decisively by the Supreme Court in *Ahmed Mahad (formerly AM (Ethiopia)) v ECO* [2009] UKSC 16, [2010] 2 All ER 535. In that decision Lords Hope, Rodger, Collins and Kerr concurred with Lord Brown's observation at [10] that:

> There is really no dispute about the proper approach to the construction of the Rules. As Lord Hoffmann said in *Odelola v Secretary of State for the Home Department* [[2009] UKHL 25, [4]]: Like any other question of construction, this [whether a rule change applies to all undetermined applications or only to subsequent applications] depends upon the language of the rule, construed against the relevant background. That involves a consideration of the immigration rules as a whole and the function which they serve in the administration of immigration policy.
> That is entirely consistent with what Buxton LJ (collecting together a number of dicta from past cases concerning the status of the rules) had said in *Odelola* in the Court of Appeal [[2008] EWCA Civ 308; [2009] 1 WLR 126] and, indeed, with what Laws LJ said (before the

---

[16] At the point of writing the appeals provisions contained in section 15 IA 2014 have not yet been brought into force. It should be noted that s 15 repeals the ground of appeal applicable on the basis that a decision is 'not in accordance with the immigration rules'. See further chapter 16.

House of Lords decision in *Odelola*) in the present case. Essentially it comes to this. The Rules are not to be construed with all the strictness applicable to the construction of a statute or a statutory instrument but, instead, sensibly according to the natural and ordinary meaning of the words used, recognising that they are statements of the Secretary of State's administrative policy. The respondent's counsel readily accepted that what she meant in her written case by the proposition 'the question of interpretation is ... what the Secretary of State intended his policy to be' was that the court's task is to discover from the words used in the Rules what the Secretary of State must be taken to have intended. After all, under section 3(2) of the IA 1971, the Secretary of State has to lay the Rules before Parliament which then has the opportunity to disapprove them. True, as I observed in Odelola (para 33): 'the question is what the Secretary of State intended. The rules are her rules'. But that intention is to be discerned objectively from the language used, not divined by reference to supposed policy considerations. Still less is the Secretary of State's intention to be discovered from the Immigration Directorates' Instructions (IDIs) issued intermittently to guide immigration officers in their application of the rules. IDIs are given pursuant to paragraph 1(3) of Schedule 2 to the 1971 Act which provides that:

> In the exercise of their functions under this Act immigration officers shall act in accordance with such instructions (not inconsistent with the immigration rules) as may be given them by the Secretary of State.

The proper interpretation of the rules 'depends on the language of the rule, construed against the relevant background' and demands consideration of the Immigration Rules as a whole and the function they aim to serve in the administration of immigration policy. Guidance, assurances given in ministerial correspondence and ministerial statements to Parliament are all relevant to the interpretation of ambiguous immigration rules: *Adedoyin* v *SSHD* [2010] EWCA Civ 773. 7.33

As applications are decided in accordance with the rules at the date of the decision (*Odelola*), it is therefore essential to be aware of, and able to access, the rules at the relevant date, to consult the archives available on the Home Office website and to be aware of the existence and relevance of transitional provisions. 7.34

D3. Guidance

The Home Office publishes internal guidance and instructions for decision makers and external guidance for applicants. Internal instructions relating to immigration, long referred to as 'Immigration Directorate Instructions' (IDIs) are now generally found within Modernised Guidance (MG). Relevant guidance is also contained within the Enforcement Instructions and Guidance (EIG), the Asylum Policy Instructions (APIs) and the European Casework Instructions (ECIs). 7.35

The power to issue these Instructions is provided at Schedule 2, para 1(3) to the IA 1971. The guidance contained within instructions cannot fetter the rights provided for by legislation or the Immigration Rules. However, where the instructions set out policies more generous than those provided by either legislation or the Immigration Rules, the failure to apply the policy will provide grounds for an appellant to challenge a decision as not being in accordance with the law. 7.36

D4. Discretion Outside the Immigration Rules

7.37   The Secretary of State may waive the application of the Immigration Rules, either because of compassionate circumstances in a specific case or via a general practice or concession. Where the Secretary of State has ignored such a general practice, or policy, to waive a requirement of the rules, it may be possible to challenge the resulting decision as being not in accordance with the law on grounds of unfairness, illegality or unreasonableness. It must be noted that the fact that the concession or practice in question is not contained within a published policy presents no bar to challenge (*R (otao Rashid) v SSHD* [2004] EWHC 2465 (Admin), All ER (D) 316 (Oct)).

7.38   The relevant policy is that in place at the time of the decision (see *R (otao Amirthanathan) v SSHD* [2002] EWHC 2595, [2003] All ER (D) 29 (May); see also *R (otao Joseph) v SSHD* [2002] EWHC 758 (Admin) as another example. In general, once the policy is no longer in existence, it cannot in the absence of explicit and unqualified promise be relied upon in order to challenge a decision: *R (otao Joseph) v SSHD* [2002] EWHC 758. Application of the '*Rashid* principle' represents an exception to this rule. In *R (otao Rashid) v SSHD* [2004] EWHC 2465 (Admin), Davis J ordered the SSHD to grant indefinite leave to the claimant who had been denied the benefit of a policy, notwithstanding the fact that it had been withdrawn because subsequent refusal to permit leave to remain constituted conspicuous unfairness arising from maladministration, the Secretary of State having failed to take adequate steps to ensure that departmental staff were aware of the policy and applied it. The decision was upheld by the Court of Appeal in *R (otao Rashid) v SSHD* [2005] EWCA Civ 744, [2005] INLR 550, and further delineation of the applicable principles was provided by Carnwath LJ in *R (otao S) v SSHD* [2007] EWCA Civ 546, [2007] INLR 450.

E. Sources of Domestic Nationality Law

E1. Statute: BNA 1981

7.39   Albeit the regime has been frequently modified by amending and/or supplementary legislation, the foundational basis of current British nationality law is BNA 1981, the analogue in nationality law of IA 1971.

7.40   Under the statutory structure concerning British citizenship provided by BNA 1981, individuals become entitled to citizenship by one of four routes: birth or adoption (section 1), descent (section 2), registration (sections 3–5 and 10) or naturalisation (section 6). Beyond this, the narrowing of entitlement to the right of abode in the UK has left a number of persons who possess some status as 'British' without British citizenship and the accompanying right of abode: (i) some British Overseas Territories citizens who have not over time acquired British citizenship, in particular those linked to the UK Sovereign Base areas in Cyprus excluded from transition to British citizenship under section 3 of the British Overseas Territories Act 2002; (ii) British overseas citizens; (iii) British nationals (overseas); (iv) British protected persons; or (v) British subjects.

7.41   Like aliens, those persons who possess a 'citizenship status' but are denied a right of abode are subject to immigration control. Section 3(1) IA 1971, as amended by section 39

BNA 1981 and paragraphs 43 and 44(1) Schedule 14 IAA 1999, provides that a person who is not a British citizen shall not enter the UK unless given leave to do so in accordance with the provisions of or made under the IA 1971, that he may be given leave to enter or remain for a limited or for an indefinite period and that if he is given leave to enter or to remain in the UK, it may be given subject to conditions restricting his employment or occupation or requiring him to register with the police.

The general requirements for British citizenship, or other forms of British citizenship status can be found in the more broadly based works concerning British nationality law identified in chapter 11. The focus of this work is particularly upon the subcategories of case in which the acquisition of British citizenship by registration, naturalisation or other means involves the exercise of a relatively broad judgment, which might be termed discretionary, by the Secretary of State.[17] The most notable examples are cases within the following categories: **7.42**

Registration: in a number of circumstances, the registration of an individual as a British national is subject to broad discretionary power on the part of Secretary of State. Under section 3(1) BNA 1981, if whilst a person is a minor an application is made for that person's registration as a British citizen, the Secretary of State 'may, if he [or she] thinks fit, cause him [or her] to be registered as such a citizen'. By section 4A BNA 1981, the Secretary of State 'may if he [or she] thinks fit cause [a British Overseas Territories citizen] to be ... registered [as a British citizen]', so long as the circumstances identified in section 4A BNA 1981 are not present.

Naturalisation: section 6(1) BNA 1981 provides that if on an application for naturalisation as a British citizen made by a person of full age and capacity, the Secretary of State is satisfied that the applicant fulfils the requirements of Schedule 1 BNA 1981 for naturalisation and thinks it fit to do so, he or she may grant a certificate of naturalisation as a British citizen. Where the applicant is married to or the civil partner of a British citizen, section 6(2) of the BNA 1981 applies. Subparagraph 1 of Schedule 1 BNA 1981 sets out requirements of presence and status in the UK, 'good character', 'sufficient knowledge of the English, Welsh or Scottish Gaelic language' and sufficient knowledge of life in the UK;

Resumption following renunciation: section 12 BNA 1981 provides the mechanism by which a British citizen 'of full age and capacity' may renounce British citizenship in a prescribed manner, upon which Secretary of State 'shall cause the declaration to be registered' so long as the Secretary of State is satisfied that the person who made it will not be left without other citizenship or nationality. If that person does not acquire some such citizenship or nationality within six months from that date, he or she shall remain a British citizen and be deemed to have remained a British citizen continuously. The Secretary of State may withhold registration of an act of renunciation 'made during any war in which Her Majesty may be engaged in right of Her Majesty's government in the United Kingdom.' Section 13 BNA 1981 provides for resumption of citizenship after renunciation in certain

---

[17] The term 'broad discretion' is a relative one and is necessarily somewhat imprecise in definition. In the present context, it has been employed to separate areas of broader discretion from others in which relatively hard-edged standards are provided. An example of decision-making from others where the discretionary power is more circumscribed—for example being limited to waiver of one particular requirement as for example s 4(4) BNA 1981, which permits the SSHD to disregard some of the requirements otherwise imposed by s 4(2) BNA 1981 as to presence in the UK and immigration status, or an otherwise excessive periods of absence from the UK.

circumstances. Under section 13(1), a person is entitled to resume citizenship as of right on one occasion only—where he or she is 'of full capacity' and the renunciation 'was necessary to enable him to retain or acquire some other citizenship or nationality'. Otherwise, under section 13(3), if a person of full capacity who ceased to be a British citizen through renunciation applies to the Secretary of State for registration as a British citizen, the Secretary of State 'may, if he thinks fit, cause him to be registered as such a citizen'.

Another focus of the work is upon the very broad powers of the Secretary of State to remove British citizenship (which also extend to other statuses connected to the UK).

7.43 Part 2 of the Borders, Citizenship, and Immigration Act 2009 (BCIA 2009), received Royal Assent on 21 July 2009, with an indication by the then government that its provisions as regards naturalisation would be introduced no sooner than July 2011. Those provisions have never come into force. Were this to occur it would bring about substantial change to the law governing naturalisation, amending section 6 BNA 1981 and Schedule 1 to that Act. The aim of these amendments was to remake the law of naturalisation treating the acquisition of British citizenship by naturalisation as the culmination of a complex process of 'earned citizenship'. However, this change was not accompanied by any of the amendments to immigration law which would have been necessary to begin to render a new scheme functional, and the provisions of Part 2 of the BCIA 2009 therefore looked, in the words of a leading expert, 'particularly unfamiliar, if not incomprehensible, using terms such as 'probationary citizenship' [a particularised form of leave to remain] as an immigration status not yet in existence in [UK] immigration law'.[18] A particular aim, explicit in the Green Paper concerning British citizenship that preceded the BCIA 2009 was to reduce the pool of persons with leave to remain in the UK but without citizenship by channelling immigrants through a series of tests for naturalisation and ending the right to remain in the event of failure.[19] As at the date of writing, the bringing into force of Part 2 BCIA 2009 at any point in the immediate future appears unlikely. The Immigration Act 2014 contains nothing suggesting an intention to bring Part 2 BCIA into force.

F. Control by the Court

7.44 An important feature of domestic law is the role of the Court in reviewing administrative action in its judicial review jurisdiction[20]. This is explored more fully in the domestic context in chapter 16, and in the EU and ECHR contexts in chapters 14 and 15, respectively.

---

[18] L Fransman, *British Nationality Law* (3rd edn, London, Bloomsbury, 2011) 414.
[19] Home Office Border and Immigration Agency, *The Path to Citizenship: Next Steps in Reforming the Immigration System*, February 2008.
[20] See further W Wade and C Forsyth, *Administrative Law*, (10th edn, Oxford, OUP, 2009); H Woolf, J Jowell, A le Sueur, C Donnelly, I Hare, *De Smith's Judicial Review*, (7th edn, London, Sweet and Maxwell, 2013); M Fordham, *Judicial Review Handbook* (6th edn, Oxford, Hart Publishing), in particular Part C, P45–P63.

Part C
Deportation, Removal and Exclusion

8

Deportation

Contents

- A. Introduction 8.1
- B. International Law 8.2
  - B1. General International Law 8.2
  - B2. International Human Rights Law 8.5
  - B3. Hybrid Instruments 8.10
  - B4. Council of Europe Instruments 8.14
- C. EU Law 8.17
- D. Domestic Law 8.19
  - D1. Prerogative 8.19
  - D2. Statute 8.20
  - D3. Statutory Instrument 8.32
    - The Immigration (European Economic Area) Regulations 2006 ...... 8.32
  - D4. Immigration Rules 8.34
  - D5. Published Guidance 8.35
- E. Discussion 8.36
  - E1. Foundations of Deportation Law 8.36
  - E2. Liability to Deportation 8.37
    - Scope of the Group of Persons Liable to Deportation 8.37
    - Definition of 'British Citizen' for the Purposes
      of Immunity from Deportation 8.38
    - The Limited Application of Sections 3(5)(b) and 3(6) IA 1971 ..... 8.39
    - The Importance of Section 3(5)(a) IA 1971 and its Relationship to
      UKBA 2007 .... 8.40
    - Liability to Deportation a Necessary Prerequisite to Exercise
      of Deportation 8.41
    - Exemptions from Liability 8.42
    - Duration of Liability to Deportation 8.43
  - E3. Liability to Deportation by the Application of
    Sections 32–33 UKBA 2007 ('Automatic Deportation' Cases) 8.46
  - E4. Liability to Deportation under Section 3(5)(a) IA 1971
    (Non-'Automatic Deportation' Cases) 8.50
  - E5. The section 5(1) IA 1971 Power to Make a Deportation Order 8.57
    - The Effect of Sections 32–33 UKBA 2007 .... 8.57
    - Exercise of the Section 5(1) IA 1971 Power where
      Section 32 UKBA 2007 Does Not Apply 8.62
    - Public Law 8.67
    - Restrictions Related to Republic of Ireland Citizens/EEA Nationals
      and Family Members/Turkish Workers and Family Members 8.68
    - Restrictions Regarding the Deportation of Family Members
      of Deportees 8.69
    - Other Matters Relevant to Decision Making: The Scope
      of Consideration Where Liability Arises under Section 3(6) IA 1971 .... 8.70
    - Article 8 ECHR in Section 5(1) IA 1971 Deportation Cases 8.83
    - The Effect of the New Part 5A NIAA 2002 .... 8.105
    - The Effect of Further Amendment to the Rules 8.108

E6. Taking a Decision under the Section 32 UKBA 2007 Duty 8.109
The Effect of the Application of the UKBA 2007 Scheme on the
Secretary of State 8.109
The Effect of Application of the UKBA 2007 in the Context
of Subsequent Challenge 8.112
E7. Notifying a Decision to Exercise the Section 5(1) IA 1971 Power
(or Act upon the Section 32 UKBA 2007 Duty) 8.118
E8. Appeal from a Decision under Section 5(1) IA 1971 or Section 32
UKBA 2007 .... 8.120
E9. Making an Order 8.121
E10. Application for Revocation 8.124
E11. Appeal against Refusal of Revocation 8.131
E12. Effects of the Deportation Process 8.132
Effects Relating to Detention 8.132
Exclusion 8.133
Effect on Existing Leave to Enter/Remain 8.134

A. Introduction

8.1 Deportation is a statutory power of the Secretary of State for the Home Department. An individual may by its exercise be required to leave, or removed from, the UK, and barred from returning either for a fixed period or indefinitely. The power is applicable to aliens in particular circumstances defined by statute. The current statutory provision has been in existence since the passage of IA 1971, with the change of greatest contemporary significance being insertion with effect from 1 August 2008 of a subsidiary scheme for those defined as 'foreign criminals' under the UK Borders Act 2007 (UKBA 2007).

B. International Law

B1. General International Law

8.2 As related in chapter 2, international law is in general not directly applicable in the UK. It can be relied upon directly only to the extent that a relevant norm has been incorporated domestically by statute, or otherwise informs the common law. However, international law may possess significance even without incorporation, for instance, where it assists interpretation of domestic law or shapes the exercise of discretion. On one level, reflecting the more traditional role of international law as the law of states, a right or duty will vest primarily in the state: it will be a state of nationality which possesses the right to protect its national against abuse by the UK, or a state to which an individual is removed in the course of deportation, or who is left in that state by action of the UK, which may complain of an international law wrong to it if it is not obliged by that law to accept an individual's return or presence. Yet, there is now a greater role for the individual in international law and this—including but not limited to international human rights law—provides significant protections accruing directly to the individual.

Expulsion and exclusion of aliens are in general recognised as being within the 8.3
ambit of a State's established rights (see chapter 2, section K(i)). However, the broad
discretion is not an absolute one, and the UK must not abuse its rights in international
law by acting arbitrarily in taking its decision to expel an alien, or acting unreasonably
in the manner in which it effects an expulsion. An expulsion or exclusion that defied
the UK's own law would necessarily breach the UK's duties to a state of nationality, as
illustrated in the *Boffolo* arbitration identified in chapter 2 at paragraph 2.46. Other
matters, such as a substantial and unjustified default in procedural rights, might
render a decision arbitrary: this category is not, on present authority, a closed one,
and judgment is fact-sensitive: see chapter 2 and, in relation to ICCPR, chapter 3,
paragraphs 3.29–3.32. There may be considerable parallels between the position in
general international law and that in international human rights law, in that a sufficient breach of internationally recognised human rights by a country of sojourn
such as the UK may represent a breach of international law duties owed to the state
of nationality of the individual, and also a breach of an individual's rights protected
under international human rights law.

Further distinct issues may arise where deportation procedures are engaged as a consequence of citizenship or right of abode being withdrawn. Deprivation of citizenship 8.4
or right of abode is addressed separately in chapter 12. However, deportation following
directly from a deprivation of nationality is likely to be viewed as part of a composite,
internally linked, sequence of actions.

B2. International Human Rights Law

A wider survey of the main international human rights law provisions relevant to immigration and nationality law is at chapter 3. A summary of those relevant to deportation 8.5
and contained within instruments ratified by the UK is set out for reference below.

First, a range of particularly important human rights protections apply under the 8.6
ICCPR to prevent return to a place in which relevant risk can be shown to arise:

(i) Article 6 ICCPR prohibits arbitrary deprivation of life, and sending an individual by way of deportation to a situation in which there are substantial grounds to believe that the deportee would face such a deprivation would breach that protection;
(ii) by Article 7 ICCPR, deportation to a situation in which there are substantial grounds to believe that the deportee would face torture, or cruel or inhuman or degrading treatment is prohibited;
(iii) Article 8 ICCPR marks the condemnation of slavery by the international community, and deportation to a situation in which there are substantial grounds to believe that the deportee would face being made a slave would constitute a breach;
(iv) by Article 9 ICCPR, arbitrary arrest or detention is prohibited. Deportation where there are substantial grounds to believe that the deportee would face such treatment is barred by this provision.

Second, an important parallel protection directed at return to a setting of relevant 8.7
risk of torture is brought into being by CAT. Deportation to a state in which 'there are

substantial grounds for believing' that the deportee would face torture as defined in that instrument would contravene Article 3(1) CAT.

8.8 Third, ICCPR provides a series of important basic standards relevant to deportation, largely if not entirely independent of the circumstances to which an individual would be returned:

(i) Deportation action will breach Article 12(4) ICCPR if: (a) the UK is the affected individual's 'own country' for purposes of that provision; (b) the effect of deportation would be to expel that individual from, or prevent his or her return to, the UK; and (c) the action would be arbitrary.

(ii) Deportation action will breach Article 13 ICCPR if: (a) the individual is an alien, not a British national; (b) he or she is lawfully present in the UK; and (c) the decision is not reached in accordance with applicable legal standards ('in accordance with law').

(iii) Save where 'compelling reasons of national security otherwise require', deportation action will breach Article 13 ICCPR if: (a) the affected individual is not permitted to submit representations setting out why he or she should not be expelled ('reasons against his expulsion'); and/or (b) is not permitted effective review of the decision before 'the competent authority or a person or persons especially designated by the competent authority'; and/or (c) is not permitted representation for the purpose of pursuing such review.

(iv) Action by the state in this context will breach Article 17 ICCPR, read in conjunction with Article 23(1) ICCPR, if it amounts to 'arbitrary or unlawful' interference with the protected interests of 'privacy, family, home', against which the domestic law does not provide protection.

(v) Article 2 ICCPR is breached where the state fails to 'respect and ensure' the rights protected by ICCPR 'without distinction of any kind', such as 'race, colour, sex, language, religion, political or other opinion, national or social origin, property, birth or other status', or where the state fails to ensure an effective remedy for the breach.

(vi) Finally, Article 3 ICCPR marks the equal right of men and women to civil and political rights provided under ICCPR. Gender discrimination in relevant respects is therefore barred under ICCPR.

8.9 Fourth, and finally, beyond ICCPR, a range of other, broader, international human rights norms are applicable to deportation action. These include, inter alia, the following:

(i) Deportation action which is discriminatory on the basis of race would breach Article 5(d) CERD.

(ii) Such action representing discrimination against a woman or women would breach Article 1 CEDAW.

(iii) Article 3(1) CRC provides that in an action concerning children, 'the best interests of the child must be a primary consideration' and the subsequent paragraph states that subscribing states 'undertake to ensure the child such protection and care as is necessary for his or her well-being'. These provisions and Article 9 CRC (regarding family unity) become relevant where a child is affected by deportation measures.

(iv) Persons to whom the CRPD applies are protected by Article 18(1)(d) not only from arbitrary deprivation of entry to 'their own country' (recalling the language of Article 12(4) ICCPR), but also from deprivation of entry to 'their own' country on any basis which, though not arbitrary, rests 'on the basis of disability'.

B3. Hybrid Instruments

Some of the instruments set out in chapter 4 may be relevant to deportation in the UK. Under IRL, an individual who is a 'refugee' in Article 1A(2) CSR terms is entitled to certain protections. Where he or she is lawfully present, then: 8.10

(i) by Article 32(1) CSR, the refugee is protected from expulsion (as in a deportation process), save on one of the two permitted grounds, namely, national security or public order;
(ii) where a refugee faces expulsion on one or both of the two permitted grounds, then by Article 32(2) CSR expulsion is permitted 'only in pursuance of a decision reached in accordance with due process of law' and is subject to procedural rights including entitlement 'to submit evidence to clear himself [herself], and to appeal to and be represented for the purpose before competent authority or a person or persons specially designated by the competent authority';
(iii) finally, where a lawfully present refugee is to be expelled for a permitted reason notwithstanding any representation to the competent authority, he or she is entitled to 'a reasonable period within which to seek legal admission into another country' under Article 32(3) CSR.

By Article 33(1) CSR, a refugee, regardless of the lawfulness of his or her presence, is entitled to protection from expulsion or *refoulement* 'in any manner whatsoever to the frontiers of territories where his life or freedom would be threatened' on account of a relevant matter, save where the exception in Article 33(2) CSR applies, because there are reasonable grounds for regarding the refugee as a danger to the security of the UK or because he or she 'convicted by a final judgment of a particularly serious crime, constitutes a danger to the community of the United Kingdom'. 8.11

Under the CSSP, a stateless person as defined therein is, if lawfully present, entitled to protections equivalent to those afforded a refugee under Article 32 CSR: 8.12

(i) by Article 31(1) CSSP, the lawfully present stateless person is entitled to protection from expulsion (implicitly including expulsion in conjunction with deportation) on any ground apart from national security or public order;
(ii) if a stateless person faces expulsion on the grounds of national security or public order, then by Article 32(2) CSSP expulsion is permitted 'only in pursuance of a decision reached in accordance with due process of law', subject to procedural rights by which he or she 'shall be allowed to submit evidence to clear himself [herself], and to appeal to and be represented for the purpose before competent authority or a person or persons specially designated by the competent authority';
(iii) by Article 32(3) CSSP, a lawfully present stateless person facing expulsion, notwithstanding any representation to the competent authority, is entitled to 'a reasonable period within which to seek legal admission into another country';

Part C – Deportation, Removal and Exclusion

In contrast to the protection from *refoulement* provided under Article 33 CSR, a stateless person (who is not also a refugee and is entitled to protection separately as such under CSR) has no protection from expulsion unless he or she is lawfully present.

8.13 The deportation-relevant obligations of the UK under the Protocol to Prevent, Suppress and Punish Trafficking in Persons, especially Women and Children 2000 (PPSPTP) are still more limited. Under Article 8(2) PPSPTP, where the UK authorities apply deportation measures to a victim of trafficking (VoT), as defined in Article 3 PPSPTP, and the effect of this is to return the VoT to a country of nationality or in which he or she had a right of permanent residence, then the authorities must give 'due regard' in the context of return to the safety of the VoT, and must also give due regard to 'the status of any legal proceedings related to the fact that the person is a [VoT]' and return 'shall preferably be voluntary'. The provisions for VoTs under PPSPTP should be seen in conjunction with those provided by Council of Europe and EU instruments. Article 8(6) PPSPTP provides that the PPSPTP 'shall be without prejudice to any applicable bilateral or multilateral agreement or arrangement that governs, in whole or in part, the return of victims of trafficking in persons'.

B4. Council of Europe Instruments

8.14 Two instruments introduced at chapter 5 are relevant to deportation. First, under the ECHR, certain very important human rights protections obstruct return to a place in which relevant risk can be shown to arise:

(i) Article 2 ECHR prohibits deprivation of life 'save in the execution of a sentence of a court' following conviction of a capital crime. Where substantial grounds show the existence of a real risk of breach of Article 2 ECHR in a country to which deportation would take place, such deportation is prohibited by Article 2 ECHR.

(ii) Article 3 ECHR prohibits torture or inhuman or degrading treatment or punishment. If by 'substantial grounds' the 'existence of a real risk' of any of the prohibited ill-treatments on return is shown, Article 3 ECHR prohibits deportation.

(iii) Article 4 ECHR prohibits slavery or servitude. Where 'substantial grounds' show the existence of a real risk of any of the prohibited ill-treatments on return, deportation is not permitted.

(iv) Article 5 ECHR bars deprivation of liberty, save in specified cases and in accordance with the law. Where in a particular case substantial grounds show the existence of a real risk of any of the prohibited ill-treatments, then Article 5 ECHR prohibits deportation.

(v) Article 6 ECHR specifies fair trial protections. Deportation to 'real risk' of a 'flagrant denial of justice' would violate the article and is prohibited.

(vi) Article 7 ECHR prohibits 'punishment without law'. Substantial grounds showing the 'real risk' of a 'flagrant breach' on return would mean that deportation breached Article 7 ECHR.

(vii) Article 8 ECHR relevantly protects the right to respect for private and family life and home. Deportation is barred where substantial grounds showing the 'real

risk' of a 'flagrant breach' of Article 8 ECHR arise in the place to which a deportee would have to go.
(viii) In the same way, substantial evidence showing 'real risk' on return of a 'flagrant breach' of protection of freedom of thought, conscience and religion (Article 9 ECHR), of freedom of expression (Article 10 ECHR), of freedom of peaceful assembly and/or association with others (Article 10 ECHR) or of the right to marry and found a family (Article 11 ECHR) would bar deportation.

8.15 Second, ECHR protections may bar the removal of an individual from the UK, in pursuance of the deportation process, by reason of the interference that this would represent to his or her protected interests in the UK. Other articles might be engaged, but the majority of such cases focus upon the right to respect for private and/or family life and/or home under Article 8 ECHR. Deportation is barred where this would represent an interference with relevant right(s) disproportionate to the legitimate public interest engaged.

8.16 Third, deportation may not be consistent with the CATHB.

(i) Article 10(2) CATHB requires the UK, if the competent authorities have reasonable grounds to believe that a person has been a VoT, to refrain from removing that person until the identification process as a victim of a trafficking offence, as provided for in Article 18 CATHB, has been completed.
(ii) Article 13 CATHB requires the UK to 'provide in its internal law a recovery and reflection period of at least 30 days' when there are reasonable grounds to believe that the person concerned is a VoT. During that period, Article 13(2) CATHB provides that removal cannot be enforced.
(iii) Under Article 14 CATHB, the UK is required to issue a renewable residence permit to a VoT where a stay 'is necessary owing to his or her personal situation' and/or 'for the purpose of cooperation with the competent authorities in investigation or criminal proceedings relating to trafficking'.

C. EU Law

8.17 Directive 2004/38/EC of 29 April 2004, Chapter VI ('Restrictions on the right of entry and the right of residence on grounds of public policy, public security or public health') sets out the EU law provisions relevant to deportation from the UK of EU citizens or family members. This has been outlined in chapter 6 above, and the relevant provisions are set out in full at Appendix A.

8.18 On 14 October 2011 the UK opted in to Directive 2011/36/EU of 5 April 2011 on preventing and combatting trafficking in human beings and protecting its victims. This indicates by Article 12(3) that 'Member States shall ensure that victims of trafficking in human beings receive appropriate protection on the basis of an individual risk assessment, inter alia, by having access to witness protection programmes or other similar measures, if appropriate and in accordance with the grounds defined by national law or procedures'. This may affect the lawfulness of deportation action against a VoT.

D. Domestic Law

D1. Prerogative

8.19 Deportation has long been regulated either by statute or by Order made in the exercise of a statutory power, and in the light of *R (Munir) v SSHD* [2012] UKSC 32, [2012] 1 WLR 2192 and *R (Alvi) v SSHD* [2012] UKSC 33, [2012] 1 WLR 2208, it seems likely that the power of the Secretary of State to order that an individual be deported effectively rests upon statute alone.

D2. Statute

8.20 Liability to deportation is delineated by sections 3(5)–(6) IA 1971:

> 3. (5) A person who is not a British citizen is liable to deportation from the United Kingdom if—
>   (a) The Secretary of State deems his deportation to be conducive to the public good; or
>   (b) Another person to whose family he belongs is or has been ordered to be deported.
> (6) Without prejudice to the operation of section (5) above, a person who is not a British citizen shall also be liable to deportation from the United Kingdom if, after he has attained the age of seventeen, he is convicted of an offence for which he is punishable with imprisonment and on his conviction he is recommended for deportation by a court empowered by this Act to do so.

8.21 Although section 3(6) IA 1971 has not been repealed, enactment under UKBA 2007 of a scheme for 'mandatory deportation' has substantially reduced the scope for its operation. In *R v Kluxen* [2010] EWCA (Crim) 1081, [2011] 1 WLR 218, the Court of Appeal, Criminal Division considered the circumstances in which a court should recommend an offender's deportation and found: (i) (at [9]) that following the coming into force of the relevant provisions of UKBA 2007, it was in general no longer appropriate for a court to recommend the deportation of a 'foreign criminal' as defined in that Act; and (ii) (at [27]–[28]), observing that 'conducive' liability to deportation under section 3(5)(a) IA 1971 remained available, 'it will rarely be appropriate to recommend the deportation of an offender who is not a British Citizen, but to whom [UKBA 2007 does not apply]; and that this is so whether or not the offender is a citizen of the EU'.

8.22 Section 5 IA 1971 sets out further provision, including section 5(1) IA 1971 by which the Secretary of State is empowered to make a deportation order against a person who is liable to deportation under the provisions at section 3 IA 1971 delineating the extent of that liability:

> 5. Procedure for, and further provisions as to, deportation
> (1) Where a person is under section 3(5) or (6) above liable to deportation, then subject to the following provisions of this Act the Secretary of State may make a deportation order against him, that is to say an order requiring him to leave and prohibiting him from entering the United Kingdom; and a deportation order against a person shall invalidate any leave to enter or remain in the United Kingdom given him before the order is made or while it is in force.

(2) A deportation order against a person may at any time be revoked by a further order of the Secretary of State, and shall cease to have effect if he becomes a British citizen.

Sections 5(3) and 5(4) IA 1971, which are rarely used in practice, provide for the deportation of members of the family of a principal subject of deportation. Further provisions in the same section are as follows:

(5) The provisions of Schedule 3 to this Act shall have effect with respect to the removal from the United Kingdom of persons against whom deportation orders are in force and with respect to the detention or control of persons in connection with deportation.

(6) Where a person is liable to deportation under section 3(5) or (6) above but, without a deportation order being made against him, leaves the United Kingdom to live permanently abroad, the Secretary of State may make payments of such amounts as he may determine to meet that person's expenses in so leaving the United Kingdom, including travelling expenses for members of his family or household.

8.23 Subparagraph 1(1) of Schedule 3 to IA 1971 sets out subsidiary provisions regarding removal:

Removal of persons liable to deportation

1(1) Where a deportation order is in force against any person, the Secretary of State may give directions for his removal to a country or territory specified in the directions being either—
(a) a country of which he is a national or citizen; or
(b) a country or territory to which there is reason to believe that he will be admitted.

Other provisions in that Schedule set out further specifications regarding matters such as directions for removal of deportees, detention or control pending deportation, powers of courts pending deportation, and the effect of appeals.

8.24 A particularly important feature of the more recent law is the statutory scheme for 'automatic deportation' under UKBA 2007. Section 32 UKBA 2007 requires the Secretary of State (by section 32(5)) to make a deportation order (under IA 1971) against someone who is a 'foreign criminal' as defined at section 32(1) UKBA 2007:

32 Automatic deportation
(1) In this section 'foreign criminal' means a person—
(a) who is not a British citizen,
(b) who is convicted in the United Kingdom of an offence, and
(c) to whom Condition 1 or 2 applies.
(2) Condition 1 is that the person is sentenced to a period of imprisonment of at least 12 months.
(3) Condition 2 is that—
(a) the offence is specified by order of the Secretary of State under section 72(4)(a) of the Nationality, Immigration and Asylum Act 2002 (c. 41) (serious criminal), and
(b) the person is sentenced to a period of imprisonment.
(4) For the purpose of section 3(5)(a) of the Immigration Act 1971 (c. 77), the deportation of a foreign criminal is conducive to the public good.
(5) The Secretary of State must make a deportation order in respect of a foreign criminal (subject to section 33).

8.25 Section 33 UKBA 2007 sets out exceptions to the section 32(5) duty to make a deportation order, and the effect where one of those exceptions arises.

Part C – Deportation, Removal and Exclusion

33 Exceptions

Section 32(4) and (5)—

do not apply where an exception in this section applies (subject to section (7) below)…

(2) Exception 1 is where removal of the foreign criminal in pursuance of the deportation order would breach—
   (a) a person's Convention rights, or
   (b) the United Kingdom's obligations under the Refugee Convention.
(3) Exception 2 is where the Secretary of State thinks that the foreign criminal was under the age of 18 on the date of conviction.
(4) Exception 3 is where the removal of the foreign criminal from the United Kingdom in pursuance of a deportation order would breach rights of the foreign criminal under the Community treaties.
(5) Exception 4 is where the foreign criminal—
   (a) is the subject of a certificate under section 2 or 70 of the Extradition Act 2003 (c. 41),
   (b) is in custody pursuant to arrest under section 5 of that Act,
   (c) is the subject of a provisional warrant under section 73 of that Act,
   (d) is the subject of an authority to proceed under section 7 of the Extradition Act 1989 (c. 33) or an order under paragraph 4(2) of Schedule 1 to that Act, or
   (e) is the subject of a provisional warrant under section 8 of that Act or of a warrant under paragraph 5(1)(b) of Schedule 1 to that Act.
(6) Exception 5 is where any of the following has effect in respect of the foreign criminal—
   (a) a hospital order or guardianship order under section 37 of the Mental Health Act 1983 (c. 20),
   (b) a hospital direction under section 45A of that Act,
   (c) a transfer direction under section 47 of that Act,
   (d) a compulsion order under section 57A of the Criminal Procedure (Scotland) Act 1995 (c. 46),
   (e) a guardianship order under section 58 of that Act,
   (f) a hospital direction under section 59A of that Act,
   (g) a transfer for treatment direction under section 136 of the Mental Health (Care and Treatment) (Scotland) Act 2003 (asp 13), or
(7) The application of an exception—
   (a) does not prevent the making of a deportation order;
   (b) results in it being assumed neither that deportation of the person concerned is conducive to the public good nor that it is not conducive to the public good;
   but section 32(4) applies despite the application of Exception 1 or 4.

8.26 By section 34(1) UKBA 2007, a deportation order required to be made by section 32(5) must be made 'at a time chosen by the Secretary of State': That is, it need not be made as soon as the statutory conditions for the duty on the Secretary of State are satisfied. However, the making of an order is restrained by section 34(2) where 'an appeal or further appeal against the conviction or sentence by reference to which the order is to be made—(a) has been instituted and neither withdrawn nor determined, or (b) could be brought', some terms therein being interpreted at section 34(3).

8.27 By section 34(4) UKBA 2007, a power is given to the Secretary of State to withdraw a decision that section 32(5) applies, or to revoke a deportation order made by reference to that provision, and then to take action under other provisions (for instance by making a new deportation order under section 5(1) IA 1971 without reference to UKBA 2007) or to take a fresh decision that section 32(5) UKBA 2007 applies and issue a new deportation order under that provision.

Deportation

8.28 Some important interpretative provisions are set out in section 38 UKBA 2007. Under section 38(3), 'convicted' for purposes of section 32 does not include a person subject to an order under section 5 Criminal Procedure (Insanity) Act 1964 (which applies where either a special verdict is returned holding that the accused is not guilty by reason of insanity, or findings are recorded that the accused is under a disability and that he did the act or made the omission charged against him). Under section 38(1) UKBA 2007, the phrase 'person who is sentenced to a period of imprisonment of at least 12 months':

(1) (a) does not include a reference to a person who receives a suspended sentence (unless a court subsequently orders that the sentence or any part of it (of whatever length) is to take effect),
(b) does not include a reference to a person who is sentenced to a period of imprisonment of at least 12 months only by virtue of being sentenced to consecutive sentences amounting in aggregate to more than 12 months,
(c) includes a reference to a person who is sentenced to detention, or ordered or directed to be detained, in an institution other than a prison (including, in particular, a hospital or an institution for young offenders) for at least 12 months, and
(d) includes a reference to a person who is sentenced to imprisonment or detention, or ordered or directed to be detained, for an indeterminate period (provided that it may last for 12 months).

8.25 Section 38(2) UKBA 2007 provides that the definition of 'person who is sentenced to a period of imprisonment' for relevant purposes:

(2) (a) does not include a reference to a person who receives a suspended sentence (unless a court subsequently orders that the sentence or any part of it is to take effect), and
(b) includes a reference to a person who is sentenced to detention, or ordered or directed to be detained, in an institution other than a prison (including, in particular, a hospital or an institution for young offenders).

8.30 Section 38(4) UKBA 2007 provides that in sections 32 and 33 UKBA 2007:

38. (4) (a) 'British citizen' has the same meaning as in section 3(5) of the Immigration Act 1971 (c. 77) (and section 3(8) (burden of proof) shall apply),
(b) 'Convention rights' has the same meaning as in the Human Rights Act 1998 (c. 42),
(c) 'deportation order' means an order under section 5, and by virtue of section 3(5) [IA 1971], and
(d) 'the Refugee Convention' means [CSR].

8.31 The scheme was brought into force on 1 August 2008 by section 59 UKBA 2007 read with the UK Borders Act 2007 (Commencement No 3 and Transitional Provisions) Order 2008, SI 2008/1818, by which it applies in the case of:

(i) any person convicted and sentenced to imprisonment of 12 months or more before 30 October 2007, who meets the definition of a 'foreign criminal' as defined in section 32(1) UKBA 2007, if still in custody on 1 August 2008 or in respect of whom sentence is suspended at the time of commencement, unless notice has already been given of a decision taken under section 5(1) IA 1971 (by the Order, paragraph 3);
(ii) any person convicted between 30 October 2007 and 1 August 2008, who meets the definition of a 'foreign criminal' as defined in section 32(1) UKBA 2007, if

still in custody on 1 August 2008 or in respect of whom sentence is suspended at the time of commencement, unless notice has already been given of a decision taken under section 5(1) IA 1971 (not expressly provided for on the face of the Order, but found to be within the reach of the provision by Nicol J in *Hussein v* [2009] EWHC 2492 (Admin), [2010] Imm AR 320 and the Court of Appeal in *AT (Pakistan) and another v SSHD* [2010] EWCA Civ 567, [2010] Imm AR 675);

(iii) any person convicted and sentenced to imprisonment of 12 months or more on or after 1 August 2008, who otherwise meets the definition of 'foreign criminal' in section 32(1) UKBA 2007 (by the Order, paragraph 2).

D3. Statutory Instrument

The Immigration (European Economic Area) Regulations 2006

8.32 The Immigration (European Economic Area) Regulations 2006, SI 2006/1003, at Part 4 seek to transpose Chapter VI of Directive 2004/38/EC of 29 April 2004. In particular, Regulation 19 provides as follows in relation to exclusion from the UK:

Exclusion and removal from the United Kingdom
19(1) A person is not entitled to be admitted to the United Kingdom by virtue of regulation 11 if his exclusion is justified on grounds of public policy, public security or public health in accordance with regulation 21.
  (1A) A person is not entitled to be admitted to the United Kingdom by virtue of regulation 11 if that person is subject to a deportation or exclusion order, except where the person is temporarily admitted pursuant to regulation 29AA.
  (1AB) A person is not entitled to be admitted to the United Kingdom by virtue of regulation 11 if the Secretary of State considers there to be reasonable grounds to suspect that his admission would lead to the abuse of a right to reside in accordance with regulation 21B(1)
  (1B) If the Secretary of State considers that the exclusion of an EEA national or the family member of an EEA national is justified on the grounds of public policy, public security or public health in accordance with regulation 21 the Secretary of State may make an order for the purpose of these Regulations prohibiting that person from entering the United Kingdom.
  …

(3) Subject to paragraphs (4) and (5), a person who has been admitted to, or acquired a right to reside in, the United Kingdom under these Regulations may be removed from the United Kingdom if—
  (a) that person does not have or ceases to have a right to reside under these Regulations;
  (b) the Secretary of State has decided that the person's removal is justified on grounds of public policy, public security or public health in accordance with regulation 21; or
  (c) the Secretary of State has decided that the person's removal is justified on grounds of abuse of rights in accordance with regulation 21B(2).
(4) A person must not be removed under paragraph (3) as the automatic consequence of having recourse to the social assistance system of the United Kingdom.
(5) A person must not be removed under paragraph (3) if he has a right to remain in the United Kingdom by virtue of leave granted under the 1971 Act unless his removal is

justified on the grounds of public policy, public security or public health in accordance with regulation 21.

A provisional right of residence is now provided prior to and during the exercise of the right of appeal. Regulation 15B provides for a conditional right of residence similar to that under sections 3C and 3D of the Immigration Act 1971 pending an appeal against the decision taken on the grounds of public policy security or health or abuse of rights, but has the effect of the time pending the appeal on that decision not constituting residence unless the decision on appeal goes in favour of the appellant. In the context of likely delays pending appeal and consequent integrative links being formed possibly leading to acquisition of higher degrees of protection in Union law, this provision should be interpreted in the context of preamble (16) of the Directive 2004/38/EC.

Regulation 20A provides for cancellation of a right of residence in circumstances where a person is at large and cannot be removed (presumably by operation of Article 3 ECHR) and has the effect of preventing that person from acquiring further degrees of protection from expulsion. This provision may raise issues of possible non-compliance with procedural guarantees of Articles 30 and 31 of Directive 2004/38/EC.

8.33

20A. (1) Where the conditions in paragraph (2) are met the Secretary of State may cancel a person's right to reside in the United Kingdom pursuant to these Regulations.
   (2) The conditions in this paragraph are met where—
      (a) a person has a right to reside in the United Kingdom as a result of these Regulations;
      (b) the Secretary of State has decided that the cancellation of that person's right to reside in the United Kingdom is justified on grounds of public policy, public security or public health in accordance with regulation 21 or on grounds of abuse of rights in accordance with regulation 21B(2);
      (c) the circumstances are such that the Secretary of State cannot make a decision under regulation 20(1); and
      (d) it is not possible for the Secretary of State to remove the person from the United Kingdom pursuant to regulation 19(3)(b) or (c).

Regulation 21A applies a different standard of protection from exclusion to persons with derivative rights of residence under the Immigration (European Economic Area) Regulations 2006 (SI 2006/1003)—i.e. those not expressly included in the Directive 2004/38/EC—deeming them subject to expulsion measures where this is 'conducive to the public good'. There is a strong argument that this is not a lawful approach—see further Chapter 6. The issue of application of Regulation 21A to *Ruiz Zambrano* cases is clearly in doubt as the Upper Tribunal made an order for reference for a preliminary ruling to CJEU on whether and if so, under what circumstances is expulsion of a parent permissible where they have a right of residence following *Ruiz Zambrano* principles on 4 June 2014 now Case C-304/14 *Secretary of State for the Home Department v CS*. Regulation 21B introduces the concept of abuse of rights:

21B. (1) The abuse of a right to reside includes—
      (a) engaging in conduct which appears to be intended to circumvent the requirement to be a qualified person;
      (b) attempting to enter the United Kingdom within 12 months of being removed pursuant to regulation 19(3)(a), where the person attempting to do so is unable to provide evidence that, upon re-entry to the United Kingdom, the

conditions for any right to reside, other than the initial right of residence under regulation 13, will be met;

(c) entering, attempting to enter or assisting another person to enter or attempt to enter, a marriage or civil partnership of convenience; or

(d) fraudulently obtaining or attempting to obtain, or assisting another to obtain or attempt to obtain, a right to reside.

(2) The Secretary of State may take an EEA decision on the grounds of abuse of rights where there are reasonable grounds to suspect the abuse of a right to reside and it is proportionate to do so.

(3) Where these Regulations provide that an EEA decision taken on the grounds of abuse in the preceding twelve months affects a person's right to reside, the person who is the subject of that decision may apply to the Secretary of State to have the effect of that decision set aside on grounds that there has been a material change in the circumstances which justified that decision.

(4) An application under paragraph (3) may only be made whilst the applicant is outside the United Kingdom.

(5) This regulation may not be invoked systematically.

(6) In this regulation, 'a right to reside' means a right to reside under these Regulations.

Regulation 21(2) provides that an exclusion decision taken on the grounds of public policy, public security or public health may not be taken to serve economic ends. Regulation 21(3) provides that a person with a permanent right of residence may not be the subject of such a decision 'except on serious grounds of public policy or public security'. Regulation 21 further provides that:

21(4) A relevant decision may not be taken except on imperative grounds of public security in respect of an EEA national who—

(a) has resided in the United Kingdom for a continuous period of at least ten years prior to the relevant decision; or

(b) is under the age of 18, unless the relevant decision is necessary in his best interests, as provided for in the Convention on the Rights of the Child adopted by the General Assembly of the United Nations on 20th November 1989.

(5) Where a relevant decision is taken on grounds of public policy or public security it shall, in addition to complying with the preceding paragraphs of this regulation, be taken in accordance with the following principles—

(a) the decision must comply with the principle of proportionality;

(b) the decision must be based exclusively on the personal conduct of the person concerned;

(c) the personal conduct of the person concerned must represent a genuine, present and sufficiently serious threat affecting one of the fundamental interests of society;

(d) matters isolated from the particulars of the case or which relate to considerations of general prevention do not justify the decision;

(e) a person's previous criminal convictions do not in themselves justify the decision.

(6) Before taking a relevant decision on the grounds of public policy or public security in relation to a person who is resident in the United Kingdom the decision maker must take account of considerations such as the age, state of health, family and economic situation of the person, the person's length of residence in the United Kingdom, the person's social and cultural integration into the United Kingdom and the extent of the person's links with his country of origin.

Regulation 21(7) further delineates the 'public health' ground. In closing this section, an important general point arises. While the Regulations provide for powers to detain a person pending deportation, and refusal of admission and exclusion where the deportation order is in force and import specific powers under Schedule 2 to the Immigration Act 1971 (see Regulations 22-24), it is important to note that a person who was subject to a deportation order made outwith the Regulations, but later acquired a status under the Regulations (e.g. by acquiring a status of a family member of a Union citizen, or by his or her state of nationality becoming a member state of the EU) cannot be excluded or denied entry under those orders (see interaction between definition of deportation order under Regulation 2, and Regulations 191A, 19(3)(b) and 24(3), and original provisions of Article 27 of Directive 2004/38/EC).

D4. Immigration Rules

The relevant passages of the Immigration Rules HC 395, which address deportation matters in Part 13, have been extensively altered in recent years. As at 1 October 2014 their content is as follows. This is set out in full, including paragraphs identified as 'DELETED' and anomalies such as headings to which no operative paragraphs apply, essentially to illustrate the present state of the Immigration Rules in relation to deportation:

8.34

    A deportation order
- A362. Where Article 8 is raised in the context of deportation under Part 13 of these Rules, the claim under Article 8 will only succeed where the requirements of these rules as at 28 July 2014 are met, regardless of when the notice of intention to deport or the deportation order, as appropriate, was served.
- 362. A deportation order requires the subject to leave the United Kingdom and authorises his detention until he is removed. It also prohibits him from re-entering the country for as long as it is in force and invalidates any leave to enter or remain in the United Kingdom given him before the Order is made or while it is in force.
- 363. The circumstances in which a person is liable to deportation include:
  - (i) where the Secretary of State deems the person's deportation to be conducive to the public good;
  - (ii) where the person is the spouse or civil partner or child under 18 of a person ordered to be deported; and
  - (iii) where a court recommends deportation in the case of a person over the age of 17 who has been convicted of an offence punishable with imprisonment.
- 363A. Prior to 2 October 2000, a person would have been liable to deportation in certain circumstances in which he is now liable to administrative removal. However, such a person remains liable to deportation, rather than administrative removal where:
  - (i) a decision to make a deportation order against him was taken before 2 October 2000; or
  - (ii) the person has made a valid application under the Immigration (Regularisation Period for Overstayers) Regulations 2000.

    Deportation of family members
- 364. DELETED
- 364A. DELETED
- 365. Section 5 of the Immigration Act 1971 gives the Secretary of State power in certain circumstances to make a deportation order against the spouse, civil partner or child of a person against whom a deportation order has been made. The Secretary of State will not normally decide to deport the spouse or civil partner of a deportee where:
  - (i) he has qualified for settlement in his own right; or

Part C – Deportation, Removal and Exclusion

      (ii)   he has been living apart from the deportee.
366. The Secretary of State will not normally decide to deport the child of a deportee where:
      (i)   he and his mother or father are living apart from the deportee; or
      (ii)   he has left home and established himself on an independent basis; or
      (iii)   he married or formed a civil partnership before deportation came into prospect.
367. DELETED
368. Where the Secretary of State decides that it would be appropriate to deport a member of a family as such, the decision, and the right of appeal, will be notified and it will at the same time be explained that it is open to the member of the family to leave the country voluntarily if he does not wish to appeal or if he appeals and his appeal is dismissed.
Right of appeal against destination
369. DELETED
Restricted right of appeal against deportation in cases of breach of limited leave
370. DELETED
Exemption to the restricted right of appeal
371. DELETED
372. DELETED
A deportation order made on the recommendation of a Court
373. DELETED
Where deportation is deemed to be conducive to the public good
374. DELETED
375. DELETED
Hearing of appeals
376. DELETED
377. DELETED
378. A deportation order may not be made while it is still open to the person to appeal against the Secretary of State's decision, or while an appeal is pending except where the Secretary of State is required to make the deportation order in respect of a foreign criminal under section 32(5) of the UK Borders Act 2007 or where the Secretary of State has certified a protection and/or a human rights claim under section 94 or section 94B of the Nationality, Immigration and Asylum Act 2002. There is no appeal within the immigration appeal system against the making of a deportation order on the recommendation of a court; but there is a right of appeal to a higher court against the recommendation itself. A deportation order may not be made while it is still open to the person to appeal against the relevant conviction, sentence or recommendation, or while such an appeal is pending.
Persons who have claimed asylum
379. DELETED
379A. DELETED
380. DELETED
Procedure
381. When a decision to make a deportation order has been taken (otherwise than on the recommendation of a court) a notice will be given to the person concerned informing him of the decision and of his right of appeal.
382. Following the issue of such a notice the Secretary of State may authorise detention or make an order restricting a person as to residence, employment or occupation and requiring him to report to the police, pending the making of a deportation order.
383. DELETED
384. If a notice of appeal is given within the period allowed, a summary of the facts of the case on the basis of which the decision was taken will be sent to the appropriate appellate authorities, who will notify the appellant of the arrangements for the appeal to be heard.
Arrangements for removal 5

385. A person against whom a deportation order has been made will normally be removed from the United Kingdom. The power is to be exercised so as to secure the person's return to the country of which he is a national, or which has most recently provided him with a travel document, unless he can show that another country will receive him. In considering any departure from the normal arrangements, regard will be had to the public interest generally, and to any additional expense that may fall on public funds.

386. The person will not be removed as the subject of a deportation order while an appeal may be brought against the decision or such an appeal has been brought and has not yet been concluded. This paragraph does not apply if there is no right to appeal the decision, or if the right to appeal is exercisable only after the person has left the United Kingdom, or if a decision is taken to certify an appeal that is in progress such that the appeal can only be continued after the person has left the United Kingdom.

Supervised departure

387. DELETED

Returned deportees

388. Where a person returns to this country when a deportation order is in force against him, he may be deported under the original order. The Secretary of State will consider every such case in the light of all the relevant circumstances before deciding whether to enforce the order.

Returned family members

389. Persons deported in the circumstances set out in paragraphs 365-368 above (deportation of family members) may be able to seek re-admission to the United Kingdom under the Immigration Rules where:
   (i) a child reaches 18 (when he ceases to be subject to the deportation order); or
   (ii) in the case of a spouse or civil partner, the marriage or civil partnership comes to an end.

Revocation of deportation order

390. An application for revocation of a deportation order will be considered in the light of all the circumstances including the following: 6
   (i) the grounds on which the order was made;
   (ii) any representations made in support of revocation;
   (iii) the interests of the community, including the maintenance of an effective immigration control;
   (iv) the interests of the applicant, including any compassionate circumstances.

390A. Where paragraph 398 applies the Secretary of State will consider whether paragraph 399 or 399A applies and, if it does not, it will only be in exceptional circumstances that the public interest in maintaining the deportation order will be outweighed by other factors.

391. In the case of a person who has been deported following conviction for a criminal offence, the continuation of a deportation order against that person will be the proper course:
   (a) in the case of a conviction for an offence for which the person was sentenced to a period of imprisonment of less than 4 years, unless 10 years have elapsed since the making of the deportation order, or
   (b) in the case of a conviction for an offence for which the person was sentenced to a period of imprisonment of at least 4 years, at any time,

Unless, in either case, the continuation would be contrary to the Human Rights Convention or the Convention and Protocol Relating to the Status of Refugees, or there are other exceptional circumstances that mean the continuation is outweighed by compelling factors.

391A. In other cases, revocation of the order will not normally be authorised unless the situation has been materially altered, either by a change of circumstances since the order was made, or by fresh information coming to light which was not before the appellate authorities or the Secretary of State. The passage of time since the person was deported may also in itself amount to such a change of circumstances as to warrant revocation of the order.

392. Revocation of a deportation order does not entitle the person concerned to re-enter the United Kingdom; it renders him eligible to apply for admission under the Immigration Rules. Application for revocation of the order may be made to the Entry Clearance Officer or direct to the Home Office.

Rights of appeal in relation to a decision not to revoke a deportation order

393. DELETED
394. DELETED
395. There may be a right of appeal against refusal to revoke a deportation order. Where an appeal does lie the right of appeal will be notified at the same time as the decision to refuse to revoke the order. 7
396. Where a person is liable to deportation the presumption shall be that the public interest requires deportation. It is in the public interest to deport where the Secretary of State must make a deportation order in accordance with section 32 of the UK Borders Act 2007.
397. A deportation order will not be made if the person's removal pursuant to the order would be contrary to the UK's obligations under the Refugee Convention or the Human Rights Convention. Where deportation would not be contrary to these obligations, it will only be in exceptional circumstances that the public interest in deportation is outweighed.

Deportation and Article 8

A398. These rules apply where:
   (a) a foreign criminal liable to deportation claims that his deportation would be contrary to the United Kingdom's obligations under Article 8 of the Human Rights Convention;
   (b) a foreign criminal applies for a deportation order made against him to be revoked.
398. Where a person claims that their deportation would be contrary to the UK's obligations under Article 8 of the Human Rights Convention, and
   (a) the deportation of the person from the UK is conducive to the public good and in the public interest because they have been convicted of an offence for which they have been sentenced to a period of imprisonment of at least 4 years;
   (b) the deportation of the person from the UK is conducive to the public good and in the public interest because they have been convicted of an offence for which they have been sentenced to a period of imprisonment of less than 4 years but at least 12 months; or
   (c) the deportation of the person from the UK is conducive to the public good and in the public interest because, in the view of the Secretary of State, their offending has caused serious harm or they are a persistent offender who shows a particular disregard for the law,
   the Secretary of State in assessing that claim will consider whether paragraph 399 or 399A applies and, if it does not, the public interest in deportation will only be outweighed by other factors where there are very compelling circumstances over and above those described in paragraphs 399 and 399A.
399. This paragraph applies where paragraph 398 (b) or (c) applies if—
   (a) the person has a genuine and subsisting parental relationship with a child under the age of 18 years who is in the UK, and

(i) the child is a British Citizen; or (ii) the child has lived in the UK continuously for at least the 7 years immediately preceding the date of the immigration decision; and in either case (a) it would be unduly harsh for the child to live in the country to which the person is to be 8 deported; and (b) it would be unduly harsh for the child to remain in the UK without the person who is to be deported; or

(b) the person has a genuine and subsisting relationship with a partner who is in the UK and is a British Citizen or settled in the UK, and
   (i) the relationship was formed at a time when the person (deportee) was in the UK lawfully and their immigration status was not precarious; and
   (ii) it would be unduly harsh for that partner to live in the country to which the person is to be deported, because of compelling circumstances over and above those described in paragraph EX.2. of Appendix FM; and
   (iii) it would be unduly harsh for that partner to remain in the UK without the person who is to be deported.

399A. This paragraph applies where paragraph 398(b) or (c) applies if—
(a) the person has been lawfully resident in the UK for most of his life; and
(b) he is socially and culturally integrated in the UK; and
(c) there would be very significant obstacles to his integration into the country to which it is proposed he is deported.

399B. Where an Article 8 claim from a foreign criminal is successful:
(a) in the case of a person who is in the UK unlawfully or whose leave to enter or remain has been cancelled by a deportation order, limited leave may be granted for periods not exceeding 30 months and subject to such conditions as the Secretary of State considers appropriate;
(b) in the case of a person who has not been served with a deportation order, any limited leave to enter or remain may be curtailed to a period not exceeding 30 months and conditions may be varied to such conditions as the Secretary of State considers appropriate;
(c) indefinite leave to enter or remain may be revoked under section 76 of the 2002 Act and limited leave to enter or remain granted for a period not exceeding 30 months subject to such conditions as the Secretary of State considers appropriate;
(d) revocation of a deportation order does not confer entry clearance or leave to enter or remain or re-instate any previous leave.

399C. Where a foreign criminal who has previously been granted a period of limited leave under this Part applies for further limited leave or indefinite leave to remain his deportation remains conducive to the public good and in the public interest notwithstanding the previous grant of leave.

399D. Where a foreign criminal has been deported and enters the United Kingdom in breach of a deportation order enforcement of the deportation order is in the public interest and will be implemented unless there are very exceptional circumstances.

D5. Published Guidance

The Secretary of State publishes guidance concerning the exercise of executive powers in relation to deportation. The main current guidance concerning deportation as at 1 October 2014, 'Immigration Directorate Instructions—Chapter 13: Criminality Guidance in Article 8 ECHR Cases' (Version 5.0, 28 July 2014) as the title suggests, focuses upon a single aspect of deportation which has been the focus of much executive activity. The scheme for automatic deportation under Part 5 UKBA 2007 is the

8.35

subject of another relatively detailed guidance, 'Automatic deportation' (Version 9.0, 24 February 2014). Outside these areas of administrative focus a substantial part of this area of the law is not covered by current guidance.

E. Discussion

E1. Foundations of Deportation Law

8.36   The retreat of prerogative powers in relation to deportation has long been tangible, and statute appears to provide the sole basis for deportation in the UK. *R (Munir) v SSHD* [2012] UKSC 32, [2012] 1 WLR 2192 and *R (Alvi) v SSHD* [2012] UKSC 33, [2012] 1 WLR 2208 appear now to have established that the deportation power of the Secretary of State rests entirely upon statute; that is, upon sections 3 and 5 IA 1971. The exclusive focus upon statue lends additional impetus, if needed, for firm understanding of the parameters of the statutory scheme. The description below seeks to outline the scheme and to identify matters of significance at each stage thereof.

E2. Liability to Deportation

Scope of the Group of Persons Liable to Deportation

8.37   The scope of the group whose members are 'liable to' deportation is established by sections 3(5)–(6) IA 1971 by which deportation is applicable to any 'person who is not a British citizen' if:

(i) the Secretary of State deems his or her deportation to be 'conducive to the public good' (section 3(5)(a) IA 1971);
(ii) another person to whose family he or she belongs is the subject of a deportation order (section 3(5)(b) IA 1971);
(iii) he or she has, after attaining the age of 17, been convicted of an offence punishable by imprisonment and on conviction recommended for deportation by a relevant court (section 3(6) IA 1971).

Definition of 'British Citizen' for the Purposes of Immunity from Deportation

8.38   The definition of 'British citizen' in the context of immunity from deportation under section 2 IA 1971 includes some persons who do not in fact hold British citizenship, including any Commonwealth citizen who on 1 January 1983 (when BNA 1981 came into force) had the right of abode in the UK. Such persons are immune to deportation. However, immunity to deportation does not attach to persons who hold a British nationality status other than that of British citizen, as a British Overseas Territories Citizen, British Overseas Citizen, British National (Overseas), British protected person or British subject. They may be deported, as Ognall J confirmed in the case of a British Overseas citizen in *R v IAT ex p*

Sunsara [1995] Imm AR 15, QBD. This remains the case even if no other nationality is possessed, though in the event of expulsion from the UK of someone possessing no nationality, or no nationality apart from that of the UK, another state may feel no legal obligation or inclination to re-admit that individual: *R v CIO Gatwick Airport ex p. Singh (Harjendar)* [1987] Imm AR 346; *Patel v SSHD* [1993] Imm AR 392.

The Limited Application of Sections 3(5)(b) and 3(6) IA 1971

8.39 The application of section 3(6) IA 1971 appears likely to be limited in future, as following *R v Kluxen* [2010] EWCA Crim 1081, [2011] 1 WLR 218, the role of the criminal courts in this respect is viewed as having become obsolete, by reason of the coming into force of the 'automatic deportation' scheme in UKBA 2007. The relevance of section 3(6) IA 1971 is therefore greatly reduced. As to the power to deport family members under section 3(5)(b) IA 1971, the Secretary of State in practice exercises a substantial degree of restraint in the use of his or her wide statutory power: see para 8.69 below. Most deportation cases will therefore engage section 3(5)(a) IA 1971.

The Importance of Section 3(5)(a) IA 1971 and its Relationship to UKBA 2007

8.40 Section 3(5)(a) IA 1971 requires a decision by the Secretary of State as to satisfaction of the condition precedent, that the deportation of the individual in question 'is conducive to the public good'. However, the requirement for such a decision is in some cases removed, since the coming into force of provisions establishing the 'automatic deportation' scheme in section 32(4) UKBA 2007, which deems deportation to be conducive in every case relating to an individual meeting the definition of a 'foreign criminal' in section 32(1)–(3) UKBA 2007, save where 'an exception' applies under section 33 UKBA 2007. If an exception applies, then by section 33(7)(b) UKBA 2007, it is 'assumed neither that the deportation of the person concerned is conducive to the public good nor that it is not conducive to the public good.' If interpreted as a deeming provision imposing a neutral view (deportation being neither conducive nor the contrary) section 33(7)(b) UKBA 2007 would appear to impose an obstacle to a new deportation order being made without an intervening change in circumstances, because the section 3(5)(a) IA 1971 condition (the Secretary of State deems deportation conducive to the public good) could not be met lawfully in defiance of statutory deeming that deportation was not conducive. An alternative interpretation may be possible. If section 33(7)(b) UKBA 2007 is not interpreted as a deeming provision imposing a neutral view, it would remove immediate liability (because the positive deeming by section 32(4) UKBA 2007 would be displaced), but it would remain open to the Secretary of State to exercise his or her judgment as to whether the section 3(5)(a) IA 1971 condition (conduciveness to the public good) was met, and then, whether to exercise the discretionary power at section 5 IA 1971. However if the statutory exception found to exist is exception 1 (ECHR or CSR) or 4 (EU law) then the deeming of deportation as conducive under section 32(4) UKBA 2007 remains in place, even if the deportation order is revoked. In this case the continued deeming means that the section 3(5)(a) IA 1971 test need not be revisited, prior to any further decision of the Secretary of State to exercise the statutory discretion under section 5 IA 1971.

Part C – Deportation, Removal and Exclusion

Liability to Deportation a Necessary Prerequisite to Exercise of Deportation

8.41 Wherever liability to deportation under section 3 IA 1971 is not established, then the condition precedent to exercise of section 5(1) IA 1971 ('Where a person is under section 3(5) or (6) above liable to deportation, then subject to the following provisions of this Act the Secretary of State may make a deportation order against him') will not have been satisfied, and no order can be made.

Exemptions from Liability

8.42 Members of certain categories are exempt from liability to deportation:

(i) Citizens of the Republic of Ireland or of a Commonwealth country, as identified in section 37 of and Schedule 3 to the BNA 1981, are by section 7 of the IA 1971 exempted from liability to deportation if ordinarily resident in the UK for at least five years, excluding periods of imprisonment or detention of more than six months, on 1 January 1973, the date on which the IA 1971 came into force. Unusually, overstayers are not treated as having lost ordinary residence by reason of the cessation of leave to remain (section 7(2) IA 1971). The burden of proof in such a case lies with the claimant, not with the Secretary of State (sections 3(8) and 7(5) IA 1971).

(ii) By section 8(1) IA 1971, certain seamen or aircrew arriving at a place in the UK under an engagement involving departure as a seaman or aircrew member are exempt, though only in the particular circumstances specified within that provision.

(iii) Some diplomats or international functionaries and their family members are exempt from liability to deportation. By section 8(2) IA 1971, the Secretary of State may exempt 'any person or class of person, either unconditionally or subject to such conditions as may be imposed' from provisions of that Act otherwise bearing on those who are not British citizens. Section 8(3)–(3A) and the Immigration (Exemption from Control) Order 1972, SI 1972/1613, give full immunity from deportation to some diplomats and international functionaries, and their family members, whilst permitting deportation of others on 'conducive to the public good' grounds. In *R v SSHD ex p Bagga and others* [1991] 1 QB 485, the Court of Appeal found that persons in the UK for the purpose of employment in a foreign mission were not susceptible to immigration control, but that those who had ceased such employment became subject to control.

(iv) Certain military personnel are exempt. By section 8(4) of the IA 1971, exemption from liability to deportation applies to all non-British citizen members of the British armed forces so long as they are subject to service law, to members of the armed services of Commonwealth, colonial, protectorate or British protected states training, or about to undergo training, with British forces in the UK, and to members of visiting forces or international headquarters or defence organisations.

Duration of Liability to Deportation

8.43 Statutory liability to deportation under section 32(4) UKBA 2007 does not lapse with time and may remain in force indefinitely. The passage of substantial time or change in circumstances might, however, be a factor relevant to whether, where section 32(4) UKBA 2007 does not apply, the Secretary of State may sustainably continue to treat deportation as conducive to the public good so as to create liability to deportation under section 3(5)(a) IA 1971.

Acquisition of British citizenship would seem to terminate liability to deportation because a necessary condition for that liability under section 3 IA 1971 is removed by the grant of citizenship, though section 5(2) IA 1971 provides that a deportation order, once made, 'shall cease to have effect' if an individual becomes a British citizen, not that any deportation order lapses. In *R (George) v SSHD* [2012] [2014] UKSC 28, [2014] 1 WLR 1831 the Supreme Court held that the term 'invalidates' in section 5(1) IA 1971 did not imply a temporary, reversible state, providing a possible parallel to the concept of 'ceasing to have effect'. But the best answer might appear that once an individual is a British citizen, where that occurs whilst a deportation order is outstanding, any deportation order, whether or not it has 'ceased to have effect' would be unlawful and should if necessary be revoked. If citizenship is then removed, under one of the powers examined at chapter 12, or lost by other means such as renunciation, a deportation order could once more be made in the case of an individual at that time liable to deportation. 8.44

If liability arises under section 3(5)(a) IA 1971 because the Secretary of State deems deportation conducive to the public good, then it is open to the Secretary of State to reconsider and by a contrary conclusion to remove the individual's liability to deportation. The scope for (re)consideration cuts both ways and subject to ordinary public law principles, which (in very brief summary) require the avoidance of illegality, irrationality or unfairness,[1] the Secretary of State may also decide that deportation is conducive, having previously formed the opposite view. 8.45

E3. Liability to Deportation by the Application of Sections 32–33 UKBA 2007 ('Automatic Deportation' Cases)

There is a subgroup in respect of whom liability to deportation under section 3(5)(a) IA 1971 does not depend upon a judgment by the Secretary of State that deportation 'is conducive to the public good', because deportation is by statute deemed conducive to the public good. The group affected consists of those designated 'foreign criminals' under section 32(1) UKBA 2007. They are defined as persons who are not British citizens, and have been convicted of a relevant offence in the UK and sentenced either to (a) a period of imprisonment of at least 12 months (section 32(2) of the UKBA 2007), or (b) a period of imprisonment of any length linked to an offence specified by the Secretary of State under section 72(4)(a) NIAA 2002. The relevant provisions (and details of commencement and transitional arrangements) have been set out at paragraphs 8.24–8.31 above. Under section 32(4) UKBA 2007, deportation is deemed to be conducive to the public good in such a case: this deeming serves to ensure that all such cases come within the statutory criterion for liability to deportation under section 8.46

---

[1] This conventional threefold summary is not exhaustive and its components are not mutually exclusive: see M Fordham, *Judicial Review Handbook* (6th edn, Oxford, Hart Publishing, 2012) 487. The public law wrongs justifying intervention are more fully examined in that work at Part C, P45–P63.

3(5)(a) IA 1971. The deeming provision in section 32(4) UKBA 2007 does not dovetail precisely with section 3(5)(a) IA 1971: the former provides that 'the deportation of a foreign criminal *is conducive* to the public good', whereas the latter requires that 'the Secretary of State deems his deportation to be conducive'. But the inconsistency may be inconsequential: the statutory intention seems clear and it is difficult to see how the Secretary of State, faced with the statutory deeming that something is so, could reasonably take a contrary view.

8.47 By section 33(1) UKBA 2007, the deeming provision in section 32(4) UKBA 2007 is disapplied where one of the six exceptions identified in section 33(2)–(6A) UKBA 2007 applies. In such a case, section 33(7)(b) UKBA 2007 provides that the application of an exception 'results in it being assumed neither that deportation of the person concerned is conducive to the public good nor that it is not conducive to the public good', save that if the applicable exception is Exception 1 (removal would breach ECHR rights incorporated by the HRA 1998 or the CSR) or Exception 4 (removal would breach EU law under the Treaties), then the deeming provision will continue to apply. As already noted at paragraph 8.40 above, section 33(7)(b) UKBA 2007 might be interpreted either as preventing a new deportation order or as leaving it open to the Secretary of State to consider operating the IA 1971 structure after UKBA 2007 is disapplied.

8.48 The effect of UKBA 2007 at the stage of liability to deportation can therefore be summarised as follows:

(i) In the case of a 'foreign criminal' as defined in section 32(1) UKBA 2007, if no section 33 UKBA 2007 exception applies, deportation is deemed to be conducive under section 32(4) UKBA 2007 and liability to deportation under section 3(5)(a) IA 1971 is established.
(ii) In the case of a section 32(1) UKBA 2007 'foreign criminal' in relation to whom Exception 1 or Exception 4 in section 33 UKBA 2007 applies, deportation continues to be deemed conducive under section 32(4) UKBA 2007. Liability to deportation under section 3(5)(a) IA 1971 therefore subsists.
(iii) In the case of a 'foreign criminal' in relation to whom another section 33 UKBA 2007 exception (Exception 2 or 3, or 4 or 6) applies, the section 32(4) UKBA 2007 deeming provision is disapplied. Under section 32(7) UKBA 2007, it is instead assumed neither that deportation is or that it is not conducive to the public good. The effect of this has been considered at paragraph 8.40 above.

8.49 Under section 33(1)(b) UKBA 2007, the deeming provision in section 32(4) UKBA 2007 is also disapplied where an exception from deportation arises under section 7 or 8 IA 1971. The relevant categories are identified at 8.42 above.

E4. Liability to Deportation under Section 3(5)(a) IA 1971 (Non-'Automatic Deportation' Cases)

8.50 In relation to all section 3(5)(a) IA 1971 cases to which section 32 UKBA 2007 does not apply, the existence of liability is established by the Secretary of State deeming deportation to be conducive to the public good. This formula does not admit absolute freedom of decision by the Secretary of State. However, it does create a substantial sphere of discretionary judgment regarding what is or is not conducive, the exercise of which will generally be difficult to challenge by judicial review or on appeal (there is of course no statutory appeal against a decision that liability to deportation arises, but under the arrangements presently provided by Part 5 NIAA 2002, though likely to be removed when changes to the statutory appeals structure introduced by IA 2014, a deportation decision could be challenged as 'not in accordance with the law' by reason of the decision power under section 5(1) IA 1971 being exercised unlawfully in the absence of liability to deportation). The cases, most of which predate the NIAA 2002 appeals provisions, reflect this.

At one end of the spectrum are security-related cases. Many of these, though not all, have been related to terrorism. In *R v Secretary of State for Home Affairs ex p Hosenball* [1977] 1 WLR 766, [1977] 3 All ER 452, the applicant was a journalist and citizen of the USA who worked as an investigative journalist in the UK and faced deportation because it was reported that he had obtained for publication information harmful to the interests of the UK. He sought unsuccessfully to challenge the fairness of the decision to deport him, not per se the decision that his deportation would be conducive to the public good. The House of Lords in *SSHD v Rehman* [2001] UKHL 47. [2003] AC 153 approved a wide definition of the 'public good' as encompassing national security, interstate relations or other political reasons. In terrorism-related cases, support for relevant activities taking place entirely outside the UK has been held by the Court of Appeal to justify liability to deportation being imposed: *Raghbir Singh v SSHD* [1996] Imm AR 507.

8.51

Beyond such 'political cases', it is clear that 'conducive to the public good' under section 3(5)(a) IA 1971 may encompass criminal conduct proven by conviction. The Court of Appeal has held that the facts of offending in a particular case rather than the general category best identifies the presence or absence of material to satisfy the test: *R v IAT ex p Florent* [1985] Imm AR 141. In the case of offences treated as particularly repugnant by the Secretary of State (on the facts, incest), the Court of Appeal has held the public interest in deterrence of others sufficient, without risk of reoffending, to justify liability to deportation being imposed: *Goremsandhu v SSHD* [1996] Imm AR 250. In *B v SSHD* [2000] EWCA Civ 158, [2000] INLR 361 [32], per Sedley LJ, it was observed that 'it is clear that sufficiently serious offending, with or without a propensity to reoffend, can make deportation under s 3(5) Immigration Act 1971 appropriate. Deportation, in other words, is authorised by law in cases of this kind'. In relation to criminality it is likely (following *N (Kenya v SSHD* [2004] EWCA Civ 1094, [2004] INLR 612 and other decisions concerning deportation and Article 8 ECHR, including *OH (Serbia) v SSHD* [2008] EWCA Civ 694, [2009] INLR 109) that separate elements of the public interest may be identified as (i) prevention of reoffending, (ii) deterrence of others, and (iii) the expression of repugnance at criminal activity. The imposition of liability to deportation has also been upheld where law enforcement agencies sought the retention of an individual in the UK: the decision of the Secretary of State was held lawful by the Court of Appeal even where the decision of the Secretary of State in *CM v SSHD* [1997] Imm AR 336 was held to be sustainable notwithstanding the fact that the Secretary of State had received representations from the police, who were keen to avert deportation because the prospective deportee had addressed drug dependence, assisted the police and was 'still of significant value as an informer'. In *R v SSHD ex p Figueiredo* [1993] Imm AR 606, the Secretary of State was held by Hutchison J to be entitled to take a decision that deportation was conducive to the public good, notwithstanding a considered decision in

8.52

Part C – Deportation, Removal and Exclusion

the Crown Court not to make a recommendation for deportation. In *M v SSHD* [2003] EWCA Civ 146, [2003] 1 WLR 1980, the Court of Appeal confirmed that the Secretary of State was not prevented from imposing liability to deportation by reference to section 5(1)(a) IA 1971 where the Court of Appeal Criminal Division on appeal had set aside an earlier recommendation for deportation in the Crown Court, but equally found that the Secretary of State had to engage with the fact of the decision in the Court of Appeal and that, in the absence of this, the decision was unsustainable. Laws LJ (with whom Ward and Jonathan Parker LJJ concurred) concluded at [19] that:

> [W]hen he comes to his own jurisdiction under s 3(5)(a) in a case such as this, the Secretary of State has to consider the prior reasoning of the criminal court and explain, however shortly, what he makes of it. He may simply state that he agrees with it. In that case he would of course make no decision to deport under s 3(5)(a). If he disagrees with it, he must explain, however shortly, why he disagrees with it. This seems to me to be no more than an elementary application of the Secretary of State's duties of fairness and good administration imposed upon him by the common law. The immigrant/defendant *ex hypothesi* has persuaded the criminal court distinctly to decide, on reasoned grounds, that there should be no s 6(1) recommendation. Whether the matter is put in terms of a legitimate expectation, ordinary fairness, or the obligation to take a rational approach to the duties of good administration, it seems to be clear that in this specific situation the law imposes upon the Secretary of State a duty to explain—as I have said however shortly—why he is taking a different view from that of the criminal court.

In *DA (Colombia) v SSHD* [2009] EWCA Civ 682, the Court of Appeal distinguished *M v SSHD*, dismissing the appeal before it on the basis that where a trial judge obviously departed from the area of recognised expertise of the criminal court (and trespassed upon that of the Secretary of State), the duty to consider and set out reasons addressing his conclusion fell away. Since the coming into force of UKBA 2007 and the guidance in *R v Kluxen* [2010] EWCA Crim 1081, [2011] 1 WLR 218, cases in which there is a recommendation will be fewer, and the absence of a recommendation will no longer represent a significant factor for consideration later by the Secretary of State.

8.53 Recent developments have extended substantially the use of section 3(5)(a) IA 1971 beyond cases in which there is a criminal conviction to cases in which convictions may be for relatively minor offences or even absent, in what could be called 'suspicion' or 'criminal association' liability. Under a scheme known as Operation Nexus, operated by the Home Office with the Metropolitan Police, it appears that anyone arrested by the latter, whether or not ultimately charged with any offence, is checked against Home Office databases, and deportation action has been initiated in a substantial number of cases based upon cautions or simple allegations of criminality or bad association. Aided by statutory amendment under section 140 Legal Aid, Sentencing and Punishment of Offenders Act 2012 (LASPO), which has added a new section 56A UKBA 2007 disapplying the Rehabilitation of Offenders Act 1974 in the immigration and nationality context so that convictions (or cautions) of any age may be relied upon by the Secretary of State, there has in recent years been increasingly systematic use of section 3(5)(a) IA 1971 based upon allegations of criminal conduct or association, without any or significant conviction, sometimes supported only by hearsay or anonymous evidence. In some cases there may be substantial issues of fairness given the nature of the evidence, and it is questionable whether the Secretary of State may lawfully base 'conducive' decision making on evidence of low probity or not going to any matter of sufficient weight, regardless of the openness of evidential standards in the Tribunal. The risk of injustice in this area is exacerbated by the withdrawal of public funding from most deportation appeals after April 2013 under measures introduced by LASPO 2012 and may be increased further by additional measures under IA 2014 reducing the coherence and accessibility of appeal procedures and access to appeal prior to removal: these are considered further in chapter 16.

Section 3(5)(a) IA 1971 may also apply where there is no criminal conviction or association, but there is other conduct of a relevant type. Imposition of liability by the Secretary of State was upheld in *R v IAT ex p Cheema, Ullah and Kawol* [1982] Imm AR 124, the conduct concerned in each case being participation in a marriage of convenience, an action identified by the Court of Appeal in judicial review appeals as undermining the key social institution of marriage. Lord Lane CJ, with whom Ackner and Oliver LJJ agreed, stated that: 'What we have to determine ... is whether there are proper grounds upon which the Secretary of State could reasonably come to the conclusion that the continued presence of these men in the United Kingdom was not conducive to the public good.' By contrast, in *R v IAT ex p Ahmud Khan* [1982] Imm AR 134, the Court of Appeal quashed and remitted another decision on the basis that the Tribunal's findings did not make out the ingredients of a marriage of convenience. In *R v IAT ex p Ghazi Khan* [1983] Imm AR 32, Stephen Brown J on judicial review quashed a decision of the Tribunal dismissing an appeal from the Secretary of State's decision to deport the applicant on the basis of concealment of a material fact on entry and alleged marriage of convenience, because the concealment was insufficient to ground liability to deportation and, even if migration to the UK had been a reason for the marriage, the findings of fact in relation to the marriage did not establish absence of intention to cohabit permanently. Later, in *Khawaja v SHHD* [1983] UKHL 8, [1984] AC 74 (albeit prior to important changes which transferred some categories of case from deportation to administrative removal), the House of Lords assumed illegal entry by deception to justify deportation. Lord Bridge, at [91], observed that the law as it then stood contained poor alternatives to the use of liability to deportation where entry had been secured by fraud, but that: 'On the other hand, the power given to the Secretary of State to deem deportation to be conducive to the public good seems to me to be intended for cases where the continued presence of the deportee would be objectionable on some positive and specific ground ... I cannot suppose that this power was ever intended to be invoked as a means of deporting a perfectly respectable established resident on grounds arising from the circumstances of his original entry.' Post-*Khawaja*, the *Ghazi Khan* decision was distinguished and *ex p Cheema* was followed in a case involving knowing entry into a bigamous marriage with a British citizen in order to obtain leave to remain: *Genc v SSHD* [1984] Imm AR 180.

8.54

Perhaps because appeals have long focused upon the decision to make a deportation order, not the decision that liability to deportation arises under section 3(5)(a) IA 1971 by reason of deportation being conducive to the public good, there is no authority establishing an outer boundary to the scope of liability by reason of conduciveness. In *R (V) v AIT* [2009] EWHC 1902 (Admin), Hickinbottom J refused a prospective deportee's application for judicial review of a refusal by the Asylum and Immigration Tribunal to dispose of appeal proceedings on the basis of abuse of process where the Secretary of State relied upon evidence of involvement in a criminal gang, including evidence of participation in the crime in respect of which acquittal had been directed in the Crown Court, and past criminal convictions. Hickinbottom J found at [36]–[48]

8.55

that the analysis of the evidence, and the weight to be attached to each item, would be a matter for the Tribunal, and that no basis for summary disposal was made out. The decision primarily concerned the scope for summary resolution of appeals based upon abuse of process findings and not a challenge to the Secretary of State's conclusion as regards liability to deportation under section 3(5)(a). It is not authority for an expansive approach to the 'conducive to the public good' formula in section 3(5)(a) IA 1971.[2] Despite the importance of the provision, the limits to the application of section 3(5)(a) IA 1971 have yet to be established with any certainty. Even if the new section 56A UKBA 2007 has in this context enabled reference to convictions and cautions which could not otherwise be made, the ability to make reference to these does not expand the limits of section 3(5)(a) IA 1971 itself.

8.56 In principle, the decision that an individual is liable to deportation may be subject to judicial review on public law grounds. In practice, such challenges have been so rare that individual examples are difficult to find. Reasons for this probably include: (i) the breadth of the section 3(1)(a) IA 1971 condition, which reduces the scope for viable challenge: (ii) the fact that challenges have tended to be directed instead against decisions to make a deportation order under section 5(1) IA 1971 rather than the liability decision; and (iii) the existence, under Part 5 NIAA 2002 and earlier provisions, of statutory appeal against decisions to make a deportation order, of a possible alternative remedy to any public law challenge addressing a section 3(5)–(6) IA 1971 designation. The absence of separate challenge has tended to obscure the real existence of a two-stage statutory process. However, the ongoing elimination of most standards expressly applicable to section 5(1) IA 1971 power (save as regards Article 8 ECHR), and anticipated changes under IA 2014 regarding the availability and nature of appeal, may in the future increase the public law focus upon section 3(5)(a) IA 1971.

E5. The section 5(1) IA 1971 Power to Make a Deportation Order

The Effect of Sections 32–33 UKBA 2007

8.57 Whilst section 5(1) IA 1971 provides a power, not a duty, to make a deportation order, in a case concerning a 'foreign criminal' as defined in section 32(1)–(3) UKBA 2007, there is no discretion: section 32(5) UKBA 2007 provides that a deportation order *must be made* by the Secretary of State in such a case. Whilst the Secretary of State is by section 34(1) UKBA 2007 given some discretion as to the *timing* of a deportation order being made, and by section 34(2) is restrained from acting whilst a criminal appeal might be brought or is pending, he or she must make a deportation order if section 32(5) UKBA 2007 remains applicable. This order will however be made under section 5(1) IA 1971: the UKBA 2007 did not create a freestanding power to make a deportation order, instead utilising the section 5(1) IA 1971 power which was already in existence.

---

[2] Further, from a judgment in further judicial review proceedings, it appears that the Secretary of State subsequently withdrew the deportation decision and restored indefinite leave to remain, recognising that reference to spent convictions and unproven allegations contravened her then policy: *R (V) v SSHD* [2013] EWHC 765 (Admin).

8.58 Section 33(1)(b) UKBA 2007 disapplies the deeming provision at section 32(4) UKBA 2007 if an exception from deportation arises under section 7 or 8 IA 1971. The relevant categories are identified at 8.42 above.

8.59 Section 32(5) UKBA 2007 is disapplied by section 33(1) UKBA 2007 if one of the exceptions designated in section 33(2)–(6A) UKBA 2007 applies. But if the exception is a contemplated breach of Exception 1 (ECHR or CSR) or Exception 4 (EU treaty law), then, as already seen, liability to deportation is sustained (section 33(7) UKBA 2007) and 'the application of an exception … does not prevent the making of a deportation order'. In such a case, the section 32(5) UKBA 2007 duty upon the Secretary of State to make a deportation order is removed by section 33(1) UKBA 2007, so the Secretary of State is left to decide whether or not to make a deportation order under the section 5(1) IA 1971 discretionary power. If a deportation order is made, then the breach of the ECHR, the CSR or EU treaty law is presumably avoided because the order is recognised as inexecutable. In the event of a change of circumstances removing the anticipated breach of the ECHR, the CSR or EU treaty law, such an order presumably could then be executed.

8.60 If section 32(5) UKBA 2007 is disapplied by a section 33 UKBA 2007 exception which is *not* Exception 1 or Exception 4, then liability to deportation under section 3(5)(a) IA 1971 is displaced. Without liability to deportation, section 5(1) IA 1971 does not permit the making of an order. So, unless liability to deportation arises once more, there remains no basis upon which section 5(1) IA 1971 gives the power to make a deportation order. It follows that section 33(7)(a) UKBA 2007, providing that the application of an exception does not prevent the making of a deportation order, is effective only if liability to deportation arises.

8.61 In summary, therefore:

(i) If section 32(1) UKBA 2007 applies and no section 33 UKBA 2007 exception is shown, then section 32(5) requires the Secretary of State to make a deportation order under section 5(1) IA 1971.

(ii) If section 32(1) UKBA 2007 applies and so does Exception 1 or Exception 4 under section 33 UKBA 2007, then (liability to deportation being still in place by reason of section 33(7) UKBA 2007) the making of a deportation order is not prevented (section 33(7)(a) UKBA 2007), but the section 32(5) UKBA 2007 duty to make an order is disapplied (section 33(1)(a) UKBA 2007). In the absence of a duty, the Secretary of State may consider the use of the discretion to make an order under section 5(1) IA 1971, notwithstanding that removal in pursuance of enforcement of any such order would breach the ECHR, the CSR or EU treaty rights (so that such an order will presumably not be executed, at least so long as removal would breach the relevant rights).

(iii) If section 32(1) UKBA 2007 applies and so does a section 33 UKBA 2007 exception apart from Exception 1 or Exception 4, then (liability to deportation under section 3(5)(a) IA 1971 being removed by reason of section 33(7)(b) UKBA 2007) the making of a deportation order under section 5(1) is prevented, unless liability to deportation arises.

Exercise of the Section 5(1) IA 1971 Power where Section 32 UKBA 2007 Does Not Apply

8.62 As just seen, section 32(5) UKBA 2007 in some circumstances displaces the exercise of a discretion by the Secretary of State, substituting a duty to make a deportation order.

Part C – Deportation, Removal and Exclusion

8.63 In all other cases in which section 5(1) IA 1971 creates a power (which requires the prior existence of statutory liability to deportation under section 3(5) or 3(6) IA 1971), the Secretary of State may consider whether to exercise that power so long as liability to deportation remains.

8.64 In *R v SSHD ex p Vladic* [1998] Imm AR 542, the Court of Appeal identified the process of decision by the Secretary of State as involving two stages: 'The legislation does not expressly confer on the Secretary of State a power to decide to deport; that the Secretary of State has such a power and the process of deportation is a two stage procedure follows necessarily from other provisions in the 1971 Act and in particular those relating to appeals in deportation cases.' The respective stages identified in *Vladic* are as follows:

(i) At the first stage, a decision is taken as to whether a deportation order should be made. In a case to which section 32 UKBA 2007 may apply, the first stage of the decision involves the decision by the Secretary of State as to whether the conditions precedent for this are met, rather than whether a discretionary power should be exercised. If it is concluded that section 32 UKBA 2007 does apply, then no discretion remains: the duty imposed by section 32(5) to make a deportation order necessarily eliminates any discretionary element. In any other event, the Secretary of State must decide whether to exercise the section 5(1) IA 1971 discretion.

(ii) At the second stage, a deportation order is 'made' or 'taken'. This is considered to occur at the moment when it is signed: *Peerbocus v SSHD* [1987] Imm AR 331; *R v SSHD ex p Sanusi* [1999] INLR 198. Where there has been a statutory appeal against, or judicial review proceedings directed at, the decision to make a deportation order, then whether the second stage is reached will logically depend upon the outcome of that appeal.

A third stage might arise where there has to be consideration as to whether an order should be revoked: a deportation order, whether taken under section 5(1) IA 1971 alone or whether under that provision in conjunction with section 32 UKBA 2007, may be revoked at any time by the Secretary of State, exercising the relevant power under section 6(2) IA 1971.

8.65 The first stage of the process is a critical point: it is the point of potential exercise of the discretionary power under section 5(1) IA 1971. This has been the link in the chain latterly appealable under Part 5 of NIAA 2002. The second, administrative, stage generally follows from the first without any further intervening decision. The Court in *Vladic* (which was decided when persons who would now be susceptible to administrative removal as overstayers or illegal entrants were subject to deportation) considered that the Secretary of State was not required to wait until a proposed deportee had become liable to deportation prior to deciding whether to deport him or her. In practice, there seems no reason why the Secretary of State should not adopt a preliminary intention to exercise the discretionary power if and when liability to deportation is established, so long as he or she does not breach the principles of public law, for example, by taking a deportation decision when there is no power to do so, enforcing an unfair procedure or failing to keep an open mind.

8.66 The Secretary of State has indicated certain procedural standards at paragraphs 381–2 and 384 Immigration Rules HC 395. Paragraph 381 provides that where a decision to make a deportation order has been taken otherwise than on the recommendation of a court, a notice will be given to the person concerned informing him or her of the decision and of his or her right of appeal. The wording of the passage in brackets ('otherwise than on the recommendation of a court'), which on a direct reading suggests that no notice is needed where the decision *is* taken 'on the recommendation of a court', is inapposite, probably reflecting confusion on the part of the drafter between the recommendation of a court in a relevant case, of which no separate notice is given in the immigration administration context, and a subsequent decision of the Secretary of State as to deportation, in relation to which written notice is a requirement, as set out below.[3] Paragraph 384 provides that where notice of appeal is received in response, 'a summary of the facts of the case on the basis of which the decision was taken will be sent to the appropriate appellate authorities, who will notify the appellant of the arrangements for the appeal to be heard'.

Public Law

As with any decision of the Secretary of State deeming deportation conducive to the public good for purposes of section 3(5)(a) IA 1971, the exercise of the power under section 5(1) IA 1971 to make a deportation order must be exercised in accordance with established principles of public law, that is, without illegality, irrationality or unfairness.[4] In *R v Secretary of State for Home Affairs ex p Hosenball* [1977] 1 WLR 766, [1977] 3 All ER 452, the Court of Appeal expressly accepted that public law standards of fairness applied even to cases stated to concern matters of national security. In *R v SSHD ex p Malhi* [1991] 1 QB 194, endorsed by the House of Lords in *Oladehinde v IAT* [1990] UKHL 11, [1991] 1 AC 254, it was held that an adjudicator hearing an appeal under the now-abolished section 15 IA 1971 was not entitled to investigate the propriety of the procedures leading up to the Secretary of State's decision to make a deportation order, but that decision turned on the expressly limited statutory jurisdiction of adjudicators at the time rather than broader public law standards. As a matter of general public law, it is well established that statutory powers must be exercised reasonably and otherwise in compliance with the principles established by public law. In relation to a decision under the Immigration Rules HC 395, Sullivan J observed in *R (otao Forrester) v SSHD* [2008] EWHC 2307 (Admin) [7] that:

8.67

> In terms of the rules it can fairly be said that the decision was impeccable. That, of course, is not the end of the matter. The defendant is given a discretion, and she is given a discretion on the basis that it will be exercised with a modicum of intelligence, common sense and humanity.

---

[3] The confusion appears to infect the Rules at a number of points. Paragraph 378 HC 395 states that: 'There is no appeal within the immigration appeal system against the making of a deportation order on a recommendation of a court.' This is plainly erroneous if intended to apply to a decision of the Secretary of State to make a deportation order after the recommendation of a court, as s 82(2)(j) of the NIAA 2002 expressly provides a statutory appeal right in those circumstances. What is probably meant is the truism that appeal does not lie in the immigration appeal system against the decision of a criminal court to make a recommendation.

[4] This conventional threefold summary is not exhaustive and its components are not mutually exclusive: as previously, see Fordham (n 1) 487 and the categorisation of public law wrongs justifying intervention examined in that work at P45–P63.

Part C – Deportation, Removal and Exclusion

A discretionary power must be exercised consistently with domestic law, including incorporated international instruments and EU law. The exercise of discretion may be affected by relevant norms of international law even where that law is not incorporated into domestic law by statute: see paragraphs 2.17–22 above.

Restrictions Related to Republic of Ireland Citizens/EEA Nationals and Family Members/Turkish Workers and Family Members

8.68 A number of groups benefit from particular restraints upon the exercise of the section 5(1) IA 1971 power:

(i) Citizens of the Republic of Ireland do not have complete exemption from liability, but their liability is limited as a result of bilateral agreement between the UK and that Republic. Since 19 February 2007, individuals holding either sole or dual Republic of Ireland nationality will as a matter of government policy be considered for deportation only where (a) a court has recommended this in sentencing and the Secretary of State decides in the exercise of discretion to act upon the recommendation, or (b) the Secretary of State concludes that 'the most exceptional circumstances' justify deportation in the public interest. This does not protect non-EEA nationals who are the dependants of Irish nationals. The applicable policy guidance[5] states that whilst 'Irish nationality does not provide automatic exemption from deportation regardless of individual circumstances', it will be 'rare' that cases will be sufficiently exceptional to justify deportation. It also states that:

> As a guide, deportation is still considered if an offence involves national security matters, or crimes that pose a serious risk to the safety of the public or a section of the public. For example, [in the case of] a person convicted and serving a custodial sentence of 10 years or more for [terrorism, murder, or serious sexual or violent offending].

(ii) Whilst their regime is less generous than that applicable to Republic of Ireland nationals, other EEA citizens benefit from binding restrictions on the exercise by the Secretary of State upon his or her deportation powers under the Immigration (EEA) Regulations 2006, SI 2006/1003. Under regulation 19(3)(b), an EEA national, or the family member of such a person, who otherwise possesses a right to reside in the UK under those Regulations may be removed if 'the Secretary of State has decided that his removal is justified on the grounds of public policy, public security, or public health in accordance with regulation 21'. Regulation 19(5) applies the same stricture where the EEA national or family member possesses leave to enter or remain under the IA 1971. Under regulation 21, further restrictions are created: a decision may not be taken 'to serve economic ends' (regulation 21(2)), may not be taken in respect of a person with a permanent right of residence under regulation 15 except on the serious grounds of public policy or public security (regulation 21(3)) and may not be taken except on the imperative grounds of public security in respect of an EEA national who has accumulated 10

---

[5] Criminal Casework, European Economic Area (EEA) foreign national offender (FNO) cases, v3.0, 27 January 2014, 2 and 7–8.

years' continuous residence or is under 18 and removal is in his or her best interests (regulation 21(4)). Other restrictions, considered below, concern the process of decision making in EEA cases rather than the scope of the power.

(iii) In *R v Kluxen*, the Court of Appeal Criminal Division referred to 'the Secretary of State's policy that no citizen of the European Economic Area will be removed unless the prison sentence imposed is two years or more'. This would extend to Republic of Ireland nationals as well as nationals of other EEA states.

(iv) Turkish workers and their family members enjoying rights under the Turkey-EEC Association Agreement and decisions of the Association Council are treated as regards deportation in the same way as EEA nationals and family members: *Nazli and others (External relations)* [2000] EUECJ C-340/97, [2000] ECR I-957.

In *Al-Sabah v IAT* [1992] Imm AR 223, the Court of Appeal rejected, as had Brooke J below at [1992] Imm AR 25, the submission on behalf of a Kuwaiti national that wording in the then-current version of the Immigration Rules requiring 'consistent and fair' decision making as regards deportation required him to be treated as though he were protected by provisions relating to citizens of states within the then EEC, in essence finding that the difference in treatment between EEC and non-EEC cases did not amount to prohibited discrimination and that the decision was neither irrational nor unfair.

Restrictions Regarding the Deportation of Family Members of Deportees

Section 3(5)(b) IA 1971, as already seen, creates a wide-ranging liability to deportation in respect of family members of persons 'ordered to be deported', defined in section 5(4) IA 1971 as spouses or civil partners and minor children. Under section 5(3) IA 1971, a deportation order shall not be made against the family member of another person if more than eight weeks have elapsed since the other person left the UK, following the making of a deportation order against him, and an order shall also cease to have effect if that person ceases to be a relevant family member or the deportation order against the primary target for deportation ceases to have effect. By paragraph 365 Immigration Rules HC 395, it is stated that the Secretary of State will not 'normally' decide to deport the spouse or civil partner of a deportee where the former (a) has separately qualified for settlement, or (b) has been living apart from the deportee. By paragraph 366, the power of deportation will not 'normally' be exercised against the child of a deportee where (a) the child and other parent are living separately from the deportee, or (b) the child has left home and established himself or herself independently, or (c) the child married or entered into a civil partnership 'before deportation came into prospect'.[6]

8.69

Other Matters Relevant to Decision Making: The Scope of Consideration Where Liability Arises under Section 3(6) IA 1971

In a recommendation case, in which liability to deportation arises by reference to section 3(6) IA 1971, it has been held that the existence of the recommendation does

8.70

---

[6] Because this restraint is located in the Immigration Rules, general terms will be interpreted in line with para 6 of the Rules unless another meaning has expressly or implicitly been applied.

Part C – Deportation, Removal and Exclusion

not eliminate the need for separate consideration of the section 5(1) discretion by the Secretary of State. In *M v SSHD* [2003] EWCA Civ 146, [2003] 1 WLR 1980, the Court of Appeal confirmed this, referring at [20] to the fact that 'the scope of considerations to be had in mind by the criminal court under s 6(1) [IA 1971] was significantly different from those to be confronted by the Secretary of State under s 3(5)(a) (or, indeed, s 3(6))'. It considered that the Secretary of State was not prevented from imposing detention liability by reference to section 5(1)(a) IA 1971 where the Court of Appeal Criminal Division on appeal had set aside an earlier recommendation for deportation in the Crown Court. As to the matters to be considered by the Secretary of State but not in the Crown Court post UKBA 2007, in *R v Kluxen* [2010] EWCA Crim 1081, [2011] 1 WLR 218, the Court of Appeal Criminal Division summarised at [29]–[32] the 'five matters which in our judgement should *not* be taken into account on the rare occasions when a recommendation for deportation is being considered' (emphasis added), these being: (a) ECHR rights, which are left for separate consideration by the Secretary of State; (b) the possible effect of a recommendation on innocent persons not before the Court, such as family members; (c) the political (or human rights) situation in the country to which the offender may be deported and in EU cases; (d) Article 28 of Directive 2004/38, which is held to refer only to the subsequent immigration decision; and (e) the Immigration (European Economic Area) Regulations 2006, SI 2006/1003.

8.71 The Immigration Rules formerly provided some guidance as to matters to consider, but it appears that this has now been removed, with the provision of new guidance as to policy in paragraphs 398–400 expressly restricted by paragraph 398 to cases 'where a person claims that … deportation would be contrary to the UK's obligations under [Article 8 ECHR]'. Oddly two paragraphs appear in the Rules which might otherwise be thought to represent a sketchy guidance in this respect, namely paragraphs 395 and 396, but the heading above these is 'Rights of appeal in relation to a decision not to revoke a deportation order', and paragraph 395 relates to refusals to revoke deportation orders. Paragraphs 396 and 397 read as follows:

> 396. Where a person is liable to deportation the presumption shall be that the public interest requires deportation. It is in the public interest to deport where the Secretary of State must make a deportation order in accordance with section 32 of the UK Borders Act 2007.
> 397. A deportation order will not be made if the person's removal pursuant to the order would be contrary to the UK's obligations under the Refugee Convention or the Human Rights Convention. Where deportation would not be contrary to these obligations, it will only be in exceptional circumstances that the public interest in deportation is outweighed.

If this is in fact the location of the Secretary of State's guidance as to when the power under section 5(1) IA 1971 will be exercised, then there is no overall lacuna, but the applicable standards are extremely vague—a presumption in favour of deportation where discretion has to be exercised (paragraph 396, first sentence), the bar to making an order if that would breach 'the UK's obligations under' the ECHR or the CSR (paragraph 397, first sentence), and otherwise a requirement for unspecified 'exceptional circumstances', in the absence of which the public interest in deportation will not be outweighed (paragraph 397, second sentence). The 'presumption' at paragraph 396 and the requirement for 'exceptional circumstances [save in the ECHR or the CSR]' cases would then presumably have to be read consistently with each other, an exercise which invites the question as to what is added to paragraph 397 by the first sentence of paragraph 396. And even treating these provisions as consistent with each other, their application depends upon broad concepts: what is the relevant content of 'the public interest in deportation' in a case, such as a non-criminal case, in which the nature of the public interest may not be clear at all, or the weight of relevant factors may be weak, and what are 'exceptional circumstances' in this context? The problems attached to the phrase are well illustrated in the separate Article 8 ECHR context by Sales J in *R (Nagre) v SSHD* [2013] EWHC 720 (Admin) and by Lord Dyson MR in *MF (Nigeria) v SSHD* [2013] EWCA Civ 1192, [2014] 1 WLR 544. A question remains as to whether the Secretary of State's policy adequately recognises the existence (in non-UKBA 2007 cases) of a statutory discretion, not a duty, and whether, even if that question is answered positively, the exercise of the discretion may be unduly fettered. If the public interest in deportation is identifiably very weak, for example, can it legitimately be said that 'exceptional factors' are required to outweigh this?

It is important to recognise that the paucity of clear guidance regarding the matters to be taken into consideration, save for Article 8 ECHR, does not alter the discretionary nature of the decision provided for by statute or fetter the ordinary requirements of lawfulness under public law. Whilst the absence of a declared policy renders it difficult to anticipate every circumstance which might constrain the Secretary of State's exercise of the power, in principle the Secretary of State must still deal with this factor in a legally adequate manner. Just as it would be a misdirection to mistake a duty, such as that imposed by section 32 UKBA 2007, for a power, so too would the fettering of a discretionary power established by Parliament represent a public law error. As the Asylum and Immigration Tribunal observed in *EO (Deportation Appeals: Scope and Process) Turkey* [2007] UKAIT 00062, [2007] Imm AR 645, [2008] INLR 177 [10]: 8.72

> A decision to make a deportation order against an individual is an exercise of the Secretary of State's discretion. It is clearly amenable to challenge under a number of the grounds set out in s 84(1). If the Secretary of State purports to decide to deport a person who is not in truth liable to deportation, there may be a successful appeal on (at least) the grounds that the decision is not in accordance with the Immigration Rules and is 'otherwise not in accordance with the law'. If, in making his decision, he fails to comply with generally-applicable rules of administrative law, there may perhaps be a successful appeal on the ground that the decision was 'otherwise not in accordance with the law'. So much is clear.

That decision was tested on appeal to the Court of Appeal and upheld: [2008] EWCA Civ 671, [2008] INLR 295.

Lawfulness in this context requires, inter alia, fairness and the consideration of all relevant matters and the setting aside of irrelevant ones. In a substantial number of cases, it has been held that such considerations applied to deportation relevant decisions. In *R v SSHD ex p Urmaza* [1996] COD 479 it was held by Sedley J that 'A decision maker can be held in public law to his policy, with departure requiring the articulation of a good reason, given (i) the principle of consistency (and avoidance of arbitrariness), (ii) the duty to have regard to relevancies, (iii) the avoidance of over-rigidity, and (iv) the need to give effect to legitimate expectations.' For instance, in *R v SSHD ex p Amankwah* [1994] Imm AR 240, a deportation decision was quashed by Popplewell J on the basis of failure by the decision maker to advert to relevant policy guidance. In *SL (Vietnam) v SSHD* [2010] EWCA Civ 225, [2010] INLR 651, a majority in the Court of Appeal found a decision flawed by reason of failure to consider past mistakes by the Secretary of State 8.73

in the application of policy, and in *AF (Jamaica) v SSHD* [2009] EWCA Civ 240 and *SS (India) v SSHD* [2010] EWCA Civ 388, the Court of Appeal found that a failure to consider policies in force at relevant dates, though subsequently withdrawn, vitiated the decisions challenged on appeal. However, the duty to consider policy does not mean that its content will necessarily dictate the outcome of every decision,[7] and a carefully reasoned disapplication of a particular policy was upheld by the Court of Appeal, reversing the decision below, in *R v SSHD ex p Hastrup* [1996] EWCA Civ 1333, [1996] Imm AR 616. The Court of Appeal in *SSHD v HH (Iraq)* [2009] EWCA Civ 727, [2010] INLR 78 upheld a decision of the Tribunal that a deportation decision was unlawful because it was inconsistent with the then policy of not sending deportees to active war zones. At [14], Sedley LJ, with whom Toulson and Rimer LJJ agreed, rejected the submission that the failure to apply the policy was immaterial because, if required to apply it, the Secretary of State would have been prompted thereby to withdraw it: 'This is, with respect, a remarkable submission. It implies that policies may be torn up whenever the policy-maker finds them inconvenient or embarrassing. For my part I do not believe that the important power of government to make and remake policy is exercised in this way.' Toulson LJ added at [18] that 'it is trite public law that a decision maker must take into account all material considerations, and it must be a material consideration when deciding whether to make a deportation order that the making of such an order would contravene the minister's stated public policy'.

8.74 In *Saribal v SSHD* [2002] EWHC 1542 (Admin), [2002] INLR 596, Moses J quashed the decision of the Secretary of State because the latter had failed to carry out sufficient investigation into the facts before concluding that a previous positive adjudication in the tribunal had been obtained by fraud, as had been alleged in a BBC broadcast, finding that for this purpose, the Secretary of State should have considered whether evidence accumulated since the tribunal's determination satisfied the requirements of relevance, credibility and previous unavailability in *Ladd v Marshall* [1954] EWCA Civ 1, [1954] 1 WLR 1489. In *M v SSHD* [2003] EWCA Civ 146, [2003] 1 WLR 1980, the Court of Appeal found a deportation decision, liability being established on a 'conducive to the public good' basis, to be unlawful because the reasons for it did not show adequate engagement with the fact of a previous successful appeal in the Court of Appeal Criminal Division against the making of a recommendation for deportation. More recently, in *R (otao Poyraz) v SSHD* [2014] UKUT 151 (IAC), the Upper Tribunal refused judicial review of the Secretary of State's conduct in taking a decision many years after conviction, and without good reason for delay, not on the merits but because it considered that an impending appeal in the Tribunal represented a suitable alternative remedy: in that case, the Secretary of State had through serious failures by her own agents delayed the decision to deport the applicant until more than 10 years after the applicant's release from custody, without any intervening factors providing justification for the decision.

8.75 So, a deportation decision taken in the exercise of the Secretary of State's section 5(1) IA 1971 discretion may be unlawful by reference to general public law considerations.

---

[7] This limitation—that policy may be departed from, where sufficient justification is shown—is necessary to the ability of an individual making representations to the Secretary of State to ask not for the application of policy, but for departure from it on the basis of the particular circumstances of the case.

But going beyond that, what general standard is applied by the Secretary of State in deciding whether to exercise the discretion?

In practice, it is difficult to detect any coherent standard, at least in non-EEA cases. Beyond paragraphs 397–8 Immigration Rules, which as already noted are, perhaps mistakenly on the part of the Secretary of State, related in the published text to revocation rather than to the taking of decisions under section 5(1) IA 1971, the sole matters expressly set out in the Immigration Rules relate to Article 8 ECHR, and the Secretary of State has published guidance in the Immigration Directorate Instructions, relating to Chapter 13 of the Rules, which exclusively addresses Article 8 ECHR.[8] It can no doubt be safely presumed, on the basis of various binding legal commitments (and the possibly misplaced commitment at paragraph 397 Immigration Rules), that the Secretary of State would not exercise the discretion in favour of deportation if this would, for instance, breach ECHR protections incorporated into domestic law by the HRA1998, or those CSR protections which are enforceable by reference to paragraph 334 Immigration Rules HC 395 and section 2 Asylum and Immigration Appeals Act 1993 or as part of EU law. But these do not identify any coherent scheme for exercise of discretion in other cases, and the absence of this is surprising given judicial encouragement for the establishment of policies as desirable and sometimes necessary for the lawful exercise of discretion.

8.76

Some separate guidance is in existence as regards deportation in EEA cases,[9] which is also covered by statutory regulations: in EEA cases, permissible grounds for exclusion are, as has already been seen, limited to 'public policy, public security, or public health' by regulation 19 of the Immigration (EEA) Regulations 2006, SI 2006/1003, and in relation to matters requiring consideration, regulation 21 further provides a clear identification of the parameters in relevant cases, namely that a decision 'must comply with the principle of proportionality', must be 'based exclusively on the personal conduct of the person concerned' and 'must represent a genuine, present and sufficiently serious threat affecting one of the fundamental interests of society' where 'matters isolated from the particulars of the case or which relate to considerations of general prevention' and 'a person's previous criminal convictions do not in themselves' justify the decision. Under Regulation 19(6):

8.77

> Before taking a relevant decision on the grounds of public policy or public security in relation to a person who is resident in the United Kingdom the decision maker must take account of considerations such as the age, state of health, family and economic situation of the person, the person's length of residence in the United Kingdom, the person's social and cultural integration into the United Kingdom and the extent of the person's links with his country of origin.

Regulation 19(7) limits severely the scope for reliance upon 'public health' as a reason for exclusion.

The absence of a clear general standard in non-EEA cases, and the doubt as to whether paragraphs 396–97 Immigration Rules are simply misplaced within the Rules, might be thought to undermine the aim of fairness and consistency present in the

8.78

---

[8] Immigration Directorate Instructions/Chapter 13: Criminality Guidance in Article 8 ECHR Cases, v 4.0, 8 May 2013.
[9] Criminal Casework/European Economic Area (EEA) Foreign National Offender (FNO) Cases, v 3, 27 January 2014.

Part C – Deportation, Removal and Exclusion

public law cases and specifically adumbrated in Immigration Rules until relatively recently, at paragraph 364, now withdrawn:

> The aim is an exercise of the power of deportation which is consistent and fair as between one person and another, although one case will rarely be identical with another in all material respects.

8.79 The achievement of consistent and fair application of the section 5(1) IA 1971 discretion would appear to be handicapped by the absence of cogent policy guidance: as Lord Woolf MR observed in *R v Home Secretary ex p Venables* [1998] AC 407, 432G–H of a wide discretion as regards the release of life prisoners: 'It is the type of discretion which calls out for the development of policy as to the way it will in general be exercised. This should assist in providing consistency and certainty which are highly desirable in any area involving the administration of justice where fairness is particularly important.' More recently, in *R (Lumba) v SSHD* [2011] UKSC 12, [2012] 1 AC 245 at [36], Lord Dyson endorsed a statement by Stanley Burnton J in an earlier case to the effect that 'it is in general inconsistent with the constitutional imperative that statute law be made known for the government to withhold information about its policy relating to the exercise of a power conferred by statute'. Although dissenting on other issues, Lord Phillips at [302] also emphasised the need for policy where a significant discretion arose:

> Under principles of public law, it was necessary for the Secretary of State to have policies in relation to the exercise of her powers of detention of immigrants and that those policies had to be published. This necessity springs from the standards of administration that public law requires and by the requirement of article 5 that detention should be lawful and not arbitrary … Unless there were uniformly applied practices, decisions would be inconsistent and arbitrary. Established principles of public law also required that the Secretary of State's policies should be published. Immigrants needed to be able to ascertain her policies in order to know whether or not the decisions that affected them were open to challenge.

8.80 The absence of a policy (or the incompleteness and sometime incoherence of such policy material as can be assembled or deduced) means that in practice, the relevant factors have to be determined on a case-by-case basis. It can be deduced that the concrete ingredients of a public interest in removal have to be weighed against the countervailing public interests and private interests of the potential deportee or other affected by the decision. This process may resemble that embarked upon in relation to Article 8 ECHR, but in law cannot be assumed to be identical to it, thus fettering application of the underlying statutory discretion. In *Singh (Bakhtaur) v IAT* [1986] UKHL 11, [1986] 1 WLR 910, a Sikh musician had overstayed his leave to enter and remain in the UK. Deportation under section 5(1) IA 1971 at that time also extended to overstayers, who presently are instead subject to administrative removal. The appellant successfully challenged by judicial review the decision of the tribunal that the interest of members of the Sikh community who benefitted from his music making was not a relevant consideration, Lord Bridge observing that:

> If, therefore, some interest of third parties which is known to the Secretary of State and which would be adversely affected by deportation is in truth relevant to the proper exercise of the discretion, a decision made without taking it into account would in any event be open to challenge by judicial review and consequently would be open, in the case of an overstayer, to appeal under s 19(1) as being 'not in accordance with the law' quite apart from the immigration rules … to construe the rules in the sense for which the respondent contends would not only conflict with

the general law but would also be ineffective to restrict the relevant matters which the appellate authorities may, and indeed must, take into consideration.

Lord Bridge rejected the submission that this risked admitting improper considerations, such as the threat of labour unrest in the event of an individual being deported:

> The only matters which the law requires, or indeed permits, to be taken into consideration either by the Secretary of State or by the appellate authorities in deciding whether or not in any particular case to make a deportation order are matters relevant to the proper exercise of the statutory discretion. Extraneous threats to instigate industrial action could only exert an improper pressure on the Secretary of State and if he allowed himself to be influenced by them, he would be taking into account wholly irrelevant considerations. It is not fanciful to imagine other, less dramatic situations, in which consideration of the political implications or repercussions of a decision for or against deportation in a particular case might not be relevant to the proper exercise of the statutory discretion. But to attempt to draw in the abstract precise boundary lines which, in this sensitive area of administration, separate the relevant from the irrelevant would be both an unprofitable and a dangerous exercise. Relevance can only be determined in relation to the facts of particular cases.

What are the factors likely to be of relevance when the Secretary of State considers the exercise of decision under section 5(1) IA 1971? Without attempting a comprehensive list, the following reflections are offered: **8.81**

(i) The Secretary of State must deal in legally adequate fashion with the fact that section 5(1) IA 1971 creates a discretion rather than imposing a duty. Amongst the public law considerations attending this will be the prohibition upon action fettering the discretion provided by Parliament, and duties both to consider any relevant matter and to ignore any irrelevant one. In the absence of express guidance as to what constitutes relevant considerations, these will have to be determined on a case-by-case basis, as indicated by Lord Bridge in *Singh (Bakhtaur)*. However, it seems possible that some assistance might be gleaned from past rules or published guidance in the UK, or from analogical reference to the treatment of the same issues in comparative, international or regional contexts (so long as the difference in context and limitations of the exercise are not lost sight of).

(ii) Where the Secretary of State has put in place policy or guidance, under the Immigration Rules or elsewhere, and this is itself lawful, the decision maker must consider it and apply it, save where a legally adequate reason not to do so arises: amongst the cases at paragraphs 8.73 above, *R v SSHD ex p Amankwah* [1994] Imm AR 240; *SL (Vietnam) v SSHD* [2010] EWCA Civ 225, [2010] INLR 651; *AF (Jamaica) v SSHD* [2009] EWCA Civ 240; *SS (India) v SSHD* [2010] EWCA Civ 388; and *R v SSHD ex p Hastrup* [1996] EWCA Civ 1333, [1996] Imm AR 616 all fall into this category. At present, such guidance as exists applies primarily to the treatment of Article 8 ECHR within and/or without the Immigration Rules and to EEA cases.

(iii) The Secretary of State should be assumed not to intend to breach other rights protected by the ECHR, CSR or EU law—as by contravening duties imposed upon him or her by the HRA 1998 in relation to ECHR rights domesticated thereunder, or refugee protections under the CSR as incorporated into domestic or EU instruments. If paragraph 397 Immigration Rules is read as part of his or her policy, this confirms his or her intention, but in the contrary case he or she

Part C – Deportation, Removal and Exclusion

would in any event not be freed from other obligations as regards the ECHR and the CSR. He or she is particularly tied as regards those provisions of the ECHR expressly incorporated into domestic law by HRA 1998, and the provisions of the CSR incorporated into domestic and/or EU law.

(iv) Amongst the applicable provisions of the ECHR, Articles 3 and 8 may have particular relevance. The scope of these rights has been delineated in chapter 5 above. Some further considerations as regards Article 8 ECHR and deportation that are specific to the UK are examined at paragraphs 8.101–115 below.

(v) The Secretary of State will inter alia be bound by section 55 Borders Citizenship and Immigration Act 2009 ('Duty regarding the welfare of children'), and in a case in which Article 8 ECHR or the principal obligation in Article 3 CRC is engaged will be bound, for the reasons set out in *ZH (Tanzania) v SSHD* [2011] UKSC 4, [2011] 2 AC 166, to treat the 'the best interests of the child' as 'a primary consideration' in relation to relevant actions. Even without the aid of that important decision, the Court of Appeal in *SS (India) v SSHD* [2010] EWCA Civ 388 found the decision below to be unsustainable in part through failure to give sufficient attention to the position of children.

(vi) Beyond the provisions of the ECHR, the CSR and the CRC already referred to, customary international law or unincorporated treaty obligations may inform the exercise of a statutory discretion, as identified in chapter 2 above.

(vii) One factor of obvious relevance in many cases is criminal offending, whether the appeal is a 'conducive to the public good' case under section 3(5)(a) IA 1971 or an exceptional case in which a recommendation has been made by a criminal court notwithstanding the creation of the UKBA 2007 regime for automatic deportation. This has been most extensively considered in the context of Article 8 ECHR, but where the statutory discretion is considered independently, it is difficult to see a logical basis for different treatment. In *OH (Serbia) v SSHD* [2008] EWCA Civ 694, [2009] INLR 109, Wilson LJ, with whom Pill and Maurice Kay LJJ agreed, considered the import of the earlier decision in *N (Kenya) v SSHD* [2004] EWCA Civ 1094, [2004] INLR 612, a case arising after a particularly abhorrent series of offences. In *OH (Serbia)*, Wilson LJ concluded at [15] that:

> From the above passages in *N (Kenya)* I collect the following propositions:
> (a) The risk of reoffending is one facet of the public interest but, in the case of very serious crimes, not the most important facet.
> (b) Another important facet is the need to deter foreign nationals from committing serious crimes by leading them to understand that, whatever the other circumstances, one consequence of them may well be deportation.
> (c) A further important facet is the role of a deportation order as an expression of society's revulsion at serious crimes and in building public confidence in the treatment of foreign citizens who have committed serious crimes.
> (d) Primary responsibility for the public interest, whose view of it is likely to be wider and better informed than that of a tribunal, resides in the respondent and accordingly a tribunal hearing an appeal against a decision to deport should not only consider for itself all the facets of the public interest but should weigh, as a linked but independent feature, the approach to them adopted by the respondent in the context of the facts of the case. Speaking for myself, I would not however describe the tribunal's duty in this regard as being higher than 'to weigh' this feature.

Accordingly, the past commission of a criminal offence: (i) will require consideration to three public interest matters in relation to any ensuing deportation: (a) the prevention of re-offending, (b) the deterrence of others from committing offences, and (c) the expression of society's revulsion at crime; and (ii) the view of the Secretary of State regarding the public interest is a matter which is weighed independently of the tribunal's consideration of an offence, but on appeal an appellate tribunal takes its own view, having carried out that weighing process. Although the original enlargement of those principles in *N (Kenya)* might have been thought to be limited to particularly appalling crimes, as in that case, in practice the principle has now come to be virtually universal in cases of contemplated deportation after offending—though a rational treatment of the principle requires it to be applied to the particular facts of each case, including the seriousness and reasons for the offending and the situation of the offender. The *N (Kenya)* approach generally continues to be cited as the correct approach to offending in deportation decisions rather than as a special approach in cases of the most serious offending. In *SE (Zimbabwe) v SSHD* [2014] EWCA Civ 256, it was summarised at [32] by Jackson LJ, with whom Elias and Beatson LJJ concurred, approving Counsel's submission, that 'the decision-maker must consider three separate aspects of the criminal offence. These are (i) the risk of re-offending, (ii) the need to deter others and (iii) the need to express society's revulsion at the criminality. I agree with that analysis'. The treatment of this requirement need not be formulaic: in *PK (Congo) v SSHD* [2013] EWCA Civ 1500, Longmore LJ observed at [24] that: 'It is unnecessary for tribunals formalistically to quote the judgment in *OH (Serbia)* and then apply it mechanistically in every case but they must at least engage meaningfully with the three-fold criteria of risk of re-offending, the need for deterrence and public revulsion in relation to serious criminal activity.' However, the applicable factors are policy-related and the Court of Appeal in *RU (Bangladesh) v SSHD* [2011] EWCA Civ 651 found that the Tribunal had erred in stating that it did 'not accept that his deportation would act in any meaningful way as a deterrent to others, as the appellant is an individual and there is no reason why any other prospective offender would have any knowledge whatsoever of his deportation', indicating exclusive focus upon the individual case to the detriment of the broader public interest considerations;

(viii) An important consideration in a criminal case will be the context to the offence disclosed by the sentencing remarks of the trial judge and other relevant material. Where a recommendation for deportation has been made or there was a reasoned decision to refrain from making a recommendation within the sphere of expertise of the trial court, this will also require consideration. But given the coming into force of the UKBA 2007 automatic deportation scheme from 2008 and the subsequent decision of the Court of Appeal Criminal Division in *R v Kluxen* [2010] EWCA (Crim) 1081, [2011] 1 WLR 218, the absence of a recommendation by a trial judge will in general carry relatively little weight, as Sedley LJ indicated in the judgment of the Court in *Gurung v SSHD* [2012] EWCA Civ 62 [23].

(ix) A useful account of the principles in a criminal case is set out in *Masih (deportation —public interest—basic principles) Pakistan* [2012] UKUT 46 (IAC). The

Tribunal in that decision sought to provide guidance for adjudication in such cases:

2. *It should not be necessary... for panels dealing with such cases to carry out the review of the authorities over six pages out of the panel's 18-page decision. What is needed, where as usual in a case of this kind there is no dispute about the requirements of the law, is to show that the basic principles have been understood, and applied to the individual facts of the case in hand.*

3. *In our view those basic principles, on the public interest side of the balancing exercise, are as follows; we have set out the authorities on which they are based in foot-notes, to make it clear that there is no need for further reference to them by panels:*
   a) In a case of automatic deportation, full account must be taken of the strong public interest in removing foreign citizens convicted of serious offences, which lies not only in the prevention of further offences on the part of the individual concerned, but in deterring others from committing them in the first place;
   b) Deportation of foreign criminals expresses society's condemnation of serious criminal activity and promotes public confidence in the treatment of foreign citizens who have committed them;
   c) The starting-point for assessing the facts of the offence of which an individual has been committed, and their effect on others, and on the public as a whole, must be the view taken by the sentencing judge;
   d) The appeal has to be dealt with on the basis of the situation at the date of the hearing;
   e) Full account should also be taken of any developments since sentence was passed, for example the result of any disciplinary adjudications in prison or detention, or any OASys or licence report...

In *Singh v SSHD* [2014] EWCA Civ 932 the Court of Appeal emphasised that the *Masih* standards were not limited to application in UKBA 2007 cases, and that where a criminal element arose on the facts they applied in IA 1971 deportations generally.

(x) Where a number of individuals have similar facts, then the Immigration Rules no longer provide express recognition of an interest in consistent and fair treatment as between cases, as formerly set out in paragraph 364. But it is difficult to see that such considerations have ceased to be relevant, so as to bar any submission, for instance, that a minor participant in a joint enterprise should not face deportation where a more significant participant, without other distinction, does not face deportation: *R v SSHD ex p Yasin* [1995] Imm AR 118.

(xi) In considering whether a deportation decision should be taken, the Secretary of State has since 1 October 2012 been able to take into account any past conviction or caution, regardless of the formerly applicable provisions of the Rehabilitation of Offenders Act (ROA) 1974 by reason of section 56A UKBA 2007 inserted by section 140 LASPO 2012. But the divorce between the ROA 1974 regime and the Secretary of State's discretionary decision making does not create relevance or weight where this does not otherwise exist, and in some respects creates new difficulties for the Secretary of State, who has to deal with material reasonably and fairly, and without other public law error. For example, it would be surprising if he or she were permitted to rely upon very old or *de minimis* material.

8.82 Paragraph 378 Immigration Rules HC 395 provides that once the decision to make a deportation order has been taken, the order may not be made whilst appeal might be entered or is pending.

Article 8 ECHR in Section 5(1) IA 1971 Deportation Cases

Since the coming into force of the HRA 1998, and particularly in recent years, there has been considerable focus, in the jurisprudence and in public debate surrounding immigration, deportation, and human rights, upon Article 8 ECHR, source of the right to respect for private and family life and home, and of a qualified protection from interference with the exercise of that right. The concentration upon this area has been so acute that it risks hiding the fact, which should be self-evident, that other important considerations may arise in deportation cases. Virtually the only matters now dealt with expressly in the Immigration Rules HC 395 and the policy of the Secretary of State are Article 8 ECHR and CSR. In the case of the former there has been concerted political and legislative pressure upon the independence of judgment by the judicial branch.

8.83

Given this context it is important to recognise that, though article 8 ECHR by its incorporation under HRA 1998 represents the most immediate embodiment of relevant principles in domestic law, equivalent rights exist in almost all developed countries and in many others. Such rights represent an important manifestation of the human rights regimes constructed after the Second World War in the wake of the abuses against humanity conducted by Nazi, Fascist, and other regimes. As seen in chapter 3, UDHR provides inter alia by Article 12 that 'No one shall be subjected to arbitrary interference with his privacy, family, home or correspondence,' and by Article 16(3) that 'The family is the natural and fundamental group unit of society and is entitled to protection by society and the State', and ICCPR set out relevant protections at Articles 17 and 23. Provision for the protection or promotion of family life is made in every regional human rights convention: for example by the American Convention on Human Rights 1969, at Articles 11 and 17, and the African Charter on Human and Peoples' Rights 1981, Article 18. Against this background, Article 7 of the Charter of Fundamental Rights of the European Union ('Everyone has the right to respect for his or her private and family life, home and communications.') reinforces a well-established pattern of respect for relevant rights. Writing extra-judicially before HRA 1998 made Article 8 ECHR directly applicable in the United Kingdom, Sir John Laws described articles 8 ECHR as being amongst '…rights [which] have become an axiom, or series of axioms, about whose desirability there can be no serious argument… given the nature of the ideals enshrined in the [ECHR]… to deny it is by necessary implication to assert a totalitarian position in which individuals are subservient to the ends of the state.'[10]

8.84

This section addresses Article 8 ECHR as applicable in relation to deportation. An account of the content of Article 8 ECHR as established primarily by decisions of the Strasbourg Court has been set out in chapter 5 above. This chapter seeks to give adequate attention to other considerations which may have been neglected, but an account of the treatment of Article 8 ECHR in deportation decisions in the UK forms a necessary part of any account of the law relating to deportation from the UK.

8.85

Deportation is not undertaken to satisfy international obligations of the UK to other states by extradition of criminals or suspected criminals, and the Supreme Court has indicated that deportation cannot be equated with extradition in the context of Article 8 ECHR. A starting point, therefore, is the distinction to be drawn as to application of

8.86

---

[10] Laws, Sir John, 'Is the High Court the guardian of fundamental constitutional rights?' [1993] *Public Law* 59–79, 59.

Article 8 ECHR between deportation and extradition cases. In *Norris v Government of the United States of America (No 2)* [2010] UKSC 9, [2010] 2 AC 487, Lord Phillips observed at [51], in a speech with which all other members of the Court agreed, that it was 'certainly not right to equate extradition with expulsion or deportation in this context'. This was reiterated in two cases heard together by the Supreme Court: in *BH and another v The Lord Advocate and another (Scotland)* [2012] UKSC 24 and *HH v Deputy Prosecutor of the Italian Republic, Genoa* [2012] UKSC 25, [2013] 1 AC 338. The distinction between deportation and extradition reflects the differing public interests invoked in each case, though a common feature as regards Article 8 ECHR is the need for a weighing of the applicable public interest against the relevant Article 8 ECHR interests. As Lord Hope put it in the *BH* case at [49]:

> I cannot agree therefore with the proposition that the approach adopted to article 8 rights in extradition cases must be radically different from that adopted in deportation or expulsion cases. The public interest in giving effect to a request for extradition is a constant factor in cases of that kind. Great weight will always have to be given to it, and the more serious the offence the greater will be that weight. The public interest in immigration control lacks the treaty base which is at the heart of the extradition process. But, the question, so far as the article 8 right is concerned, is the same in both cases. How is one to balance two powerful and competing interests?

8.87 In relation to deportation, the Strasbourg Court has in a number of important decisions, including but not limited to *Boultif v Switzerland* no 54273/00 [2001] ECHR 497, (2001) 33 EHRR 50; *Üner v The Netherlands* no 46410/99 [2006] ECHR 873, (2007) 45 EHRR 14; and *Maslov v Austria* [GC] no 1638/03 [2008] ECHR 546, [2009] INLR 47, established a list of key factors to be considered in any assessment concerning the proportionality of a deportation or other exclusion decision otherwise breaching Article 8 ECHR. The body of standards that this has produced is outlined in chapter 5 above. What is set out here is a separate supplementary account of the means by which those standards are applied in the UK in the context of deportation.

8.88 In *R (Razgar) v SSHD* [2004] UKHL 27, [2004] 2 AC 368, Lord Bingham at [17] identified five questions to be addressed in Article 8 ECHR cases. Although these are identified as questions for 'the reviewing court', they also identify the questions which on a primary decision the Secretary of State must confront:

> In a case where removal is resisted in reliance on article 8 [the questions which would have to be answered by an adjudicator] are likely to be:
> (1) Will the proposed removal be an interference by a public authority with the exercise of the applicant's right to respect for his private or (as the case may be) family life?
> (2) If so, will such interference have consequences of such gravity as potentially to engage the operation of article 8?
> (3) If so, is such interference in accordance with the law?
> (4) If so, is such interference necessary in a democratic society in the interests of national security, public safety or the economic well-being of the country, for the prevention of disorder or crime, for the protection of health or morals, or for the protection of the rights and freedoms of others?
> (5) If so, is such interference proportionate to the legitimate public end sought to be achieved?

8.89 As to the second question, as to whether Article 8 ECHR is engaged, in *AG (Eritrea) v SSHD* [2007] EWCA Civ 801, [2008] 2 All ER 28 at [28], Sedley LJ, delivering the judgment of the court (the other members of the panel being Maurice Kay and Lawrence Collins LJJ), confirmed as regards the second question raised by Lord Bingham in *Razgar* that:

> 28. It follows, in our judgment, that while an interference with private or family life must be real if it is to engage art. 8(1), the threshold of engagement (the 'minimum level') is not a specially high one. Once the article is engaged, the focus moves, as Lord Bingham's remaining questions indicate, to the process of justification under art. 8(2). It is this which, in all cases which engage article 8(1), will determine whether there has been a breach of the article.

In *Huang v SSHD; Kashmiri v SSHD* [2007] UKHL 11, [2007] 2 AC 167, the House of Lords reviewed the approach required of an immigration appellate body in relation to the fifth of Lord Bingham's questions in *Razgar*, that of proportionality. Lord Bingham delivering the judgment of the Committee endorsed, at [19], the statement in *Razgar* that proportionality 'must always involve the striking of a fair balance between the rights of the individual and the interests of the community which is inherent in the whole of the Convention'. At [20] Lord Bingham concluded as regards proportionality, that: **8.90**

> 20. In an article 8 case where this question is reached, the ultimate question for the appellate immigration authority is whether the refusal of leave to enter or remain, in circumstances where the life of the family cannot reasonably be expected to be enjoyed elsewhere, taking full account of all considerations weighing in favour of the refusal, prejudices the family life of the applicant in a manner sufficiently serious to amount to a breach of the fundamental right protected by article 8. If the answer to this question is affirmative, the refusal is unlawful and the authority must so decide. It is not necessary that the appellate immigration authority, directing itself along the lines indicated in this opinion, need ask in addition whether the case meets a test of exceptionality. The suggestion that it should is based on an observation of Lord Bingham in *Razgar* above, [20]. He was there expressing an expectation, shared with the Immigration Appeal Tribunal, that the number of claimants not covered by the Rules and supplementary directions but entitled to succeed under article 8 would be a very small minority. That is still his expectation. But he was not purporting to lay down a legal test.

In *Beoku-Betts v SSHD* [2008] UKHL 39, [2009] 1 AC 115, Lord Brown, with whom the other members of their Lordships' House agreed, concluded that in a deportation or removal case in which relevant family life arose, the correct approach was to take account of the impact of the proposed removal upon all those sharing that family life. **8.91**

In another decision, *Chikwamba v SSHD* [2008] UKHL 40, [2008] 1 WLR 1420, Lord Brown, delivering the primary speech in the House, with which the other members of the House concurred, recorded at [4] that: 'Rather it seems to me that only comparatively rarely, certainly in family cases involving children, should an article 8 appeal be dismissed on the basis that it would be proportionate and more appropriate for the appellant to apply for leave from abroad.' He rejected the proposition that persons who could expect to be granted entry clearance and leave to enter should be removed from the UK purely to penalise 'queue-jumping', and the House found the policy of routinely doing so to be disproportionate. This principle was recently applied in *R (otao Zhang) v SSHD* [2013] EWHC 891 (Admin), [2014] 2 All ER 560 in relation to prohibition to switching. In *Treebhowan (Mauritius) v SSHD; Hayat (Pakistan) v SSHD* [2012] EWCA Civ 1054 the Court of Appeal adopted and applied the same approach as formulated by Sullivan LJ in *MA (Pakistan) v SSHD* [2009] EWCA Civ 953, by which, where Article 8 ECHR was engaged, it would be a disproportionate interference with family or private life to enforce such a policy unless there was 'a sensible reason for doing so.' The Court **8.92** of Appeal accepted that there was such a reason where there had been a temporary purpose to entry. Elias LJ at [30] set out an analysis of the effect of the cases, with which Sir David Keene and Maurice Kay LJ concurred:

> 30. In my judgment, the effect of these decisions can be summarised as follows:
> a) Where an applicant who does not have lawful entry clearance pursues an Article 8 claim, a dismissal of the claim on the procedural ground that the policy requires that the applicant should have made the application from his home state may (but not necessarily will) constitute a disruption of family or private life sufficient to engage Article 8, particularly where children are adversely affected.
> b) Where Article 8 is engaged, it will be a disproportionate interference with family or private life to enforce such a policy unless, to use the language of Sullivan LJ, there is a sensible reason for doing so.
> c) Whether it is sensible to enforce that policy will necessarily be fact sensitive; Lord Brown identified certain potentially relevant factors in *Chikwamba*. They will include the prospective length and degree of disruption of family life and whether other members of the family are settled in the UK.
> d) Where Article 8 is engaged and there is no sensible reason for enforcing the policy, the decision maker should determine the Article 8 claim on its substantive merits, having regard to all material factors, notwithstanding that the applicant has no lawful entry clearance.
> e) It will be a very rare case where it is appropriate for the Court of Appeal, having concluded that a lower tribunal has disproportionately interfered with Article 8 rights in enforcing the policy, to make the substantive Article 8 decision for itself. *Chikwamba* was such an exceptional case. Logically the court would have to be satisfied that there is only one proper answer to the Article 8 question before substituting its own finding on this factual question.
> f) Nothing in *Chikwamba* was intended to alter the way the courts should approach substantive Article 8 issues as laid down in such well known cases as *Razgar* and *Huang*.
> g) Although the cases do not say this in terms, in my judgment if the Secretary of State has no sensible reason for requiring the application to be made from the home state, the fact that he has failed to do so should not thereafter carry any weight in the substantive Article 8 balancing exercise.

8.93 Later, in *EB (Kosovo)* [2008] UKHL 41, [2009] 1 AC 1159, Lord Bingham at [12] observed that:

> [T]he appellate immigration authority must make its own judgment and that judgment will be strongly influenced by the particular facts and circumstances of the particular case. The authority will, of course, take note of factors which have, or have not, weighed with the Strasbourg court. It will, for example, recognise that it will rarely be proportionate to uphold an order for removal of a spouse if there is a close and genuine bond with the other spouse and that spouse cannot reasonably be expected to follow the removed spouse to the country of removal, or if the effect of the order is to sever a genuine and subsisting relationship between parent and child. But cases will not ordinarily raise such stark choices, and there is in general no alternative to making a careful and informed evaluation of the facts of the particular case. The search for a hard-edged or bright-line rule to be applied to the generality of cases is incompatible with the difficult evaluative exercise which article 8 requires.

8.94 It is clear that the interests of children play an important role in Article 8 ECHR, which in *ZH (Tanzania) v SSHD* [2011] UKSC 4, [2011] 2 AC 166 was held to invoke other international human rights standards including the 'best interests' protection in Article 3 CRC. The Supreme Court has further elaborated and applied those standards in the context of extradition in *BH and another v The Lord Advocate and another (Scotland)* [2012] UKSC

24; and *HH v Deputy Prosecutor of the Italian Republic, Genoa* [2012] UKSC 25, [2013] 1 AC 338 respectively. Whilst these are distinguishable as to the application of article 8 ECHR, they provide valuable illustration as to the 'best interests' approach.

As per the observation of Lord Bingham in the *EB (Kosovo)* case at [12], rejecting 'The search for a hard-edged or bright-line rule to be applied to the generality of cases', individual cases are highly fact-specific. Religious and community work of positive value is, however, something that the Court of Appeal has found directly relevant to the Article 8 ECHR proportionality assessment: in *UE (Nigeria) and others v SSHD* [2010] EWCA Civ 975, [2011] 2 All ER 352, per Sir David Keene at [18]:

8.95

> [A] public interest in the retention in this country of someone who is of considerable value to the community can properly be seen as relevant to the exercise of immigration control. It goes to the weight to be attached to that side of the scales in the proportionality exercise. The weight attached to the public interest in removal of the person in question is not some fixed immutable amount. It may vary from case to case, and where someone is of great value to the community in this country, there exists a factor which reduces the importance of maintaining firm immigration control in his individual case. The weight to be given to that aim is correspondingly less.

Richards LJ put it differently at [39]–[41], but it is clear that he too considered that contribution to the community could be a relevant and proper consideration in the judicial assessment of proportionality. Ward LJ indicated at [46] that:

> I too would allow the appeal and remit the matter back for further consideration. Insofar as a difference of emphasis can be detected in the judgments of my Lords, their dicta seem to me with respect to be obiter and I prefer therefore to say no more about it.

Various measures were incorporated into the Immigration Rules HC 395 as from 9 July 2012 by means of a Statement of Changes in Immigration Rules HC 194 setting how the Secretary of State intended to apply Article 8 ECHR obligations within the Immigration Rules. Despite the fact that Article 8 ECHR is an international standard and is effectively incorporated by statute into domestic law, unfortunate suggestions were made that, in the light of the amended Rules: 'The Secretary of State would expect the Court to defer to the view endorsed by Parliament on how, broadly, public policy considerations are weighed against individual family and private life rights, when assessing Article 8 in any individual case. That is, save in a narrow group of cases where it is found that the consequences of the immigration decision are exceptional.'[11] However, the position of the Secretary of State has modified over time. In *R (Nagre) v SSHD* [2013] EWHC 720 (Admin), Sales J rejected a challenge to the lawfulness of the new provisions, noting the concession for the Secretary of State by her Counsel that the new provisions did not reconstitute a test of exceptionality and were not exhaustive of all matters which might in a particular case require consideration in relation to Article 8 ECHR:

8.96

> 32. Ms Giovannetti made clear for the Secretary of State that in these proceedings it is not contended that the effect of the new rules is to restore an exceptional circumstances test equivalent to that rejected by the House of Lords in [*Huang v SSHD; Kashmiri v SSHD* [2007] UKHL 11; [2007] 2 AC 167] (by reference to the old Immigration Rules) and by the Upper Tribunal in [*Izuazu (Article 8—New Rules) Nigeria* [2013] UKUT 45

---

[11] The Secretary of State's submission recorded in *Izuazu (Article 8—New Rules) Nigeria* [2013] UKUT 45 (IAC), Imm AR 13 [49].

Part C – Deportation, Removal and Exclusion

(IAC), Imm AR 13] (by reference to the new rules), by contrast with the position argued unsuccessfully by the Secretary of State in *Izuazu*—see [28], [47]–[50] and [58]. Rather, the Secretary of State accepts that the consideration of possible Article 8 claims arising outside the new rules involves broader consideration of cases by reference to the general factors and approach set out in the new guidance on her residual discretion set out above.

33. The Secretary of State does not contend that the new rules completely cover every conceivable case in which a foreign national may have a good claim for leave to remain under Article 8 … it is possible to envisage cases where they would not …

34. In cases where consideration of the new rules does not fully dispose of a claim based on Article 8, the Secretary of State will be obliged to consider granting leave to remain outside the Rules. If she does not, where there is an appeal the First-Tier Tribunal will be obliged to consider allowing the appeal, and where there is no appeal, judicial review will lie.

35. The important points for present purposes are that there is full coverage of an individual's rights under Article 8 in all cases by a combination of the new rules and (so far as may be necessary) under the Secretary of State's residual discretion to grant leave to remain outside the Rules and that, consequent upon this feature of the overall legal framework, there is no legal requirement that the new rules themselves provide for leave to remain to be granted under the Rules in *every* case where Article 8 gives rise to a good claim for an individual to be allowed to remain. This had always been the position in relation to the operation of the regime of immigration control prior to the introduction of the new rules, and the introduction of the new rules has not changed these basic features of the regime.

8.97 *R (Nagre)* was not a deportation case. The effect of changes to the Immigration Rules under HC 194 as regards deportation was considered by the Court of Appeal in *MF (Nigeria) v SSHD* [2013] EWCA Civ 1192, [2014] 1 WLR 544. Then as now, the relevant standards provided under the altered Immigration Rules are those set out in paragraphs 398–99A HC 395. These are examined below.

8.98 The key provisions relating to Article 8 ECHR and deportation in the altered Immigration Rules read, at the date of the decision in *MF (Nigeria)*, as follows:

398. Where a person claims that their deportation would be contrary to the UK's obligations under Article 8 of the Human Rights Convention, and
    (a) the deportation of the person from the UK is conducive to the public good because they have been convicted of an offence for which they have been sentenced to a period of imprisonment of at least 4 years;
    (b) the deportation of the person from the UK is conducive to the public good because they have been convicted of an offence for which they have been sentenced to a period of imprisonment of less than 4 years but at least 12 months; or
    (c) the deportation of the person from the UK is conducive to the public good because, in the view of the Secretary of State, their offending has caused serious harm or they are a persistent offender who shows a particular disregard for the law,
the Secretary of State in assessing that claim will consider whether paragraph 399 or 399A applies and, if it does not, it will only be in exceptional circumstances that the public interest in deportation will be outweighed by other factors.

399. This paragraph applies where paragraph 398(b) or (c) applies if—
    (a) the person has a genuine and subsisting parental relationship with a child under the age of 18 years who is in the UK, and
        (i) the child is a British Citizen; or
        (ii) the child has lived in the UK continuously for at least the 7 years immediately preceding the date of the immigration decision; and in either case

(a) it would not be reasonable to expect the child to leave the UK; and
(b) there is no other family member who is able to care for the child in the UK; or

(b) the person has a genuine and subsisting relationship with a partner who is in the UK and is a British Citizen, settled in the UK, or in the UK with refugee leave or humanitarian protection, and
(i) the person has lived in the UK with valid leave continuously for at least the 15 years immediately preceding the date of the immigration decision (discounting any period of imprisonment); and
(ii) there are insurmountable obstacles to family life with that partner continuing outside the UK.

399A. This paragraph applies where paragraph 398(b) or (c) applies if—
(a) the person has lived continuously in the UK for at least 20 years immediately preceding the date of the immigration decision (discounting any period of imprisonment) and he has no ties (including social, cultural or family) with the country to which he would have to go if required to leave the UK; or
(b) the person is aged under 25 years, he has spent at least half of his life living continuously in the UK immediately preceding the date of the immigration decision (discounting any period of imprisonment) and he has no ties (including social, cultural or family) with the country to which he would have to go if required to leave the UK.

These standards did not cover all deportation cases, and after subsequent amendment there remains the possibility of deportation decisions being taken either without these Rules having application, because none of the conditions precedent in the Rules is met, or alternatively, the Rules not being decisive because of the need to look to Article 8 ECHR outwith the Rules. In either case any decision would require to be based upon Article 8 ECHR principles as well established by the ECtHR and domestic jurisprudence. **8.99**

The scope of the provisions is defined in the Immigration Rules themselves by the effective identification of two groups, namely: **8.100**

(i) those whose deportation is conducive to the public good because they have been convicted of an offence and received a custodial sentence of at least 12 months (within this group is a subgroup of those whose sentence is four years or more) (paragraph 398(a)–(b));
(ii) those whose deportation of the person from the UK 'is conducive to the public good because, in the view of the Secretary of State, their offending has caused serious harm or they are a persistent offender who shows particular disregard for the law' (paragraph 398(c)).

The first group (defined by conviction and custodial sentence of 'at least 12 months') would coincide with those who come within the UKBA 2007 'automatic deportation' scheme by virtue of section 32(1) in conjunction with 'condition 1' (sentenced to imprisonment of 12 months or more) in section 32(2) UKBA 2007, but excludes those others brought within the scheme under 'condition 2' (offence specified by order and sentenced to imprisonment of any length), save where the sentence is 12 months or more. The second group (defined by offending which has caused serious harm or persistent offending showing particular disregard for the law) is uniquely defined: it is not coextensive with the larger group of those liable to deportation under section 3(1)(a) IA 1971, but forms a subset thereof. A public law consequence of this is that the lawfulness of application of the paragraph 398 strictures, if dependent upon paragraph 398(c), might be challenged on the basis that the Secretary of State's view that an individual's 'offending has caused serious harm' or that he or she is 'a persistent offender who shows particular disregard for the law' is unsustainable.

8.101 There has now been extensive reflection and decision both judicially and on the part of the Secretary of State, which can be traced through a substantial number of decisions (most notably *MF (Article 8—New Rules) Nigeria* [2012] UKUT 393 (IAC); *Izuazu (Article 8—New Rules) Nigeria* [2013] UKUT 45 (IAC), Imm AR 13; *Ogundimu (Article 8—New Rules) Nigeria* [2013] UKUT 60 (IAC); *R (Nagre) v SSHD* [2013] EWHC 720 (Admin); *Green (Article 8—New Rules) Jamaica* [2013] UKUT 254 (IAC); and *MF (Nigeria) v SSHD* [2013] EWCA Civ 1192, [2014] 1 WLR 544). In effect, this appears to have established that the Secretary of State's approach to Article 8 ECHR expressed in the Immigration Rules supplants the established approach, but that where the Immigration Rules do not point to a grant of leave, the tribunal must then consider the established approach to Article 8 ECHR. The cases also show senior courts as seeking interpretations of the Rules, which, wherever possible, admit access to scrutiny on the established basis within the Rules themselves, whilst preserving recourse to established principles where these are not fully expressed.

8.102 Where an individual is not caught by any of the paragraph 398 HC 395 criteria, consideration of Article 8 ECHR then generally moves outwith the Rules. In *Nagre* Sales J at [30] accepted that this would be necessary unless the Rules provided exhaustively for the consideration of relevant Article 8 ECHR issues:

> 30. I agree with the guidance given by the Upper Tribunal in [*Izuazu (Article 8—new rules) Nigeria* [2013] UKUT 45 (IAC)] at paras [40]-[43], as follows:
>
> "40. We accordingly further endorse the Upper Tribunal's observation in [*MF (Article 8 – new rules) Nigeria* [2012] UKUT 00393 (IAC)] that judges called on to make decisions about the application of Article 8 in cases to which the new rules apply, should proceed by first considering whether a claimant is able to benefit under the applicable provisions of the Immigration Rules designed to address Article 8 claims. If he or she does, there will be no need to go on to consider Article 8 generally. The appeal can be allowed because the decision is not in accordance with the rules.
>
> 41. Where the claimant does not meet the requirements of the rules it will be necessary for the judge to go on to make an assessment of Article 8 applying the criteria established by law.
>
> 42. When considering whether the immigration decision is a justified interference with the right to family and/or private life, the provisions of the rules or other relevant statement of policy may again re-enter the debate but this time as part of the proportionality evaluation. Here the judge will be asking whether the interference was a proportionate means of achieving the legitimate aim in question and a fair balance as to the competing interests.
>
> 43. The weight to be attached to any reason for rejection of the human rights claim indicated by particular provisions of the rules will depend both on the particular facts found by the judge in the case in hand and the extent that the rules themselves reflect criteria approved in the previous case law of the Human Rights Court at Strasbourg and the higher courts in the United Kingdom."
>
> The only slight modification I would make, for the purposes of clarity, is to say that if, after the process of applying the new rules and finding that the claim for leave to remain under them fails, the relevant official or tribunal judge considers it is clear that the consideration under the Rules has fully addressed any family life or private life issues arising under Article 8, it would be sufficient

Deportation

simply to say that; they would not have to go on, in addition, to consider the case separately from the Rules. If there is no arguable case that there may be good grounds for granting leave to remain outside the Rules by reference to Article 8, there would be no point in introducing full separate consideration of Article 8 again after having reached a decision on application of the Rules.

The key decision in the context of deportation is that of the Court of Appeal in *MF (Nigeria) v SSHD* [2013] EWCA Civ 1192, [2014] 1 WLR 544, in which the Master of the Rolls' Court considered aspects of the new scheme for Article 8 ECHR under the Immigration Rules as applicable in deportation cases. Lord Dyson MR, giving the judgment of the Court, noted at [39] that Counsel for the Secretary of State both disclaimed restoration of an 'exceptionality' test and conceded that the new Rules 'should be interpreted consistently with' the absence of an exceptionality test. Emphasising the explicit contemplation at paragraph 398 Immigration Rules of a weighing process, he concluded at [43] that the word 'exceptional' indicated the general need for compelling reasons outweighing the public interest in deportation, which was a factor to be taken into account in that process. Accordingly: **8.103**

> 44. We would, therefore, hold that the new rules are a complete code and that the exceptional circumstances to be considered in the balancing exercise involve the application of a proportionality test as required by the Strasbourg jurisprudence. We accordingly respectfully do not agree with the UT that the decision-maker is not 'mandated or directed' to take all the relevant article 8 criteria into account ([38]).
> 45. Even if we were wrong about that, it would be necessary to apply a proportionality test outside the new rules as was done by the UT. Either way, the result should be the same. In these circumstances, it is a sterile question whether this is required by the new rules or it is a requirement of the general law. What matters is that it is required to be carried out if paragraphs 399 or 399A do not apply.

As to 'insurmountable obstacles', a phrase employed in the Immigration Rules in paragraph 339(b) (citing a need for 'insurmountable obstacles to family life with that partner continuing outside the UK), the Court observed at [49] that:

> 49. In view of the concession made before the UT, the question of the meaning of 'insurmountable obstacles' does not arise. We did, however, hear argument on the point. We would observe that, if 'insurmountable' obstacles are literally obstacles which it is *impossible* to surmount, their scope is very limited indeed. We shall confine ourselves to saying that we incline to the view that, for the reasons stated in detail by the UT in *Izuazu* at paragraphs 53 to 59, such a stringent approach would be contrary to article 8.

Lord Dyson in *MF (Nigeria)* attached substantial importance to the words 'exceptional circumstances', which are set within the phrase 'it will only be in exceptional circumstances that the public interest in deportation will be outweighed by other factors' at the close of para 398 Immigration Rules HC 395, as it then stood. At [16] he noted, referring to the guidance of the Secretray of State concerning the application of para 398, that: **8.104**

> 16. On the other hand, the document issued in March 2013 defines exceptional circumstances and states that, in determining whether a case is exceptional, all relevant factors in favour of and against deportation are to be considered under the new rules. On this approach, it is difficult to see what scope there is for any consideration outside the new rules: ie they provide a complete code.

At [44] he concluded that the breadth to be found at that point in the Rules meant that they could in relation to deportation be treated as a complete code:

> We would, therefore, hold that the new rules are a complete code and that the exceptional circumstances to be considered in the balancing exercise involve the application of a proportionality test as

required by the Strasbourg jurisprudence. We accordingly respectfully do not agree with the UT that the decision-maker is not 'mandated or directed' to take all the relevant article 8 criteria into account…

The applicable principles, as they apply in non-deportation cases, have since been further examined in a number of important decisions including those of the Court of Appeal in *Haleemudeen v SSHD* [2014] EWCA Civ 558 and *R (MM & Ors) v SSHD* (Rev 1) [2014] EWCA Civ 985 and the decision of Michael Fordham QC sitting as a High Court Deputy Judge in *R (Ganesabalan) v SSHD* [2014] EWHC 2712 (Admin).

The Effect of the New Part 5A NIAA 2002

8.105 Section 19 IA 2014 added to NIAA 2002 a number of provisions relating to the interpretation of article 8 ECHR:

PART 5A

ARTICLE 8 OF THE ECHR: PUBLIC INTEREST CONSIDERATIONS

117A Application of this Part
(1) This Part applies where a court or tribunal is required to determine whether a decision made under the Immigration Acts—
  (a) breaches a person's right to respect for private and family life under Article 8, and
  (b) as a result would be unlawful under section 6 of the Human Rights Act 1998.
(2) In considering the public interest question, the court or tribunal must (in particular) have regard—
  (a) in all cases, to the considerations listed in section 117B, and
  (b) in cases concerning the deportation of foreign criminals, to the considerations listed in section 117C.
(3) In subsection (2), 'the public interest question' means the question of whether an interference with a person's right to respect for private and family life is justified under Article 8(2).
17B Article 8: public interest considerations applicable in all cases
(1) The maintenance of effective immigration controls is in the public interest.
(2) It is in the public interest, and in particular in the interests of the economic well-being of the United Kingdom, that persons who seek to enter or remain in the United Kingdom are able to speak English, because persons who can speak English—
  (a) are less of a burden on taxpayers, and
  (b) are better able to integrate into society.
(3) It is in the public interest, and in particular in the interests of the economic well-being of the United Kingdom, that persons who seek to enter or remain in the United Kingdom are financially independent, because such persons—
  (a) are not a burden on taxpayers, and
  (b) are better able to integrate into society.
(4) Little weight should be given to—
  (a) a private life, or
  (b) a relationship formed with a qualifying partner, that is established by a person at a time when the person is in the United Kingdom unlawfully.
(5) Little weight should be given to a private life established by a person at a time when the person's immigration status is precarious.
(6) In the case of a person who is not liable to deportation, the public interest does not require the person's removal where—
  (a) the person has a genuine and subsisting parental relationship with a qualifying child, and
  (b) it would not be reasonable to expect the child to leave the United Kingdom.

17C Article 8: additional considerations in cases involving foreign criminals
(1) The deportation of foreign criminals is in the public interest.
(2) The more serious the offence committed by a foreign criminal, the greater is the public interest in deportation of the criminal.
(3) In the case of a foreign criminal ('C') who has not been sentenced to a period of imprisonment of four years or more, the public interest requires C's deportation unless Exception 1 or Exception 2 applies.
(4) Exception 1 applies where—
　(a) C has been lawfully resident in the United Kingdom for most of C's life,
　(b) C is socially and culturally integrated in the United Kingdom, and
　(c) there would be very significant obstacles to C's integration into the country to which C is proposed to be deported.
(5) Exception 2 applies where C has a genuine and subsisting relationship with a qualifying partner, or a genuine and subsisting parental relationship with a qualifying child, and the effect of C's deportation on the partner or child would be unduly harsh.
(6) In the case of a foreign criminal who has been sentenced to a period of imprisonment of at least four years, the public interest requires deportation unless there are very compelling circumstances, over and above those described in Exceptions 1 and 2.
(7) The considerations in subsections (1) to (6) are to be taken into account where a court or tribunal is considering a decision to deport a foreign criminal only to the extent that the reason for the decision was the offence or offences for which the criminal has been convicted.

This provision entered into force on 28 July 2014 by the Immigration Act 2014 (Commencement No 1, Transitory and Saving Provisions) Order 2014, [3].

8.106 The provision is in essence an extension of the endeavour pursued through changes to the Immigration Rules by HC 194 in July 2012. Sections 117B and 117C NIAA 2002 set out highly proscriptive, if often apparently trite, standards: for instance, 'The maintenance of effective immigration controls is in the public interest' (section 117B(1) NIAA 2002) and 'the deportation of foreign criminals is in the public interest' (section 117C(1) NIAA 2002).

8.107 Though some of the standards identified in the new Part 5A NIAA 2002 positively identify matters of assistance to claimants in many cases, such as ability in English language (although the exclusion of Welsh and Scots Gaelic is striking in this context, and raises legal as well as political questions), overall, the new Part 5A NIAA 2002 might seem designed to force courts and tribunals to attach greater weight to factors that the Secretary of State will routinely rely upon when defending deportation decisions. This would represent in effect a continuation of the strategy initially stated to be attached to the July 2012 amendments to the Immigration Rules HC 395. It seems likely that senior courts will interpret this provision in a manner which is consistent with the continued application of Article 8 ECHR through HRA 1998, which as noted previously has been identified by Laws LJ, with subsequent endorsement in the Supreme Court, as a 'constitutional statute'. In general, interpreted in such a way, the language might be read as general abjuration not preventing independent consideration as to whether, on the facts of any given case, weight should be attached to the factors identified therein. However, in general, the language requires consideration without requiring that, on the facts of any given case, weight be attached to the factors identified therein. An obvious if also unfortunate precursor is section 8 Asylum and Immigration (Treatment of Claimants etc) Act 2004, which 'in determining whether to believe a statement made by or on behalf of a person who makes an asylum claim or a human rights claim, a deciding authority [including a tribunal] shall take account, as damaging the claimant's credibility, of any behaviour [listed below]'. In *JT (Cameroon) v SSHD* [2008] EWCA Civ 878, [2009] 1 WLR 1411, the Court of Appeal in respect of that provision noted the potential for offence against the 'constitutional principle' of judicial independence. Pill LJ, with whom Laws and Carnwath LJJ concurred, was not prepared to 'read the word "shall" as meaning "may"', but found that 'the section 8 factors shall be taken into account ... but the section does not dictate that relevant damage to credibility inevitably results'. Laws LJ, with whom Carnwath LJ agreed, indicated that he would incline to read the word 'potentially' into the words of the section before the word 'damaging'. Insofar as the language of Part 5A only requires judicial notice to be taken of trite factors without interference in the judicial task of weighing relevant interests, its effect is unobjectionable. If and where the language may imply something further, it appears open to reading in a way which protects the critical value of judicial independence. The gradual alteration of the position of the Secretary of State since the *Izuazu* proceedings, and the approach taken to the Immigration Rules by superior courts in *Nagre* and *MF (Nigeria)*, tend to support the viability of the view that the new Part 5A NIAA 2002 is likely in practice to be interpreted consistently with the protection of judicial independence in deportation appeals.

The Effect of Further Amendment to the Rules

8.108   Further changes to the Rules, applicable from 28 July 2014, have since the decision in *MF (Nigeria)* been made by means of a new Statement of Changes in Immigration Rules HC 532 published on 10 July 2014. Changes which have come into effect are shown in the quotation from the Rules at paragraph 8.34 above. A change of particular noteworthiness is the following:

> 22. In paragraph 398, for 'it will only be in exceptional circumstances that the public interest in deportation will be outweighed by other factors' substitute 'the public interest in deportation will only be outweighed by other factors where there are very compelling circumstances over and above those described in paragraphs 399 and 399A'.

There is as yet no judicial interpretation of the phrase 'over and above those described in [the exceptions]', which mirrors language at new section 117C(6) NIAA 2002. The new formula might be interpreted as simply emphasising the trite point that where a sentence is lengthy, reflecting a more significant incident or pattern of offending, the interest protected by Article 8 ECHR must be of greater weight if the public interest is to be offset. Equally, if treated as creating an elevation of the requirements in the Rules beyond that supported by known Article 8 ECHR principles, it may end the continuing relevance of the conclusion in *MF (Nigeria)* that the Rules on the point of deportation and Article 8 ECHR represented 'a complete code', requiring acknowledgement of a need to look at Article 8 ECHR outwith the Rules in some cases.

E6. Taking a Decision under the Section 32 UKBA 2007 Duty

The Effect of the Application of the UKBA 2007 Scheme on the Secretary of State

8.109   Where section 32(1)–(3) UKBA 2007 applies, the Secretary of State by section 32(5) UKBA 2007 must make a deportation order, unless an exception identified in section

33(1) UKBA 2007 applies. Where the duty falls away because one of the section 33 UKBA 2007 exceptions arises, consideration may be given to the exercise of the section 5(1) IA 1971 discretionary power, applying the principles just examined, so long as a lawful basis for liability to deportation remains.

Section 34(1)–(2) UKBA 2007 allows the Secretary of State some control over the timing of a deportation order being made, and in particular restrains the making of an order until such time as any criminal appeal process is resolved. Paragraph 378 Immigration Rules HC 395 provides that once the decision to make a deportation order has been taken, the order may not be made whilst appeal might be entered or is pending, but makes an exception of orders under section 32 UKBA 2007, which may be made as soon as section 34(1)–(2) UKBA 2007 allows. 8.110

Where an individual is caught by the section 32 UKBA 2007 scheme and no exception is shown, then the Secretary of State's view of the individual case becomes in essence irrelevant. This also makes a difference to the contemplated deportee and his or her representatives, because the useful ground for representations is limited to those matters which are directed at whether a section 33 UKBA 2007 exception arises, although other representations may be raised on the basis that they might become relevant if and when an exception is shown, and the questions of liability to deportation under section 3(5)(a) IA 1971 and/or of section 5(1) IA 1971 discretion on the part of the Secretary of State is revived. 8.111

The Effect of Application of UKBA 2007 in the Context of Subsequent Challenge

In practice, the key current question for individuals in relation to deportation decisions taken by reference to UKBA 2007 is whether different standards apply on legal challenge to such decisions—largely pursued under the present NIAA 2002 appeals scheme, though theoretically susceptible to judicial review challenge in the absence of appeal or other alternative remedy. 8.112

In some respects, the difference is obvious and has already been identified. Challenge to the lawfulness of imposition of liability under section 3(5)(a) IA 1971 and/or the exercise of a discretion to deport under section 5(1) IA 1971 is in essence forestalled by the deeming provisions at section 32(4) and/or (5) IA 1971 so long as these are applicable. Beyond this, the matters to be considered on appeal had until recently been treated as effectively similar to those considered on appeal in a discretionary case, with Article 8 ECHR being in practice central to most cases. 8.113

However, it has subsequently come to be adjudged that the fact of a deportation being ordered under the UKBA 2007 scheme makes a substantial difference to the treatment of Article 8 ECHR on appeal. In *Gurung v SSHD* [2012] EWCA Civ 62, Sedley LJ, with whom Rix and McFarlane LJJ agreed, at [7] referred to *OH (Serbia) v SSHD* [2008] EWCA Civ 694, recording that 'until the enactment and coming into force of [the automatic deportation scheme under the UKBA 2007], appeals against deportation orders had a unique layer of complexity: tribunals were required to have regard, in addition to the regular article 8 factors, to the Home Secretary's own estimation of the public interest' and then endorsed the proposition in *RU (Bangladesh) v SSHD* [2012] EWCA Civ 651 that in a UKBA 2007 case, an appellant could not argue that his deportation was not 8.114

conducive to the public good, the deeming provision in section 32(4) UKBA 2007 precluding this, and that consideration where Article 8 ECHR was raised would go directly to the question of whether there was in contemplation a relevant breach, the elements of the public interest identified in *OH (Serbia)* continuing to have relevance in this case.

8.115 The Court of Appeal in *Gurung* went on to observe that:

> 11. The public interest is not only to be treated as by definition served, subject to the United Kingdom's international obligations, by deporting foreign criminals; it is also among the factors capable of affecting the proportionality of deporting them if this arises. This means that, while the public interest in deportation has already been established by legislation, its content and extent in the particular case have to be separately evaluated, initially by the Home Secretary and thereafter if necessary by the tribunal, if the proportionality of deportation comes into question.
>
> 12. The tribunal should accordingly entertain both sides' submissions on the public interest, along with such elements as the nature and gravity of the offence; but the fact that one estimation of the public interest (or of any other element) is the Home Secretary's, whether leaning towards or against deportation in the particular case, commands no additional weight. To let it do so—as counsel for the Home Secretary have implicitly recognised—would be to upset the equal footing on which the Crown and the individual come before this country's tribunals and courts, not least when Parliament has already decided where, other things being equal, the public interest lies. It would also impinge on the independence and impartiality of the tribunal by requiring it to defer to one side's judgment of a material question.

8.116 In *Richards v SSHD* [2013] EWCA Civ 244, Laws LJ, with whom Hallett and Rimer LJJ agreed, observed at [21] that:

> 21. What in my judgment needs emphasis is that the strong public interest in deporting foreign criminals is now not merely the policy of the Secretary of State but the judgment of Parliament. That gives it special weight, which the courts ought to recognise, as no doubt the Strasbourg court will. This approach sits with the well-established approach to proportionality questions in European Union law where Acts of the primary legislator enjoy a wider margin of discretion.

Later, in *SS (Nigeria) v SSHD* [2013] EWCA Civ 550, [2014] 1 WLR 998, the Court of Appeal considered the appeal from a decision of the tribunal in a section 32 UKBA 2007 deportation case contested on the basis that exception 1 applied because removal would represent a disproportionate breach of Article 8 ECHR. The Court held that:

> 53. The importance of the moral and political character of the policy shows that the two drivers of the decision-maker's margin of discretion—the policy's nature and its source—operate in tandem. An Act of Parliament is anyway to be specially respected; but all the more so when it declares policy of this kind. In this case, the policy is general and overarching. It is circumscribed only by five carefully drawn exceptions, of which the first is violation of a person's Convention/Refugee Convention rights. (The others concern minors, EU cases, extradition cases and cases involving persons subject to orders under mental health legislation.) Clearly, Parliament in the 2007 Act has attached very great weight to the policy as a well justified imperative for the protection of the public and to reflect the public's proper condemnation of serious wrongdoers. Sedley LJ was with respect right to state that 'in the case of a "foreign criminal" the Act places in the proportionality scales a markedly greater weight than in other cases'.

Deportation

54. I would draw particular attention to the provision contained in s.33(7): 'section 32(4) applies despite the application of Exception 1...', that is to say, a foreign criminal's deportation remains conducive to the public good notwithstanding his successful reliance on Article 8. I said at paragraph 46 that while the authorities demonstrate that there is no rule of exceptionality for Article 8, they also clearly show that the more pressing the public interest in removal or deportation, the stronger must be the claim under Article 8 if it is to prevail. The pressing nature of the public interest here is vividly informed by the fact that by Parliament's express declaration the public interest is injured if the criminal's deportation is not effected. Such a result could in my judgment only be justified by a very strong claim indeed.

The effect of this decision is controversial, for a number of reasons: 8.117

(i) First, the approach in *SS (Nigeria)* risks ignoring the practical purpose of the section 32(4) UKBA 2007 deeming provision which is to ensure that section 3(5)(a) IA 1971 is satisfied, enabling the UKBA 2007 scheme to operate without individual deeming by the Secretary of State.

(ii) Second, if deeming under section 32(4) UKBA 2007 is to give additional weight to the public interest in deportation in the context of proportionality, then it is difficult to see how this is not counterweighted in an Article 8 ECHR case by section 33(1) UKBA 2007, by which Parliament provided expressly that cases in which removal would create a breach of the ECHR or the CSR are to be treated as an exception and section 32(5) disapplied.

(iii) Third, a conclusion that Parliament can, without amendment to 'constitutional statutes' such as the HRA 1998, modify a judicial exercise concerning proportionality under Article 8 ECHR by a change in the means by which policy is expressed would appear to conflict with authoritative guidance of the House of Lords in *SSHD v Huang* [2007] UKHL 11, [2007] 2 AC 167 [15]–[18] concerning the role of statutory tribunals, the nature and effect of 'democratic approval' by the legislature in different contexts, and the nature of the proportionality exercise. This remains the fundamental authority in this area. And the democratic importance of proportionality of restraint as regards fundamental rights, implicit in that decision, is widely recognised. Since the decision in *Huang*, Aharon Barak, former President of the Supreme Court of Israel, has analysed at length the components of proportionality common to many or all democratic constitutions and has noted that whilst relevant public interests may provide a justification for limiting the application of particular rights: 'The notion of "limits on limitations" is of utmost importance. It lies at the very foundation of constitutional democracy. It is the legal basis for the limitation of the legislative power in relation to the limitation of human rights. In the same way that human rights require a thorough study, so too do their limitations.'[12] On that approach, the protection of the weighing task from excessive influence by the Executive represents an essential safeguard for the liberty of the individual.

---

[12] A Barak, *Proportionality: Constitutional Rights and their Limitations* (Cambridge, Cambridge University Press, 2012) 167.

(iv) Fourth, Article 8 ECHR is, and separate from domestic incorporation remains, part of an international instrument with the purpose of establishing minimum protections for fundamental rights exercisable across many states. Its application does not seem obviously dependent upon whether applicable standards in a Member State are set by legislation, policy or another method.

(v) Finally, there may be some doubt that the decisions cited in *SS (Nigeria)* support the proposition that additional weight is entered into one side of the weighing exercise. In *SE (Zimbabwe) v SSHD* [2014] EWCA Civ 256, Jackson LJ, effectively delivering the judgment of the Court, observed at [58] that:

> I can see that the decision in *SS (Nigeria)* does give rise to difficult issues, which might merit further argument in an appropriate case. One important issue concerns the extent to which Parliament can pre-empt the operation of the evaluative exercise under ECHR article 8, by enshrining a particular policy objective in primary legislation. It may be said that the conclusions of the court in *SS (Nigeria)* go some way beyond *AP (Trinidad & Tobago) v SSHD* [2011] EWCA Civ 551 and the other authorities to which Laws LJ refers. But none of these issues are matters for this court.

This suggests that the point may ultimately have to be resolved outside the UK, although one significant reason for doubt concerning the proposition that extra weight attaches to the deemed public interest in an Article 8 ECHR assessment is the apparent inconsistency of this with the decision making of the House of Lords and Supreme Court over a considerable period.

E7. Notifying a Decision to Exercise the Section 5(1) IA 1971 Power (or Act upon the Section 32 UKBA 2007 Duty)

8.118 There is no direct and overarching requirement for written notice of a decision to deport a non-citizen. Indeed, as already seen, paragraph 381 Immigration Rules HC 381 seems to state the opposite proposition. In practice, however, a duty to give notice in writing arises in most cases because certain decisions are appealable by statute and there is a requirement for service in those cases. Under regulation 4 Immigration (Notices) Regulations 2003, SI 2003/658, a decision maker must give notice in writing to a person of any immigration decision or EEA decision taken in respect of him or her which is appealable. Regulation 5 sets out requirements as regards contents, including 'a statement of the reasons for the decision'. A decision to make a deportation order under section 5(1) IA 1971 (save for a UKBA 2007 decision) or to refuse to revoke a deportation order under section 5(2) IA 1971 is, subject to specified exceptions, an appealable immigration decision in relevant terms, by reference to section 82(2)(j)–(k) NIAA 2002, and so will come within the category of decisions of which notice in writing must be given. In the case of a decision applying section 32(5) UKBA 2007, this also attracts a requirement of written notice as a consequence of section 82(3A) NIAA 2002, by which a decision that section 32(5) UKBA 2007 applies is appealable.

8.119 Were the present, somewhat contingent, requirement for notice in writing to be modified or removed, it seems unlikely that the courts would support any general practice by the Secretary of State of failing to serve decisions upon those affected while expecting them to be treated as effective by the courts, or even a limited practice to this effect unsupported by very good reason. The application to this context of the principles expressed by Lord Steyn in *R (otao Anufrijeva) v SSHD and another* [2003] UKHL 36, [2004] AC 604 would suggest that a decision is effective only when served on the affected individual or his or her representative. However, it is also established that a failure by the representative might deny an intended deportee knowledge of a decision, as in the student case of *Al-Medawi v SSHD* [1989] UKHL 7, [1990] 1 AC 876. Under regulation 7(2)–(3), a notice of decision may in very limited circumstances be served 'on the file', where an individual's location is unknown, and then provided to the subject once that person is located.

E8. Appeal from a Decision Under Section 5(1) IA 1971 or Section 32 UKBA 2007

Under section 82(2)(j) NIAA 2002, as presently in force, a decision to make a deportation order under section 5(1) IA 1971 is appealable by reference to any of the matters identified in section 84 NIAA 2002, including in section 84(1)(e) 'that the decision is otherwise not in accordance with the law'. This provision is disapplied in the case of decisions made by reference to section 32(5) UKBA 2007 by section 82(3A) NIAA 2002, but the decision that section 32(5) UKBA 2007 applies is itself made an appealable decision by the same provision. Amendments to the NIAA 2002 under the IA 2014 will remove both provisions, substituting a new section 82 NIAA 2002 right to appeal a 'decision to refuse a human rights claim' or a protection claim. It appears that this is intended to apply to deportation cases where an HRA 1998 or CSR claim is made in support of representations against deportation. At the same time, changes to section 84 NIAA 2002 will seek to greatly restrict the grounds available in a statutory appeal, in essence to the HRA 1998, the CSR and humanitarian protection entitlement under the EU Qualification Directive. Further, under section 94B NIAA 2002, the Secretary of State will be able to certify claims made by a 'foreign criminal' (as defined in the new Part 5A NIAA 2002) on the basis that removal prior to the conduct of his or her appeal 'would not be unlawful under section 6 [HRA 1998]', in that the subject would not face 'a real risk of serious irreversible harm' if removed to the relevant location. Although issues of broader lawfulness may now shift so as to be considered more frequently under Article 8 ECHR—Lord Bingham's third question in *R (Razgar) v SSHD* [2004] UKHL 27, [2004] 2 AC 368 [17] is whether a decision which interfered with Article 8 ECHR is 'in accordance with the law'—restrictions on appeals are likely to reduce the extent to which appeal allows all relevant legal issues to be determined and to increase the need for satellite judicial review litigation. The IA 2014 has in effect reversed the progress made up to the NIAA 2002 in producing a relatively self-sufficient appeals system able to resolve almost all legal issues arising in the context of deportation. Appeals and judicial review prior to and following the IA 2014 are further addressed in chapter 16.

8.120

E9. Making an Order

The basic statutory structure of the IA 1971 creates, as was identified by the Court of Appeal *R v SSHD ex p Vladic* [1998] Imm AR 542 (see paragraph 8.82 above), a two-

8.121

Part C – Deportation, Removal and Exclusion

stage system, in which the taking of the decision is a largely administrative step undertaken presently after any appeal is resolved against a prospective deportee. There may be constraints on the timing of a deportation order being made. Under paragraph 378 Immigration Rules HC 195, it is said that such an order may not be made:

a. whilst it is still open to that person to appeal the decision to deport that individual or where appeal is pending, save where the Secretary of State is subject to the duty under section 32(5) of the IA 1971; or
b. where it is still open to the prospective deportee to appeal the relevant '[criminal] conviction, sentence, or recommendation [for deportation]', or such an appeal is pending.

The latter provision follows, or mirrors, section 6(6) IA 1971, by which in a recommendation case a deportation order may not be made whilst appeal against the recommendation or conviction could be made or is pending. The language does not expressly prevent the making of a *decision to deport* someone before any appeal against conviction, sentence or recommendation is concluded, which would seem more sensible than preventing only the making of the order. However, it may be that established public law principles would apply in the event of, for example, a decision to deport someone which gives inadequate or no consideration to the existence of an outstanding appeal against a criminal conviction, sentence or recommendation which is a condition precedent for the exercise of deportation powers or is otherwise relevant as to a deportation decision, as opposed to an order. Further, it is very difficult to see how the Secretary of State could rationally depend upon a decision in his or her favour in statutory immigration appeal proceedings, where a subsequent event such as a success on appeal in criminal proceedings by the deportee has materially changed the situation. In that event, the intention visible in paragraph 378 HC 195—of avoiding premature action where important matters remain to be decided—may be of assistance, though there is a marked shortage of decided authority on the meaning and effect of this. For example, it is not clear whether one or both of the phrases 'it is still open to the person to appeal' or 'an appeal is pending' includes (as regards either statutory appeal against deportation or appeal against the criminal conviction, sentence or recommendation) not only periods within which an appeal notice or application for permission to appeal could be made as of right, or following the grant of permission to appeal, but also those periods where an out-of-time application matched with a request for extension of time could be made. In an asylum support case, the Court of Appeal in *R (otao Erdogan) v SSHD* [2004] EWCA Civ 1087, [2004] All ER (D) 421 (Jul) has held, per Newman J at [16], that: 'As a matter of general approach to time limits in connection with an appeal, it seems to me that, since an application for permission to appeal within a statutory time limit exists as a statutory right, it has a character which an application made out of time does not.' If applied to paragraph 378, this would suggest that it should be read as barring the making of an order where a period for appeal or application by right had not been exhausted or where an out-of-time application had been admitted, but not otherwise.

8.122 In a UKBA 2007 case, under section 34(2) UKBA 2007, a deportation order may not be made under section 32(5) UKBA 2007 'while an appeal or further appeal against the conviction or sentence by reference to which the order is to be made—(a) has been instituted and neither withdrawn nor determined, or (b) could be brought', section 34(3) UKBA 2007 discounting the possibility of appeal out of time with permission or appeal where a person has informed the Secretary of State in writing that he or she does not intend to appeal.

The making of a deportation decision may be delegated by the Secretary of State to a more junior official. The decision does not have to be taken by the Secretary of State in person and, as the House of Lords confirmed in *Oladehinde v IAT* [1990] UKHL 11, [1991] 1 AC 254, may be taken by an official he or she has duly authorised for this purpose, in accordance with the principle delineated in *Carltona Ltd* v *Commissioner of Works* [1943] 2 All ER 560. In practice, however, this is rarely tested, as under section 32(2) IA 1971, a document purporting to be signed on behalf of the Secretary of State will be treated as such, save where the absence of authorisation is demonstrated.

8.123

E10. Application for Revocation

Under section 5(2) IA 1971, a deportation order 'may at any time be revoked by a further order of the Secretary of State'. The revocation of a deportation order under section 5(2) IA 1971, like the initial making of an order under section 5(1) IA 1971 where the UKBA 2007 scheme does not apply, represents the exercise by the Secretary of State of a statutory discretion and is equally subject to established principles of public law. An application for revocation may overlap with the attempt to make good a fresh claim to protection of relevant human rights under paragraph 353 Immigration Rules.

8.124

The manner of exercise of the discretion is identified by guidance. Paragraph 390 Immigration Rules HC 395 provides that an application for revocation of a deportation order will be considered in the light of all the circumstances including the following:

8.125

(i) the grounds on which the order was made;
(ii) any representations made in support of revocation;
(iii) the interests of the community, including the maintenance of an effective immigration control;
(iv) the interests of the applicant, including any compassionate circumstances.

Paragraph 390A Immigration Rules provides that where paragraph 398 applies, 'the Secretary of State will consider whether paragraph 399 or 399A applies and, if it does not, it will only be in exceptional circumstances that the public interest in maintaining the deportation order will be outweighed by other factors'. This particular provision in the Immigration Rules evidently aims for a treatment of Article 8 ECHR in relation to revocation which is identical to that applicable in relation to deportation, though where an individual has left the UK, some parts of the paragraph 398 scheme may apply differently; for instance, departure will break continuous presence in the UK.

8.126

The Immigration Rules also provide other standards for decision making concerning revocation. Under paragraph 391 Immigration Rules, unless the ECHR or the CSR would otherwise be breached, continuation in force of the order is presumed to be the proper course where a person has been deported following conviction of a criminal offence and a sentence of imprisonment, as follows:

8.127

(i) where the custodial sentence was of less than four years, the presumption against revocation extends for 10 years from the date of the deportation order;

(ii) where the sentence was of four years or more, the presumption against revocation has no end date.

8.128 Where an individual is deported without there having been a relevant conviction, presumption against revocation arises, unless there has been 'material alteration':

> 391A. In other cases, revocation of the order will not normally be authorised unless the situation has been materially altered, either by a change of circumstances since the order was made, or by fresh information coming to light which was not before the appellate authorities or the Secretary of State. The passage of time since the person was deported may also in itself amount to such a change of circumstances as to warrant revocation of the order.
>
> 392. Revocation of a deportation order does not entitle the person concerned to re-enter the United Kingdom; it renders him eligible to apply for admission under the Immigration Rules. Application for revocation of the order may be made to the Entry Clearance Officer or direct to the Home Office.

8.129 In some older cases the Tribunal considered relatively short periods to be sufficient for a deportation order to be revoked or at least reviewed: *Dervish v SSHD* [1972] Imm AR 48; and *Udoh v SSHD* [1972] Imm AR 89. These related to cases in which there had been breaches of compliance with immigration control (which at that point attracted deportation rather than removal), not criminal convictions. Such cases are not of lasting value given various intervening developments, including changes to the Immigration Rules and guidance. There are few cases to provide guidance, apart from the growing body of guidance in this area related to Article 8 ECHR and covered in chapter 5, above. In *R (otao HM (Malawi)) v SSHD* [2010] EWHC 1407 (Admin), HHJ Gilbart QC quashed a decision of the Secretary of State certifying as 'clearly unfounded' under section 94 NIAA 2002 an application to revoke in which there was evidence that the prospective deportee had married his partner since an earlier adjudication, and additional medical evidence. In *Sanade and others (British Children—Zambrano—Dereci)* [2012] UKUT 00048 (IAC), the Tribunal at [125]–[128] dismissed the appeal of one prospective deportee, Walker, against deportation, the factors considered in relation to Article 8 ECHR including the poor health of his wife and mother and the impact of his removal upon his children, noting that these had been balanced against other factors, but that, despite rejection of the appeal against the deportation decision: 'Combined with the interest of the children they may carry weight in an application for revocation of the deportation order.'

8.130 In relation to Article 8 ECHR, the Strasbourg Court has on occasion been asked to consider the expected length of exclusion under a deportation order under previous provisions. In *Onur v UK*—27319/07 [2009] ECHR 289, the deportee, a Turkish national, had been deported from the UK following conviction of a number of offences, the final one resulting in a sentence of four and a half years for robbery. At [61], the Court observed that 'the Court has had regard to the duration of the deportation order. Although the Immigration Rules do not set a specific period after which revocation would be appropriate, it would appear that at the very latest the applicant would be able to apply to have the deportation order revoked ten years after his deportation'. It found no disproportionate breach of Article 8 ECHR. In *Miah v UK*—53080/07 [2010] ECHR 721, the Court found the claim inadmissible, observing at [25] that: 'Finally, while the duration of the deportation imposed on the applicant is of the same duration as that imposed in *Maslov*, it does not exclude him from the United Kingdom for as much time as he spent there and does not do so for a decisive period in his life. The Court therefore finds that the domestic authorities have not exceeded the margin of appreciation afforded to them in such cases.' Other cases concerning duration of an exclusion measure and Article 8 ECHR are digested in chapter 5.

E11. Appeal against Refusal of Revocation

Under section 82(2)(k) NIAA 2002, as presently in force, a refusal to revoke a deportation order under section 5(2) IA 1971 is appealable within the UK by reference to any of the matters identified in section 84 NIAA 2002, save in the event of certification under section 94 or 96 NIAA 2002: *R (otao BA (Nigeria)) v SSHD* [2009] UKSC 7, [2010] 1 AC 444. Amendments to the NIAA 2002 under the IA 2014 will produce a substantially different situation. Restrictions on appeals are likely to reduce the extent to which appeal allows all relevant legal issues to be determined and to increase the need for satellite judicial review litigation. The IA 2014 also seeks to reduce the degree to which appeal is exercised prior to removal from the UK. Chapter 16 below considers appeals and judicial review in greater detail.

8.131

E12. Effects of the Deportation Process

Effects Relating to Detention

Under paragraph 382 HC 395, once a notice of the Secretary of State's decision to make a deportation order has been issued, 'the Secretary of State may authorise detention or make an order restricting a person as to residence, employment or occupation and requiring him to report to the police, pending the making of a deportation order'. Paragraphs 2(1)–(3) of Schedule 3 to the IA 1971 variously provide the Secretary of State with the power to detain potential deportees following the recommendation of a court for deportation, when a decision to deport has been made, and once a deportation order has been signed.

8.132

Exclusion

An individual will be excluded from the UK as long as a deportation order continues in force. The mechanism by which this is enforced is paragraph 320(2) Immigration Rules, under which entry clearance or leave to enter will be refused where 'the person seeking entry ... is currently the subject of a deportation order'. A deportation order will cease to have effect automatically if the deportee becomes a British citizen (section 5(1) IA 1971), if he or she has been deported as a spouse but has divorced (section 5(3)–(4) IA 1971) or if he or she has been deported as a child but has reached the age of 18 (section 5(3)–(4) IA 1971). If the deportation order does not cease to have effect by one of these means, then it will have effect until such time as the subject dies (at which point he or she would cease to be a 'person' for the purposes of the IA 1971 provisions) or the order is discharged by the Secretary of State on application by the subject or of her own volition. In *Latif (s 120—Revocation of Deportation Order) Pakistan* [2012] UKUT 78 (IAC), the Tribunal held that an individual subject to a deportation order had to apply

8.133

for revocation rather than seek to raise claimed grounds for revocation in support of an appeal against automatic refusal relying on paragraph 320(2) Immigration Rules. Under paragraph 392 Immigration Rules, an application for revocation may be made either to an Entry Clearance Officer (ECO) or directly to the Home Office.

Effect on Existing Leave to Enter/Remain

8.134 Section 5(1) IA 1971 provides that a deportation order against a person shall 'invalidate any leave to enter or remain in the United Kingdom given ... before the order is made or while it is in force'. The language does not indicate that leave to remain is terminated. Where a deportation order is made and the prospective deportee then succeeds on appeal, or the deportation decision is revoked or otherwise ceases to have effect, does that revalidate any unelapsed leave to remain possessed earlier? In *R (George) v SSHD* [2012] [2014] UKSC 28, [2014] 1 WLR 1831, the Court of Appeal by a majority decision found that was so, but this was reversed by the Supreme Court on appeal at [2014] UKSC 28. Accordingly, a deportee who possesses indefinite or other leave to remain which would, save for the making of a deportation order, still be in force does not regain that leave to remain or the balance of it upon the revocation of the deportation order. Under paragraph 392 Immigration Rules, revocation of a deportation order does not entitle the subject to re-enter the UK; it simply removes to bar to an application for entry clearance.

9
Administrative Removal of Persons

Contents

A. Introduction 9.1
B. International Law 9.2
    B1. General 9.2
    B2. International Human Rights Law 9.4
    B3. Hybrid Instruments 9.9
    B4. Council of Europe Instruments 9.14
C. EU Law 9.18
D. Domestic Law 9.20
    D1. Prerogative 9.20
    D2. Statute 9.21
        Paragraphs 8–15 of Schedule 2 to the IA 1971 .... 9.25
        Section 10 IAA 1999 .... 9.29
        Section 47 IANA 2006 .... 9.32
    D3. Statutory Instrument 9.35
        The Immigration (European Economic Area) Regulations 2006 .... 9.35
    D4. Published Guidance 9.38
E. Discussion 9.39
    E1. Removal under Schedule 2 IA 1971 of Persons Refused Leave to Enter,
        Illegal Entrants, Family Members of Persons within the First Two
        Categories and Members of Maritime or Air Crews 9.39
        i. Refusal of Leave to Enter 9.40
        ii. Illegal Entrants 9.41
            Entry by Deception and Related Criminal Offences 9.47
            No Evidence of Lawful Entry (NELE) 9.51
            Entry in Breach of a Deportation Order 9.53
            Entry through the Common Travel Area (Republic of Ireland,
            the Channel Islands or the Isle of Man) 9.54
            The Consequences of Being Classified an Illegal Entrant 9.56
    E2. Removal under Section 10 IAA 1999 .... 9.59
        Overstayers 9.61
        Breach of Conditions 9.65
        Leave to Remain by Deception 9.71
        Removal Following Curtailment/Revocation of Leave 9.73
        Section 10 IAA 1999 as Substituted by Section 1 IA 2014 .... 9.80
    E3. Section 47 IANA 2006 .... 9.84
    E4. Family Members 9.87
        EEA Nationals and Their Family Members 9.95
    E5. Exercises of Statutory Removal Powers: Applicable Standards 9.97
    E6. Appeals 9.98
        The Effect of the New Part 5A NIAA 2002 .... 9.102

A. Introduction

9.1 The Secretary of State currently possesses three statutory powers concerning administrative removal (generally referred to simply as 'removal') from the UK. These can be found, respectively, in: (i) Schedule 2 to IA 1971; (ii) section 10 Immigration and Asylum Act 1999 (IAA 1999); and (iii) section 47 Immigration, Asylum and Nationality Act 2006 (IANA 2006). It appears that the IA 2014 will significantly reshape the statutory landscape when relevant provisions are brought into force (at the time of writing no date has been appointed for this). This chapter considers the current position and the likely effect of the new provisions introduced by IA 2014.

B. International Law

B1. General

9.2 International law is directly applicable in the UK to the extent that a relevant treaty norm has been incorporated domestically, or customary international law represents a source for the common law. It may possess significance without incorporation, as where it assists the interpretation of domestic law or shapes the exercise of discretion. Reflecting the more traditional role of international law as the law of states, a right or duty will vest primarily in the state: it will be a state of nationality which possesses the right to protect its national against abuse by the UK, or a state to which an individual is removed in the course of deportation, or who is left in that state by action of the UK, which may complain of an international law wrong unless it is itself obliged under international law to accept an individual's return or presence. However, there is now a greater role for the individual in international law and this—including but not limited to international human rights law—provides significant protections accruing directly to the individual.

9.3 Removal amounts to expulsion and is generally recognised to be within the state's established right to expel aliens (see chapter 2, section K). However, the broad discretion permitted by international law is not an absolute one, and as with deportation, considered in chapter 8, the UK is not permitted by international law to act arbitrarily in taking its decision to expel an alien, or to act unreasonably in the manner in which it effects an expulsion.

B2. International Human Rights Law

9.4 A detailed survey of the main international human rights law provisions is provided in chapter 3 above. Below is a summary of provisions which may be particularly relevant in a removal situation.

First, a range of important human rights protections apply under the ICCPR to prevent return to a place in which relevant risk can be shown to arise: **9.5**

(i) Article 6 ICCPR prohibits arbitrary deprivation of life, and removing an individual to a situation in which there are substantial grounds to believe that the deportee would face such a deprivation would breach that protection.
(ii) By Article 7 ICCPR, removal to a situation in which there are substantial grounds to believe that the deportee would face torture, or cruel, inhuman or degrading treatment is prohibited.
(iii) Article 8 ICCPR marks the condemnation of slavery by the international community, and removal to a situation in which there are substantial grounds to believe that the deportee would face being made a slave would constitute a breach.
(iv) By Article 9 ICCPR, arbitrary arrest or detention is prohibited. Removal where there are substantial grounds to believe that the deportee would face such treatment is barred by this provision.

Second, an important parallel protection directed at return to a setting of relevant risk of torture is brought into being by the CAT. Removal to a state in which 'there are substantial grounds for believing' that the subject would face torture as defined in that instrument would contravene Article 3(1). **9.6**

Third, ICCPR provides a series of important basic standards relevant to removal, focusing upon the nature and effect of removal from the UK rather than the circumstances to which an individual would be returned: **9.7**

(i) Removal will breach Article 12(4) ICCPR if: (a) the UK is the affected individual's 'own country' for the purposes of that provision; (b) the effect of removal would be to expel that individual from, or prevent his or her return to, the UK; and (c) the action would be arbitrary.
(ii) Removal will breach Article 13 ICCPR if: (a) the individual is an alien, not a British national; (b) he or she is lawfully present in the UK; and (c) the decision is not reached in accordance with applicable legal standards ('in accordance with law').
(iii) Save where 'compelling reasons of national security otherwise require', removal will breach Article 13 ICCPR if: (a) the affected individual is not permitted to submit representations setting out why he or she should not be expelled ('reasons against his expulsion'); and/or (b) is not permitted effective review of the decision before 'the competent authority or a person or persons especially designated by the competent authority'; and/or (c) is not permitted representation for the purpose of pursuing such review.
(iv) Action by the state in this context will breach Article 17 ICCPR, read in conjunction with Article 23(1) ICCPR, if it amounts to 'arbitrary or unlawful' interference with the protected interests of 'privacy, family, home', against which the domestic law does not provide protection.
(v) Article 2 ICCPR is breached where the state fails to 'respect and ensure' the rights protected by the ICCPR 'without distinction of any kind', such as 'race, colour, sex, language, religion, political or other opinion, national or social origin, property,

birth or other status', or where the state fails to ensure an effective remedy for the breach.

(vi) Finally, Article 3 ICCPR marks the equal right of men and women to civil and political rights provided under the ICCPR. Gender discrimination in relevant respects is therefore prohibited under the ICCPR.

9.8 Fourth, and finally, beyond the ICCPR, a range of other, broader international human rights norms are applicable to removal action:

(i) Removal which is discriminatory on the basis of race would breach Article 5(d) CERD.

(ii) Removal representing prohibited discrimination against a woman or women would breach Article 1 CEDAW;

(iii) Article 3(1) CRC provides that in an action concerning children, 'the best interests of the child must be a primary consideration' and the subsequent paragraph says that subscribing states 'undertake to ensure the child such protection and care as is necessary for his or her well-being'. These provisions and Article 9 CRC (regarding family unity) become relevant where a child is affected by removal measures.

(iv) Persons to whom the Convention on the Rights of Persons with Disabilities 2006 applies are protected by Article 18(1)(d) not only from arbitrary deprivation of entry to 'their own country' (recalling the language of Article 12(4) ICCPR) but also from deprivation of entry to 'their own' country on any basis, which, though not arbitrary, rests 'on the basis of disability'.

B3. Hybrid Instruments

9.9 Chapter 4 set out international law provisions established by three regimes referred to as 'hybrid', in that they combine the creation of rights, like the instruments seen in chapter 3 and above, with other purposes, such as the sharing of burdens amongst members of the international community. Some of those have important consequences in relation to removal. The CSR defines the term 'refugee' at Article 1A(2). Save where that status has ended in accordance with the cessation provision at Article 1C CSR or exclusion applies by reason of one of Articles 1D–1E CSR, a refugee is entitled to certain protections. Where he or she is lawfully present, then:

(i) by Article 32(1) CSR, the refugee is protected from expulsion (as in a removal process), save on the grounds of national security or public order;

(ii) where a refugee faces expulsion on one or both of the two permitted grounds, under Article 32(2) CSR, expulsion is permitted 'only in pursuance of a decision reached in accordance with due process of law' and is subject to procedural rights including entitlement 'to submit evidence to clear himself [herself], and to appeal to and be represented for the purpose before competent authority or a person or persons specially designated by the competent authority';

(iii) finally, where a lawfully present refugee is to be expelled for a permitted reason notwithstanding any representation to the competent authority, he or she is entitled to 'a reasonable period within which to seek legal admission into another country' under Article 32(3) CSR.

Administrative Removal of Persons

9.10 By Article 33(1) CSR, a refugee regardless of the lawfulness of his or her presence is entitled to protection from expulsion or *refoulement* 'in any manner whatsoever to the frontiers of territories where his life or freedom would be threatened' on account of a relevant matter, save where the exception in Article 33(2) CSR applies because there are reasonable grounds for regarding the refugee as a danger to the security of the UK, or because he or she, 'convicted by a final judgment of a particularly serious crime, constitutes a danger to the community of the UK'.

9.11 Under the CSSP, a stateless person as defined therein is, if lawfully present, entitled to protections equivalent to those afforded a refugee under Article 32 CSR:

(i) under Article 31(1) CSSP, the lawfully present stateless person is entitled to protection from expulsion (including expulsion in aid of removal) on any ground apart from national security or public order;
(ii) if a stateless person faces expulsion on the grounds of national security or public order, then by Article 32(2) CSSP, expulsion is permitted 'only in pursuance of a decision reached in accordance with due process of law', subject to procedural rights by which he or she 'shall be allowed to submit evidence to clear himself [herself], and to appeal to and be represented for the purpose before competent authority or a person or persons specially designated by the competent authority';
(iii) by Article 32(3) CSSP, a lawfully present stateless person facing expulsion notwithstanding any representation to the competent authority is entitled to 'a reasonable period within which to seek legal admission into another country';

In contrast to the protection from *refoulement* provided in Article 33 CSR, a stateless person (who is not also a refugee and is entitled to protection separately as such under CSR) has no protection from expulsion unless he or she is lawfully present.

9.12 The removal-relevant obligations of the UK under the Protocol to Prevent, Suppress and Punish Trafficking in Persons, especially Women and Children 2000 (PPSPTP) are still more limited. Under Article 8(2) PPSPTP, where the UK authorities apply removal to a VoT, as the latter term is defined in Article 3 PPSPTP, and: (a) the effect of this is to return the VoT to a country of nationality or in which he or she had a right of permanent residence; then (b) the authorities must give 'due regard' in the context of return to the safety of the VoT; and (c) must also give due regard to 'the status of any legal proceedings related to the fact that the person is a [VoT]' and (d) return shall preferably be voluntary.

9.13 These protections for VoTs should be seen in conjunction with those provided by subsequent overlapping Council of Europe and EU instruments, considered below. Article 8(6) PPSPTP provides that the PPSPTP 'shall be without prejudice to any applicable bilateral or multilateral agreement or arrangement that governs, in whole or in part, the return of victims of trafficking in persons'.

B4. Council of Europe Instruments

9.14 Two instruments introduced in chapter 5 are relevant to removal. First, under the ECHR, certain very important human rights protections obstruct return to a place in which relevant risk can be shown to arise in so-called 'foreign cases':

(i) Article 2 ECHR prohibits deprivation of life 'save in the execution of a sentence of a court' following conviction of a capital crime. Where substantial

Part C – Deportation, Removal and Exclusion

grounds show the existence of a real risk of breach of Article 2 ECHR in a country to which removal would take place, removal is prohibited by Article 2 ECHR.

(ii) Article 3 ECHR prohibits torture or inhuman or degrading treatment or punishment. If by 'substantial grounds', the 'existence of a real risk' of any of the prohibited ill-treatments on return is shown, Article 3 ECHR prohibits removal.

(iii) Article 4 ECHR prohibits slavery or servitude. Where 'substantial grounds' show the existence of a real risk of any of the prohibited ill-treatments on return, removal is not permitted.

(iv) Article 5 ECHR bars deprivation of liberty save in specified cases and in accordance with the law. Where in a particular case substantial grounds show the existence of a real risk of any of the prohibited ill-treatments, Article 5 ECHR prohibits removal.

(v) Article 6 ECHR specifies fair trial protections. Removal to 'real risk' of a 'flagrant denial of justice' would violate the article and is prohibited.

(vi) Article 7 ECHR prohibits 'punishment without law'. Substantial grounds showing the 'real risk' of a 'flagrant breach' on return would mean that removal breached Article 7 ECHR.

(vii) Article 8 ECHR relevantly protects the right to respect for private and family life and home. Removal is barred where substantial grounds showing the 'real risk' of a 'flagrant breach' of Article 8 ECHR arise in the place to which a deportee would have to go.

(viii) In the same way, substantial evidence showing 'real risk' on return of a 'flagrant breach' of protection of freedom of thought, conscience and religion (Article 9 ECHR), of freedom of expression (Article 10 ECHR), of freedom of peaceful assembly and/or association with others (Article 10 ECHR) or of the right to marry and found a family (Article 11 ECHR) would bar removal.

9.15 Second, the ECHR provides a series of important basic standards relevant to removal, focusing upon the nature and effect of removal from the UK rather than the circumstances to which an individual would be returned. Other articles might be engaged, but the majority of such cases focus upon the right to respect for a private and/or family life and/or home in the UK, which is protected under Article 8 ECHR. Removal is barred by Article 8 ECHR where this would represent an interference with relevant right(s) disproportionate to the legitimate public interest engaged (see 9.100 below for statutory judicial guidance for the balancing exercise inherent to the assessment of proportionality).

9.16 Third, removal may not be consistent with the CATHB:

(i) Article 10(2) CATHB requires the UK, if the competent authorities have reasonable grounds to believe that a person has been a VoT, to refrain from removing that person until the identification process as victim of a trafficking offence, as provided for in Article 18 CATHB, has been completed.

(ii) Article 13 CATHB requires the UK to 'provide in its internal law a recovery and reflection period of at least 30 days' when there are reasonable grounds to believe that the person concerned is a VoT. During that period, Article 13(2) CATHB, provides that removal cannot be enforced.

(iii) By Article 14 CATHB, the UK is required to issue a renewable residence permit to a VoT where a stay 'is necessary owing to his or her personal situation' and/or 'for the purpose of cooperation with the competent authorities in investigation or criminal proceedings relating to trafficking'.

In the context of removals of asylum-seekers or refugees to third countries under the Dublin regime (see chapter 6, section F2), there is tension between the Home Office policy and CATHB protections. Home Office policy (set out in 'Modernised Guidance—Victims of Human Trafficking—Competent Authority Guidance'—version 1.0 EXT) identified trafficking victims as removable under the Dublin II regime and specifically states: 'Unless the case meets Dublin II arrangements and another European Union (EU) member state is taking responsibility for the case, a competent authority must offer the victim help and protection in the UK under the convention.' However, the CATHB makes no provision for states to be relieved of their positive obligations towards victims by removal to third countries. In fact, [131]–[133] of the Explanatory Report that accompanies the CATHB states specifically that 'removal from its territory' includes third country removal in these circumstances. This understanding is reinforced at [178] of the Explanatory Report, which states that victims must not be removed from the territory during the recovery and reflection period. Phillip Mott QC, sitting as a Deputy High Court Judge in *R (otao E) v SSHD* 2012] EWHC 1927 (Admin), made reference to the issues at [54], observing that he would 'need a lot of persuading that Dublin II could relieve the Defendant of the self-imposed obligations arising from her policy of implementing the Trafficking Convention'.

9.17

C. EU Law

Chapter VI of Directive 2004/38/EC of the European Parliament and of the Council of 29 April 2004 ('Restrictions on the right of entry and the right of residence on grounds of public policy, public security or public health') contains provisions relevant to removal from the UK of EU citizens or family members. This has been outlined in chapter 6.

9.18

Directive 2011/36/EU of 5 April 2011 on preventing and combatting trafficking in human beings and protecting its victims, to which the UK opted in on 14 October 2011 (see chapter 6 above) requires by Article 12(3) that 'Member States shall ensure that victims of trafficking in human beings receive appropriate protection on the basis of an individual risk assessment, inter alia, by having access to witness protection programmes or other similar measures, if appropriate and in accordance with the grounds defined by national law or procedures'. In common with other trafficking protections, this may affect the lawfulness of deportation action against a victim of trafficking.

9.19

D. Domestic Law

D1. Prerogative

Removal in the light of *R (Munir) v SSHD* [2012] UKSC 32, [2012] 1 WLR 2192 and *R (Alvi) v SSHD* [2012] UKSC 33, [2012] 1 WLR 2208, almost certainly depends upon statute.

9.20

D2. Statute

9.21 Prior to IA 1971, domestic immigration legislation focused upon restricting entry to the UK whilst providing relatively limited powers of removal. IA 1971 introduced administrative removal, more commonly referred to as removal, as an alternative method of dealing with illegal entrants and others in breach of immigration control.

9.22 Currently, separate powers exist as regards discrete categories of persons designated as susceptible to removal, but they can be broadly split into two groups: those seeking to enter the UK ('on entry') and those already here ('after entry'). 'On entry' cases are in general covered by provisions in Schedule 2 to IA 1971. This provides for removal of individuals seeking to enter the UK but refused leave to enter or other admission at the port. It also provides for removal of 'illegal entrants', defined in section 33(1) IA 1971 as persons 'unlawfully entering or seeking to enter in breach of a deportation order or of the immigration laws, or … entering or seeking to enter by means which include deception by another person [including] … a person who has entered [in those circumstances]'.

9.23 Section 10 IAA 1999 and section 47 IANA 2006 focus upon 'after entry' removal categories, focused upon those who have in the past lawfully entered and remained in the UK in some capacity, but have either breached the conditions of leave to enter or remain, failed to depart before it expired, used deception in seeking further leave, been refused a variation of leave or had extant leave curtailed or revoked. Changes resulting from the IA 2014 are considered further below at paragraphs 9.80–9.83.

9.24 Removal of EEA nationals and family members is governed by the Immigration (European Economic Area) Regulations 2006, SI 2006/1003. Part 4 of those Regulations transposes Chapter VI of Directive 2004/38/EC of the European Parliament and of the Council of 29 April 2004.

Paragraphs 8–15 of Schedule 2 to the IA 1971

9.25 Schedule 2 to IA 1971 provides the powers for the administrative removal of persons within certain categories:

(a) those refused leave to enter (at [8] and [10]);
(b) illegal entrants (at [9] and [10]);
(c) family members of the above (at 10A]); and
(d) sea and air crews (at [12]–[15]).

9.26 Paragraph 8 of Schedule 2 refers specifically to the removal of those refused leave to enter, but also sets out provision for removal directions which is also applied to illegal entrant cases by virtue of paragraph 9(1) of Schedule 2. An immigration officer (IO) may give directions to the captain, owners or agents of a ship or aircraft for the removal of an individual from the UK to a country or territory: (i) of which he is a national or citizen; or (ii) in which he has obtained a passport or other document of identity; or (iii) in which he embarked for the UK; or (iv) to which there is reason to believe he will be admitted.[1] Any leave to enter obtained by deception is disregarded (paragraph 9(2) of Schedule 2 to IA 1971).

---

[1] There is no right of appeal under s 82(2)(h) NIAA 2002 against a decision to remove on the ground that the destination country in the decision was not one that would satisfy the IA 1971, sch 2, para 8(1)(c): *MS (Palestinian Territories) v SSHD* [2010] UKSC 25, [2010] WLR 1639.

With respect to those arriving through the Channel Tunnel, the provisions of Schedule 2 to IA 1971 are applied by Schedule 4 Channel Tunnel (International Arrangements) Order 1993, SI 1993/1813, as amended. 9.27

Section 8(1) IA 1971 provides for members of the crew[2] of a ship or aircraft to enter the UK without leave pending the departure of that ship or aircraft, if arriving in the UK as a member of a ship's crew under an engagement to leave as a member of it or in the case of aircrew to leave within seven days on that or another aircraft as a crew member. Three exceptions exist: where the individual is subject to a deportation order; where he or she has previously been refused leave to enter and not been granted leave since the refusal; or where an IO requires him or her to submit to examination. Specific provisions exist at paragraphs 12–15 enabling the removal of deserting seaman or aircrew.[3] 9.28

Section 10 IAA 1999

Section 10 IAA 1999 has been radically rewritten and replaced by section 1 IA 2014. At the time of writing, the new provision is not yet in force. For now, section 10(1) IAA 1999 provides the powers for the administrative removal of the following categories of persons: 9.29

10. Removal of certain persons unlawfully in the United Kingdom
    (1) A person who is not a British citizen may be removed from the United Kingdom, in accordance with directions given by an immigration officer, if—
       (a) having only a limited leave to enter or remain, he does not observe a condition attached to the leave or remains beyond the time limited by the leave;
       (b) he uses deception in seeking (whether successfully or not) leave to remain; or
       (ba) his indefinite leave to enter or remain has been revoked under section 76(3) of the Nationality, Immigration and Asylum Act 2002 (person ceasing to be refugee);
       (c) directions ... have been given for the removal, under this section, of a person ... to whose family he belongs.

Neither section 10 IAA 1999 nor section 47 IANA 2006 imposes upon the Secretary of State either a general obligation to take removal action in every case where an individual is, or becomes, susceptible to removal, or a duty to take a removal decision in any particular case; nor will a failure to do so affect the validity of a related immigration decision such as a refusal to grant further leave to remain. This issue was finally resolved by the Supreme Court in *Patel v SSHD, Anwar v SHDD, Alam v SSHD* [2013] UKSC 72, [2013] 3 WLR. 1517. The first group of appellants therein had made an application for further leave to remain, which was refused. No removal decision was taken. They argued (relying on the Court of Appeal decisions in *R (otao Mirza) and others v SSHD* [2011] EWCA Civ 159, [2011] Imm AR 484 and *Sapkota and another v SSHD* [2011] EWCA Civ 1320, [2012] Imm AR 254) that the decision was consequently unlawful and furthermore was an unjustified deferral of the removal decision. The Supreme Court rejected the submission holding, per Lord Carnwath at [27], that: 'The powers to issue 9.30

---

[2] Defined by s 33(1) IA 1971 as all persons actually employed in the working or service of a ship or an aircraft.
[3] For Home Office policy on deserting seamen and aircrews, see ch 6 EIG and ch 16 Immigration Directorate Instructions and Modernised Guidance with respect to aircrew.

Part C – Deportation, Removal and Exclusion

removal directions under section 10 of the 1999 Act and section 47 of the 2006 Act (like the power to issue notices under section 120 of the 2002 Act) are just that—powers.'

9.31 Similarly, when an overstayer makes an out-of-time application for leave to remain and this is refused, there is no obligation upon the Secretary of State to make a removal decision so as to engage the statutory appeal provisions: *R (otao Daley-Murdock) v SSHD* [2011] EWCA Civ 161. There are, however, certain circumstances in which the Home Office will make a removal decision upon the request of an applicant now set out in non-statutory guidance (Modernised Guidance: Requests for Removal Directions—version 5.0, 24 February 2014). At present, these circumstances apply in the following cases:

— the refused application for leave to remain included a dependent child under the age of 18 resident in the UK for three years or more;
— the applicant has a dependent child under the age of 18 who is a British citizen;
— the applicant is being supported by the Home Office or has provided evidence of being supported by a local authority (under section 21 of the National Assistance Act 1948 or section 17 of the Children Act 1989); or
— there are other exceptional and compelling reasons to make a removal decision at the time in question.

The Guidance states that

When making a decision to accept a request, you must consider:
— the need to promote the welfare of children who are in the UK
— any direct cost in supporting the applicant and dependants being met by the Home Office or a local authority (under section 21 of the National Assistance Act 1948 or section 17 of the Children Act 1989), and
— exceptional and compelling circumstances.

Section 47 IANA 2006

9.32 Section 47 IANA 2006 applies to persons with statutorily extended leave, that is, individuals who made applications to extend or vary leave to remain before the expiry of their leave, whose leave is extended by operation of law under section 3C or 3D IA 1971 once the previous leave has expired, whilst an application or appeal remains outstanding. The provision as originally enacted provides that:

47. Where a person's leave to enter or remain in the United Kingdom is extended by section 3C(2)(b) or 3D(2)(a) of the Immigration Act 1971 (extension pending appeal), the Secretary of State may decide that the person is to be removed from the United Kingdom, in accordance with directions given by an immigration officer if and when the leave ends.

9.33 The Secretary of State's view of this provision was that in response to an in-time application for further leave to remain, he or she was entitled to issue a single decision refusing the application to extend leave and deciding to remove the individual. Indeed, this appeared to be the intention of Parliament when the amendment was made to the Bill in the House of Lords.[4] However, following *Ahmadi (Section 47 Decision: Validity; Sapkota)*

---

[4] See statement of the Minister for Justice Baroness Ashton of Upholland, HL Hansard 7 February 2006, cols 520–21.

[2012] UKUT 00147 (IAC) and *Adamally and Jaferi (Section 47 Removal Decisions: Tribunal Procedures)* [2012] UKUT 00414 (IAC) in the Upper Tribunal, the Court of Appeal decided in *SSHD v Ahmadi* [2013] EWCA Civ 512, [2013] 4 All ER 442 that the provision was inadequate to achieve what Parliament had set out to accomplish and that the Secretary of State's practice of issuing combined decisions was unlawful.

A new version of subsection 47(1) IANA 2006 with a supplementary section 47(2) IANA 2006 was substituted by section 51 of the Crime and Courts Act 2013. The amending provision was brought into force on 8 May 2013.[5] This new version appears to resolve the problem identified in litigation, enabling the Secretary of State to take two decisions together in circumstances defined by statute:

9.34

47(1) Where the Secretary of State gives written notice of a pre-removal decision to the person affected, the Secretary of State may—
  (a) in the document containing that notice,
  (b) in a document enclosed in the same envelope as that document,
  (c) otherwise on the occasion when that notice is given to the person, or
  (d) at any time after that occasion but before an appeal against the pre-removal decision is brought under section 82(1) of the Nationality, Immigration and Asylum Act 2002,
also give the person written notice that the person is to be removed from the United Kingdom under this section in accordance with directions given by an immigration officer if and when the person's leave to enter or remain in the United Kingdom expires.

(1A) In subsection (1) 'pre-removal decision' means—
  (a) a decision on an application—
      (i) for variation of limited leave to enter or remain in the United Kingdom, and
      (ii) made before the leave expires,
  (b) a decision to revoke a person's leave to enter or remain in the United Kingdom, or
  (c) a decision to vary a person's leave to enter or remain in the United Kingdom where the variation will result in the person having no leave to enter or remain in the United Kingdom.

D3. Statutory Instrument

The Immigration (European Economic Area) Regulations 2006

By regulation 19(3) Immigration (European Economic Area) Regulations 2006, SI 2006/1003, a person who has been admitted to or acquired a right of residence in the UK under the Regulations may be removed if:

9.35

(a) he or she does not have or ceases to have a right to reside under the Regulations;
(b) he or she would otherwise be entitled to reside in the UK under the Regulations, but the Secretary of State has decided that his or her removal is justified on the grounds of public policy, public security or public health in accordance with regulation 21; or
(c) the Secretary of State has decided that his or her removal is justified on the grounds of abuse of rights in accordance with regulation 21B(2).

---

[5] SI 2013/1042, art 2(i).

9.36 There would appear to be a substantial case that Regulation 19(3)(a) does not constitute a lawful application of Directive 2004/38/EC in relation to cases where a person is subject to removal merely for no longer having the right to reside under the Regulations, given that Article 15(1) of the Directive applies protection of Articles 30 and 31 to all decisions 'restricting free movement of Union Citizens on the grounds other than public policy, public security or public health' and Article 31(3) expressly requires detailed considerations of proportionality stipulated in Article 28(1): 'Member State shall take account of considerations such as how long the individual concerned has resided on its territory, his/her age, state of health, family and economic situation, social and cultural integration into the host Member State and the extent of his/her links with the country of origin.' By regulation 19(4), an individual must not be removed as an automatic consequence of having recourse to the social assistance system. By regulation 19(5), he or she must not be removed whilst possessing leave under the IA 1971, save where removal is justified by reference to regulation 21 grounds of public policy, public security or public health, or one of these.

9.37 By Regulation 24(2)–(4), where a person is to be removed, he or she will be treated variously as though he or she was a person to whom section 10 (1)(a) IAA 1999 or section 3 (5)(a) IA 1971 applied, depending upon the basis for removal in any given case. Under regulation 24(5), where a person was not removed for two years after a deportation order was made, the Secretary of State must consider whether the circumstances have changed materially prior to any removal and, in light thereof, whether removal is still justified Regulation 24(6) provides that a person shall be allowed a month to leave the UK prior to removal by the state, save in 'duly substantiated' cases of urgency, persons detained pursuant to sentence or order of a court, or entry in breach of a deportation or exclusion order. Regulation 24AA enables the Secretary of State to give directions for removal of a person pending appeal against a decision under Regulation 19(3)(b), having certified that such a removal does not constitute a breach of section 6 of the Human Rights Act 1998 and may include that the person would not be at risk of 'serious irreparable harm if removed' to the proposed country or territory. While Article 31(4) of Directive 2004/38/EC does envisage the possibility of exclusion from the territory pending an appeal but notably the state cannot prevent a person defending their appeal in person, a decision to exclude a person pending such an appeal must comply with (a) the principle of proportionality in Union Law (see further Chapter 6) and (b), given that such a decision falls within the scope of Union Law (see further Chapter 16), with the provisions of the Charter of Fundamental Rights of the European Union. Of particular relevance are Articles 47, which sets high standards of protection in terms of the right to an effective remedy before a court and standards of fair trial under Article 6 ECHR; Article 41 right to good administration which includes a right to be heard before any individual measure which could affect a person adversely is taken; as well as substantive guarantees of Article 7 CFREU embodying Article 8 ECHR and Article 24 CFREU which is based on Articles 3, 9, 12 and 13 of the Convention on the Rights of the Child and ensures that children have 'right to such protection and care as is necessary for their wellbeing' as well as that their views are taken into account; that their best interests must be a primary consideration and they have a right to maintain a personal relationship and contact with both parents unless that is contrary to their interests. Given the fundamental status of citizenship of the Union and right to free movement it is in doubt whether any such decision which has the capability of undermining the substance of such rights, can be taken without very serious reasons.

D4. Published Guidance

The Secretary of State publishes extensive guidance concerning removal, set out primarily in the Enforcement Instructions and Guidance (EIG) at chapters 46-52: most particularly by Chapter 47 ('Removal of Illegal Entrants'), Chapter 50 ('Persons liable to administrative removal under section 10 (non EEA)'), Chapter 50 (EEA) ('EEA Administrative Removal'), and Chapter 53 ('Extenuating Circumstances'). Details of this guidance are examined below.

9.38

E. Discussion

E1. Removal under Schedule 2 IA 1971 of Persons Refused Leave to Enter, Illegal Entrants, Family Members of Persons within the First Two Categories and Members of Maritime or Air Crews

As already noted, three separate removal powers exist in domestic law. Schedule 2 IA 1971 applies to those refused leave to enter, illegal entrants, family members of persons within the first two categories and members of maritime or air crews.

9.39

i. Refusal of Leave to Enter

Persons refused leave to enter are susceptible to removal under the initial paragraph 8 of Schedule 2 IA 1971 power, by which directions may be given to the captain of a ship or aircraft, or the owners or agents of the same, for the removal of a person refused leave to enter. By paragraph 8(2), this must, in specified circumstances, be done within two months of the date on which leave to enter was refused. Alternatively, directions may issue under paragraph 10 of Schedule 2 IA 1971 where directions might have been given under paragraph 8, but would be impractical or ineffective, or previous directions under paragraph 8 have not been complied with. Such decisions are subject to ordinary public law principles, which (in very brief summary) require the avoidance of illegality, irrationality or unfairness.[6]

9.40

ii. Illegal Entrants

The meaning of 'illegal entrant' is given at section 33(1) IA 1971 as follows:

9.41

(1) '[E]ntrant' means a person entering or seeking to enter the United Kingdom and 'illegal entrant' means a person—
   (a) unlawfully entering or seeking to enter in breach of a deportation order or of the immigration laws, or

---

[6] This conventional three-fold summary is not exhaustive and its components are not mutually exclusive: see M Fordham, *Judicial Review Handbook* (6th edn, Oxford, Hart Publishing, 2012) 487. The public law wrongs justifying intervention are more fully examined in that work at Part C, P45–P63.

(b) entering or seeking to enter by means which include deception by another person, and includes also a person who has entered as mentioned in paragraph (a) or (b) above;

9.42 An individual is not considered to have 'entered' until he or she has disembarked from the ship or plane and has passed through border control (if there is one), and a person is deemed not to have entered the UK if detained, temporarily admitted or released while liable to detention: section 11(1) IA 1971. By reason of the wording employed in the statutory definition at section 33(1) IA 1971, however, the term 'illegal entrant' includes someone who is 'seeking to enter', that is, whose attempt at actual entry is frustrated. Section 33(1) IA 1971 defines 'the immigration laws' as meaning IA 1971 and any law for similar purposes which is for the time being or has (before or after the passing of IA 1971) been in force in any part of the UK, the Channel Islands or the Isle of Man.

9.43 The term 'unlawfully entering' employed in section 33(1) IA 1971 is a broad one. The general Home Office policy, set out at paragraph 1.2 of Chapter 1 of the Enforcement and Instructions and Guidance (EIG) ('Illegal Entrant'), is to deal with passengers seeking entry 'unlawfully' as arriving passengers seeking entry under the Immigration Rules and to refuse them as such, rather than to treat them immediately as illegal entrants. Individuals will generally be interviewed prior to designation as 'illegal entrants', and appropriate standards of procedural fairness apply to designation whether or not an interview takes place (the absence of an interview itself may indicate unfairness as not permitting a response to suspicions of illegal entry). 'Illegal entry' must relate to the latest entry or attempted entry. Paragraph 1 of Chapter 1 EIG states that:

> When interviewing a person about illegal entry, their last entry into the UK is the relevant entry. Previous entries (lawful or unlawful) are not relevant to the proof of illegal entry. Care must be exercised when interviewing a person about illegal entry. The last entry signalled in a person's passport might not be the last entry, either because the person has subsequently entered without leave, or because they last entered on or after 30 July 2000 under one of the provisions of the Immigration (Leave to Enter and Remain) Order 2000 (see 2, 3.9 and 3.12).

In paragraph 1.3 of Chapter 1 EIG ('Assessment of the strength of the illegal entry contention'), it is noted that:

> The responsibility for assessing that the illegal entry contention is sound lies with the CIO who authorises service of notice of illegal entry and subsequently, the Inspector who authorises removal.

The strength of the illegal entry contention must be able to withstand a judicial review challenge.

9.44 Those who unwittingly evade immigration control are also classified as illegal entrants, though Home Office policy recognises that the unwitting nature of their entry may be a mitigating factor. Chapter 2 EIG gives as examples those who:

(a) present a passport to the IO on arrival who fails to endorse it when an endorsement is required for leave to enter to be granted;
(b) unwittingly bypass immigration control;
(c) unwittingly enter illegally from the Republic of Ireland;
(d) are believed by the IO (albeit no deception employed) on arrival to be still employed by a foreign embassy or international organisation and therefore exempt from immigration control;

(e) are believed by the IO to be a British citizen and are allowed to pass through EU control, when in fact they are British Overseas Citizens or British Overseas Territory Citizens and do not have the right of abode.

9.45 Home Office policy, set out in paragraph 2.4 of Chapter 2 EIG, suggests that if no mitigating features exist, then a notice of illegal entry (IS151a) will be served, save that where a person would but for the unwitting illegal entry have qualified for leave to enter, it may be considered appropriate to grant leave to enter notwithstanding unwitting illegal entry.

9.46 British citizens and EEA nationals are exempt from immigration control and do not require leave to enter the UK,[7] but there are cases where an individual will present a British or EEA passport to an IO who questions the document or the status of the individual presenting it. If a foreign national enters the UK by presenting a forged British or EEA passport or a genuine one to which he or she is not entitled, then his or her entry breaches of section 3 (1)(a) IA 1971 and is an illegal entrant.[8] Where a person claims to have entered legally on a British passport and it is clear that he or she has been issued with a British passport, the burden of proof rests on the IO to prove that he or she is not entitled to British citizenship and therefore is not entitled to the passport (*R v SSHD ex p Obi* [1991] Imm AR 420, QBD).

Entry by Deception and Related Criminal Offences

9.47 Section 33 IA 1971 does not shed any light upon the definition of entering or seeking to enter by deception, other than it includes deception by another. A person can be an illegal entrant on the basis of third party deception even if he or she had no knowledge of the deception.[9] However, illegal entry by deception is criminalised by two provisions of IA 1971. First, under section 26(1)(c):[10] 'if on any such examination or otherwise he makes or causes to be made to an immigration officer or other person lawfully acting in the execution of a relevant enactment a return, statement or representation which he knows to be false or does not believe to be true.' The burden of proof rests with the IO to show that leave was obtained by deception. To prove this offence, there must be a statement of representation made. A simple failure to disclose material facts would not amount to an offence, since there is no duty of candour placed on the defendant. However, conduct and silence as to material facts may amount to a representation. Furthermore, the deception must, as was established by the House of Lords in *Khawaja v SSHD* [1983] UKHL 8, [1984] AC 74, be material to the grant of leave to enter, that is,

---

[7] The burden of proving his or her entitlement to such status is on the passenger by production of a valid passport or ID card: IA 1971, s 3(9) and SI 2006/1003, reg 11.
[8] This is not obtaining, entering or attempting to enter by deception because no leave has been granted.
[9] Para 3.4 of ch 3 EIG provides that the deception of a parent is imputed to the children; even if the children are unaware of the deception employed, they may be treated as if they were parties to the deception perpetrated by the parents. The decision to serve a notice of illegal entry on a child is discretionary—factors such as whether there is the possibility of prosecution of others for facilitation or to trigger the right of an appeal in an asylum case should be considered. S 55 of the Borders, Citizenship and Immigration Act 2009 regarding the safeguarding and promoting the welfare of children must also be considered.
[10] A summary only offence with a maximum sentence of a fine or imprisonment for not more than six months, or both.

had the person granting leave to enter known the truth, he or she would not have granted the leave (paragraph 3.1 of Chapter 3 EIG).

9.48 The second offence is created in section 24A IA 1971[11] and defines the offence, committed by a person who 'by means which include deception by him—obtains or seeks to obtain leave to enter or remain in the United Kingdom; or ... secures or seeks to secure avoidance, postponement or revocation of enforcement action against him'.

9.49 It is also an offence contrary to section 26(1)(d) IA 1971 for a person without lawful authority to alter or to use for the purposes of IA 1971 any passport, certificate of entitlement, entry clearance, work permit or other document issued or made for the purposes of IA 1971, or to have such a document in his or her possession for such use which he or she knows or has reasonable cause to believe to be false. Presenting such a document would also amount to a representation that breaches section 26(1)(c) and section 24A IA 1971 and would therefore make such a person an illegal entrant by deception (however, note the difference of presenting a British or EEA passport; see above at paragraph 9.46).

9.50 In addition to the offences dealt with above in relation to entering by deception, a further offence exists: knowingly entering the UK without leave contrary to section 24(1)(a) IA 1971, punishable by a fine or imprisonment for not more than six months, or both.

No Evidence of Lawful Entry (NELE)

9.51 'No evidence of lawful entry' is a phrase used in Home Office policy, often reduced to an acronym (NELE): ch 4 EIG. Individuals who cannot produce a passport as evidence of their lawful entry, or in respect of whom there is no trace within Home Office records are not automatically treated as illegal entrants. They may, for example, have lawfully entered through the Common Travel Area and have no evidence in their passports of this. However, where they cannot provide evidence or a credible explanation to support their claim of lawful entry and the IO is satisfied that they are an illegal entrant, an interview under caution would normally proceed (paragraph 4 of Chapter 4 EIG). In the absence of an admission from the individual that they entered illegally, the burden of proof is on the IO to a high degree of probability (Chapter 4 EIG). There are circumstances in which an individual may claim to have been given notice of leave to enter orally (Article 8(3) or 9 of the Immigration (Leave to Enter or Remain) Order 2000); the onus is then upon the individual to produce evidence of the manner and date of entry, such as a travel ticket.

9.52 Home Office policy (Chapter 4 EIG) provides for initial checks to be made in every case of application forms, screening and port records, interview records, documents on file, CID and Warehouse (Home Office computer records) for information on their method of entry. Where that is not the case, the individual should be given a method of entry questionnaire and allowed 28 days to complete and return it. In the absence of sufficient information being provided or the form not being returned at all, it will be

---

[11] An either-way offence with a maximum sentence of two years' imprisonment if tried upon indictment. *R v Nasir Ali* [2002] 2 Cr App R, the leading authority on sentencing for this offence indicates that even where a guilty plea is entered, a sentence of 9–12 months' imprisonment should be imposed, which results in these offences usually being dealt with in the Crown Court.

assumed that he or she has entered illegally and he or she will be treated accordingly. This may also be the conclusion reached where method of entry has been fully investigated but the IO is still unable to determine the individual's status.

Entry in Breach of a Deportation Order

Section 5(1) IA 1971 invalidates any leave to enter or remain given to an individual before a deportation order is made or granted while it is in force. Therefore, unless or until a deportation is revoked, any leave purportedly granted whilst it is in force is invalidated and anyone seeking or entering on such leave will be an illegal entrant. Unless an individual admits to being subject to a deportation order, the IO must prove, again to a high degree of probability, that he or she is from Home Office records. **9.53**

Entry through the Common Travel Area (Republic of Ireland, the Channel Islands or the Isle of Man)

Entry to the UK from the Republic of Ireland (ROI) is controlled by section 1(3) and (9) IA 1971 and the Immigration (Control of Entry through Republic of Ireland) Order 1972. The following categories require leave to enter on arrival from the ROI:[12] **9.54**

(a) persons who have entered the ROI unlawfully (but not those who were granted leave to enter the ROI outside the Common Travel Area, whether deception was used or not) and overstayers (SI 1972/1610, Article (3)(1)(b)(ii));
(b) those transiting through the ROI to the UK from outside the Common Travel Area who were not given leave to enter (SI 1972/1610, Article 3(1)(a));
(c) visa nationals without a valid UK visa (SI 1972/1610, Article 3(1)(b)(i));
(d) illegal entrants or overstayers from the UK who cross to the ROI and seek to come back (SI 1972/1610, Article 3(1)(b)(iii));
(e) persons subject to an exclusion or deportation order (SI 1972/1610, Article (3)(1)(b)(iv));
(f) persons previously refused leave to enter the UK and who have not since been granted leave to enter or remain in the UK (section 9(4)(b) of IA 1971).

Persons entering the UK from the Channel Islands or the Isle of Man will be illegal entrants if their presence in the previous territory was unlawful unless they are given leave to enter the UK (paragraph 4 of Schedule 4 to IA 1971). Leave to enter is required and may be refused to a person who has previously been refused leave to enter the UK and has not since been granted leave to enter or remain in the UK (section 9(4)(b) IA 1971). **9.55**

The Consequences of Being Classified an Illegal Entrant

Where an individual appears to fit the definition of an illegal entrant on one of the bases set out above, the Secretary of State possesses a discretion as to whether to treat **9.56**

---

[12] Para 2.6.1 of ch 2 EIG contains a useful flowchart.

that person as an illegal entrant. The exercise of discretion depends on whether it would be fair in all the circumstances to treat the individual as an illegal entrant and to embark upon the official process starting with service of notice to an illegal entrant (IS151A) upon him or her. In this, account must be taken of any information or representations available. The issue of whether it is appropriate to exercise discretion is distinct from the question of whether an individual is in fact an illegal entrant and Home Office records should show a separate written record of this (Chapter 7 EIG—service of notice of illegal entry). The IO has a continuing duty to consider exercising discretion to withdraw a notice of illegal entry if further information comes to light or there is a change of circumstances which means that an individual is being prejudiced as a result of the notice.

9.57 There is no right of appeal against the decision of the Secretary of State to classify an individual as an illegal entrant. It is therefore only challengeable via judicial review. Illegal entrants refused leave to enter, such as asylum-seekers, will receive removal decisions (Part 2 of IS151 or IS151B), which are appealable under the NIAA 2002 regime (see further below).

9.58 Anyone who is found to have practiced deception to gain entry to the UK or who has attempted to seek entry unlawfully or in breach of a deportation order is subject to the re-entry ban (of one, five or 10 years depending upon the circumstances) provisions contained within paragraph 320(7A) or (7B) of the Immigration Rules. Whilst subject to such a ban and for as long as it is in force, an individual is prohibited from lawfully seeking entry to the UK.

E2. Removal under Section 10 IAA 1999

9.59 As noted above, section 10 IAA 1999 empowers the removal of a person who is not a British citizen where:

(a) having only a limited leave to enter or remain, he does not observe a condition attached to the leave or remains beyond the time limited by the leave;
(b) he uses deception in seeking (whether successfully or not) leave to remain; or
(ba) his indefinite leave to enter or remain has been revoked under section 76(3) of the Nationality, Immigration and Asylum Act 2002 (person ceasing to be refugee);
(c) directions ... have been given for the removal, under this section, of a person ... to whose family he belongs.

There may be overlap with Schedule 2 to IA 1971 where a person has been granted leave to remain but can still be treated as an illegal entrant—see paragraph 3.10 of Chapter 3 EIG. The exercise of the power is tritely an exercise of discretion and must be entered into, and completed, subject to ordinary public law principles, in brief summary avoiding illegality, irrationality or unfairness.[13] A recent affirmation of the application of such principles to a section 10 IAA 1999 decision can be seen in *R (otao Thapa) v SSHD* [2014] EWHC 659 (Admin), per Helen Mountfield QC sitting as a

---

[13] This conventional threefold summary is not exhaustive and its components are not mutually exclusive: see Fordham (n 6) 487. The public law wrongs justifying intervention are more fully examined in that work at Part C, P45–P63.

High Court Deputy Judge ('The Claimant's case, in short, is that the fact of a discretion triggers a duty to exercise it, and be seen to do so, fairly and rationally').

Entry clearance granted from abroad has the effect of leave to enter. An IO at the port of entry then conducts an examination to check documents and whether there are any change of circumstances (section 3A(3) IA 1971, inserted by the IAA 1999 and the Orders[14] made further to it). Anyone who obtains entry clearance by deception will have committed an offence under section 24A IA 1971. Whether or not the deception was practised upon an Entry Clearance Officer (ECO) or the IO is immaterial.[15]

9.60

Overstayers

Individuals who remain in the UK after the expiry of their leave are liable to administrative removal under section 10 IAA 1999.[16] However, if they have submitted an application to vary their leave before the expiry of their current leave and their leave expires before a decision is made, they do not become an overstayer by virtue of section 3C IA 1971. Their leave becomes automatically extended, including any conditions attached to it, until the time limit for appealing any negative decision expires. Of course, if they properly lodge a notice of appeal with the Tribunal, then the leave is again automatically extended until such time as the in-country appeal is disposed of and/or appeal rights are exhausted (leave lapses if the individual leaves the UK: section 3C(3)). Leave is not statutorily extended in cases that only attract an out-of-country appeal.

9.61

Overstaying must be proved by evidence, such as passport, Home Office file, landing card or an individual's own admission under caution. As with illegal entrants above, those granted leave to enter orally or through a responsible third party, the burden is upon them to produce some evidence of the date and manner of entry.

9.62

Where the Secretary of State relies on allegations of misconduct in removal proceedings, the same principles apply as to proof of conduct and the assessment of risk to the public as in deportation cases; see *Farquharson (Removal—Proof of Conduct)* [2013] UKUT 00146 (IAC) with reference to *Bah* [2012] UKUT 196 (IAC). It was also confirmed in *Farquharson* that a criminal charge that has not resulted in a conviction is not a criminal record; but the acts that lead to the charge may be established as conduct. If the Secretary of State seeks to rely on the contents of police CRIS reports, then the actual documents, as opposed to statements referring to them, should be produced to the individual in good time to prepare for any appeal.

9.63

British citizens, those with the right of abode, EEA nationals and their dependants (save for those subject to expulsion or exclusion—see further below), those exempt from immigration control under section 8 IA 1971 and Irish and Commonwealth citizens

9.64

---

[14] Immigration (Leave to Enter and Remain) Order 2000, SI 2000/1161.
[15] Para 3.12 of ch 3 EIG. Caseworkers can assume illegal entry without an interview under caution and serve notices only where there is clear evidence of illegal entry and the facts are not in dispute. Interviews are required where verbal deception is suspected or prosecution intended.
[16] When the IAA 1999 was brought in, s 9 of the Act allowed overstayers a short window (8 February to 1 October 2000 inclusive) in which to regularise their stay. Directions for removal could not be made against an individual who had made such an application and if the application was refused, he or she would continue to have an in-country right of appeal against the decision to make a deportation order (since that was the consequence for overstayers before the IAA 1999).

who were ordinarily resident in the UK on 1 January 1973 and have been ordinarily resident in the UK for the last five years at the date of the decision to remove cannot be administratively removed from the UK.

Breach of Conditions

9.65 Under section 3(1)(c) IA 1971, the Secretary of State is empowered to attach one or more of five conditions to an individual's limited leave:

> 3(1)(c) if he is given limited leave to enter or remain in the United Kingdom, it may be given subject to all or any of the following conditions, namely—
> (i) a condition restricting his employment or occupation in the United Kingdom;
> (ia) a condition restricting his studies in the United Kingdom;
> (ii) a condition requiring him to maintain and accommodate himself, and any dependants of his, without recourse to public funds;
> (iii) a condition requiring him to register with the police;
> (iv) a condition requiring him to report to an immigration officer or the Secretary of State; and
> (v) a condition about residence.

Where a person is found to be breaching any of the conditions attached to his or her leave, he or she may face a section 10 IANA 1999 enforcement action.

9.66 Paragraph 50.6 of Chapter 50 EIG states that where an individual has worked contrary to the conditions of his or her leave, the breach must be sufficiently grave in order to warrant removal action.[17] It further states that there must be firm and recent evidence of such a breach. The policy provides that evidence is to include one of the following: either an admission under caution, a statement by the employer, documentary evidence (eg, payslips, National Insurance records or tax records) or a statement by an IO or police officer to the effect that he or she has seen the individual preferably on two or more occasions, or on a single occasion over a sustained period, or wearing the employer's uniform. Where a person has both overstayed and has worked in breach of the conditions of his or her leave, the policy dictates that he or she should not be made subject to section 10 for both, but only as an overstayer, unless he or she claims to have made in-time applications that cannot be substantiated.

9.67 Students over the age of 16 are permitted to work part time during term (subject to limitation upon hours), full time in vacations, and where work is a placement as part of the course or is as a student union sabbatical officer (subject to limitation to two years).[18] A student found to have worked in excess of these hours may be subject to administrative removal for breaching relevant conditions. A student who has stopped attending his or her course but who continues to work within the hours permitted may well have his or her leave curtailed, but he or she cannot be removed for breaching his or her conditions: *R (otao Zhou) v SSHD* [2003] EWCA Civ 51. In *R (otao Zahid) v SSHD* [2013] EWHC 4290 (Admin), a decision was taken to remove a student seen by an IO and suspected of working in breach of his Tier 4 visa. He was detained and removal directions were put in place. He made an unparticularised Article 8 ECHR claim and notified the Secretary of State of an intention to initiate

---

[17] See also *R (otao Lim) v SSHD* [2006] EWHC 3004 (Admin), [2006] All ER (D) 410 (Nov).
[18] See para 50.7 of ch 50 EIG for a full breakdown.

judicial review proceedings. He was then removed without notice in spite of the Secretary of State's confirmation that removal would not take place prior to the hearing. His Article 8 ECHR claim was later refused and was certified as clearly unfounded. The claimant issued judicial review proceedings seeking a declaration that his removal was unlawful and requiring his return to the UK and/or damages. The Court held, applying *R (otao Lim) v SSHD* [2007] EWCA Civ 773, [2008] INLR 60, that, notwithstanding the failure to give notice of his removal and to respond to the Article 8 claim, there was nothing exceptional about his case that justified his application for judicial review, and that the claimant's out-of-country appeal was an effective remedy. However, it further found the without-notice removal to be unlawful, particularly in light of the confirmation that he would not be removed. He was entitled to damages, the court's provisional view considering *R (otao Shaw) v SSHD* [2013] EWHC 42 (Admin) being that the sum would be less than £2,000.

9.68 Work permits are not required by those working wholly on offshore oil rigs as the Immigration Acts do not apply to the continental shelf, and immigration control cannot consequently be exercised in offshore waters.

9.69 A person who is subject to the condition of no recourse to public funds and is found to be in receipt of one may be subject to a section 10 enforcement action. The endorsement in his or her passport must expressly state that public funds are prohibited for a breach to be found (at paragraph 50.11 of Chapter 50 EIG). In order for action to commence, there must be either an admission under caution or a statement from an official at the relevant benefit agency confirming that public funds have been claimed.

9.70 Having knowingly overstayed or breached a condition also amounts to a criminal offence further to section 24(1)(b) IA 1971.

Leave to Remain by Deception

9.71 Under section 10 IANA 1999, removal may only be used against a person who has used deception in seeking or obtaining leave to remain since 1 October 1996,[19] since that is when the criminal offence was first introduced.[20]

9.72 The evidence of deception must be to a high degree of probability, the burden of proof being upon the Secretary of State: *Khawaja v SSHD* [1983] UKHL 8, [1984] AC 74. Paragraph 50.12 of Chapter 50 EIG states that the evidence should be clear and unambiguous if action is to be initiated. The policy further states at Chapter 3 EIG, in identical terms to the policy regarding illegal entry by deception, that the deception must be 'material', which reflects the House of Lords' conclusion in *Khawaja*. As an example of materiality, the policy states that 'in other words, had the officer known the truth, the leave would not have been given'. The Secretary of State's policy appears to indicate that the 'whether successfully or not' part of the statutory provision may not be relied upon in practice. Relevant deception is not just deception related to the current application, as historic deception practised in previous applications may be relied upon: *R (otao Fazal-E-Haq) v SSHD* [2009] EWHC 357 (Admin); and *R (otao Alapati) v SSHD* [2009] EWHC 3712.

---

[19] Deception pre-dating 1 October 1996 is to be considered for possible deportation action on non-conducive grounds under s 3 (5)(a) IA 1971.
[20] It was later replaced by s 24A IA 1971 (as inserted by IAA 1999).

Part C – Deportation, Removal and Exclusion

Removal Following Curtailment/Revocation of Leave

9.73 As set out above, section 10(1)(ba) IAA 1999 allows for the removal of individuals where indefinite leave to remain has been revoked pursuant to section 76(3) NIAA 2002 upon an individual ceasing to qualify for recognition as a refugee. These provisions are further reflected in paragraphs 323, 322, 339A and 399G of the Immigration Rules, which provide for additional circumstances, with reference to the general grounds for refusal, in which leave to remain may be curtailed.

9.74 Curtailment of leave is a discretionary power; the Secretary of State's policy acknowledges that leave should not be automatically curtailed because one or more of the criteria set out in the Rules is met, notwithstanding other circumstances (Modernised Guidance, ('Curtailment of Leave'), version 10.0, valid from 11 February 2014, page 6). In cases of false representation or non-disclosure of material facts, the Home Office will consider whether it can be treated as a removal case under section 10 IAA 1999 on the grounds of deception before curtailing leave. If it is decided that a section 10 IAA 1999 decision on the grounds of deception is justified, then the decision would invalidate any remaining leave that has been obtained by the deception. Page 9 of the Modernised Guidance, provides that leave must not be curtailed under this category if the undisclosed facts would not have affected the original decision to grant leave.

9.75 With respect to a failure to comply with conditions, the breach must be of sufficient gravity to warrant curtailment. Where the breach is minor, leave must not be curtailed if it would be disproportionate (Modernised Guidance, page 12).

9.76 With respect to claiming public funds, where a condition of an individual's leave restricted his or her access to public funds, then doing so could amount to a breach of conditions. Mitigating factors must be taken into account when deciding whether curtailment is appropriate—for example, benefits may have only been claimed for a short period in the case of emergency or loss of employment outside the individual's control. In such cases, it may be appropriate for the decision maker to use his or her discretion.

9.77 With respect to conduct, character and associations, conduct and convictions that do not reach the deportation threshold may be taken into account, but the evidence must be reliable to justify curtailment on this basis (Modernised Guidance, Curtailment of Leave, version 10.0, page 16).

9.78 In addition to the reasons set out in paragraph 323 Immigration Rules HC 395 for curtailment, specific provisions exist for the curtailment of point-based system leave where certain requirements have not been realised (paragraphs 323A–323C HC 395).

9.79 If leave is curtailed so that there is no leave to remain, the decision attracts a right of appeal (section 82(2)(e) NIAA 2002). So too, pursuant to section 82(2)(f) NIAA 2002, does a decision to revoke indefinite leave to remain under section 76(3) NIAA 2002. Now that section 47 IANA 2006 has been amended, a simultaneous removal decision can be taken at the same time as the decision to curtail and therefore any appeal would consider both the decision to curtail leave in the first place and the decision to remove within the same proceedings.

Section 10 IAA 1999 as Substituted by Section 1 IA 2014

9.80 The new section 10 IAA 1999 looks quite different from its current incarnation. Reference to overstaying, breaching conditions or using deception has been stripped away by section 10(1) of the new provision, as substituted by section 1 IA 2014 (on a date to be appointed). The new section 10(1) simply states that: 'A person may be removed from the United Kingdom under the authority of the Secretary of State or an immigration officer if the person requires leave to enter or remain in the United Kingdom but does not have it.'

Section 10(2)–(6) deals with the removal of family members, discussed below in section E4. Section 10(7)–(9) deals with directions for removal and collateral powers of detention, drawing from Schedule 2 IA 1971. Section 10(10) allows the Secretary of State to use regulations to make further provision for the time period during which a family member may be removed and the service of a notice to a family member. A requirement for the primary individual facing removal to be given notice is, on the facts of the Act, noticeably absent. Prior to the Act passing, a government factsheet of 10 October 2013 said that the purpose of this clause (as it then was) is to streamline and simplify decision making by having a single decision informing a person that he or she has no leave and that he or she is liable to removal. Therefore, it appears that the government does intend to inform individuals about decisions, but despite amendments to the bill being tabled to put the requirement of notice to be given to the primary individual on a statutory footing, no such amendments were accepted. In response to amendments tabled to clause 1 of the bill in response to concerns raised by the Immigration Law Practitioners' Association (ILPA) on clause 1 of the bill, Lord Taylor of Holbeach stated:

9.81

> I can confirm to my noble friend Lady Hamwee, and indeed to other noble Lords, that such people will all receive notice of the decision in writing, in accordance with Section 4 of the Immigration Act 1971, so it is unnecessary to place an additional notice requirement within this clause. This notice will inform them of the decision on leave, of their liability to be removed if they do not depart voluntarily, and the proposed destination for any enforced removal.[21]

In the same response, Lord Taylor made it clear that an individual will be given a minimum of 72 hours to raise any asylum, human rights or EU law reasons why he or she should not be removed before any removal can be enforced. Ultimately the proposed amendment was withdrawn in both the Commons and the Lords, and thus there is still no provision on the face of the Act that a person must be given notice of his or her removal. However, the giving of notice of a decision is, as Lord Steyn said in *R (Anufrijeva) v SSHD* [2003] UKHL 36, [2004] 1 AC 604 [26], a constitutional principle: 'Notice of a decision is required before it can have the character of a determination with legal effect because the individual concerned must be in a position to challenge the decision in the courts if he or she wishes to do so. This is not a technical rule. It is simply an application of the right of access to justice. That is a fundamental and constitutional principle of our legal system.'

9.82

Whereas section 10 IAA 1999 currently provides for removal decisions to be taken in respect of those who have breached conditions or have used deception without the need to curtail their leave first, since the removal decision invalidates any leave to remain, it would appear from the new provisions that the Secretary of State, or an IO, would have to make a decision curtailing any extant leave on the basis of some wrongdoing and at the same time notify him or her of the liability of removal. However, notice of removal given to family members invalidates any leave to enter or remain they may have (section 1(6) IA 2014).

9.83

---

[21] Hansard 3 March 2014, col 1119.

Part C – Deportation, Removal and Exclusion

E3. Section 47 IANA 2006

9.84 As set out above, this provision was amended by section 51(3) of the Crime and Courts Act 2013 in light of litigation culminating in *R (otao Ahmadi) v SSHD* [2013] EWCA Civ 512, [2013] 4 All ER 442 to allow the Secretary of State to make an administrative removal decision at the same time as refusing to vary or curtail leave. The refusal decision does not have to be included with the decision refusing or curtailing leave; however, a section 47 decision cannot be made once an appeal against the refusal or curtailment decision has been lodged. The Upper Tribunal has very recently considered the new provision, issuing a 'recorded' decision in *Castro and another v SSHD (Removals: Section 47 (as Amended)) Philippines* [2014] UKUT 234 (IAC). The provision continues to provide a power, not a duty, and the Secretary of State or the IO must act compatibly with general public law standards.

9.85 In addition, since the Court of Appeal's decision in *Ahmadi*, the Administrative Court in *R (otao Hashemi) v The Upper Tribunal (IAC) and another* [2013] EWHC 2316 (Admin) has refused to entertain a challenge to the removal of an individual brought about by the use of section 47 IANA 2006 prior to the 8 May 2013 amendment. Hickinbottom J accepted that a simultaneous decision refusing further leave and to remove the claimant was ineffective for the reasons set out in *Ahmadi*, and that the claimant had been removed as the result of a process that was prima facie unlawful and deprived him of the in-country right of appeal attached to a section 10 removal decision in his case. However, the Tribunal had not been told of this prior to the decision refusing permission to appeal sought on other grounds, undermining the late challenge, and relief was withheld in the exercise of discretion.

9.86 Currently, a section 47 IANA 2006 removal decision triggers an additional right of appeal under section 82(2)(ha) NIAA 2002. In such a case, the issues arising from both the variation and removal decision will be considered together in a single appeal before the Tribunal. Any removal decision taken simultaneously under the original enactment of section 47 is ordinarily withdrawn by the Secretary of State on appeal, in lieu of which appeal against the removal decision will be allowed. A decision on an appeal that a section 47 removal decision is unlawful does not vitiate the immigration decision (on the facts of the case, refusing variation of limited leave) notified at the same time and dealt with together on appeal (*Rahman v SSHD* [2014] EWCA Civ 11).

E4. Family Members

9.87 The statutory removal provisions also provide for the removal of spouses and dependent children. Not all of them, however, will be removable—for example, if the spouse or child is a British or EEA national. As to the removal of adult children under section 10(1)(c) IAA 1999 (prior to the amendments made by section 1 IA 2014), see *Ahmad (Removal of Children over 18: Pakistan)* [2012] UKUT 267 (IAC), [2013] Imm AR 1, where the Upper Tribunal held:

> There is no power under the provisions of section 10(1)(c) of the Immigration and Asylum Act 1999 to remove children who are over the age of 18 years as the family members of an adult being removed under section 10(1)(b) of that Act.

Paragraph 50.13 of Chapter 50 EIG provides further categories within which removal action will not normally be taken. With regard to spouses, where a spouse has either qualified for settlement in his or her own right or has been living apart from the primary target for removal, action will not normally be pursued. With regard to children, where living apart from the parent or in the UK for some time and nearing the age of 18, or established independently of the family home, or married before removal became a prospect then, under the relevant policy, the following factors should be taken into account: **9.88**

(a) the best interests of the child;
(b) the ability of the spouse to maintain himself or herself and any children without being a long-term burden on public funds;
(c) the effect on a school-age child's education;
(d) the practicality of any plans for the care and maintenance of the child in the UK if one or both of his or her parents were removed; and
(e) any representations made on behalf of the spouse or child.

Written notice as the family member of a person to be removed (Parts 1 and 2 of IS151A) must be served on each individual family member. Paragraph 50.13 of Chapter 50 EIG states that the warning should be given as early as possible and ideally before the principal is removed. If notice has not been given to the family member within eight weeks of the principal being removed, then removal under section 10(1)(c) IAA 1999 is not possible. Section 10 (1)(c) IAA 1999 also requires directions to have been given to the principal person before a direction can be given to his or her family member; however, the removal *decisions* can be made at the same time: *RJ (India) v SSHD* [2012] EWCA Civ 1865, [2012] All ER (D) 48 (Dec). As to service, written notice may be served by first-class post to the last known address of the person concerned and a dated copy placed on the Home Office file. Removal action is not possible if the person ceases to be a family member of the principal. **9.89**

Section 1(2) IA 2014 (not yet in force as at date of writing) provides for the removal of a family member of a person (P) who is liable to be or has been removed from the UK under section 1(1) of the same Act, providing he or she has been given written notice of the intention to remove him or her. There are three conditions to meet: (i) being a 'family member' as defined in section 1(3) IA 2014; (ii) not having leave in his or her own right (section 1(4) IA 2014); and finally (iii) not being a British citizen or entitled to enter or remain on the basis of an EU right or provision (section 1(5) IA 2014). To be considered a family member of P, he or she must be: **9.90**

(a) P's partner;
(b) P's child, or a child living in the same household as P in circumstances where P has care of the child;
(c) P's parent (where P is a child); or
(d) an adult dependant relative of P.

The definition of 'family member' in (b) above is not without its problems, since the definition of 'a child living in the same household as P where P has care of the child' is imprecise and creates the risk of removal of a child where someone else has parental responsibility, and could also cause problems with children in the care of a local authority. **9.91**

9.92 As for the immigration status of the family member, the second condition requires that where he or she has leave to enter or remain, it is on the basis of his or her family life with P. Alternatively, where he or she does not have leave to enter or remain, *in the opinion of* the Secretary of State or immigration officer, he or she would not, on making an application for leave, be granted in his or her own right, but would be granted leave on the basis of his or her family life with P. This requires a hugely subjective and speculative test, which we can see as producing uncertain results that will vary widely. This presents a very risky and uncertain future for many family members.

9.93 Section 2 IA 2014 (not yet in force) inserts a new section 78A into the NIAA 2002 and provides that where a child is being removed as part of a family unit, it cannot be done until 28 days following the date when all appeal rights were exhausted. However, under section 78A (4)(a), this does not stop the making a removal directions and taking other interim and preparatory action during the 28-day period.

9.94 Section 3 IA 2014 (not yet in force) inserts a new section 54A in the Borders, Citizenship and Immigration Act 2009 that puts the Independent Family Returns Panel on a statutory footing. However, under section 54A(4), the Secretary of State may by regulations make provision about the additional functions of the Panel, its status and constitution, appointment of its members, payment and allowances of its members, and any other matters in connection with its establishment and operation. Therefore, the *independence* of the Panel is questionable.

EEA Nationals and Their Family Members

9.95 After engaging with the criteria necessary for the removal of an EEA national or his or her family member under regulation 19(3)(a) and (c), the decision maker must also consider whether it is proportionate to proceed with removal in all the circumstances of the case (paragraph 3 of Chapter 50 EIG).

9.96 The consequences of being administratively removed for not exercising Treaty rights is a re-entry ban for the next 12 months, unless it can be demonstrated that Treaty rights will be exercised immediately upon re-entry. It is arguable that the Directive 2004/38/EC may not have envisaged a re-entry ban if the person was expelled for reasons other than public policy or security as the exclusion orders are only mentioned in that context in Article 32).

E5. Exercises of Statutory Removal Powers: Applicable Standards

9.97 What are the factors likely to be of relevance when the Secretary of State or an IO considers the exercise of discretionary removal powers under any of the powers above: Schedule 2 IA 1971, section 10 IAA 1999 or section 47 IANA 2006? In general, the following matters all apply:

(i) The decision maker must deal in legally adequate fashion with the fact that the removal provisions create a discretion rather than imposing a duty. He or she must act consistently with established public law standards.

(ii) Where the decision maker has put in place policy or guidance as to how discretion will be exercised and this is itself lawful, he or she must in general consider this and apply it, save where a legally adequate reason not to do so arises.

(iii) The decision maker is bound by rights protected by the HRA 1998 in relation to ECHR rights domesticated thereunder, or refugee protections under the CSR as incorporated into domestic or EU instruments.
(iv) Amongst the applicable provisions of ECHR, Articles 3 and 8 may have particular relevance. The scope of these rights has been delineated in chapter 5 above. Some further considerations as regards Article 8 ECHR and deportation, specific to the UK, are examined in paragraphs 8.101–8.115 in chapter 8.
(v) The decision maker will inter alia be bound by section 55 Borders Citizenship and Immigration Act 2009 ('Duty regarding the welfare of children') and in a case in which Article 8 ECHR or the principal obligation in Article 3 CRC is engaged will be bound, for the reasons set out in *ZH (Tanzania) v SSHD* [2011] UKSC 4, [2011] 2 AC 166, to treat the 'the best interests of the child' as 'a primary consideration' in relation to relevant actions.
(vi) Where it applies, the decision maker must comply with the relevant EU law standards.
(vii) Beyond the provisions of the ECHR, the CSR and the CRC already referred to, customary international law or unincorporated treaty obligations of the UK may inform the exercise of a statutory discretion, as identified in chapter 2 above.

E6. Appeals

The appeals regime will be changed enormously by the IA 2014; appeals and judicial review prior to and following the IA 2014 are further addressed in chapter 16. Currently, a decision to administratively remove an individual from the UK attracts a right of appeal to the First Tier Tribunal, Immigration and Asylum Chamber. Whether a decision taken by the Secretary of State is an appealable one, namely an 'immigration decision' as defined by section 82(1) NIAA 2002, and whether that appeal will be heard in-country or out-of-country is determined by the regime contained within NIAA 2002. Further information regarding the notices given to individuals are contained in Chapters 7, 8 and 51 EIG.   9.98

With respect to both illegal entrants and those subject to administrative removal for immigration infractions or removal pursuant to section 47, the first notice that is served is an IS151A Part 1,[22] which simply informs the individual that he or she is being treated as an illegal entrant and is liable to removal. A short statement of reasons should also be included (regulation 5(1)(a) Immigration (Notices) Regulations 2003). This is not an appealable decision. The notice that follows is the decision to remove: the 'immigration decision'. There is no specified timeframe in which the immigration decision must be made (subject to unreasonable delay), but Home Office policy states that it is best practice to serve the IS151A Part 1 and the immigration decision together (paragraph 51.2 of Chapter 51 of the EIG). An IS151A Part 2 is served on those who can only appeal from outside the UK and IS151B (where an asylum or human rights claim has been refused) informs the individual that a decision has been taken to remove him or her from the   9.99

---

[22] Seaman are served with form IS85B.

UK, but that he or she can exercise an in-country right of appeal. IS151D is the actual removal direction; again, this is not an appealable decision, but contains the information of the actual date, time, method and destination for removal. Although an IS151A Part 2 and IS151B can specify multiple destinations for removal, for example, where nationality is disputed or for dual nationals, IS151D must only specify one country to which removal will actually be effected (paragraph 7.1 of Chapter 7 EIG).

9.100 A removal decision pursuant to section 10(1)(b) because an individual has obtained leave to remain by deception (for example by stating that he or she intended to study at a college that was later found to be bogus) does not amount to a 'variation decision' for purposes of section 82(2)(e) NIAA 2002 (*R (otao Ali) v SSHD* [2009] EWHC 2126 (Admin)).

9.101 Where a person is subject to a removal order for breaching a condition, he or she has no right of appeal in country if the alternative remedy of an out-of-country appeal provides adequate protection: see *R (otao Lim) v SSHD* [2007] EWCA Civ 773, [2007] All ER (D) 402 (Jul); *R (otao Saleh) v SSHD* [2008] EWHC 3196 (Admin), [2008] All ER (D) 15 (Dec); *R (otao RK (Nepal)) v SSHD* [2009] EWCA Civ 359, [2009] All ER (D) 226 (Apr).

The Effect of the New Part 5A NIAA 2002

9.102 Section 19 IA 2014 added to NIAA 2002 a number of provisions relating to the interpretation of Article 8 ECHR:

PART 5A

ARTICLE 8 OF THE ECHR: PUBLIC INTEREST CONSIDERATIONS

117A Application of this Part
(1) This Part applies where a court or tribunal is required to determine whether a decision made under the Immigration Acts—
   (a) breaches a person's right to respect for private and family life under Article 8, and
   (b) as a result would be unlawful under section 6 of the Human Rights Act 1998.
(2) In considering the public interest question, the court or tribunal must (in particular) have regard—
   (a) in all cases, to the considerations listed in section 117B, and
   (b) in cases concerning the deportation of foreign criminals, to the considerations listed in section 117C.
(3) In subsection (2), 'the public interest question' means the question of whether an interference with a person's right to respect for private and family life is justified under Article 8(2).

117B Article 8: public interest considerations applicable in all cases
(1) The maintenance of effective immigration controls is in the public interest.
(2) It is in the public interest, and in particular in the interests of the economic well-being of the United Kingdom, that persons who seek to enter or remain in the United Kingdom are able to speak English, because persons who can speak English—
   (a) are less of a burden on taxpayers, and
   (b) are better able to integrate into society.

(3) It is in the public interest, and in particular in the interests of the economic well-being of the United Kingdom, that persons who seek to enter or remain in the United Kingdom are financially independent, because such persons—
   (a) are not a burden on taxpayers, and
   (b) are better able to integrate into society.
(4) Little weight should be given to—
   (a) a private life, or
   (b) a relationship formed with a qualifying partner,
   that is established by a person at a time when the person is in the United Kingdom unlawfully.
(5) Little weight should be given to a private life established by a person at a time when the person's immigration status is precarious.
(6) In the case of a person who is not liable to deportation, the public interest does not require the person's removal where—
   (a) the person has a genuine and subsisting parental relationship with a qualifying child, and
   (b) it would not be reasonable to expect the child to leave the United Kingdom.

This provision entered into force on 28 July 2014 by the Immigration Act 2014 (Commencement No 1, Transitory and Saving Provisions) Order 2014, [3].

As has been stated in chapter 8, to which these changes are also relevant, this provision is in essence an extension of the endeavour pursued in July 2012 through changes to the Immigration Rules by HC 194, of seeking to pressurise decisions on Article 8 ECHR in the immigration context. Section 117B NIAA 2002 sets out proscriptive, if often apparently trite, generic standards. On the language issue the exclusion of Welsh and Scots Gaelic would appear problematic, raising legal as well as political questions. 9.103

It seems likely that senior courts will interpret this provision in a manner which is consistent with the continued application of Article 8 ECHR through HRA 1998. In general, the language might be read as general abjuration not preventing independent consideration as to whether, on the facts of any given case, weight should be attached to the factors identified therein. An obvious if unfortunate precursor is section 8 Asylum and Immigration (Treatment of Claimants etc) Act 2004, which 'in determining whether to believe a statement made by or on behalf of a person who makes an asylum claim or a human rights claim, a deciding authority [including a tribunal] shall take account, as damaging the claimant's credibility, of any behaviour [listed below]'. In *JT (Cameroon) v SSHD* [2008] EWCA Civ 878, [2009] 1 WLR 1411, the Court of Appeal in respect of that provision noted the potential for offence against the 'constitutional principle' of judicial independence. Pill LJ, with whom Laws and Carnwath LJJ concurred, was not prepared to 'read the word "shall" as meaning "may"', but found that 'the section 8 factors shall be taken into account … but the section does not dictate that relevant damage to credibility inevitably results'. Laws LJ, with whom Carnwath LJ agreed, indicated that he would incline to read the word 'potentially' into the words of the section before the word 'damaging'. Insofar as the language of Part 5A only requires judicial notice to be taken of trite factors without interference in the judicial task of weighing relevant interests, its effect is unobjectionable. If and where the language may imply something further, it appears open to reading in a way which protects the critical value of judicial independence. 9.104

10

Exclusion from the UK

Contents

A.	Introduction	10.1
B.	International Law	10.2
	B1. General International Law	10.2
	B2. International Human Rights Law	10.5
	B3. Hybrid Instruments	10.10
	B4. Council of Europe Instruments	10.12
C.	EU Law	10.16
D.	Domestic Law	10.17
	D1. Prerogative	10.17
	D2. Statute	10.18
	D3. Statutory Instrument	10.21
	The Immigration (European Economic Area) Regulations 2006	10.21
	D4. The Immigration Rules	10.22
	D5. Guidance	10.29
E.	Discussion	10.30
	E1. Introduction	10.30
F.	Exclusion Decision	10.71
	Revocation	10.91
G.	Exclusion under the EEA Regime	10.97

A. Introduction

In the modern period it has been accepted that one of the primary powers of a sovereign state is control over the entry of aliens into its territory, in particular where the state considers the person's presence to be contradictory to 'peace, order and good governance'[1] or to its own social and economic interest. Exclusion of an alien or of a national without right of abode may take a variety of forms in practice, from the refusal to grant entry clearance on an application made at an overseas post to a refusal of leave to enter at the frontier. Exclusion is applicable to aliens, or to others not possessing

10.1

---

[1] *Attorney General for Canada v Cain* [1906] AC 542, 546.

right of abode in the UK,[2] by the exercise of discretion in line with the Immigration Rules HC 395 and a shifting body of subsidiary policy.

B. International Law

B1. General International Law

10.2 It is well established as a matter of international law that a state must admit its own nationals to its territory if required to do so by another state. Related to this, there is a widespread practice by which a national is held entitled to enter his or her own state of nationality. The European Court of Justice affirmed in *Van Duyn v Home Office (Workers)* [1974] EUECJ R-41/74, [1974] ECR 1337 that 'it is a principle of international law, which the EEC treaty cannot be assumed to disregard in the relations between member states, that a state is precluded from refusing its own nationals the right of entry or residence'. The relevant principles are examined in chapter 2. The UK in domestic law restricts right of abode to British citizens and some others, a practice which the Court of Appeal upheld in *R v SSHD ex p Thakrar* [1974] QB 684 (CA).

10.3 By contrast to the position of nationals, there is no general right in international law to enter a country of which one is not a national. In *Attorney General for Canada v Cain* [1906] AC 542, Lord Atkinson in the Privy Council observed at 546A–B that:

> One of the rights possessed by the supreme power in every State is the right to refuse to permit an alien to enter that State, to annex what conditions it pleases to the permission to enter it, and to expel or deport from the State, at pleasure, even a friendly alien, especially if it considers his presence in the State opposed to its peace, order, and good government, or to its social or material interests.

10.4 Exclusion of aliens is today generally recognised in international law as being within the ambit of a state's established attributes, as set out in chapter 2, section K. The broad discretion is not an absolute one, and the UK must not abuse its rights in international law by acting arbitrarily in excluding an alien. As with other areas examined in this work, a relationship of mutual reinforcement may exist as between the position in general international law and that in international human rights law.

B2. International Human Rights Law

10.5 Article 13 UDHR provides that 'Everyone has the right to leave any country, including his own, and to return to his country' and, as set out in chapter 3, Article 12(4)

---

[2] The UK has not extended the right of abode to all those persons it treats as being its nationals. Under s 2 of the IA 1971, the right of abode is granted to those who are British citizens and to a limited range of other persons. A wider treatment is provided by the leading work on British nationality law, Fransman's *British Nationality Law*, and another good treatment may be found in the most recent edition of *Halsbury's Laws of England*: Laurie Fransman QC, *British Nationality Law* (3rd edn, London, Bloomsbury Professional, 2011); Lord Mackay of Clashfern (ed), *Halsbury's Laws of England* (London, Butterworths, 2012).

ICCPR provides that: 'No-one shall be arbitrarily deprived of the right to enter his own country.'

First, a range of important human rights protections apply under the ICCPR to prevent return to a place in which relevant risk can be shown to arise. These might be engaged in certain very exceptional situations, such as exclusion at the border which would force an applicant to return to a situation against which he or she is entitled to protection: 10.6

(i) Article 6 ICCPR prohibits arbitrary deprivation of life, and sending an individual by way of exclusion to a situation in which there are substantial grounds to believe that he or she would face such a deprivation would breach that protection;

(ii) under Article 7 ICCPR, exclusion to a situation in which there are substantial grounds to believe that the deportee would face torture, or cruel or inhuman or degrading treatment, is prohibited;

(iii) Article 8 ICCPR marks the condemnation of slavery by the international community, and exclusion to a situation in which there are substantial grounds to believe that the deportee would face being made a slave would constitute a breach;

(iv) under Article 9 ICCPR, arbitrary arrest or detention is prohibited. Exclusion where there are substantial grounds to believe that the subject would face such treatment is barred by this provision.

Second, an important parallel protection directed at return to a setting of relevant risk is brought into being by the CAT. Exclusion at the border resulting in return to a state in which 'there are substantial grounds for believing' that the deportee would face torture, as defined in the CAT, would contravene Article 3(1) CAT. 10.7

Third, the ICCPR provides a series of important basic standards relevant to exclusion depending upon the subject's links to the UK, and not dependent upon the circumstances to which an individual would be exposed elsewhere: 10.8

(i) Exclusion action will breach Article 12(4) ICCPR: if (a) the UK is the affected individual's 'own country' for purposes of that paragraph; (b) the effect of exclusion would be to expel that individual from, or prevent his or her return to, the UK; and (c) the action would be arbitrary.

(ii) Action by the state in this context will breach Article 17 ICCPR, read in conjunction with Article 23(1) ICCPR, if it amounts to 'arbitrary or unlawful' interference with the protected interests of 'privacy, family, home'.

(iii) Article 2 ICCPR will be breached where the state fails to 'respect and ensure' the rights protected by the ICCPR 'without distinction of any kind', such as 'race, colour, sex, language, religion, political or other opinion, national or social origin, property, birth or other status', or where the state fails to ensure an effective remedy for breach.

(iv) Article 3 ICCPR identifies equal right of men and women to civil and political rights provided under the ICCPR, which would be breached by unjustified gender discrimination (against a members of either gender) in relation to a protected right.

Fourth, and finally, beyond the ICCPR, a range of other, broader international human rights norms may be applicable to exclusion action. These include, inter alia, the following: 10.9

(i) Exclusion action which is discriminatory on the basis of race would breach Article 5(d) CERD.

(ii) Exclusion action amounting to gender discrimination against a woman or women would breach Article 1 CEDAW.

Part C – Deportation, Removal and Exclusion

(iii) In an 'action concerning children', Article 3(1) CRC provides that 'the best interests of the child must be a primary consideration', and the subsequent paragraph states that subscribing states 'undertake to ensure the child such protection and care as is necessary for his or her well-being'. These provisions and Article 9 CRC (regarding family unity) are relevant where a child is affected by exclusion.

(iv) Persons to whom the CRPD applies are protected by Article 18(1)(d) not only from arbitrary deprivation of entry to 'their own country' (recalling the language of Article 12(4) ICCPR) but also from deprivation of entry to 'their own' country on any basis which, though not arbitrary, rests 'on the basis of disability'.

B3. Hybrid Instruments

10.10 Chapter four set out international law provisions established by three regimes referred to as 'hybrid' in that they combine the creation of human rights, like the instruments seen in chapter 2 and above, in combination with other purposes, such as the sharing of burdens amongst members of the international community. Some of those may have important consequences in relation to exclusion. The CSR defines the term 'refugee' in Article 1A(2). Save where that status has ended in accordance with the cessation provision in Article 1C CSR or exclusion applies by reason of one of Articles 1D–1E CSR, a refugee is entitled to certain protections. A refugee under the CSR has no right of travel to or entry into the UK by reason of that international status, but a return to a country of feared persecution following exclusion at the border might engage CSR, as well as the international human rights instruments identified above.

10.11 A stateless person under the CSSP has no right of travel to or entry into the UK by reason of his or her particular international status under the CSSP, but a return to prohibited treatment following exclusion at the border might engage either the CSR or the international human rights instruments identified above.

B4. Council of Europe Instruments

10.12 Two instruments introduced in chapter 5 are relevant to exclusion. First, under the ECHR, a refusal at the frontier leading to return to prohibited treatment might engage certain very important human rights protections:

(i) Article 2 ECHR prohibits deprivation of life 'save in the execution of a sentence of a court' following conviction of a capital crime. Where substantial grounds show the existence of a real risk of breach of Article 2 ECHR, action is prohibited by article 2 ECHR;

(ii) Article 3 ECHR prohibits torture or inhuman or degrading treatment or punishment. If by 'substantial grounds' the 'existence of a real risk' of any of the prohibited ill-treatments on return is shown, Article 3 ECHR prohibits relevant action.

(iii) Article 4 ECHR prohibits slavery or servitude. Where 'substantial grounds' show the existence of a real risk of any of the prohibited ill-treatments on return, exclusion is not permitted.

(iv) Article 5 ECHR bars deprivation of liberty save in specified cases and in accordance with the law. Where in a particular case substantial grounds show the existence of a real risk of any of the prohibited ill-treatments, then article 5 ECHR prohibits deportation.

(v) Article 6 ECHR specifies fair trial protections. Deportation to 'real risk' of a 'flagrant denial of justice' would violate the article and is prohibited.

(vi) Article 7 ECHR prohibits 'punishment without law.' Substantial grounds showing the 'real risk' of a 'flagrant breach' on return would mean that deportation breached article 7 ECHR.

(vii) Article 8 ECHR relevantly protects the right to respect for private and family life and home. Deportation is barred where substantial grounds showing the 'real risk' of a 'flagrant breach' of Article 8 ECHR arise in the place to which a deportee would have to go.

(viii) In the same way, substantial evidence showing 'real risk' on return of a 'flagrant breach' of protection of freedom of thought, conscience and religion (Article 9 ECHR), of freedom of expression (Article 10 ECHR), of freedom of peaceful assembly and/or association with others (Article 10 ECHR), or of the right to marry and found a family (article 11 ECHR) would bar exclusion.

Second, ECHR protections may bar the exclusion of an individual from the UK by reason of the interference that this would represent to his or her protected interests in the UK. Other articles might be engaged, but the majority of such cases focus upon the right to respect for private and/or family life and/or home under Article 8 ECHR. Deportation is barred where this would represent an interference with relevant right(s) disproportionate to the legitimate public interest engaged. **10.13**

Third, exclusion at the frontier may not be consistent with the Council of Europe CATHB. Article 10(2) CATHB requires the UK, if the competent authorities have reasonable grounds to believe that a person has been a VoT, to refrain from removing that person until the identification process as a victim of a trafficking offence, as provided for in Article 18 CATHB, has been completed. **10.14**

Council of Europe Member States, especially those in the Mediterranean, have in recent years seen significant increases in the number of arrivals of migrants by sea. Following a number of high-profile disasters in the course of attempts by migrants to enter Europe by sea, the Council of Europe on 21 June 2011 adopted Resolution 1821 (2011) of the Parliamentary Assembly of the Council of Europe on the interception and rescue at sea of asylum-seekers, refugees and irregular migrants. **10.15**

C. EU Law

Chapter VI of Directive 2004/38/EC of 29 April 2004 ('Restrictions on the right of entry and the right of residence on grounds of public policy, public security or public health') sets out the EU law provisions relevant to exclusion from the UK of EU citizens or family members. This is outlined in chapter 6. The Directive creates rights which apply to EEA nationals[3] and their family members regardless of whether or not they themselves are EEA nationals. Directive 2004/38/EC reasserts that EEA nationals, and their direct family members, derive a right of entry. Unlike other non-nationals, there is a duty upon the UK to admit them, save in certain prescribed circumstances. **10.16**

---

[3] EEA countries include the 28 Member States of the EU, Norway, Liechtenstein, Iceland and Switzerland.

D. Domestic Law

D1. Prerogative

10.17 The power of the Secretary of State to exclude an individual from the UK is no longer attributable, if it was previously, to prerogative power: *R (Munir) v SSHD* [2012] UKSC 32, [2012] 1 WLR 2192; and *R (Alvi) v SSHD* [2012] UKSC 33, [2012] 1 WLR 2208.

D2. Statute

10.18 Section 3(1) IA 1971 provides that, except as otherwise provided by or under that Act, where a person is not a British citizen, he or she shall not enter the UK unless given leave to do so in accordance with the provisions of, or made under, the Act; he or she may be given leave to enter (or, when already there, leave to remain) either for a limited or for an indefinite period; and if he or she is given limited leave to enter or remain, it may be given subject to conditions restricting his or her employment and studies in the UK. Section 3(2) IA 1971 provides that the Secretary of State may do so by the laying of a statement of Immigration Rules HC 395 before Parliament.

10.19 The basic principle of immigration control in the UK is the exclusionary principle: everyone is excluded from entry or residence, unless expressly exempted by law or given permission to reside. Section 1 IA 1971 provides that:

1(1) All those who are in this Act expressed to have the right of abode in the UK shall be free to live in and to come and go into and from, the UK …
(2) Those not having that right may live, work and settle in the UK by permission and subject to such regulation and control of their entry into, stay in and departure from the UK as is imposed by this Act.

10.20 The Secretary of State retains a statutory discretion to exclude those subject to immigration control under IA 1971. This discretion is exercised in the main through the General Grounds of Refusal, set out at Part 9 of the Immigration Rules, but it has been held that an inherent statutory discretion is retained. This is exercised directly by the Secretary of State, ordinarily on the grounds that the presence of the individual is 'non-conducive to the public good'. Where the Secretary of State has personally directed exclusion, leave to enter must be refused.

D3. Statutory Instrument

The Immigration (European Economic Area) Regulations 2006

10.21 The Immigration (European Economic Area) Regulations 2006, SI 2006/1003, at Part 4 seek to transpose Chapter VI of Directive 2004/38/EC of 29 April 2004. In particular, Regulation 19 provides as follows in relation to exclusion from the UK:

Exclusion and removal from the United Kingdom

19(1) A person is not entitled to be admitted to the United Kingdom by virtue of regulation 11 if his exclusion is justified on grounds of public policy, public security or public health in accordance with regulation 21.

(1A) A person is not entitled to be admitted to the United Kingdom by virtue of regulation 11 if that person is subject to a deportation or exclusion order, except where the person is temporarily admitted pursuant to regulation 29AA.

(1AB) A person is not entitled to be admitted to the United Kingdom by virtue of regulation 11 if the Secretary of State considers there to be reasonable grounds to suspect that his admission would lead to the abuse of a right to reside in accordance with regulation 21B(1)

(1B) If the Secretary of State considers that the exclusion of an EEA national or the family member of an EEA national is justified on the grounds of public policy, public security or public health in accordance with regulation 21 the Secretary of State may make an order for the purpose of these Regulations prohibiting that person from entering the United Kingdom.

…

D4. The Immigration Rules

10.22 The relevant passages in the Immigration Rules have been extensively altered in recent years.

10.23 Ordinarily, a person who does not meet the requirements of the Immigration Rules is to be refused entry. For those seeking entry or residence in accordance with the Immigration Rules, the Secretary of State retains additional powers to exclude, contained within paragraphs 320–323 of the Rules and section S-EC of Appendix FM to those Rules. The Secretary of State provides detailed guidance to ECOs concerning the use of the powers contained within those paragraphs, and the guidance is mainly available at the Home Office website. It now forms a growing part of the Home Office system of control of entry, and the requirements are regularly changed.[4]

10.24 The criteria are separated into mandatory grounds (those which specify that, where they apply, entry must be refused by the decision maker) and discretionary grounds (those that specify that entry should normally be refused), and ECOs are obliged to consider the criteria in respect of all applications made for entry clearance. Where a discretionary ground has been applied without the exercise of discretion, the subsequent decision may be unlawful.[5]

10.25 Paragraph 320 applies to those who seek entry clearance or leave to enter where entry clearance has not previously been obtained, other than as family members under Appendix FM:

320. In addition to the grounds of refusal of entry clearance or leave to enter set out in Parts 2–8 of these Rules, and subject to paragraph 321 below, the following grounds for the refusal of entry clearance or leave to enter apply:

Grounds on which entry clearance or leave to enter the United Kingdom is to be refused

(1) the fact that entry is being sought for a purpose not covered by these Rules;
(2) the fact that the person seeking entry to the United Kingdom:
(a) is currently the subject of a deportation order; or

---

[4] See www.ukba.homeoffice.gov.uk.
[5] See ch 11 below for discussion on appropriate remedies.

Part C – Deportation, Removal and Exclusion

- (b) has been convicted of an offence for which they have been sentenced to a period of imprisonment of at least 4 years; or
- (c) has been convicted of an offence for which they have been sentenced to a period of imprisonment of at least 12 months but less than 4 years, unless a period of 10 years has passed since the end of the sentence; or
- (d) has been convicted of an offence for which they have been sentenced to a period of imprisonment of less than 12 months, unless a period of 5 years has passed since the end of the sentence.

Where this paragraph applies, unless refusal would be contrary to the Human Rights Convention or the Convention and Protocol Relating to the Status of Refugees, it will only be in exceptional circumstances that the public interest in maintaining refusal will be outweighed by compelling factors.

- (3) failure by the person seeking entry to the United Kingdom to produce to the Immigration Officer a valid national passport or other document satisfactorily establishing his identity and nationality;
- (4) failure to satisfy the Immigration Officer, in the case of a person arriving in the United Kingdom or seeking entry through the Channel Tunnel with the intention of entering any other part of the common travel area, that he is acceptable to the immigration authorities there;
- (5) failure, in the case of a visa national, to produce to the Immigration Officer a passport or other identity document endorsed with a valid and current United Kingdom entry clearance issued for the purpose for which entry is sought;
- (6) where the Secretary of State has personally directed that the exclusion of a person from the United Kingdom is conducive to the public good;
- (7) save in relation to a person settled in the United Kingdom or where the Immigration Officer is satisfied that there are strong compassionate reasons justifying admission, confirmation from the Medical Inspector that, for medical reasons, it is undesirable to admit a person seeking leave to enter the United Kingdom.
- (7A) where false representations have been made or false documents or information have been submitted (whether or not material to the application, and whether or not to the applicant's knowledge), or material facts have not been disclosed, in relation to the application *or* in order to obtain documents from the Secretary of State or a third party required in support of the application.
- (7B) where the applicant has previously breached the UK's immigration laws (and was 18 or over at the time of his most recent breach) by:
  - (a) Overstaying;
  - (b) breaching a condition attached to his leave;
  - (c) being an Illegal Entrant;
  - (d) using Deception in an application for entry clearance, leave to enter or remain, or in order to obtain documents from the Secretary of State or a third party required in support of the application (whether successful or not);

  unless the applicant:

  - (i) Overstayed for 90 days or less and left the UK voluntarily, not at the expense (directly or indirectly) of the Secretary of State;
  - (ii) used Deception in an application for entry clearance more than 10 years ago;
  - (iii) left the UK voluntarily, not at the expense (directly or indirectly) of the Secretary of State, more than 12 months ago;
  - (iv) left the UK voluntarily, at the expense (directly or indirectly) of the Secretary of State, more than 2 years ago; and the date the person left the UK was no more than 6 months after the date on which the person was given notice of the removal

decision, or no more than 6 months after the date on which the person no longer had a pending appeal; whichever is the later;
- (v) left the UK voluntarily, at the expense (directly or indirectly) of the Secretary of State, more than 5 years ago;
- (vi) was removed or deported from the UK more than 10 years ago; or
- (vii) left or was removed from the UK as a condition of a caution issued in accordance with section 22 of the Criminal Justice Act 2003 more than 5 years ago.

Where more than one breach of the UK's immigration laws has occurred, only the breach which leads to the longest period of absence from the UK will be relevant under this paragraph.

(7D) failure, without providing a reasonable explanation, to comply with a request made on behalf of the Entry Clearance Officer to attend for interview.

Grounds on which entry clearance or leave to enter the United Kingdom should normally be refused

- (8) failure by a person arriving in the United Kingdom to furnish the Immigration Officer with such information as may be required for the purpose of deciding whether he requires leave to enter and, if so, whether and on what terms leave should be given;
- (8A) where the person seeking leave is outside the United Kingdom, failure by him to supply any information, documents, copy documents or medical report requested by an Immigration Officer;
- (9) failure by a person seeking leave to enter as a returning resident to satisfy the Immigration Officer that he meets the requirements of paragraph 18 of these Rules, or that he seeks leave to enter for the same purpose as that for which his earlier leave was granted;
- (10) production by the person seeking leave to enter the United Kingdom of a national passport or travel document issued by a territorial entity or authority which is not recognised by Her Majesty's Government as a state or is not dealt with as a government by them, or which does not accept valid United Kingdom passports for the purpose of its own immigration control; or a passport or travel document which does not comply with international passport practice;
- (11) where the applicant has previously contrived in a significant way to frustrate the intentions of the Rules by:
  - (i) overstaying; or
  - (ii) breaching a condition attached to his leave; or
  - (iii) being an illegal entrant; or
  - (iv) using deception in an application for entry clearance, leave to enter or remain or in order to obtain documents from the Secretary of State or a third party required in support of the application (whether successful or not); and

there are other aggravating circumstances, such as absconding, not meeting temporary admission/reporting restrictions or bail conditions, using an assumed identity or multiple identities, switching nationality, making frivolous applications or not complying with the re-documentation process.
- (12) DELETED
- (13) failure, except by a person eligible for admission to the United Kingdom for settlement, to satisfy the Immigration Officer that he will be admitted to another country after a stay in the United Kingdom;
- (14) refusal by a sponsor of a person seeking leave to enter the United Kingdom to give, if requested to do so, an undertaking in writing to be responsible for that person's maintenance and accommodation for the period of any leave granted;
- (16) failure, in the case of a child under the age of 18 years seeking leave to enter the United Kingdom otherwise than in conjunction with an application made by his parent(s) or legal guardian to provide the Immigration Officer, if required to do so, with written consent to the application from his parent(s) or legal guardian; save that the requirement as to written

Part C – Deportation, Removal and Exclusion

consent does not apply in the case of a child seeking admission to the United Kingdom as an asylum-seeker;

(17) save in relation to a person settled in the United Kingdom, refusal to undergo a medical examination when required to do so by the Immigration Officer;

(18) DELETED

(18A) within the 12 months prior to the date on which the application is decided, the person has been convicted of or admitted an offence for which they received a non-custodial sentence or other out of court disposal that is recorded on their criminal record;

(18B) in the view of the Secretary of State:
  (a) the person's offending has caused serious harm; or
  (b) the person is a persistent offender who shows a particular disregard for the law.

(19) The immigration officer deems the exclusion of the person from the United Kingdom to be conducive to the public good. For example, because the person's conduct (including convictions which do not fall within paragraph 320(2)), character, associations, or other reasons, make it undesirable to grant them leave to enter.

(20) failure by a person seeking entry into the United Kingdom to comply with a requirement relating to the provision of physical data to which he is subject by regulations made under section 126 of the Nationality, Immigration and Asylum Act 2002.

(21) DELETED

(22) where one or more relevant NHS body has notified the Secretary of State that the person seeking entry or leave to enter has failed to pay a charge or charges with a total value of at least £1,000 in accordance with the relevant NHS regulations on charges to overseas visitors.

Refusal of leave to enter in *relation* to a person in possession of an entry clearance

321. A person seeking leave to enter the United Kingdom who holds an entry clearance which was duly issued to him and is still current may be refused leave to enter only where the Immigration Officer is satisfied that:
  (i) false representations were made or false documents or information were submitted (whether or not material to the application, and whether or not to the holder's knowledge), or material facts were not disclosed, in relation to the application for entry clearance; or in order to obtain documents from the Secretary of State or a third party required in support of the application;
  (ii) `a change of circumstances since it was issued has removed the basis of the holder's claim to admission, except where the change of circumstances amounts solely to the person becoming over age for entry in one of the categories contained in paragraphs 296–316 of these Rules since the issue of the entry clearance; or
  (iii) on grounds which would have led to a refusal under paragraphs 320(2), 320(6), 320(18A), 320(18B) or 320(19) (except where this sub-paragraph applies in respect of an entry clearance issued under Appendix Armed Forces it is to be read as if for 'paragraphs 320(2), 320(6), 320(18A), 320(18B) or 320(19)' it said 'paragraph 8(a), (b), (c) or (g) and paragraph 9(d)').

Grounds on which leave to enter or remain which is in force is to be cancelled at port or while the holder is outside the United Kingdom

321A. The following grounds for the cancellation of a person's leave to enter or remain which is in force on his arrival in, or whilst he is outside, the United Kingdom apply:

(1) there has been such a change in the circumstances of that person's case since the leave was given, that it should be cancelled; or

(2) false representations were made or false documents were submitted (whether or not material to the application, and whether or not to the holder's knowledge), or material facts were

not disclosed, in relation to the application for leave; or in order to obtain documents from the Secretary of State or a third party required in support of the application or,

(3) save in relation to a person settled in the United Kingdom or where the Immigration Officer or the Secretary of State is satisfied that there are strong compassionate reasons justifying admission, where it is apparent that, for medical reasons, it is undesirable to admit that person to the United Kingdom; or

(4) where the Secretary of State has personally directed that the exclusion of that person from the United Kingdom is conducive to the public good; or

(4A) grounds which would have led to a refusal under paragraphs 320(2), 320(6), 320(18A), 320(18B) or 320(19) if the person concerned were making a new application for leave to enter or remain (except where this sub-paragraph applies in respect of leave to enter or remain granted under Appendix Armed Forces it is to be read as if for 'paragraphs 320(2), 320(6), 320(18A), 320(18B) or 320(19)' it said 'paragraph 8(a), (b), (c) or (g) and paragraph 9(d)'); or

(5) the Immigration Officer or the Secretary of State deems the exclusion of the person from the United Kingdom to be conducive to the public good. For example, because the person's conduct (including convictions which do not fall within paragraph 320(2)), character, associations, or other reasons, make it undesirable to grant them leave to enter the United Kingdom; or

(6) where that person is outside the United Kingdom, failure by that person to supply any information, documents, copy documents or medical report requested by an Immigration Officer or the Secretary of State.

Refusal of leave to remain, variation of leave to enter or remain or curtailment of leave

322. In addition to the grounds for refusal of extension of stay set out in Parts 2–8 of these Rules, the following provisions apply in relation to the refusal of an application for leave to remain, variation of leave to enter or remain or, where appropriate, the curtailment of leave:

Grounds on which leave to remain and variation of leave to enter or remain in the United Kingdom are to be refused

(1) the fact that variation of leave to enter or remain is being sought for a purpose not covered by these Rules;

(1A) where false representations have been made or false documents or information have been submitted (whether or not material to the application, and whether or not to the applicant's knowledge), or material facts have not been disclosed, in relation to the application or in order to obtain documents from the Secretary of State or a third party required in support of the application;

(1B) the applicant is, at the date of application, the subject of a deportation order or a decision to make a deportation order;

(1C) where the person is seeking indefinite leave to enter or remain:
    (i) they have been convicted of an offence for which they have been sentenced to imprisonment for at least 4 years; or
    (ii) they have been convicted of an offence for which they have been sentenced to imprisonment for at least 12 months but less than 4 years, unless a period of 15 years has passed since the end of the sentence; or
    (iii) they have been convicted of an offence for which they have been sentenced to imprisonment for less than 12 months, unless a period of 7 years has passed since the end of the sentence; or
    (iv) they have, within the 24 months prior to the date on which the application is decided, been convicted of or admitted an offence for which they have received

Part C – Deportation, Removal and Exclusion

a non-custodial sentence or other out of court disposal that is recorded on their criminal record.
(1D) DELETED

Grounds on which leave to remain and variation of leave to enter or remain in the United Kingdom should normally be refused

(2) the making of false representations or the failure to disclose any material fact for the purpose of obtaining leave to enter or a previous variation of leave or in order to obtain documents from the Secretary of State or a third party required in support of the application for leave to enter or a previous variation of leave;

(2A) the making of false representations or the failure to disclose any material fact for the purpose of obtaining a document from the Secretary of State that indicates the person has a right to reside in the United Kingdom;

(3) failure to comply with any conditions attached to the grant of leave to enter or remain;

(4) failure by the person concerned to maintain or accommodate himself and any dependants without recourse to public funds;

(5) the undesirability of permitting the person concerned to remain in the United Kingdom in the light of his conduct (including convictions which do not fall within paragraph 322(1C), character or associations or the fact that he represents a threat to national security;

(5A) it is undesirable to permit the person concerned to enter or remain in the United Kingdom because, in the view of the Secretary of State:
(a) their offending has caused serious harm; or
(b) they are a persistent offender who shows a particular disregard for the law;

(6) refusal by a sponsor of the person concerned to give, if requested to do so, an undertaking in writing to be responsible for his maintenance and accommodation in the United Kingdom or failure to honour such an undertaking once given;

(7) failure by the person concerned to honour any declaration or undertaking given orally or in writing as to the intended duration and/or purpose of his stay;

(8) failure, except by a person who qualifies for settlement in the United Kingdom or by the spouse or civil partner of a person settled in the United Kingdom, to satisfy the Secretary of State that he will be returnable to another country if allowed to remain in the United Kingdom for a further period;

(9) failure by an applicant to produce within a reasonable time information, documents or other evidence required by the Secretary of State to establish his claim to remain under these Rules;

(10) failure, without providing a reasonable explanation, to comply with a request made on behalf of the Secretary of State to attend for interview;

(11) failure, in the case of a child under the age of 18 years seeking a variation of his leave to enter or remain in the United Kingdom otherwise than in conjunction with an application by his parent(s) or legal guardian, to provide the Secretary of State, if required to do so, with written consent to the application from his parent(s) or legal guardian; save that the requirement as to written consent does not apply in the case of a child who has been admitted to the United Kingdom as an asylum-seeker.

(12) where one or more relevant NHS body has notified the Secretary of State that the person seeking leave to remain or a variation of leave to enter or remain has failed to pay a charge or charges with a total value of at least £1000 in accordance with the relevant NHS regulations on charges to overseas visitors.

Paragraphs 323–323C provide similar grounds for curtailment of existing leave to remain.

10.26 Appendix FM to the Immigration Rules, which was brought into force on 9 July 2012, introduced specific grounds on which those seeking to enter the UK as family members of those settled in the UK (refugees and those with Humanitarian Protection are to be equated with those otherwise deemed settled)[6] may be excluded, despite otherwise qualifying for entry. Sections S-EC 1.1–1.8 provide the grounds on which a person must be excluded on grounds of suitability:

S-EC.1.1. The applicant will be refused entry clearance on grounds of suitability if any of paragraphs S-EC.1.2. to 1.8. apply.

S-EC.1.2. The Secretary of State has personally directed that the exclusion of the applicant from the UK is conducive to the public good.

S-EC.1.3. The applicant is currently the subject of a deportation order.

S-EC.1.4. The exclusion of the applicant from the UK is conducive to the public good because they have:
  (a) been convicted of an offence for which they have been sentenced to a period of imprisonment of at least 4 years; or
  (b) been convicted of an offence for which they have been sentenced to a period of imprisonment of at least 12 months but less than 4 years, unless a period of 10 years has passed since the end of the sentence; or
  (c) been convicted of an offence for which they have been sentenced to a period of imprisonment of less than 12 months, unless a period of 5 years has passed since the end of the sentence.

Where this paragraph applies, unless refusal would be contrary to the Human Rights Convention or the Convention and Protocol Relating to the Status of Refugees, it will only be in exceptional circumstances that the public interest in maintaining refusal will be outweighed by compelling factors.

S-EC.1.5. The exclusion of the applicant from the UK is conducive to the public good because, for example, the applicant's conduct (including convictions which do not fall within paragraph S-EC.1.4.), character, associations, or other reasons, make it undesirable to grant them entry clearance.

S-EC.1.6. The applicant has failed without reasonable excuse to comply with a requirement to:
  (a) attend an interview;
  (b) provide information;
  (c) provide physical data; or
  (d) undergo a medical examination or provide a medical report.

S-EC.1.7. It is undesirable to grant entry clearance to the applicant for medical reasons.

S-EC.1.8. The applicant left or was removed from the UK as a condition of a caution issued in accordance with section 22 of the Criminal Justice Act 2003 less than 5 years prior to the date on which the application is decided.

10.27 There is a considerable overlap between the mandatory suitability criteria and the General Grounds for Refusal. The contents are thus liable to be interpreted in the same way.

10.28 Paragraphs 320(6) and S-EC.1.5 oblige the Secretary of State to exclude a person whose presence he or she deems not to be conducive to the public good. However, unlike paragraph 320(2), exclusion is not here expressed as subject to the provisions of the ECHR. This is discussed in more detail below.[7] Where an exclusion order has not been made, a person may be excluded by an ECO or IO under paragraph 320(19), one of the discretionary grounds of refusal. This is discussed in more detail below.

---

[6] Paragraph E-ECP.2.1.
[7] See section E.

D5. Guidance

10.29 The Secretary of State publishes guidance for caseworkers indicating the manner in which the relevant powers should be exercised. It is difficult to provide a full account of this as the pace of change is substantial and ongoing reorganisation of government information online has created additional confusion. As to the application of the General Grounds for Refusal under the Immigration Rules HC 395, the present casework guidance, divided into a number of internal sections (including discrete sections relating to entry clearance applications and leave to remain applications respectively), is within the General Grounds for Refusal (Modernised Guidance), which was last updated on 30 April 2014 and is available online. As regards the 'suitability' criteria under Appendix FM, the latest guidance appears to be the Immigration Directorate Instruction (IDI), 'Family Members under the Immigration Rules', last updated in October 2013. The exercise of exclusion powers is addressed in the 'Modernised Guidance: Exclusion Decisions and Exclusion Orders' which provides guidance on the use of these powers (29 January 2014) (www.gov.uk/government/publications/exclusion-decisions-and-exclusion-orders).

E. Discussion

E1. Introduction

10.30 The primary bases of exclusion from the UK are those set out in Part 9 of the Immigration Rules under the heading 'General Grounds for Refusal'. These have already been quoted at length, by reason of their importance, in paragraph 10.25 above. They are addressed sequentially below. The list of grounds is differentiated by the headings: paragraphs 320(1)–(7D) are cited as grounds of mandatory refusal, paragraphs 320(8)–(22) as cases in which entry clearance or leave to enter 'should normally be refused.' In each case the burden of proof lies on the decision maker: *JC (Part 9 HC395, burden of proof) China* [2007] UKAIT 00027, [10] and *NA & Others (Cambridge College of Learning) Pakistan* [2009] UKAIT 00031, [98]–[102].

10.31 Leave to enter or entry clearance will be refused by reference to paragraph 320(1) HC 395 if entry is sought for a reason that is not covered by the Immigration Rules. The Rules are progressively more narrowly drafted, so that certain persons are excluded; for example, there is no longer a rule permitting entry to highly skilled migrants unless they have already secured sponsored employment or have sufficient funds to invest in a business. Nor is there a route of entry for non-traditional family members of those with limited leave to remain. However, contrary to the placement of the criteria within the mandatory grounds for refusal, there is nothing preventing the exercise of discretion outside of the Immigration Rules and, indeed, particularly in the latter case, such discretion is occasionally exercised.

10.32 Nonetheless, refusals of application for entry clearance outside the scope of the Immigration Rules will be on the basis that entry is for a reason not covered by the Immigration Rules. Section 88(2)(d) Nationality Immigration and Asylum Act 2002

(NIAA 2002) removes the right of appeal against such decisions, unless human rights arguments are engaged (section 88(2) (d) NIAA 2002).

10.33 Refusal of entry to those subject to a current deportation order has long formed a ground for refusal. As discussed previously, the effect of a deportation order is to prohibit entry until and unless it is revoked (see chapter 8 above). However, in the case of persons deported as family members under section 3(5)(b) IA 1971, they may not be excluded from return, in the case of spouses, if the marriage has come to an end or, in the case of children, once they reach their majority (paragraph 389 of the Immigration Rules).

10.34 A deportation order will cease to have effect automatically if the deportee becomes a British citizen (section 5(1) IA 1971), if he or she has been deported as a spouse but has divorced (section 5(3)–(4) IA 1971), or if he or she has been deported as a child, but has reached the age of 18 (section 5(3)–(4) IA 1971). In all other circumstances, a deportation order remains in place until an application for revocation is made. Under paragraph 392 of the Immigration Rules, an application for revocation may be made either to an ECO or directly to the Home Office. In *Latif (Section 120—Revocation of Deportation Order) Pakistan* [2012] UKUT 78 (IAC), the Tribunal held that an individual subject to a deportation order had to apply for revocation rather than seek to raise claimed grounds for revocation in support of an appeal against automatic refusal relying on paragraph 320(2) Immigration Rules.

10.35 Mandatory entry bans for those sentenced to any period of imprisonment under paragraph 320(2) and S-EC.1.4 were inserted in January 2013.[8] Imprisonment and other criminality had previously been a discretionary criteria for refusal, subject to a conviction becoming 'spent'. Since January 2013, convictions resulting in periods of imprisonment of four years or more are never capable of becoming 'spent' for immigration purposes, and thus refusal is mandatory. The provision will apply to all new applications, regardless of whether the applicant has previously entered the UK. Thus, an applicant with a positive immigration history may still be excluded on the grounds of an earlier criminal conviction.

10.36 Convictions for less than four years, but more than 12 months will result in applications for entry being refused for 10 years. The 10 years runs from the end of the sentence, and not simply the custodial element of that sentence. A person sentenced to less than 12 months' immediate imprisonment will similarly be banned for five years from the conclusion of his or her sentence.

10.37 The exclusion is mandatory, whether the conviction and sentence occurs in the UK or overseas (paragraph 6 of the Immigration Rules). The only condition regarding overseas convictions is that there must be an equivalent criminal offence; convictions for homosexuality in certain countries, for example, will not cause the exclusion of an applicant (see Modernised Guidance: General Grounds for Refusal). However, it will be no excuse for an applicant to note that in the UK the offence would attract a lesser sentence (see Modernised Guidance: General Grounds for Refusal).

10.38 All such decisions must take account of the ECHR, although the provision is tautologically difficult. The exclusion of persons with the relevant conviction is said to be

---

[8] From 1 October 2012, certain immigration decisions were exempt from the provisions of s 4 of the Rehabilitation of Offenders Act 1974, meaning that the concept of a conviction becoming 'spent' no longer applies to such decisions.

mandatory, but clearly is subject, by importation of the provisions of Article 8 ECHR, to a public interest justification. The Secretary of State's policy documents suggest that refusal of entry must result in a situation that is, in the words of the Modernised Guidance: General Grounds for Refusal, 'unjustifiably harsh' and provides a non-exhaustive list of examples:

(a) Since conviction, the passage of time or the personal circumstances of the person have significantly changed such that maintaining a refusal would be so perverse as to undermine confidence in the immigration system
(b) The person concerned intends to make a significant investment in the UK. For example, buying or heavily investing in a major company, so by refusing entry it would not be in the national interest
(c) There is reliable evidence to suggest the conviction was politically motivated.

10.39 Paragraph 320(3) provides that a person attempting to enter without producing a valid passport or identity document falls to be excluded. There is, however, no mandatory format for the identity document. In *AM (Section 88(2): 'Immigration Document') Somalia* [2009] UKAIT 00008, the Tribunal confirmed that validity of a document was a question of fact. If the document appeared to be genuinely issued and established the identity and nationality, it did not need to be a document whose purpose was to ensure passage across borders. Any document which was issued to establish identity would therefore suffice.

10.40 No similar provision appears in the suitability criteria. However, paragraph 34 of the Immigration Rules requires anyone seeking entry for longer than six months to have entry clearance endorsed in a valid passport or identity document. Therefore, although the suitability grounds will not apply, they are unlikely to be granted entry without such a document.

10.41 Paragraph 320(4) provides for mandatory refusal of an individual arriving in the UK or seeking entry through the Channel Tunnel 'with the intention of entering any other part of the common travel area' if he or she is not acceptable to the immigration authorities in the area to which transit is proposed. The next paragraph, 320(5), requires refusal if entry clearance obtained in advance of travel is required and no passport or other identity document endorsed with a valid entry clearance is shown on arrival. Paragraph 320(6) requires refusal where 'the Secretary of State has personally directed that the exclusion of a person from the United Kingdom is conducive to the public good'. The powers of the Secretary of State to give such directions are addressed at section E in this chapter. Paragraphs 320(7) and S-EC.1.7 give the Secretary of State limited powers to exclude a person on medical grounds. There must be a confirmation from an approved Medical Officer that such exclusion is desirable for medical reasons. Appendix T of the Immigration Rules now makes it mandatory for persons from certain countries to undergo a tuberculosis screening if they seek entry for more than six months.[9] The list is subject to regular change.

---

[9] At the time of writing, those countries from which applicants had to undergo mandatory tuberculosis screening were: Afghanistan, Angola, Armenia, Azerbaijan, Bangladesh, Benin, Bolivia, Botswana, Brunei Darussalam, Burkina Faso, Burundi, Cambodia, Cape Verde, the Central African Republic, Chad, Cameroon, China, Congo, Congo Democratic Republic, Côte d'Ivoire, Djibouti, Dominican Republic, Ecuador, Equatorial Guinea, Eritrea, Ethiopia, Gabon, Gambia, Georgia, Ghana, Guatemala, Guinea, Guinea Bissau, Guyana, Haiti, Hong Kong and Macau, India, Indonesia, Kazakhstan, Kenya, Kiribati, Korea, the Democratic Republic of Korea, Kyrgyzstan, Laos, Lesotho, Liberia, Madagascar, Malawi, Malaysia, Mali, the Marshall

Paragraph 320(7A) gives the Secretary of State the power to exclude persons who have used deception in the application being decided. Deception is evidenced by the production of false documents, or the making of false representations, or the omission of information that is material to the outcome of the application. The act of deception may be by the applicant, or by any other, with or without the applicant's knowledge and regardless of the purpose of the fraud. For example, an applicant who submits a document relating to his or her employment in good faith may be excluded if the document contains fraudulent information, even if the fraud was perpetrated by his or her employer in order to deceive the tax authorities without the knowledge of the applicant. Although there is a right of appeal against such decisions, an appeal will not succeed on the basis that the appellant had no knowledge of the deception. 10.42

Paragraph S-EC.2.2 provides that an application will normally be refused where deception, fraud or material non-disclosure has been used in relation to the application. The deception, fraud or material non-disclosure must have been perpetrated in relation to the application being decided; there is therefore no ban for historical deception. 10.43

The action/inaction must be deliberately deceptive. Innocent misrepresentations will not justify the applicant's exclusion.[10] This extends to the actions of a third party; an employer who makes an innocent mistake in information provided may make representations that are untrue, but without the intent to deceive, the errors cannot justify exclusion on the grounds of paragraph 320(7A). 10.44

In *AA (Nigeria)* [2010] EWCA Civ 773, the appellant on an application for leave to remain had ticked 'no' in response to the question on the form as to whether he had any criminal convictions in the UK. In fact, he had three traffic convictions, but claimed not to know that they were relevant for the purposes of the application. The lower courts had found that his intent was irrelevant; once established that the representation was not true, the decision maker was obliged to refuse the application. The Court of Appeal held at [76]–[77]: 10.45

76. Dishonesty or deception is needed, albeit not necessarily that of the applicant himself, to render a 'false representation' a ground for mandatory refusal.
77. If it were otherwise, then an applicant whose false representation was in no way dishonest would not only suffer mandatory refusal but would also be barred from re-entry for ten years if he was removed or deported. That might not in itself be so very severe a rule, if only because the applicant always has the option of voluntary departure. If, however, he has to be assisted at the expense of the Secretary of State, then the ban is for five years. Most seriously of all, however, is the possibility, on the Secretary of State's interpretation, that an applicant for entry clearance (not this case) who had made an entirely innocent misrepresentation, innocent not only so far as his personal honesty is concerned but also in its origins, would be barred from re-entry under paragraph 320(7B)(ii) for ten years, even if he left the UK voluntarily.

Islands, Mauritania, Micronesia, Moldova, Mongolia, Morocco, Mozambique, Namibia, Nepal, Niger, Nigeria, Pakistan, Palau, Papua New Guinea, Panama, Paraguay, Peru, the Russian Federation, Rwanda, Sao Tome and Principe, Senegal, Sierra Leone, the Solomon Islands, Somalia, South Africa, South Sudan, Sudan, Tajikistan, Swaziland, Tanzania, Timor Leste, Togo, Thailand, the Philippines, Turkmenistan, Tuvalu, Uganda, Uzbekistan, Vanuatu, Vietnam, Zambia and Zimbabwe.

[10] *AA (Nigeria) v Secretary of State for the Home Department* [2010] EWCA Civ 773 (6 July 2010), per Rix LJ, *Ahmed (General Grounds of Refusal—Material Non-disclosure) Pakistan* [2011] UKUT 351 (IAC) (9 September 2011).

10.46 Dishonesty must also be present in the case of material non-disclosure. In *Ahmed (General Grounds of Refusal—Material Non-disclosure) Pakistan* [2011] UKUT 351 (IAC), Judge McKee held 'material non-disclosure' and 'false representations' to be opposite sides of the same coin. An innocent omission will equally not justify the application of paragraph 320(7A).

10.47 Where entry clearance operated as leave to enter, it can only be cancelled where the failure to disclose was 'material' and leave had been obtained 'as a result of the failure to disclose material facts'. The Court of Appeal in *Sukhjinder Kaur* [1998] Imm AR 1 (CA) held 'Material' to mean that the facts not disclosed would have been capable of influencing the decision. Thus, the decision maker must show that the applicant has failed to disclose facts that they knew to be relevant to the consideration of their application.

10.48 Paragraphs 320(7A) and (7B) are often read together. Paragraph 320(7B) creates what are commonly, if mistakenly, known as re-entry bans.[11] An applicant for entry with previous, specified breaches of immigration laws must be excluded for set periods of time. Unlike paragraph 320(7A), the breach must be knowingly made by the applicant. Therefore, the use of deception/misrepresentation in an earlier application is insufficient to justify the applicant's exclusion; the decision maker must prove that the applicant was complicit. The Tribunal has held that the use of deception in this case requires that the act is done with the deliberate intent of securing advantage in immigration terms (*Ozhogina and Tarasova (Deception within Para 320(7B)—Nannies) Russia* [2011] UKUT 00197 (IAC), per Burton J).

10.49 Exclusion is fixed for mandatory terms. Those who have breached the immigration laws by overstaying for more than 90 days, breaching the conditions of their stay, or entering illegally must be excluded for a minimum of 12 months, unless they left at the public expense. Those using deception or who were removed or deported will be excluded for a period of 10 years. Note that the time begins to run from the time that the person left the UK, not the date of issue of any notice. The Rules now give added incentive to those who leave promptly following any such breach (paragraph 320(7B)(i) and (iv)).

10.50 There is no equivalent mandatory provision in the suitability criteria under Appendix FM. As noted above, there is no provision for mandatory exclusion for historical deception.

10.51 Exclusion under paragraph 320(7B) does not apply when any of the matters at 320(7C) arise.

10.52 Paragraph 320(7B)(vii) and S-EC.1.8 provide that a person who was removed or left as a condition of a caution under section 22 of the Criminal Justice Act 2003 will be excluded from re-entry until five years have passed. Since the coming into force of section 134 of the Legal Aid, Sentencing and Punishment of Offenders Act 2012,[12] the Secretary of State has had the power to make it a specific condition of a caution that a foreign offender leave the country, either voluntarily or at the public expense. The stated purpose is to bring about the removal of offenders who are foreign nationals and to prohibit their return within a set period.

10.53 Cautions of this nature may only be made against 'relevant offenders' who are defined as those foreign national offenders against whom removal directions or a deportation order has

---

[11] The exclusion grounds do not apply only to those who have previously been in the UK. Those who used deception in previous applications and were unsuccessful are also caught by the provisions of para 320(7B).
[12] This came into force on 8 April 2013.

been made (section 134(3G) LASPO). A caution must be accepted by the offender in place of a prosecution and conviction. Many are not aware of the long-term impact of these cautions.

Paragraph 320(7D), the final mandatory ground, provides for mandatory refusal in the event of failure, without reasonable excuse, to comply with a request to attend for interview as requested by the Entry Clearance Officer. As with other grounds this may be distinct from any reservation concerning the substance of the application.

Paragraph 320(8)–(22) of the Immigration Rules applies a presumption in favour of exclusion. Since the grounds are discretionary, challenge can be made by way of appeal, if an appeal right exists, and a tribunal judge may direct entry, notwithstanding the existence of factors falling within the definitions. In *RM (Kwok On Tong: HC395 para 320) India* [2006] UKAIT 00039, the Tribunal confirmed that since the powers exercised under paragraph 320(8) onwards are discretionary, whilst a judge must have regard to the decision, if he or she determines that the discretion should have been exercised differently, the appeal may be allowed. However, if all factors were known to the decision maker and no reference is made to paragraph 320, the judge is entitled to consider that those matters are not in issue. If new facts are found that may give rise to the application of the discretionary grounds, the judge may allow the presenting officer the opportunity to address those issues.

10.54

Paragraphs 320(8) and (8A) give the IO the opportunity to exclude an applicant for failure to provide documents additional to those specified in the Immigration Rules or guidance, which have been requested by the IO or the ECO. Such further information must be relevant to the decision being taken. Paragraph 320(8) is often cited in relation to 'genuineness' challenges: for example, in relation to applications under the points-based scheme, an IO may request significant further documentation from an applicant to prove that he or she is a 'genuine entrepreneur/student'. Failure to provide that documentation may result in the exclusion of an applicant, notwithstanding that all the 'specified documents' have been provided.[13] Paragraph 320(9) provides for discretionary refusal where a person who has been outside the United Kingdom for less than 2 years, and who had indefinite leave to enter or remain on departure, seeks admission as a returning resident under paragraph 18 Immigration Rules HC 395 but cannot demonstrate that the requirements of that rule are met 'or that he seeks leave to enter for the same purpose as that for which his earlier leave was granted.' The final clause is obscure given that indefinite leave generally does not have a fixed purpose attached to it and that paragraph 18(iv) HC 395 requires that admission is being sought 'for settlement', which may itself be considered to differ from 'the purpose for which ... earlier leave was granted.' There appears to be no jurisprudence on the point.

10.55

By paragraph 320(10), discretionary refusal may be applied where an individual produces a national passport or travel document issued by a territorial entity or authority which is not recognised by Her Majesty's Government as a state or is not dealt with as a government by them, or which does not accept valid United Kingdom passports for the purpose of its own immigration control; or a passport or travel document which does not comply with international passport practice. The primary current entities not recognised by the UK government in this context are the Republic of China (Taiwan), and the Turkish Republic of Northern Cyprus (TRNC). Passports issued in the past by royalist authorities in Yemen are also not recognised. In such cases refusal does

10.56

---

[13] See, for example, the provisions of para 245DD(h) and (i).

Part C – Deportation, Removal and Exclusion

not follow automatically. The relevant guidance, at Entry Clearance Guidance ECB08, provides that generally 'Entry clearances should not therefore be put in such passports or travel documents' but also that 'However, this does not mean that an entry clearance may not be issued. If the requirements of the Immigration Rules are met, an entry clearance must be issued on an EU Uniform Format Form (EU UFF).' Paragraph 320(11) gives the Secretary of State a wide discretion to exclude those he or she considers to have breached immigration laws. Following a series of challenges to the unfettered nature of the provision, the Secretary of State published guidance to ECOs as to the proper application of the provision.

10.57 A person will therefore be considered to have 'contrived in a significant way to frustrate the intentions of the rules' when he or she has previously done one or more of the following things, and there are aggravating circumstances which also contravened the immigration laws:

(a) been an illegal entrant;
(b) overstayed;
(c) breached a condition of their leave;
(d) used deception in an application for leave;
(e) obtained benefits, including NHS treatment.

10.58 The aggravating circumstances, which must exist in order for the provision to be relied upon, include the following:

(a) absconding/breaching temporary admission or bail conditions;
(b) working in breach of visitor conditions;
(c) receiving benefits to which the applicant is not entitled;
(d) resisting removal;
(e) entering into sham marriages;
(f) using multiple identities;
(g) frivolous applications designed to frustrate removal;
(h) facilitating immigration offending, including by harbouring offenders;
(i) people smuggling.

10.59 Each decision must be taken on its merits and the complicity or otherwise of the individual considered. However, unlike the provisions of paragraph 320(7B) above, the provision can be used to exclude persons who breached the law whilst a minor.

10.60 Kenneth Parker J in *PS (Paragraph 320(11) Discretion: Care Needed) India* [2010] UKUT 440 (IAC) emphasised the need for the decision maker to take into account the public interest in encouraging those who are unlawfully in the UK to regularise their status. There was thus a need to use the power sparingly and only where the circumstances were truly said to be aggravating.

10.61 Paragraph 320(13) provides for discretionary refusal if a person not eligible for admission to the UK for settlement cannot satisfy the Immigration Officer that he or she will be admissible to another country after a stay in the UK. The obvious purpose is to avoid admission of persons for temporary stay in circumstances which suggest that they may become 'stranded' in the UK. Paragraph 320(14) and S-EC.2.4 give the Secretary of State power to exclude a person for whom a sponsorship undertaking is not given. Prior to July 2012, there was no provision of the Immigration Rules which mandated the giving of a sponsorship undertaking in all cases. Paragraph EC-DR.3.2 now requires an undertaking to be signed by the sponsor of an adult dependant relative where the sponsor is a British citizen or is settled in the UK.[14]

In addition, paragraph 35 of the Immigration Rules gives the Secretary of State the power to request that any sponsor of a person seeking leave to enter or remain may be asked to sign an undertaking in writing 'to be responsible for that person's maintenance, accommodation and (as appropriate) personal care for the period of any leave granted, including any further variation or for a period of 5 years from date of grant where indefinite leave to enter or remain is granted'. The undertaking permits the Secretary of State, the Department of Social Security or the Department of Health to recover from the sponsor any amounts paid out in benefits (defined within paragraph 35 of the Immigration Rules as income support or asylum support) to the applicant within that period. Failure to maintain the person is also an offence under section 105 of the Social Security Administration Act 1992 and/or under section 108 IAA 1999 if, as a consequence, asylum support and/or income support is provided to, or in respect of, that person. Paragraph 320(16) provides for discretionary refusal of an application made by a child under the age of 18 years seeking leave to enter the United Kingdom otherwise than as an asylum seeker or in conjunction with an application made by his parent(s) or legal guardian, where no parent(s) or legal guardian has given written consent. By paragraph 320(17) refusal may be entered (unless the applicant is settled in the UK) by reason of refusal to undergo a medical examination when required to do so by the IO. A striking absence is specific reference to the possibility of reasonable excuse for refusal, as at paragraph 320(7D), but the presentation of such an excuse presumably would represent a powerful reason to refrain from the use of a discretionary refusal power on this basis. 10.62

Paragraph 320(18) and S-EC.2.5(a) give the Secretary of State broad discretionary powers to exclude those with sentences which do not cross the criminality threshold set above in paragraph 10.36. A person would normally be excluded if he or she has been convicted of any offence within the last 12 months. 10.63

Paragraph 320(18A)–(18B) and S-EC.2.5(b) provide a discretionary power to exclude a person whose offending the Secretary of State deems to have caused serious harm or is persistent. Serious harm is deemed inclusive of, but limited to, causing death or serious injury to an individual or group (Modernised Guidance: General Grounds for Refusal, 30 April 2014). The guidance given to caseworkers requires consideration not simply of the offence the person was convicted of, but also the circumstances surrounding the offence and the consequences thereof. Examples given include dangerous driving and the supply of drugs, where the consequences are death or injury. 10.64

Persistent offenders are those whose offending constitutes a series of offences, which, by reason of extent, seriousness and impact of the offences, represent a pattern of escalation.[15] 10.65

The guidance specifically references the need to balance the assessment with the family and private life of an individual. 10.66

In *F (Paragraph 320(8)—Type of Leave) USA* [2013] UKUT 00309 (IAC), the appellant had sought leave to enter as a spouse. He had a relevant conviction, after which the Tribunal at first instance found he had been fully rehabilitated and thus presented 10.67

---

[14] 'Settled' for these purposes means in possession of indefinite leave to remain or permanent residence. Refugees and those with humanitarian protection may also sponsor their adult dependant relatives, but are not required to sign the sponsorship declaration.
[15] *Supra.*

no danger to the community. His application was refused in reliance on paragraph 320(18) alone. His appeal was upheld at first instance on the basis that his rights under Article 8 ECHR would be breached. The respondent appealed. The Upper Tribunal accepted that there was an error of law, noting that in such an appeal, a grant of leave to enter or remain on the basis of Article 8 ECHR would not result in leave under the Immigration Rules and thus would impact any extension applications.[16] The Upper Tribunal noted that there was a two-stage process:[17]

> 8. Thus, the sub-paragraph requires an assessment to be made as a precondition to its applicability. If the individual in question has been convicted of a relevant offence, para 18 does not apply if the Immigration Officer (here including Entry Clearance Officers) 'is satisfied that admission would be justified for strong compassionate reasons'. If he is not so satisfied, sub-paragraph 18 applies, and sub-paragraph 18 imports, as we have said, a discretion. To put the matter shortly, if there are strong compassionate reasons, the sub-paragraph has no application; if there are, exclusion is still not mandatory.

10.68 In addition to the Secretary of State's residual statutory powers, paragraph 320(19) permits an ECO to exclude an applicant if he or she deems that exclusion is conducive to the public good. Such a decision does not require the direct intervention of the Secretary of State. The Entry Clearance Guidance suggests that the threshold is a high one;[18] there must be reason to suspect that the applicant will be a threat to national security, has committed war crimes, crimes against humanity, is subject to a UN[19] or EU[20] travel ban or that the presence of the applicant in the UK could lead to a breach of public order. However, the Court of Appeal has in *CB (United States of America) v Entry Clearance Officer (Los Angeles)* [2008] EWCA Civ 1539 held by a majority (Laws and Richards LJJ; Carnwath LJ dissenting) that the judgment of the public interest by the Secretary of State (although in the case the decision was that of an ECO) required the attachment of weight in an assessment, drawing a parallel with the earlier decision in *N (Kenya v SSHD* [2004] EWCA Civ 1094, [2004] INLR 612 as regards deportation cases: on the facts in *CB*, the ECO had refused entry clearance to the rapper Snoop Dogg pointing to an incident of confrontation between police and some of the rapper's entourage at Heathrow Airport some time earlier.

10.69 In *R (otao Naik) v SSHD* [2011] EWCA Civ 1546, the Court of Appeal rejected an appeal from a decision of Cranston J refusing judicial review of exclusion by an Islamic speaker of Indian nationality. In *R (otao Ivlev) v Entry Clearance Officer New York* [2013] EWHC 1162 (Admin), the claimant, a Russian lawyer based in the US, faced charges of embezzlement, fraud, money laundering and tax evasion. Trials of his co-accused were widely criticised as politically motivated and unfair and their convictions had been appealed. He sought entry clearance as a Tier 1 (General) Migrant under the Immigration Rules. Sales J upheld the decision to exclude under paragraph 320(19), noting that the UK immigration authorities were not in a position to undertake an

---

[16] Paragraph E-ILRP requires an applicant to have had leave to remain as a spouse for a continuous period of 60 months. Those with discretionary leave to enter/remain will not be entitled to settle unless they have resided continuously in the UK for 120 months.
[17] See also *Cahonyo, R (otao) v Entry Clearance Officer* [2013] EWHC 365 (Admin).
[18] *Supra.*
[19] A ban is made following a UN Security Council Resolution.
[20] Imposed on third-country nationals as a restrictive measure pursuant to Art 11 of the TEU.

independent trial of the evidence against the claimant in order to ascertain whether the discretion should be exercised in his favour.

A successful challenge to a deportation order issued where admission was allowed, immigration staff having not been notified of an exclusion order made by the Secretary of State, may be seen in *Mahajna v Home Secretary (Deportation Hate Speech— Unacceptable Behaviour)* [2012] UKUT B1 (IAC), which concerned an Islamic speaker of Israeli nationality and Palestinian background.

10.70

Paragraph 320(20) provides for refusal by reason of failure to comply with requirements under section 126 NIAA 2002 for provision of biometric data. As with paragraph 320(17), addressed already, there is no specific reference to the possibility of reasonable excuse, but such an excuse would almost certainly present a barrier to the use of discretionary power to refuse. Finally, paragraph 320(22) permits refusal where 'a relevant NHS body has notified the Secretary of State' of an outstanding charge or charges under 'the relevant NHS regulations' totalling at least £1000.

Paragraph 321(i) sets out provision for discretionary refusal of leave to enter to persons already in possession of entry clearance, in the event of false representations or submission of false documents or information or material non-disclosure in relation to the entry clearance application, or to obtain documents from the Secretary of State or a third party required in support of the application. Paragraph 321(ii) provides for refusal of leave to enter where there has been a change of circumstances since the issuance of entry clearance removing the basis for issuance, apart from an applicant whose application was filed in a category limited to persons under 18 passing that age: an example might be the closure of a sponsoring organisation or loss of a sponsorship licence. Paragraph 321(iii) brings to bear, in the context of leave to enter to an applicant possessing a valid entry clearance, certain grounds already specified in paragraph 320, with particular provision as regards specified armed forces cases.

Para 321A provides grounds on which leave to enter 'is to be cancelled at port or while the holder is outside the UK', the grounds substantially overlapping with those addressed above.

F. Exclusion Decision

In addition to the general grounds of refusal, the Secretary of State has broad powers of exclusion for non-EEA nationals.[21] These may be exercised by the Secretary of State alone, not by those working on his or her behalf, and thus can only be revoked by him or her. The use of exclusion powers is designed to replicate the powers to deport and thus to prevent a foreign national offender from entering, or re-entering, the UK.[22] The guidance issued by the Secretary of State states:

10.71

> The power to exclude a person from the UK is currently exercised by the Home Secretary. It is a non-statutory power and potentially very broad. The exclusion remains in place until it is revoked by the Home Secretary.[23]

---

[21] IA 1971, s 3.
[22] Modernised Guidance: Exclusion Decisions and Exclusion orders provides guidance on the use of these powers (29 January 2014).
[23] ibid.

10.72 The assertion that the power is independent of statute is erroneous. For it to be true, it would have to be shown that this was an area in which prerogative powers subsisted notwithstanding IA 1971 and the decisions of the Supreme Court in *R (Munir) v SSHD* [2012] UKSC 32, [2012] 1 WLR 2192 and *R (Alvi) v SSHD* [2012] UKSC 33, [2012] 1 WLR 2208. However, the mistake in the guidance as to the basis of the power does not prove that the power itself does not exist. In fact, the Secretary of State's power of exclusion is statutory and emanates from section 3 IA 1971, read together with paragraph 1(3) Schedule 2 IA 1971.

10.73 The existence of these powers outside the Immigration Rules has been held to be lawful. In *Cakani v SSHD* [2013] EWHC 16 (Admin), the claimant, a failed asylum-seeker, had been removed under the Facilitated Returns Scheme following conviction of possession of a false passport with intent to use it. He received a six-month sentence and was not deported, not having met the automatic deportation threshold and the discretionary powers under the IA 1971 having not been utilised.[24] He made an application for entry, which was refused on the basis that, amongst other reasons, the Secretary of State had personally directed his exclusion from the UK. He sought to challenge the exclusion decision on the basis that the Secretary of State had no residual exclusionary discretion. At [46]–[48], Ingrid Simler QC, sitting as a Deputy High Court Judge, rejected the claim:

> 46. I cannot accept these arguments. Paragraph 320(6) of the Immigration Rules undoubtedly assumes the existence of a practice or power to exclude, but the power itself derives from the general powers of the 1971 Act rather than from any specific authorisation in the rules themselves.
>
> 47. The focus of sections 1 and 3 of the 1971 Act is on the control of entry into and stay in the UK by those without the right of abode in the UK, conferring powers to exercise such control in the broadest terms. The 1971 Act also empowers the Secretary of State to give instructions to immigration officers (who exercise functions under the Act) that are not inconsistent with the Immigration Rules: Schedule 2 paragraph 1(3). These provisions are amply wide enough to confer the necessary power on the Secretary of State to make an exclusion decision in respect of a foreign national who is outside the UK. Furthermore, given the terms of paragraph 320(6) of the Immigration Rules, it cannot be said that the making of such a decision is inconsistent with the Immigration Rules. To the contrary, the Immigration Rules expressly envisage that the Secretary of State may personally make a decision that exclusion of a person is conducive to the public good.
>
> 48. Further, there is nothing in the judgments of the Supreme Court in *Alvi* and *Munir* that suggests that the Immigration Rules must themselves spell out in detail the circumstances when a decision to exclude will be revoked. *Alvi* and *Munir* require no more than that when guidance is issued on how a discretion within the Immigration Rules is to be exercised, and where that guidance contains a requirement that compels a particular outcome (as opposed to simply advising or recommending that particular factors be considered) then that requirement is a rule for the purposes of section 3(2) of the 1971 Act and must be laid before Parliament to be effective.

10.74 Paragraph 30A(iii) of the Immigration Rules now provides that an entry clearance may be revoked if the ECO is satisfied that the holder's exclusion from the UK would be conducive to the public good.[25] Under paragraph 320(6), entry clearance must be refused

---

[24] See ch 8 above.
[25] HC 395, para 30A, inserted by HC 329, 3 June 1996.

where the Secretary of State has personally directed that the exclusion of a person would be conducive to the public good.

10.75 The most common use of exclusion decisions is against those who agree to voluntarily leave the UK at the end of a criminal sentence. In agreeing to benefit from the Facilitated Return Scheme, applicants are obliged to sign a waiver, acknowledging that although they are not being deported, they may subsequently be excluded on the basis that their presence is deemed to be non-conducive to the public good. Guidance issued to the Criminal Casework Directorate suggests that 'major area(s) of future use' of the exclusion power will target foreign national prisoners who have taken up the offer of assistance and who have left the country as part of the Facilitated Return Scheme.[26] The power, which was used sparingly until 2006, has been used more frequently since that date.

10.76 Prior to January 2013, exclusion decisions relied predominantly on criteria set out in paragraph 391 of the Immigration Rules relating to the continued exclusion of a person who had been deported.[27] Exclusion was therefore appropriate in the case of a conviction capable of becoming spent under the Rehabilitation of Offenders Act 1974, ie, a sentence of 30 months' imprisonment or less, for a minimum of 10 years following the conviction of a relevant offence and, in the case of a conviction not capable of becoming spent, indefinitely. The criteria were subject to rights under both the 1951 Refugee Convention and the ECHR.[28]

10.77 Decisions to exclude are now based predominantly on criminality and thus are to be considered in line with the UK visa and immigration guidance on criminality. Applicants with convictions resulting in sentences of imprisonment over 12 months are likely to be considered for exclusion. A decision may be taken against a person who meets the deportation criteria, namely that his or her presence in the UK would not be conducive to the public good. Any such decision must be balanced against any compassionate circumstances.

10.78 The Secretary of State has a number of policies that are relevant in broader circumstances, but are applicable to the exercise of his or her exclusionary powers, to which he or she may turn. One such policy document, the 'List of Unacceptable Behaviours', introduced in August 2005 after the bombings on London transport to target those who would 'foment terrorism or provoke others to terrorist acts',[29] lists actions which the Secretary of State will use his or her exclusionary powers to prevent. The policy has been reviewed and now forms part of the 'Prevent Strategy',[30] which aims to respond to the threat posed by terrorism. The policy documents provides:

> A non-British citizen, whether in the UK or abroad, engages in unacceptable behaviour if he/she uses any means or medium including:
>
> Writing, producing, publishing or distributing material;
> Public speaking including preaching
> Running a website; or
> Using a position of responsibility such as teacher, community or youth leader

---

[26] Criminal Casework Directorate Process Communication 18/06 (B27-30).
[27] See ch 8 above.
[28] Modernised Guidance (n 22).
[29] Initially announced by a press release on behalf of the Home Secretary, Charles Clarke (Home Office press notice 118-05) in 2008.
[30] Published by the Home Secretary, Theresa May, in June 2011.

Part C – Deportation, Removal and Exclusion

To express views which:

Foment, justify or glorify terrorist violence in furtherance of particular beliefs;
Seek to provoke others to terrorist acts;
Foment other serious criminal activity or seek to provoke others to serious criminal acts or;
Foster hatred which might lead to inter-community violence in the UK.

This list is indicative, rather than exhaustive; types of behaviour not on the list may also be deemed unacceptable.

10.79 Exclusion is also likely to be pursued where the person is a member of a proscribed terrorist group,[31] a person who is suspected of war crimes, or crimes against humanity, or whose presence might lead to an infringement of UK laws.

10.80 Decisions are taken on a personal basis. There is not, and cannot be, any broad application or principle to an exclusion decision. To be lawful, a decision must encompass circumstances wider than a particular conviction; any decision that suggests a blanket ban on account of convictions of a specified length or nature is erroneous.

10.81 A decision to exclude is not an immigration decision as defined by section 82(1) NIAA 2002, and therefore there is no formal notice that must be issued in order to give effect to such a decision. However, the basic principles of fairness require that a person who is to be excluded is properly notified, and in practice the Secretary of State will write to inform the person. If the person is in the UK, the decision will normally be accompanied by a decision to remove, although more usually, if the Secretary of State deems the person's exclusion necessary, he or she will issue a deportation decision.

10.82 Since a decision to exclude is not an immigration decision, there is no right of appeal against such a decision. Challenge will need to be by way of judicial review.

10.83 The courts will be slow to interfere with the exercise of this discretion. In *R (Farrakhan) v SSHD* [2002] EWCA Civ 606, a decision was taken to exclude a US citizen, the leader of the Nation of Islam, who sought entry to speak to followers in the UK. His exclusion was based on fears that his presence would cause racial disharmony and potential public order offences, in light of certain statements that the Secretary of State deemed to be anti-semitic. The claimant argued that his rights to free expression were breached by so doing. In rejecting his argument, Lord Phillips MR said:

> 71. Miss Carss-Frisk submitted that there were factors in the present case which made it appropriate to accord a particularly wide margin of discretion to the Secretary of State. We agree. We would identify these factors as follows. First and foremost is the fact that this case concerns an immigration decision. As we have pointed out, the European Court of Human Rights attaches a considerable weight to the right under international law of a state to control immigration into its territory. And the weight that this carries in the present case is the greater because the Secretary of State is not motivated by the wish to prevent Mr Farrakhan from expressing his views, but by concern for public order within the United Kingdom.
>
> 72. The second factor is the fact that the decision in question is the personal decision of the Secretary of State. Nor is it a decision that he has taken lightly. The history that we have set out at the beginning of this judgment demonstrates the very detailed consideration, involving widespread consultation, that the Secretary of State has given to his decision.

---

[31] Proscribed by the Terrorism Act 2000.

73. The third factor is that the Secretary of State is far better placed to reach an informed decision as to the likely consequences of admitting Mr Farrakhan to this country than is the court.
74. The fourth factor is that the Secretary of State is democratically accountable for [the decision to exclude the Respondent from the UK]. This is underlined by the fact that section 60(9) of the 1999 Act precludes any right of appeal where the Secretary of State has certified that he has personally directed the exclusion of a person on the ground that this is conducive to the public good. Mr Blake submitted that the absence of a right of appeal required a particularly rigorous scrutiny under the process of judicial review. This submission appeared to us to be tantamount to negating the effect of section 60(9). There is no doubt that the Secretary of State's decision is subject to review, but we consider that the effect of the legislative scheme is legitimately to require the court to confer a wide margin of discretion upon the minister
75. These conclusions gain support from the approach of the House of Lords to the discretion of the Secretary of State to deport a person on grounds of national security in *SSHD v Rehman* [2001] 3 WLR 877.

10.84 The Secretary of State's decision is one which is not taken lightly; exclusion remains a rare step. The courts will accord a great deal of weight to the Secretary of State's opinion and reasoning, and only rarely will such steps be considered to have breached rights under the ECHR. The latest authority is now the decision of the Supreme Court in *R (Lord Carlile of Berriew QC and others) v SSHD* [2014] UKSC 60 delivered as this work went to print.

10.85 There has been some debate about the extent to which a right to enter can be derived from the ECHR.[32] In *Sun Myung Moon (Human Rights, Entry Clearance, Proportionality) USA* [2005] UKIAT 00112, the Tribunal found that *Farrakhan* was not authority for the proposal that the ECHR rights had an extraterritorial effect. The Tribunal accepted that Article 8 ECHR rights—family life—had been successfully argued before the Strasbourg Court, but found that the arguments were founded on the presence in the UK of a family member. Insofar as other rights were concerned, it was doubtful whether persons not physically present on territory of the UK were able to invoke the protection of the ECHR.[33]

10.86 Subsequent decisions have cast doubt on this position. The Strasbourg Court in *Cox v Turkey* (Application No 2933/03) [2010] ECHR 700, (2012) 55 EHRR 13 held that Article 10 ECHR (freedom of expression) was engaged by the ban on the re-entry of a US woman who had expressed strong views on issues of Kurdish assimilation and the treatment of Armenians. In *Women on Waves and others v Portugal*,[34] the Strasbourg Court found a violation of Article 10 ECHR when Portugal refused entry into Portuguese territorial waters to a ship bearing representatives of three groups seeking to campaign for the decriminalisation of abortion.[35] In *Nolan and K v Russia* (Application No 2512/04 of 6 July 2009), the Russian authorities considered activities such as those of the applicant for the Unification Church 'under the cover of religion, establish extensive governing structures which they use for gathering socio-political, economic, military and other information about ongoing events in Russia, indoctrinate the citizens and incite separatist tendencies'. Mr Nolan was thus prohibited from

---

[32] *Farrakhan (Human rights, Entry Clearance, Proportionality) USA* [2005] UKIAT 00112 (30 June 2005); *R (otao Lord Carlile of Berriew and others) v SSHD* [2013] EWCA Civ 199 (20 March 2013).
[33] *Sun Myung Moon (Human Rights, Entry Clearance, Proportionality) USA* [2005] UKIAT 00112 [68]–[70].
[34] Application No 31276/05, ECHR 2009, available in French and Russian only.
[35] For discussion on the balance to be struck between the protections of free expression under Art 10 of the Convention and the competing interests of national security, see *Sürek v Turkey* app no 26682/95 (1999) 7 BHRC 339; *A and others v SSHD* [2004] UKHL 56, [2005] 2 AC 68; *SSHD v Rehman* [2001] UKHL 47.

Part C – Deportation, Removal and Exclusion

re-entry to Russia. The Strasbourg Court found that the exclusion of the applicant violated Article 9 (freedom of religion).

10.87 In *R (otao Naik) v SSHD* [2011] EWCA Civ 1546, the Court of Appeal (Carnwath, Gross and Jackson LJJ) were reluctant to apply the territorial principle. Dr Naik, a lecturer on Muslim religious matters, was held entitled to rely on the Article 10 ECHR rights of his supporters in the UK to challenge the refusal to grant him entry to the UK, although his appeal was ultimately unsuccessful.

10.88 The Court of Appeal in *Naik* found that decisions of the Secretary of State to refuse entry to this country to an alien on national security or public order grounds are entitled to great weight and must, by their nature, enjoy a wide margin of appreciation (or discretion). These decisions had to be balanced against the rights of the individuals protected by the ECHR and were thus subject to review, but the Secretary of State was in a better position to consider the interests of the public than the court. At [88], Gross LJ provided a useful summary of the approach taken by the courts reviewing the decision:

> 88. Decisions of the SSHD to refuse entry to this country to an alien on national security or public order grounds are entitled to great weight and must, by their nature, enjoy a wide margin of appreciation (or discretion). Let it be accepted that such decisions, when resulting in the engagement of Article 10, warrant the most careful scrutiny on the part of the Court; crucially, even so, the decision-maker is the SSHD not the Court. As Carnwath LJ expressed it (at [62] above), the Court is not substituting its own view for that of the SSHD. The Court's task remains one of review. By way of elaboration:
>
> (a) The starting point is that the SSHD's decisions in this area are entitled to 'great weight', to adopt, with respect, Lord Bingham's wording in *A v Secretary of State for the Home Department* [2005] 2 AC 68 at [29]. For my part, I would regard this as self evident, given the subject-matter under consideration; the 'cost of failure' (see [45] above) is a most pertinent consideration. See, further, the authorities cited by Cranston J, at [43]–[46] of the judgment.
>
> (b) Given the nature of the decision, the SSHD must be accorded a wide margin of appreciation (or discretion). This is an area where, again adopting an observation of Lord Bingham (loc cit), 'reasonable and informed minds may differ'. Take, for instance, the 'Prevent' strand in the UK government's counter-terrorism strategy, to which reference was made in the evidence; judgment calls of no little difficulty will be required in determining the extent, nature and termination of engagement with those of extreme views. Further and as will be emphasised below, it is of the first importance that the Court does not substitute its views for those of the SSHD; a reminder that the SSHD enjoys a wide discretion serves as a useful warning to the Court against straying into territory more properly that of the SSHD.
>
> (c) As it seems to me (and with great respect to the extensive discussion of such matters in the literature), it matters little whether an approach which accords great weight and a wide margin of appreciation to decisions of the SSHD in this area is best described in terms of 'deference' or 'demarcation of functions'"(Lord Bingham, loc cit). The point is the same. Put simply and whether as a matter of 'deference' or 'demarcation', in areas such as national security or public order, the SSHD is likely to have advice and a perspective not or not readily available to the Court.
>
> (d) Nothing in the above observations precludes the Court from reviewing the decision of the SSHD by reference to what Carnwath LJ has termed ([62] above) 'public law and human rights principles'. Where Convention rights are involved, that review will be an 'intensive review': *A v Secretary of State for the Home Department*, supra,

headnote at p.69. Such a review would (as appropriate, see Carnwath LJ at [48] above) extend to the rationality, legality, procedural regularity and proportionality of a Ministerial decision. If it is necessary, which I am not sure it is, to add descriptive phrases to 'intensive review', then, no doubt, intensive review will involve 'the most careful scrutiny': *Cox v Turkey* [2010] Imm AR 4 at [38].

(e) But, whatever the intensity of the review, it is crucial that the Court should not substitute its views for those of the SSHD. The Court does not assume the role of the decision-maker; the Court's task is and remains one of review. It follows that a measure of judicial reserve or restraint must be prudent in this sphere—serving to underline the Court's proper role and to guard against usurping, however inadvertently, the role of the decision-maker. In any event, a Court will not lightly overturn a decision of the SSHD as to what is conducive to the public good, still less a decision made by the SSHD personally.

These issues were revisited in *R (otao Lord Carlile of Berriew and others) v SSHD* [2013] EWCA Civ 199 and thereafter on appeal to the Supreme Court: its decision is awaited.

Most challenges to exclusion arise following the refusal of an application for entry clearance or, in the case of a person with extant leave, following a decision to refuse leave to enter. Paragraph 320(6) requires an ECO or an IO to make decisions refusing entry clearance on the basis that an exclusion decision is in force. If an exclusion order is made after the person has obtained entry clearance, the normal procedure is for entry clearance to be revoked.[36]

10.89

These decisions are immigration decisions as defined in section 82(1) NIAA 2002 and thus can be appealed in the normal way to the Tribunal. Where national security issues are raised, an appeal may be heard by the Special Immigration Appeals Commission (SIAC).

10.90

Revocation

Exclusion decisions are in force until revoked by the Secretary of State, in the same manner as deportation orders. Revocation is governed by paragraphs 390 and 391 of the Immigration Rules, though a decision not to revoke an exclusion decision will not attract an appeal right, not being an immigration decision for the purposes of section 82 NIAA 2002. Challenge will be by way of judicial review.

10.91

Where a person has been sentenced to a term of imprisonment in excess of 30 months, his or her continued exclusion will be appropriate, save where there is a breach of the ECHR or in exceptional circumstances.

10.92

If a person has received a conviction that received a sentence of four years' imprisonment or less, the Secretary of State will normally to refuse to revoke an exclusion decision until a period of 10 years has passed since the making of the decision.[37] For those of longer duration, an exclusion order will not normally be revoked. A decision may be revoked earlier if:

10.93

— the decision would breach the UK's obligations under the Refugee Convention or the ECHR;
— the circumstances have significantly changed;

---

[36] Paragraph 30A, inserted by HC 329, 3 June 1996.
[37] Modernised Guidance (n 22).

Part C – Deportation, Removal and Exclusion

— fresh information that has become available since the exclusion decision suggests a change of approach.

10.94 Time runs from the date of the making of the decision to exclude, not from the date on which the sentence was passed. Such convictions never become spent insofar as the the immigration authorities are concerned. The fact that a conviction is deemed spent will therefore not be sufficient to warrant the revocation of an order.

10.95 Applications to revoke an exclusion order may be made to the Home Office directly or to the entry clearance point overseas. There is no formal procedure to be followed or application form that must be used. However, exclusion orders can only be revoked by the Secretary of State.

10.96 Revocation of an exclusion order does not guarantee re-entry into the UK. Visa nationals still require a visa to re-enter, and applications for visas will be subject to the provisions of the Immigration Rules, including those of Part 9 (General Grounds of Refusal).

G. Exclusion under the EEA Regime

10.97 Exclusion and removal of a national of an EEA state[38] or a person residing as a family member thereof is now governed by the provisions of Directive EC 2004/38, also known as the Citizen's Directive, which was transposed into domestic law by the Immigration (European Economic Area) Regulations 2006 (hereinafter the EEA Regulations). Such persons are not subject to the regime imposed by the Immigration Rules.

10.98 Article 45.3 of the TFEU establishes that the right to move to other Member States is subject to 'limitations justified on grounds of public policy, public security or public health'. While Article 45(3) TFEU applies to workers, equivolent limitations are contained in Articles 52(1) and 62 in relation to self-employed persons or service providers.

10.99 Chapter VI of the Citizen's Directive contains provisions for special measures taken by Member States against union citizens and their family members. Article 27 of the Directive provides:

1. Subject to the provisions of this Chapter, Member States may restrict the freedom of movement and residence of Union citizens and their family members, irrespective of nationality, on grounds of public policy, public security or public health. These grounds shall not be invoked to serve economic ends.

2. Measures taken on grounds of public policy or public security shall comply with the principle of proportionality and shall be based exclusively on the personal conduct of the individual concerned. Previous criminal convictions shall not in themselves constitute grounds for taking such measures.

The personal conduct of the individual concerned must represent a genuine, present and sufficiently serious threat affecting one of the fundamental interests of society. Justifications that are isolated from the particulars of the case or that rely on considerations of general prevention shall not be accepted.

---

[38] EEA countries include the 28 members of the EU, Norway, Liechtenstein, Iceland and Switzerland.

10.100 Article 27 now reflects the developments in the jurisprudence of the Court of Justice of the European Union (CJEU), formerly the European Court of Justice (ECJ). The powers to exclude are therefore not as broad as those applicable to those without EEA rights.

10.101 A decision to make an exclusion order must comply with the principle of proportionality; that is, it must be appropriate for securing the objective sought and must not go beyond what is necessary in order to obtain it.[39] Any such decision can have regard only to the circumstances relating to the individual concerned[40] and cannot incorporate any broader public interests (such as the need to deter foreign national prisoners or the fight against drugs). Previous convictions cannot of themselves found a decision to exclude.

10.102 In *Van Duyn v Home Office (No 2)* [1974] ECR 1337,[41] the ECJ considered the exclusion from the UK of a Dutch national who was associated with the Church of Scientology, then deemed an organisation whose activities were socially harmful and thus contrary to public policy. The ECJ held that the concept of public policy was to be interpreted strictly, but could be justified on the basis of clearly stated principles. Where a Member State had taken measures to combat activities of a particular organisation, exclusion of those with a current association with that organisation could be justified, although a past association was unlikely to do so.[42]

10.103 The decision must be taken as a protective measure, and therefore there must be evidence showing an individual will commit further offences or pose a risk to public security or policy in the future. In *R v Bouchereau* [1977] ECR 1999,[43] the ECJ held that criminal convictions were relevant only insofar as 'the circumstances that gave rise to them was evidence of personal conduct constituting a present threat to the requirements of public policy'.[44] Persistent petty criminality could represent a threat to public policy, irrespective of the fact that any single crime/offence, taken individually, would be insufficient to amount to a sufficiently serious threat and in that case it must be demonstrated that the personal conduct does represent a serious threat on the basis of nature, frequency and harm of the offending, *C-349/06 Polat* [2007] ECR I-08167, [35].

10.104 Enquiries may be made of other Member States as to whether a person represents a danger for public policy or public security reasons, although this may not be routine.[45] However, a person holding a residence document issued by the UK must be re-admitted, regardless of whether that document has expired, if he or she is expelled from another Member State.[46]

10.105 The threat must exist at the point that a decision is taken or is reviewed by the courts;[47] the passage of time since a relevant conviction, for example, must be considered before excluding a person who would otherwise have a right of entry. A decision to exclude following an expulsion decision taken more than two years previously must be reviewed in light of any potential change of circumstances, and the Secretary of State

---

[39] Case 55/94 *Gebhard v Consigol dell' Ordine degli Advocat AE Procuratori di Milano* [1995] ECR I-4165.
[40] Article 27.2 of Directive 2004/38; reg 21(5) of the EEA Regulations (see also Case C-67/74 *Bonsignore* [1975] ECR 297).
[41] Case 41/74 *Van Duyn v Home Office (No 2)* [1974] ECR 1337.
[42] ibid 24.
[43] Case 30/77 *R v Bouchereau* [1977] ECR 1999.
[44] ibid [28].
[45] Article 27(3) of Directive 2004/38.
[46] ibid Art 27(4).
[47] ibid Art 27(2); reg 21(5) of the EEA Regulations; Joined Cases C-484 and C-493//01 *Orafanopoulos and Oliveri* [2005] 1 CMLR 18, [2004] ECR I-5757, [2004] ECR I-5257, [2004] EUECJ C-482/01; *R v Bouchereau* (n 44).

must be satisfied that the person continues to represent a genuine and current threat to public policy or public security.

10.106 Exclusion decisions made under the Immigration Rules cease to apply to a person who subsequently acquires an EEA right of residence. Those with potential rights of entry—extended or other family members defined by Article 3 of the Directive and regulation 8 of the EEA Regulations—must have their claims examined in accordance with the process and criteria of the Directive/EEA Regulations. Whilst the existence of an exclusion order or a deportation order made under the IA 1971 may be a relevant factor, a separate EEA decision under regulation 19 of the EEA Regulations must be taken for the individual to be lawfully excluded.

10.107 Such a decision is subject to the additional requirements of regulation 21, which sets out criteria for decisions taken on public policy or public security grounds:

   (a) A decision may not be taken to serve economic ends.
   (b) A decision may not be taken in respect of a person with a permanent right of residence except on serious grounds of public policy or public security.
   (c) A relevant decision may not be taken except on imperative grounds of public security in respect of an EEA national who—
       — has resided in the UK for a continuous period of at least ten years prior to the relevant decision; or
       — is under the age of 18, unless the relevant decision is necessary in his best interests,

   a. Where a relevant decision is taken on grounds of public policy or public security it shall, in addition to complying with the preceding paragraphs of this regulation, be taken in accordance with the following principles—
   b. principle of proportionality;
   c. must be based exclusively on the personal conduct of the person concerned;
   d. the personal conduct of the person concerned must represent a genuine, present and sufficiently serious threat affecting one of the fundamental interests of society;
   e. matters which relate to considerations of general prevention do not justify the decision;
   f. a person's previous criminal convictions do not in themselves justify the decision.

Before taking a relevant decision on the grounds of public policy or public security in relation to a person who is resident in the UK, the decision maker must take account of considerations such as the age, state of health, family and economic situation of the person, the person's length of residence in the UK, the person's social and cultural integration into the UK, and the extent of the person's links with his or her country of origin.

10.108 The exclusion measure must be taken in order to protect a fundamental interest of society. In *GW (EEA Regulation 21: 'Fundamental Interests') Netherlands* [2009] UKAIT 00050 [17], the Tribunal held that those fundamental interests were to be governed by the laws of the host state:

> In a society as closely regulated as the United Kingdom is, but probably in any society governed by the rule of law, it is one of the functions of legal regulation to protect the fundamental interests of society. If one wants to discover what interests are regarded as fundamental in a society it is appropriate to look at the legal provisions in that society. It is therefore highly unlikely that a matter which is not governed by law is a matter which is properly regarded as the fundamental interests of that society.

10.109 The *GW (Netherlands)* case concerned the exclusion of a Dutch Member of Parliament, who had voiced strong criticism of the presence and standing of Islam in Europe and, to quote [3] of the decision, 'expresses his views in a manner which any right thinking person would regard as offensive to the religion of Islam and its founder'. He sought entry to show a film he had made expressing these views, which the Secretary of State considered would 'threaten community harmony, and therefore public security in the UK'. Having attempted to enter the UK, he was refused entry at port and was duly removed. He appealed. The Secretary of State maintained that if permitted entry, there was a possibility that he would commit a public order offence. In addition, there was said to be a risk that his presence and activities would lead to inter-community violence. The Secretary of State asked for deference to her views on this, in line with the Court of Appeal authority in *Farrakhan*.[48] In distinguishing *Farrakhan*, the Tribunal expressed concerns about the evidence upon which the Secretary of State's decision was based; GW had previously entered the UK and no public order offences or community violence had been noted. The Tribunal further distinguished the legal situation: Farrakhan, as an American citizen, had no right to enter the UK, whereas GW, as an European citizen, had an underlying right to enter. In determining whether his exclusion was a proportionate response in line with regulation 21 of the EEA Regulations, the Tribunal was obliged to consider whether there was a necessary infringement in his human rights—here his rights to free expression under Article 10 ECHR. Whilst Article 10 is a qualified right, the evidence produced fell well short of demonstrating a need to exclude GW such as to trump his free movement rights.

Regulation 19 now also requires the Secretary of State to consider new regulation 21B (which came into force on 1 January 2014),[49] which additionally permits the Secretary of State to exclude those who are considered to have abused their EEA rights of residence, or if there are reasonable grounds to suspect that admission would lead to the abuse of those rights. An abuse is considered to be:[50]

10.110

(a) conduct designed to circumvent the need to be a qualified person;
(b) attempting to re-enter the UK within 12 months of being removed, where the person is unable to show that he or she would be a qualified person or a family member of a qualified person/person with permanent residence;
(c) entering or attempting to enter into a marriage of convenience;
(d) using fraud to obtain or assist another to obtain the right to reside.

Regulation 21B permits the Secretary of State to exclude a person where there are reasonable grounds to suspect that the person has abused the rights of residence, for up to 12 months, unless that person can show that there has been a material change in his or her circumstances. Such a change in circumstances requires proof that the individual will be a qualified person on entry, or a family member thereof. The effect is to remove the initial right of residence, provided for under regulation 13 and Article 6 of the Directive, from those whom the Secretary of State deems abusive. The new provisions in relation to abuse of rights extend the exclusion provisions of the Directive 2004/38/EC on grounds of public policy security or health and enable the Secretary of State to refuse admission, cancel a right of residence and potentially exclude a person for 12 months

10.111

---

[48] *Supra*, para 10.82.
[49] Introduced by the Immigration (European Economic Area) (Amendment) (No 2) Regulations 2013, SI 2013/3032.
[50] Enforcement Instructions and Guidance, ch 50.

on the grounds of 'reasonable suspicion' of abuse of rights. Whilst a member state is entitled to engage mechanisms for prevention of abuse of rights where there is well founded suspicion of the same, there is no authority that the state in fact is left power enabling it to take the actions proposed by current amendments. The express wording of Article 35 of the Directive 2004/38/EC is that the member state may 'adopt the necessary measures to refuse, terminate or withdraw any right conferred by this Directive in the case of abuse of rights or fraud' subject to proportionality requirement and the procedural safeguards of Articles 30 and 31 (thus by way of Article 31(3) directly importing detailed considerations on proportionality under Article 28—requiring account to be taken 'of considerations such as how long the individual concerned has resided on its territory, his/her age, state of health, family and economic situation, social and cultural integration into the host Member State and the extent of his/her links with the country of origin). This clearly does not envisage such actions on the basis merely of 'reasonable suspicion'. EU law requires clear proof of both objective circumstances and intention for abuse of rights. Most recently in Case *C- 456/12 O & B v Minister voor Immigratie, Integratie en Asiel*, Judgment of 12 March 2014, para 58 Court of Justice of the European Union stated that "Proof of such an abuse [of rights] requires, first, a combination of objective circumstances in which, despite formal observance of the conditions laid down by the European Union rules, the purpose of those rules has not been achieved, and, secondly, a subjective element consisting in the intention to obtain an advantage from the European Union rules by artificially creating the conditions laid down for obtaining it". If Union citizens and their family members obtain a right of residence in a member state other than their own this does not constitute abuse as they are benefiting from an advantage inherent in the exercise of right of free movement irrespective of the purpose of the their move (*C-212/97 Centros Ltd v Erhvervsog Selskabsstyrelsen* [1999] ECR I-01459, para 27; *C-109/01 Secretary of State for the Home Department v Hacene Akrich* [2003] ECR I-09607 para 55; *C-1/05 Yunying Jia v Migrationsverket* [2007] ECR I-00001, para 31).

10.112   Article 32 of the Directive provides:

1. Persons excluded on grounds of public policy or public security may submit an application for lifting of the exclusion order after a reasonable period, depending on the circumstances, and in any event after three years from enforcement of the final exclusion order which had been validly adopted in accordance with Community law, by putting forward arguments to establish that there had been a material change in the circumstances which justified the decision ordering their exclusion.

The Member State shall reach a decision on this application within six months of its submission.

2. The persons referred to in paragraph 1 shall have no right of entry to the territory of the Member State while the application is being considered.

10.113   Entry in breach of an exclusion order will not constitute the exercising of rights under the EU Treaties and thus, under Regulation 24, such a person may be removed as an illegal entrant under Schedule 2, IA 1971.[51]

---

[51] See ch 9 above.

Exclusion from the UK

10.114 Exclusion orders and the decision not to revoke exclusion orders are EEA decisions for the purposes of the EEA Regulations[52] and therefore, unlike non-EEA cases, attract a right of appeal.[53] However, the Regulation holds that this right of appeal may only be exercised on production of a valid EEA identity document in the case of an EEA national, or a valid national identity document and proof of his or her relationship to the EEA national. If the person is outside of the country when the decision is made, the right of appeal cannot be exercised in-country.[54] It is doubtful that limitation on the right of appeal in the absence of specified documents is lawful in the light of authority that the requirement for an identification document is not absolute where identity can be established on other basis *Case C-459/99 MRAX v Belgian State* [2002] ECR I-659, [62] and *Case C-215/03 Oulane v Minister voor Vreemdelingenzaken en Integratie* [2005] ECR I-01215, [20]-[24], as well as absence of authority for such a limitation of a right of appeal in Directive 2004/38/EC.

10.115 Where a person is excluded from the UK pending appeal, they may apply to SSHD to be present to make submissions in person for that appeal under Regulation 29AA and the Secretary of State must grant them temporary admission "except when P's appearance may cause serious troubles to public policy or public security" (Reg. 29AA(3)). The admission must take into account the dates of the appeal and may be removed pending subsequent stages of the redress procedure and re-admitted for those. However, under regulation 29AA(6), 'upon such admission P is to be treated as if P were a person refused leave to enter under the 1971 Act for the purposes of paragraphs 8, 10, 10A, 11, 16 to 18 and 21 to 24 of Schedule 23 to the 1971 Act'.

---

[52] Regulation 2 defines an 'EEA decision' as decisions concerning a person's right to be admitted into the UK, amongst others.
[53] Regulation 26. A person has a right of appeal against an EEA decision.
[54] Regulation 27(1)(aa).

Part D
Denial and Deprivation of Citizenship

11
Denial of British Citizenship

Contents

A. Introduction 11.1
B. International Law 11.3
    B1. General International Law 11.3
    B2. International Human Rights Law 11.5
    B3. Hybrid Instruments 11.10
    B4. Council of Europe Instruments 11.12
C. EU Law 11.14
D. Domestic Law 11.15
    D1. Prerogative 11.15
    D2. Statute 11.16
    D3. Statutory Instrument 11.21
    D4. Published Guidance 11.22
E. Discussion 11.24
    E1. The Acquisition of British Citizenship 11.24
    E2. Litigation Concerning Refusal to Grant British Citizenship 11.38
        Discretionary Decisions Not Concerning 'Good Character' 11.38
        'Good Character' Decisions 11.39

A. Introduction

11.1 Decisions regarding the grant or denial of British citizenship status are taken by the Secretary of State applying British nationality law, which is primarily set out in BNA 1981. A short introductory account of that law is set out in chapter 7 above, and a much fuller treatment of British nationality law is provided by the leading work on the subject, Fransman's *British Nationality Law*, and the most recent edition of *Halsbury's Laws of England*.[1] This chapter considers the denial of British citizenship status, with a focus upon cases in which the Secretary of State is empowered to exercise relatively broad judgment.

11.2 Some concepts mentioned in this chapter require definition. 'Nationality' is the term denoting attachment to a state for the purposes of international law and reflects a concept which has evolved from the earlier categorisation of any given individual as either a 'subject', identifying status as the subject of a sovereign power, generally a monarch in the pre-modern and early modern period, or as the converse, namely an 'alien'. Nationality is determined by municipal law, the domestic law of a state, but international tribunals

---

[1] Laurie Fransman QC, *British Nationality Law* (3rd edn, London, Bloomsbury Professional, 2011); Lord Mackay of Clashfern (ed), *Halsbury's Laws of England* (London, Butterworths, 2012).

and other states will consider norms of international law in relation to any question of recognition under international law of the nationality status identified by municipal law. The possession of nationality is generally evidenced by possession and presentation of a passport. In common parlance in the UK, 'nationality' is often used synonymously with another familiar phrase, namely 'citizenship'. But the latter term in the UK denotes a status created under domestic law that indicates nationality but is not possessed by all those who do, or may, possess the nationality of the UK. As is illustrated elsewhere—see chapters 1 and 7 and the broader works on British nationality law identified above—the edges of the nationality associated with the UK have come to be poorly defined, whilst British citizenship and some other subcategories of relevant citizenship are by contrast closely defined by statute and, particularly in the case of British citizenship, identify those expressly granted certain important rights under domestic law.

B. International Law

B1. General International Law

11.3   In chapter 2, it was indicated that international law in general may not be directly relied upon in the UK. International law applies to the extent that customary international law forms part of or a source for the common law, or, as to treaties, a relevant norm has been incorporated domestically, or is relevant in some other way, for instance, by assisting the interpretation of domestic law or shaping the exercise of discretion.

11.4   The League of Nations Convention on Certain Questions Relating to the Conflict of Nationality Laws 1930 (CCQRCNL) provides by Article 1 that: 'It is for each State to determine under its own law who are its nationals. This law shall be recognised by other States in so far as it is consistent with international conventions, international custom, and the principles of law generally recognised with regard to nationality.' A relatively limited range of international norms may be applicable in the context of denial of nationality. In particular, norms of non-discrimination and avoidance of statelessness have gradually developed and, as already observed, in the *Barcelona Traction* case, *Belgium v Spain (Second Phase)* [1970] ICJ Reports 3 [33]–[34], the International Court of Justice held that core protections of individuals constituted *erga omnes* norms, including protection from racial discrimination. A racially based pattern or practice of exclusion from nationality (or a similar pattern based on some other form of prohibited discrimination) would breach the protected norms.

B2. International Human Rights Law

11.5   A wider survey of the main international human rights law provisions relevant to immigration and nationality law can be found in chapter 3. The precursor of other post-war instruments is of course Article 15 1948 UDHR, which, whilst not having binding effect upon states, asserted the human right to possess a nationality and not to be arbitrarily deprived of nationality or denied the right to change nationality. This has been understood as a statement of principle which does not impose a duty on the UK or any other particular state to afford nationality to a specific individual or group. A summary of

Denial of British Citizenship

other standards relevant to denial of nationality and contained within instruments ratified by the UK is set out below.

First, the ICCPR does not contain a direct descendant of Article 15 UDHR that is applicable generally, but does provide a protective norm concerning children: Article 24(3) ICCPR provides that 'every child has the right to acquire a nationality', imposing duties upon states, though the UN Human Rights Committee in the General Comment cited in chapter 3 has indicated that this 'does not necessarily make it an obligation to give their nationality to every child born in their territory'. 11.6

Two other primary ICCPR norms might be relevant: 11.7

(i) Action by the state in the context of nationality might in some circumstances be said to breach Article 17 ICCPR, read in conjunction with Article 23(1) ICCPR, if it amounts to 'arbitrary or unlawful' interference with the protected interests of 'privacy, family, home', and the law does not provide protection against this. In *R v SSHD ex p Montana* [2001] 1 WLR 552 [18]–[20], the Court of Appeal found that Article 8 ECHR, the ECHR provision closely analogous to Article 23(1) ICCPR, was not in the circumstances of the case engaged by the withholding of citizenship, though the decision on its face would not prevent relevant provisions being raised on different, more conducive facts. In *Genovese v Malta* no 53124/09 [2011] ECHR 1590, (2014) 58 EHRR 25, the European Court of Human Rights at [30] referred to earlier decisions and observed of Article 8 ECHR that 'The provisions of Article 8 do not, however, guarantee a right to acquire a particular nationality or citizenship. Nevertheless, the Court has previously stated that it cannot be ruled out that an arbitrary denial of citizenship might in certain circumstances raise an issue under Article 8 of the Convention because of the impact of such a denial on the private life of the individual', and the potential application of Article 8 ECHR was supported by Blake J in *MH and others v SSHD* [2008] EWHC 2525 (Admin) [54]–[62] and by Ouseley J in *AHK and others v SSHD* [2013] EWHC 1426 (Admin), refusing judicial review of refusals of naturalisation in which no or minimal grounds for concluding that applicants were not of 'good character' had been shown beyond that assertion, and public interest immunity certificates were upheld. Referring to *Genovese*, Ouseley J noted, at [45], that: 'A submission that the mere nature or degree of effect of a refusal of naturalisation, without some further quality of arbitrariness or discrimination, suffices to engage Article 8 seems to me ill-founded on this ECtHR jurisprudence.'

(ii) A denial of nationality (for example, the refusal of an application for naturalisation or registration) does not under domestic law entail departure or expulsion from the territory, for example, by terminating subsisting leave to enter or remain in the UK. If it did, then the much more extensive ICCPR norms concerning expulsion, perhaps most significantly the protection against arbitrary deprivation of the right to enter his or her own country identified at Article 12(4) ICCPR, would potentially come to bear.

Separate non-discrimination norms within the ICCPR may apply in relation to substantive rights under that instrument: 11.8

(i) Article 2(1) ICCPR is breached where the state fails to 'respect and ensure' the rights protected by the ICCPR 'without distinction of any kind', such as 'race, colour, sex, language, religion, political or other opinion, national or social origin, property, birth or other status', or where the state fails to ensure an effective remedy for breach.

(ii) Article 3 ICCPR reflects the undertaking of States Parties to ensure the equal right of men and women to civil and political rights provided under the ICCPR.

11.9 Beyond the ICCPR, a range of other, broader, international human rights norms may be applicable to denial of nationality. These include, inter alia, the following:

(i) Action concerning the right to nationality which is discriminatory on the basis of race would breach Article 5(d)(iii) CERD and could, depending upon the facts, also breach Article 5(d)(i)–(ii) CERD if rights to freedom of movement and residence or to leave or return to 'one's [own] country' are encroached upon.

(ii) A 'distinction, exclusion or restriction made on the basis of sex which has the effect or purpose of impairing or nullifying the recognition, enjoyment or exercise by women, irrespective of their marital status, on a basis of equality of men and women, of human rights and fundamental freedoms in the political, economic, social, cultural, civil or any other field' would breach Article 1 CEDAW.

(iii) In an 'action concerning children', Article 3(1) CRC requires that 'the best interests of the child shall be a primary consideration'. This and Article 9 CRC (regarding family unity) may be relevant where a child is the subject of or is affected by denial of nationality.

(iv) Persons to whom the CRPD applies are by Article 18 CRPD entitled to 'a nationality, on an equal basis with others' by the specific means described therein, including 'the right to acquire and change a nationality' (Article 18(a)) and protection from deprivation of entry to 'their own' country on any basis 'arbitrarily or on the basis of disability'.

B3. Hybrid Instruments

11.10 Chapter 4 set out international law provisions established by three regimes referred to as 'hybrid', in that they combine the creation of human rights, like the instruments seen in chapter 2 and above, in combination with other purposes. The CSR and the CSSP in general have little to say regarding denial of nationality, save that each provides that States Parties 'shall as far as possible facilitate the assimilation and naturalisation' of those within its regime, in particular by '[making] every effort to expedite naturalisation proceedings and to reduce as far as possible the charges and cost of such proceedings': the relevant provisions are Article 34 CSR and Article 32 CSSP. Neither provision is explicitly incorporated into domestic law.

11.11 The CRS provides a number of relevant protections:

(i) Under Article 1 CRS, a Contracting State shall grant its nationality to a person born in its territory who would otherwise be stateless, subject to relevant requirements.

(ii) Under Article 2 CRS, a foundling found in the territory of a Contracting State shall, in the absence of proof to the contrary, be considered to have been born within that territory of parents possessing the nationality of that state.

(iii) Article 3 CRS provides that birth on a British registered ship or aircraft triggers the other provisions of the Convention (so that, for instance, a child born on a British registered aircraft who would otherwise be stateless is entitled to the benefit of Article 1 CRS).

(iv) Under Article 4 CRS, a Contracting State 'shall grant its nationality to a person, not born in the territory of a Contracting State, who would otherwise be stateless, if the nationality of one of his parents at the time of the person's birth was that of that State', subject to relevant requirements.[2]

B4. Council of Europe Instruments

Two instruments introduced in chapter 5 are relevant to denial of nationality. Under the ECHR, certain human rights protections might in appropriate circumstances apply. The most significant of these is Article 8 ECHR. Article 8 ECHR relevantly protects the right to respect for private and family life. This does not directly cite a right to nationality, but the effect of uncertainty or insecurity created or contributed to by nationality-related action has in some circumstances, as set out in chapter 5, been found to engage Article 8 ECHR. In *R v SSHD ex p Montana* [2001] 1 WLR 552 [18]–[20], the Court of Appeal found on the facts that Article 8 ECHR was not in the circumstances of the case engaged, alone or in conjunction with Article 14 ECHR, by the withholding of citizenship, but did not reject the possibility of engagement in an appropriate case. In *Genovese v Malta* no 53124/09 [2011] ECHR 1590, (2014) 58 EHRR 25, the European Court of Human Rights confirmed that 'it cannot be ruled out that an arbitrary denial of citizenship might in certain circumstances raise an issue under Article 8 of the Convention because of the impact of such a denial on the private life of the individual'. In *AHK and others v SSHD* [2013] EWHC 1426 (Admin), Ouseley J referred to *Genovese* and earlier decisions, apparently accepting that 'some further quality of arbitrariness or discrimination' in a nationality decision might engage Article 8 ECHR.

11.12

The ECN 1997 has been signed but not ratified by the UK. Under Article 18 VCLT, a state which has signed but not ratified a treaty is obliged to 'refrain, in good faith, from acts that would defeat the object and purpose of the treaty'. The obligation is, however, a relatively limited one. Were the UK to ratify this provision, then under Article 6 ECN, the UK would be bound to facilitate in its internal law the acquisition of nationality for persons falling within the categories designated there, leaving relevant criteria to be determined by domestic law, and to meet the procedural standards in Chapter IV: Article 10 ECN requiring a decision within a reasonable time, Article 11 ECN reasons in writing with decisions, Article 12 ECN admissibility of 'administrative or judicial review' under municipal law and Article 13 ECN that fees for nationality-related applications be reasonable and not constitute 'an obstacle' to applicants.

11.13

---

[2] The UK has taken steps in its nationality law to comply with the CRS requirements, notably at sch 2 BNA 1981.

C. EU Law

11.14 In Case C-135/08 *Rottmann (European Citizenship)* [2010] OJ C113/4, [2010] QB 761, the Court of Justice of the European Union at [39] observed that 'according to established case-law, it is for each Member State, having due regard to Community law, to lay down the conditions for the acquisition and loss of nationality', but also went on to note at [45] that 'Thus, the Member States must, when exercising their powers in the sphere of nationality, have due regard to European Union law', so that EU law procedural standards come to bear. This has been rejected domestically in *G1 (Sudan) v SSHD* [2012] EWCA Civ 867, [2013] QB 1008. Chapter 6 further addresses this, and the effect of EU law in the context of denial of nationality is considered in section E below.

D. Domestic Law

D1. Prerogative

11.15 An important distinction between the nationality and immigration laws of the UK is that whereas IA 1971 provides under section 3(2) that the Secretary of State shall 'from time to time (and as soon as may be) lay before Parliament statements of the rules, or of any changes in the rules, laid down by him as to the practice to be followed in the administration of this Act for regulating the entry into and stay in the United Kingdom of persons required by this Act to have leave to enter, including any rules as to the period for which leave is to be given and the conditions to be attached in different circumstances', it does not treat nationality as being within the span of material set down in the Rules, providing only that 'account may be taken of citizenship or nationality'. The Supreme Court has held in *R (Munir) v SSHD* [2012] UKSC 32, [2012] 1 WLR 2192 and *R (Alvi) v SSHD* [2012] UKSC 33, [2012] 1 WLR 22 that the exercise of power by SSHD by reference to the prerogative has been abrogated or suspended in the field of immigration control since the coming into force of IA 1971. BNA 1981, the cornerstone of UK nationality law, does not on its face set down any requirement parallel to that applied in the immigration context by section 3(2) IA 1971. Accordingly, the prerogative cannot be positively identified as excluded by statute, although, as set out below, the primary powers exercised by the Secretary of State in relation to nationality are statutory ones. A more detailed account of prerogative powers is given in chapter 7.

D2. Statute

11.16 Under section 2(1)(a) IA 1971, as amended with effect from 1 January 1983 by section 39(2) BNA 1981, any British citizen possesses the right of abode in the UK. A second route to right of abode applies to certain Commonwealth citizens. Under section 2(1)(b) IA 1971, as amended by BNA 1981, entitlement to the right of abode extends to Commonwealth citizens who immediately before the commencement BNA 1981 on

1 January 1983 were Commonwealth citizens with the right of abode under section 2(1) IA 1971 and who have not in the meantime ceased to be Commonwealth citizens.

11.17 Part 1 BNA 1981 sets out the various bases on which individuals may be entitled to citizenship, which are:

(i) by birth or adoption (section 1 BNA 1981);
(ii) by descent (section 2 BNA 1981);
(iii) in the case of minors, by registration (sections 3–5 and 10 BNA 1981);
(iv) in the case of adults, by naturalisation (section 6 and Schedule 1 BNA 1981).

11.18 In the adjudication of challenges to refusal of naturalisation or registration, it has been held repeatedly that the grant of British citizenship by naturalisation under section 6(1) BNA 1981 is not itself a fundamental human right: *R v SSHD ex p Fayed (No 2)* [2000] EWCA Civ 523, [2001] Imm AR 134 [93]; *R (AHK and others) v SSHD* [2009] EWCA Civ 287 [10]. As Blake J stated, referring to authority, in *MH and others v SSHD* [2008] EWHC 2525 (Admin) at [41]: 'In general terms ... no claimant [under section 6(1) BNA 1981] has a right to British citizenship, but only a right to have an application fairly considered under the statutory scheme.' That said, in *R v SSHD ex p Fayed* [1996] EWCA Civ 946, [1997] 1 All ER 228, Phillips LJ at 251d–e stated that:

> An applicant for citizenship has not at risk any vested right ... The right for which he applies is, however, a right of great importance. It carries with it the rights of freedom of movement and establishment enjoyed by members of the European Community. It exempts from visa requirements in many parts of the world. It carries a right to vote. It is a legitimate aspiration for one who has established his home in this country, the more so if he has children here who have British Nationality and if his wife is a British National.
>
> There is another side to the coin. The refusal of British Nationality to one who has, apparently, satisfied all the technical requirements of Section 6 is likely to carry the natural implication, both in this country and abroad, that he has attributes of background, character or conduct that are disreputable.

In the context of deprivation of nationality, McCombe LJ in *L1 v SSHD* [2013] EWCA Civ 906 observed at [41] that 'without being excessively emotional about the privileges of British citizenship, the issue was as to a fundamental matter of the appellant's personal status'.

11.19 As set out in chapter 7, domestic anti-discrimination law now applies to the administration of the Secretary of State's nationality functions. Under section 19B(1) Race Relations Act 1976 (RRA 1976): 'It is unlawful for a public authority in carrying out any functions of the authority to do any act which constitutes discrimination.' Discrimination under section 1 RRA 1976 means treating another person on racial grounds less favourably than he or she treats or would treat other persons, or applying to a person a requirement or condition which is or would be applied equally to persons not of the same racial group as that other, but which indirectly discriminates in the manner delineated in the statute. The term 'racial grounds' in section 3(1) RRA 1976 means colour, race, nationality, or ethnic or national origins. As a result of this, 'when considering the grant of British citizenship, the Secretary of State may not discriminate on grounds of race, as defined by the 1976 Act', as Burnett J noted in *R (otao Ramalingum) v SSHD* [2009] EWHC 453 (Admin) [9].

11.20 BCIA 2009 received Royal Assent on 21 July 2009, with an indication by the then government that extensive provisions as regards naturalisation in Part 2 BCIA 2009, amending BNA 1981, would be introduced no sooner than July 2011. The aim of these amendments was to remake the law of naturalisation treating the acquisition of British citizenship by naturalisation as the culmination of a complex process of 'earned citizenship'. This change, however, was not accompanied by any of the amendments to immigration law which would have been necessary to begin to render a new scheme functional, and the provisions of Part 2 BCIA 2009 therefore looked 'particularly unfamiliar, if not incomprehensible'.[3] The new provisions were never brought into force and no further steps have been taken to make this possible. At the date of writing, the bringing into force of Part 2 BCIA 2009 at any point in the immediate future appears unlikely.

D3. Statutory Instrument

11.21 The contribution of statutory instruments to the operation of British nationality law is notably small, though they are not excluded as a matter of legal principle. Perhaps the primary context in which they arise in relation to acquisition of nationality (irrelevant to the issues in this book and noted only as a phenomenon) is that they designate specific forms of service to Her Majesty's Government which enable a person to claim British citizenship by descent on the basis of birth outside the UK whilst a parent is engaged in government service.

D4. Published Guidance

11.22 Decisions of the Secretary of State on applications for citizenship must be taken consistently with the powers set out in Part 1 BNA 1981, which frequently require that consideration be given to the exercise of discretion. In contradistinction to immigration law, there is no direct equivalent in nationality law to the Immigration Rules HC 395. There is, however, extensive non-statutory guidance in this area, provided by the Nationality Instructions (NIs).[4] These are used by UK Border Agency staff deciding applications for citizenship. At present, the contents are arranged into two volumes, which are subdivided into chapters and sections as follows:

— Volume 1 of the NIs contains the primary instructions. At the time of writing, these were split into 57 chapters, each dealing with a different subject matter, and in general are more focused upon standards for decisions under BNA 1981 than are the chapters in Volume 2.
— Volume 2 was at the time of writing divided into 54 chapters, which provide general information, including some interesting historical material, to be used alongside the primary instructions.

11.23 The primary basis for decision making in relation to nationality therefore depends upon the satisfaction of statutory requirements, primarily set down in BNA 1981, where issues of elucidation may be assisted to a greater of lesser degree by the NIs.

---

[3] Fransman (n 1) 414.
[4] www.ukba.homeoffice.gov.uk/policyandlaw/guidance/nationalityinstructions.

E. Discussion

E1. The Acquisition of British Citizenship

As seen above, the acquisition of nationality is an area in which international law imposes a limited range of standards, but some duties are created, including the following: **11.24**

(i) customary international law and international human rights law respectively contain and have further elucidated or extended strong non-discrimination norms applicable to the grant or withholding of nationality in any manner which constitutes relevant discrimination on the basis of, inter alia, race discrimination, gender and disability;

(ii) within international refugee and statelessness law, Article 34 CSR and Article 32 CSSP emphasise the desirability of assimilation of refugees and stateless persons respectively to nationality of the country in which they have obtained protection;

(iii) international human rights law and the international law concerning statelessness have prescribed individually and cumulatively significant protections for children, including the 'best interests' principle in Article 3 CRC and the provisions of the CRS concerning children who otherwise would be left stateless;

(iv) the denial of nationality may in principle have effects which impinge upon protections applicable to private or family life or home under Articles 17 and 23(1) ICCPR and Article 8 ECHR, and hence create ground for the application of the relatively wide anti-discrimination provisions in Articles 2(1) and 3 ICCPR and/or Article 14 ECHR. However, whether this situation arises in practice will depend upon the factual situation;

(v) the denial of nationality if linked to expulsion or exclusion from the territory may breach rights of entry to or presence in 'his [or her] own' country, perhaps most importantly that provided in Article 12(4) ICCPR, and create ground for the application of Articles 2(1) and 3 ICCPR. Whether this situation arises in practice will depend upon the factual situation.

EU law may create procedural rights, if not substantive ones. On this issue, the law must be regarded as in flux. In *Rottmann (European Citizenship)* (see paragraph 11.14 above), the effect of application of EU law was said to be as follows: **11.25**

> 56. … it is, however, for the national court to ascertain whether the withdrawal decision at issue in the main proceedings observes the principle of proportionality so far as concerns the consequences it entails for the situation of the person concerned in the light of European Union law, in addition, where appropriate, to examination of the proportionality of the decision in the light of national law.
>
> 57. Having regard to the importance which primary law attaches to the status of citizen of the Union, when examining a decision withdrawing naturalisation it is necessary, therefore, to take into account the consequences that the decision entails for the person concerned and, if relevant, for the members of his family with regard to the loss of the rights enjoyed by every citizen of the Union. In this respect it is necessary to establish, in particular, whether that loss is justified in relation to the gravity of the offence committed by that person, to the lapse of time between the naturalisation decision and the withdrawal decision and to whether it is possible for that person to recover his original nationality.

Whilst the subject matter of that case was deprivation of nationality entailing loss of attached rights rather than refusal to grant naturalisation to which rights attached, no clear distinction between the two was elucidated by the Court. An earlier decision of the Court of Justice, Case C-192/99 *Kaur (European Citizenship)* [2001] 2 CMLR 505, turned on the finding that the claimant, a citizen of the Commonwealth and the UK given no right of abode in the UK under IA 1971, was covered by a UK declaration on accession to the European legal order excluding her from the definition of 'national' for the purposes of EU law, so that she had at no stage been a person to whom relevant entitlements attached. It did not test an application for naturalisation or registration as a British citizen. And whilst the *Rottmann* decision has in *G1 (Sudan) v SSHD* [2012] EWCA Civ 867, [2013] QB 1008 been criticised and said to be of no practical effect, as regards domestic decision making, the issue appears far from finally settled.

11.26 That said, even if EU procedural law applied to decisions concerning British citizenship, the effect of this in the context of denial of citizenship might be relatively minimal. It is difficult to see that substantial weight would not be put on the ability of the state to set and apply its standards for the grant of citizenship, as opposed to its withdrawal, so that quite weighty matters would probably be needed to indicate a different outcome in a denial case. A more intrusive approach would in effect create a discrete EU citizenship law regime substantially displacing national regimes.

11.27 Returning to domestic law, the requirements for British citizenship, or other forms of British citizenship status, are a matter of British nationality law and can be found in both of the sources identified in paragraph 11.1 above. The focus of this work is upon the more circumscribed, but still very significant, range of cases under BNA 1981 in which the acquisition of British citizenship by registration, naturalisation or other means is subject to the exercise of discretionary judgment by the Secretary of State.

11.28 It is an important feature of the statutory scheme that some bases of entitlement involve no judgment on the part of the Secretary of State. For instance, a person entitled to British citizenship by birth or adoption under section 1 BNA 1981 or by descent under section 2 BNA 1981 cannot lawfully be denied recognition of citizenship. Under other provisions, however, the Secretary of State is for example instructed to register an individual as a British citizen (in the case of a minor under section 3 BNA 1981) 'if he thinks fit'. In sections 6(1) and 6(2) BNA 1981, the Secretary of State is empowered to grant naturalisation as a British citizen if the statutory requirements are met (save in respect of any provision which may be waived), but, even if all relevant requirements are met, is required to grant naturalisation only if 'he thinks fit' to do so. Further, at some points in his or her decision making, broad assessments have to be made by the Secretary of State as to whether to exercise a statutory discretion to waive requirements (paragraph 2 of Schedule 1 to the BNA 1981). Even beyond the features of the scheme which are strictly discretionary, there are others, such as the requirement for 'good character' on the part of any child of 10 or more ('adult or young person') seeking registration, or any adult seeking naturalisation, which call for broad judgment. Whilst in principle the 'good character' requirement is non-discretionary, in practice it requires an assessment of sufficient breadth that a large element of judgment is required.

11.29 Important loci of discretion or broad judgement in relation to the grant of British citizenship include the following:

(i) Registration: in a number of circumstances, the registration of an individual as a British citizen is subject to broad discretionary power on the part of the Secretary of State. Under section 3(1) BNA 1981, if whilst a person is a minor an application is made for that person's registration as a British citizen, the Secretary of State 'may, if he [or she] thinks fit, cause him [or her] to be registered as such a citizen'. Analogously, under section 4A BNA 1981, the Secretary of State 'may if he [or she] thinks fit cause [a British overseas territories citizen] to be … registered [as a British citizen]', so long as the circumstances identified in section 4A BNA 1981 are not present. Under section 41A BNA 1981, an application for registration of an 'adult or young person', described as a person who has attained the age of 10 years at the time of the application being made, 'must not be granted unless the Secretary of State is satisfied that the adult or young person is of good character'.

(ii) Naturalisation: section 6(1) BNA 1981 provides that: 'If, on an application for naturalisation as a British citizen made by a person of full age and capacity, the Secretary of State is satisfied that the applicant fulfils the requirements of Schedule 1 BNA 1981 for naturalisation and thinks it fit to do so, he or she may grant a certificate of naturalisation as a British citizen.' Section 6(2) BNA 1981 applies the same formula to the particular situation in which an applicant is married to, or the civil partner of, a British citizen. Paragraph 1 of Schedule 1 to BNA 1981 then sets out requirements in relation to section 6(1) BNA 1981 which specify: (a) minimum periods of presence and status in the UK; (b) being of 'good character'; (c) having 'sufficient knowledge of the English, Welsh or Scottish Gaelic language'; (d) having sufficient knowledge of life in the UK; and (e) having an intention to make the UK his or her home or (if more than one home is maintained) his or her principal home (or to be abroad for purposes of Crown service or service under a relevant international organisation or company or association established in the UK). Paragraph 2 of Schedule 1, however, provides that: 'If in the special circumstances of any particular case the Secretary of State thinks fit, he may for the purposes of paragraph 1 do all or any of the following things.' It sets out permissions given to the Secretary of State to: (a) treat the applicant as fulfilling the requirement for a minimum period of time and status in the UK, where presence would otherwise be insufficient, or count towards admissible time in the UK periods which would otherwise be inadmissible; (b) disregard any restriction upon his or her presence so long as this is not in place on the date of application; (c) treat the applicant as having not been in breach of Immigration Rules in the previous five years when in fact the contrary was factually the case; and (d) waive the requirements for 'sufficient knowledge of the English, Welsh or Scottish Gaelic language' and/or 'sufficient knowledge of life in the United Kingdom' if it is concluded that by reason of the applicant's age or physical or mental condition, it would be unreasonable to insist upon satisfaction of these or either of them.

(iii) Resumption following renunciation: section 12 BNA 1981 provides the mechanism by which a British citizen 'of full age and capacity' may renounce British citizenship in a prescribed manner, upon which the Secretary of State 'shall cause the declaration to be registered' so long as the Secretary of State is satisfied that the person who made it will not be left without other citizenship or nationality. If that person does not acquire some such citizenship or nationality within six months from that date, he or she shall remain a British citizen and shall be deemed to have remained a British citizen continuously. The Secretary of State may withhold registration of an act of renunciation 'made during any war in which Her Majesty may be engaged in right of Her Majesty's government in the United Kingdom'. Section 13 BNA 1981 provides for resumption of citizenship after renunciation in certain circumstances. Under section 13(1) BNA 1981, a person is entitled to resume citizenship as of right, on one occasion only, where he or she is 'of full capacity' and the renunciation 'was necessary to enable him [or her] to retain or acquire some other citizenship or nationality'. Otherwise, under section 13(3) BNA 1981, if a person of full capacity who ceased to be a British citizen through renunciation applies to the Secretary of State for registration as a British citizen, the Secretary of State 'may, if he thinks fit, cause him to be registered as such a citizen'.

11.30 Given the extent of statutory discretion given to the Secretary of State (and/or, in the case of the good character requirement, the breadth of judgment or appraisal required), it is very understandable that a substantial body of guidance has developed in the NIs. To take one very important example, the policy of the Secretary of State regarding 'good character' is set out in her Nationality Instructions at 'Chapter 18, Annex D—The Good Character Requirement', most recently revised on 2 October 2013. This extends to 32 pages, but at section 1.3 ('Aspects of the requirement') summarises the matters which normally justify refusal:

> 1.3 Aspects of the Requirement
>
> The decision maker will not normally consider a person to be of good character if there is information to suggest:
>
> a. They have not respected and/or are not prepared to abide by the law. For example, they have been convicted of a crime or there are reasonable grounds to suspect (i.e. it is more likely than not) they have been involved in crime. For further information on the criminality element, see section 2—Criminal Convictions (General Approach), section 3—Non-Custodial Sentences and Other Out of Court Disposals and section 4—Other Criminal & Suspected Criminal Activity; or
> b. They have been involved in or associated with war crimes, crimes against humanity or genocide, terrorism or other actions that are considered not to be conducive to the public good. For further information on this particular element, see section 5—War Crimes, Terrorism and Other Non-conducive Activity; or
> c. Their financial affairs were not in appropriate order. For example, they have failed to pay taxes for which they were liable. For further information on the financial aspect, see section 6—Financial Soundness; or
> d. Their activities were notorious and cast serious doubt on their standing in the local community. For further information on notoriety, see section 7—Notoriety; or
> e. They had been deliberately dishonest or deceptive in their dealings with the UK Government. For further information on dishonesty and deception, see section 8—Deception & Dishonesty; or
> f. They have assisted in the evasion of immigration control; or
> g. They have previously been deprived of citizenship. For further information on these two points, see section 9—Immigration Related Issues.
>
> This is a non-exhaustive list.
>
> If the person does not clearly fall into one of the categories outlined above but there are doubts about their character, the decision maker may still refuse the application. They may also request an interview in order to make an overall assessment.

Whilst the list is stated to be 'non-exhaustive', a consistent level of gravity appears to be reflected in the items given and it would appear arguable that any extension should respect the *ejusdem generis* principles and should not reduce the minimal level of gravity reflected in the matters itemised in the NI.

The extent of the guidance in the NIs, and its liability to change, renders it impossible to provide any broad survey here. However, an understanding of the legal status of the NIs is important in the present context. As guidance, these may indicate the approach to be exercised in relation to discretion or judgment under BNA 1981, but at the same time may not fetter the scope of a power thereof or be used to justify failure to examine a particular application on its merits.   **11.31**

Like the deeming of deportation as conducive to the public good under section 3(5)(a) IA 1971 or the discretionary power to make a deportation order under section 5(1) IA 1971 (addressed in chapter 8), the various discretions in relation to the grant of nationality must be exercised in accordance with the established principles of public law, that is (in very brief summary), without illegality, irrationality or fairness.[5] As Sullivan J observed in *R (otao Forrester) v SSHD* [2008] EWHC 2307 (Admin) [7]: 'The defendant is given a discretion, and she is given a discretion on the basis that it will be exercised with a modicum of intelligence, common sense and humanity.'   **11.32**

Further, policy guidance such as is provided by the NIs must be legitimate given the statutory framework within which discretion is exercised: as Lord Dyson indicated in *R (Lumba) v SSHD* [2012] UKSC 12, [2012] 1 AC 245 at [35]: 'The individual has a basic public law right to have his or her case considered under whatever policy the executive thinks fit to adopt provided that the adopted policy is a lawful exercise of the discretion conferred by the statute.' The guidance must allow the consideration of each case on its merits and with a view to the possibility of exceptional circumstances not canvassed or expressly excluded by the written policy material. In *R (Lumba)* Lord Dyson at [21] noted that 'it is a well-established principle of public law that a policy should not be so rigid as to amount to a fetter on the discretion of decision-makers'. In *R v SSHD ex p Venables and Thompson* [1997] UKHL 25, [1998] AC 407, Lord Browne-Wilkinson, citing the leading text *De Smith, Woolf and Jowell: Judicial Review of Administrative Action*:   **11.33**

> When Parliament confers a discretionary power exercisable from time to time over a period, such power must be exercised on each occasion in the light of the circumstances at that time. In consequence, the person on whom the power is conferred cannot fetter the future exercise of his discretion by committing himself now as to the way in which he will exercise his power in the future. He cannot exercise the power *nunc pro tunc*. By the same token, the person on whom the power has been conferred cannot fetter the way he will use that power by ruling out of consideration on the future exercise of that power factors which may then be relevant to such exercise.
>
> These considerations do not preclude the person on whom the power is conferred from developing and applying a policy as to the approach which he will adopt in the generality of cases: see *Rex v Port of London Authority, Ex parte Kynoch Ltd* [1919] 1 K.B. 176; *British Oxygen Company Ltd v Board of Trade* [1971] AC 610. But the position is different if the policy adopted is such as

---

[5] This conventional three-fold summary is not exhaustive and its components are not mutually exclusive: see M Fordham, *Judicial Review Handbook* (6th edn, Oxford, Hart Publishing, 2012) 487. The public law wrongs justifying intervention are more fully examined in that work at Part C, P45–P63. See further chapter 16.

to preclude the person on whom the power is conferred from departing from the policy or from taking into account circumstances which are relevant to the particular case in relation to which the discretion is being exercised. If such an inflexible and invariable policy is adopted, both the policy and the decisions taken pursuant to it will be unlawful: see generally *de Smith, Woolf and Jowell: Judicial Review of Administrative Action*, 5th ed. (1995), para 11.004 et seq, pp 506 et seq.

11.34 Policy guidance, such as is provided by the NIs in the present context, cannot be employed as a means to escape normal public law constraints upon the exercise of discretion.[6] And, as already noted, a discretionary power must be exercised consistently with domestic law including incorporated international instruments and EU law, and the exercise of a discretion may be affected by relevant norms of international law even where that law is not incorporated into domestic law by statute: see paragraph 2.17 in chapter 2 above.

11.35 One important restraint is that whilst the Secretary of State, as already seen, in respect to certain immigration powers is protected by section 19D(1) RRA 1976 from the requirement not to discriminate on the basis of nationality or ethnic or national origin otherwise imposed by sections 1(1)(a) and 19B RRA 1976, read together, this immunity does not extend to the exercise of nationality law powers under BNA 1981. Section 44(1) BNA 1981 provides that any discretion vested in the decision maker under BNA 1981 'shall be exercised without regard to the race, colour, or religion of any person who may be affected by its exercise'. In *R (Ramalingum) v SSHD* [2009] EWHC 453 (Admin), this was tested, Burnett J concluding at [14]–[17] that on the facts, refusal to register the child as a British national under section 3(1) BNA 1981 on the basis that her parents were not British citizens was based on a proper consideration and did not show prohibited discrimination on the basis of national origin.

11.36 No appeal rights have been provided in relation to nationality decisions, and so such decisions may be challenged only by judicial review. The original section 44(2) BNA 1981, repealed with effect from 7 November 2002 by section 162(2)(b) NIAA 2002, provided that decision makers were not required to provide 'any reason for the grant or refusal of any application under this Act the decision on which is at … discretion' and that 'the decision of the Secretary of State or a Governor or Lieutenant-Governor on any such application shall not be subject to appeal to, or review in, any court'. In *R v SSHD ex p Fayed* [1996] EWCA Civ 946, [1998] 1 WLR 763, the Court of Appeal found that the denial of citizenship was a decision so serious that the achievement of natural justice required it to ignore section 44(2) BNA 1981 and to consider the exercise of its judicial review powers in relation to a refusal of naturalisation. Lord Woolf MR, with whom Phillips LJ concurred, observed at 773e–f that:

> It is obvious that the refusal of their application has damaging implications for the Fayeds. This is a matter which is for them, because of their high public profile, of particular significance. The damage is the greater because it is not in dispute that they comply with the formal requirements other than that of good character the relevance of which to the refusal is not known.

---

[6] See ibid, 50.4, 522–25; H Woolf, J Jowell and A Le Sueur, *De Smith's Judicial Review* (7th edn, London, Sweet & Maxwell, 2013) ch 9; W Wade and C Forsyth, *Administrative Law* (10th edn, Oxford, Oxford University Press, 2009) 270–76; P Craig, *Administrative Law* (7th edn, London, Sweet & Maxwell, 2012) chs 17–18.

Apart from the damaging effect on their reputation of having their application refused the refusal has deprived them of the benefits of citizenship. The benefits are substantial. Besides the intangible benefit of being a citizen of a country which is their and their families' home, there are the tangible benefits which include freedom from immigration control, citizenship of the European Union and the rights which accompany that citizenship, the right to vote and the right to stand in Parliamentary elections. The decisions of the Minister are therefore classically ones which but for section 44(2) would involve an obligation on the Minister making the decision to give the Fayeds an opportunity to be heard before that decision was reached.

The fact that the Secretary of State may refuse an application because he is not satisfied that the applicant fulfils the rather nebulous requirement of good character or 'if he thinks fit' underlines the need for an obligation of fairness. Except where non-compliance with a formal requirement other than that of good character, is being relied on, unless the applicant knows the areas of concern which could result in the application being refused in many cases, and especially this case, it will be impossible for him to make out his case. The result could be grossly unfair.

This decision was appealed to the House of Lords, but in 1997 a new Secretary of State indicated his view that the giving of reasons was appropriate, and withdrew the appeal to the House of Lords so that the decision of the Court of Appeal stood. In due course, the original section 44(2) BNA 1981 was repealed. Since then, it has been clear that decisions by the Secretary of State in relation to nationality are susceptible to judicial review.

In *MH and others v SSHD* [2008] EWHC 2525 (Admin), Blake J, in judicial review proceedings directed at decisions in which the Secretary of State maintained that public interest prevented reasons from being given for refusals of naturalisation based upon failure to show good character, invited the Attorney General to appoint special advocates to represent nine claimants in judicial review proceedings. On appeal, in *SSHD v AHK and others* [2009] EWCA Civ 287, the Court (Sir Anthony Clarke MR, Jacob and Maurice Kay LJJ) upheld the decision below, setting out a number of principles including the following, at [37]:   **11.37**

> We now first set out the principles which it appears to us should be adopted and then explain the reasons for some of them in the light of the submissions which were made to us.
>
> i) The general principles are that a person whose application for citizenship is refused is entitled to be told the reasons for the decision to refuse and that a claimant who challenges a refusal to grant British nationality on the grounds set out above is entitled to see all the material which the Secretary of State considered when reaching her decision and/or upon which she relies, whether favourable or unfavourable to the applicant.
>
> ii) There are some exceptions to those general principles. They apply or, depending upon the circumstances, may apply to a case in which the Secretary of State (a) refuses an application for British nationality on the ground that she is not satisfied that the applicant is of good character and (b) refuses to disclose to the applicant for judicial review some or all of the material upon which she relied ('the material') and/or refuses to give any, alternatively any further, reasons on public interest grounds, including in particular on the ground that to do so would put national security at risk.
>
> iii) In case (b), the Secretary of State should consider with counsel, who should consider the issue dispassionately, whether it is appropriate for the trial judge to have the assistance of a special advocate.

E2. Litigation Concerning Refusal to Grant British Citizenship

Discretionary Decisions Not Concerning 'Good Character'

11.38   A number of cases have arisen in relation to the exercise of discretion to grant citizenship by registration under BNA 1981:

(i) In *R v SSHD ex p Montana* [2001] 1 WLR 552, the appellant was a British citizen who challenged a decision not to register as a British citizen his young son J, who had been born out of wedlock and so did not have British citizenship by descent. J lived in Norway with his mother, following the end of her relationship with the appellant, and she opposed J's registration as a British citizen on the basis that she feared this would enable the appellant to remove J to the UK without her consent. Registration was refused on the basis of absence of close links by residence in the UK and future intentions to live in the UK, and by reason of the absence of agreement between the parents. This was challenged on the basis that the decision breached Article 8 ECHR and that legitimate expectation arose. The Court (Schiemann and Tuckey LJJ and Sir Swinton Thomas) concluded that in some circumstances Article 8 ECHR might be engaged by refusal of citizenship, but that this did not arise on the facts of the appeal, that the withholding of registration was not unlawful through the failure to put the parties into the position which would have prevailed had the appellant been married to J's mother, in which case J would have acquired British nationality by descent, and that the decision was neither perverse nor contrary to legitimate expectation.

(ii) In *R (Ramalingum) v SSHD* [2009] EWHC 453 (Admin), Burnett J found that refusal to register a child as a British national under section 3(1) BNA 1981, where a reason for refusal was that her parents were not yet able to apply for naturalisation, did not show prohibited discrimination on the basis of national origin, concluding at [15] that the treatment of the claimant was based upon legitimate interests in family cohesion and closeness of family ties to the UK, given that the child, if granted registration, would be the only British citizen in the family and that her parents had not been in a position to apply for naturalisation at the same time as that of the application entered for the child.

(iii) The decision of Singh J in *R (otao Vagh) v SSHD* [2012] EWHC 1841 (Admin) arose on a challenge to the Secretary of State's refusal to register as a British citizen, under section 4B BNA 1981, an adult of Indian national background who was a British Overseas Citizen under BNA 1981, and therefore was not accorded right of abode under IA 1971. The applicant had recently acquired and used an Indian passport, and had failed to prove notwithstanding this that she was not an Indian national, and so was entitled to registration as a British national under section 4B BNA 1981. Her secondary argument that the barrier to her achieving British citizenship was unlawful, as perpetuating a historical injustice, also failed. The decision was upheld by the Court of Appeal in *R (otao Vagh) v SSHD* [2013] EWCA Civ 1253.

(iv) In *Kasonga and another, Re Judicial Review* [2013] ScotCS CSOH 152, linked applications had been made for the naturalisation of the mother of two teenage children and for the registration of the children as British citizens. The mother's application was refused because of unspent convictions for driving without 'L-plates' whilst a learner driver and of driving without insurance. This decision was not challenged, but the refusal to register the children as British citizens was challenged by petition in the Outer House of the Court of Session. The applicable guidance provided that: 'It will rarely be right to register a child neither of whose parents is or is about to become a British citizen. However, each case should be considered on its merits, and there may be exceptional circumstances to justify registration in a particular case, such as for example ... older teenagers who have spent most of their life here.' Lord Glennie rejected the application, considering that, in the case of an older teenager who had spent just over half his life in the UK, 'most' was not to be interpreted as 'more than half', and that his 14-year-old sister, who had spent a greater proportion of her life in the UK, was not an 'older teenager'.

'Good Character' Decisions

A striking feature of the litigation relating to refusal to grant British citizenship is the degree to which it has focused upon the 'good character' requirement. This is a requirement of Schedule 1 BNA 1981 as regards adults and section 41A BNA 1981 as regards children aged 10–17 inclusive, and there is no statutory power to waive it. Under section 6(1), the Secretary of State must be 'satisfied that the applicant fulfils' relevant requirements and then 'may, if he thinks fit', grant naturalisation, a formulation which has been read as placing the onus on an applicant to satisfy the Secretary of State on this score, as Pitchford LJ, with whom Moore-Bick LJJ agreed, observed in *R (otao DA (Iran)) v SSHD* [2014] EWCA Civ 654 [9]: 'The onus was upon the appellant to establish his good character for the purpose of section 6(1) of and schedule 1 to the 1981 Act.'

11.39

The phrase 'good character' provides a starting point, so that what is involved on the part of the Secretary of State involves a judgment rather than a discretion, but the breadth of the statutory language at this point means that the process of consideration and judgment may be a very open-textured one, with public law characteristics quite similar to those which would apply to a straightforward statutory discretion. In *R v SSHD ex p Fayed* [1996] EWCA Civ 946, [1998] 1 WLR 763, Lord Woolf MR at 773f–g observed of the test that 'the rather nebulous requirement of good character or "if he thinks fit" underlines the need for an obligation of fairness'. In subsequent proceedings pursued by the same claimant, in *R v SSHD ex p Al Fayed (No 2)* [2000] EWCA Civ 523, [2001] Imm AR 134, Nourse LJ (with whom Kennedy and Rix LJJ agreed) referred to the earlier observation by Lord Woolf:

11.40

> Lord Woolf MR referred in passing to the requirement of good character as being a rather nebulous one. By that he meant that good character is a concept that cannot be defined as a single standard to which all rational beings would subscribe. He did not mean that it was incapable of definition by a reasonable decision-maker in relation to the circumstances of a particular case. Nor is it an objection that a decision may be based on a higher standard of good character than other reasonable decision-makers might have adopted. Certainly, it is no part of the function of the courts to discourage ministers of the Crown from adopting a high standard in matters which have been assigned to their judgment by Parliament, provided only that it is one which can reasonably be adopted in the circumstances.

Part D – Denial and Deprivation of Citizenship

11.41 The detailed guidance of the Secretary of State, in force since 9 December 2013, is at Annex D to Chapter 18 NIs, which, as already noted, lists as areas of focus matters related to criminal conviction or proven or suspected criminal conduct, war crimes, terrorism and 'other non-conducive activity', financial soundness, 'notoriety', 'deception and dishonesty' and matters relating to an individual's immigration or nationality history, with limited scope identified for exceptional grants.[7]

11.42 It is clear that the Secretary of State is permitted substantial flexibility in appraisal of cases, but that as a matter of public law he or she must act fairly and not adopt a strained or unnatural standard. As cases differ factually, it cannot be said that there is a fixed line. However, some basic principles may be deduced from the decided cases and publicly accessible material:

(i) In *R v SSHD ex p Fayed (No 2)* [2000] EWCA Civ 523, [2001] Imm AR 134, the Court of Appeal in earlier litigation having found that fairness required the giving of reasons for refusals of naturalisation, a different panel of the Court found that refusal by the Secretary of State based upon the applicant's interference with a safe deposit box belonging to a personal and commercial rival held in a bank under the applicant's control, and admission to the making of secret payments to Members of Parliament, was not impeachable on the basis of accusations of bias.

(ii) In January 2001, the former Treasury Solicitor, Sir Anthony Hammond KCB QC, was asked to carry out an official *Review of the Circumstances Surrounding an Application for Naturalisation by Mr S P Hinduja in 1998*.[8] Mr SP Hinduja and his brother Mr GP Hinduja had applied for, and been granted, naturalisation as British citizens. It was alleged that there had been political interference on the Hinduja's behalf. In the course of his enquiries, Sir Anthony examined the handling of applications made by SP and GP Hinduja. He saw intelligence material and recorded that during the relevant period:

> [T]he Secret Intelligence Service ... has accumulated a certain amount of intelligence about the Hindujas' business activities abroad. It would not be appropriate for me to describe in detail the nature of this material. Suffice it to say that it raised the possibility that they had been involved in a number of dubious practices, in some cases potentially amounting to illegal activities, but that [the evidence was not] conclusive.

Of the application by Mr GP Hinduja, Sir Anthony concluded that:

> The only issue which I think calls for comment is whether it was right to conclude that the 'good character' requirement was satisfied, in view of the Bofors[9] scandal and of the somewhat unenthusiastic terms of the [responsible Foreign and Commonwealth Office officer] ... Whether the application should have been refused on the basis that the scandal cast doubt on whether Mr Hinduja satisfied the 'good character' requirement is a matter

---

[7] Nationality Instructions: Chapter 18, Annex D—The Good Character Requirement v4.0 (02 October 2013).
[8] HC 287, ordered to be printed 9th March 2001.
[9] The Bofors scandal related to alleged bribery in relation to an arms contract between Swedish armaments manufacturing firm Bofors and the Indian Defence Ministry. Charges against the Hinduja brothers relating to the Bofors allegations were later (in 2005) quashed by the Delhi High Court for lack of evidence: 'Hinduja brothers cleared of arms scandal charges after 14 years', Randeep Ramesh, The Guardian, 1 June 2005, www.theguardian.com/world/2005/jun/01/armstrade.india.

of judgment ... It seems to me that, in all the circumstances, it was a reasonable judgment by officials that the application should not be refused on that ground.[10]

In relation to the application by Mr SP Hinduja, Sir Anthony concluded that:

> [T]he information available in the Secret Intelligence Service was undoubtedly relevant to the issue of whether the [good character test] was satisfied ... my own view is that, because of its speculative and inconclusive nature, the conclusion would probably have been that its existence did not of itself justify a refusal to grant naturalisation.

(iii) In *R (otao Messaoudi) v SSHD* [2003] EWHC 1834 (Admin), Newman J adjourned a substantive application for judicial review directed at the speed and/or manner of processing of the application for naturalisation, on which no decision had been reached: 'There has been a Metropolitan Police interview, but there are still investigations which the Secretary of State is entitled to make under section 6 and Schedule 1 of the Act. Until such times as he has considered them he is not in a position to make a fully considered decision. As it stands ... if there was to be a decision now, bearing in mind the Secretary of State cannot be satisfied of the matters under Schedule 1 [BNA 1981] about which he needs to be satisfied, if forced to make a decision, it would be an adverse one. Nothing is to be gained from that. Thus the only question is: what can be gained by way of understanding or indication as to when it will be considered and decided upon because there are personal circumstances surrounding the application which do give rise to a sense of urgency on the part of the claimant?' The Court declined to intervene in the absence of evidence of abuse of power;

(iv) The judgment of Langstaff J in *R (Al-Tamimi) v SSHD* [2007] EWHC 1962 (Admin) was given in dismissing a renewed oral application, by the applicant without representation, for permission to apply for judicial review of a decision to refuse naturalisation. The applicant was Iraqi. Naturalisation was refused by the Secretary of State in 2006 on the basis that he was not satisfied that the good character requirement was met, adding without further expansion: 'This is because of your past relationship with the Directorate of General Intelligence (the DGI).' In the acknowledgment of service, this was expanded with the statement that the Secretary of State had been told by government agencies that the applicant had been an agent of the DGI since 1999 or earlier, might well still be and had declined when requested to end that relationship. The applicant disputed the statement advanced regarding his alleged relationship with the DGI, but was refused permission on the basis that post-decision rebuttal evidence would not show that the Secretary of State had erred in law by the refusal to naturalise the applicant.

(v) In *R (Thamby) v SSHD* [2011] EWHC 1763 (Admin), the claimant had been a supporter of the Liberation Tigers of Tamil Eelam (LTTE). Sales J at [47] recorded Counsel for the Secretary of State as denying that in policy or practice, 'membership of or support for the LTTE for any period of time will always mean that a claimant for naturalisation will be regarded as not being of "good character" for the purposes of the 1981 Act. The question in each case will be

---

[10] Para 4.9.

whether there has been a sufficient level of support given to the LTTE, with awareness that it used war crimes and crimes against humanity as a material part of its mode of operation, as to raise serious doubts about the commitment of the claimant to respect the values of British society'. The Court accepted (at [50]) that on the facts on the case, 'the period and nature of the support provided by [the claimant to] the LTTE was such as to give rise to serious doubt about his good character (in particular, about his respect for the values of British society) for the purposes of [BNA 1981]' but found at [73] that the claimant had not attempted to mislead and had not been given a fair opportunity to address the concerns of the Secretary of State.

(vi) In *SSHD v SK (Sri Lanka)* [2012] EWCA Civ 16, the Court of Appeal overturned a decision below in favour of the applicant, who had been an armed combatant for the LTTE involved in incidents in which prisoners of war had been killed, concluding that the failure to argue exclusion from refugee status on the basis of Article 1F CSR in earlier asylum proceedings did not prevent the Secretary of State from relying upon the applicant's past LTTE involvement as a basis for concluding that he was not of good character for the purposes of naturalisation: per Stanley Burnton LJ (with whom Hallett and Richards LJJ concurred), on the facts of the case, the Secretary of State 'was entitled to conclude that the respondent, if not involved in war crimes, in the sense of personally carrying out such murders, was associated with such crimes', particularly given that the applicant was also an active member of the LTTE, an organisation which carried out acts of terrorism; in addition, the applicant had answered falsely by denying in the application form that the LTTE was an organisation that had been concerned in terrorism (at [39]–[40]).

(vii) In *AHK and others v SSHD* [2012] EWHC 1117 (Admin) and in a later decision in relation to the same parties, *AHK and others v SSHD* [2013] EWHC 1426 (Admin), Ouseley J considered the mechanism of dealing with cases in which the reasons for refusal of naturalisation were said to be absence of good character, but undisclosable for national security reasons, holding that refusals could stand where they were based on incompletely disclosed reasons which were protected under Public Interest Immunity certificates;

(viii) In *PRC, Re Judicial Review* [2013] ScotCS CSOH 128, Lord Bannatyne refused a petition for judicial review, rejecting the argument that refusal of naturalisation on the basis of failure to disclose a conviction in an earlier, but relatively recent, application should have been offset by a duty on the part of the Secretary of State to afford the petitioner a chance to explain or correct the omission.

(ix) In *R (otao Amirifard) v SSHD* [2013] EWHC 279 (Admin), the claimant was an Iranian recognised as a refugee in the UK who had as a national service conscript been posted to the Iranian prison service, where serious abuses known to him were consistently taking place. Lang J found that the Secretary of State was entitled to rely upon association or involvement in crimes against humanity which fell short of personal responsibility, notwithstanding mitigating circumstances. The decision was upheld on appeal in *R (otao DA (Iran) v SSHD* [2014] EWCA Civ 654.

(x) In *R (Hiri) v SSHD* [2014] EWHC 254 (Admin), the claimant was a former British Army soldier of good report refused naturalisation because of an unspent conviction for speeding. Lang J quashed the refusal on the basis that the examination had failed to look at all aspects of the claimant's character and to consider the particular nature of unspent convictions. She concluded that 'criminal convictions are relevant to the assessment of character, but they are likely to vary greatly in significance, depending upon the nature of the offence and the length of time which has elapsed since its commission, as well as any pattern of repeat offending' (at [35]) and (at [36]) that the Secretary of State is 'entitled to adopt a policy on the way in which criminal convictions will normally be considered by her caseworkers, but it should not be applied mechanistically and inflexibly. There has to be a comprehensive assessment of each claimant's character, as an individual, which involves an exercise of judgment, not just ticking boxes on a form'.

What the cases appear to show is that: 11.43

(i) 'good character' may be displaced without, for example, the fixed requirement that there be a criminal conviction, but an adequate factual basis is in any case required (*Fayed (No 2)*, the Hinduja enquiry, *Thamby, SK (Sri Lanka), PRC, DA (Iran), Hiri*);
(ii) in appropriate circumstances, special steps may be taken to reflect the invocation of investigation or security-sensitive material (*Messaudi, AHK*);
(iii) notwithstanding the breadth of the power given to the Secretary of State, it must be exercised fairly (*Thamby, Hiri*);
(iv) the Secretary of State may rely upon his or her policy, but must not do so mechanistically or inflexibly (*Hiri*).

12

Deprivation of British Citizenship or Right of Abode

Contents

A. Introduction 12.1

B. International Law 12.3
    B1. General International Law 12.3
    B2. International Human Rights Law 12.8
    B3. Hybrid Instruments 12.12
    B4. Council of Europe Instruments 12.15

C. EU Law 12.17

D. Domestic Law 12.18
    D1. Prerogative 12.18
    D2. Statute 12.19
    D3. Statutory Instrument 12.23
    D4. Published Guidance 12.24

E. Discussion 12.25
    E1. Voidability of the Original Grant of Citizenship Status 12.25
    E2. The Deprivation Power 12.35
    E3. Deprivation by Reason of Fraud, False Representation or Concealment of a Material Fact 12.38
    E3. Deprivation as Conducive to the Public Good 12.49
        The New IA 2014 Provision 12.61
    E4. Appeals 12.67

A. Introduction

Decisions regarding the deprivation of British citizenship status or right of abode are taken by the Secretary of State, utilising statutory powers. This chapter addresses both deprivation of British citizenship, a consequence of which will in most cases be loss of the statutory right of abode provided to British citizens by section 2(1) IA 1971 and deprivation of the right of abode where this is given by statute. In the former case, the loss of British citizenship under domestic law will mean the loss of British nationality for the purposes of international law. **12.1**

The power to remove British citizenship is provided at section 40 BNA 1981. In the case of deprivation of the right of abode bestowed by section 2(1)(b) IA 1971 upon someone who is not a British citizen, the power of deprivation is found in section 2A IA 1971. There is no power to strip the right of abode from someone who continues to be a British citizen. Each power is applicable only in particular circumstances, defined by statute. **12.2**

B. International Law

B1. General International Law

12.3   General international law as it applies to the subject matter of this book is examined in chapter 2. An outline of its application to the denial of British citizenship is found in chapter 11 (paragraphs 11.3–4). As is further explained in chapter 2, as an essentially dualist system, the application of international law in the English legal order is governed by the principles of non-justiciability and the absence of direct effect.[1]

12.4   The determination of nationality is generally a matter for nation states. CCQRCNL provides at Article 1 thereof that: 'It is for each State to determine under its own law who are its nationals. This ... shall be recognised by other States in so far as it is consistent with international conventions, international custom, and the principles of law generally recognised with regard to nationality.' In specific contexts, different principles apply: for instance, in the international law of statelessness, a stateless person is defined for purposes of CSSP by the domestic position alone, without considering questions of international recognition, because as set out at paragraphs 2.31 and 4.88 the key question for the purposes of that regime is not whether or not to recognise a nationality attributed by domestic law of a state, but what the authorities of that state hold as to an individual's nationality.

12.5   There is no evidence for the existence of a current general norm of international law prohibiting deprivation of nationality, even where this imposes statelessness upon the subject. However, the Human Rights Council of the UN has recently stated that international law, whilst not prohibiting deprivation, does impose certain norms upon it, in particular requiring avoidance of arbitrary conduct by states:

> Therefore, loss or deprivation of nationality must meet certain conditions in order to comply with international law, in particular the prohibition of arbitrary deprivation of nationality. These conditions include serving a legitimate purpose, being the least intrusive instrument to achieve the desired result and being proportional to the interest to be protected.[2]

On this approach, arbitrary deprivation of nationality would constitute a breach of international law. The concept of arbitrariness has been examined in chapter 3 above in the context of international human rights law. The Human Rights Council refers in this context to a recent report of the UN Working Group on Arbitrary Detention:[3]

> 61. The notion of 'arbitrary' *stricto sensu* includes both the requirement that a particular form of deprivation of liberty is taken in accordance with the applicable law and procedure and that it is proportional to the aim sought, reasonable and necessary. The drafting history of article 9 of the International Covenant on Civil and Political Rights 'confirms that "arbitrariness" is not to be equated with "against the law", but must be interpreted more broadly to include elements of inappropriateness, injustice, lack of predictability and due process of law'.

---

[1] *JH Rayner (Mincing Lane) v Department of Trade and Industry* [1990] 2 AC 418 HL.
[2] UN Human Rights Council, *Human Rights and Arbitrary Deprivation of Nationality: Report of the Secretary-General*, 19 December 2013, A/HRC/25/28.
[3] United Nations Human Rights Council, *Report of the Working Group on Arbitrary Detention*, 24 December 2012, A/HRC/22/24 [61].

Deprivation of nationality will result in statelessness where an individual deprived of British nationality (as by deprivation of British citizenship) has no other nationality. Where an individual is not made stateless, this does not render legitimate a process which was arbitrary in any of the respects canvassed above. But where statelessness does follow from a deprivation of nationality, the consequences for the individual and for the state may be less serious by reason of the existence of another state of nationality obliged to admit its national to its territory. In addition, a substantial number of states, including the UK, are bound by the CRS, the relevance of which is examined below. 12.6

Although there is no customary law norm prohibiting deprivation of nationality, even where statelessness may result (though norms established by the CRS binding upon States Parties thereto may do this, or greatly limit the scope for deprivation), customary law norms restrict the conduct of states as regards their nationals abroad. The admission of a British citizen to the territory of another state on the basis of British nationality, where he or she is not a national of that state and so does not have a general right of entrance and residence to it, creates a relationship between the two states within which the UK has a duty not to impinge upon the sovereignty of the other state by frustrating its ability to expel an alien who entered its territory as a British citizen. 12.7

B2. International Human Rights Law

A wider survey of the main international human rights law provisions relevant to immigration and nationality law can be found in chapter 3. Article 15 UDHR, whilst not having binding effect upon states, asserted the human right to possess a nationality and not to be arbitrarily deprived of nationality or denied the right to change nationality. This provision, and the equivalent provisions in later instruments, is to be understood as a statement of principle which does not impose a duty on another particular state to afford nationality to a specific individual or group. Other standards relevant to deprivation of nationality and contained within instruments ratified by the UK are summarised below. 12.8

First, the ICCPR does not directly protect the possession of nationality itself, but a primary value of nationality is the right to enter and reside, and it provides important standards in this context: 12.9

(i) most particularly, under Article 12(4), the ICCPR provides a protection against arbitrary deprivation of the right to enter (or remain in) his or her own country;

(ii) as regards children, Article 24(3) ICCPR provides that 'every child has the right to acquire a nationality', imposing duties upon states, though the UN Human Rights Committee in the General Comment cited at chapter 3 has indicated that this 'does not necessarily make it an obligation to give their nationality to every child born in their territory'. The deprivation of nationality applied to a child and rendering that child stateless might cause this provision, individually or with others, to be engaged;

(iii) action by the state in the context of nationality might in some circumstances be said to breach Article 17 ICCPR, read in conjunction with Article 23(1) ICCPR, if it amounts to 'arbitrary or unlawful' interference with the protected interests of 'privacy, family, home', and the law does not provide protection against this. As noted earlier in the context of denial of nationality, in *R v SSHD ex p Montana* [2001] 1 WLR 552 [18]–[20], the Court of Appeal found that Article 8 ECHR, the ECHR provision closely analogous to Articles 17 and 23(1) ICCPR, was not in the circumstances of the case engaged by the withholding of citizenship, though the decision on its face would not prevent relevant provisions being raised on different, more conducive facts. In *Genovese v Malta* no 53124/09, [2011] ECHR 1590, (2014) 58 EHRR 25, the ECtHR at [30] referred to earlier decisions and observed of Article 8 ECHR that: 'The provisions of Article 8 do not, however, guarantee a right to acquire a particular nationality or citizenship. Nevertheless, the Court has previously stated that it cannot be ruled out that an arbitrary denial of citizenship might in certain circumstances raise an issue under Article 8 of the Convention because of the impact of such a denial on the private life of the individual.' The potential application of Article 8 ECHR was supported by Blake J in *MH and others v SSHD* [2008] EWHC 2525 (Admin) [54]–[62] and by Ouseley J in *AHK and others v SSHD* [2013] EWHC 1426 (Admin), refusing judicial review of refusals of naturalisation in which no or minimal grounds for concluding that applicants were not of 'good character' had been shown beyond that assertion, and public interest immunity certificates were upheld. Referring to *Genovese*, Ouseley J noted at [45] that: 'A submission that the mere nature or degree of effect of a refusal of naturalisation, without some further quality of arbitrariness or discrimination, suffices to engage Article 8 seems to me ill-founded on this ECtHR jurisprudence.'

12.10 Separate non-discrimination norms within the ICCPR may apply in relation to substantive rights under that instrument:

(i) Article 2(1) ICCPR is breached where the state fails to 'respect and ensure' the rights protected by the ICCPR 'without distinction of any kind', such as 'race, colour, sex, language, religion, political or other opinion, national or social origin, property, birth or other status', or where the state fails to ensure an effective remedy for the breach.

(ii) Article 3 ICCPR reflects the undertaking of States Parties to ensure the equal right of men and women to civil and political rights provided under the ICCPR.

12.11 Beyond the ICCPR, a range of other, broader, international human rights norms may be applicable to deprivation of nationality. *Inter alia*:

(i) Action concerning the right to nationality which is discriminatory on the basis of race would breach Article 5(d)(iii) CERD and could, depending upon the facts, also breach Article 5(d)(i)–(ii) CERD 66 if rights to freedom of movement and residence, or to leave or return to 'one's [own] country' are encroached upon.

(ii) A 'distinction, exclusion or restriction made on the basis of sex which has the effect or purpose of impairing or nullifying the recognition, enjoyment or exercise by women, irrespective of their marital status, on a basis of equality of men and women, of human rights and fundamental freedoms in the political, economic, social, cultural, civil or any other field' would breach Article 1 CEDAW.

(iii) In an 'action concerning children', Article 3(1) CRC requires that 'the best interests of the child shall be a primary consideration'. This and Article 9 CRC (regarding family unity) may be relevant where a child is the subject of, or is affected by, deprivation of nationality.

(iv) Persons to whom the CRPD applies are under Article 18 CRPD entitled to 'a nationality, on an equal basis with others' by the specific means described therein, including 'the right to acquire and change a nationality' (Article 18(a) CRPD) and protection from deprivation of entry to 'their own' country on any basis 'arbitrarily or on the basis of disability'.

B3. Hybrid Instruments

12.12 Chapter 4 contains a wider survey of 'hybrid'[4] international law provisions. In general, the CSR and the CSSP do not cover deprivation of nationality, though an arbitrary deprivation of nationality by one state may entitle an individual to refugee status in another, where Article 1A(2) CSR is otherwise satisfied and entitlement under the CSR has not ceased or been excluded. Although the CSSP does not bear directly on relevant questions, the definition of statelessness generally used in the context of protection against deprivation of citizenship (under Article 1(1) CSSP, 'the term "stateless person" means a person who is not considered as a national by any State under the operation of its law'.) This differs from the definition in the CCQRCNL of the approach to be adopted to questions of international law recognition of domestic decisions (see para 12.4 above).

12.13 The CRS provides a number of relevant protections. In the paper already referred to (paragraph 12.5 above), the UN Human Rights Council, having noted that international law required that 'loss or deprivation of nationality must meet certain conditions in order to comply with international law', went on to observe that 'Where loss or deprivation of nationality leads to statelessness, the impact on the individual is particularly severe' and that:

> International law therefore strictly limits the circumstances in which loss or deprivation of nationality leading to statelessness can be recognized as serving a legitimate purpose. The 1961 Convention on the Reduction of Statelessness (1961 Convention) and the 1997 European Convention on Nationality both accept that statelessness may, exceptionally, result from the loss or deprivation of nationality in response to its fraudulent acquisition. The 1961 Convention establishes a set of basic rules which prohibit loss or deprivation of nationality where the result is to leave an individual stateless. The 1961 Convention contains a limitative set of exceptions to these rules, recognizing a narrow set of circumstances in which loss or deprivation of nationality leading to statelessness may serve a legitimate purpose. Even in such cases, however, the loss or deprivation of nationality must satisfy the principle of proportionality. The consequences of any withdrawal of nationality must be carefully weighed against the gravity of the behaviour or offence for which the withdrawal of nationality is prescribed. Given

---

[4] Reference to these instruments as 'hybrid' denotes their combination of human rights with other purposes.

the severity of the consequences where statelessness results, it may be difficult to justify loss or deprivation resulting in statelessness in terms of proportionality.[5]

12.14 The CRS provides that:

Article 8

1. A Contracting State shall not deprive a person of his nationality if such deprivation would render him stateless.
2. Notwithstanding the provisions of paragraph 1 of this article, a person may be deprived of the nationality of a Contracting State:
   ...
   (b) where the nationality has been obtained by misrepresentation or fraud.
3. Notwithstanding the provisions of paragraph 1 of this article, a Contracting State may retain the right to deprive a person of his nationality, if at the time of signature, ratification or accession it specifies its retention of such right on one or more of the following grounds, being grounds existing in its national law at that time:
   (a) that, inconsistently with his duty of loyalty to the Contracting State, the person
      (i) has, in disregard of an express prohibition by the Contracting State rendered or continued to render services to, or received or continued to receive emoluments from, another State, or
      (ii) has conducted himself in a manner seriously prejudicial to the vital interests of the State;
   (b) that the person has taken an oath, or made a formal declaration, of allegiance to another State, or given definite evidence of his determination to repudiate his allegiance to the Contracting State.
4. A Contracting State shall not exercise a power of deprivation permitted by paragraphs 2 or 3 of this article except in accordance with law, which shall provide for the person concerned the right to a fair hearing by a court or other independent body.

Article 9

A Contracting State may not deprive any person or group of persons of their nationality on racial, ethnic, religious or political grounds.

B4. Council of Europe Instruments

12.15 As with denial of citizenship (see paragraphs 11.12 et seq), Article 8 ECHR, explored in more detail in chapter 5, is the most significant Council of Europe instrument relevant to deprivation of citizenship or right of abode. Article 8 ECHR protects the right to respect for private and family life, it does not directly cite a right to nationality, but the effect of uncertainty or insecurity created or contributed to by nationality-related action has in some circumstances been found to engage Article 8 ECHR (see paragraphs 5.184–187). In *R v SSHD ex p Montana* [2001] 1 WLR 552 [18]–[20], the Court of Appeal found on the facts that Article 8 ECHR was not in the circumstances

---

[5] United Nations Human Rights Council, *Report of the Working Group on Arbitrary Detention*, 24 December 2012, A/HRC/22/24.

of the case engaged, alone or in conjunction with Article 14 ECHR by the withholding of citizenship, but did not reject the possibility of engagement in an appropriate case. In *Genovese v Malta* no 53124/09, [2011] ECHR 1590, (2014) 58 EHRR 25, the European Court of Human Rights confirmed that 'it cannot be ruled out that an arbitrary denial of citizenship might in certain circumstances raise an issue under Article 8 of the Convention because of the impact of such a denial on the private life of the individual'. In *AHK and others v SSHD* [2013] EWHC 1426 (Admin), Ouseley J referred to *Genovese* and earlier decisions, apparently accepting that 'some further quality of arbitrariness or discrimination' in a nationality decision might engage Article 8 ECHR.

The ECN has been signed but not ratified by the UK. By Article 18 VCLT, a state which has signed a treaty but not yet ratified it is obliged to 'refrain, in good faith, from acts that would defeat the object and purpose of the treaty', at least where the signatory has not disavowed the intention to ratify the treaty in due course. This obligation is, however, of extremely limited effect. Were the UK to ratify ECN, then its conduct could be engaged in significant respects: 12.16

(i) first, it would be bound as to the content of its internal law under Article 4 ECN, by which 'The rules on nationality of each State Party shall be based on the following principles', these being the right of every person to a nationality, the avoidance of statelessness and the prohibition on arbitrary deprivation of nationality;

(ii) second, by Article 7(1) ECN, the UK would be limited in the circumstances in which its internal law could provide for deprivation of nationality to voluntary acquisition of another nationality; acquisition of the nationality of the State Party by means of fraudulent conduct, false information or concealment of any relevant fact attributable to the applicant; voluntary service in a foreign military force; conduct seriously prejudicial to the vital interests of the State Party; lack of a genuine link between the State Party and a national habitually residing abroad; where it is established during the minority of a child that the preconditions laid down by internal law which led to the *ex lege* acquisition of the nationality of the State Party are no longer fulfilled; and adoption of a child if the child acquires or possesses the foreign nationality of one or both of the adopting parents.

C. EU Law

In Case C-135/08 *Rottmann (European Citizenship)* [2010] OJ C113/4, [2010] QB 761, the Court of Justice of the European Union recognized that the determination of nationality was a matter for the Member States but that they must have 'due regard' to EU law when exercising their powers in the sphere of nationality such that EU law procedural standards come to bear (at [39] and [45]). This has been rejected in the domestic context in *G1 (Sudan) v SSHD* [2012] EWCA Civ 867, [2013] QB 1008. Chapter 6 further addresses this, and the effect of EU law in the context of deprivation of nationality is considered in section E below. 12.17

D. Domestic Law

D1. Prerogative

12.18   The distinction between the nationality and immigration laws of the UK in relation to the application of prerogative powers is explored at paragraph 11.15. In summary, the power in section 3(2) IA 1971 for the Secretary of State to make Immigration Rules does not treat nationality as being within the span of material set down in the Rules, providing only that 'account may be taken of citizenship or nationality'. The Supreme Court has held in *R (Munir) v SSHD* [2012] UKSC 32, [2012] 1 WLR 2192 and *R (Alvi) v SSHD* [2012] UKSC 33, [2012] 1 WLR 22 that the exercise of power by the SSHD by reference to the prerogative has been abrogated or suspended in the field of immigration control since the coming into force of IA 1971. BNA 1981, the cornerstone of UK nationality law, does not on its face set down any requirement parallel to that applied in the immigration context by section 3(2) IA 1971.

D2. Statute

12.19   As currently in force, section 40(1) BNA 1981 defines 'citizenship status' as including status as a British citizen, and a number of other forms of status, some of which, including British citizenship, fall within the definition of British nationality. It further provides that:

> 40(2)   The Secretary of State may by order deprive a person of a citizenship status if the Secretary of State is satisfied that deprivation is conducive to the public good.
> (3)   The Secretary of State may by order deprive a person of a citizenship status which results from his registration or naturalisation if the Secretary of State is satisfied that the registration or naturalisation was obtained by means of—
>   (a)   fraud,
>   (b)   false representation, or
>   (c)   concealment of a material fact.
> (4)   The Secretary of State may not make an order under subsection (2) if he is satisfied that the order would make a person stateless.

Section 40(5) BNA 2001 provides that prior to any order for deprivation of nationality being made, a written notice must be given to that person stating that the Secretary of State has decided to make an order, the reasons for that decision and the route of appeal open to the subject of the order. Under section 40(6) BNA 2001, where a person acquired a citizenship status by the operation of a law which applied to him or her because of his or her registration or naturalisation under an enactment having effect before commencement, the Secretary of State may by order deprive the person of the citizenship status if the Secretary of State is satisfied that the registration or naturalisation was obtained by means of fraud, false representation or concealment of a material fact.

12.20   Section 2(1)(b) IA 1971, as amended, bestowed the right of abode upon Commonwealth citizens who already possessed such right immediately prior to the coming into force of BNA 1981. Section 2A IA 1971, inserted by section 57(1) Immigration, Asylum and Nationality Act 2006, provides that in such cases the right of abode may be removed, on conditions parallel to that in section 40(2) BNA 1981:

2A(1) The Secretary of State may by order remove from a specified person a right of abode in the United Kingdom which he has under section 2(1)(b).
(2) The Secretary of State may make an order under subsection (1) in respect of a person only if the Secretary of State thinks that it would be conducive to the public good for the person to be excluded or removed from the United Kingdom.
(3) An order under subsection (1) may be revoked by order of the Secretary of State.
(4) While an order under subsection (1) has effect in relation to a person—
   (a) section 2(2) shall not apply to him, and
   (b) any certificate of entitlement granted to him shall have no effect.

There is no power to exile someone who remains a British citizen by denying the right of abode.

Section 66(1) IA 2014 has now added a new subsection 40(4A) BNA 1981 after section 40(4) BNA 1981. The new provision provides that: **12.21**

[40](4A) But that does not prevent the Secretary of State from making an order under subsection (2) to deprive a person of a citizenship status if—
   (a) the citizenship status results from the person's naturalisation,
   (b) the Secretary of State is satisfied that the deprivation is conducive to the public good because the person, while having that citizenship status, has conducted him or herself in a manner which is seriously prejudicial to the vital interests of the United Kingdom, any of the Islands, or any British overseas territory, and
   (c) the Secretary of State has reasonable grounds for believing that the person is able, under the law of a country or territory outside the United Kingdom, to become a national of such a country or territory.

Section 66(2) IA 2014 additionally provides that:

In deciding whether to make an order under [section 40(2) BNA 1981] in a case which falls within subsection (4A) of that Act, the Secretary of State may take account of the manner in which a person conducted him or herself before this section came into force.

Additionally, under section 66(3) IA 2014 a new section 40B BNA 1981 has been added to BNA 1981. This requires the Secretary of State to arrange for a regular review of the operation of the power of deprivation introduced by section 66 IA 2014. The reports of those reviews must by new section 40B(5) be laid before each House of Parliament, though by section 40B(6) 'the Secretary of State may, after consultation with the person who produced the report, exclude a part of the report from the copy laid before Parliament if the Secretary of State is of the opinion that it would be contrary to the public interest or prejudicial to national security for that part of the report to be made public.' The new subsection 40(4A) and section 40B BNA 1981 entered into force on 28 July 2014: Immigration Act 2014 (Commencement No 1, Transitory and Saving Provisions) Order 2014 (SI 2014/1820), at [3(t)].

As set out below, a question arises as to whether a grant of citizenship obtained by deception is void or voidable, so that, because an individual has either never truly had British citizenship or the Secretary of State has some power to void it without reference to BNA 1981, no deprivation proceeding is necessary. **12.22**

D3. Statutory Instrument

12.23 As noted in chapter 11, the contribution of statutory instruments to the operation of British nationality law is small. They play no significant role in relation to deprivation of citizenship itself, though they are significant in the context of associated matters, such as appeals procedure rules.

D4. Published Guidance

12.24 Extensive non-statutory guidance in relation to nationality law and practice is provided by the NIs.[6] Within this, deprivation of nationality and nullity/voidability are addressed in Chapter 55, last updated on 17 March 2014, and deprivation of the right of abode in Chapter 57 of volume 1 of the NIs, last updated on 29 November 2013.

E. Discussion

E1. Voidability of the Original Grant of Citizenship Status

12.25 Prior to examining the law relating to the deprivation of British citizenship, it is worth dealing with a question which may arise in some cases as to whether deprivation by the Secretary of State is necessary, where British citizenship or other status has been obtained by deception or omission. On the understanding applied in those cases, the Secretary of State and the recipient of naturalisation or registration as a British citizen do not share a common understanding where there has been material deception or omission by the party making the application, so that the transaction is void or voidable: either it has never in fact taken place or the Secretary of State may treat it as never having taken place.

12.26 Over time, there has been a trickle of cases in which the Secretary of State, rather than exercising statutory powers to withdraw a citizenship status granted on the basis of misleading information or omission, has instead maintained that the original grant of nationality was void (or voidable), so that the grant could be treated as not having taken place at all: *R v SSHD ex p Sultan Mahmood* [1981] QB 59; *R v SSHD ex p Parvaz Akhtar* [1981] QB 46; *R v SSHD ex p Naheed Ejaz* [1994] QB 496, [1994] 2 All ER 436; and *Bibi v ECO* [2007] EWCA Civ 740, [2008] INLR 683.

12.27 The first two cases involved impersonation of others in order to obtain documentation as holders of citizenship. In each case, it was held that no citizenship had been acquired. In the third case, *Ejaz*, the Court of Appeal overturned a refusal to declare that the applicant was a British citizen where she had obtained British citizenship in reliance upon her husband's being a British citizen, whilst in fact her husband was not—he had

---

[6] www.ukba.homeoffice.gov.uk/policyandlaw/guidance/nationalityinstructions.

impersonated another person who was. The court left open whether the applicant had been aware of her husband's fraud, but held that she remained a British citizen until deprived of citizenship under section 40 BNA 1981. At 506D–G, Stuart-Smith distinguished *ex p Sultan Mahmood* and *ex p Parvaz Akhtar*, and rejected the submission advanced in favour of the applicant's citizenship being void:

> The uncertainty arises because if at any time a precedent fact is discovered to be incorrect, no matter how long after the registration or naturalisation, the effect will be as if the registration or naturalisation had never been granted. This has the inevitable consequence of affecting the status of others, such as children. This is highly undesirable where questions of status are concerned. While the construction contended for by the applicant does not eliminate all uncertainty, since the status is defeasible under section 40, such a construction gives rise to much less uncertainty since the section does not operate retrospectively.

> By depriving the Secretary of State of the wide discretion that he is granted under section 40, it seems to me that great injustice could be done. For example, however innocent the mistake may have been, if there is error in relation to precedent fact such as age, the registration or naturalisation is null and void. In many instances deprivation of British citizenship may render the person stateless. Although it is only in the case of persons sentenced to 12 months' imprisonment or more that section 40(5)(b) provides an absolute bar on the Secretary of State's power to deprive a person of British citizenship on that ground if it appears to the Secretary of State that the result will be to make him stateless, it seems to me that this consequence must be one of the considerations which the Secretary of State should take into account in the exercise of his discretion under section 40.

However, he noted at 507B–C that a grant of citizenship could be treated as void if the person to whom it was made was not the person described in the registration or certificate of naturalisation, the grant of citizenship in any other case, as in the earlier ones, conferring nothing. Balcombe LJ concurred. Peter Gibson LJ at 508C–E, agreed, also indicating that:

> If one asks why Parliament should have chosen to allow a mistaken registration or certificate of naturalisation validity unless and until the Secretary of State successfully invokes section 40, the answer would appear to lie in the fact that status is conferred by the registration or certification. Status may affect persons other than the person registered or certified to be naturalised. It may well have been thought to be intolerable that, for example, an innocent mistake as to the age or capacity of the person registered or certified to be naturalised, should, when the mistake comes to light perhaps many years later, have the effect of rendering the registration or naturalisation void ab initio with dire consequences for those whose status is derived from that person.

In *Bibi*, the applicants, who were not British citizens, claimed the right of abode in the UK. They were the widow and children, resident in Bangladesh, of a man who had earlier registered as a British citizen by impersonating a person entitled to do so when he himself was not. Wilson LJ, with whom Sedley LJ and Sir Mark Potter P agreed, found at [20] that: 12.28

> In my view the decision in *Naheed Ejaz* is a useful reminder of the limited circumstances in which the verdict of the law is that citizenship never existed. Without having made any misrepresentation about her own identity the applicant in that case had successfully applied for a certificate of naturalisation … If, in the present case, the appellants had already obtained registration in their own names as British citizens or had already secured a grant of certificates of naturalisation in their own names as such citizens, even if only by virtue of their having falsely

claimed that Mr Jabbar, their late husband and father, was a British citizen, they would have been British citizens albeit at risk of deprivation. So the focus remains directly on the citizenship or otherwise of Mr Jabbar. In this regard the decisions in *Sultan Mahmood* and *Parvaz Akhtar* are in my view directly in point and compel the conclusion that, because he applied for registration in a false identity, there was never a grant to Mr Jabbar of UK (or thus, later, British) citizenship. Had the result been otherwise, a paradox would arise in that the appellants, who have not been registered or naturalised and do not seek registration or naturalisation, would not even be at such risk of deprivation and subsequent removal as was the applicant in *Naheed Ejaz*.

12.29 In recent years, the effect of the earlier decisions has been tested, particularly by reference to a substantial number of individuals who, often as children or very young men, obtained refugee status or leave to remain prior to 1999 on the basis of claims to originate in Kosovo, were permitted to remain and were ultimately granted naturalisation. Years later, evidence emerged in many cases of birth in Albania rather than Kosovo. In *R otao Krasniqi and Kadria v SSHD* [2010] EWHC 3405 (Admin), HHJ Gore QC, sitting as a Deputy High Court Judge, considered the authorities and at [32] rejected the submission that the Court could distinguish between cases in which an applicant impersonated another extant individual and those in which a wholly false identity was invented. At [33], he advanced seven broad propositions, essentially concluding that the key to whether an initial grant of naturalisation was void depended upon matters of fact and degree.[7]

12.30 The NIs set out a notably wide account of the circumstances in which 'nullity action' is called for, rather than deprivation, stating at 55.1.3 as to the distinction between deprivation and nullity that, in addition to cases in which enquiries reveal that the individual seeking naturalisation or registration is already a British citizen, 'nullity action' will be appropriate where:

  a) the applicant has given false information or concealed information concerning his or her identity, for example, by using a false name, giving a false date or place of birth, or claiming a false nationality or concealing his or her nationality status. In this scenario, whether nullity action is appropriate will depend on the nature, quality and extent of any fraud, deception or concealment;
  b) the applicant has created an entirely new false identity;
  c) the applicant is using someone else's identity (ie, impersonation).

This guidance clearly looks to the decision in *Krasniqi and Kadria*, and suffers from the same problem of opacity, with an additional difficulty of imperfect rendering of that decision. This in effect designates almost any case in which another 'identity', whether that of an individual being impersonated or that of an imaginary individual, is given (the limiting factors of 'nature, quality, and extent of any fraud' being restricted to one of three factors likely to be read as alternatives) as a nullity case. On this point, the NIs do not serve the function of providing guidance as to the manner of exercise of a discretion; they simply seek to describe the common law position: here the NIs are entirely secondary to the common law and come close to being guesswork once they move from the facts of the decided cases. Part 2 of Chapter 55 of the NIs, on the basis for nullity action, cites the cases to

---

[7] Permission to appeal on a narrow point was refused by Sullivan LJ in *R otao Krasniqi and Kadria* [2011] EWCA Civ 696.

that point and provides examples of what are said to be nullity and non-nullity cases respectively. The only example of a case in which nullity is said not to arise, at 55.9.7, is one in which the individual had changed his or her name by deed poll to that under which he or she applied for citizenship and had failed to disclose his or her name prior to the change and facts relevant to that identity.

The subject has been re-examined in a very recent decision. In *R (otao Kaziu, Bakijasi and Hysaj) v SSHD* [2014] EWHC 832 (Admin), Ouseley J noted the inflexibility of effect attached to voidability (which he referred to as nullity), noting at [39] that: 'There is good reason, in my judgment, to take a narrow view of those cases which cannot fall within the scope of the statutory provisions for deprivation of nationality.' However, he found that he was bound by earlier decisions of the Court of Appeal and that these obliged him to acknowledge the existence of a class of case in which the grant of nationality is void: **12.31**

42. I turn to consider the narrow category of cases to which nullification can apply. In my view, it comes down to what can be summed up in the word 'impersonation', though that begs some questions. It obviously relates to the individuals who made the false representations about their own identity.

43. What underlies the Court of Appeal decisions is the concept that X cannot obtain nationality by fraudulently claiming to be Y. The way Sullivan LJ expressed it in *Kadria and Krasniqi* above captures the essence of the point. However, what that case did not have to deal with, and none of the other cases did either, is precisely what is it that makes the grant to X not the grant to Y. What aspects of the person have to be false to create a nullity, given that fraud and falsehoods in the application do not of themselves do so, since they are the very essence of deprivation proceedings? The Court of Appeal gave no guidelines, apart from saying that it was obvious when they were crossed, and they were crossed in *Mahmood* and *Akhtar*.

44. Although I agree with the result of HHJ Gore's judgment in *Kadria and Krasniqi*, I consider that his approach was too broad, as to how in practice a case of nullification was to be distinguished from a case of deprivation. His listed factors do not sufficiently distinguish between nullification and deprivation; the question is not one of degree, nor of the nature, quality, extent or frequency or circumstances of the deceit, in the broad way he suggests. Although he is right that it is the attributes of the person which matter, those attributes have to be carefully defined; it is not just any matter which can be described as an attribute of a person or of his identity which matters in this context, since that blurs or removes the crucial distinction between nullification and deprivation. For example, sexuality may be core to personal identity in one sense, yet a false story of sexuality leading to persecution does not go to identity for naturalisation purposes.

…

46. The key characteristics of identity in this context, to my mind, are name, date of birth, and nationality, or country and place of birth, if the latter is used instead of the former. This reflects the information on the certificate, and the basis upon which the earlier cases were decided. These are necessary ingredients for the SSHD to check the identity of someone who seeks naturalisation. Mr Knafler's suggested distinction between falsely using the identity of a real person, dead or alive, and falsely using a fictitious identity, in which only the latter created a nullity of the naturalisation is not rational. It is not supported by authority, and has been rejected whenever raised.

47. It is also clear that the grant has to have been obtained by fraud. So not uncommon innocent errors in the detail of date of birth, perhaps of name, or the innocent use of

pseudonyms, misunderstandings as to nationality, or country and place of birth do not make a nullity of citizenship. The fraud must also have been material to the grant.

12.32 Ouseley J noted at [48] that the agreed position of the parties was that whether a grant of citizenship is a nullity is a question of precedent fact, or simply fact, for the Court, and not one for the Secretary of State to be reviewed on the basis of reasonableness. Whilst the point was not argued, Ouseley J considered that in a relationship case, such as X naturalising as the wife of Y, the relationship must in fact exist, this being a question of precedent fact ([52]). As to the position of third parties who had obtained nationality on the basis of a relationship with someone whose own nationality was void, he considered that no clear guidance was offered by the cases and that the position was 'problematic':

> 55. [T]here is no clear and logical dividing line. The decisions more obviously seek a pragmatic limit to the logical effects of the nullification of citizenship on dependants. Such a pragmatic approach befits giving limited scope to nullification and a wide right of appeal in respect of deprivation. If nullification survives, as I hold it does, this case by case pragmatism leads to uncertainty in application of the concept and is unsatisfactory. Either nullification of one citizenship should nullify the citizenship of those whose citizenship had depended on its validity, or it should go no further than the impersonator's citizenship. Half-way pragmatism, which may or may not apply to a given case, simply illustrates the difficulty of the concept.

12.33 The judgment notes the paradox that neither the Secretary of State nor the courts have treated leave to enter or remain as void on the basis of factors cited as rendering nationality void. Ouseley J felt compelled by reason of the Court of Appeal decisions to reject 'powerful' submissions by Counsel for the claimants directed against the arising of voidability in the context of nationality.[8]

12.34 Despite this recent decision, some doubt must attach to prospects for the continuing application of the concept of voidability in nationality cases, at least beyond the clearest cases of impersonation (and subject to the problems of definition thereof which have bedevilled adjudication in this area), given intervening developments in public law. In *Khawaja v SSHD* [1983] UKHL 8, [1984] AC 74, a case concerned with whether entry by deception was 'illegal entry' for the purposes of section 33 IA 1971, Lord Bridge of Harwich at 118A–D doubted the usefulness of voidability in an immigration context:

> To say that the fraud 'vitiates' the leave or that the leave is not 'in accordance with the Act' is, with respect, to state a conclusion without explaining the steps by which it is reached. Since we are here concerned with purely statutory law, I think there are dangers in introducing maxims of the common law as to the effect of fraud on common law transactions and still greater dangers in seeking to apply the concepts of 'void' and 'voidable'. In a number of recent cases in your Lordships' House it has been pointed out that these transplants from the field of contract do not readily take root in the field of public law. This is well illustrated in the judgment of the Court of Appeal in the instant case of *Khawaja* [1982] 1 WLR 625, where Donaldson LJ, as he then was, spoke of the appellant's leave to enter as being 'voidable ab initio' (at p 630G), which I find, with respect, an impossibly difficult legal category to comprehend.

---

[8] At the time of writing, it was understood that Ouseley J had on the papers granted permission to appeal to the Court of Appeal.

The arguments against voidability, including that based on the desirability of consistency as between leave to enter or remain, on the one hand, and nationality, on the other hand, are obvious in cases such as those before Ouseley J: he explicitly acknowledged the power of the arguments addressed to him. Against this, an argument for eliminating voidability entirely must address questions which may arise along a spectrum of cases: for instance, if A, standing in a passport queue, drops her passport, and B, standing behind her in sight of A and the Immigration Officer, picks it up from the floor and presents it to the Immigration Officer as her own, the brief and ineffective impersonation surely cannot create a situation in which B must be stripped of the nationality belonging to A by exercise of section 40 BNA 1981. It may be that, instead, the law should be clarified by statute or that interpretation of the law in this area should be more sensitive to the facts of particular cases, as the decision in *Krasniqi and Kadria v SSHD* hinted at, in which case the consequential question would be at what point the line would fall to be drawn. For now, the reported Court of Appeal decisions and the recent decision of Ouseley J provide clear binding precedent, but as Ouseley J clearly contemplated, the law in this area may be due for renewed scrutiny at a senior level.

E2. The Deprivation Power

12.35 In chapter 8 of this book, the law relating to deportation of non-citizens is reviewed. Under that law, section 3(5)–(6) IA 1971 defines those liable to deportation, whilst section 5(1)–(2) IA 1971 gives the Secretary of State the power to make a deportation order against someone who is liable thereto. The UKBA 2007 scheme operates within the parameters of the pre-established statutory powers, whilst in specified cases substituting a duty for the discretionary power of the Secretary of State.

12.36 By contrast with the deportation power, there is a single stage involved in the exercise of the powers of deprivation of nationality, or of right of abode, given respectively by section 40(2)–(3) BNA 1981 and section 2A IA 1971. In the case of section 40(2) 1971, the condition precedent is that 'the Secretary of State is satisfied that deprivation is conducive to the public good' (and it is disapplied by section 40(4) if satisfied 'that the order would make a person stateless', although, the new section 40(4A) BNA 1981 will, in respect of the cases to which it applies, reduce the scope of the restriction denationalization by the UK where statelessness would ensue under section 40(4) BNA 1981). Section 2A IA 1971 enables the Secretary of State to remove the statutory right of abode where it is 'conducive to the public good for the person to be excluded or removed from the United Kingdom.' Section 40(3) BNA 1981 provides that the Secretary of State may deprive of British citizenship (or other citizenship status) a person who has gained that status through registration or naturalisation if the Secretary of State is satisfied that the status was obtained by fraud, false representation or concealment of a material fact.

12.37 In public law terms, it is doubtful that much is lost through adoption of a structure different from the two-stage IA 1971 scheme for deportation. In each case, there is, subject to the arising of certain conditions, a discretionary power. In each case, two essential issues arise: first, whether the conditions for existence of the discretion themselves arise; and, second, the exercise of that power. The power must be exercised in accordance with the established principles of public law, that is (in summary), without illegality, irrationality or procedural impropriety.[9]

E3. Deprivation by Reason of Fraud, False Representation or Concealment of a Material Fact

12.38 Although there has been a longstanding power to derive an individual of nationality or citizenship status obtained by deception, this had for some decades, and until relatively recently, been little used. In what might be called the modern era of immigration control and nationality law, since IA 1971 and BNA 1981 respectively, the number of cases would appear to have been zero between 1983 and 2009. In that year, 30 decisions were taken under section 40(3) BNA 1981,[10] all or almost all prompted by the identification of large numbers of cases in which men who had obtained refugee status or exceptional leave to remain as Kosovars during a period of most acute conflict in that territory a decade earlier were put forward as sponsors on applications for entry clearance to the UK as spouses, and the documents presented suggested that they in fact were of Albanian rather than Yugoslav national origin.

12.39 The process of deprivation is set out at Part B of the NI, at 55.6 ('Process Overview'). The www.gov.uk website contains forms for recording investigation results and sample letters giving notice to potential subjects, inviting representations within 21 days, as well as sample decision letters.[11] In this context, 21 days may represent a relatively short space of time, and any decision refusing a reasonable request for extension in the absence of good reason might endanger the fairness of the process: such decisions in the operation of the process are of course subject to judicial review if appeal does not provide an alternative remedy.

12.40 In any deprivation based on section 40(3) BNA 1981, the actual existence of 'fraud, false representation, or concealment' represents a condition precedent for exercise of the power. The statutory language, which requires that the Secretary of State be satisfied that registration or naturalisation was obtained by means of one of the three sanctioned forms of conduct, has in *Arusha and Demushi (Deprivation of Citizenship—Delay) Albania* [2012] UKUT 80 (IAC) [11]–[14] been held by the Tribunal not to exclude it from deciding itself, with the burden of proof upon the Secretary of State both whether the necessary condition(s) for deprivation have been shown to be present and whether the exercise of discretion to deprive is consistent with the relevant standards of the ECHR and EU law, and supported by the circumstances.

12.41 In this context, the NIs attempt an interpretation of the statutory language, stating at 55.4 that 'false representation' denotes 'a representation which was dishonestly made on the applicant's part i.e. an innocent mistake would not give rise to a power to order deprivation under this provision', and 'concealment of any material fact'

---

[9] This conventional threefold summary is not exhaustive and its components are not mutually exclusive: see M Fordham, *Judicial Review Handbook* (6th edn, Oxford, Hart Publishing, 2012) 487. The public law wrongs justifying intervention are more fully examined in that work at Part C, P45–P63.
[10] Freedom of Information response to authors.
[11] https://www.gov.uk/government/publications/chapter-55-deprivation-section-40-and-nullity-nationality-instructions.

means concealment which was material to the process by which British citizenship was obtained, no requirement for dishonesty being specified. 'Fraud' is defined as either false representation or concealment of any material fact, and so adds nothing to the scope of the overall formula.

As to the mental element of these conditions, the condition of 'fraud' would appear on its face to require a finding of dishonesty. In relation to 'false representation', the Court of Appeal in *AA (Nigeria) v SSHD* [2010] EWCA Civ 773, [2011] 1 WLR 564 at [65]–[76] distinguished the earlier decision of a different panel of the Court in *Tahzeem Akhtar v IAT* [1991] Imm AR 326, 332–33 that the term 'false representation' covered an innocent if factually incorrect representation as well as a dishonest one, and found that the requirement for 'false representation' under the exclusion clauses of the Immigration Rules was satisfied only where dishonesty was shown. Whilst that case, like *Akhtar v IAT*, concerned interpretation of the Immigration Rules, there would seem to be substantial room for argument that the principle applies equally to section 40(3) BNA 1981, something which for present purposes also reflects the approach taken in the policy of the Secretary of State at 55.4.1. Whether 'concealment of any material fact' must be dishonest is less clear, and the policy of the Secretary of State at 55.4.2 does not specify any requirement that concealment be dishonest. **12.42**

'Materiality' is defined at 55.7.1–2 in terms of whether the relevant facts 'would have' affected the decision to grant citizenship, examples including undisclosed convictions, a marriage or civil partnership found to be invalid or void, or false details given in relation to an earlier immigration or asylum application leading to a grant of status to a person 'who would not otherwise have qualified', so that, for example, the Secretary of State would appear not to envision deprivation where an individual from Kosovo, who would have qualified as a refugee at the relevant time in his or her own identity, had given false identity details. If fraud, false representation or concealment did not have a direct impact upon the grant of citizenship, then the NIs at 55.7.3–4 envision that 'it will not be appropriate to pursue deprivation action'.[12] The NIs also state, at 55.7.6, that 'where fraud postdates the application for British citizenship it will not be appropriate to pursue deprivation action', that 'If a person has been resident in the United Kingdom for more than 14 years we will not normally deprive of citizenship', that a person who was a minor at the date of application for citizenship would not be liable to exercise of the discretion, and that where a person who acquired indefinite leave to remain as a minor where the false representation, concealment of material fact or fraud arose at that stage and acquisition of citizenship ultimately followed this, discretionary deprivation will not follow. These concessions are subject to the caveat that where the public interest indicates deprivation, this will be pursued.[13] The Secretary of State indicates at 55.7.6 **12.43**

---

[12] This probably mis-states the law, expressing the absence of satisfaction of the statutory conditions or any of them as a reason for not exercising a discretionary power which on a correct understanding does not exist. If the registration or naturalisation was not 'obtained by' one of the three enumerated means, then section 40(3) BNA 1981 creates no power to remove nationality. It illustrates the importance of returning to the source of the statutory power rather than assuming that this is correctly understood or described in the guidance.

[13] Of the four subcategories, the first (fraud after application) seems to be properly understood as indicative of failure of satisfaction of the statutory conditions or any of them, because the registration or naturalisation was not 'obtained by' one of the three enumerated means, unless what is meant is fraud entered into by an individual in relation to some enquiry after the application is made but before the process is concluded.

that an individual will 'not normally' be deprived of British citizenship after more than 14 years' residence, but that in particular circumstances deprivation would be pursued.

12.44 The NIs appear to indicate at 55.7.7 that deprivation will be pursued only where the applicant or someone else acted deliberately: 'The caseworker should be satisfied that there was an intention to deceive: an innocent error or genuine omission should not lead to deprivation.' Where deception is entered into on behalf of a child or in the context of a family application, caseworkers are instructed at 55.7.8 to assume, inter alia, that a child was 'not complicit in any deception by their parent or guardian', but this does not allow conduct after reaching 18 to be treated as not responsible for deception, and the guidance envisions treating with caution claims to be without responsibility through acting on the advice of others, and the assumption of complicity where a family application has been made unless 'sufficient evidence in mitigation' is provided. This last scenario may ignore the unbalanced position within families, and in particular the frequent domination of women by men in some cultures. It also appears unnecessary, given that the statute does not require personal responsibility for fraud, false representation or concealment of a material fact, simply that someone has acted deliberately and that the Secretary of State 'is satisfied that the registration or naturalisation was obtained by [such] means'.

12.45 The Nis, however, now set out at 55.7.10 clear guidance to caseworkers as to the exercise of the discretionary power where such a power arises: 'The caseworker should consider whether deprivation would be seen to be a balanced and reasonable step to take, taking into account the seriousness of the fraud, misrepresentation or concealment, the level of evidence for this, and what information was available to UKBA at the time of consideration.' The guidance also adds the proviso that 'evidence that was before the Secretary of State at the time of application but was disregarded or mishandled should not in general be used at a later stage to deprive of nationality. However, where it is in the public interest to deprive despite the presence of this factor, it will not prevent the deprivation'. In complex cases, examination of the relevant records, obtained by subject access request, may be fruitful in identifying documents seen at the time of a final decision and reflections upon different aspects of a particular case recorded in minutes or memoranda. 'Mitigating factors' are identified at 55.7.11 and, subject to the reservation that 'All adults are expected to take responsibility for the information they provided', expressly may include:

(i) relevant evidence of 'mental or physical impairment that can clearly be shown to have impacted on the subject's judgement at the time the material fraud took place' or of 'some form of coercion that indicates that the subject was not able to make independent decisions at the time the material fraud took place'(at 55.7.11.3–5);

(ii) any foreseeable breach of ECHR rights: 'the impact of deprivation on the individual's rights under [the ECHR]. In particular you should consider whether deprivation and/or removal would interfere with the person's private and family life and, if so, whether such action would nevertheless be proportionate'.

Where fraud postdates the conclusion of the application process, no discretionary power is created and no amount of 'public interest' will suffice to create one.

The guidance records that: 'In some cases it might be appropriate to remove citizenship but allow the person to remain in the UK. In such cases you should consider granting leave in accordance with guidance on family and private life' (at 55.7.11.6);

(iii) the impact of deprivation upon rights under EU law including 'where the person previously held another EU citizenship and would need time to resume it' or 'where the person is living in another European country, exercising a treaty right, and so would need time to regularise their stay' or 'where a person was exercising EU rights as a student overseas and would need time to complete his or her course' (at 55.7.11.7);

(iv) the guidance does not expressly exclude any particular factor which would otherwise be relevant, and one factor which may require consideration, if not adequately incorporated by reference to the ECHR, is whether the decision renders an individual stateless and, if so, what rights of access he or she has to the territory of any state. The imposition of statelessness is expressly permitted by Article 8(2)(b) CRS 'where the nationality has been obtained by misrepresentation or fraud' as an exception to the normal principle, given in Article 8(1) CRS, that a State Party 'shall not deprive a person of his nationality if such deprivation would render him stateless'. But it would follow from statelessness that no country would have a binding duty to admit the subject of deprivation.

12.46 Under the heading 'Evidence' at 55.7.12.1, the guidance invites the caseworker to test the strength of evidence, 55.7.12.2 noting that: 'The UKBA does not wish to pursue deprivation where this is likely to be unsuccessful on appeal as this would not be an effective use of public resources.'

12.47 In the *Arusha and Demushi (Deprivation of Citizenship—Delay) Albania* [2012] UKUT 80 (IAC) [11]–[14], appeal, the Tribunal upheld a first instance decision finding that the Secretary of State had not demonstrated that nationality had been obtained by fraud, false representation or concealment. In *Deliallisi (British Citizen: Deprivation Appeal: Scope) Albania* [2013] UKUT 439 (IAC), the Tribunal held at [54]–[63] that appeals should be considered in light of 'reasonably foreseeable consequences of deprivation, which may, depending on the facts, include removal'. It set aside the decision at first instance, dismissing the appeals, but on reconsideration substituted its own decision to the same effect, though following consideration of Article 8 ECHR matters not canvassed earlier.

12.48 The statute does not prevent the Secretary of State from making an order under section 40(3) BNA 1981 where the individual affected has never had other nationality, or has lost that nationality, so that deprivation would render him or her stateless.

E3. Deprivation as Conducive to the Public Good

12.49 The power presently provided to the Secretary of State by section 40(2) BNA 1981 is an extensive one by which any British citizen, or person possessing some other British 'citizenship status' as defined therein, may be deprived of that status by an order of the Secretary of State provided that the holder of that office is satisfied that deprivation 'is conducive to the public good'. An individual possessing the right of abode under section

2(1) IA 1971 may be deprived thereof if the Secretary of State 'thinks that it would be conducive to the public good for the person to be excluded or removed from the United Kingdom'.

12.50 Both of these powers acquired their present form by legislation introduced after the terrorist attacks carried out or attempted in London in July 2005. In the case of deprivation of citizenship, section 4 NIAA 2002, which came into force on 1 April 2003, substituted a new section 40(2) BNA 1981, which provided that: 'The Secretary of State may by order deprive a person of a citizenship status if the Secretary of State is satisfied that the person has done anything seriously prejudicial to the vital interest of: (a) the United Kingdom, or (b) a British overseas territory.' NIAA 2002 broadened the scope of the power so that it extended to all British citizens, including those who had become such by birth or descent rather than by registration or naturalisation. The effect of this as understood at that time would have been mitigated by the exigency of the 'seriously prejudicial to the vital interest' test. But the regime for deportation on the grounds of conduct provided by the amended section 40(2) BNA 1981 was subsequently broadened once more by section 56(1) IANA 2006. In apparent reaction to the lack of success in the litigation leading to a decision of the Court of Appeal in *SSHD v Hicks (David)* [2006] EWCA Civ 400, this substituted for the 'seriously prejudicial to the vital interest' test, which was in force for only three years and three months, the 'conducive to the public good' test. Section 57(1) IANA 2006 inserted the new section 2A IA 1971 to provide an equivalent position as regards deprivation of the right of abode.

12.51 These changes represented a serious increase in the potential range and penetration of the statutory regime for deprivation of nationality (effectively extended to the right of abode), which is unprecedented in modern peacetime legislation. In its report issued whilst the legislative process was ongoing, the Parliamentary Joint Committee on Human Rights concluded that both provisions were seriously flawed. As regards deprivation of citizenship, it held:

> [T]hat the new test for deprivation of citizenship contains insufficient guarantees against arbitrariness in its exercise in light of (i) the significant reduction in the threshold, (ii) the lack of requirement of objectively reasonable grounds for the Secretary of State's belief, and (iii) the arbitrariness of the definition of the class affected, and that it therefore gives rise to a risk of incompatibility with a number of human rights standards.[14]

In relation to the power to deprive an individual of the right of abode, the Committee considered the same problems to arise as had been pointed to in relation to nationality deprivation, and that the breadth of the provision meant that:

> [T]here are not at present sufficient guarantees against arbitrariness in the exercise of the power to deprive of a right of abode, and that therefore the power as currently set out gives rise to a substantial risk of incompatibility with various human rights. However, in the Committee's view, if these two concerns were addressed, the availability of a full right of appeal in relation to this power would provide a sufficient guarantee.[15]

---

[14] House of Lords and House of Commons Joint Committee on Human Rights: Counter-Terrorism Policy and Human Rights: Terrorism Bill and Related Matters, Third Report of Session 2005–06 (HL paper 75-I, HC 561-I) 7.
[15] ibid.

12.52 The Home Office at the time of enactment had indicated that its new powers would be used in conjunction with a list of 'unacceptable behaviours' published just over a month after the second of the July 2005 terrorist incidents, initially addressed to non-citizens. The list sanctioned the use of 'any means ... to express views which ... foment, justify or glorify terrorist violence in furtherance of particular beliefs; seek to provoke others to terrorist acts; foment other serious criminal activity or seek to provoke others to serious criminal acts; foster hatred that might lead to inter-community violence in the UK'.[16] The Home Office indicated to the Joint Committee on Human Rights its vision as being that 'individuals subject to these powers will in most cases subsequently be liable for deportation for conduct covered by the list of unacceptable behaviours'.[17]

12.53 The NIs at paragraph 55.4.4 of Chapter 55 define 'conduciveness to the public good' as meaning 'depriving in the public interest on the grounds of involvement in terrorism, espionage, serious organised crime, war crimes, or unacceptable behaviours'. This very broad definition provides some limitation on the extent of reach of the statutory power, but the degree of limitation is minimal, given the breadth of the terms used and the absence of any permanent underpinning to this, given that the NIs are a document which may be altered at will by the Secretary of State without public consultation or recourse to Parliament. The section 40(2) BNA 1981 power appears to have been used on 27 occasions since it took its present form, 24 of those since the change of government in May 2010.[18] However, the exercise of the power is shrouded in secrecy and the Secretary of State has chosen to defend litigation brought by journalists seeking matters as basic as the number of times on which the power has been exercised: see *The Home Office v The Information Commissioner and Cobain (Information rights: Freedom of information—absolute exemptions)* [2014] UKUT 306 (AAC). As to published guidance there is no other guidance of any significance in the NIs as regards deprivation on a 'conducive' basis: the absence of this represents a marked contrast with the position as regards the section 40(3) BNA 1981 power, in relation to which, as has been seen, there is detailed guidance, and also with, for instance, the guidance concerning exercise of the power to grant naturalisation, referred to in the previous chapter.

12.54 A feature of the use of section 40(2) BNA 1981 which might not have been anticipated at the time of the legislative changes broadening the scope of the power is that it has been predominantly applied to individuals whilst they are outside the UK. A total of 15 out of 17 or 18 individuals identified by the Bureau of Investigative Journalism were outside the UK at the time that section 40(2) BNA 1981 was exercised.[19] In *L1 v SSHD* [2013] EWCA Civ 906, Laws LJ observed at [5] that:

> 5. As it clearly shows, when the Secretary of State made the decision to deprive the appellant of his citizenship on 6 July 2010, it was known to her that the appellant was in Sudan; and indeed the decision to make and give notice of the decision was advisedly postponed until he had left the United Kingdom to travel to Sudan. The court's concern was that this appeared to

---

[16] www.telegraph.co.uk/news/uknews/1496902/What-is-meant-by-unacceptable-behaviour.html
[17] n 14 above, para 106.
[18] Bureau of Investigative Journalism, 10 June 2014, www.thebureauinvestigates.com/category/projects/deprivation-citizenship.
[19] Patrick Galey and Alice K Ross, 'Interactive: The 53 Britons Stripped of Their Nationality', Bureau of Investigative Journalism, 3 June 2014, www.thebureauinvestigates.com/2014/06/03/interactive-the-53-britons-stripped-of-their-nationality.

constitute a deliberate manipulation of provisions in the SIAC (Procedure) Rules 2003 relating to notice undertaken for the purpose of obstructing the appellant's statutory right of appeal or making it more difficult to exercise.

McCombe LJ added at [39] that the Secretary of State had 'for her own understandable reasons (as presented to us) sought to circumvent the obvious intent of the Act and regulations as to service of the notice, in the hope that a means of service, arguably within the letter of the rules (as to which I express no concluded view), but clearly not within their spirit, would suffice as a manner of compliance with the service requirements.

12.55 In the case of deprivation of the right of abode, guidance is set out in the Nationality Instructions at Chapter 57 ('Right of Abode') volume 1, section 6. The guidance does not repeat the definition of 'conduciveness to the public good' provided in the guidance relating to deprivation of nationality. Instead, it contains a short reference at paragraph 6.2 to statements made by ministers during the passage of IANA 2006:

> 6.2 Ministers suggested ... that such action may be appropriate where the person—
> — has encouraged or assisted others to commit acts of terrorism;
> — has committed war crimes, public order offences or other serious crime; or
> — has carried out acts seriously prejudicial to vital national interests, including espionage and acts of terrorism directed at the United Kingdom or an allied power.

The guidance further states at paragraph 6.4 that: 'Cases in which there may be a possibility of deprivation of right of abode will be scarce.' It does not appear that the statutory power has been used.

12.56 As to the persons who were subjects of decisions, two have successfully appealed to the SIAC on the basis that the making of the order was barred by section 40(4) BNA 1981 because it would render them stateless (including one since extradited to the US and the subject in the *B2* appeal now reversed on appeal to the Court of Appeal, who has been granted permission to appeal to the Supreme Court),[20] two have apparently been killed in drone strikes, and one has succeeded in reversing the SIAC's adverse decision on appeal to the Court of Appeal and has seen that decision sustained in the Supreme Court, but within weeks was the subject of a new decision under the same section and would appear a likely target for the new power given to the Secretary of State by the IA 2014.

12.57 Because the statutory scheme is so strikingly free from other restraints, one particular matter has come to have considerable prominence in the appeals that have come before the SIAC, including every successful appeal. Section 40(4) BNA 1981 provides that the Secretary of State may not make an order under section 40(2) depriving an individual of citizenship status if he or she is 'satisfied that the order would make a person stateless'.

12.58 As to the scope of this protection, the SIAC in *Abu Hamza v SSHD* [2010] UKSIAC 23/2005 (5 November 2010) considered whether 'stateless' in section 40(4) BNA 1981 meant de jure and not de facto stateless, the term 'de jure stateless' in this context referring to the definition in Article 1(1) CSSP: 'a person not considered a national by any State under the operation of its laws'. The SIAC observed that the UK was a party to

---

[20] *Abu Hamza v SSHD* [2010] UKSIAC 23/2005 (5 November 2010) and *B2 v SSHD (Deportation— Preliminary Issue— Allowed)* [2012] UKSIAC 114/2012 (26 July 2012), appealed in *B2 v SSHD* [2013] EWCA Civ 616. Appeal to the Supreme Court from the latter decision is to take place in November 2014.

the CSSP and that no agreed delineation of the scope of de facto statelessness had been established, concluding at [5] that:

> [I]t is hardly likely that Parliament intended to link the prohibition on the making of a deprivation order to an undefined status which has never been the subject of international agreement. The obvious, and, we are satisfied, only proper conclusion is that Parliament intended that the Secretary of State should not make a deprivation order in respect of a person if satisfied that the effect would be that he would therefore be made a person who is not considered as a national by any state under the operation of its law—the definition in Article 1.1 of the 1954 Convention. Such an interpretation has the advantage of aligning domestic law with the United Kingdom's international obligations.

The SIAC has since followed the earlier conclusion in *Al Jedda v SSHD* [2008] UKSIAC 66/2008 (23 May 2008) [4] that it was for the appellant to show that he or she would be made stateless on the balance of probabilities, the possession or otherwise of a foreign nationality being a conditional precedent. In the *Abu Hamza v SSHD* case, the SIAC found that the appellant had lost his previous Egyptian nationality and so would be made stateless by removal of British citizenship (and hence British nationality). On the approach to be followed in assessing whether statelessness arose, the SIAC found that the question was focused upon the effect, not the reasonableness, of foreign laws concerning nationality: 'The Secretary of State and SIAC [are] not concerned with the reasonableness of the laws of a foreign state or of decisions made under them to deprive a person of his nationality, but with their effect.'

12.59 In *Al-Jedda v SSHD* [2009] UKSIAC 66/2008 (7 April 2009) on the first consideration of that case by the SIAC, the primary question was whether the subject's Iraqi nationality, which had been lost when he was granted naturalisation in the UK in 2000, had been automatically restored to him by Iraqi legislation enacted following the fall of Saddam Hussein in March 2003. The SIAC held that the subject's Iraqi nationality had been restored at some point after 2003. On subsequent appeal to the Court of Appeal, this decision was set aside for procedural reasons and rehearing of the appeal by SIAC was ordered. On completing the rehearing, the SIAC once more held that Iraqi nationality had been restored. The reheard appeal was successfully appealed to the Court of Appeal, which in *Al-Jedda v SSHD* (Rev 2) [2012] EWCA Civ 358 held that the SIAC had erred in its approach to the evidence of Iraqi law and that on a correct approach, Mr al-Jedda was not an Iraqi citizen because the relevant Iraqi laws would require him to apply for restoration of his nationality, something he had not done. As Richards LJ observed at [117]: 'It is unnecessary to decide whether any application, once made, has to be granted if the basic conditions are fulfilled or whether there exists a residual discretion to refuse it. What matters is that an application has to be made if Iraqi nationality is to be restored.' The Supreme Court in *SSHD v Al-Jedda* [2013] UKSC 62, [2014] 1 AC 253 confirmed the correctness of this interpretation.

12.60 There remains a pending appeal to the Supreme Court from the decision of the Court of Appeal in *B2 v SSHD* [2013] EWCA Civ 616. In these proceedings, the Court considered the appeal of the Secretary of State from a decision of the SIAC, concluding that a British citizen, identified only as B2, would be made stateless by a deprivation of his British citizenship, so that a deprivation order could not be made. B2 had been born in Vietnam in 1983. Shortly thereafter his family relocated to Hong Kong. In 1989 the family came to the UK and in 1995 its members, including B2, applied successfully to naturalise as British citizens. B2 subsequently travelled to Yemen, where it was believed that he received terrorist training. In 2011 the Secretary of State made an order under section 40(2) BNA 1981 depriving B2 of British citizenship on conducive grounds. The SIAC allowed his appeal on the basis that the effect of the Secretary of State's decision would be to render him stateless, so that section 40(4) prevented an order being made. The decision turned upon the absence of willingness of the Vietnamese executive, to which all relevant decisions concerning nationality were allocated by the Vietnamese laws in question, itself to accept that B2 was a national of Vietnam as the Secretary of State maintained. The Court of Appeal decided that B2 was not stateless because the refusal of the Vietnamese state to acknowledge his nationality was in the Court's view arbitrary. This decision of the Court is, on its face, difficult to reconcile with the principle stated by the SIAC in the *Abu Hamza v SSHD* decision, based upon the definition of statelessness in Article 1 CSSP ('is not considered as a national by any State under the operation of its law'), which purposefully incorporates not only the content of national law but also 'the operation' thereof, and which, as set out in chapters two and three, purposefully looks not at whether the position of the state (here Vietnam) should be recognised under international law, but simply whether Vietnam, 'rightly or wrongly' in the view of the international community, repudiates the obligations otherwise imposed upon a state of nationality. The appeal of B2 from that decision is to be heard by the Supreme Court in November 2014.

The New IA 2014 Provision

12.61 The new provision in section 40(4A) BNA 1981 allows the Secretary of State to circumvent the section 40(4) BNA 1981 restriction in a limited subset of cases in which the subject is a naturalised British citizen and two conditions are met:

(i) the Secretary of State is satisfied that the deprivation is conducive to the public good because the person, while having that citizenship status, has conducted himself or herself in a manner which is seriously prejudicial to the vital interests of the UK, any of the islands or any British overseas territory (section 40(4A)(b)); and

(ii) the Secretary of State has reasonable grounds for believing that the person is able, under the law of a country or territory outside the UK, to become a national of such a country or territory (section 40(4A)(c)).

12.62 This represents a direct attempt to avoid the obstacle to deprivation of nationality raised in *Al-Jedda*. No new provision as regards deprivation of nationality was contained in the original Immigration Bill presented to Parliament. At the Second Reading in the House of Commons, a new clause 60 was introduced by government amendment, which would have modified section 40 BNA 1981 by adding a new section 40(4A) resembling the new provision, but without the additional condition requiring reasonable grounds for belief that a person is able to acquire another nationality in section 40(4A)(c). An amendment brought about in the House of Lords threatened to reroute consideration of the proposed change to a cross-parliamentary committee. The safeguard in section 40(4A)(c) BNA 1981 was brought about upon the Bill's return to the Commons by a compromise in the light of that amendment.

The original proposal was characterised by Lord Pannick in the House of Lords as 'unacceptable'. Addressing the final form of the Bill prior to its passage, he noted a number of observations and enquiries: **12.63**

> I have written to the Minister giving him notice of a number of assurances that I seek and which I consider are important to the understanding of the protections which are contained in the new paragraph. The first is this. I understand that the reasonableness of the Secretary of State's conclusion that another nationality is open to the individual will be open to challenge in the Special Immigration Appeals Commission, and that SIAC will have the power to determine whether the Secretary of State does have reasonable grounds for her belief that the individual is able to become a national of another country. I understand from the Minister's opening remarks that he agrees with that.
>
> The second assurance I seek is this. Does the Minister agree that the material which is relevant to the Secretary of State's decision on this point—that is, the ability to acquire another nationality—would be very unlikely to be secret? The material would be provided to the applicant's lawyers so that it could be fully debated in any appeal to SIAC. I would be grateful if he could confirm that.
>
> Thirdly, am I correct in my understanding that the new provision means that the Secretary of State has no power to take away British citizenship if the matter depends on a discretionary judgment by the foreign state? I think that the words in the new paragraph, 'able to become', must mean that the matter is in the hands of the individual, who needs only to apply to the foreign state, pay the relevant fee, provide the relevant documents and show their entitlement. The paragraph does not say 'able to apply'. There is good reason to interpret this provision narrowly: namely, to prevent deprivation of British citizenship where it would leave people in limbo, with the risk of statelessness if the foreign country decides not to exercise any discretion in favour of the applicant. I therefore think that this provision means that at the time of deprivation of British citizenship, the individual must have a right to citizenship under the law of the foreign country. Does the Minister agree?
>
> I seek reassurance on a fourth point. I think that the word 'able', which is the word in the new paragraph, must mean that there is no practical impediment to obtaining the foreign citizenship. For example, if there is reason to think that the foreign state will not apply its own laws, or will not do so within a reasonable time, the Secretary of State simply could not remove British citizenship. Does the Minister agree?
>
> Fifthly, the word 'able', as well as general principles of public law must mean that the Secretary of State could not exercise this new power to take away British citizenship where, although the person is entitled to acquire the foreign citizenship, there is good reason for their being unwilling to do so. An obvious example is where the individual is a member of a group that is persecuted in the country concerned. Does the Minister agree that it would be wholly wrong and unlawful for the Secretary of State, if she accepts that those are the facts, nevertheless to go ahead and deprive that person of British citizenship?
>
> Sixthly and finally, I think that the word 'able' and the general requirement that the Minister must exercise her power in a reasonable manner must mean that the courts would apply a 'reasonable link' test. By that, I mean that the clause could not be applied by reference to an individual's rights to acquire citizenship in a country with which he or she has no close link other than an entitlement to nationality. For example, surely the Secretary of State could not rely on the entitlement of a Jewish man or woman to citizenship of the state of Israel under the law of return if the individual has no other link with the state of Israel; or rely on a wife's right to acquire the citizenship of her husband in a country that she has never visited. I have not thought up these examples. I take them from the judgment of Lord Wilson for the Supreme

Court in the *Al-Jedda* case last October, at paragraph 23. Therefore, the sixth question is: does the Minister agree in principle that there must be a 'reasonable link' test implicit in this paragraph, so that the clause could not be used in circumstances that would, in the absence of a reasonable link, be wholly unreasonable?[21]

12.64 Lord Hope welcomed the reaching of compromise whilst inviting the Minister to indicate whether the final provision was consistent with the international obligations of the UK. He noted, referring to the CRS, that:

The phrase 'the vital interests' is a precise quotation from Article 7(1)(d) of the convention and one can see how closely tied the wording of the statute is to that of the convention. It is important that the wording should be narrowly framed in order to meet what the preamble and Article 4 were talking about, but that has another significance when one looks at how the wording will work in practice. It is well known that the courts will construe legislation on the assumption that Parliament has intended to legislate in accordance with this country's international obligations. One would expect a court to have regard to the wording of the convention and to construe the words narrowly. They are narrowly worded but they will be narrowly construed, too. The key words already identified are 'is able'. It is not 'maybe' or a possibility; it is 'is', in the present tense. 'Able' is itself a powerful word, and the new Section refers to being able to become a national of a country, not to an ability to apply or be considered.[22]

12.65 Closing the debate, the Minister (Lord Taylor of Holbeach) responded to some points raised by members of the House. Only a part of his speech, containing some important answers, can be set out here:

Perhaps most important is the whole question of the meaning of 'reasonable grounds to believe' and whether those reasonable grounds of belief are appropriate for determining the ability of a person to acquire another nationality. The Home Secretary's decision must be 'reasonable' based on the evidence available to her on the nationality laws of those countries and the person's circumstances. That will include having regard to any practical arrangements, but those will vary from case to case, and it is not possible or appropriate to speculate about what weight those issues would carry in a particular case. 'Satisfied' has been interpreted to mean that SIAC decides for itself whether a person is a dual national. In some circumstances a person, after being deprived of British citizenship, may take steps which guarantee that another country will not recognise him or her as a national. The appeal should therefore review the decision at the time it was made, which is why the phrase 'reasonable grounds to believe' instead of 'satisfied' is used.

Both the noble Lord, Lord Pannick, and the noble Baroness, Lady Kennedy of The Shaws, asked what the position would be if the foreign state had some discretion in whether to approve an individual's request for citizenship. I think that the noble Baroness went as far as to say that she thought that there were likely to be grounds for discretion in almost any case. The clause refers to whether under the laws of a country or territory a person is able to acquire the nationality of that country. The key issue will be whether the Secretary of State reasonably believes that they are able to acquire the nationality. It does not say that the person must have a right—an automatic entitlement—to that other nationality. Where there is a discretionary judgment there may be reasonable grounds to believe that the discretion will be exercised. However, reasonableness would require something more than saying that the person should apply for the exercise of a general discretion to grant citizenship to any country that has such discretion.

---

[21] HL Hansard 12 May 2014, cols 1674–75.
[22] ibid col 1680.

I hope I make myself clear on that. The Home Secretary must have reasonable grounds to believe that, at the end of any application process—if one is required—the person will become a national of another country.

The noble Lord, Lord Pannick, asked whether there was a reasonable link test, which would mean, for example, that the use of the power would be limited to cases where the person would be reacquiring a citizenship that they once held. In most cases, the decision will be made on the Secretary of State's assessment of whether the person can reacquire a nationality that has previously been held by that individual. But we cannot rule out circumstances in which a person has recourse to a nationality that they have not held recently. As we have noted, the nationality laws of other countries can be very complex and any decision will be entirely case-specific. We cannot speculate on the way in which an overseas jurisdiction would act under its own laws. The duty of the Home Secretary will be to take a decision on whether she reasonably believes that the person is able under the law of another country to acquire another nationality.

The noble Baroness, Lady Smith, raised the question of what would happen in the event that the other citizenship is not granted and the other individual is abroad. The prime consideration for the Home Secretary is the operation of the law within those countries. However, as part of the assessment made by the Home Secretary, she will have regard to the practicalities associated with acquiring that citizenship. As I set out earlier, the Home Secretary will consider the evidence available to her on the relevant nationality laws of those countries and the person's circumstances; she will not be permitted to take deprivation action when she does not have reason to believe that the person has a right in law to become a national of that country. The nationality laws of other countries can be complex, and every case will be different. We do not propose to issue guidelines, but the independent reviewer will look at how the power is used in practice and Parliament will have his report and be able to debate it.

…

The noble Baroness, Lady Smith, asked whether it was about the ability to seek or to acquire. The whole point is that it is about the ability to acquire another nationality. She asked me to clarify when a person need only have the ability to seek another nationality rather than acquiring it. The terms of the clause are clear: the Home Secretary must reasonably believe that the person can, under the law of another country, gain the nationality of that country. The Secretary of State will make the decision based on the information that she has before her. We cannot have time limits, as the onus is on the individual to take the necessary action. As I said when I spoke earlier, these are dangerous individuals—and I am sure that the noble Baroness will understand the reason for us debating these issues today—who are likely to seek to create barriers to acquiring citizenship.

The noble Baroness also asked whether we should have consulted other countries about the introduction of the power. She suggested that we needed to do so, but we cannot prejudge which countries will be involved in future deprivation decisions. The circumstances of each case will be different, and it would be impossible to consult all countries on a theoretical question. We need to act in the interests of the national security of the United Kingdom, and what is important is that it is clear that we are acting within our international obligations and under the law. In the context of an individual case, we would not rule out consulting another country, but that must not be a requirement.

The noble Baroness, Lady Smith, and, indeed, my noble friend Lord Macdonald of River Glaven asked about comparisons with states which also have deprivation laws. We cannot compare a carefully considered decision about an individual who presents a real national security risk to the UK with provisions in states where there has been mass deprivation on the basis of ethnicity, for example. My noble friend Lord Macdonald and others also asked whether the UK would have to admit people who had been refused while they were abroad. Noble Lords have repeated the view of Professor Goodwin-Gill that other states would be entitled to return deprived individuals. I have said in previous debates that we do not agree with this. The UK has a very limited obligation to readmit people we have deprived and there is no general obligation in international law in this regard.[23]

12.66 The new provision might reasonably appear to breach the obligations of the UK under Article 8(3) CRS, because while this allowed a state to 'retain' the power to deprive an individual of nationality, the conception of 'retention' of a particular power, interpreted according to established principles, does not self-evidently coincide with 'regaining' or 'recreating' that power after it has been removed by the amendment of domestic law. Given that Article 8 CSR has not been incorporated into domestic law, this does not weaken the binding domestic law character of the new section 40(4A) BNA 1981, but the principles of CRS may in due course inform renewed domestic litigation in this complex area.

E4. Appeals

12.67 Under section 40(5) BNA 1981, the Secretary of State must give written notice to a person in relation to whom the making of an order under section 40 BNA 1981 is proposed, and that notice must state that the Secretary of State has decided to make an order, set out the reasons for the order and indicate the addressee's right of appeal under section 40A(1) BNA 1981 or section 2B Special Immigration Appeals Commission Act 1997. Under section 40A(1) BNA 1981, a person given notice may appeal to the First-Tier Tribunal. This provision is set aside by section 40A(2) BNA 1981 if the Secretary of State certifies that it was taken wholly or partly in reliance on information which in his or her opinion should not be made public in the interests of national security, or in the interests of the relationship between the UK and another country, or otherwise in the public interest. In that event, the right of appeal is to the SIAC under section 2B Special Immigration Appeals Commission Act 1997. Section 40A(3) BNA 1981, which applies to appeals to the Tribunal and the Commission, provides that some of the provisions of Part V NIAA 2002 which apply to appeals against immigration and asylum decisions shall apply to an appeal to the Tribunal against a deprivation decision, one of which, by virtue of section 2B 1997 Act, also applies to an appeal to the Commission: section 87 (which permits the Tribunal/Commission to give a direction for the purpose of giving effect to its decision).

12.68 There has been no successful appeal on the merits against any decision of the Secretary of State employing section 40(2) BNA 1981. This reflects the limited number of cases and of appeals, the difficulties of advancing appeals in a security context where the Secretary of State may rely upon evidence never disclosed to the appellant or his or her representatives, but perhaps also the sheer breadth of the 'conducive to the public good' test. Serious concerns have been raised concerning problems of recourse: to take one example, in February 2013, the ILPA complained to the Office of the UN High

---

[23] HL Hansard 12 May 2014, cols 1685–88.

Commissioner for Human Rights regarding the breadth of the 'conducive to the public good' test and the absence of procedural protections for persons left outside the UK by a deprivation of nationality.[24]

Section 57(2) IANA 2006 amended section 82(2) NIAA 2002 so as to provide a right of appeal against a decision to deprive an individual of right of abode by exercise of the section 2A IA 1971 power. It appears, however, that this appeal right will be lost when section 15(2) IA 2014 substitutes a new section 82 NIAA 2002 severely limiting appeal rights. From that point, the sole recourse in such a case would be judicial review. This outcome as regards deprivation of the right of abode cases produces a result inconsistent with the continuation of appeals in section 40(2) BNA 1981 cases, which are independent of the NIAA 2002 appeals provisions which appear to face radical amendment provisions at section 15 IA 2014. As of 1 October no date has been appointed for that change.

12.69

---

[24] ILPA, 14 February 2013, Arbitrary Deprivation of Nationality: Submission of the Immigration Law Practitioners' Association to the UN Office of the High Commissioner for Human Rights.

Part E
Procedure and Remedies

13

International Remedies

Contents

A. Introduction..13.1
B. UN Charter-Based Bodies...13.5
   B1. Universal Periodic Review 13.9
   B2. The Advisory Committee 13.14
   B3. Complaints Procedure 13.15
   B4. Special Procedures..13.20
C. UN Treaty-Based Bodies 13.33

A. Introduction

Remedies at an international level may become relevant to an act of expulsion or exclusion from the UK or to executive action concerning nationality. These may, depending upon the particular circumstances of the case, be accessed either separately or in parallel with domestic remedies. Raising a case or particular issue internationally may also contribute to improving policy and law concerned with the protection of rights associated with the subject matter of this work. In general, it might be observed that the greater the degree of effective reference to such bodies, the broader will be the scope for increased future effectiveness as protectors of relevant norms. 13.1

The modern international framework regulating human rights and public international law norms has developed markedly since its inception. Unlike the more conventional dynamic, where natural or legal persons seek an international remedy for wrongdoing by their *country of origin*, in expulsion and exclusion cases, the remedy is often sought against the actions or omissions of a *host state*, in this case the UK. 13.2

For the purposes of this chapter, the key bodies and institutions are those concerned with the promotion and protection of human rights under the auspices of the UN. This chapter should therefore be considered alongside chapters 2 and 3. Remedies available at a European level are subsequently dealt with in chapters 14 and 15. 13.3

In general terms, the UN human rights framework can be split into two categories: bodies and functions established through the UN Charter ('Charter-based' bodies) and those created directly through UN treaties ('treaty-based' bodies). Both categories can have a role to play in matters relating to expulsion, exclusion and nationality. Some remedies are, however, more suited than others to particular situations. For example, where removal directions have been set and time is limited, the most appropriate avenue is likely to be through the Special Procedures of the UN Charter-based bodies, where an urgent action can be made by a Special Rapporteur to the UK government. Cases that raise discrimination against women or concern persons with disabilities are likely to be suited to the treaty-based bodies, two of which deal with these precise issues and are 13.4

able to accept individual petitions, the UK having taken action to enable this in these two particular cases.

B. UN Charter-Based Bodies

13.5 The UN Charter established a court, the International Court of Justice (ICJ), concerned with legal disputes between Member States and legal questions generally. Legal disputes can only be brought by states, not individuals, while legal questions can be brought only by specific organs or specialised agencies of the UN. As such, the ICJ does not offer a direct remedy to those facing expulsion, exclusion or the deprivation of nationality.

13.6 In 1946, the UN created a body exclusively concerned with safeguarding and promoting fundamental human rights, the UN Commission on Human Rights (hereinafter the Commission). On 15 March 2006, it was replaced by the UN Human Rights Council (hereinafter the Council), which remains the key UN human rights body.[1] Its purpose and utility could not be clearer: 'All victims of human rights abuses should be able to look to the Human Rights Council as a forum and a springboard for action.'[2]

13.7 The Council seeks to strengthen the promotion and protection of human rights around the world, addressing situations of human rights violations and making recommendations on them.[3] A total of 47 states are members of the Council, each elected via the UN General Assembly.

13.8 The Council seeks to achieve its goals through three main forums:

(i) the Universal Periodic Review (UPR) mechanism;
(ii) the Advisory Committee; and
(iii) the Complaint Procedure.

B1. Universal Periodic Review

13.9 Under the UPR process, the Council is tasked with reviewing the human rights record and situation in every Member State of the UN. Specifically, it is required to:

> [U]ndertake a universal periodic review, based on objective and reliable information, of the fulfilment by each State of its human rights obligations and commitments in a manner which ensures universality of coverage and equal treatment with respect to all States.[4]

13.10 Member States are reviewed every four and a half years. Under the UPR process, they are subject to review by the UPR Working Group. The Working Group meets three times

---

[1] UN General Assembly Resolution A/RES/60/251 (15 March 2006).
[2] Ban Ki-Moon, UN Secretary General, 12 March 2007, Opening of 4th Human Rights Council Session, www.ohchr.org/en/hrbodies/hrc/pages/hrcindex.aspx.
[3] Office of the High Commissioner for Human Rights, www.ohchr.org/EN/HRBodies/HRC/Pages/HRCIndex.aspx. See further *Institution Building of the Human Rights Council*, UN Human Rights Council Resolution A/HRC/RES/5/1 (18 June 2007) for a summary of the Council's functions and procedures.
[4] Office of the High Commissioner for Human Rights: Basic Facts about the UPR. Available online: www.ohchr.org/en/hrbodies/upr/pages/BasicFacts.aspx.

a year and holds sessions, during which Member States' compliance with human rights obligations is considered. The review includes scrutiny of information provided by the state under review (often via a 'national report'); information from other UN bodies and mechanisms (for example, via the Special Procedures and human rights treaties monitoring bodies, as outlined below); and from other stakeholders, including national human rights institutions and NGOs. Dialogue between the Working Group, representatives of the Member State under review and other states occurs during the review, with questions asked and points clarified.

At the end of the review, the Working Group drafts a Report, which summarises proceedings and makes various recommendations, which the Member State under review is required to implement before the next review. Documentation arising from the process is available via the Council's website, including video coverage of the proceedings themselves and a diary outlining future sessions and countries subject to review.[5]   13.11

Issues relating to expulsion, exclusion and the deprivation of nationality all featured in the UK's second UPR in 2012. NGOs, including the Poppy Project, Amnesty International, Freedom from Torture, the Gatwick Detainees Welfare Group, the Equal Rights Trust, and Redress provided submissions to the Working Group. Topics covered included: 13.12

(i) the absence of a separate legal framework for the recognition and protection of victims of human trafficking;
(ii) failings within the National Referral Mechanism (NRM), which was previously used to identify VoTs;
(iii) the increase in the use of immigration detention and the flaws within that system;
(iv) the impact legal aid cuts had on the ability of asylum-seekers to secure representation or advice;
(v) the lack of a mechanism to identify stateless persons.[6]

Organs of the UN, such as the United Nations High Commissioner for Refugees (UNHCR), the CEDAW Committee and the Special Rapporteur on the Human Rights of Migrants, also expressed concern on various matters, not least the risk of arbitrary detention for stateless persons, de facto indefinite detention of migrants, and the importance of implementing Asylum Gender Guidelines. The Working Group's report concluded by listing a number of recommendations put forward to Member States, such as the need to protect children and families of migrants (Morocco); take measures to ensure trafficked people have access to support and services (Greece); publish conclusions of an inquiry into the death of an Angolan national whilst being deported (Angola); prevent indefinite detention of migrants (Chile); and abandon unreflective the use of diplomatic assurances   13.13

---

[5] Office of the High Commissioner for Human Rights, www.ohchr.org/EN/HRBodies/UPR/Pages/UPRMain.aspx.

[6] Summary Prepared by the Office of the High Commissioner for Human Rights in Accordance with Paragraph 5 of the Annex to Human Rights Council Resolution 16/21, United Kingdom of Great Britain and Northern Ireland, A/HRC/WG.6/13/GBR/3 (9 March 2012). Available at: www.refworld.org/docid/5007e80e2.html.

that individuals will not be mistreated or tortured if involuntarily transferred to another country (Nicaragua).[7]

B2. The Advisory Committee

13.14 The Human Rights Council Advisory Committee[8] acts as a 'think-tank', providing expert advice and research on thematic human rights issues.

B3. Complaints Procedure

13.15 Importantly, the Council has a complaints procedure, which is also provided for under UN Human Rights Council Resolution 5/1:

> The complaint procedure of the Human Rights Council addresses consistent patterns of gross and reliably attested violations of all human rights and fundamental freedoms occurring in any part of the world under any circumstances.[9]

'Patterns of gross ... violations' describes circumstances severe enough that they can 'no longer [be] regarded as falling exclusively within the domestic jurisdiction of States'.[10] A 'pattern' seems to require several victims, and a certain number of breaches, spread over a period of time.[11] Any individual, group or NGO can submit a complaint—referred to as a communication— where they claim to be victims of human rights violations or have direct, reliable knowledge of such violations. However, the need to show a pattern suggests that coordination with other practitioners facing similar issues is key in bringing a successful communication.

13.16 Communications are confidential in an attempt to enhance state cooperation and can be made irrespective of whether the state complained of has ratified the relevant human rights treaties.[12]

13.17 Whilst no complaint appears to have been made against the UK's approach to exclusion, expulsion or the withdrawal of nationality (at least none that have been made public), complaints have been made against countries from which people flee persecution or risk being sent back to, including Iraq, Iran and Eritrea.[13]

---

[7] Report of the Working Group on the Universal Periodic Review, United Kingdom of Great Britain and Northern Ireland A/HRC/21/9 (6 July 2012). Available at: www.refworld.org/docid/506d88d227.html.

[8] Established under UN Human Rights Council Resolution 5/1, adopted on 18 June 2007. Available at: www.ohchr.org/EN/HRBodies/HRC/AdvisoryCommittee/Pages/AboutAC.aspx.

[9] ibid.

[10] See discussion of the *travaux préparatoires* of the complaints procedure under the now defunct UN Commission on Human Rights, in OHCHR Complaint Procedure of the Human Rights Council, Frequently Asked Questions. Available at: www.ohchr.org/EN/HRBodies/HRC/ComplaintProcedure/Pages/HRCComplaintProcedureIndex.aspx.

[11] ibid.

[12] See: www.ohchr.org/en/HRBodies/HRC/ComplaintProcedure/Pages/HRCComplaintProcedureIndex.aspx.

[13] See: www.ohchr.org/Documents/HRBodies/HRCouncil/SituationsconsideredHRCJan2013.pdf.

Communications can be sent by post or email.[14] In order for a communication to be considered, it must first be deemed admissible. Specifically, it must: 13.18

(i) be in writing, in one of the six official UN languages;
(ii) include a description of the facts complained about, including the names of alleged victims, dates, events and locations, with as much detail as possible, but on no more than 15 pages;
(iii) not manifestly politically motivated;
(iv) not based exclusively on reports from the media;
(v) not already being considered by another UN or regional human rights body;
(vi) not use abusive or insulting language; and
(vii) domestic remedies must already have been exhausted, unless they would be ineffective or unreasonably long to secure.

An initial screening of the communication is undertaken by the Chairperson of the Working Group on Communications, along with the Secretariat. If the admissibility criteria appear to be met, the communication is provided to the state in question for a response. A further three stages are then followed. First, the Working Group as a whole considers the communication and determines whether the admissibility and 'consistent pattern' criteria are met. If they are, the second stage follows, where the communication is referred to the Working Group on Situations. This Working Group then decides whether to discontinue the communication, keep the situation under review or inform the Human Rights Council. Finally, during the forth stage, the Human Rights Council determines whether to keep the situation under review (either by seeking further information from the state or appointing an independent expert to monitor and report on the situation), discontinue the matter or recommend the Officer for the High Commissioner for Human Rights (OHCHR) to provide technical, capacity-building assistance, or advisory services to the state in question. 13.19

B4. Special Procedures

Special procedures—the provision of experts tasked with reporting and advising on thematic and country-specific human rights situations—are seen as a core component of the UN human rights machinery. They work individually as Special Rapporteurs or Independent Experts, or within a Working Group of five, drawn from each regional group of the UN. There are currently 14 country mandates and 37 thematic mandates. The remit of Special Procedures is broad: 13.20

> [They] undertake country visits; act on individual cases and concerns of a broader, structural nature by sending communications to States and others in which they bring alleged violations or abuses to their attention; conduct thematic studies and convene expert consultations,

---

[14] Addresses can be found on the website for the Office of the High Commissioner for Human Rights: www.ohchr.org/EN/HRBodies/HRC/ComplaintProcedure/Pages/HRCComplaintProcedureIndex.aspx.

contribute to the development of international human rights standards, engage in advocacy, raise public awareness, and provide advice for technical cooperation.[15]

13.21 The ability to act in individual cases is particularly relevant insofar as expulsion and exclusion cases are concerned. The thematic mandates provide for a Special Rapporteur on the Human Rights of Migrants and a Special Rapporteur on Torture and Other Cruel, Inhuman or Degrading Treatment or Punishment, both clearly having a potential interest in the subject matter of this book.

13.22 The Special Rapporteur on the Human Rights of Migrants was established in 1999.[16] The mandate has developed over the years since then into the following:

(i) examining limitations on the protection of human rights of migrants, in particular, women, children and those undocumented or in precarious circumstances;
(ii) requesting and receiving information concerning violations of migrants' human rights;
(iii) making recommendations as to preventing and remedying such violations;
(iv) promoting the application of relevant international norms and standards applying to migrants;
(v) considering the gender dimension to such situations, giving special consideration to multiple discrimination and violence against women;
(vi) giving emphasis to practical solutions that seek to implement the rights protected under the Special Rapporteur's mandate, including the identification of best practice;
(vii) reporting to the Council and the General Assembly.

13.23 The Special Rapporteur's objectives are realised through:

(i) addressing individual allegations of human rights violations, received through urgent appeals and communications;
(ii) conducting in-country visits;
(iii) attending and participating in conferences, seminars and panels; and
(iv) reporting annually to the Council and, when required, the General Assembly.

13.24 The first objective is particularly relevant. There are two avenues for addressing individual allegations: Letters of Allegation and Urgent Appeals. Like under the Council's complaints mechanism, communications can be sent to the Special Rapporteur in respect of individual cases and general situations. Communications must comply with conditions that broadly reflect the admissibility criteria under the Council's communications process, with one important difference: domestic remedies do not need to be exhausted before submitting a communication. Urgent Appeals concern:

> [C]ases where the alleged violations are time-sensitive in terms of [i]nvolving loss of life, life-threatening situations or either imminent or ongoing damage of a very grave nature to victims that cannot be addressed in a timely manner by letters of allegations.[17]

---

[15] OHCHR, Special Procedures of the Human Rights Council. Available at: www.ohchr.org/EN/HRBodies/SP/Pages/Introduction.aspx.
[16] UN Commission on Human Rights Resolution 1999/44 (1999). For further details, see the Special Rapporteur's website: www.ohchr.org/EN/Issues/Migration/SRMigrants/Pages/SRMigrantsIndex.aspx.
[17] See: www.ohchr.org/EN/Issues/Migration/SRMigrants/Pages/Communications.aspx.

13.25 The procedure for submitting a communication is far from onerous, simply requiring the completion of a questionnaire available on the Special Rapporteur's website.[18] The information required in the questionnaire includes details of the reported victim and the perpetrator, the incident complained about, the action or inaction of the national authorities and international bodies (if utilised), and the source of the information. Communications can be made in writing or via email.[19]

13.26 Upon receipt of a communication, the Special Rapporteur can enter into correspondence with the government in question, clarify the allegation(s) and work towards preventing or investigating the allegations. Communication can be taken forward by the Special Rapporteur acting alone or in conjunction with other Special Rapporteurs or Working Groups where their mandates overlap.

13.27 The Special Rapporteur on the Human Rights of Migrants conducted a country visit to the UK in June 2009. During the visit, he met with officials from various government departments, UNICEF and the UNHCR. He also met with migrants and visited Immigration Removal Centres at Dover and Gosport. Whilst welcoming various government practices in the sphere of immigration, he highlighted major challenges, not least indefinite periods of detention of asylum-seekers or those who could not be removed to third countries. Once such example pointed to was Ahmed Daq, a Somali national detained for over three years with no prospect of deportation.[20] The Special Rapporteur also expressed concern over exclusion and deprivation of nationality on 'national security' grounds. Depriving third country nationals married to British nationals of leave to remain, and the lowering of the threshold required to deprive someone of their British nationality—to where doing so is conducive to the public good—were two such examples.[21]

13.28 The Special Rapporteur has sent allegation letters and requests for urgent action to the UK government. For example, in 2007 the Special Rapporteur sent an allegation letter regarding changes to the Highly Skilled Migrant Programme (HSMP) and raising concerns for those who were already in the UK on that basis, but may fall short of the later, more stringent requirements. The UK government provided a detailed response to the allegation, highlighting the background to the amendments and the fact there would be transitional arrangements in place.[22] Also in 2007, the Special Rapporteur (in conjunction with the Special Rapporteur on Torture—see below) sent an urgent appeal to the UK government in respect of AMK, a Cameroonian national detained at Oakington Immigration Reception Centre. AMK asserted that he had been tortured in his home country and had claimed asylum on account of political persecution. His claim had been refused and his appeal rights were exhausted. The Special Rapporteurs raised concern for his physical and moral integrity if he were forcibly returned to Cameroon

---

[18] ibid.
[19] Addresses can be found on the website for the Special Rapporteur on the Human Rights of Migrants: www.ohchr.org/EN/Issues/Migration/SRMigrants/Pages/Communications.aspx.
[20] Report of Special Rapporteur on the Human Rights of Migrants, Jorge Bustamante, Mission to the United Kingdom of Great Britain and Northern Ireland, A/HRC/14/30/Add.3 (16 March 2010) 14. Available at: www.refworld.org/pdfid/4c0623e92.pdf.
[21] ibid 17.
[22] Human Rights Council, Report Submitted by the Special Rapporteur on the Human Rights of Migrants, Jorge G. Bustamante A/HRC/7/12/Add.1 (5 March 2008) 39–40. Available at: www.refworld.org/docid/47d647462.html.

(he was due to be removed the day after the urgent action). The UK government provided a detailed response, outlining the standard of proof required in asylum cases, the procedural history of AMK's case and the fact that the Foreign and Commonwealth Office follow the human rights situation around the world, pass information to the Home Office where there are allegations that returnees have been mistreated and, where appropriate, make discreet enquiries through NGOs or third parties.[23]

13.29   The mandate of the Special Rapporteur on torture and other cruel inhuman or degrading treatment or punishment largely reflects that of the Special Rapporteur on the Human Rights of Migrants. This includes a communication procedure. Urgent appeals include cases where an individual is to be deported imminently to a country where he or she is at risk of torture. Allegation letters appear to be more focused on less time-sensitive cases, where they show systemic patterns of torture.

13.30   Upon receipt, the Special Rapporteur will write to the Minister of Foreign Affairs of the country concerned, urging the government to ensure the individual's physical and mental integrity.[24]

13.31   Communications can be made in writing or via email, using a model questionnaire.[25]

13.32   The Special Rapporteur on Torture has yet to conduct a country visit to the UK; no request for such a visit is pending. He has, however, dealt with communications from individuals who assert they are at risk of ill-treatment through expulsion from the UK. For example, he recently issued an Urgent Action to the UK government in respect of three Sri Lankan nationals of Tamil ethnicity identified as X, Y, and Z, due to be involuntarily returned to their country of origin. Each asserted that he was at risk of torture. The UK government responded to the Urgent Action, confirming such cases were carefully considered and that a number of the individuals concerned had secured injunctions preventing their removal. The Special Rapporteur in return underlined the prohibition on extradition, expulsion or *refoulement* where doing so would expose an individual to the danger of torture or cruel, inhuman or degrading treatment/punishment, and stressed that the use of diplomatic assurances did not override the obligations of states under international human rights law or the principle of *non-refoulement*.[26]

C. UN Treaty-Based Bodies

13.33   The second avenue for remedies within the UN human rights framework rests with the treaty-based bodies, also referred to as treaty-monitoring bodies. These bodies are normally established and provided for within the treaty itself or an additional related treaty. Their role is to monitor the application of their respective treaties by each State Party to that treaty.

---

[23] ibid 41–43.
[24] See: www.ohchr.org/EN/Issues/Torture/SRTorture/Pages/Appeals.aspx.
[25] Addresses can be found on the website for the Special Rapporteur on Torture: www.ohchr.org/EN/Issues/Torture/SRTorture/Pages/Appeals.aspx.
[26] Report of the Special Rapporteur on torture and other cruel, inhuman or degrading treatment or punishment, Juan E Mendez, Observations on Communications Transmitted to Governments and Replies Received, A/HRC/22/53/Add.4 (12 March 2013).

International Remedies

For the purposes of this chapter, the treaty-monitoring bodies of relevance are: **13.34**

(i) the Human Rights Committee, the treaty-based body of the ICCPR;[27]
(ii) the Committee on Economic, Social and Cultural Rights, the treaty-based body of the International Covenant on Economic, Social and Cultural Rights;[28]
(iii) the Committee on the Elimination of Racial Discrimination, the treaty based body of the CERD;[29]
(iv) the Committee on the Elimination of Discrimination against Women, the treaty-based body of the CEDAW;[30]
(v) the Committee against Torture, the treaty-based body of the CAT;[31]
(vi) the Committee on the Rights of the Child, the treaty-based body of the CRC;[32] and
(vii) the Committee on the Rights of Persons with Disabilities, the treaty-based body of the CRPD.[33]

All of the above treaties—the core international human rights treaties—touch on rights that may be compromised or violated in cases of expulsion and exclusion. The UK is a State Party to each of these treaties and is bound under international law to protect the rights therein.   **13.35**

Each of the treaty bodies monitors compliance with its respective treaty provisions in a number of ways, including a periodic review process. The reporting procedure provides another opportunity for NGOs and professional bodies to highlight human rights concerns applying to those subject to expulsion or exclusion from the UK. One way to do this would be through liaising with others who intend on submitting reports to the respective bodies.   **13.36**

Matters concerning expulsion and exclusion often feature in the reporting process. For example, during the UK government's sixth periodic review under the ICCPR, consideration was given to the removal of suspected terrorists from the UK. The UN Human Rights Committee raised concern over the UK government's previous (but recent) position that suspected terrorists could be returned in certain circumstances without appropriate safeguards prohibiting ill-treatment. Whilst that position was rejected by the European Court of Human Rights in *Saadi v Italy* (Application No 37201/06),[34] the Committee also raised concerns over the use of diplomatic assurances, especially where the country in question was know to use torture systematically, where clear and transparent practices and judicial oversight were required prior to any such removal, and where removal was deemed appropriate, effective monitoring in the country   **13.37**

---

[27] 999 UNTS 171, 16 December 1966 (entered into force 23 March 1976).
[28] 993 UNTS 3, 16 December 1966 (entered into force 3 January 1976).
[29] 660 UNTS 195, 21 December 1965 (entered into force 4 January 1969).
[30] 2131 UNTS 83, 10 December 1999 (entered into force 22 December 2000).
[31] 1465 UNTS 85, 10 December 1984 (entered into force 26 June 1987).
[32] 1577 UNTS 3, 20 November 1989 (entered into force 2 September 1990).
[33] 2515 UNTS 3, 30 March 2007 (entered into force 3 May 2008).
[34] Intervening in an Italian case, the UK government in *Saadi* argued for a reappraisal of the approach taken in expulsion cases concerning suspected terrorists that raised Art 3 ECHR. First, the threat posed by the individual subject to exclusion should be weighed against the risk and nature of potential ill-treatment on return. Second, in such cases, the standard of proof required to prevent expulsion on Art 3 ECHR grounds should be increased and they would need to show that ill-treatment was 'more likely than not'. The European Court of Human Rights' Grand Chamber rejected both arguments.

Part E – Procedure and Remedies

of origin was important.³⁵ The UK government was required to address these issues directly, which it did in a subsequent report to the Human Rights Committee.³⁶

13.38   Seven of the treaty bodies above—the Human Rights Committee, the CERD, the Committee against Torture, the CEDAW, the CRPD and the Committee on Enforced Disappearances—are currently able to receive complaints by individuals in certain circumstances. In order for individuals to be able to access the complaints procedure, the state they seek to bring the complaint against must have recognised the treaty bodies' authority to consider individual complaints. Authority normally derives from a provision within the treaty concerned or the ratification of a supplementary treaty.

13.39   The complaints procedure for each of the treaty bodies varies and each body's own protocol and guidance should be considered before making a complaint. Generally speaking, the bodies' approaches reflect in a number of respects those provided for under the Council's procedure, as detailed above: they must be in writing in one of the UN languages; provide the victim's details (including authorisation) and all the facts surrounding the violation complained of; specify the treaty articles that are deemed to have been violated; the remedies sought; steps taken to exhaust domestic remedies; confirmation as to whether other international remedies have been utilised; and contain copies of documents relied upon. However, the Council's 'patterns of gross violations' test does not apply. No particular format need be used, although a number of the treaty bodies provide model-complaint forms on their websites.

13.40   Like the Council's procedure, treaty bodies considering individual complaints first determine whether the complaint is admissible, not least whether:

(i) the complainant has given authorisation and, if not, the reasons for not doing so (for example, if he or she is imprisoned);

(ii) the complainant is the alleged victim insofar as he or she is personally and directly affected;

(iii) the complaint corresponds with rights protected under the treaty body petitioned;

(iv) the treaty body is being invited to review facts and evidence already determined by a national court (treaty bodies consider violations of treaty provisions and do not act as appellate courts);

(v) the complaint has sufficient detail to be substantiated;

(vi) the complaint arises on or after the date the relevant treaty body acquired jurisdiction to consider complaints from the State Party in question;

(vii) the complaint has been subject to review from another international body, such as the European Court of Human Rights. If it has, the treaty body will not consider the communication further;

(viii) domestic remedies have been exhausted. Again, the treaty body will not consider a communication where there is a failure first to exhaust domestic remedies

---

³⁵ Concluding observations of the Human Rights Committee, United Kingdom of Great Britain and Northern Ireland, CCPR/C/GBR/CO/6 (30 July 2008) 3.

³⁶ See Information received from the United Kingdom of Great Britain and Northern Ireland on the Implementation of the Concluding Observations of the Human Rights Committee CCPR/C/GBR/CO/6/Add.1 (3 November 2009) 5–6.

International Remedies

unless such remedies have been unreasonably prolonged or would be ineffective. Complaints should be submitted as soon as possible after domestic remedies are exhausted; some treaty bodies specify timeframes by which complaints must be submitted;

(ix) the complaint is subject to a reservation by the state concerned, either in relation to the right deemed to have been violated or the remit of the treaty body concerned; and

(x) the complaint is frivolous or vexatious.

Once a complaint is deemed admissible, it is registered. Treaty bodies can determine admissibility and the substantive merits of a complaint separately or at the same time. **13.41**

A number of the treaty bodies provide for 'interim measures', actions aimed at preventing irreparable harm, which can be sought prior to the complaint being finally determined. **13.42**

Upon registration, the complaint is normally forwarded to the State Party in question, which usually has six months to respond to the allegations. The complainant then has an opportunity to respond to the state's observations. Finally, the treaty body makes a decision through a written determination, confirming whether there have been treaty violations as alleged and, if so, outlining recommendations for the State Party to follow. Recommendations are not legally binding as such, but nevertheless do represent an authoritative interpretation of the treaty in question. The decision is sent to both the complainant and the State Party. Where violations have been found, the state is invited to respond within 180 days, providing details of how the recommendations have been followed. Failure to do so can trigger further proceedings via the follow-up procedure. Dialogue between the treaty body and the State Party can follow, with the case remaining open until an appropriate outcome is secured. A copy is then uploaded onto the Office of the High Commissioner for Human Rights' website and becomes part of the treaty body jurisprudence. **13.43**

The UK has only opted into the complaints procedure for two of the seven treaties, namely the CEDAW and the CRPD. The UK's unwillingness to accede to other individual complaints mechanisms remains a bone of contention with a number of those bodies, including the Human Rights Committee, which has consistently recommended the UK's ratification of the Optional Protocol. The last recommendation arose during the UK's seventh periodic review by the Human Rights Committee in 2013. The following response was provided: **13.44**

> 192. The UK Government remains to be convinced of the added practical value to people in the United Kingdom of rights of individual petition to the United Nations. The United Nations committees that consider petitions are not courts, and they cannot award damages or produce a legal ruling on the meaning of the law, whereas the United Kingdom has strong and effective laws under which individuals may seek remedies in the courts or in tribunals if they feel that their rights have been breached. In 2004, the Government acceded to the Optional Protocol to the Convention on the Elimination of All Forms of Discrimination against Women (OP-CEDAW). One of the reasons for doing so was to enable consideration, on a more empirical basis, of the merits of the right of individual petition more generally. In 2009, the UK ratified the Optional Protocol to the United Nations Convention on the Rights of Persons with Disabilities. To date the UK's experience under both protocols has not provided sufficient empirical evidence to

decide either way on the value of other individual complaint mechanisms. We will need further evidence, over a longer period, to establish what the practical benefits are.[37]

13.45 Time will tell whether that further evidence will ever materialise. Accession to the Optional Protocol in particular would be beneficial to those subject to exclusion or expulsion, not least because of Articles 12 and 13 ICCPR.[38] See further chapter 3.

13.46 To date, only three complaints against the UK government have been scrutinised by the CEDAW and, even then, only on admissibility grounds. Interestingly, all three cases concern immigration-related matters.

13.47 The first case, *NSF v UK* (10/2005, 30 May 2007, CEDAW/C/38/D/10/2005), concerned a Pakistani asylum-seeker fearing domestic violence on return to Pakistan. Interim measures—the prevention of deportation pending the outcome of proceedings before the Committee—were requested by the complainant and sought by the Committee. In response to the UK government's contention that no provision of the Convention had been particularised by the complainant, the Committee confirmed that discrimination against women included gender-based violence. Nonetheless, because no specific allegation of sex discrimination had been dealt with at the domestic level, the Committee concluded that domestic remedies had not been exhausted, making the complaint inadmissible.

13.48 The second case, *Constance Ragan Salgado v UK* (11/2006, 22 January 2007, CEDAW/C/37/D/11/2006), raised questions of discrimination and nationality. The complainant was a British national unable to pass that nationality on to her eldest son by descent; he has been born in Colombia and his father was a Colombian national. The British Nationality Act 1948 only provided for British nationality by descent from a father, not a mother. The complainant alleged that clear discrimination was only partially remedied by subsequent legislation, through the British Nationality Acts of 1981 and 2002, and in any event her son was unable to register as British national because of his age. The Committee concluded that the discrimination complained of finished in 1979, with the establishment of government policy allowing British women to register their minor children as British citizens. That policy pre-dated the establishment of the Optional Protocol, which in turn established the Committee, and therefore the complaint was inadmissible *ratione temporis*.

13.49 In *JS v UK* (38/2012, 27 November 2012, CEDAW/C/53/D/38/2012), the complainant, an Indian national, also complained of discrimination in the acquisition of British nationality because this had not been passed to him because of his mother's gender. The

---

[37] Human Rights Committee, Consideration of Reports Submitted by States Parties under Article 40 of the Convention, Seventh Periodic Report, United Kingdom (29 December 2012), CCPR/C/GBR/7. Available at: http://tbinternet.ohchr.org/_layouts/TreatyBodyExternal/Countries.aspx.
[38] Article 12 ICCPR reads: '1. Everyone lawfully within the territory of a State shall, within that territory, have the right to liberty of movement and freedom to choose his residence. 2. Everyone shall be free to leave any country, including his own. 3. The above-mentioned rights shall not be subject to any restrictions except those which are provided by law, are necessary to protect national security, public order (ordre public), public health or morals or the rights and freedoms of others, and are consistent with the other rights recognized in the present Covenant. 4. No one shall be arbitrarily deprived of the right to enter his own country.' Article 13 ICCPR reads: 'An alien lawfully in the territory of a State Party to the present Covenant may be expelled therefrom only in pursuance of a decision reached in accordance with law and shall, except where compelling reasons of national security otherwise require, be allowed to submit the reasons against his expulsion and to have his case reviewed by, and be represented for the purpose before, the competent authority or a person or persons especially designated by the competent authority.'

complainant had made an application for citizenship with the Home Office in 2010 and had not exhausted domestic remedies against the refusal of that application on account of his limited financial means. Concluding that the pursuit of domestic remedies had been possible and that such remedies would not be unreasonably prolonged or unlikely to bring about effective relief, the Committee found the complaint inadmissible.

13.50 To date, only one communication involving the UK government has been considered by the CRPD (*Kenneth McAlpine v UK* (6/2011, 13 November 2012, CRPD/C/8/D/6/2011)). This was not relevant to any immigration or nationality matter, concerning disability discrimination within the workplace.

14

Remedies under EU Law

Contents

A. Introduction 14.1
B. General Principles of EU Law and EU Fundamental Rights
   Affecting Remedies 14.7
   B1. Equivalence and Effectiveness 14.8
   B2. Effective Judicial Protection and Fundamental Rights 14.12
C. Remedies Provided by EU Secondary Legislation 14.15
D. State Liability in Damages for Breach of EU Law 14.28
E. Preliminary References 14.36
   E1. Discretionary References 14.42
   E2. Mandatory References 14.44
   E3. Making a Reference 14.46

A. Introduction

Individuals whose cases fall within the scope of EU law[1] may seek to avail themselves of appropriate remedies. Given that decisions on expulsion and exclusion and the denial or deprivation of nationality are made by the authorities of the member states themselves, individuals do not have standing before the EU courts in the subject area of this work.[2] However, if a violation of rights protected by EU law is caused by domestic legislative, administrative or judicial action, a complainant may seek a remedy before the national courts. This may be a remedy prescribed by EU law or otherwise regulated by general remedial principles of EU law. Accordingly, the focus of this chapter is on EU remedies before domestic courts for violations of EU rights by UK legislative, administrative, and—in certain limited circumstances—judicial actions or omissions.   **14.1**

The EU Treaties contain no express provisions dealing with remedies and EU law does not generally stipulate the remedies that a national court should provide for its breach. Thus, in general terms—and with particular exceptions set out in EU secondary legislation[3]—remedies and procedural rules are a matter for domestic law. However, there is a tension between the principle of 'national procedural autonomy' and the effective enforcement of EU substantive rights. Thus, within its scope, EU law has developed an overall supervisory framework by requiring national laws to provide a system of domestic remedies to guarantee the effectiveness of substantive EU rights. In addition,   **14.2**

---

[1] For a detailed account of the meaning of the 'scope of EU law', see ch 6.
[2] The EU courts (the CJEU and the General Court) have jurisdiction to judicially review the legality of acts of the EU institutions. There are strict standing requirements for individuals: Art 263 TFEU.
[3] See section C below.

14.3 EU law has developed its own free-standing remedy, namely, the right to damages against a Member State for particularly serious breaches of EU law.

14.3 The central principles of EU law that affect domestic remedies are those of equivalence and effectiveness. Equivalence is essentially a requirement of non-discrimination that seeks to ensure that EU rights are not treated less favourably than comparable rights in domestic law. Effectiveness requires national authorities (including courts and tribunals) to ensure the proper protection of EU rights by providing for appropriate remedies. These are 'general principles' of EU law[4] and are outlined in more detail below. National remedies may also be affected by other general principles of EU law such as, in particular, proportionality. Further, since the entry into force of the Treaty of Lisbon on 1 December 2009, the CFREU is now binding within the scope of EU law and may separately affect national remedies.[5]

14.4 Further, whilst not strictly a remedy under EU law, the preliminary reference procedure enables a dialogue between the national courts and the CJEU in which the national courts can refer questions on the interpretation and/or validity of EU law for an answer by the CJEU.

14.5 As is always the case with EU law, these principles apply only if a case falls within the scope of EU law. The scope of EU law is examined elsewhere in this work.[6]

14.6 The chapter considers first the general principles of EU law that affect the provision of remedies in domestic law for the violation of EU rights, then those instances in which remedies are provided by EU law, and closes with an examination of the preliminary reference procedure.

B. General Principles of EU Law and EU Fundamental Rights Affecting Remedies

14.7 As noted above, the principles described below apply to national procedures and remedies which are within the scope of EU law. Of most relevance to remedies are the twin principles of effectiveness and equivalence and fundamental rights, including the right to an effective remedy or effective judicial protection. These are analysed below in turn.

B1. Equivalence and Effectiveness

14.8 The general principle of equivalence requires, in the context of remedies, that domestic remedies available for breaches of EU rights should not be less favourable than those for comparable national rights: Case 326/96 *Levez v TJ Jennings (Harlow Pools) Ltd* [1998] ECR I-7835, [1999] 2 CMLR 363 [39]. In *Levez*, the CJEU held that determining whether the general principle of equivalence was breached was a question for the

---
[4] See further ch 6.
[5] See ch 6 for a discussion of the CFREU.
[6] See ch 6.

national courts and the burden of proving a breach of the principle of equivalence was on the party who sought to benefit from the application of the principle.

In order to successfully invoke the principle, there must be a comparator remedy in national law. In the absence of a proper comparator, there can be no infringement of the principle. Rights are considered comparable where there are similar objectives and similar essential characteristics (see, eg, Case C-261/95 *Palmisani v INPS* [1997] ECR I-4025 [38]; Case C-78/98 *Preston* [2000] ECR I-3201 [63]; and *Matra Communication SAS v Home Office* [1999] EWCA Civ 860, [1999] 1 WLR 1646, at 1658.

14.9

The question of equivalence in the remedial context was considered by the Supreme Court in *FA (Iraq) v SSHD* [2011] UKSC 22, [2011] 3 CMLR 23. The appellant, a national of Iraq, had claimed asylum and humanitarian protection, and the Secretary of State had refused both his applications. The appellant then argued that as a matter of the general principle of equivalence, he was entitled to an appeal against the refusal of the humanitarian protection claim since, given that an asylum claim attracted a right of appeal, the entirely EU-based claim for humanitarian protection was subjected to less favourable treatment. The Secretary of State argued that the asylum claim was not a proper comparator since it too was in part based on EU law. The Court of Appeal found that the asylum and humanitarian protection claims were comparable, and that the absence of an appeal right in the latter case constituted less favourable treatment. On the Secretary of State's appeal, the Supreme Court made a reference to the CJEU under Article 267 TFEU.[7] The Court asked whether for the purposes of equivalence under EU law, the comparator must be purely domestic (or whether, as in the case of the asylum right, it could be a mixture of EU and domestic rights). In the event, the Secretary of State settled the claim and the reference was withdrawn.

14.10

The general principle of effectiveness requires the full and effective protection of substantive EU rights. In the context of remedies, this demands national law to provide for appropriate remedies for the violation of EU rights. In practical terms, this may mean, for example, the provision of effective judicial review, compensation or interim relief. It precludes national laws which render the exercise of EU rights impossible or excessively difficult (see, eg, Case 33/76 *Rewe-Zentralfinanz eG and Rewe- Zentral AG v Landwirtschaftskammer für das Saarland* [1976] ECR 1989).

14.11

B2. Effective Judicial Protection and Fundamental Rights

The Treaty of Lisbon inserted Article 19(1) into the TEU. It provides for a specific obligation on Member States to provide adequate remedies to ensure effective judicial protection:

14.12

> Member States shall provide remedies sufficient to ensure effective legal protection in the fields covered by Union law

The obligation to ensure effective judicial protection is further reinforced by Article 47(1) CFREU, which provides that: 'Everyone whose rights and freedoms guaranteed by laws of the Union are violated has the right to an effective remedy before a tribunal.'

14.13

---

[7] See section E below for an examination of the preliminary reference procedure.

Part E – Procedure and Remedies

14.14 The broad wording of Articles 19 TEU and 47 CFREU may indicate a shift towards greater scrutiny of national procedural rules and remedies. The CJEU has applied Article 47 CFREU to domestic remedies in certain circumstances: see, eg, Case C-439/08 *VEBIC* [2011] 4 CMLR 12 and Case C-279/09 *DEB* [2011] CMLR 21. In terms of the subject matter of this work, for (at least) two reasons, reliance on EU due process rights is more favourable than equivalent rights under the ECHR and the HRA 1998. First, the exclusion of the rights protected by Article 6 ECHR from immigration and asylum claims does not apply to Article 47 CFREU (which is expressed as applying to 'everyone') and, second, EU law requires more potent remedial action for its violation than does the ECHR. The violation of a right protected by the HRA 1998 will lead, at best, to the domestic courts issuing a declaration of incompatibility, an essentially discretionary remedy, whereas the violation of EU rights requires that conflicting national provisions be disapplied.

C. Remedies Provided by EU Secondary Legislation

14.15 Despite the general principle noted above that EU law does not provide specific remedies, in certain cases touching upon the subject area of this work, EU secondary legislation provides for specific remedial action to be implemented by Member States. Of relevance to the subject matter of this work, in particular, Directive 2004/38/EC (the Citizens' Directive),[8] Directive 2005/85/EC (the Asylum Procedures Directive)[9] and the Dublin III Regulation[10] contain specific remedial provisions. They are examined below in turn.

14.16 Article 30 Citizens' Directive obliges the citizen to be notified in writing of any decision taken under Article 27(1) and be 'informed, precisely and in full, of the public policy, public security or public health grounds on which the decision taken in their case is based, unless this is contrary to the interests of State security' as well as their rights of appeal and a period by which they are required to leave the EU, save for 'duly substantiated cases of urgency'.

14.17 Article 31 Citizens' Directive provides for a right of appeal on substantive and procedural grounds against a decision to expel or exclude the citizen on the grounds of public policy, public security or public health:

1. The persons concerned shall have access to judicial and, where appropriate, administrative redress procedures in the host Member State to appeal against or seek review of any decision taken against them on the grounds of public policy, public security or public health.
2. Where the application for appeal against or judicial review of the expulsion decision is accompanied by an application for an interim order to suspend enforcement of that decision,

---

[8] Directive 2004/38 of the European Parliament and of the Council of 29 April 2004 on the right of citizens of the Union and their family members to move and reside freely within the territory of the Member States amending Regulation (EEC) No 1612/68 and repealing Directives 64/221/EEC, 68/360/EEC, 72/194/EEC, 73/148/EEC, 75/34/EEC, 75/35/EEC, 90/364/EEC, 90/365/EEC and 93/96/EEC [2004] OJ L229/35.

[9] Council Directive 2005/85/EC of 1 December 2005 on minimum standards of procedures in Member States for granting and withdrawing refugee status [2005] OJ L326/13.

[10] Regulation 604/2013.

actual removal from the territory may not take place until such time as the decision on the interim order has been taken, except:
— where the expulsion decision is based on a previous judicial decision; or
— where the persons concerned have had previous access to judicial review; or
— where the expulsion decision is based on imperative grounds of public security under Article 28(3).

3. The redress procedures shall allow for an examination of the legality of the decision, as well as of the facts and circumstances on which the proposed measure is based. They shall ensure that the decision is not disproportionate, particularly in view of the requirements laid down in Article 28.

4. Member States may exclude the individual concerned from their territory pending the redress procedure, but they may not prevent the individual from submitting his/her defence in person, except when his/her appearance may cause serious troubles to public policy or public security or when the appeal or judicial review concerns a denial of entry to the territory.

Thus, Article 31 stipulates the procedural safeguards for judicial and administrative redress which must allow for the determination of interim measures preventing expulsion and 'allow for an examination of the legality of the decision, as well as of the facts and circumstances on which the proposed measure is based': Article 31(3) Citizens' Directive. The requirement for a full merits review would therefore appear to exclude judicial review from satisfying the remedial requirements of the Citizens' Directive. Member States may 'exclude the individual concerned from their territory pending the redress procedure, but they may not prevent the individual from submitting his/her defence in person, except when his/her appearance may cause serious troubles to public policy or public security or when the appeal or judicial review concerns a denial of entry to the territory': Article 31(4). 14.18

In the case of exclusion orders, there must be an opportunity to apply to re-enter within a reasonable time and no later than three years from enforcement by arguing a material change in circumstances, but during the determination of the application which must be decided within six months, there is no right of re-entry: Article 32 Citizens' Directive. 14.19

Article 35 permits the Member States to 'adopt the necessary measures to refuse, terminate or withdraw any right conferred by this Directive in the case of abuse of rights or fraud, such as marriages of convenience', which must be proportionate and subject to the procedural safeguards provided for in Articles 30 and 31. 14.20

In Case C-300/11 *ZZ (France) v SSHD* (judgment of 4 June 2013), the CJEU examined the effect of Article 30(2) Citizens' Directive. Article 30(2) permits Member States to limit disclosure in national security cases. In *ZZ*, the Home Office limited the disclosure of the grounds upon which an decision taken under Article 27 Citizens' Directive (refusal of entry) was taken. In the original proceedings, the decision of the SIAC noted that 'little of the case against ZZ' had been disclosed to him and that those elements 'did not really engage with the critical issues', but was satisfied that non-disclosure was necessary in the interests of national security. The Court of Appeal referred the question as to whether and to what extent Articles 30(2) and 31 Citizens' Directive read in the light of Article 47 CFREU, which guaranteed the right to an effective remedy before a national authority and the right to a fair trial, permitted the essence of the public security grounds which constituted the basis of a decision refusing an EU citizen entry 14.21

not to be disclosed precisely and in full. The CJEU ruled that as a derogation from the general principle of notification in Article 30 Citizens' Directive, non-disclosure must be interpreted strictly and so as to respect the essence of the fundamental right enshrined in Article 47 CFREU. Further, the restriction on disclosure must be subject to the principle of proportionality, so the limitation must be necessary and genuinely meet the objectives of general interest. Thus, the CJEU concluded that the national court was required to:

> [E]nsure that failure by the competent national authority to disclose to the person concerned, precisely and in full, the grounds on which a decision taken under article 27 [Citizens'] Directive is based and to disclose the related evidence to him is limited to that which is strictly necessary, and that he is informed, in any event, of the essence of those grounds in a manner which takes due account of the necessary confidentiality of the evidence.

14.22 The judgment is clear that the national authority must determine that state security would in fact be compromised by precise and full disclosure of reasons, but there is 'no presumption that the reasons invoked by a national authority exist and are valid' (*ZZ* at [61]). It is further clear that the essence or 'gist' as it has become known domestically of the case against the EU citizen must be disclosed. Thus, 'the necessary protection of state security cannot have the effect of denying the person concerned his right to be heard and, therefore, of rendering his right of redress as provided for in article 31 of that Directive ineffective' (*ZZ* at [63]).

14.23 When the matter was examined by the Court of Appeal (*ZZ v SSHD* [2014] EWCA Civ 7), it was remitted to the SIAC, the impact of CJEU judgment having been interpreted as limited in effect to disclosure of the essence of the basis of the decision. Richards LJ noted that ZZ would be assisted on appeal to the SIAC by the more recent judgment of the General Court in Joined Cases C-584/10 P, C-593/10 and C-595/10 P *European Commission v UK (Kadi (No 2))* at [141], in which the General Court endorsed Mr Kadi's argument that the allegation that he had been the owner in Albania of several firms which funnelled money to extremists or employed those extremists in positions where they controlled the funds of those firms 'is insufficiently detailed and specific given that it contains no indication of the identity of the firms concerned, of when the alleged conduct took place and of the identity of the "extremists" who allegedly benefited from that conduct'.

14.24 Given that these remedial provisions are contained in directives, the form and method of their implementation are left to the Member States (see Article 288 TFEU). Their domestic implementation is considered in chapter 16.

14.25 In the asylum context, the Procedures Directive (Directive 2005/85/EC)[11] provides under Article 39 that asylum applicants shall have an effective remedy before a court or tribunal in relation to decisions on their asylum application (Article 39(1)). It does not require the remedy to be suspensive of removal (Article 39(3)(a). Article 23 Procedures Directive provides for the procedures applicable to the examination of asylum claims. In Case C175/11 *HID, BA v Refugee Applications Commissioner, Refugee Appeals Tribunal, Minister for Justice, Equality and Law Reform, Ireland* (31 January 2013), the

---

[11] Council Directive 2005/85/EC of 1 December 2005 on minimum standards on procedures in Member States for granting and withdrawing refugee status [2005] OJ L326/13. The UK has not opted into the recast Procedures Directive (2013/32/EU) and accordingly Directive 2005/85/EC continues to apply.

CJEU ruled that the requirements of Article 23 of Directive 2005/85 apply to prioritised procedures for determining a claim for international protection, such that individuals 'must enjoy a sufficient period of time within which to gather and present the necessary material in support of their application, thus allowing the determining authority to carry out a fair and comprehensive examination of those applications and to ensure that the applicants are not exposed to any dangers in their country of origin' (at [75]). This is of particular relevance in the context of the detained fast track in the UK.

The Dublin regime provides for redress against a transfer decision taken by a host Member State. Article 27 (remedies) Dublin III Regulation reads: 14.26

1. The applicant … shall have the right to an effective remedy, in the form of an appeal or a review, in fact and in law, against a transfer decision, before a court or tribunal.
2. Member States shall provide for a reasonable period of time within which the person concerned may exercise his or her right to an effective remedy pursuant to paragraph 1.
3. For the purposes of appeals against, or reviews of, transfer decisions, Member States shall provide in their national law that:
   (a) the appeal or review confers upon the person concerned the right to remain in the Member State concerned pending the outcome of the appeal or review; or
   (b) the transfer is automatically suspended and such suspension lapses after a certain reasonable period of time, during which a court or a tribunal, after a close and rigorous scrutiny, shall have taken a decision whether to grant suspensive effect to an appeal or review; or
   (c) the person concerned has the opportunity to request within a reasonable period of time a court or tribunal to suspend the implementation of the transfer decision pending the outcome of his or her appeal or review. Member States shall ensure that an effective remedy is in place by suspending the transfer until the decision on the first suspension request is taken. Any decision on whether to suspend the implementation of the transfer decision shall be taken within a reasonable period of time, while permitting a close and rigorous scrutiny of the suspension request. A decision not to suspend the implementation of the transfer decision shall state the reasons on which it is based.
4. Member States may provide that the competent authorities may decide, acting ex officio, to suspend the implementation of the transfer decision pending the outcome of the appeal or review.
5. Member States shall ensure that the person concerned has access to legal assistance and, where necessary, to linguistic assistance.
6. Member States shall ensure that legal assistance is granted on request free of charge where the person concerned cannot afford the costs involved. Member States may provide that, as regards fees and other costs, the treatment of applicants shall not be more favourable than the treatment generally accorded to their nationals in matters pertaining to legal assistance.

Without arbitrarily restricting access to legal assistance, Member States may provide that free legal assistance and representation not be granted where the appeal or review is considered by the competent authority or a court or tribunal to have no tangible prospect of success.

Where a decision not to grant free legal assistance and representation pursuant to this paragraph is taken by an authority other than a court or tribunal, Member States shall provide the right to an effective remedy before a court or tribunal to challenge that decision.

In complying with the requirements set out in this paragraph, Member States shall ensure that legal assistance and representation is not arbitrarily restricted and that the applicant's effective access to justice is not hindered.

Legal assistance shall include at least the preparation of the required procedural documents and representation before a court or tribunal and may be restricted to legal advisors or counsellors specifically designated by national law to provide assistance and representation.

Procedures for access to legal assistance shall be laid down in national law.

14.27 Thus, the Dublin III Regulation requires Member States to provide a full merits review of a transfer decision that is suspensive of removal. This means that the situation whereby procedural challenges are excluded from review under the Dublin II regime (see, eg, Case C-394/12 *Abdullahi v Bundesasylamt*, 10 December 2013) cannot be applicable to transfer decisions since 1 January 2014 and are susceptible to a full merits challenge. As there appears to be no specific implementation of Dublin III in the UK, the challenges can still be brought by way of judicial review; however, this is subject to the proviso that such a review would be compliant with Article 27 and includes a review of facts.

D. State Liability in Damages for Breach of EU Law

14.28 In addition to the specific remedial provisions contained in EU secondary legislation, the CJEU has developed a general EU remedy for compensation for its breach. In the seminal Joined Cases C-9/90 *Francovich and Bonifaci v Italy* [1991] ECR I-5357, the CJEU first outlined the basis on which Member States may be liable in damages for violations of EU law. The Court derived the principle from the duty of sincere cooperation contained in Article 4(3) TEU and the general principle of effectiveness. The scope of the principle was developed in the later case of *Brasserie du Pêcheur and Factortame*: Joined Cases C-46 and C-48/93 *Brasserie du Pêcheur SA v Germany, R v Secretary of State for Transport ex p Factortame Ltd* [1996] ECR I-1029. See also Joined Cases C-178–79, C-188–90/94 *Dillenkofer v Germany* [1996] ECR I-4845. Interpretation of the principle of reparation in this context may include an obligation to 'nullify' the unlawful consequences of a breach of EU law which is not limited to an award of damages: Case C-201/02 *R (otao) Delena Wells v Secretary of State for Transport, Local Government and the Regions* [2004] ECR 1-723 [64] and [68]. In practice this means that the full range of orders available in domestic law may be remedies for breaches of EU law.

14.29 In circumstances in which Member States have a discretion over how to act,[12] the CJEU has specified the following conditions necessary to found state liability in damages: (1) the rule of law infringed must have been intended to confer rights on individuals; (2) the breach of such rule must have been 'sufficiently serious'; and (3) there must have been a 'direct causal link' between the breach and the damage sustained: [1996] ECR I-1029 [48]–[51].

14.30 Rights that are directly effective are likely to satisfy the first condition, but rights that are not directly effective may also suffice (as in *Francovich* itself). In each case there must

---

[12] Where there is no discretion and where, for example, a Member State has failed to transpose a directive, it appears that the requirement that the breach be sufficiently serious is met automatically: see, eg, Cases C-258–59/90 *Pasquerias De Bermeo SA and Naviera Laida SA v Commission* [1992] ECR I-2901; and Case C-5/94 *Hedley Lomas* [1996] ECR I-2553.

be an intention to confer rights even if the relevant EU legislation is not sufficiently clear/unconditional to be self-executing.[13]

14.31 The House of Lords in *R v Secretary of State for Transport ex p Factortame (No 5)* [1999] UKHL 44, [2000] 1 AC 524 at 554 provided important guidance on the meaning of the second requirement, namely that the breach be sufficiently serious. Whilst finding that no factor is necessarily decisive, Lord Clyde set out eight factors of relevance:

i. the importance of the EU right or principle that has been breached;
ii. the clarity and precision of the rule breached;
iii the degree of excusability of an error of law;
iv. the existence of any relevant judgment on the point;
v. whether the infringer was acting deliberately or involuntarily in breaching EU law;
vi. the behaviour of the infringer after it has become evident that an infringement has occurred;
vii. the identity of the persons affected by the breach;
viii. the position (if any) taken by any of the EU institutions in the matter.

14.32 The third condition for *Francovich* liability is a causation requirement similar to that applicable in the English law of tort.

14.33 In Case C-224/01 *Kobler* [2004] QB 848, the CJEU found for the first time that the failure of a national court to apply EU law correctly could render a Member State liable for damages under the *Francovich* principle. However, the Court held that Member State liability for damages for judicial error would be exceptional and limited to cases 'where the court has manifestly infringed the applicable law' (at [53]). Damages on the *Francovich/Kobler* principle were sought in *Cooper v Attorney General* [2010] EWCA Civ 464, [2011] QB 976. The claim was based on the failure of domestic courts to remedy decisions infringing an EU directive, including the failure to make a reference. Although at first instance and on appeal to the Court of Appeal, it was found that there had been judicial errors—including the failure to make a reference—these errors were not sufficiently serious to give rise to state liability in damages. It was held that in declining to make a reference, the court in question had given a considered judgment. The fact that it was ultimately incorrect did not constitute a manifest breach of EU law.

14.34 In relation to the procedure for commencing claims in respect of EU damages, state liability for damages for a breach of EU law is generally understood as a breach of statutory duty.[14] Accordingly, the limitation principles applicable to the law of tort apply so that there is a limitation period of six years 'from the date on which the cause of action accrued'.[15]

14.35 *Francovich* damages may in theory be sought in relation to decisions within the subject matter of this work. However, as seen above, the circumstances in which a breach

---

[13] However, the question of whether the provisions are intended to confer rights on individuals is not always clear and, since there is no comprehensive guidance from the CJEU, the question is likely to be answered on a case-by-case basis.

[14] See Hobhouse LJ in the Divisional Court in *Factortame (No 5)* [1998] 1 CMLR 1353. The case was appealed unsuccessfully to the Court of Appeal and the House of Lords, but the basis of state liability in domestic law was not addressed. This does not exclude, however, a claim being brought by judicial review.

[15] Limitation Act 1980, s 2.

Part E – Procedure and Remedies

will be sufficiently serious to found an EU law damages claim will be limited. In practice, the domestic courts have been reluctant to make a finding that there had been a serious breach of EU law—see, eg, *R (otao Negassi* and *another) v SSHD* [2013] EWCA Civ 151, [2013] 2 CMLR 45; *AB and another v Home Office* [2012] EWHC 226, [2012] 4 All ER 276.

E. Preliminary References

14.36   As noted above, the preliminary reference procedure is not strictly an EU remedy. However, it is relevant to practitioners within the subject matter of this work who may seek to obtain clarification from the CJEU on a point of EU law in the context of domestic remedies. Indeed, preliminary rulings delivered by the CJEU, which are directly effective, often constitute an important source of rights for individuals before the domestic courts and administrative authorities.

14.37   The legal basis for the preliminary reference procedure is set out in Article 267 TFEU and Article 19 TEU. Article 267 TFEU provides as follows:

> The Court of Justice of the European Union shall have jurisdiction to give preliminary rulings concerning:
> (a) the interpretation of the Treaties;
> (b) the validity and interpretation of acts of the institutions, bodies, offices or agencies of the Union.
>
> Where such a question is raised before any court or tribunal of a Member State,[16] that court or tribunal may, if it considers that a decision on the question is necessary to enable it to give judgment, request the Court to give a ruling thereon.
>
> Where any such question is raised in a case pending before a court or tribunal of a Member State against whose decisions there is no judicial remedy under national law, that court or tribunal shall bring the matter before the Court of Justice.
>
> If such a question is raised in a case pending before a court or tribunal of a Member State with regard to a person in custody, the Court of Justice of the European Union shall act with the minimum of delay.[17]

14.38   Article 19 TEU provides as follows:

> 1. The Court of Justice of the European Union shall include the Court of Justice, the General Court and specialised courts. It shall ensure that the interpretation and application of the Treaties the law is observed.
>
> …

---

[16] The expression 'court or tribunal' is widely construed: see Case C-54/96 *Dorsch Consult* [1997] ECR I-4961.

[17] Article 267(4) TFEU was added by the Treaty of Lisbon. Articles 105 and 107 Rules of Procedure of the Court of Justice provide for expedited and urgent procedures, respectively. See further 'Recommendations to national courts and tribunals in relation to the initiation of preliminary ruling proceedings', 6 November 2012, 2012/C 338/01, paras 37–40. These procedures may be of relevance to practitioners whose clients face expulsion.

3. The Court of Justice of the European Union shall, in accordance with the Treaties: ... (b) give preliminary rulings, at the request of courts or tribunals of the Member States, on the interpretation of Union law or the validity of acts adopted by the institutions.

14.39 Thus, pursuant to Article 267 TFEU and Article 19(3)(b) TEU, the national courts may refer relevant questions of law for determination by the CJEU. Following changes brought about by the Treaty of Lisbon, all national courts and tribunals, not just those of last instance,[18] may now refer questions relating to asylum and immigration.

14.40 As seen in the text of Article 267 TFEU, the national courts generally have a discretion over whether to refer a question; however, national courts of last instance have a duty to refer where a decision on the question of law is necessary to enable that court to give judgment.

14.41 The jurisdiction of the CJEU under Article 267 TFEU is limited to: (1) interpretation of the EU Treaties; and (2) interpretation and validity of acts of the EU institutions, bodies, offices or agencies. Generally, there is a division of responsibility between the CJEU, which should determine the legal questions asked within the frame of reference set out in Article 267, and the national court, which should adjudicate on the facts and apply the CJEU's decision on the interpretation and/or validity of EU law to those facts.[19] The CJEU may not determine the validity of national law.

E1. Discretionary References

14.42 As seen above, Article 267 TFEU does not require national courts of first instance to make a reference, since there is judicial remedy from decisions of first instance courts in seeking of permission to appeal.

14.43 The guidance provided in the 2012 'Recommendations to national courts and tribunals in relation to the initiation of preliminary ruling procedures' provides the following:

> [A] national court or tribunal may, in particular where it considers that sufficient guidance is given by the case-law of the Court of Justice, itself decide on the correct interpretation of European Union law and its application to the factual situation before it. However, a reference for a preliminary ruling may prove particularly useful when there is a new question of interpretation of general interest for the uniform application of European Union law, or where existing case-law does not appear to be applicable to a new set of facts.[20]

E2. Mandatory References

14.44 The Supreme Court, as the final appellate court, has a general duty to refer questions to the CJEU where a reference is necessary to enable it to give judgment. However, this is

---

[18] Prior to Lisbon, under the former Art 68 EC (introduced by the Treaty of Amsterdam), what is now Art 267 was modified in its application so that the power of making a reference in respect of certain decisions (eg, in the field of asylum and immigration) was confined to national courts against whose decisions there is no judicial remedy in national law. Article 68 EC was repealed by the Treaty of Lisbon.

[19] However, the line is at times blurred and the CJEU has been known to make findings akin to those on the facts.

[20] 'Recommendations to national courts and tribunals in relation to the initiation of preliminary ruling procedures', 6 November 2012 (2012/C 338/1), para 13.

Part E – Procedure and Remedies

subject to the *acte clair* doctrine. The doctrine provides that a national court need not make a reference where the 'the correct application of [EU] law [is] so obvious as to leave no scope for any reasonable doubt as to the manner in which the question raised is to be resolved': Case 283/81 *CILFIT* [1982] ECR 3415 [16]. In *R v International Stock Exchange ex p Else* [1993] QB 534, Lord Bingham MR, applying *CILFIT*, characterised acte clair as denoting positive response as to whether any issue in question could be resolved 'with complete confidence' and 'with no real doubt' (at 545).

14.45 In addition to the Supreme Court, the Court of Appeal or first instance courts may also have a duty to refer insofar as they are deciding a question against which—as a result of that decision—it is not possible to seek permission to appeal to a higher court.

E3. Making a Reference

14.46 The point at which a reference can, or should, be made will depend primarily on whether sufficient factual and legal findings have been made in order for the court to determine whether a decision by the CJEU is necessary to enable it to give judgment. Accordingly, in judicial review proceedings, it will be rare that a decision will be made to refer a question at or before the permission stage. The Upper Tribunal will often have sufficient material before it to be competent to make a reference.

14.47 In the Administrative Court and the Court of Appeal, the procedure for seeking a reference is regulated by Part 68 CPR. In the Supreme Court it is regulated by rule 42 Supreme Court Rules[21] and Practice Direction 11. References have been made by the Upper Tribunal and although there is no reference to the preliminary ruling procedure in the procedure rules of the Upper Tribunal, the format is in practice the same as in the Administrative Court and the Court of Appeal.

14.48 A reference may be made on application by one or both parties prior to the substantive hearing, on application by one or both parties at the hearing itself, or by the judge of his or her own motion.

14.49 In summary, the reference takes the form of an order which stays further proceedings until the answers to the questions referred are handed down by the CJEU and specifies any interim relief. In a schedule to the order, the questions referred are set out along with a statement of case. The reference is made only after it is in fact sent to the CJEU. The judgment itself does not amount to the making of a reference.

14.50 It should be noted that there is considerable delay involved in obtaining a preliminary ruling from the CJEU. In 2012, the average delay was nearly 16 months.[22] There are two accelerated procedures for consideration of references for a preliminary ruling normally instigated on the part of the referring court or exceptionally on the motion of the President of the Court under the Rules of Procedure of the Court of Justice of 25 September 2012: first, expedition under Article 105 'where the nature of the case requires that it be dealt with within a short time'; and, second, the urgent procedure under Article 107 where the reference raises one or more questions in the areas covered by the Area of Freedom Security and Justice (Title V of Part 3 TFEU) and thus refers

---

[21] SI 2009/1603.
[22] Court of Justice of the European Union Annual Report 2012, para 2.

to matters within the scope of this book in relation to issues involving international protection.

14.51 The European Commission may commence infringement proceedings in cases where it believes that a member country is failing to fulfil its obligations under EU law. Under Article 268 TFEU, the Commission is responsible for ensuring that EU law is applied correctly. While much of the time the Commission will be acting of its own motion, anyone can make a complaint to the Commission in the belief that EU law has been breached. There are no limitations on standing. This route will not result in a speedy remedy as the Commission will go through an investigation and issue a reasoned opinion inviting the Member State to respond and eventually consider whether to bring proceedings. Whether or not to act is solely within the competence of the Commission.

15

Council of Europe Remedies

Contents

A. Introduction 15.1
B. Application to the ECtHR 15.3
    B1. Background 15.3
    B2. Composition of the ECtHR and its Administration 15.11
    B3. ECtHR Procedure 15.21
    B4. Applying to the ECtHR 15.29
    B5. Admissibility Criteria 15.36
    B6. Striking Out 15.48
    B7. Applying to the ECtHR: Interim Remedies under Rule 39 .... 15.50
    B8. Legal Aid 15.60
    B9. Just Satisfaction: Compensation and Costs 15.64
    B10. Finality and Execution of Judgments 15.68
C. GRETA 15.71

A. Introduction

An account was given in chapter 5 of Council of Europe instruments including the ECHR, ECN (which the UK has not ratified) and CATHB. This chapter describes remedies available through the Council of Europe or its institutions. **15.1**

The primary Council of Europe remedy likely to be considered in relation to expulsion or exclusion, or relevant nationality decisions is application to the ECtHR at Strasbourg. This, however, is not the sole relevant remedy. In chapter 12, attention was given, in the context of international human rights law, to treaty-based monitoring bodies. In relation to the CATHB, the Council of Europe supports a body created under the CATHB for the purpose of monitoring implementation of the treaty, namely the Group of Experts on Action against Trafficking in Human Beings (GRETA). **15.2**

B. Application to the ECtHR

B1. Background

The existence of the ECtHR was brought about by section II of the ECHR, Article 19 thereof setting out that: 'To ensure the observance of the engagements undertaken by the High Contracting parties in the Convention and the protocols thereto, there shall be set up a European Court of Human Rights ... [which] shall function on a permanent basis.' **15.3**

Part E – Procedure and Remedies

15.4　The ECtHR's jurisdiction, under Article 32 ECHR, 'shall extend to all matters concerning the interpretation and application of [the ECHR] and the protocols thereto', subject to this arising by one of the means (inter-state case, individual application or advisory opinion) provided in Articles 33, 34 and 47 respectively. The ECtHR's procedures are delineated by its own Rules of Court,[1] most recently updated on 1 January 2014, and by a number of Practice Directions.[2]

15.5　A right of individual petition to the ECtHR for those within the jurisdiction of the UK has existed since 14 January 1966. Engagement of the ECtHR was relatively limited for some years thereafter, with very few cases reaching it. Originally, supervision of the ECHR was undertaken by the Committee of Ministers of the Council of Europe, a political body formed of the Minister for Foreign Affairs of each Contracting State, assisted by the European Commission on Human Rights, and with recourse to the ECtHR only in rare cases. On 1 November 1998, the original two-tier organisational structure was replaced by a single court, the European Commission on Human Rights being abolished. The Committee of Ministers no longer has a role in determining violations of the ECHR, but retains supervision of the enforcement of judgments of the ECtHR.[3]

15.6　Thereafter, many of the principal rights enshrined in the ECHR were incorporated into domestic law by the HRA 1998. It was intended that the HRA 1998 would provide domestic remedies for human rights violations, and this is now frequently the case;[4] however, it has not obviated the need in certain circumstances to apply to the ECtHR seeking to remedy a violation of rights contained in the ECHR or to protect against the serious risk of a future violation.

15.7　In recent years there have been a number of reforms to the organisation and procedure of the ECtHR. Protocol 14 to the ECHR entered into force on 1 June 2010. It sought specifically to address the excessive caseload of the ECtHR by introducing new powers to permit the consideration of admissibility by single judges and to enforce altered admissibility criterion.

15.8　On 19–20 April 2012, the UK Chairmanship of the Committee of Ministers organised a conference at Brighton to consider reform of the ECtHR. The declaration adopted by that conference[5] formed the basis of a new Protocol 15 to the ECHR. Protocol 15 introduces reference in the ECHR to the principle of subsidiarity and the doctrine of margin of appreciation. Its reforms will also include a reduction in the limitation period within which an application may be made to the ECtHR from six to four months and the abolition of the right of parties to object to the relinquishment of a case to the Grand Chamber.[6] At the time of writing, Protocol 15 to the ECHR has not yet entered into force.

15.9　The Brighton conference also discussed a proposal to extend the jurisdiction of the ECtHR to give advisory opinions, which Article 47 presently enables only where a

---

[1] www.echr.coe.int/Documents/Rules_Court_ENG.pdf.
[2] www.echr.coe.int/Pages/home.aspx?p=basictexts/rules&c=#n1347877334990_pointer.
[3] See section B10 below.
[4] The right to an effective remedy for the violation of a substantive Convention right (Art 13 ECHR) was not therefore incorporated into the HRA 1998. See para 5.203 for a discussion of the application of Art 13 ECHR to the subject matter of this work.
[5] The Brighton Declaration of the High Level Conference on the Future of the European Court of Human Rights, 19 and 20 April 2012, www.echr.coe.int/Documents/2012_Brighton_FinalDeclaration_ENG.pdf.
[6] For the text of Protocol 15, see: www.echr.coe.int/Documents/Protocol_15_ENG.pdf.

request is made by the Committee of Ministers of the Council of Europe.[7] Since then, the Committee of Ministers has adopted Protocol 16 to the ECHR. Protocol 16 will establish a mechanism to permit national courts and tribunals at the highest level to request the ECtHR to give advisory opinions on questions of principle relating to the interpretation or application of the rights and freedoms enshrined in the ECHR and its protocols. At the time of writing, Protocol 16 has not entered into force.

The Rules of Court were most recently amended on 1 January 2014 to include expanded rules dictating the form and content required of applications to the ECtHR.[8]   15.10

B2. Composition of the ECtHR and its Administration

Each Contracting State is represented by a judge at the ECtHR: Article 20 ECHR. Presently, there are 47 judges, reflecting the 47 Contracting States. Judges are elected by the Parliamentary Assembly of the Council of Europe from a shortlist of three candidates proposed by Contracting States: Article 22 ECHR. Under Article 23 ECHR, judges of the ECtHR hold office for a non-renewable term of nine years, subject to retirement at the age of 70.   15.11

The Plenary Court consists of all 47 judges of the ECtHR. It has no judicial capacity, but under Article 25 ECHR, it possesses important administrative functions, namely, the election of its own president and vice-president, the establishment of Chambers, the adoption of the Rules of Court, and the election of a Registrar and Deputy Registrars.   15.12

The judicial work of the ECtHR under Article 26 ECHR may be accomplished by one or more of its judges acting as single judges, as a Committee (three judges), a Chamber (seven judges) or the Grand Chamber (17 judges).   15.13

Under Article 26(3) ECHR, a single judge shall not examine any application against his or her own State Party of nationality. A single judge may declare individual cases inadmissible or strike cases off the list, such decisions being final ones: Article 27(1)–(2) ECHR. Cases not declared inadmissible or struck off the ECtHR's list by a single judge are referred to a Committee or Chamber: Article 27(3) ECHR.   15.14

Where examination by a Committee or Chamber is found to be justified, a Judge Rapporteur is designated to examine the application: rules 49(1)–(2) Rules of Court. Under rule 49(3) Rules of Court, a Judge Rapporteur, in the examination of an application: 15.15

(a) may request the parties to submit, within a specified time, any factual information, documents or other material which they consider to be relevant;
(b) shall, subject to the President of the Section directing that the case be considered by a Chamber or a Committee, decide whether the application is to be considered by a single-judge formation, by a Committee or by a Chamber;
(c) shall submit such reports, drafts and other documents as may assist the Chamber or the Committee or the respective President in carrying out their functions.

---

[7] The proposal was originally made in the report to the Committee of Ministers of the Group of Wise Persons, set up under the Action Plan adopted at the Third Summit of Heads of State and Government of the Member States of the Council of Europe (Warsaw, 16–17 May 2005).
[8] See, in particular r 47 Rules of Court.

Part E – Procedure and Remedies

15.16 Committees are established by Chambers for a fixed term. The Chamber will also determine the composition of judges to sit on the Committee. Committees are empowered in the event of unanimity to declare a case inadmissible or to strike it out of its list of cases or declare a case admissible and provide a judgment on the merits, provided that the underlying question is already the subject of well-established case law: Article 28 ECHR.

15.17 Chambers are established by the Plenary Court for a fixed term. Chambers are competent to determine the admissibility and merits of all applications to the ECtHR: Article 29 ECHR.

15.18 The Grand Chamber is the highest judicial body under the ECHR. Its composition includes the President and Vice-President and the Presidents of the Chambers. The national judge of a respondent state must always sit; therefore, if not already appointed to the Grand Chamber, he or she replaces one of the appointed judges. The Grand Chamber's role is to determine complex cases in situations where a Chamber has relinquished jurisdiction pursuant to rule 72 Rules of Court (where a case raises a serious question affecting the interpretation of the Convention or where a decision may be inconsistent with a previous decision), or where a reference to the Grand Chamber has been accepted upon the request of either/both of the parties (rule 73 Rules of Court). Where the Grand Chamber is seised of a case, rule 71 Rules of Court confers on the Grand Chamber all the powers of the Chamber over hearings.

15.19 Where a party wishes to request that a case be referred to the Grand Chamber, he or she must file such a request at the Registry within three months of the date of the judgment of a Chamber. The request must specify the serious question affecting the interpretation or application of the ECHR or the 'serious issue of general importance' which warrants consideration by the Grand Chamber: rule 73(1) Rules of Court. A panel of five judges of the Grand Chamber decide whether or not to accept the request. If the request is refused, the reasons need not be given. Where accepted, a judgment shall be delivered by the Grand Chamber: rule 73(2)–(3) Rules of Court.

15.20 Under Article 24(1), the administration of the ECtHR's business is undertaken by the Registry, headed by the Registrar and Deputy Registrars elected by the Plenary Court under Article 25(e).

B3. ECtHR Procedure

15.21 The procedure of the ECtHR is governed by the Rules of Court and various Practice Directions: Article 25 ECHR and rule 32 Rules of Court. The official languages of the ECtHR are English and French: rule 34 Rules of Court. An overview of the procedure before the ECtHR is set out below, followed by a more detailed examination of certain procedural factors of particular relevance to individual applicants and their representatives in mounting an application to the Court.

15.22 The basic procedural steps are as follows:

(i) A case may be initiated in one of two ways: first, by the filing of an application with the Registry; and, second, it may also commence with an application for an interim measure pursuant to rule 39 Rules of Court only. Once the application has been decided, the party is given the opportunity to file a full application with the court, but does not have to do so, for instance, in the event that the Rule 39 measure is refused.

(ii) The application will be registered and a decision made as to whether the case may be determined (on admissibility) by a single judge or examined by a Committee or Chamber.

(iii) A single judge may determine that the application is inadmissible or should be struck out. If he or she does not determine the application on admissibility, it will pass to a Committee or Chamber.

(iv) If examination by a Committee or Chamber seems justified, the President of the relevant section will appoint a Judge Rapporteur, who examines the application and decides whether to refer it to a Committee or Chamber.

(v) If referred to a Committee, it may determine the application on the grounds of admissibility or merits (the latter if it is following a clear line of authority). If there is no unanimous vote on admissibility and/or merits in the Committee, it will be examined by a Chamber.

(vi) If referred to a Chamber by the Judge Rapporteur or forwarded by a Committee, the Chamber may then find the application to be inadmissible or, if admissible, may 'communicate' the application to the respondent government and may ask the government specific questions. The government may then submit its observations on the application and its answers to any questions. In certain circumstances, the Chamber may also relinquish jurisdiction to the Grand Chamber.

(vii) If the Chamber does not relinquish jurisdiction, it will then examine the application and provide a judgment on admissibility and/or merits. This may exceptionally involve the establishment of facts, separate from the statement of facts supplied with the application. See further paragraph 15.25 below.

(viii) If a Chamber relinquishes jurisdiction or a reference is accepted by the Grand Chamber following the judgment of a Chamber, the Grand Chamber will determine the application. In general the Grand Chamber will not revisit an earlier admissibility decision, but Article 38(4) ECHR has been held to permit this as it enables the Court to dismiss applications that it considers inadmissible 'at any stage of the proceedings': *Odièvre v France* [GC] no 42326/98; [2003] ECHR 86, (2004) 38 EHRR 43 [22].

The sequence in which cases are dealt with is a matter for the discretion of the court depending on the importance and urgency of the issues involved: rule 41 Rules of Court. **15.23**

An oral hearing may be held, but in Chamber judgments this is only exceptionally the case (rule 59(3)–(4) Rules of Court). Hearings take place in public (unless the Chamber decides there are exceptional circumstances: rule 63 Rules of Court). Decisions are made following private deliberation by a majority vote. In the case of a tie, the President has the casting vote. **15.24**

If a case is found to be admissible, the Rules of Court empower the ECtHR to make findings of fact and obtain evidence. These powers are contained in the Annex to the Rules. The powers are rarely used and the court will generally rely upon findings of fact made by domestic courts in preceding domestic proceedings, only questioning such findings in exceptional cases. However, the ECtHR will often rely on evidence contained in reports by international organisations or NGOs. **15.25**

15.26 Following a finding of admissibility, Article 39(1) ECHR and rule 62 Rules of Court empower the Registrar, acting on the instructions of the President of a Chamber, to enter into contact with the parties with a view to securing a friendly settlement. The negotiations are confidential and without prejudice to the parties' positions in contentious proceedings. Where a friendly settlement is secured, the Court will strike the application out of its list in a decision: Article 39(3) ECHR. Where an applicant has refused the terms of a friendly settlement, the respondent state may file a request with the Court to strike the case out of its list. The request is accompanied by a declaration that there has been a violation of the ECHR and an undertaking to provide redress. Where the Court is satisfied that the unilateral declaration provides sufficient protection of human rights, it may strike the case out of its list: rule 62A Rules of Court. Although potentially unsatisfactory for applicants, the unilateral declaration procedure is frequently used. In *Rantsev v Cyprus and Russia* (2010) ECHR 25965/04, (2010) 51 EHRR 1, a relatively rare example of the ECtHR declining to strike out an application following unilateral declaration by a defendant state, it was successfully argued on behalf of the applicant that the unilateral declaration provided by Cyprus should not cause the application to be struck out because the case was of wider general importance.

15.27 Third party intervention by State Parties is governed by Article 36 ECHR, which provides that any state, one of whose nationals is an applicant, shall have the right to submit written comments and to take part in hearings, and that in any other case, the President of the Court may, 'in the interest of the proper administration of justice, invite any High Contracting Party which is not a party to the proceedings or any person concerned who is not the applicant to submit written comments or take part in hearings'. In all cases before a Chamber or the Grand Chamber, the Council of Europe Commissioner for Human Rights may submit written comments and take part in hearings.

15.28 If a state, one of whose nationals is an applicant, wishes to intervene, it must advise the Registry of this intention within 12 weeks of communication of the case: rule 44 Rules of Court. Any other Contracting State and any other person concerned may also seek to intervene. Requests for leave under Article 36(2) ECHR must be reasoned and should also be submitted within 12 weeks of the date of communication. The grant of leave to intervene may be subject to conditions such as limits on the length of submissions.

B4. Applying to the ECtHR

15.29 The making of individual applications is enabled by Article 34 ECHR: 'The Court may receive applications from any person, nongovernmental organisation or group of individuals claiming to be the victim of a violation by one of the High Contracting Parties of the rights set forth in the Convention or the Protocols thereto. The High Contracting Parties undertake not to hinder in any way the effective exercise of this right.' After the application has been filed, applicants are expected to be represented, save where the President of a Chamber exceptionally decides otherwise: rule 36(2) Rules of Court.

15.30 To be admissible, an application must satisfy a number of criteria. Of particular importance are the conditions that an applicant must be a 'victim' as defined by the ECHR, must have exhausted available effective domestic remedies, must have properly completed the relevant forms and must have made the application within the six months from 'the date on which the final [domestic] decision' was taken: Article 35 ECHR.

The procedural requirements with which the contents of the application must comply are set out in rule 47 Rules of Court. Further details are found in the ECtHR's Practice Direction concerning the Institution of Proceedings.[9] Failure to comply with the procedural requirements contained in rule 47 will result in the application not being examined: rule 47(5)(1) Rules of Court. Rule 47(1) specifies that the application must be made on the application form provided by the Registry and must contain: 15.31

(a) the name, date of birth, nationality and address of the applicant and, where the applicant is a legal person, the full name, date of incorporation or registration, the official registration number (if any) and the official address;
(b) the name, occupation, address, telephone and fax numbers and e-mail address of the representative, if any;
(c) the name of the Contracting Party or Parties against which the application is made;
(d) a concise and legible statement of the facts;
(e) a concise and legible statement of the alleged violation(s) of the Convention and the relevant arguments; and
(f) a concise and legible statement confirming the applicant's compliance with the admissibility criteria laid down in Article 35 § 1 of the Convention.

The procedural requirements in rule 47(1) are stated as aiming to 'enable the Court to determine the nature and scope of the application without recourse to any other document' (rule 47(2)(a)). However, applicants are permitted to supplement the application form by appending no more than 20 additional pages of written submissions on the facts and violations of ECHR alleged in the application (rule 47(2)(b)). 15.32

The application form must be signed by the applicant or the applicant's representative and accompanied by the following documents (rule 47(3)(1)): 15.33

(a) copies of documents relating to the decisions or measures complained of, judicial or otherwise;
(b) copies of documents and decisions showing that the applicant has complied with the exhaustion of domestic remedies requirement and the time-limit contained in Article 35 § 1 of the Convention;
(c) where appropriate, copies of documents relating to any other procedure of international investigation or settlement;
(d) where represented, the original of the power of attorney or form of authority signed by the applicant.

The documents deposited with the Registry, save documents related to any attempt to reach a friendly settlement, are open to the public: rule 33 Rules of Court. If an applicant does not wish to have his or her identity disclosed to the public, this must be indicated in the application to the Court. Rule 47(4) requires applicants requesting anonymity to submit a statement of reasons for 'justifying such a departure from the normal rule of public access to information'. It also specifies that the ECtHR may grant anonymity of its own motion. A Practice Direction on Requests for Anonymity supplements rules 33 and 47.[10] 15.34

---

[9] www.echr.coe.int/Documents/PD_institution_proceedings_ENG.pdf.
[10] www.echr.coe.int/Documents/PD_anonymity_ENG.pdf.

15.35　Following the instigation of proceedings, the requirements of form and content with which pleadings must comply are set out in the Practice Direction on Written Pleadings.[11] Rule 38 Rules of Court requires pleadings to be lodged within time limits.

B5. Admissibility Criteria

15.36　The primary admissibility criterion under Article 34 is that the applicant must be a 'victim' of a violation of ECHR. Under Article 34, the applicant may be a person or persons, or an NGO or association. The term 'person' is not defined, but may include children and other individuals who may lack capacity under domestic law. The next of kin of an applicant who dies following the instigation of proceedings may continue the proceedings in the deceased's name.[12]

15.37　In addition to demonstrating victim status, an applicant must also show that the subject matter of the application falls within the material scope of the ECHR and that the events complained of took place within the jurisdiction of the ECHR after the UK's acceptance of the right of individual petition on 14 January 1966.

15.38　An application to the ECtHR must be made within the time limit permitted under the ECHR. Under Article 35 ECHR this means that the application must be brought within a six month time limit from the final domestic decision, or, if that decision was not published, the day on which the applicant or, if represented, his or her lawyer was informed of it. In the absence of a domestic remedy, the time runs from the date on which the act under challenge took place or the date on which the applicant was affected by, became aware or could have become aware of the act under challenge. Time runs with the exhaustion of effective remedies and the pursuing of further ineffective remedies does not stop time from running. The time stops on the date on which the application form is posted or on the date of arrival of a fax. The ECHR does not allow the ECtHR or any respondent state to waive the six-month limitation period.

15.39　Article 35 ECHR further requires the exhaustion of domestic remedies: 'The Court may only deal with the matter after all domestic remedies have been exhausted, according to the generally recognised rules of international law, and within a period of six months from the date on which the final decision was taken.' The relevant date for the assessment of satisfaction of this admissibility criterion is the date of the admissibility decision rather than the date of application: *Luberti v Italy* no 9019/80 [1984] ECHR 3, (1984) 6 EHRR 440. Under Article 35(2) ECHR, it will not deal with any application submitted under Article 34 that is anonymous (in such a case, it cannot be established that the applicant is a 'victim') or is 'substantially the same as a matter that has already been examined by the Court or has already been submitted to another procedure of international investigation or settlement and contains no relevant new information'.

15.40　The exhaustion of domestic remedies requires that complaints that are substantively the same as those that will be made to the ECtHR are made to domestic authorities and that, in so doing, there is compliance with the relevant domestic procedural

---

[11] www.echr.coe.int/Documents/PD_written_pleadings_ENG.pdf.
[12] For a fuller account of the requirement of victim status, see R Clayton QC and H Tomlinson QC *The Law of Human Rights*, (2nd edn, Oxford, Oxford University Press, 2009) 22.15, p 2005 et seq.

requirements. Thus, an applicant who has failed to comply with the national time limits cannot benefit from his or her omission to found an admissible application to the ECtHR: *Barberá, Messegué and Jabardo v Spain* no 10590/83 [1988] ECHR 25, (1989) 11 EHRR 360.

15.41 The risk of unfairness in enforcement of the requirement that domestic remedies be exhausted is ameliorated by the interpretation of the duty as applicable only where alternative remedies are effective, in that they are 'available and sufficient': *McFarlane v Ireland* no 31333/06 [2010] ECHR 1272 [107]. There is no requirement that remedies be pursued if they offer no realistic prospect of success.[13] Remedies that are not sufficiently certain both in theory and in practice, by preventing the violation or its continuation or providing adequate redress for a violation that has already occurred, will lack the requisite accessibility and effectiveness. The burden of proving that these conditions are satisfied rests on the respondent state: *McFarlane* [107]. However, the existence of doubts as to the effectiveness of national remedies or lack of financial means does not obviate the exhaustion requirement.[14] Further, a discretionary remedy is not effective: *Agee v UK* (1976) 7 DR 164. Thus, a declaration of incompatibility under section 4 HRA 1998 is not an effective remedy since it is not binding on the parties and does not constitute a duty to amend legislation.

15.42 In immigration and asylum cases, applicants will be expected to use the available statutory appeal rights and/or judicial review. Where there are low merits, the domestic remedy should be pursued. Refusal of legal aid will not absolve an applicant for failure to exhaust domestic remedies unless it may be demonstrated that it was otherwise impossible for domestic remedies to be pursued (ie, the applicant could not litigate in person). In general, where there is a prospect of success, an individual will be expected to apply to the Court of Appeal. An appeal to the Supreme Court will only be expected where, rarely, there is a point of law of general public importance which it is reasonable to pursue. Article 35 has 'close affinity' with Article 13 ECHR, which guarantees the existence of an effective domestic remedy in relation to the violation of Convention rights: *Diallo v Czech Republic* no 20493/07 [2011] ECHR 1015 [53]. There is no need to exhaust remedies which do not have automatic suspensive effect as interpreted under Article 13 ECHR: *Diallo* [78].

15.43 Under Article 35(3) ECHR:

(3) The Court shall declare inadmissible any individual application submitted under Article 34 if it considers that:
   (a) the application is incompatible with the provisions of the Convention or the Protocols thereto, manifestly ill-founded, or an abuse of the right of individual application; or
   (b) the applicant has not suffered a significant disadvantage, unless respect for human rights as defined in the Convention and the Protocols thereto requires an examination

---

[13] It may be possible to demonstrate this by documenting the opinion of Counsel that a case has no prospect of success in the domestic courts.

[14] See, eg, *FA v UK* no 20658/11 (ECtHR (admissibility decision), 10 September 2013), where Counsel's opinion that judicial review proceedings would offer better prospects of success in a trafficking case was insufficient to demonstrate that the applicant had exhausted all available and sufficient remedies pursuant to Art 35.

15.44 Further, an application will not be admissible if it is incompatible with the provisions of the ECHR and its Protocols, is manifestly ill-founded or is an abuse of the right of individual application (Article 35(3)(a) ECHR). Abusive applications may include those which are made repeatedly or those based on deliberately untrue or incomplete facts. As for the criterion that an application not be 'manifestly ill-founded', the test appears to be akin to a 'strong prima facie case'.[15] However, since decisions on admissibility and merits are now generally taken together, this ground of admissibility is now invoked less often.

15.45 The final admissibility criterion (Article 35(3)(b) ECHR) indicates that an application will not be received where the applicant has not suffered a significant disadvantage, unless respect for human rights as defined in the ECHR requires an examination of the application on the merits and provided that no case may be rejected on this ground which has not been duly considered by a domestic tribunal. This was introduced by Protocol 14 to the ECHR as a response to the excessive caseload pressure on the Court.[16]

15.46 Article 35(3)(b) is intended to be a additional filter excluding unmeritorious cases. There are, however, two caveats to the requirement that a case be rejected as inadmissible where the applicant has not suffered a significant loss. The first safeguard relates to general human rights protection: it exists to permit the Court to examine a case whose individual merits alone do not justify substantive determination, but which discloses a broader point of principle that is important in relation to the interpretation and/or application of the ECHR. The second has regard to the individual interests of the applicant. It seeks to avoid the situation in which there has been no proper judicial (domestic or supranational) consideration of the alleged rights violation.[17]

15.47 Preliminary evaluation of the use of the Article 35(3)(b) provision by the Steering Committee for Human Rights suggests that its use has been limited.[18]

B6. Striking Out

15.48 Article 36 ECHR governs the ECtHR's power to strike cases out of its list:

1. The Court may at any stage of the proceedings decide to strike an application out of its list of cases where the circumstances lead to the conclusion that
    (a) the applicant does not intend to pursue his application; or
    (b) the matter has been resolved; or
    (c) for any other reason established by the Court, it is no longer justified to continue the examination of the application.

---

[15] Clayton (n 12) 23.80, p 2079.
[16] See further the 'Explanatory Report to Protocol No 14 to the Convention for the Protection of Human Rights and Fundamental Freedoms, Amending the Control System of the Convention': http://conventions.coe.int/treaty/EN/reports/html/194.htm.
[17] The Brighton Declaration of the High Level Conference on the Future of the European Court of Human Rights called for the deletion of the second safeguard clause: para 15. This has been replicated in Protocol 15: www.echr.coe.int/Documents/Protocol_15_ENG.pdf.
[18] 'CCDH Report Containing Elements to Contribute to the Evaluation of the Effects of Protocol No. 14 to the Convention and the Implementation of the Interlaken and Izmir Declarations on the Court's Situation', CDDH(2012)R76 Addendum II, 30 November 2012.

However, the Court shall continue the examination of the application if respect for human rights as defined in the Convention and the Protocols thereto so requires.

2. The Court may decide to restore an application to its list of cases if it considers that the circumstances justify such a course.

As to Article 36(1)(a) ECHR, the applicant must be unequivocal in his or her decision not to pursue the application. Similarly, Article 36(1)(b) ECHR requires it to be manifest that the circumstances that gave rise to the application are no longer present and that the effects of a possible violation have been redressed. In relation to Article 36(1)(c) ECHR, the ECtHR has a broad discretion to strike out. This may occur where, for example, a respondent state had admitted full liability or has settled the case such that the applicant has lost victim status. The ECtHR may strike cases out irrespective of the wishes of individual applicants.   **15.49**

B7. Applying to the ECtHR: Interim Remedies under Rule 39

Rule 39 Rules of Court contains the ECtHR's rules on interim relief: **15.50**

1. The Chamber or, where appropriate, the President of the Section or a duty judge appointed pursuant to paragraph 4 of this Rule may, at the request of a party or of any other person concerned, or of their own motion, indicate to the parties any interim measure which they consider should be adopted in the interests of the parties or of the proper conduct of the proceedings.

Rule 39 permits the Chamber, its President or a Chamber Vice-President appointed as a duty judge to indicate to the parties any interim measures that it considers should be adopted. The indication may be given in response to a request from a party to the proceedings or of its own motion.   **15.51**

The ECtHR will grant interim relief against a Contracting State where it considers that the applicant faces an 'imminent risk of irreparable damage' if the measure is not applied: *Mamatkulov and Abdurasulovic v Turkey* nos 46827/99 and 46951/99 [2003] ECHR 68, 41 EHRR 494 [104]. According to the Grand Chamber in *Paladi v Moldova* no 39806/05 [2009] ECHR 450, (2008) 47 EHRR 15 [88], the purpose of interim measures pursuant to Rule 39 is to ensure 'the effectiveness of the right of individual petition' and to preserve 'the Court's ability to render such a judgment [on the merits of the complaint] after an effective examination of the complaint' (at [89]). The measure is granted in order to avoid 'irreversible situations that would prevent the Court from ... securing to the applicant the practical and effective benefit of the Convention rights asserted': *Mamatkulov and Abdurasulovic* [125].   **15.52**

The Court has granted interim measures preventing removal pursuant to Rule 39 in cases involving imminent mental harm (*Balogun v UK* no 60286/09; [2012] ECHR 614, (2013) 56 EHRR 3 [4]) and involving the risk of an imminent violation of Article 8 ECHR (*Nunez v Norway* no 55597/09 [2011] ECHR 1047, (2014) 58 EHRR 17 [4]; and *Eskinazi and Chelouche v Turkey* no 14600/05 (6 December 2005)).   **15.53**

In expulsion cases, an interim measure may also be necessary in order to prevent other forms of harm not directly related to removal. For instance, the Court indicated to the Dutch government in two asylum cases that applicants would need to be provided   **15.54** with adequate accommodation pending the outcome of the proceedings before the Court: *Abdilahi Abdulwahidi v The Netherlands* no 21741/07 (ECtHR, 12 November 2013); *Alif v The Netherlands* no 60915/09 (ECtHR, 24 May 2011) [25]. In *Aleksanyan v Russia* no 46468/06 [2008] ECHR 1745, an application concerning the detention of a visually impaired and HIV-positive lawyer suffering from various medical issues in detention, the ECtHR at [4] indicated to the Russian government by way of an interim measure that it should provide the applicant with medical treatment in detention.

15.55 Requests for interim remedies are frequently made in the context of expulsion in immigration cases. They should be made in accordance with the guidance set out in the Practice Direction on Requests for Interim Measures.[19] In particular, this requires applications to be made by fax or letter and applicants to state the reasons why interim relief is required. This includes the grounds on which the particular fears are based, the nature of the alleged risks and the provisions of ECHR which are alleged to have been violated.

15.56 In relation to supporting documentation, the Practice Direction on Requests for Interim Measures states that:

> A mere reference to submissions in other documents or domestic proceedings is not sufficient. It is essential that requests be accompanied by all necessary supporting documents, in particular relevant domestic court, tribunal or other decisions, together with any other material which is considered to substantiate the applicant's allegations.

15.57 In cases involving expulsion, details of the expected date and time of removal, the applicant's address or place of detention and his or her ECtHR case reference number should be provided. In terms of the urgency of applications for interim relief in expulsion cases, the Practice Direction on Requests for Interim Measures states that:

> Requests for interim measures should normally be received as soon as possible after the final domestic decision has been taken, in order to enable the Court and its Registry to have sufficient time to examine the matter. The Court may not be able to deal with requests in removal cases received less than a working day before the planned time of removal

> Where the final domestic decision is imminent and there is a risk of immediate enforcement, especially in extradition or deportation cases, applicants and their representatives should submit the request for interim measures without waiting for that decision, indicating clearly the date on which it will be taken and that the request is subject to the final domestic decision being negative.

15.58 However, applicants facing expulsion should pursue all domestic remedies that may be capable of suspending removal before applying to the ECtHR for interim relief. Where there is a domestic recourse still available, the court will not apply rule 39 to suspend removal.

15.59 An indication under rule 39 is not formally binding on the respondent state. However, the ECtHR has held that failure to comply with an indication as to interim relief is a violation of the duty of Contracting States not to hinder the exercise of individual petition under Article 34 ECHR. The UK has generally complied with indications.

---

[19] www.echr.coe.int/Documents/PD_interim_measures_ENG.pdf. See also the further information provided by the Registry at: www.echr.coe.int/Pages/home.aspx?p=applicants&c=#n1365511916164_pointer.

B8. Legal Aid

Applicants may request legal aid from the ECtHR as part of the initial application. Legal aid is available from the moment when observations in writing on the admissibility of an application are received from the respondent state or where the time limit for their submission has expired: rule 100 Rules of Court. 15.60

The conditions on which legal aid shall be granted are set out in rule 101 Rules of Court, which provides that: 15.61

> Legal aid shall be granted only where the President of the Chamber is satisfied:
>
> (a) that it is necessary for the proper conduct of the case before the Chamber;
> (b) that the applicant has insufficient means to meet all or part of the costs entailed.

The assessment of (in)sufficient means is conducted by the ECtHR on the basis of a declaration of means certified by, in the case of the UK, the Legal Aid Agency: rule 102(1) Rules of Court. 15.62

Once a decision to grant legal aid is made by the President of the Chamber is made, the Registry fixes the levels of grant: rule 104 Rules of Court. 15.63

B9. Just Satisfaction: Compensation and Costs

Article 41 ECHR provides: 15.64

> If the Court finds that there has been a violation of the Convention or the Protocols thereto, and if the internal law of the High Contracting Party concerned allows only partial reparation to be made, the Court shall, if necessary, afford just satisfaction to the injured party.

Applicants may recover compensation and reasonable costs from the respondent as 'just satisfaction' under Article 41 ECHR.[20] Compensation may be for pecuniary and non-pecuniary loss. This is in addition to a declaration of a violation of a right protected by the ECHR. Frequently, however, the Court finds that the finding of a violation is just satisfaction of itself such that compensation and/or costs are not warranted. 15.65

Importantly, the ECtHR has no power either to over-rule the decisions of domestic courts and tribunals or to annul the decisions of domestic administrative authorities. However, it may indicate the measures it considers to be necessary to rectify the violation. 15.66

Where the Court finds it necessary to rule on compensation and/or costs, it may adjourn the matter and invite settlement: rule 75 Rules of Court. Absent an agreement which the Court finds to be equitable, the applicant may be required to submit representations on the nature of the loss. Claims for costs require a detailed breakdown to be submitted to the Court. The quantum of both compensation and costs ordered by the Court are modest. 15.67

B10. Finality and Execution of Judgments

Judgments of the Grand Chamber are final with immediate effect: Article 44(1) ECHR. Chamber judgments become final: (a) when the parties declare that they will not request 15.68

---

[20] States may not, however, recover their costs from individual applicants.

that the case be referred to the Grand Chamber; or (b) three months after the date of the judgment, if reference of the case to the Grand Chamber has not been requested; or (c) when the panel of the Grand Chamber rejects the request to refer under Article 43: Article 44(2) ECHR.

15.69 Article 46 ECHR provides the following on the binding force and execution of judgments of the ECtHR:

1. The High Contracting Parties undertake to abide by the final judgment of the Court in any case to which they are parties.
2. The final judgment of the Court shall be transmitted to the Committee of Ministers, which shall supervise its execution.
3. If the Committee of Ministers considers that the supervision of the execution of a final judgment is hindered by a problem of interpretation of the judgment, it may refer the matter to the Court for a ruling on the question of interpretation. A referral decision shall require a majority vote of two thirds of the representatives entitled to sit on the committee.
4. If the Committee of Ministers considers that a High Contracting Party refuses to abide by a final judgment in a case to which it is a party, it may, after serving formal notice on that Party and by decision adopted by a majority vote of two thirds of the representatives entitled to sit on the committee, refer to the Court the question whether that Party has failed to fulfil its obligation under paragraph 1.
5. If the Court finds a violation of paragraph 1, it shall refer the case to the Committee of Ministers for consideration of the measures to be taken. If the Court finds no violation of paragraph 1, it shall refer the case to the Committee of Ministers, which shall close its examination of the case.

15.70 The execution of judgments is essentially a political matter, supervised by the Committee of Ministers of the Council of Europe. It is a matter for the respondent state to decide how to implement the decision of the ECtHR.[21] Following conveyance of a judgment to it, the Committee of Ministers requests the respondent state to inform it of the measures to be taken to remedy the violation. When satisfied that all the necessary remedial measures have been undertaken, the Committee of Ministers adopts a resolution to that effect.

C. GRETA

15.71 Chapter VII CATHB concerns the monitoring mechanism set up under that convention. This was brought into being under Article 36 CATHB:

Article 36—Group of experts on action against trafficking in human beings

1. The Group of experts on action against trafficking in human beings (hereinafter referred to as 'GRETA'), shall monitor the implementation of this Convention by the Parties.
2. GRETA shall be composed of a minimum of 10 members and a maximum of 15 members, taking into account a gender and geographical balance, as well as a multidisciplinary expertise. They shall be elected by the Committee of the Parties for a term of office of

---

[21] Subject to decisions under the 'pilot judgment' procedure where the ECtHR gives specific indications of the measures to be taken to comply with its judgments in the case of systemic or structural deficiencies: see r 61 of the Rules of Court.

4 years, renewable once, chosen from amongst nationals of the States Parties to this Convention.
3. The election of the members of GRETA shall be based on the following principles:
   (a) they shall be chosen from among persons of high moral character, known for their recognised competence in the fields of Human Rights, assistance and protection of victims and of action against trafficking in human beings or having professional experience in the areas covered by this Convention;
   (b) they shall sit in their individual capacity and shall be independent and impartial in the exercise of their functions and shall be available to carry out their duties in an effective manner;
   (c) no two members of GRETA may be nationals of the same State;
   (d) they should represent the main legal systems.
4. The election procedure of the members of GRETA shall be determined by the Committee of Ministers, after consulting with and obtaining the unanimous consent of the Parties to the Convention, within a period of one year following the entry into force of this Convention. GRETA shall adopt its own rules of procedure.

GRETA is responsible for monitoring implementation of CATHB by the parties. It regularly publishes reports evaluating the measures taken by the parties and invites those which do not fully respect the measures contained in the Convention to step up their action. The evaluation procedure is divided into cycles. At the beginning of each, GRETA will define the provisions to be monitored and will determine the most appropriate means to carry out the evaluation. This is likely to commence by requesting the parties to complete a questionnaire to be followed up with additional requests for information. If GRETA considers it necessary, it may also request information from civil society bodies and/or organise country visits in order to obtain more information. GRETA will then produce a report in draft upon which comments are invited from the State Party. Once comments have been received, GRETA will prepare its final report and conclusions, which will be sent at the same time to the State Party concerned and the Committee of the Parties. GRETA's final report, together with the comments of the State Party, is then published. GRETA is independent and its reports are not susceptible to modification by the Committee of the Parties which represents the State Parties. Details of GRETA's activities are provided on its website.[22]

15.72

The Committee of the Parties may adopt recommendations indicating the measures to be taken by the Party concerned to implement GRETA's conclusions, if necessary setting a date for submitting information on their implementation, and promoting cooperation to ensure the proper implementation of the Convention.

15.73

Unlike some treaty-based monitoring bodies, GRETA does not entertain individual petitions, though individual cases may be considered in conjunction with its overall purpose of monitoring compliance with the CATHB. Its reports may be a source of support regarding issues of compliance by the UK with the CATHB.

15.74

---

[22] www.coe.int/t/dghl/monitoring/trafficking/Docs/Monitoring/GRETA_en.asp.

16

Domestic Remedies

Contents

A.	Introduction	16.1
B.	Appeals	16.6
	B1. The Structure of the Appeals System: Overview	16.6
	B2. Procedure Rules and Practice Directions	16.10
	B3. The DFT Procedure	16.17
	B4. Onward Appeals	16.21
	Upper Tribunal	16.21
	The Court of Appeal and the Supreme Court	16.25
	B5. Appeal Rights: The Impact of IA 2014	16.29
	B6. NIAA 2002 before IA 2014: Overview	16.30
	B7. Appealable Decisions under NIAA 2002 before IA 2014	16.35
	B8. Grounds of Appeal under NIAA 2002 before IA 2014	16.43
	B9. The Claimed Rationale behind IA 2014	16.45
	B10. Appealable Decisions under NIAA 2002 as Amended by IA 2014	16.46
	B11. Grounds of Appeal in NIAA 2002 as Amended by IA 2014	16.51
	B12. IA 2014: Other Changes to Appeals	16.54
	B13. IA 2014: Administrative Review	16.58
	B14. Appeal Rights: EEA Appeals	16.59
	B15. The One-Stop Procedure under NIAA 2002	16.72
C.	Appeals in National Security Cases: The SIAC	16.75
	C1. Background	16.75
	C2. Certification and Grounds	16.80
	C3. Appeals in the SIAC	16.83
	C4. Closed Material, Special Advocates and Disclosure	16.90
	C5. Procedure in Deportation Appeals	16.104
	C6. Onward Appeal to the Court of Appeal	16.112
D.	Judicial Review	16.113
	D1. Basic Principles	16.113
	Amenability to Review and Standing	16.114
	Heads of Review	16.119
	Remedies	16.122
	D2. Damages and Other Relief under the HRA 1998	16.125
	D3. Procedure—Administrative Court	16.128
	D4. Costs in the Administrative Court	16.140
	D5. Transfer to the Upper Tribunal	16.143
	D6. Procedure in the Upper Tribunal	16.151
	D7. Specific Types of Judicial Review Application Relating to Expulsion, Exclusion, Denial or Deprivation of Nationality	16.161
	Non-suspensive Appeals Challenging Removal Directions	16.162

A. Introduction

16.1 In principle the lawfulness of any administrative decision relating to expulsion or exclusion from the territory of the UK and/or denial or deprivation of citizenship may be challenged on established public law grounds, which (in summary) require the avoidance of illegality, irrationality or unfairness.[1] Such challenge is, in the absence of alternative remedy, possible by judicial review, considered in the High Court, the Administrative Court or the Upper Tribunal (Immigration and Asylum Chamber). In some cases, however, there will be an alternative remedy, such as a statutory appeal or internal review providing an effective remedy.

16.2 Judicial review is the means by which the judiciary supervise administrative action. In *Council of Civil Service Unions v Minister for the Civil Service* [1985] AC 374, 408E, Lord Diplock observed that: 'Judicial review ... provides the means by which judicial control of administrative action is exercised.' It has also been described as 'the rule of law in action: a fundamental and inalienable constitutional protection'.[2] The court has found legislation purporting to exclude judicial review to be ineffective in ousting the supervisory jurisdiction of the High Court in *Anisminic Ltd v Foreign Compensation Commission* [1969] 2 AC 147, holding judicial review to be available despite language asserting that decisions of the defendant tribunal were 'not to be called into question in any legal proceedings whatsoever'; and in *R v SSHD ex p Fayed* [1996] EWCA Civ 946, [1998] 1 WLR 763, reviewing refusal of naturalisation despite an apparent ouster by Parliament according to which such decisions should 'not be subject to ... review in, any court'.

16.3 By contrast to judicial review, which rests on the fundamental principles of the underlying constitution, rights to appeal or review are created by statute. In general, nationality decisions are not appealable. By contrast, certain immigration decisions attract statutory appeal rights. The immigration appeals system, though much altered in recent years, has in essence rested since 1 April 2003 upon the NIAA 2002. Appeals in migration cases are now governed by Part V NIAA 2002.[3] At the time of writing, NIAA 2002 remains the central statute governing migration appeals in the UK.

16.4 The entry into force of IA 2004 will significantly alter the system of migration appeals. A summary of the changes is included below.

16.5 This chapter will first examine the appeals regimes, including the appeals structure and appeal rights under NIAA 2002 and IA 2014, and will examine the regime for national security cases in the SIAC, before turning to consider judicial review in the Administrative Court and the Upper Tribunal.

---

[1] This conventional three-fold summary is not exhaustive and its components are not mutually exclusive: see M Fordham, *Judicial Review Handbook* (6th edn, Oxford, Hart Publishing, 2012) 487. The public law wrongs justifying intervention are more fully examined in that work at Part C, P45–P63. On judicial review and administrative law more widely, see H Woolf, J Jowell, A Le Sueur, C Donnelly and I Hare, *De Smith's Judicial Review* (7th edn, London, Sweet & Maxwell, 2013); W Wade and C Forsyth, *Administrative Law* (10th edn, Oxford, Oxford University Press, 2009) 270–76; P Craig, *Administrative Law* (7th edn, London, Sweet & Maxwell, 2012).

[2] Fordham (n 1) Part A, P1, 5. See also Woolf et al (n 1).

[3] Appeals in EEA cases are governed by regs 25–30 Immigration (EEA) Regulations 2006, which refer back to the NIAA 2002. In national security cases, appeals are governed by ss 2 and 2B SIACA 1997.

B. Appeals

B1. The Structure of the Appeals System: Overview

16.6 The appellate authority has evolved over the years from adjudicators and the Immigration Appeal Tribunal to the Asylum and Immigration Tribunal, and from 15 February 2010, pursuant to section 3 of the Tribunals, Courts and Enforcement Act 2007 (TCEA 2007), a two-tier tribunal structure has been in place. This two-tier tribunal structure is composed of the First-Tier Tribunal and the Upper Tribunal, each organised into chambers according to a specific legal area. The Immigration and Asylum Chamber (IAC) deals with immigration matters.

16.7 The First-Tier Tribunal hears appeals against appealable immigration decisions, apart from cases involving issues of national security, which are heard by the SIAC. Whilst remaining part of the First-Tier Tribunal, there is a separate accelerated procedure subject to separate procedure rules applicable to cases subjected to the Detained Fast Track (DFT) procedure. Appeals may either take place whilst the appellant remains in the UK or, in the case of appeals from decisions of entry clearance officers and appeals that are not suspensive of expulsion, where the appellant is present in his or her country of origin.

16.8 There is a right of appeal from the First-Tier Tribunal to the Upper Tribunal on a point of law. If following a refusal of permission by the First-Tier, the Upper Tribunal refuses permission to appeal, an applicant may apply for judicial review of the refusal of permission (on limited grounds).

16.9 A further right of appeal from the Upper Tribunal to the Court of Appeal exists ('a second appeal') with the permission of either the Upper Tribunal or the Court of Appeal if it is considered that the appeal would raise some important point of principle or practice or there is some other compelling reason for the appeal to be heard.[4] Following the Supreme Court's decision in *R (Cart) v Upper Tribunal* [2011] UKSC 28, [2011] 2 WLR 36, the test to be applied in applications for judicial review of the Upper Tribunal's decision to refuse permission to appeal is analogous.

B2. Procedure Rules and Practice Directions

16.10 Immigration appeals in the First-Tier Tribunal (IAC) are governed by the Tribunal Procedure (First-tier Tribunal) (Immigration and Asylum Chamber) Rules 2014. The Schedule of Fast Track Rules, appended to the 2014 Rules, identifies the operative regime for cases under the DFT procedure in the First-Tier Tribunal. Appeals in the Upper Tribunal are governed by the amended Tribunal Procedure (Upper Tribunal)

---

[4] CPR 52.13: '(1) Permission is required from the Court of Appeal for any appeal to that court from a decision of the County Court or the High Court which was itself made on appeal. (2) The Court of Appeal will not give permission unless it considers that—(a) the appeal would raise an important point of principle or practice; or (b) there is some other compelling reason for the Court of Appeal to hear it.'

Part E – Procedure and Remedies

Rules 2008. The procedure rules are supplemented by Practice Directions and Practice Statements.[5]

16.11 In-country appeals to the First-Tier Tribunal are commenced by filing a notice of appeal.[6] The current form is IAFT-1. The in-country appeal must be brought within fourteen days after the notice of the decision appealed is sent to the potential appellant (rule 19(2) Tribunal Procedure (First-tier Tribunal) (Immigration and Asylum Chamber) Rules 2014).

16.12 Appeals instituted from outside of the UK are commenced by filing a notice of appeal (rule 19(3) Procedure Rules), currently on Form IAFT-3. This must be done within 28 days from receipt of the notice of the immigration decision (rule 19(3)(b) Tribunal Procedure (First-tier Tribunal) (Immigration and Asylum Chamber) Rules 2014).

16.13 The calculation of time is dictated by rule 11 Tribunal Procedure (First-tier Tribunal) (Immigration and Asylum Chamber) Rules 2014 by which an act required to be on or by a particular day must be done by midnight on that day (in the absence of contrary direction), and where the time period ends on a day which is not a 'working day' under the Rules, the act is done in time if done on the next day. Where a notice of an immigration decision is defective such that it does not comply with the Immigration and Asylum Appeals (Notices) regulations 2000, time does not run against an appellant (*DJ (Defective Notice of Decision) Iraq* [2004] UKIAT 00194).

16.14 The First-Tier Tribunal has the power to extend time for filing the notice of appeal, by virtue of rule 20(4) Procedure Rules, if it is satisfied that it would be unjust not to do so.

16.15 A fee is payable with the appeal unless the appellant is exempt. For example, those facing removal and those in receipt of legal aid are exempt.

16.16 Applications to the First-Tier Tribunal for permission to appeal to the Upper Tribunal are currently commenced on Form IAFT-4. These must be submitted 'so that it is received no later than 14 days after the date on which the party working the application was served with written reasons for the decision' (rule 33(2) Procedure Rules) or where an appellant is outside the UK, the time limit for that person sending or delivering an application is 28 days (rule 33(3) Procedure Rules). In all circumstances these are calendar days. Once again, the First-Tier Tribunal has the power to extend time if satisfied that by reasons of special circumstances it would be unjust not to do so (rule 4(3)(a) Procedure Rules).

B3. The DFT Procedure

16.17 Where asylum claimants are detained whilst their claim is being processed, their appeals are expedited under the DFT procedures. The relevant procedure rules are contained in the Schedule of Fast Track Rules, appended to the Tribunal Procedure Rules.

---

[5] Which can be found at www.justice.gov.uk/tribunals/immigration-asylum-upper/rules-and-legislation.
[6] Rule 19 Tribunal Procedure (First-tier Tribunal) (Immigration and Asylum Chamber) Rules 2014.

16.18 Where an individual is subject to the DFT procedure, a decision on his or her claim should be made within three days of arrival, and notice of appeal must be made not later than two working days after the day on which the relevant immigration decision was served (rule 5(1) Schedule of Fast Track Rules). The test for extension of this time limit is whether it is in the interests of justice to do so (Rule 5(2) Schedule of Fast Track Rules). The Secretary of State must then file within two days of service upon him or her of the notice of appeal the following documents (rule 7 Schedule of Fast Track Rules): the notice of the decision to which the notice of appeal relates and any other document served on the appellant giving reasons for that decision; any statement of evidence form completed by the appellant; a record of an interview with the appellant in relation to the decision being appealed; any other unpublished document which is referred to in any of the aforementioned documents or relied upon by him or her; the notice of any other immigration decision made in relation to the appellant in respect of which he or she has a right of appeal under section 82 NIAA 2002. The appeal hearing is to be fixed no later than two days after the Secretary of State has filed the documents required of him or her by rule 7 or as soon as practicable thereafter.

16.19 The Tribunal has the power to: (i) adjourn the hearing within the fast track procedure (rule 12 Schedule of Fast Track Rules); or (ii) remove the case from the fast track procedure altogether (rule 4 Schedule of Fast Track Rules). The Tribunal may only adjourn the hearing in two scenarios: (i) the Tribunal is satisfied that the appeal or application cannot be justly determined on the date within the timescale provided for, normally, not more than 10 days after the date on which the appeal or application is listed for hearing, by which it can be justly determined (rule 12(b) Schedule of Fast Track Rules). Transfers out of the fast-track procedure can only take place in two scenarios: (i) if all parties consent (rule 4(1)(a) Schedule of Fast Track Rules); (ii) if the Tribunal is satisfied the appeal or application cannot be justly determined (rule 14(1)(b) Schedule of Fast Track Rules).

16.20 The Tribunal is expected to serve its determination of the appeal on both parties no later than two days after the day upon which the hearing concluded (rule 10(2) Schedule of Fast Track Rules). Any application for permission to appeal must be sent or delivered to the Tribunal so that it is received no later than three days after the date on which the party was served with the written decision (rule 11 Schedule of Fast Track Rules).

B4. Onward Appeals

Upper Tribunal

16.21 Unsuccessful appellants in the First-Tier Tribunal may appeal against any decision that is not excluded by section 11 TCEA 2007.[7] The success of the appeal is dependent upon

---

[7] This includes: (i) refusals of bail; (ii) procedural, ancillary or preliminary decisions; (iii) decisions by the First-Tier Tribunal not to self-review; (iv) decisions by the First-Tier Tribunal not to take action in light of self-review; (v) decisions to set aside earlier decision of the First-Tier Tribunal; (vi) decisions to refer or not refer a matter to the Upper Tribunal; (vii) decisions already set aside by the First-Tier Tribunal.

the demonstration of the existence of a material error of law (section 11(1) TCEA 2007). A non-exhaustive list of potential material errors of law was provided by Brooke LJ in the Court of Appeal in *R (Iran) v SSHD* [2005] EWCA Civ 982, [2005] Imm AR 535 [9]:

(i) Making perverse or irrational findings on a matter or matters that were material to the outcome (material matters);
(ii) Failing to give reasons or any adequate reasons for findings on material matters;
(iii) Failing to take into account and/or resolve conflicts of fact or opinion on material matters;
(iv) Giving weight to immaterial matters;
(v) Making a material misdirection of law on any material matter;
(vi) Committing or permitting a procedural or other irregularity capable of making a material difference to the outcome or the fairness of the proceedings;
(vii) Making a mistake as to a material fact which could be established by objective and uncontentious evidence, where the appellant and/or his advisers were not responsible for the mistake, and where unfairness resulted from the fact that a mistake was made.

16.22   Upon receipt of the application for permission to appeal, the First-Tier Tribunal will first consider whether to itself review the decision against which an appeal is being sought (section 9 TCEA 2007). The test on review will be whether the error of law deprived a party of a fair hearing or other opportunity to put their case or there are 'highly compelling reasons' why the matter should be re-decided by the First-Tier Tribunal. If the First-Tier Tribunal decides to review or, having reviewed the decision, decides to leave it substantially the same, the First-Tier Tribunal then has to go on and decide whether to grant permission to appeal to the Upper Tribunal.

16.23   Permission must be sought from the First-Tier Tribunal before being sought in turn, after refusal by the First-Tier Tribunal, from the Upper Tribunal (rule 21(2) Tribunal Procedure (Upper Tribunal) Rules 2008, SI 2008/2698). The application must be made seven working days after the date on which the First-Tier Tribunal's refusal was sent to the appellant (rule 21(3)(aa)(i) Tribunal Procedure (Upper Tribunal) Rules 2008)[8] or 56 days where the appellant is outside the UK. The Upper Tribunal has discretion to extend time (rule 5(3)(a) Tribunal Procedure (Upper Tribunal) Rules 2008), but any application for permission to appeal made out-of-time must be accompanied by a request for an extension of time and an explanation as to why the time limits were not complied with (rule 21(6)(a) Tribunal Procedure (Upper Tribunal) Rules 2008).

16.24   If the Upper Tribunal finds a material error of law, it can: (i) remit the case back to the First-Tier Tribunal with directions for its reconsideration; or (ii) re-make the decision itself, whereby it will have the power to make any decision the First-Tier Tribunal could have made.

The Court of Appeal and the Supreme Court

16.25   An application for permission to appeal to the Court of Appeal must first be made to the Upper Tribunal before seeking permission to appeal directly from the Court of Appeal.

---

[8] Note that if the decision was sent electronically or delivered personally, the application for permission to appeal must be received by the Upper Tribunal no later than five working days after the date on which the notice of refusal of permission was sent to the appellant, by virtue of r 21(3A)(a).

As outlined in paragraph 16.9 above, the test to be applied is the 'second appeals' test established in *R (Cart)*. This states that permission to appeal to the Court of Appeal should not be granted unless: (a) the proposed appeal would raise some important point of principle or practice; or (b) there is some other compelling reason for the relevant appellate court to hear the appeal.

Carnwarth LJ has clarified in *PR (Sri Lanka), SS (Bangladesh) and TC (Zimbabwe)* [2011] EWCA Civ 988, [2012] 1 WLR 73 at [36] that '"compelling" means legally compelling rather than compelling, perhaps from a political or emotional point of view, although such considerations may exceptionally add weight to the legal arguments' (see also *JD (Congo)* [2012] EWCA Civ 327, [2012] 1 WLR 3273 in which the Court of Appeal tempered the conclusion of the court in *PR (Sri Lanka)* by finding that whilst stringent, the test of 'compelling reasons' was sufficiently flexible to take into account the particular factual circumstances of the case). 16.26

If permission to appeal is granted, but the appeal to the Court of Appeal is dismissed, an application may be made for permission to appeal to the Supreme Court. Permission is granted where, in the opinion of the Justices, the application raises an arguable point of law of general public importance which ought to be considered by the Supreme Court at that time, bearing in mind that the matter will already have been the subject of judicial decision and may have already been reviewed on appeal. An appeal panel, consisting of no fewer than three Justices will consider applications for permission, and will do so generally without a hearing. 16.27

Those unable to obtain an effective remedy from the domestic courts may apply to the ECtHR: see further, chapter 15. 16.28

B5. Appeal Rights: The Impact of IA 2014

NIAA 2002 provides for rights of appeal, in circumstances set out in section 82, and grounds of appeal, prescribed in section 84. However, IA 2014, which received the royal assent on 14 May 2014, will lead to the wholesale reform of the appeals system.[9] Most notably, it inserts into NIAA 2002 new and more restrictive versions of sections 82 and 84 and repeals sections 83 and 83A. It also has significant effects on deportation appeals. At this time of flux, it is important that practitioners are aware of both sets of provisions: ie NIAA 2002 before IA 2014 and NIAA 2002 after IA 2014. This section covers both scenarios. 16.29

B6. NIAA 2002 before IA 2014: Overview

There is no right of appeal against a decision refusing applications for leave to remain from illegal entrants, overstayers or those in breach of conditions who had 16.30

---

[9] At the time of writing, the central appeals provisions of IA 2014 have entered into force in respect of Tier 4 student applications and deportation decisions only.

no leave at the date of the application. However, irregular migrants, liable to summary removal by directions given by an immigration officer (section 10 IAA 1999), have a right of appeal against the decision to remove them.[10] Therefore, every migrant who is subject to a removal decision has a right of appeal, although this may be restricted by certification.

16.31 Migrants whose deportation is recommended by a criminal court (section 6 IA 1971) and those whose deportation is deemed by the Secretary of State to be conducive to the public good (section 3(5) IA 1971) have a right of appeal under section 82(2)(j) NIAA 2002. Since the Secretary of State is required to make a deportation order where the circumstances listed in section 32 UKBA 2007 prevail, such a decision will attract a right of appeal under the NIAA 2002 (section 32(5) UKBA 2007 and section 82(2)(j) of the NIAA 2002). In sum, therefore, those subject to a deportation decision have a right of appeal.

16.32 Whether an appeal suspends expulsion is determined by sections 92–98 NIAA 2002. Section 92 NIAA 2002 establishes a presumption that an appeal can only be pursued from outside the UK unless that section says otherwise. In order to determine whether the hearing of the appeal will be inside the UK, one must look at the type of decision being appealed and the type of claim being made. In respect of irregular migrants, under section 92(1), a right of appeal may be exercised only after removal, save where an asylum or human rights claim has been made (section 92(1) and (4)(a) NIAA 2002) or where there is a claim that a decision breaches EU law (sections 92(1) and (4)(b) NIAA 2002). The exercise of an appeal right suspends expulsion in deportation cases (section 92(1) and (2) NIAA 2002). However, the Secretary of State may extinguish an in-country appeal right by certifying a claim on the grounds listed in NIAA 2002, namely that the claim is clearly unfounded (section 94), that there is a safe country of origin (section 94A), or where there was an earlier right of appeal on the same matter (section 96). In addition, NIAA 2002, as amended by section 7 IANA 2006, includes a power to certify an in-country right of appeal, under section 97A NIAA 2002, where Secretary of State certifies that deportation is on the basis of national security. Where an appeal raises human rights grounds, they will be heard prior to removal unless the Secretary of State certifies that removal will not breach the UK's human rights obligations under the ECHR.

16.33 Section 40A BNA 1981 provides a right of appeal against a decision to make an order depriving an individual of citizenship. The Secretary of State must notify the individual of his or her decision to deprive him or her of citizenship (section 40(5) BNA 1981). The person given the notice of appeal may appeal against the decision before the order is made (section 40A BNA 1981).

16.34 There is no right of appeal against the refusal to register a person as a British citizen, and an application for judicial review is the only avenue to remedy.

---

[10] An appeal against leave to enter is not an appeal against removal directions, even though the notice of decision may include such directions.

B7. Appealable Decisions under NIAA 2002 before IA 2014

Section 82 NIAA 2002 provides the following exhaustive list of decisions which attract a right of appeal: 16.35

— refusal of leave to enter the UK (section 82(2)(a));
— refusal of entry clearance (section 82(2)(b));
— refusal of a certificate of entitlement under section 10 NIAA 2002 (section 82(2)(c));
— refusal to vary a person's leave to enter or remain in the UK if the result of the refusal is that the person has no leave to enter or remain (section 82(2)(d));
— variation of a person's leave to enter or remain in the UK if when the variation takes effect, the person has no leave to enter or remain (section 82(2)(e));
— revocation under section 76 NIAA 2002 of indefinite leave to enter or remain in the UK (section 82(2)(f));
— a decision that a person is to be removed from the UK by way of directions under section 10(1)(a), (b) or (c) IAA 1999 (section 82(2)(g));
— a decision that an illegal entrant is to be removed from the UK by way of directions under paragraphs 8–10 of Schedule 2 to the IA 1971 (section 82(2)(h));
— a decision that a person is to be removed by way of directions under section 47 IANA 2006 (section 82(2)(ha));
— a decision that a person is to be removed from the UK by way of directions given by virtue of paragraph 10A of Schedule 2 IA 1971 (section 82(2)(i));
— a decision that a person is to be removed from the UK by way of directions under paragraph 12(2) of Schedule 2 IA 1971 (section 82(2)(ia));
— a decision to make an order under section 2A IA 1971 (section 82(2)(ib));
— a decision to make a deportation order under section 5(1) IA 1971 (section 82(2)(j)) and refusal to revoke a deportation order under section 5(2) IA 1971 (ie, the decision to make a deportation order following a court recommendation) (section 82(2)(k)).

The right of appeal under section 82 is limited by the provisions in sections 88 and 91 NIAA 2002, which exclude the following types of case from the right of appeal: 16.36

(a) Decisions taken on the grounds that the applicant or his or her dependant: (i) does not satisfy a requirement as to age, nationality or citizenship specified in the Immigration Rules (section 88(2)(a) NIAA 2002); (ii) does not have an immigration document (section 88(2)(b) NIAA 2002); (iii) is seeking to be in the UK for a period longer than that permitted by the Immigration Rules (section 88(2)(c) NIAA 2002); (iv) is seeking to enter of remain in the UK for a purpose other than one permitted by the Immigration Rules (section 88(2)(d) NIAA 2002); or (v) has failed to supply a medical report or medical certificate in accordance with a requirement of the Immigration Rules (section 88(2)(ba) NIAA 2002).
(b) Refusal of entry clearance unless entering as the dependant of a person in circumstances prescribed by the relevant regulations (section 88A(1) NIAA 2002). The relevant regulations can be found in the Immigration, Asylum and Nationality 2006 (Commencement No 8 and Transitional and Saving Provisions)

Order 2008, SI 2008/310. The effect of the regulations are that only points-based system and visit visa applicants are prevented from appealing against refusals of entry clearance.

16.37 These limitations do not apply to appeals on grounds of race discrimination, in-country asylum or human rights (section 88(4) NIAA 2002).

16.38 Sections 83 and 83A NIAA 2002 also create rights of appeal specific to asylum and humanitarian protection appeals.

16.39 Section 83 NIAA 2002, stipulates that a refusal of a claim for asylum is appealable if the person has been refused asylum, but has been granted leave to enter or remain for a period exceeding one year or for periods exceeding one year in aggregate. The refusal of asylum does not itself attract a right of appeal as it is not an 'immigration decision' pursuant to section 82. A person refused asylum without being granted or having had leave to enter or remain for more than a year may only appeal if, as well as being refused asylum, he or she is the subject of an immigration decision within the meaning of section 82(2) NIAA 2002.

16.40 Section 83A NIAA 2002 provides a right of appeal where the Secretary of State decides that an individual is no longer entitled to refugee status, but he or she has leave to remain in the UK otherwise than as a refugee.

16.41 The appeals system is different for EEA nationals who have rights of appeal by virtue of EU instruments implemented into domestic law: see section B14.

16.42 There is also a right of appeal (to the SIAC) against a decision by the Secretary of State to certify as clearly unfounded a human rights claim by a person against whom the Secretary of State has made a decision to make a deportation order which he or she has certified as taken on the ground that the person's removal from the UK would be in the interests of national security (section 97A(3) NIAA 2002, inserted by section 7 IANA 2006).

B8. Grounds of Appeal under NIAA 2002 before IA 2014

16.43 Another development brought about by NIAA 2002 was the statutory definition of the grounds that can be relied upon when appealing section 82 immigration decisions. These grounds are set out at section 84. At least one of these grounds must be relied upon when bringing an appeal against a section 82 decision. They are:

— not in accordance with the Immigration Rules (section 84(1)(a) NIAA 2002);
— unlawful by virtue of section 19(b) RRA 1976 (discrimination by public authorities) (section 84(1)(b) NIAA 2002);
— unlawful by virtue of section 6 HRA 1998 in terms of being incompatible with an individual's rights under the ECHR (section 84(1)(c) NIAA 2002);
— where an individual is an EEA national or family member and the decision breaches the his or her rights under EU Treaties in respect of entry to or residence in the UK (section 84(1)(d) NIAA 2002);
— where the decision not in accordance with the law (section 84(1)(e) NIAA 2002);
— where the person taking the decision should have exercised a discretion conferred by the Immigration Rules differently (section 84(1)(f) NIAA 2002);

— where the removal of an individual from the UK as a consequence of immigration decision would breach the UK's obligation under the Refugee Convention or would be unlawful under section 6 HRA 1998 (section 84(1)(g) NIAA 2002).

Decisions under sections 83 and 83A are appealable only on Refugee Convention and humanitarian protection grounds, by virtue of section 83(3) and 83(4). **16.44**

B9. The Claimed Rationale behind IA 2014

In outlining the objective behind the IA 2014, Lord Taylor of Holbeach, the Conservative Home Office Minister, said at the second reading of the then Immigration Bill in the House of Lords on 10 February 2014: **16.45**

> We are simplifying an overly complex system that forces people to bring expensive and time-consuming appeals. These reforms will incentivise those who wish to make claims to do so at the earliest opportunity and will strengthen the adverse consequences for those who make claims too late, in order to obstruct the removal process. We recognise that many appeals are allowed under the current system and there will be legitimate concerns. Many appeals are allowed because we take a different view from the courts on Article 8. The Bill will require the courts to put the public interest at the heart of their consideration of Article 8. We are achieving this in a way wholly compatible with the convention and fully maintaining our duty to promote and safeguard the best interests of children.
>
> Many appeals are allowed because of administrative errors in decision-making. We believe that an administrative review can better correct those errors. We will debate the merits of the administrative review in Committee, but it has proven effective at resolving entry-clearance removals since 2008. A 28-day administrative process is substantially quicker and cheaper than the average 12 weeks it now takes to appeal via the tribunal and all the costs that this incurs.

B10. Appealable Decisions under NIAA 2002 as Amended by IA 2014

The previous list of immigration decisions in section 82 has been replaced by a far more limited list. The new section 82, incorporated into NIAA 2002 by virtue of section 15 IA 2014, removes the right to appeal against the 17 immigration decisions in the old section 82. **16.46**

The only remaining rights of appeal are against: (i) refusal of a 'protection claim' (section 82(1)(a)); (ii) refusal of a human rights claim (section 82(1)(b));[11] or (iii) a decision to revoke a person's protection status (section 82(1)(c)). **16.47**

---

[11] Section 82(1)(b) NIAA 2002 as amended by s 15 IA 2014 requires a 'human rights claim' to have been made by an applicant and refused by SSHD. At the time of writing, 'human rights claim' is defined in s 113 NIAA 2002 as follows: '"human rights claim" means a claim made by a person to the Secretary of State at a place designated by the Secretary of State that to remove the person from or require him to leave the United Kingdom would be unlawful under section 6 of the Human Rights Act 1998 (c 42) (public authority not to act contrary to Convention) as being incompatible with his Convention rights.' IA 2014 (paragraph 53 Schedule 9) amends the definition substantively by adding to it a claim that a refusal of entry to the United Kingdom breaches section 6 HRA 1998. However, the amendment will not provide an

16.48 A 'protection claim' is defined in section 82(2)(a) NIAA 2002 as a claim made by a person that his or her removal from the UK would breach the country's obligations under the Refugee Convention or would breach its obligations in relation to persons eligible for a grant of humanitarian protection. Section 82(2)(b) defines when a protection claim is refused, namely whether the Secretary of State either decides that an individual's removal would not breach the UK's obligations under the Refugee Convention or its obligations in relation to persons eligible for a grant of humanitarian protection. A person with protection status is defined in section 82(2)(c) as a person who has been granted leave to enter or remain as a refugee or as someone eligible for humanitarian protection.

16.49 IA 2014 (by virtue of section 15, once in force) also repeals sections 83 and 83A NIAA 2002. These sections also created rights of appeal specific to asylum and humanitarian protection appeals (see paras 16.38-39 above).

16.50 The rights of appeal in respect of EEA decisions, as seen below, derive from the EEA Regulations and are not repealed by IA 2014.

B11. Grounds of Appeal in NIAA 2002 as Amended by IA 2014

16.51 In tandem with the significant reduction to the rights of appeal available, IA equally reduces and limits grounds of appeal. As with rights of appeal, there are now just three grounds of appeal.

16.52 If an appeal is brought under section 82(1)(a), that is, in respect of a refusal of a protection claim, then there are three possible grounds of appeal: (i) that removal from the UK would breach the UK's obligations under the Refugee Convention (section 84(1)(a)); (ii) that removal from the UK would breach the UK's obligations in relation to persons eligible for a grant of humanitarian protection (section 84(1)(b)); (iii) that removal from the UK would be unlawful under section 6 HRA 1998.

16.53 Given that IA 2014 repeals the grounds of appeal that permitted the First-tier Tribunal to examine a decision's correct application of the relevant law (including public law principles) (ie the 'not in accordance with the Immigration Rules' and 'not in accordance with the law' grounds of challenge—see para 16.43), it is unclear if and how such issues may be argued on appeal once the appeals provisions of IA 2014 enter into force. However, it is suggested that these issues may still be litigated under Article 8 ECHR. This is because in order to comply with human rights, a decision must be 'in accordance with the law' (this is expressly the third stage of the House of Lords' famous

---

in-country right of appeal from refusals of entry engaging human rights since the new section 92(4) NIAA 2002 provides that an appeal from human rights claim made from outside the UK must be brought out-of-country (see further para 16.56 below). It should also be noted that section 12 Immigration, Asylum and Nationality Act 2006 provides an amended definition of 'human rights claim' in section 113 NIAA 2002 but this section has not yet (at the time of writing) been brought into force. Section 12 provides: '"human rights claim"—(a) means a claim made by a person that to remove him from or require him to leave the United Kingdom would be unlawful under section 6 of the Human Rights Act 1998 (c 42) (public authority not to act contrary to Convention) as being incompatible with his Convention rights, but (b) does not include a claim which, having regard to a former claim, falls to be disregarded for the purposes of this Part in accordance with immigration rules.' It is as yet unclear which definition of 'human rights claim' IA 2014 is intended to amend.

Razgar test: *R (Razgar) v SSHD* [2004] UKHL 27, [2004] 2 AC 368). Arguably, therefore, a decision that involves human rights (eg a refusal of a spouse visa or indefinite leave to remain on the grounds of long residence) that is not in accordance with the Immigration Rules or public law principles will be unlawful on the basis of the third stage of the *Razgar* test. In such circumstances it will not be necessary to show that the decision is disproportionate under the fifth stage of *Razgar*. This question will doubtlessly be subject of litigation.

B12. IA 2014: Other Changes to Appeals

The effect of the changes to the rights and grounds of appeal in IA 2014 will be to vastly reduce the number of appeals brought to the First-tier Tribunal. Many individuals with leave to remain, in particular economic migrants such as students and workers, will no longer have a right of appeal. The only remedy available to these groups will be administrative review (see below) or judicial review. However, importantly individuals whose only remedy is judicial review will not have their leave to remain extended by statute (section 3C IA 1971) whilst the judicial review is pending. On the other hand, overstayers and others without immigration status but with family or private life in the UK will now have a right of appeal upon refusal of an application made on that basis (subject to the Secretary of State's certification powers under sections 94 and 96 NIAA 2002, which are retained by IA 2014—see para 16.32).[12] A summary of further changes IA 2014 makes to the appeals system is provided below.   **16.54**

Matters arising after decision: section 85 NIAA 2002 is amended by section 15(5) IA 2014 so that the Tribunal may only consider matters arising after the decision being appealed with the Secretary of State's consent. A 'new matter' is defined in the new section 85(6) as a ground of appeal of a kind listed in section 84, and the Secretary of State has not previously considered the matter in the context of a section 82(1) decision or a section 120 statement.   **16.55**

Location of appeal: section 17 IA 2014 amends section 92 NIAA 2002 in respect of the location from which an appeal must be brought. Per section 92(2)(a) and (b) NIAA 2002, section 92(3)(a) and (b) NIAA 2002) appeals under sections 32(1)(a) and (b) can be brought in-country unless the Secretary of State certifies the appeal under section 94(1) or (7) or unless paragraph 5(3)(a), 10(3), 15(3) or 19(b) of Schedule 3 to the Asylum and Immigration (Treatment of Claimants etc) Act 2004 applies. A section 82(1)(b) appeal must be brought out of country if the claim to which the appeal relates was made whilst the appellant was out of the country: section 92(4). Section 82(1)(c) appeals must be brought in-country if the decision to which the appeal relates was made while the appellant was in the UK, and out-of-country if the appellant was outside the UK when the decision was made.   **16.56**

Certification in deportation cases: the IA 2014 has brought into force[13] new provisions in relation to whether a person liable to deportation may bring an appeal, having made   **16.57**

---

[12] This resolves the notorious difficulties in obtaining a right of appeal experienced by overstayers since the decision in *R (Daley-Murdoch) v SSHD* [2011] EWCA Civ 161, [2011] WLR D 56.

[13] Brought into force on 28 July 2014 by the first commencement order under IA 2014 (The Immigration Act 2014 (Commencement No. 1, Transitory and Saving Provisions) Order 2014). There are, therefore, com-

a human rights claim, from within the UK. The new section is section 94B NIAA 2002, incorporated into that Act by section 17 IA 2014. Section 94B(2) IA 2014 gives the Secretary of State the power to certify the human rights claim made by a person liable to deportation[14] if he or she 'considers that, despite the appeals process not having been begun or not having been exhausted, removal of P [a person liable to deportation] to the country or territory to which P is proposed to be removed, pending the outcome of an appeal to P's claim, would not be unlawful under section 6 HRA 1998.' The grounds for certification are set out in section 94B(3) NIAA 2002, namely whether P would 'before the appeals process is exhausted, face a real risk of serious irreversible harm if removed to the country or territory to which P is proposed to be removed'. From the wording of section 94B it is clear that the Home Office's interpretation of the power is that absent a real risk of 'serious irreversible harm', certification will comply with the ECHR. The test of 'serious irreversible harm' appears to originate from the jurisprudence of the ECtHR, in particular indications under Rule 39 (see further chapter 15) and in the case of *De Souza Ribeiro v France* [GC] no 22689/07 [2012] ECHR 2066. The *De Souza Ribeiro* case distinguishes between claims that expulsion pending appeal will violate Article 3 ECHR and those that claim Article 8 will be violated (at [82]–[83]). The ECtHR concluded that 'where expulsions are challenged on the basis of alleged interference with private and family life, it is not imperative, in order to be effective, that it should have automatic suspensive effect' (at [83]). Accordingly, this appears to support the Home Office position, however, in *Nunez v Norway* no 55597/09 [2011] ECHR 1047, (2014) 58 EHRR 17, the ECtHR found that separation of the person liable to deportation from her children would cause 'irreversible harm' such that interim urgent relief was appropriate under Rule 39. Undoubtedly there will be litigation on the application of section 94B.

B13. IA 2014: Administrative Review

16.58 It is the present government's stated intention that the new appeals system is to be supplemented by a system of administrative review of decisions that individuals assert have been wrongly made, but in relation to which they no longer, by virtue IA 2014, have a right of appeal.[15] A limited system of administrative review presently operates in

---

plex transitional provisions. The effect of the first commencement order on deportation appeals in practice is, however, to remove an in-country appeal as of right from deportation decisions, as well as from human rights and EEA claims in the deportation context. It affects both EEA and non-EEA appeals. It is unclear what the effect of s 94B on pending appeals will be. UKVI guidance appears to suggest that the powers can be used before the appeal process has been exhausted, however, on the face of the provisions existing appeal rights do not appear to be affected. This is likely to be the subject of litigation.

[14] Section 94B(1) applies expressly to conducive deportations under section 3(5)(a) IA 1971 and court recommended deportations under section 3(6) IA 1971. By virtue of s 32(4) UKBA 2007, which deems automatic deportation to be conducive to the public good for the purposes of section 3(5)(a) IA 1971, section 94B(1) would appear also to apply to automatic deportation under UKBA 2007.

[15] At the time of writing the Immigration Rules have been updated to include provisions on administrative review. Appendix Administrative Review sets out the procedure. Rules 34M to 34Y set out the powers of the Home Office.

relation to some decisions under NIAA 2002 before IA 2014, but this is to be extended greatly once IA 2014 comes into force.

16.59 The statement of intent on administrative review produced by the government in support of the passage IA 2014 discloses the following principles.

16.60 Administrative review will resolve case-working errors:

— where it is alleged that the Home Office has applied the wrong immigration rules;
— where it is alleged that the Home Office has not applied the immigration rules correctly;
— where it is alleged that the Home Office has added up points to be awarded under the Immigration Rules incorrectly;
— where it is alleged that there has been an error in calculating the correct period of immigration leave;
— where it is alleged that the Home Office has granted the wrong type of immigration leave;
— where the Home Office has not considered all the evidence that was submitted;
— where a challenge is made to the exercise of discretion or where credibility is an issue. The test on review would be only whether the original decision was unreasonable/perverse, not a new credibility decision;
— where the application is refused on the basis that the documents supporting the application did not meet the requirements of the Immigration Rules or were not genuine;
— where the Home Office has not applied the evidential flexibility policy correctly (a process by which an applicant is asked to correct minor omissions in an application before the application is decided).

16.61 Post-decision evidence cannot be submitted at the administrative review stage. The only exception to this will be where the new evidence is relied upon to demonstrate that a previously submitted document is genuine or meets the requirements of the Immigration Rules.

16.62 Human rights grounds cannot be raised as part of the administrative review process. The government has indicated that it is necessary for an individual to instead make a separate human rights application or asylum claim.

16.63 An individual can only request one administrative review of a refusal decision, unless the decision is maintained on different grounds. In that case, an individual can request a further administrative review.

16.64 Valid requests for administrative review (of a decision that is eligible for it) that are in-time and are accompanied by payment are suspensive of removal.

16.65 There will be a charge for requesting an administrative review, although the statement document indicates that this will not be more than £80.

16.66 The time limits that apply to requests for administrative review are 14 calender days from receipt of the refusal decision unless an individual is in detention when it will be seven days.

16.67 The Home Office has indicated that it will have a service standard of completing administrative reviews within 28 days.

16.68 Within a year of the administrative review process being established, the Secretary of State is required to ask the independent chief inspector to include a review of the administrative review process in his or her inspection plan (section 16 IA 2014).

B14. Appeal Rights: EEA Appeals

16.69 As noted above, the appeals system is different for EEA nationals. EEA decisions[16] are treated as immigration decisions under section 82 NIAA 2002. A ground of appeal under EEA law grounds can be raised by virtue of section 84. This is preserved by IA 2014.[17] An EEA national or family member of an EEA national may also appeal to the First-Tier Tribunal or the SIAC against an EEA decision by virtue of regulation 26 of the Immigration (European Economic Area) Regulations 2006 (the EEA Regulations).[18]

16.70 An EEA decision is defined in regulation 2 EEA Regulations as a decision made under those regulations concerning a person's:

— entitlement to admission to the UK;
— entitlement to be issued with, have renewed or not have revoked a registration certificate, residence card, derivative residence card, document certifying permanent residence or permanent residence card;
— removal from the UK;
— right to reside in the UK being cancelled, pursuant to regulation 20A.

16.71 There are some limitations to the right of appeal under the EEA Regulations. An EEA national may not appeal under the EEA regulations unless he or she produces a valid national identity card or passport issued by an EEA state, and a person claiming to have a relationship to the EEA national must produce a passport and either an EEA family permit or the requisite proof that he or she is related to the EEA national. The Secretary of State may certify a ground under regulation 26(5) if it has been considered in a previous appeal, whether brought under the EEA Regulations or section 82(1) NIAA 2002.

B15. The One-Stop Procedure under NIAA 2002

16.72 Section 120 NIAA 2002 requires an appellant who is given a one-stop warning (a section 120 notice) by the Home Office to declare any additional grounds for being allowed to stay in the UK other than those raised in his or her application (section 120(2)(c)). This is done in a one-stop statement.

16.73 If an individual fails, without good reason, to provide all of his or her reasons in response to a section 120 notice, a later application may be certified under section 96(2) with the consequence that he or she may lose his or her right to appeal.

---

[16] Made after 1 April 2003.
[17] The venue of appeals in EEA deportation cases is, however, altered by IA 2014. See para 16.59.
[18] The appeal rights under the EEA Regulations derive from Directive 2004/38/EC of 30 April 2004 on the right of citizens of the Union and their family members to move and reside freely within the territory of the Member States [2004] OJ L158/77, which the EEA Regulations have transposed into domestic law. The appeal rights provided by Directive 2004/38/EC are considered in ch 14.

In *Lamichhane v SSHD* [2012] EWCA Civ 260, [2012] 1 WLR 3064, the Court of Appeal held that the Secretary of State is not under a legal duty to serve a section 120 notice. An appellant on whom no section 120 notice has been served cannot raise before the First-Tier Tribunal any ground for the grant of leave to remain different from that which was the subject of the Secretary of State's decision being appealed against.

16.74

C. Appeals in National Security Cases: The SIAC

C1. Background

The SIAC is a superior court of record established by section 1(3) Special Immigration Appeals Commission Act 1997, added by the Anti-terrorism, Crime and Security Act 2001 (ATCSA 2001).

16.75

Its purpose is to hear appeals relating to those individuals who are excluded from the normal appeals system on the grounds of national security or some other protected public interest. These individuals are excluded by means of certification by the Secretary of State.

16.76

The SIAC was established in response to the judgment of the ECtHR in *Chahal v UK* (1996) 22 EHRR 413, which held that the predecessor extra-statutory advisory procedure did not satisfy the procedural fairness requirements of Articles 5(4), 3 and 13 ECHR.

16.77

The SIAC is governed by SIACA 1997. The relevant procedure rules are found in the Special Immigration Appeals Commission (Procedure) Rules 2003, SI 2003/1034 as amended (hereinafter the SIAC Procedure Rules), created under section 5 SIACA 1997.

16.78

Until March 2005, the SIAC had responsibility for adjudicating challenges to detention under Part 4 ATCSA 2001. However, following the judgment in *A and others v SSHD* [2004] UKHL 56, [2005] 2 AC 68 and the lapsing and repeal of the scheme by which by which a person could be certified as 'a suspected international terrorist' and detained under IA 1971 if he or she could not be deported from the UK, the SIAC no longer deals with these types of cases.

16.79

C2. Certification and Grounds

The Secretary of State can certify any of the following decisions:[19]

16.80

— a decision listed under section 82 NIAA 2002;
— (prior to the entry into force of IA 2014) the rejection of an asylum claim under section 83(2) NIAA 2002;[20]

---

[19] Appeal then lies to the SIAC by virtue of s 97 NIAA 2002, reg 28 EEA Regulations 2006 and s 40A BNA 1981.
[20] Section 83 NIAA 2002 is repealed by IA 2014.

— (prior to the entry into force of IA 2014) the decision to curtail or to refuse to extend limited leave following a decision that a person is not a refugee under section 83A NIAA 2002;[21]
— EEA decisions;
— a decision to deprive a person of citizenship under section 40 BNA 1981.

16.81 Certification can take place on the following grounds:

— the decision was taken wholly or partly (or given wholly or partly in accordance with a direction of the Secretary of State which identifies the person to whom the decision relates) in the interests of national security; or
— the decision was taken wholly or partly (or given wholly or partly in accordance with a direction of the Secretary of State which identifies the person to whom the decision relates) in the interests of the relationship between the UK and another country; or
— the decision was taken wholly or partly in reliance on information which in the Secretary of State's opinion should not be made public in the above interests or otherwise in the public interest.

16.82 The decision to certify must be taken by the Secretary of State acting in person (section 97(4) NIAA 2002; regulation 28(5) EEA Regulations) apart from in cases of deprivation of citizenship.

C3. Appeals in the SIAC

16.83 An appeal may be made to SIAC against a decision that could be appealed under section 82 NIAA 2002 (and, prior to the entry into force of the appeals provisions of IA 2014, sections 83 and and 83A NIAA 2002) but for the certification of that appeal under s 97 NIAA (section 2(1) SIACA 1997) (see section C2). The available grounds of appeal in the SIAC are the same grounds that can be advanced in normal appeals to the First-Tier Tribunal under section 84 NIAA 2002 (section 2(2)(e) SIACA 1997). The mirroring provisions in SIACA 1997 mean that once the appeals provisions of IA 2014 enter into force rights and grounds of appeal will be limited in the SIAC as in the First-tier Tribunal.

16.84 Many other provisions IA 1971 and NIAA 2002 apply to SIAC proceedings. These include, among others, the continuation of leave whilst an appeal is pending (sections 3C and 3D IA 1971) and the matters and evidence to be considered at an appeal hearing. The same general principles of law apply in SIAC appeals as in normal appeals subject to SIAC's statutory rules on evidence and disclosure.

16.85 Prior to the entry into force of IA 2014, there was a limitation on the right to appeal in-country in deportation cases where issues relating to national security are raised (section 97A NIAA 2002, which qualifies the SIACA 1997). The right of appeal was non-suspensive apart from in cases where human rights claims are made or where EEA nationals made claims under EU law. Even in human rights cases, the Secretary of State

---

[21] Section 83A NIAA 2002 is repealed by IA 2014.

can certify that a person's removal from the UK would not breach the ECHR, but the decision to issue such a certificate gives rise to an in-country right of appeal (section 97(3) NIAA 2002).

16.86 Following the entry into force of section 18 IA 2014,[22] which inserts a new section 2E into SIACA 1997, the jurisdiction of the SIAC in relation to deportation decisions that have been certified under sections 97 or 97A(1) NIAA 2002 is limited to the principles that would apply in judicial review (section 2E(3)).

16.87 Panels in SIAC appeals consist of three members. One must hold or have held high judicial office or be or have been a member of the Judicial Committee of the Privy Council; one must be or have been a judge of the First-Tier Tribunal or the Upper Tribunal; the qualifications of the final member are not defined by statute, but the person is generally someone with experience of national security matters.

16.88 The Lord Chancellor appoints a chairman, who must preside at sittings of the SIAC and report its decisions, although this responsibility can be delegated to another member nominated by the chairman.

16.89 The chairman alone or a single member of the panel can exercise a number of the SIAC's powers, including giving directions for hearing, deciding applications for permission to vary grounds of appeal, extending time limits, granting bail, deciding applications for leave to appeal to the Court of Appeal, issuing witness summons and making orders for failure to comply with directions.

C4. Closed Material, Special Advocates and Disclosure

16.90 One of the unique features of the SIAC is that section 5(3) of the SIACA 1997 legislates that proceedings can take place without the appellant being given all the evidence upon which the Secretary of State relies (section 5(3) NIAA 2002).

16.91 The material that is not seen by the appellant and his or her legal representatives is called 'closed material' (sections 5(3) and 6 SIACA 1997 and rule 37 SIAC Procedure Rules). Hearings, or parts of hearings, that relate to the 'closed material' will also take place without the appellant and his or her legal representatives being present.

16.92 In SIAC proceedings, the Home Office may not rely on 'closed material' unless a special advocate has been appointed (rule 37(2) SIAC Procedure Rules).

16.93 A special advocate is a barrister appointed by the Attorney General (section 6 SIACA 1997; rule 34 SIAC Procedure Rules). An appellant can select his or her special advocate from a list of those who are members of the Attorney General's panel. The Attorney General normally permits two special advocates to be appointed for SIAC cases: a leader and a junior.

16.94 Rule 35 sets out the special advocate's role. He or she must 'represent the interests of the appellant' by: (i) making submissions to the SIAC at any hearings from which the appellant and his or her representatives are excluded; (ii) adducing evidence and cross-examining witnesses at any such hearing; (iii) making written submissions to the SIAC.

16.95 The special advocate is not a party to proceedings (rule 32 SIAC Procedure Rules). He or she is also not responsible to the person whose interests he or she is appointed to

---

[22] At the point of writing, section 18 IA 2014 has not entered into force.

represent (section 6(4) SIACA 1997). He or she is not able to take instructions from that person, but rather must use his or her judgment in determining how best to present the appellant's case whilst representing the appellant's interests. For example, if he or she considers that the closed material received is insufficient for the SIAC to determine the outcome of the appeal justly, he or she can seek further closed disclosure.[23]

16.96 Before closed material is received, the special advocate may communicate with the appellant and his or her representatives. This communication may include meeting in person to discuss the case. The special advocate cannot communicate with the appellant after the receipt of closed material (or after seeing the closed material in the context of another case),[24] apart from to acknowledge receipt of communications, unless the SIAC grants permission. The Secretary of State must be notified of the request and can object to the request on public interest grounds—it is then for the SIAC to adjudicate as to whether the special advocate should be permitted to communicate with the appellant (rules 36(4) and (5) SIAC Procedure Rules).

16.97 After receipt of closed material, the special advocate can communicate with the SIAC, the Secretary of State, the Attorney General and any other person with whom it is necessary to communicate in relation to administrative matters (apart from the appellant and his or her representative, unless with permission) (rule 36(3) SIAC Procedure Rules).

16.98 According to rule 4 SIAC Procedure Rules, the SIAC 'shall secure' that information is not disclosed contrary to the interests of national security, the international relations of the UK, the detection and prevention of crime or in any other circumstances where disclosure is likely to harm the public interest.

16.99 The Secretary of State must conduct an 'exculpatory review' in every case before the SIAC, that is, he or she should disclose anything touching on the general issue of what is relevant to the risk of ill-treatment prohibited by Article 3 ECHR. This includes material which adversely affects his or her case or supports the appellant's case (rule 2 SIAC Procedure Rules). This exculpatory material must be filed by the Secretary of State when he or she files a statement opposing the appeal (rule 10 SIAC Procedure Rules). When the appellant serves a statement, the Secretary of State must then make a reasonable search for exculpatory material and notify the appellant of the extent of that search. Reasonable search is defined with reference to the following factors, outlined in rule 10A(3) SIAC Procedure Rules: the number of documents involved, the nature and complexity of the proceedings, whether the documents are in the control of the Secretary of State, the ease and expense of retrieval of any particular document and the significance of any document which is likely to be located during the search. The duty to make this search is continuing.

16.100 Rules 37 and 38 SIAC Procedure Rules sets out the procedure for disclosure of closed material. Under rule 38, the special advocate, once he or she has assessed the closed material, will file and serve on the Secretary of State a written submission with requests for onward disclosure of closed material to the appellant. The Secretary of State will

---

[23] The SIAC itself is required by r 4(3) SIAC Procedure Rules 2003 to satisfy itself that the material available to it enables it properly to determine the proceedings.

[24] In which case, the appellant can choose a different special advocate, may forego communication with the special advocate or, if two special advocates have been appointed, can communicate with one and not the other, provided that the one with whom he or she communicates has not seen the evidence.

respond to these requests in writing. The special advocate has the opportunity to reply in writing. Any outstanding issues in relation to disclosure are then first generally discussed at a meeting between the special advocate and legal representatives for the Secretary of State and then, if there are still matters that remain unresolved, the matter can go to a hearing. In advance of the hearing, the special advocate and the Secretary of State must file a schedule identifying the issues (rule 38(4)(c) SIAC Procedure Rules).

The test that the SIAC will apply is whether it considers that disclosure would be contrary to the public interest. If it rules against the Secretary of State's objections, the Secretary of State is under no obligation to disclose the material, although the SIAC can direct that he or she cannot rely on that material. 16.101

One of the functions of the special advocate is to try to persuade the SIAC, in appropriate circumstances, that closed material can and should be disclosed to the appellant—this can be done in a number of creative ways, including arguing that closed material can be summarised or redacted. 16.102

The CJEU has ruled that a summary or 'gist' of the case against an individual whose case is in the SIAC must be provided to EU nationals: Case C-300/11 *ZZ (France) v SSHD* (judgment of 4 June 2013) and, as applied in the Court of Appeal: *ZZ v SSHD* [2014] EWCA Civ 7 (see further chapter 14). The minimum level of disclosure requirement also applies in relation to individuals challenging the imposition of control orders (or their successor, terrorism prevention and investigation measures): *A v UK* [GC] no 3455/05, (2009) 49 EHRR 29 and *SSHD v AF* [2009] UKHL 28, [2010] 2 AC 269. However, non-EU nationals facing deportation are not entitled to a gist of the case against them: *Tariq v Home Office* [2011] UKSC 35, [2012] 1 AC 452. 16.103

C5. Procedure in Deportation Appeals

The vast majority of appeals before the SIAC are national security deportation cases. Appeals against a decision to make a deportation order in the SIAC begin by giving notice of appeal to the SIAC and the Secretary of Statute under rule 7 SIAC Procedure Rules within five days of the appellant being served with the decision if the appellant is in detention, 10 days if he or she not in detention, or 28 days if he or she is outside the UK (rule 8 SIAC Procedure Rules). The SIAC can extend the time limit for starting an appeal. If an individual is in detention, notice can be served on the person with custody of him or her, who is obliged to forward the notice to the SIAC, and the SIAC will then serve the notice on the Secretary of State. 16.104

The notice of appeal must set out the grounds for appeal and give reasons in support of the grounds (rule 9 SIAC Procedure Rules). A copy of the notice of decision must be attached to the notice of appeal, together with a statement of reasons for the decision, if available. The SIAC has the power to strike out an appeal if does not disclose a reasonable ground for bringing the appeal or if it appears to be an abuse of process. An appellant may withdraw his or her appeal orally or in writing. 16.105

There is then a directions hearing in the SIAC (rule 9A SIAC Procedure Rules). At this hearing, the SIAC is likely to set a timetable for the progress of the case. Directions are likely to be set in respect of: (i) a date by which the Secretary of State should file and serve the statement of evidence on which he or she relies in opposi- 16.106

tion of the appeal, as well as exculpatory material; (ii) a date by which the appellant should file and serve statement of evidence upon which he or she relies; (iii) a date by which the Secretary of State should file any evidence in response; (iv) a date by which the Secretary of State will serve closed material on the special advocate; (v) when the special advocate should serve his or her submissions in respect of disclosure and when the Secretary of State should respond; (vi) when skeleton arguments should be filed and served; and (vii) a date of hearing. The parties and the special advocate can apply to the court for directions between the first directions hearing and the substantive hearing. Rule 40 SIAC Procedure Rules outlines the available sanctions for breach of directions.

16.107 As with the First-Tier Tribunal, the SIAC has the power to issue a summons requiring any person in the UK to attend a hearing as a witness and at the hearing to answer questions or produce documents which relate to an issue in the case.

16.108 If closed material has been served, then, as a matter of practice, appeal hearings involve an open session, which both parties and the special advocate attend. This is then followed by a closed session during which the appellant and his or her legal representatives are not present.

16.109 The SIAC will first determine whether a person is a danger to national security and, if it considers that he or she is, will then consider whether his or her expulsion is lawful. The term 'safety on return' is used to describe the assessment of whether a person is at risk of ill-treatment in breach of his or her human rights if returned.

16.110 When the SIAC considers the issue of safety on return, it does so with reference to the Refugee Convention, the Qualification Directive, the ECHR and the relevant Immigration Rules.

16.111 The SIAC must give a written determination of its decisions by virtue of rule 47(3) SIAC Procedure Rules. Where the Secretary of State has relied on closed material, an open judgment and a closed judgment will be given. Before the open judgment is served on the appellant, he or she is given five days to check it and he or she can apply to the SIAC to amend the judgment if it is considered that it contains materials which should not be open. In the same way, the special advocate may, at any time, apply to the SIAC for material in the closed judgment to be placed in the open judgment.

C6. Onward Appeal to the Court of Appeal

16.112 An appellant may appeal a determination of the SIAC to the Court of Appeal on a question of law material to the determination by virtue of section 7 SIACA 1997. An application for permission to appeal must first be made to the SIAC. The procedure is set out in rule 27 SIAC Procedure Rules 2003. The application must be filed no later than five days after the service of the SIAC's determination if the appellant is in immigration detention and 10 days if not. The 10-day time limit applies if the Secretary of State wishes to apply for permission to appeal. The SIAC may decide the application without a hearing unless it considers that special circumstances make a hearing necessary or desirable. If it refuses permission, a party can apply directly to the Court of Appeal. The relevant provisions are in Part 52 CPR. The question for the Court of Appeal in any appeal will be whether there has been an error of law.

D. Judicial Review

D1. Basic Principles

Judicial review is the procedure by which the legality of the decisions of the government and other public bodies can be challenged in the Administrative Court, a branch of the Queen's Bench Division of the High Court of Justice, and now, in many immigration decisions, by the Upper Tribunal. The aim of this section is to focus on the aspects of judicial review relevant to the subject matter of the work (administrative decisions on expulsion, exclusion, denial or deprivation of nationality).[25]

16.113

Amenability to Review and Standing

Judicial review is concerned with the propriety of the decision-making process rather than the merits of the decision itself.[26] It can be brought against: (i) public bodies in the performance (or non-performance) of their public functions; (ii) lower courts; and (iii) tribunals. It is a residual remedy and thus cannot be used where there is an equally effective remedy available. However, many decisions in immigration law are not appealable[27] and therefore judicial review is often the only means by which a challenge to a flawed decision can be brought.

16.114

In immigration cases, it is clear that the decisions and omissions of the Home Office or its agencies and officials are challengeable by way of judicial review. Prerogative decisions of the Secretary of State are also reviewable. As are policies, procedures, the Immigration Rules and statutory instruments.

16.115

An applicant must have standing to apply for judicial review. Section 31(3) Senior Courts Act (SCA) 1981 (Part 54 CPR) stipulates a test of 'sufficient interest' in the matter to which the application relates. In immigration law cases, this will not generally be an issue.

16.116

It is useful to note that there is now a well-established precedent that campaigning organisations and public interest groups can have sufficient standing as a result of the purpose of their establishment and the cause or constituents they represent. For example, see: *R v Secretary of State for Foreign and Commonwealth Affairs ex p World Development Movement Ltd* [1995] 1 WLR 386 (DC); *Equal Opportunities Commission v Secretary of State for Employment* [1995] 1 AC 1 (HL); *R (on the application of Corner House Research and another) v Director of the Serious Fraud Office* [2008] EWHC 714 (Admin).

16.117

Claims should also be served on interested parties, who are defined in CPR Part 54(2)(1)(f) as anyone 'who is directly affected by the claim.' Further, public interest groups and other such bodies can also intervene in judicial review cases, by virtue of CPR 54.17.

16.118

---

[25] For a full account of judicial review practice and procedure, see: Fordham (n 1). For an account of EU law principles as they apply to English judicial review, see R Gordon QC and R Moffatt, *EU Law in Judicial Review* (Oxford, Oxford University Press, 2014).
[26] See, eg, *Chief Constable of North Wales Police v Evans* [1982] 1 WLR 1155, per Lord Brightman at 1173.
[27] The changes to the appeals structure enacted by the IA 2014 will substantially reduce the number of appealable decisions.

Heads of Review

16.119 The main heads of judicial review were outlined by Lord Diplock in his now famous dicta in *Council of Civil Service Unions v Minister for the Civil Service (GCHQ)* [1985] AC 374 (HL), namely, illegality, irrationality and procedural impropriety. These are umbrella terms that cover a number of different principles upon which the exercise of discretionary power may be subject to review.

16.120 Breaches of an individual's rights under the ECHR, as incorporated by the HRA 1998, can be challenged through judicial review. In *SSHD v Nasseri* [2009] UKHL 23, [2010] 1 AC 1, as was noted by Lord Hoffmann at [14], when the breach of a right protected by the ECHR is in issue 'an impeccable decision-making process by the Secretary of State will be of no avail if she actually gets the answer wrong.' However, the standard ultimately remains one of review of legality and the primary decision maker is accorded a margin of appreciation. Thus, in *R (A) v The Chief Constable of Kent Constabulary* [2013] EWCA Civ 1706, [2014] BMLR 22 it was held (per Beatson LJ at [39]) that where the relevant factors had been properly considered by the decision maker, a broad margin of appreciation would be accorded his or her view, however, where there had been no, or no proper, consideration of relevant factors, the decision-maker's view should carry little weight and the court must make up its own mind. Provided, therefore, that the decision-making process has been lawful in public law terms and the decision is not irrational, the court in judicial review will be most likely to find that the decision was within the reasonable range of responses open to the decision-maker even if it does not agree with the outcome. Similarly, breaches of rights protected by EU law may also be challenged through judicial review.

16.121 Proportionality is the relevant principle applicable under HRA 1998 and rights protected by EU law. It not been established as a free-standing ground of judicial review for purely domestic cases, although the common law recognises a sliding scale of intensity of review (*R v Minister of Defence ex p Smith* [1996] QB 517 (CA)).

Remedies

16.122 All remedies in judicial review are discretionary, which means that even if a claimant established that the decision maker has acted unlawfully, the court may decide not to grant him or her relief.

16.123 An applicant for judicial review may seek one or more of the following remedies:

— A 'quashing order', quashing the targeted decision. The court will usually quash the decision and remit the matter back to the decision maker to reconsider lawfully. In rare cases, the court may take the decision itself.

— A 'prohibitory order', preventing the public body from acting or continuing to act ultra vires or contrary to natural justice.

— A 'mandatory order', compelling the public body to perform a public law duty imposed by law. The courts are reluctant to grant mandatory orders, as it is assumed that, following a ruling that a decision is unlawful, the defendant will comply with the court's ruling lawfully.

— A declaration, which is a statement of the legal position. This does not question the exercise of a power.
— An injunction, ordering a party to perform or refrain from performing a specific act.
— Damages—a claim for judicial review cannot have as its sole purpose the seeking of damages, but damages are available in judicial review if they could have been awarded in an ordinary claim.

Applications can be made for interim orders at any stage of the proceedings, although these are usually made before or at the permission stage. The Administrative Court has the power to grant interim remedies in accordance with CPR Part 23 (see further, in relation to injunctions against expulsion, 16.168 et seq below). 16.124

D2. Damages and Other Relief under the HRA 1998

A person who is a 'victim' of an act which is incompatible with ECHR rights can claim compensation or other remedy, or rely on the Convention right concerned in legal proceedings (by effect of section 7(1) HRA 1998). 'Victim' is a far narrower requirement of standing than that required in judicial review (of 'sufficient interest'). By effect of section 7(7) HRA 1998, the term is given the same meaning as it has in Article 34 ECHR (where the right of petition extends to 'any person, non-governmental organisation or group of individuals claiming to be the victim of a violation'). 16.125

By virtue of section 8(1) HRA 1998, a court may grant any relief, remedy or order within its powers in relation to any act or proposed act of a public authority which would be incompatible with rights under the ECHR. Section 8(2) HRA 1998 enables any court (with the power to do so) to award damages or to order the payment of compensation. 16.126

The level of damages is not necessarily limited to levels comparable to those awarded by the Strasbourg Court (see further, chapter 15) and, in appropriate cases (such as breach of the right to liberty protected by Article 5), will by guided by comparison with the levels awarded in tort claims (*Anufrijeva v London Borough of Southwark* [2003] EWCA Civ 1406, [2004] QB 1124 [74]). 16.127

D3. Procedure—Administrative Court

Applications for judicial review have traditionally always been brought in the Administrative Court (Queen's Bench Division of the High Court) by virtue of section 38(3) of the County Courts Act (CCA) 1984. The situation has changed since the establishment of the Upper Tribunal. 16.128

Those intending to apply for judicial review should comply with the Pre-Action Protocol for Judicial Review before issuing proceedings.[28] Where the defendant has no legal power to change the decision being challenged or in urgent applications, claims can be issued without compliance, although the party's conduct in this regard 16.129

---

[28] Accessible at www.justice.gov.uk/courts/procedure-rules/civil/protocol/prot_jrv.

Part E – Procedure and Remedies

may be a relevant consideration when the issue of costs is decided at the conclusion of proceedings. The Protocol requires that the intending claimant should send a letter before claim to the defendant, identifying the matter to be challenged, summarising the grounds upon which the challenge is brought, outlining what action is sought and the timeframe for response. Proposed defendants should normally be given 14 days to reply.

16.130 The first stage in an application for judicial review is an application for permission to apply for judicial review. A claim for judicial review is generally made using Form N461. Rule 54.6 CPR, paragraph 15 Practice Direction 16 and Practice Direction 54A stipulate what information must be contained on a judicial review claim form. In compliance with paragraph 5.9 of Practice Direction 54A and rule 54.6(2) CPR, two copies of a paginated and indexed bundle containing all the required documents must be filed when the claim is issued. The form to be used for applications for urgent consideration is N463, although note the relevant procedure in the Upper Tribunal for immigration cases is at para 16.168 et seq below.

16.131 The claim form must be filed promptly and in any event not later than three months after the grounds to make the claim arose: CPR 54.5(1). The time does not run from the date when the claimant first learnt of the decision, even where there are exceptional circumstances for the claimant's delay in becoming aware of the decision. However, such matters may be relevant to the separate question of whether an extension of the time limit should be granted: *R v Secretary of State for Transport ex p Presvac Engineering Ltd* (1992) Admin LR 121, 133D–H (CA).

16.132 The time limit may not be extended by agreement between the parties: CPR 54.5(2). The court can grant an extension of time under CPR 3.1(2)(a).

16.133 The claim form and appended documentation must be served on the defendant and interested parties within seven days after the date of issue: CPR 54.7.

16.134 Any person served with the claim form must file an acknowledgement of service on Form N462 within 21 days after service if they wish to take part in the proceedings: CPR 54.8(2)(a). This must be served on the claimant and the interested parties within seven days after the date it is filed: CPR 54.8(2)(b). A party that does not file an acknowledgment of service is not allowed to take part in the permission hearing unless the court allows it to: CPR 54.9(1). For specific principles applicable to immigration cases, please see section D5 below.

16.135 If permission is granted, the matter will proceed to substantive hearing in relation to the grounds upon which permission was granted. A judge usually considers the question of permission on the papers. The test for granting permission is whether, on the material available to the judge and without going into the matter in depth, there is an arguable case for granting the relief claimed: *Inland Revenue Commissioners v National Federation of Self-Employed and Small Businesses Ltd* [1982] AC 617 (HL). It was articulated in *R v SSHD ex p Rukshanda Begum* [1990] COD 107, 108 (CA) as whether 'there is a point fit for further investigation on a full inter partes basis with all such evidence as is necessary on the facts and all such argument as is necessary on the law'.

16.136 If permission is refused, one of two things will happen. Where an application for permission is refused on the papers, a claimant may request that the matter of permission be reconsidered at an oral hearing: CPR 54.12(3). This application must be made within seven days of the refusal of permission. The defendant and the interested parties are not expected to attend the hearing unless so directed by the court (paragraph 8.5 Practice Direction 54A). However, for claims issued on or after 1 July 2013, a judge deciding the matter on the papers now has the power to consider that the application is 'totally without merit', in which case a claimant is prevented from renewing the matter at an oral hearing: CPR 54.12(7).

Where permission is granted, the matter will proceed to a substantive hearing unless settlement is reached before the date of that hearing. The defendant or any other person served with the claim form who wishes to contest the claim must file and serve detailed grounds and written evidence relied upon within 35 days after service of the order giving permission: CPR 54.14. **16.137**

The claimant must file and serve a skeleton argument not less than 21 working days before the hearing date: paragraph 15.1 Practice Direction 54A. It must be accompanied by a paginated and indexed bundle of all relevant documentation. Other parties must file and serve their skeleton arguments not less than 14 working days before the hearing date (paragraph 15.2 Practice Direction 54A). **16.138**

Where the parties to an application for judicial review agree terms settling the case which renders a substantive hearing unnecessary, it is possible to obtain an order from the court to put that agreement into effect without the need to attend a hearing. The procedure is outlined paragraph 17 Practice Direction 54A. **16.139**

D4. Costs in the Administrative Court

A detailed overview of the law on the costs in judicial review cases is beyond the scope of this book. However, the general principle can be found in CPR Part 44.2: **16.140**

(1) The court has discretion as to—
   (a) whether costs are payable by one party to another;
   (b) the amount of those costs; and
   (c) when they are to be paid.
(2) If the court decides to make an order about costs—
   (a) the general rule is that the unsuccessful party will be ordered to pay the costs of the successful party; but
   (b) the court may make a different order.

CPR 44.3(4)–(5) provide guidance as to whether and to what degree to apply the general principle in a given case. **16.141**

Central cases are: *R (Boxall) v The Mayor and Burgesses of Waltham Forest LBC* (2000) 4 CCLR 258 (HC); *Bahta and others, R (on the application of) v SSHD and others* [2011] EWCA Civ 895, [2011] 5 Costs LR 857 (CA); and *M v London Borough of Croydon* [2012] EWCA Civ 595, [2012] 1 WLR 2607. The Administrative Court has laid down strict guidance on how costs must be claimed in judicial review proceedings:[29] an **16.142**

---

[29] At the time of writing, the most recent version of the guidance is that published in December 2013, available at www.justice.gov.uk/downloads/courts/administrative-court/aco-costs-guidance-dec-13.pdf.

attempt must be made to reach agreement before seeking a ruling, submissions must be filed and served within two weeks of the approval by the court of any consent order, and they must be limited to no more than two sides of A4 paper.

D5. Transfer to the Upper Tribunal

16.143 A growing number of complaints from members of the government and the judiciary that immigration judicial reviews were disproportionately draining the limited resources of the High Court to the detriment of both immigration and other types of cases resulted in gradual steps being taken to transfer immigration judicial reviews out of the High Court.

16.144 Lord McNally, the relevant Minister of State in the House of Lords, described the government's concern in a debate on amendments to the Crime and Courts Bill 2012 on 2 July 2012 in the following terms:

> The ability to transfer such cases would play an important role in improving access to justice. Immigration and asylum judicial review cases currently form a high proportion—around 70% of the caseload in the administrative court. The total number of these cases has doubled in the past five years, with around 8,800 being received in 2011. Many of these cases are relatively straightforward. This volume of cases is unsustainable for the administrative court. It keeps High Court judges from other complex civil and criminal cases that they should be hearing. It has created a backlog and has added to waiting times for all public law cases heard by the administrative court.

16.145 From 17 October 2011, asylum fresh claim and age assessment judicial reviews were transferred to the Upper Tribunal.

16.146 Section 22 Crime and Courts Act 2013 then provided the mechanism to transfer the majority of other immigration judicial reviews. The relevant provisions of the Crime and Courts Act 2013 came into force on 1 November 2013. In anticipation of the enactment of these provisions, the Lord Chief Justice, exercising his powers under Part 1 of Schedule 2 Constitutional Reform Act 2005 (CRA 2005) and section 18(6) TCEA 2007, gave a direction on 31 August 2013 transferring jurisdiction for most immigration judicial review applications to the Upper Tribunal. Judicial reviews in the following types of cases were to be transferred:

(a) a decision made under the Immigration Acts ... or any instrument having effect (whether wholly or partly) under an enactment within the Immigration Acts, or otherwise relating to leave to enter or remain in the United Kingdom outside the immigration rules; or

(b) a decision of the Immigration and Asylum Chamber of the First Tier Tribunal, from which no appeal lies to the Upper Tribunal.

16.147 The cases that continue to fall under the jurisdiction of the High Court include:

— challenges to the validity of legislation, including immigration rules and applications for declarations of incompatibility under section 4 HRA 1998;
— challenges to lawfulness of detention;
— challenges regarding the inclusion of sponsors on the register of sponsors;
— nationality law and citizenship challenges;

— welfare support challenges;
— challenges to the decisions of the Upper Tribunal or the SIAC.

16.148 Notwithstanding the distinction between the cases that should be issued in the Upper Tribunal and those that should begin in the High Court, it is useful to be aware of *R (on the application of Ashraf) v SSHD* [2013] EWHC 4028 (Admin), in which Cranston J gave a warning about issuing in the High Court when the aspect of the case that in jurisdictional terms should be considered by that court is unmeritorious.

16.149 The transfer of the majority of immigration judicial reviews to the Upper Tribunal led to the introduction of new statutory instruments, including the Tribunal Procedure (Amendment No 4) Rules 2013, SI 2013/2067, the First-tier Tribunal and Upper Tribunal (Chambers) (Amendment No 2) Order 2013, SI 2013/2068, and the Upper Tribunal (Immigration and Asylum) (Judicial Review) (England and Wales) Fees (Amendment) Order 2013, SI 2013/2069. Changes were also made to practice directions and new forms have been issued.

16.150 The procedure for issuing claims for judicial review in the Upper Tribunal is set out below.

D6. Procedure in the Upper Tribunal

16.151 At the time of writing, the relevant form for issuing a claim is Form T480. An application for urgent consideration must be made using Form T483. The other important forms to be aware of are:

— T482: acknowledgment of service;
— T483: application for urgent consideration;
— T484: application notice;
— T485: statement under rule 28A(2)(b) Upper Tribunal (Procedure) Rules 2008.

16.152 Applications must be issued at one of the following centres:

— Field House, London;
— Birmingham Civil Justice Centre;
— Cardiff Civil Justice Centre;
— Leeds Combined Court;
— Manchester Civil Justice Centre.

16.153 The fees for issuing are the same as for judicial review in the High Court, namely £60 for permission to apply and £215 if permission is granted.

16.154 Given that these cases are now to take place in the Upper Tribunal, its terminology should now be used—for example, 'Applicant' instead of 'Claimant', 'Respondent' instead of 'Defendant', and 'reconsideration' instead of 'renewal'.

16.155 Judicial review principles and practical considerations like time limits and the stages of a judicial review remain the same, but the applicable rules are the Upper Tribunal Rules (as amended). The most relevant rules are rules 27–33A. Rule 30 deals with decisions on permission, applications for reconsideration for permission or summary dismissal at a hearing.

16.156 Rule 30(1) states that the Upper Tribunal must send written reasons for permission (rule 30(1)(a)) or refusal of the application (rule 30(1)(b)) to the applicant and any other party that provided an acknowledgment of service to the Upper Tribunal or to any interested party.

16.157 Rule 30(4) states that in cases where permission is refused or limited permission is granted (rule 30 (3)(a)), the applicant has an option of applying for reconsideration of the decision at a hearing unless the application is deemed to be 'totally without merit'. If an application is considered to be 'totally without merit', renewal of an application is prevented by virtue of rule 30(4)(A). Rule 30(5) provides nine days for an application for reconsideration of permission in an immigration judicial review case, beginning with the date on which the notice of written decision was sent by the tribunal.

16.158 There has also been judicial guidance in relation to the service of, or failure to serve, acknowledgments of service by the Secretary of State within the required timeframe. In *R (on the application of Jasbir Singh) v SSHD* [2013] EWHC 2873 (Admin), Hickinbottom J in the Administrative Court held that although the court could not lay down general guidelines regarding applications for extensions of time, unless a claimant identified some good reason as to why such an extension would be particularly prejudicial, the first application by the Secretary of State for an extension of up to three weeks did not need to be supported by any detailed evidence or grounds and should be treated generously by the court. Subsequent applications had to be supported by a full explanation for the delay. On second and subsequent applications, the court should rigorously scrutinise the reasons for the delay, and the Secretary of State should be prepared for such applications to fail unless compelling reasons specific to the case as to why further time was needed had been provided.

16.159 The Upper Tribunal has subsequently considered the effect of the principles in *Singh* in the context of judicial reviews in its jurisdiction in *R (on the application of Kumar and another) v SSHD (Acknowledgement of Service; Tribunal Arrangements) (IJR)* [2014] UKUT 104 (IAC). The Upper Tribunal followed *Singh* and expanded on it, dispensing with the need to apply for an extension of time by setting a standard timetable of six weeks before applications for permission to bring judicial review will be considered (see [42]–[45]). Any application to extend time after that will have to comply with the requirements set out by Hickinbottom J at [25] of *Singh* by showing compelling reasons specific to the case as to why further time is needed. Applications to extend time must be made on notice to the applicant. Where no application to extend time is made, or it is refused, the Upper Tribunal will consider whether permission to bring judicial review should be granted.

16.160 Therefore, it is important to note that if an applicant needs consideration within six weeks of making a claim, he or she will need to ask for urgent consideration using Form T483 (assuming it is made in the Upper Tribunal).

D7. Specific Types of Judicial Review Application Relating to Expulsion, Exclusion, Denial or Deprivation of Nationality

16.161 There are certain types of judicial review application that will commonly occur for practitioners working within the subject matter of this book. These include judicial reviews

Non-suspensive Appeals

The Secretary of State has the power to certify certain immigration decisions with the effect that no in-country appeal can be brought to the First-Tier Tribunal (see 16.32 above). These appeals are commonly referred to as 'non-suspensive appeals'. 16.162

The only legal challenge to 'certification' is by way of judicial review proceedings unless the certificate was imposed after an in-country appeal to the First-Tier Tribunal had already been instituted. 16.163

In relation to the certification of claims as clearly unfounded under s 94 NIAA 2002, in *ZT (Kosovo) v SSHD* [2009] UKHL 6, [2009] 1 WLR 348, Lord Phillips approved the judgment of the Court of Appeal that the threshold test for determining whether a claim is clearly unfounded should be applied in the same way, whether or not the country is designated as 'safe' according to the presumption in s 94(3) and (4) NIAA 2002: 16.164

> The result cannot, for instance, depend upon whether the burden of proof is on the claimant or the Secretary of State, albeit that section 94 makes express provision in relation to the burden of proof.

The practical effect of designation is nevertheless very significant, as the Home Office certifies far more claims from designated countries as a matter of policy. 16.165

In *Razgar v SSHD (No 2)* [2003] EWCA Civ 840, [2003] Imm AR 529, [2004] UKHL 27 (17 June 2004), the Court of Appeal emphasised the 'very high threshold' that had to be met before a claim could be characterised as 'clearly unfounded', explaining that: 16.166

> The Secretary of State cannot lawfully issue such a certificate unless the claim is bound to fail … It is not sufficient that he considers that the claim is likely to fail on appeal, or even that it is very likely to fail … the court will subject the decision of the Secretary of State to the most anxious scrutiny.

In *ZT*, the House of Lords also confirmed that on judicial review of a clearly unfounded certificate, the Court will determine for itself whether an appeal would be bound to fail. Lord Phillips cited his observation in *ZL* that: 16.167

> [T]he test is an objective one: it depends not on the Home Secretary's view but upon a criterion which a court can readily re-apply once it has the materials which the Home Secretary had. A claim is either clearly unfound or it is not.

Challenging Removal Directions

Urgent applications for injunctions restraining the Secretary of State from removing an individual from the UK frequently arise in immigration law. There has recently been strong criticism by the Administrative Court of several immigration practitioners in cases including *Hamid* [2012] EWHC 3070 (Admin), *R (B and J)* [2012] EWHC 3770 (Admin), *R (Awuku) v SSHD* [2012] EWHC 3298 (Admin) and *Butt, Kiran, Siddique and Patel* [2014] EWHC 264 (Admin) which has underlined the need to ensure that the correct procedure is followed when applying for these orders from the Upper Tribunal and/or 16.168

Part E – Procedure and Remedies

the Administrative Court, in addition to the importance of complying at all times with the duty of candour. This duty, as it applies to a legal representative, was described by Lord Denning in *Rondel v Worsley* [1969] 1 AC 181 (HL) as follows (emphasis added):

> [The legal representative] has a duty to the court which is paramount. It is a mistake to suppose that he is the mouthpiece of his client to say what he wants, or his tool to do what he directs. He is none of these things. He owes allegiance to a higher cause. It is the cause of truth and justice. *He must not consciously misstate the facts. He must not knowingly conceal the truth. He must not unjustly make a charge of fraud, that is without evidence to support it. He must produce all the relevant authorities, even those that are against him. He must see that his client discloses, if ordered, the relevant documents, even those that is fatal to his case.* He must disregard the most specific instructions of his client, if they conflict with his duty to the court.

16.169 When making the application within court hours (in relation to a judicial review that should be brought in the Upper Tribunal), the claim should be issued at the Upper Tribunal. At the time of writing, the two forms that must be completed are: T480 (claim form) and T483 (application for urgent consideration). The following procedural requirements must also be met: it must be stated on the face of the application that the relevant practice direction applies; a draft order must be attached; the removal directions and documents in support of removal directions must be attached (if not, an explanation must be given as to why); and it must be specified by when the urgent application should be decided and the need for urgency must be justified.

16.170 The relevant guidance and directions that must be followed at the time of writing are: 'Immigration Judicial Reviews in the Immigration and Asylum Chamber on or after 1 November 2013' and 'Immigration Judicial Review in the IAC of the Upper Tribunal' (amended 1 November 2013).

16.171 Once the claim is issued, the practitioner must serve (by fax and post) the claim form and the request for urgent consideration on the Home Office and interested parties, putting them on notice of the application. Where an interim injunction is sought, practitioners must serve (by fax and post) the draft order and grounds for the injunction on the Home Office and the interested parties, putting them on notice of the application. It is important to keep in close telephone contact with the Home Office in order to try to get a positive result without having to seek a court order.

16.172 It is also mandatory to provide a statement: (i) explaining why the application is made urgently; (ii) stating when the decision under challenge came to the claimant/applicant's notice and justifying any delay since that date; and (iii) certifying that there is nothing in the application that the legal representative does not consider to be properly arguable. Such applications must be served on the respondent together with the application for permission.

16.173 An urgent application for a stay of removal will be considered on the papers by an Upper Tribunal judge, unless the judge adjourns the application for an oral hearing at which both sides can make submissions. Where a judge considers an urgent application on the papers and concludes that further information is needed from the respondent, the judge may telephone the Home Office and seek the further information. A note shall be kept of any information supplied. Where an urgent application is granted, the judge will draw up an order and give short reasons for it. This order will be sent to both parties. It is therefore important to give the court contact details for a fax machine that will be monitored. Upon receipt of the order, it is important to ensure that it is sent to the Home Office and that receipt is confirmed.

An urgent application that is refused on the papers may be renewed orally to an Upper Tribunal judge upon application being made promptly to the Tribunal and notice given to the respondent. The Tribunal will list such application as soon as practicable in all the circumstances of the case. Oral renewal can take place on the telephone if out of hours. **16.174**

Applications for urgent relief made before an application for judicial review has been issued should be made to the Administrative Court—this often happens, for example, when, for whatever reason, it was not possible to issue the claim before the Upper Tribunal closed and an application is being made out of hours. In those circumstances, at the time of writing, the procedure is for the practitioner to telephone security at the Royal Courts of Justice and leave his or her details for the duty clerk to contact the practitioner. There is an out-of-hours form that must be completed, a fee paid, and the clerk will invite the practitioner to send this along with all relevant documentation to him or her to be passed to the duty judge. **16.175**

Select Bibliography

International Law

Crawford, J (ed), *Brownlie's Principles of Public International Law* (8th edn, Oxford, Oxford University Press, 2012)

Goodwin-Gill, G, *International Law and the Movement of Persons between States* (Oxford, Clarendon, 1978)

Hannum, H, *The Right to Leave and Return in International Law and Practice* (Dordrecht, Martinus Nijhoff, 1987)

Jennings, R, and Watts, A (eds), *Oppenheim's International Law* (9th edn, volume 1 (*Peace*), (Oxford, Oxford University Press, 1992)

Plender, R, *International Migration Law* (Leiden, Martinus Nijhoff, 1988)

International Law in Domestic Proceedings

Fatima, S, *Using International Law in Domestic Courts* (Oxford, Hart Publishing, 2005)

Nationality and Statelessness: International Law

van Waas, L, *Nationality Matters: Statelessness under International Law* (Antwerp, Intersentia, 2008)

Weis, P, *Nationality and Statelessness in International Law* (London, Stevens, 1956)

UK Nationality Law

Fransman, L, *British Nationality Law* (3rd edn, London, Bloomsbury, 2011)

International Human Rights Law

Eide, A, and Alfredsson, G (eds), *The Universal Declaration of Human Rights: A Commentary* (Oslo, Scandinavian University Press, 1992)

Joseph, S, and Castan, M, *The International Covenant on Civil and Political Rights* (8th edn, Oxford, Oxford University Press, 2012)

Kälin, W, and Künzli, J, *The Law of Human Rights Protection* (Oxford, Oxford University Press, 2009)

Macdonald, A, *The Rights of the Child: Law and Practice* (Bristol, Jordan Publishing Limited, 2011)

Nowak, M, *The UN Covenant on Civil and Political Rights: CCPR Commentary* (2nd revised edn, Kehl am Rhein, N P Engel Verlag, 2005)

Nowak, M, and MacArthur, E, *The United Nations Convention against Torture: A Commentary* (Oxford, Oxford University Press, 2008)

International Refugee Law

Feller, E, Türk, V, and Nicholson, F, *Refugee Protection in International Law* (Cambridge, Cambridge University Press, 2003)

Goodwin-Gill, G, and McAdam, J, *The Refugee in International Law* (3rd edn, Oxford, Oxford University Press, 2011)

Hathaway, J, *The Law of Refugee Status* (Toronto, Butterworths Canada, 1992)

Hathaway, J, *The Rights of Refugees in International Law* (Cambridge, Cambridge University Press, 2005)

Hathaway, J, and Foster, M, *The Law of Refugee Status* (2nd edn, Cambridge, Cambridge University Press, 2014)

Zimmermann, A, (ed), Dörschner, J, and Machts, J (assistant eds), *The 1951 Convention Relating to the Status of Refugees and its 1967 Protocol: A Commentary* (Oxford, Oxford University Press, 2011)

International Refugee Law/United Kingdom Asylum Law

Symes, M, and Jorro, P, *Asylum Law and Practice* (2nd edn, Haywards Heath, Bloomsbury, 2010)

International Law of Human Trafficking

Chandran, P (ed), *Human Trafficking Handbook* (London, Butterworths, 2011)

Gallagher, A, *The International Law of Human Trafficking* (Cambridge, Cambridge University Press, 2012)

European Human Rights Law

Leach, P, *Taking a Case to the European Court of Human Rights* (3rd edn, Oxford, Oxford University Press, 2011)

Mole, N, and Meredith, C, *Asylum and the European Convention on Human Rights* (5th edn, Strasbourg, Council of Europe, 2010)

Reid, K, *A Practitioner's Guide to the European Convention on Human Rights* (4th edn, Sweet & Maxwell, 2012)

European Union Law

Barnard, C, *The Substantive Law of the EU: The Four Freedoms* (3rd edn, Oxford, Oxford University Press, 2010)

Craig, P, and De Búrca, G (eds), *The Evolution of EU Law* (Oxford, Oxford University Press, 2011)

O'Neil, A, *EU Law for UK Lawyers* (2nd edn, Oxford, Hart Publishing, 2011)

Peers, S, Guild, E, Acosta Arcarazo, D, Groenendijk, C, and Moreno-Lax, V, *EU Immigration and Asylum Law (Text and Commentary)* (2nd revised edn, Leiden, Martinus Nijhoff, 2012)

Rogers, N, Scannell, R, and Walsh, J, *Free Movement of Persons in the Enlarged European Union* (2nd edn, London, Sweet & Maxwell, 2012)

Judicial Review/Constitutional and Administrative Law

Barak, A, *Proportionality: Constitutional Rights and their Limitations* (Cambridge, Cambridge University Press, 2012)

Bingham, T, *The Rule of Law* (London, Allen Lane/Penguin, 2010)

Fordham, M, *Judicial Review Handbook* (6th edn, Oxford, Hart Publishing, 2012)

Wade, W, and Forsyth, C, *Administrative Law* (10th edn, Oxford, Oxford University Press, 2009)

Woolf, H, Jowell, J, Le Sueur, A, Donnelly, C, and Hare, I, *De Smith's Judicial Review* (7th edn, London, Sweet & Maxwell, 2013)

Domestic Immigration or Nationality Laws

Dubinsky, L, *Foreign National Prisoners: Law and Practice* (London, Legal Action Group, 2012)

Macdonald QC, I and Toal, R (eds), *Macdonald's Immigration Law and Practice* (8th edn, London, LexisNexis, 2010)

Lord Mackay of Clashfern (ed), *Halsbury's Laws of England* (5th edn, London, Butterworths, 2012)

Index

Abode
see **Right of abode**
Acquisition of citizenship
  anti-discrimination law, 11.35, 11.38
  appeals, 11.36
  birth or adoption, 1.21, 7.40, 11.17, 11.28
  descent, 1.21, 7.40, 11.17, 11.28, 11.38
  ECHR protection, 11.24, 11.38
  good character, 11.30, 11.37, 11.39–11.43
  guidance, 11.30–11.31, 11.33–11.34
  ICCPR protection, 11.24
  international human rights law, 11.24
  international law, 11.24
  international refugee law, 11.24
  judicial review, 11.36–11.37
  naturalisation, 1.21, 7.40, 7.42–7.43, 11.17–11.18, 11.20, 11.27–11.29, 11.38, 11.42, 12.19
  procedural rights, 11.25–11.26
  public law principles, 11.32, 11.34, 11.42
  registration 1.21, 7.40, 7.42, 11.17–11.18, 11.27–11.29, 11.38, 12.19
  resumption following renunciation, 11.29
  statelessness law, 11.24
  statutory discretionary powers, 11.22, 11.27, 11.29–11.30, 11.33–11.34
Administrative Court
  acknowledgment of service, 16.134
  arguable cases, 16.135
  claim forms, 16.131, 16.133–16.134
  costs, 16.140–16.142
  judicial review, 16.113, 16.128–16.130
  jurisdiction, 16.113
  permission refused, 16.136
  permission to apply, 16.130, 16.135, 16.137
  Pre-action Protocol, 16.129
  settlement agreement, 16.139
  skeleton arguments, 16.138
  substantive hearing, 16.135, 16.137
  time limits, 16.132
Administrative removal of persons
see **Removal**
Administrative review
  application of immigration rules, 16.60–16.61
  charges, 16.64–16.65
  economic migrants, 16.54
  evidential flexibility, 16.60
  extended system, 16.58
  further review, 16.63
  human rights grounds, 16.62
  immigration leave, 16.60
  new evidence, 16.61
  post-decision evidence, 16.61
  principles, 16.59
  removal suspended, 16.64
  review of process, 16.68
  revised scope, 16.60
  service standard, 16.67
  single application, 16.63
  time limits, 16.66
  unreasonable decisions, 16.60
Aliens
  admission, 10.3–10.4
  aliens and subjects distinguished, 1.2, 1.6
  deportation, 8.1, 8.3
  exclusion, 2.40, 2.42, 5.6, 8.3, 10.1
  expulsion, 1.4, 2.39–2.44, 5.6, 5.225, 5.228–5.233, 8.3
  see also **Expulsion of aliens**
  international law treatment, 2.24–2.25
  lawful presence, 2.51
  statutory limitations, 1.5, 1.7
Appeals
  appeal rights
    appeals outside UK, 16.32
    deportation cases, 16.31, 16.57
    EEA appeals, 16.69–16.71, 16.85
    human rights obligations, 16.32, 16.42, 16.47, 16.53
    in-country appeals, 16.32
    migrants, 16.3–16.4, 16.30–16.32, 16.54
    national security issues, 16.32
    one-step procedure, 16.72–16.74
    onward appeals, 16.8–16.9, 16.16, 16.231, 16.23–16.27
    over-stayers, 16.54
    statutory provisions, 16.5, 16.29–16.42, 16.46–16.50
  Court of Appeal, 16.9, 16.25–16.27
  Detained Fast Track Procedure (DFT), 16.7, 16.10, 16.17–16.20
  see also **Detained Fast Track Procedure (DFT)**
  deportation appeals
    deportation orders, 16.104
    directions hearing, 16.106
    notice of appeal, 16.105
    open session, 16.108
    safety on return, 16.109–16.110
    Special Immigration Appeals Commission (SIAC), 16.104–16.105
  European Court of Human Rights (ECtHR), 16.28
  First-Tier Tribunal
    see **First-Tier Tribunal**
  grounds of appeal, 16.43–16.44, 16.51, 16.53–16.54
  Immigration and Asylum Chamber (IAC), 16.6
  immigration appeals
    appeal rights, 16.5
    statutory basis, 16.3, 16.13
  location of appeal, 16.56
  new matters, 16.55
  post-decision matters, 16.55

practice directions, 16.10
practice statements, 16.10
procedural rules, 16.10–16.16
reduction in number, 16.54
respect for private and family life, 15.53–16.54
Special Immigration Appeals Commission (SIAC), 16.5, 16.42, 16.104–16.105
  see also **Special Immigration Appeals Commission (SIAC)**
statutory appeals
  effective remedy, 16.1
  immigration decisions, 16.3, 16.13
  migration cases, 16.3–16.4, 16.30–16.31
Upper Tribunal
  see **Upper Tribunal**
Area of Freedom, Security and Justice
international protection, 6.72–6.73
Asylum-seekers
Dublin III Regulation, 6.87–6.88
EU law, 6.73–6.74
refugee law, 4.5
right to effective remedy, 5.207, 5.210–5.213
  see also **Right to effective remedy**
state responsibility, 2.41
UNHCR protection, 3.42–3.43

Borders, Citizenship and Immigration Act (2009)
naturalisation, 11.20
British citizenship
acquisition of citizenship, 11.24–11.38
  see also **Acquisition of citizenship**
denial of citizenship, 11.1–11.23, 11.27, 11.35
  see also **Denial of citizenship**
deprivation of citizenship, 12.1–12.69
  see also **Deprivation of citizenship**
British nationals (overseas), 7.40, 8.38
British Overseas Citizens, 7.40, 8.38
British Overseas Territories Citizens, 7.40, 8.38
British protected persons, 7.40, 8.38
British subjects, 7.40, 8.38
earned citizenship, 7.43
executive discretion, 7.42
immigration control, 7.41
  see also **Immigration control**
probationary citizenship, 7.43
refusal to grant citizenship
  citizenship registration, 11.38
  exercise of discretion, 11.38
  good character decisions, 11.39–11.43
requirements, 7.42
resumption following renunciation, 7.42
right of abode, 1.19–1.21, 7.40–7.41, 8.38
British Nationality Act (1981)
appeal procedure, 12.67–12.68
appeal rights, 16.33
citizenship obtained by deception, 12.22
citizenship status, 12.19
Commonwealth citizens, 12.20
deprivation of citizenship, 12.2, 12.21, 12.49–12.50, 12.53–12.54, 12.56–12.57, 12.61–12.62, 12.66–12.68
deprivation of nationality, 12.19, 12.36, 12.40, 12.67

discretionary powers, 11.22, 11.27, 11.30, 11.33–11.34
entitlement to citizenship
  birth or adoption, 11.17, 11.28
  challenges, 11.18
  descent, 11.17, 11.28
  naturalisation, 11.17–11.18, 11.20, 11.28–11.29, 12.19, 12.40
  registration, 11,17–11.18, 11.29, 11.38, 12.19, 12.40
  resumption following renunciation, 11.29
evidential requirements, 12.40, 12.44, 12.46
notice requirement, 12.67
right of abode, 11.16
statelessness, 12.57–12.58
structure, 7.39–7.40

Charter of Fundamental Rights of the European Union (CFREU)
application, 6.2, 6.16–6.19, 6.28, 6.49, 6.60, 6.86, 6.88
respect for private and family life, 8.84
Children
  see also **Convention on the Rights of the Child (CRC)**
adoption, 5.201
best interests of the child, 2.22, 3.82, 5.131, 5.159–5.162, 8.9, 8.94, 9.88
citizenship
  denial, 11.9
  deprivation, 12.11
continuing to live with parents, 5.103
decision to have children, 5.110
deportation measures, 8.34, 8.69, 8.81
exclusion and expulsion, 6.63–6.64, 10.25
ICCPR protection, 3.14, 3.54–3.57
nationality issues, 3.83
parent/child relationship, 5.101–5.102
parental rights and duties, 3.82
removal provisions, 9.31, 9.87
state responsibility, 3.82
trafficking, 4.98, 5.242, 5.244
UN Committee on the Rights of the Child, 13.34
UNHRC protection, 3.56–3.57
Citizens' Directive
abuse of rights, 14.20
EEA nationals, 10.97
EU citizenship, 6.30–6.31
exclusion and expulsion provisions, 6.31, 6.35, 6.37, 6.39, 6.48–6.49, 6.51, 6.57, 10.97, 14.19–14.24
family members, 6.31–6.32, 6.35, 6.61
fraud, 14.20
free movement provisions, 6.30, 6.61–6.62, 6.59, 10.97
integration, 6.51–6.52
marriages of convenience, 14.20
procedural guarantees, 6.57, 6.59, 14.18
public health, 14.16–14.17
public policy, 14.16–14.17
public security, 14.16–14.17
remedies, 14.15–14.24

right of entry, 6.31–6.33
right of residence, 6.31–6.33, 6.35, 6.51, 6.61
third country nationals, 6.33–6.34
Citizenship
see also **EU citizenship**
acquisition of citizenship, 11.24–11.38, 12.19
see also **Acquisition of citizenship**
citizenship status, 12.19
denial of citizenship, 5.187, 11.1–11.23, 11.27, 11.35
see also **Denial of citizenship**
deprivation of citizenship, 6.1, 6.22, 12.1–12.69
see also **Deprivation of citizenship**
meaning, 2.6
Civil partnerships
deportation measures, 8.34, 8.69
Immigration Rules, 8.34
respect for private and family life, 5.105
Committee against Torture
credibility issues, 3.79–3.80
medical evidence, 3.78
procedural safeguards, 3.81
refoulement provisions, 3.72–3.74
remedies, 13.34, 13.38
risk of torture, 3.76–3.77
standard of proof, 3.75
Commonwealth citizens
denial of citizenship, 11.16
deportation, 8.42
deprivation of citizenship, 12.20
Constitutional law
citizenship, 7.4–7.5
constitutional statutes, 7.5–7.7
EU law, 7.4–7.5
exercise of powers, 7.4
free speech, 7.4
fundamental rights, 7.5–7.10
see also **Fundamental rights (UK)**
judicial review, 7.4
personal freedoms, 7.4
role of the judiciary, 7.4
state institutions/individuals relationship, 7.2–7.3, 7.5
US Constitution compared, 7.4, 7.8
written constitution, 7.2, 7.4
Convention against Torture and Other Cruel, Inhuman or Degrading Treatment (CAT)
see also **Committee against Torture**
credibility issues, 3.79–3.80
cruel, inhuman or degrading treatment, 3.73
definition of torture, 3.67, 3.72
exclusion measures, 10.7
expulsion and exclusion, 3.69
medical evidence, 3.78
past torture, 3.77
prohibition of torture, 3.68
refoulement, 3.70–3.72, 3.74–3.75, 3.81
removals, 9.6
risk of torture, 3.69, 3.72, 3.75–3.79, 8.7
scope, 3.73–3.74
standard of proof, 3.75
state complicity, 3.17

Convention for the Protection of All Persons from Enforced Disappearance (CPED)
Committee on Enforced Disappearances, 13.38
enforced disappearance, 3.88
human rights violations, 3.88
Convention on Action against Trafficking in Human Beings (CATHB)
see also **Group of Experts on Action against Trafficking in Human Beings (GRETA); International Law of Human Trafficking (ILHT); Trafficking**
aim, 5.242
children, 5.242, 5.244
definitions, 5.242, 5.244
deportations, 8.16
elements of trafficking, 5.244
exclusion measures, 10.14
non-discrimination, 5.242
people smuggling distinguished, 5.243
ratification, 5.4
recovery and reflection period, 5.246
remedies, 15.71
removals, 9.16–9.17
scope, 5.242
UK position, 5.242, 15.74
victims
consent, 5.242
expulsion, 5.245–5.246
identification, 5.245
protection, 9.16–9.17
residence permits, 5.247
Convention on the Elimination of All Forms of Discrimination against Women (CEDAW)
citizenship
denial, 11.9
deprivation, 12.11
Committee on the Elimination of Discrimination against Women, 13.34, 13.38
discrimination against women, 3.63–3.64
elimination of discrimination, 3.64
exclusion measures, 10.9
nationality rights, 3.66
prostitution, 3.65
removals, 9.8
trafficking, 3.65
Convention on the Elimination of All Forms of Racial Discrimination (CERD)
citizenship
denial, 11.9
deprivation, 12.11
Committee on the Elimination of Racial Discrimination, 13.34, 13.38
equality before the law, 3.62
equality measures, 3.60
exclusion measures, 10.9
nationality rights, 3.62
protecting domestic laws, 3.60
racial discrimination, 3.59, 3.61–3.62
removals, 9.8
Convention on the Protection of Migrant Workers (MWC)
diplomatic protection, 3.85

meaning of migrant worker, 3.85
prohibition on expulsion, 3.85
safeguards, 3.85
states of origin, 3.85
Convention on the Rights of Persons with Disabilities (CRPD)
citizenship
  denial, 11.9
  deprivation, 12.11
exclusion measures, 10.9
human dignity, 3.86
human rights protection, 3.86
liberty of movement, 3.87
persons with disabilities, 3.86–3.87
removals, 9.8
Convention on the Rights of the Child (CRC)
best interests of the child, 3.82, 8.94
child protection and care, 3.82
citizenship
  denial, 11.9
  deprivation, 12.11
family unity, 3.84
identity of the child, 3.83
nationality issues, 3.83
state responsibility, 3,82
Convention on the Reduction of Statelessness (CRS)
citizenship
  denial, 11.10–11.11
  deprivation, 12.13–12.14, 12.66
foundlings, 4.93
grant of nationality, 4.93
loss of nationality, 4.93
Convention Relating to the Status of Refugees (CSR)
alienage, 4.12–4.13, 4.12, 4.14
application, 4.9
citizenship
  denial, 11.10
  deprivation, 12.12, 12.66
country of nationality, 4.11
current fear, 4.12, 4.15
deportations, 8.10–8.11
exclusion measures, 10.10
fear of persecution, 4.11–4.12, 4.16–4.36
multi-nationality, 4.11–4.12, 4.66–4.67
persecution based on race, religion or nationality, 4.11–4.12, 4.48–4.53
refugee status
  expulsion, 4.77–4.82
  lawful presence, 4.79
  naturalisation, 4.83–4.84
  refoulement, 4.77, 4.80–4.82, 4.89
  territorial asylum, 4.77
removals, 9.9–9.10
social groups or political opinions, 4.11–4.12, 4.54–4.64
unwillingness to return to country of nationality, 4.11–4.12, 4.65
well-founded fear, 4.11–4.12, 4.37–4.47
Convention Relating to the Status of Stateless Persons (CSSP)
citizenship
  denial, 11.10
  deprivation, 12.12
exclusion measures, 10.10
expulsion, 4.90, 8.12
fundamental rights and freedoms, 4.86
lawful presence, 8.12
national security exception, 8.12
naturalisation, 4.91–4.92
non-application, 4.88
refoulement protection, 4.89–4.90
removals, 9.11
scope, 4.85–4.87
stateless persons defined, 4.87
Council of Europe
aim, 5.1
Committee of Ministers, 5.3
European Convention on Nationality, 5.4
human rights protection, 5.2, 5.4
  see also **European Convention on Human Rights (ECHR)**
human trafficking, 5.4
  see also **Convention on Action against Trafficking in Human Beings (CATHB)**
instruments
  denial of citizenship, 11.12–11.13
  deportation, 8.14–8.16
  deprivation of citizenship, 12.15–12.16
  exclusion cases, 10.12–10.15
  removal cases, 9.14–9.17
remedies
  available remedies, 15.1
  ECtHR applications, 15.2–15.10
  expulsion and exclusion cases, 15.2
  nationality decisions, 15.2
  trafficking offences, 15.2
rule of law, 5.2
state commitments, 5.3
Court of Justice of the European Union (CJEU)
exclusion decisions, 10.100
free movement provisions, 10.100
jurisdiction, 6.2, 14.37, 14.41
preliminary reference procedure, 14.36–14.50
  see also **Preliminary reference procedure**
state liability, 14.29

Denial of citizenship
British Nationality Act (1981), 11.6–11.8
Commonwealth citizens, 11.16
Council of Europe instruments, 11.12–11.13
CRS protection, 11.10–11.11
CSR protection, 11.10
CSSP protection, 11.10
domestic law
  anti-discrimination law, 11.19, 11.35
  entitlement to citizenship, 11.17–11.18
  guidance, 11.22–11.23
  naturalisation, 11.17–11.18. 11.20
  prerogative powers, 11.15
  statute law, 11.16–11.20
  statutory instrument, 11.21
ECHR protection, 11.7, 11.12

ECN provisions, 11.13
EU law, 11.14
hybrid instruments, 11.10–11.11
Immigration Act (1971), 11.6
international human rights law
  CEDAW provisions, 11.9
  CERD protection, 11.9
  CRC protection, 11.9
  CRPD provisions, 11.9
  ICCPR protection, 11.6–11.8
  UDHR protection, 11.5
international law
  erga omnes norms, 11.4
  general international law, 11.3–11.4
  international human rights law, 11.5–11.9
  racially-based exclusion, 11.4
nationality
  determination of nationality, 11.2
  meaning of nationality, 11.2
  nationality law, 11.1, 11.27
  nationality status, 11.2
right of abode, 11.16
Secretary of State's decision, 11.1

Deportation
see also **Deportation orders**
aircrew, 8.68
aliens, 8.1, 8.3
deportation appeals
  appeal pending, 8.57, 8.82
  appeal rights, 16.31, 16.57
  deportation orders, 16.104
  directions hearing, 16.106
  notice of appeal, 16.105
  open session, 16.108
  safety on return, 16.109–16.110
  Special Immigration Appeals Commission (SIAC), 16.104–16.105
certification, 16.57
children, 8.34
civil partners, 8.34, 8.69
Commonwealth citizens, 8.42
Council of Europe instruments, 8.14–8.16
deportation process, 8.132, 8.134
detention, 8.132
diplomatic staff, 8.42
domestic law
  guidance, 8.35
  prerogative powers, 8.19, 8.36
  statute law, 8.20–8.31, 8.36, 8.39–8.40
ECHR protection, 5.5, 8.14–8.15
EEA nationals, 8.68
EU law, 8.17–8.18
exclusion, 8.132–8.133
exercise of executive power, 8.35
family members, 8.22, 8.34, 8.39, 8.68–8.69
foreign criminals, 8.1, 8.21, 8.24, 8.31, 8.34, 8.40, 8.46, 8.48
freedom of assembly, 8.14
freedom of expression, 5.193, 5.196, 8.14
freedom of thought, conscience and religion, 5.189–5.190, 8.14

Immigration Act (1971), 8.20–8.23, 8.37–8.42, 8.44–8.45, 8.50–8.56, 12.35
Immigration (European Economic Area) Regulations (2006), 8.32–8.33
Immigration Rules
  see **Immigration Rules**
in-country deportation cases, 16.85
international human rights law
  best interests of the child, 8.9
  discrimination against women, 8.9
  ICCPR protection, 3.20–3.32, 8.6, 8.8–8.9
  immigration law, 8.5
  nationality law, 8.5
  non-discrimination provisions, 8.8–8.9
  torture, 8.6–8.7
international law
  deprivation of nationality, 8.4
  exercise of discretion, 8.2
  expulsion of aliens, 8.3
  general international law, 8.2
  hybrid instruments, 8.10–8.13
  influence, 8.2
  international human rights law, 8.2, 8.5–8.9
  interpreting domestic law, 8.2
international refugee law, 8.10
Irish citizens, 8.42
judicial review, 8.50, 8.55–8.56, 8.80
lawfulness requirement, 8.50, 8.72–8.75
leave to remain, 8.134
margin of discretion, 8.116
migrants, 16.31
military personnel, 8.42
national security, 16.104–16.106, 16.108–16.110
PPSTP provisions, 8.13
proportionality, 5.114
public good, 8.37, 8.40, 8.45–8.46, 8.50, 8.52, 8.54–8.55, 8.67, 8.74, 8.100, 11.32, 16.31
public interest, 8.71, 8.80–8.81, 8.104–8.108
punishment without law, 5.97
racial discrimination, 8.9
respect for private and family life, 5.114, 8.14, 8.85–8.108, 8.114, 8.116–8.117, 8.129
  see also **Respect for private and family life**
returned deportees, 8.34
revocation, 8.124–8.130
right to marry, 8.14
seamen, 8.68
Special Immigration Appeal Commission (SIAC), 16.79, 16.104–16.111
  see also **Special Immigration Appeal Commission (SIAC)**
spouses, 8.34, 8.69
statutory liability
  absence of policy, 8.80
  appeals, 8.120
  British Citizens, 8.38, 8.44
  children, 8.69, 8.81
  civil partners, 8.69
  consistency principle, 8.73, 8.79
  criminal conduct, 8.81
  discretionary power, 8.40, 8.50, 8.70–8.71, 8.79–8.80, 8.109, 8.111, 8.117, 12.37

duration of liability, 8.43–8.45
ECHR obligations, 8.71–8.72, 8.80–8.81, 8.83–8.84
EEA nationals, 8.68, 8.76–8.78, 8.81
eligible persons, 12.35, 12.37
exemptions, 8.42, 8.68
exercise of powers, 8.1, 8.40, 8.63–8.67, 8.71, 8.75, 8.81
fairness, 8.73, 8.79
family members, 8.22, 8.39, 8.68–8.69
foreign criminals, 8.46, 8.48, 8.57, 8.81
group members, 8.37
immunity, 8.38
improper considerations, 8.80
lawfulness requirement, 8.72–8.75
legitimate expectations, 8.73
limits, 8.39
necessary deportation, 8.41
non-automatic deportation, 8.50–8.55
notification requirement, 8.119–8.119
over-rigidity, 8.73
policy considerations, 8.73
previous positive adjudication, 8.74
proportionality principle, 8.77, 8.117
public good, 8.81
public health, 8.77
public interest, 8.71, 8.80–8.81
public law, 12.37
public policy, 8.77
public security, 8.77
recommendation case, 8.70
relevant factors, 8.73, 8.80–8.81
respect for private and family life, 8.71–8.72, 8.80–8.81, 8.83–8.86
right of abode, 7.25, 8.38
serious harm, 8.100
spouses, 8.69
torture, inhuman and degrading treatment, 5.36–5.38, 5.40, 5.63, 5.66, 5.74
trafficking, 8.13, 8.16
Turkish workers, 8.68
UK Borders Act (2007), 8.21, 8.24–8.31, 8.39–8.40, 8.43, 8.46–8.49, 8.53, 8.57–8.62, 8.100, 8.109–8.111, 8.114, 8.117

Deportation orders
appeal pending, 8.57, 8.110
appeal system, 16.104
consistency principle, 8.73, 8.79
detention, 8.132
discretionary power, 11.32
entry in breach, 9.53
exclusion, 8.133
exercise of power, 8.63–8.66
foreign criminals, 8.57
human rights protection, 8.71–8.72, 8.80
legal challenge, 8.112–8.114
legitimate expectations, 8.73
making of orders, 8.121–8.122
mandatory deportation, 8.57
material alteration, 8.128
procedural standards, 8.66
public interest, 8.71, 8.80

public law, 8.67, 8.75
respect for private and family life, 8.71–8.72, 8.80, 8.114, 8.116
revocation, 8.27, 8.124–8.131, 10.33–10.34
Special Immigration Appeals Commission (SIAC), 16.42
see also **Special Immigration Appeals Commission (SIAC)**
statutory provisions, 8.22, 8.24–8.26, 8.34, 8.41, 8.47, 8.56–8.57, 8.61, 8.109–8.111, 8.114, 8.117, 8.122, 12.35, 16.31
timing, 8.26, 8.57, 8.110

Deprivation of citizenship
appeals, 12.67–12.69
arbitrariness, 12.51
British Nationality Act (1981), 12.2, 12.19–12.22, 12.36, 12.40, 12.49–12.50, 12.56–12.58, 12.61–12.62, 12.66–12.68
citizenship obtained by deception, 12.22, 12.25, 12.38, 12.44
concealment, 12.40, 12.41, 12.44–12.45
Council of Europe instruments, 12.15–12.16
CRS protection, 12.13–12.14
CSR protection, 12.12
CSSP protection, 12.12
deprivation power, 12.36
deprivation process, 12.39
discretionary deprivation, 12.40, 12.43, 12.45
domestic law
    guidance, 12.24, 12.45–12.46
    prerogative powers, 12.18
    statute law, 12.19–12.22, 12.51
    statutory instrument, 12.23
ECN provisions, 12.16
EU law, 6.1, 6.22, 12.17
false representation, 12.40–12.41, 12.43–12.45, 12.47
fraud, 12.40, 12.42–12.45, 12.47
human rights standards, 12.51
hybrid instruments, 12,12–12.14
Immigration Act (1971), 12.1–12.2, 12.20
Immigration Act (2014), 12.21, 12.61–12.66
Immigration, Asylum and Nationality Act (2006), 12.50, 12.55, 12.69
international human rights law
    CEDAW provisions, 12.11
    CERD provisions, 12.11
    CRC protection, 12.11
    CRPD protection, 12.11
    ECHR protection, 12.9, 12.15
    ICCPR protection, 12.9–12.10
    UDHR protection, 12.8
international law
    arbitrary deprivation, 12.5
    customary law norms, 12.7
    determination of nationality, 12.4
    general international law, 12.3–12.7
    international human rights law, 12.8–12.11
    statelessness, 12.6–12.7
loss of citizenship, 12.1–12.2
loss of nationality, 12.1
material facts, 12.41–12.44

mental/physical impairment, 12.45
mitigating factors, 12.45
Nationality, Immigration and Asylum Act (2002), 12.50, 12.67, 12.69
notice requirement, 12.54
objectively reasonable grounds, 12.51
persons outside UK, 12.54
proportionality, 12.45
public good, 12.36, 12.49–12.50, 12.52–12.53, 12.55, 12.68
public interest, 12.45, 12.53
respect for private and family life, 12.45, 12.47
right of abode, 12.1–12.2, 12.36, 12.51, 12.55
SIAC appeals, 12.56–12.60, 12.63, 12.65, 12.67
statelessness, 12.57–12.58, 12.63
statutory powers, 12.1–12.2
terrorist activity, 12.50, 12.52, 12.56
unacceptable behaviour, 12.52
voidability of original grant
  citizenship obtained by deception, 12.25
  fraud, 12.34
  grant of naturalisation, 12.27, 12.29, 12.31–12.32
  impersonation, 12.27–12.30
  misleading information, 12.26
  necessary deprivation, 12.25
  nullity actions, 12.25, 12.30–12.34
  omission, 12.26
  refugee status, 12.29
Deprivation of nationality
  arbitrary deprivation, 2.60–2.61
  British Nationality Act (1981), 12.19, 12.36, 12.40
  conflicting nationality laws, 2.59
  customary international law, 2.58
  denationalisation, 2.59, 2.64–2.65
  deprivation power, 12.36
  dual nationality, 2.59
  ECN protection, 5.240
  effectiveness, 2.61
  EU citizenship, 6.24–6.27
  EU law remedies, 14.1
  expulsion contemplated, 2.62–2.63
  human rights, 2.60, 2.68
  Immigration Act (1971), 12.36
  internal element, 2.62
  international law, 2.62, 2.65, 2.68, 8.4
  international standards, 2.69
  persecution, 4.22
  proportionality, 6.25, 6.27
  racial discrimination, 2.60–2.61
  re-admission, 2.64, 2.67–2.68
  refugees, 4.69
  respect for private and family life, 5.184–5.186
  state control, 2.58
  statelessness, 2.59, 2.60, 2.62–2.63, 2.66–2.67
    see also **Statelessness**
  terrorist suspects, 6.27
Detained Fast Track (DFT) Procedure
  adjournment, 16.19
  asylum claimants, 16.17
  notice of appeal, 16.18
  procedural rules, 16.17–16.19
  removal from fast track, 16.19
  time limit, 16.18
  Tribunal powers, 16.19
  Tribunal determination, 16.20
Detention
  abuse of detainees, 5.41, 5.50, 5.72
  arbitrary detention, 5.85, 5.87
  fair trial, 5.90
  indefinite detention, 5.224
  terrorist suspects, 5.224
  torture prior to execution, 5.35
Disability
  see also **Convention on the Rights of Persons with Disabilities (CRPD)**
  denial of citizenship, 11.9
  human dignity, 3.86
  human rights protection, 3.86
  liberty of movement, 3.87
  persons with disabilities, 3.86–3.87
  UN Committee on the Rights of Persons with Disabilities, 13.34, 13.38
Discrimination
  acquisition of citizenship, 11.35, 11.38
  birth, 5.218, 5.220, 5.222
  colour, 5.218–5.219
  definition, 5.217
  denial of citizenship, 11.19, 11.35
  deportation, 8.8–8.9
  differential treatment, 5.217–5.220, 5.222
  discrimination against women, 3.63–3.64, 8.9, 11.9
    see also **Convention on the Elimination of All Forms of Discrimination against Women (CEDAW)**
  ECHR protection, 5.5, 5.215–5.222, 11.12
  EU law, 14.3
  exclusion cases, 5.218
  expulsion cases, 5.218
  gender discrimination, 8.8
  human rights protection, 3.7
  ICCPR protection, 3.30
  language, 5.218
  legitimate aim, 5.217
  national/ethnic origin, 5.218–5.219
  no less favourable treatment, 14.3, 14.8
  other status, 5.218, 5.221–5.222
  positive action, 5.217
  prohibited grounds, 5.217–5.218
  proportionality, 5.217
  racial discrimination, 2.60–2.61, 3.59, 3.61–3.62, 5.41, 5.218–5.219, 8.9, 11.4, 13.34, 13.38
    see also **Convention on the Elimination of All Forms of Racial Discrimination (CERD)**
  reasonable/objective justification, 5.217, 5.219, 5.222
  socio-economic rights, 4.35
Domestic law
  constitutional law, 7.2–7.10
    see also **Constitutional law**
  fundamental rights, 7.5–7.10, 7.14, 7.17, 7.25
    see also **Fundamental rights (UK)**
  immigration control, 7.5, 7.26, 7.41

503

Index

see also **Immigration control**
immigration law, 7.1, 7.22–7.23, 7.25–7.38
  see also **Immigration law**
judicial review, 7.44
  see also **Judicial review**
nationality law, 7.1, 7.39–7.43
  see also **Nationality law**
parliamentary sovereignty, 7.10–7.20
  see also **Parliamentary sovereignty**
prerogative powers, 7.21–7.24
  see also **Prerogative powers**
sources of law, 7.1, 7.25–7.34, 7.39–7.43

Domestic remedies
appeals
  see **Appeals**
expulsion and exclusion cases, 16.1
judicial review 16.1–16.2, 16.5
  see also **Judicial review**
lawfulness of administrative decisions, 16.1
public law challenges
  illegality, 16.1
  irrationality, 16.1
  unfairness, 16.1

Dublin III Regulation
asylum claims, 6.87–6.88
EU law remedies, 14.15, 14.26–14.27
fundamental rights, 6.89
reception conditions, 6.88
refoulement, 6.88
refugee status, 6.87

Effective remedy
  see **Right to effective remedy**

EU Citizenship
Citizens' Directive, 6.30–6.31
  see also **Citizens' Directive**
deprivation of citizenship, 6.22
expulsion and exclusion, 6.22, 6.28, 6.31, 6.35, 6.37, 6.39, 6.48–6.49, 6.51, 6.57–6.68
family members, 6.31–6.32, 6.35
free movement provisions, 6.20, 6.28, 6.30, 6.59
nationality
  acquisition and loss, 6.24–6.27
  possession, 6.23
procedural guarantees, 6.25
right of entry, 6.31–6.33
right of residence, 6.31–6.33, 6.35
Treaty rights, 6.36–6.38

EU fundamental rights
asylum, 6.19
Charter of Fundamental Rights of the European Union, 6.2, 6.16–6.19, 6.28, 6.49, 6.60
ECHR protection, 6.19
  see also **European Convention on Human Rights (ECHR)**
fair trial, 6.19
immigration, 6.19
private and family life, 6.19
right to dignity, 6.19
right to good administration, 6.19
scope of protection, 6.16
torture, inhuman and degrading treatment, 6.19

EU law
application, 6.4, 6.10
citizenship
  acquisition, 11.25–11.26
  denial, 11.14
  deprivation, 6.1, 6.22, 12.17
CJEU decisions, 6.2
deportation, 8.17–8.18
derived rights, 6.60
derogation, 6.15
direct effect, 6.2, 6.9–6.10
enforcement, 1.23
EU law remedies
  access to national courts, 14.1–14.2
  appropriate remedies, 14.3, 14.11
  Asylum Procedures Directive, 14.15, 14.25
  Citizens' Directive, 14.15–14.24
    see also **Citizens' Directive**
  compensation, 14.11
  damages, 14.2
  deprivation of nationality, 14.1
  Dublin III Regulation, 14.15, 14.26–14.27
  due process rights, 14.14
  effectiveness principle, 14.3, 14.11, 14.13
  equivalence principle, 14.3, 14.8–14.10
  European Commission proceedings, 14.51
  EU Treaties, 14.2
  expulsion and exclusion cases, 14.1
  fundamental rights protection, 14.13
  general principles, 14.3, 14.5–14.14
  human rights protection, 14.14
  interim relief, 14.11, 14.18
  judicial protection, 14.12–14.13
  judicial review, 14.11, 14.17–14.18
  Member State decisions, 14.1
  no less favourable treatment, 14.3, 14.8
  non-discrimination requirement, 14.3
  preliminary reference procedure, 14.4, 14.6
    see also **Preliminary reference procedure**
  scrutiny of national procedure, 14.14
  secondary legislation, 14.2, 14.15
  standing (*locus standi*), 14.1
  state liability, 14.2
    see also **State liability**
  subsidiarity principle, 15.8
  supervisory framework, 14.2
  violation of rights
    administrative action, 14.1
    domestic legislation, 14.1
    domestic remedies, 14.1–14.3, 14.6, 14.14
    enforcement, 14.2
    judicial action, 14.1
    procedural autonomy, 14.2
exclusion and expulsion provisions
  absence from host state, 6.55
  automatic expulsion, 6.46
  children, 6.63–6.64
  Citizens' Directive, 6.31
  compliance, 6.49, 6.68
  derived rights, 6.60, 6.62–6.64, 6.66–6.67, 6.70
  EU citizens, 6.28, 6.31, 6.35–6.37, 6.39, 6.48–6.49, 6.51, 6.57–6.68

504

exclusion measures, 10.16
family members, 6.31–6.32, 6.35, 6.58
free movement rights, 6.30
fundamental rights, 6.28
imperative grounds, 6.52–6.54
minors, 6.51
periods of imprisonment, 6.56
present threat, 6.45
proportionality, 6.28, 6.37, 6.48, 6.58–6.59, 6.65
protection, 6.1, 6.3, 6.37, 6.51–6.52, 6.65, 6.67
public health, 6.28, 6.37–6.40, 6.43, 6.58–6.59, 6.62, 6.64, 6.70
public policy, 6.28, 6.37–6.41, 6.44, 6.46, 6.51, 6.58–6.59, 6.62, 6.64, 6.70
public security, 6.28, 6.37–6.42, 6.44, 6.46, 6.51, 6.58–6.59, 6.62, 6.64, 6.70
regulation, 6.72
right of entry, 6.29, 6.31–6.32
right of residence, 6.29–6.30, 6.32, 6.60, 6.63, 6.66
serious threat, 6.47, 6.52–6.53
social assistance burden, 6.58
terrorism cases, 6.50
third country nationals, 6.60
Treaty rights, 6.36–6.38, 6.63–6.64
Turkish nationals, 6.71
freedom of movement, 1.23, 6.20–6.21, 6.28, 6.30–6.35, 6.37, 6.59, 6.61–6.62, 6.59, 10.98–10.99, 10.102–10.104
see also **Free movement provisions (EU)**
fundamental rights, 6.16–6.19, 6.28, 6.49, 6.60
see also **EU fundamental rights**
general principles, 6.2, 6.11–6.15
human trafficking
 criminal offences, 6.91
 national security considerations, 6.93
 penalties, 6.92
 prevention, 6.91
 public policy, 6.93
 rights of residence, 6.93
 sanctions, 6.91
 Trafficking Directive, 6.90–6.93
 UK position, 6.90
 victims, 6.91–6.93
incorporation, 1.23, 2.5
international protection
 Area of Freedom, Security and Justice, 6.72–6.73
 asylum, 6.73–6.74
 control of external borders, 6.73
 Dublin III Regulation, 6.87–6.89
 entry conditions, 6.75
 exclusion and expulsion, 6.72
 immigration policy, 6.75
 Procedures Directive, 6.76
 Qualification Directive, 6.76–6.86
 Reception Directive, 6.76
 residence conditions, 6.75
 subsidiary protection, 6.74
 TFEU provisions, 6.73–6.76
 third country nationals, 6.72, 6.75
 trafficking, 6.75
national law conformity, 6.10

non-discrimination, 6.14
proportionality, 6.12–6.13, 6.28, 6.37
 see also **Proportionality**
remedies
 see **EU law remedies**
removals, 9.18–9.19
scope, 6.5–6.8
secondary legislation, 6.2
sources, 6.2
sovereignty, 7.18–7.19
state liability, 14.28–14.29
 see also **State liability**
supremacy, 6.9
third country agreements, 6.2
Turkish nationals, 6.69–6.71
 see also **Turkish nationals**
European Convention on Human Rights (ECHR)
additional rights protection
 expulsion of aliens, 5.225, 5.228–5.231
 expulsion of nationals, 5.225–5.227
 revocation of nationality, 5.226
 return to one's own country, 5.227
 UK position, 5.231
anti-discrimination provision, 5.5, 5.215–5.222, 11.12
application
 autonomous meaning, 5.10
 consular officials, 5.14
 customary international law, 5.13
 exercise of effective control, 5.14
 extraterritoriality, 5.14, 5.21–5.22
 immigration issues, 5.15–5.18
 interpretation, 5.10
 legal space, 5.14
 nature and extent, 5.8–5.9
 state agent authority, 5.14
 territorial jurisdiction, 5.11–5.12
 treaty law, 5.13
breaches, 16.120, 16.125–16.126
citizenship
 acquisition, 11.24, 11.38
 denial, 11.7, 11.2
 deprivation, 12.9, 12.15
declarations of incompatibility, 7.20, 14.14
deportation, 5.5, 8.14–8.15, 8.34
derogation
 anti-discrimination provision 5.5
 detention of terrorist suspects, 5.224
 freedom of speech, 5.5
 information requirement, 5.223
 public emergency, 5.223–5.224
 wartime, 5.223
exclusion decisions, 10.85–10.88, 10.92, 10.109
fair trial, 4.29, 5.85–5.94, 8.14, 9.14, 9.37, 10.12, 14.14
 see also **Fair trial**
foreign and domestic cases distinguished, 5.19–5.25
freedom of assembly and association, 5.188, 9.14, 10.12
freedom of expression, 5.188, 5.193–5.196, 10.12, 10.87, 10.109

see also **Freedom of expression**
freedom of speech, 5.5
freedom of thought, conscience and religion, 5.188–5.192, 9.14, 10.12
  see also **Freedom of thought, conscience and religion**
incorporation into UK law, 2.21, 5.7, 7.5, 8.76, 8.84, 8.96, 8.107, 15.6, 16.120
interpretation, 2.14
liberty and security of the person, 5.84–5.87, 8.14, 9.14, 10.12
  see also **Liberty and security of the person**
living instrument, 5.10
margin of appreciation, 15.8
nationality issues, 5.5
procedural safeguards
  case review, 5.232, 5.237
  expulsion of aliens, 5.232–5.233
  lawful residence, 5.235
  lawfulness requirement, 5.233–5.234
  meaning of expulsion, 5.236
  national security considerations, 5.232
  UK position, 5.238
proportionality assessment, 9.15
public authority intervention
  disproportionate interference, 8.15
  economic well-being, 5.100, 5.115, 5.127
  national security, 5.100, 5.115, 5.125, 5.127–5.128
  prevention of disorder 5.100, 5.115, 5.127–5.128
  protection of health and morals, 5.100, 5.115, 5.127–5.128
  protection of other's rights, 5.100, 5.115, 5.127
  public safety, 5.100, 5.115, 5.127
punishment without law, 5.95–5.99, 8.14, 9.14, 10.12
  see also **Punishment without law**
refoulement, 5.20, 5.23, 5.35, 5.37, 5.47
removal or exclusion, 5.5–5.6, 9.14–9.15
respect for private and family life, 3.49–3.50, 5.6, 5.24–5.25, 5.100–5.201, 8.14, 8.83–8.84, 9.14–9.15, 9.37, 9.100–9.102, 10.12, 10.85, 11.7, 11.12, 11.24, 11.38, 12.9, 12.15, 16.53–16.54
  see also **Respect for private and family life**
right to effective remedy, 5.202–5.214
  see also **Right to effective remedy**
right to life, 3.17, 5.6, 5.21, 5,26–5.33, 8.14, 9.14, 10.12
  see also **Right to life**
right to marry and found a family, 5.197–5.201, 9.14
  see also **Right to marry and found a family**
slavery, servitude and forced or compulsory labour, 5.22, 5.77–5.83, 8.14, 9.14, 10.12
  see also **Slavery, servitude and forced or compulsory labour**
subsidiarity principle, 15.8
torture, inhuman and degrading treatment, 3.17, 5.6, 5.33, 5.34–5.76, 8.14, 9.14, 10.12, 16.99
  see also **Torture, inhuman and degrading treatment**
European Convention on Nationality (ECN)
aim, 5.239

avoidance of statelessness, 5.240
competence of the state, 5.239
cooperation between states, 5.241
denial of nationality, 11.13
deprivation of citizenship, 12.16
deprivation of nationality, 5.240
general principles, 5.240
judicial review, 5.241
military service, 5.239, 5.241
multiple nationality, 5.239, 5.241
nationality rules, 5.241
non-discrimination, 5.240
procedural standards, 5.241
ratification, 5.4
right to nationality, 5.240
spouses, 5.240
state succession, 5.241
European Court of Human Rights (ECtHR)
  see also **European Court of Human Rights applications**
administration, 15.20
admissibility criterion, 15.7, 15.22, 15.26, 15.30, 15.36–15.47
advisory opinions, 15.9
appeals, 16.28
Brighton Conference, 15.8–15.9
caseload, 15.7
Chambers, 15.15, 15.17, 15.22
Committees, 15.15–15.16
enforcement of judgments, 15.5
execution of judgments, 15.69–15.70
establishment, 15.3
function, 15.3
Grand Chamber, 15.13, 15.18–15.19, 15.22
individual petition, 15.5, 15.29, 15.59
Judge Rapporteur, 15.15, 15.22
judges, 15.11–15.14
jurisdiction, 15.4, 15.9, 15.22
Plenary Court, 15.12, 15.17
procedure
  admissibility decision, 15.22, 15.26
  contact with parties, 15.26
  evidence, 15.25
  findings of fact, 15.25
  friendly settlements, 15.26
  initiation of case, 15.22
  interim relief, 15.50–15.59
  official language, 15.21
  oral hearing, 15.24
  Rules of Court, 15.10, 15.18–15.19, 15.21, 15.23–15.26, 15.31–15.32, 15.50
  sequence of cases heard, 15.23
  state intervention, 15.28
  third party intervention, 15.27
  unilateral declarations, 15.26
reforms, 15.7–15.9
European Court of Human Rights applications
abusive applications, 15.44
admissibility criterion, 15.7, 15.22, 15.26, 15.30, 15.36–15.47
advisory opinions, 15.9
alternative remedies, 15.41

anonymity, 15.34
application form, 15.33
appropriate subject matter, 15.37
asylum cases, 15.42
background, 15.3–15.10
compensation, 15.65, 15.67
costs, 15.65, 15.67
decisions
  execution of judgments, 15.69–15.70
  finality, 15.68
  immediate effect, 15.68
deposit of documents, 15.34
European Convention on Human
  Rights (ECHR)
  incompatibility, 15.43–15.44
  violations, 15.30, 15.36–15.37
exhaustion of remedies, 15.30, 15.39–15.42, 15.58
friendly settlements, 15.26
Grand Chamber, 15.13, 15.18–15.19, 15.22
ill-founded applications, 15.43–15.44
immigration cases, 15.42
individual petition, 15.5, 15.29, 15.59
interim relief
  expulsion cases, 15.54, 15.57–15.58
  indication of interim measure, 15.50, 15.59
  mental harm, 15.53
  removal cases, 15.53, 15.57
  requests, 15.50, 15.55, 15.57
  risk of irreparable damage, 15.52
  Rules of Court, 15.50–15.51
  supporting documentation, 15.56
jurisdiction, 15.4, 15.9, 15.22
just satisfaction, 15.64
legal aid, 15.42, 15.60–15.63
limitation period, 15.8, 15.30, 15.38
nature of loss, 15.67
overruling domestic courts, 15.66
pleadings, 15.35
primary remedy, 15.2
procedural rules, 15.21–15.28, 15.31–15.32
reforms, 15.7–15.9
registration, 15.22
settlement, 15.67
significant disadvantage suffered, 15.45–15.47
striking out, 15.14, 15.26, 15.48–15.49
European Economic Area (EEA)
appeal rights (EEA nationals), 16.41, 16.50, 16.69–16.71, 16.85
deportation measures, 8.32–8.33, 8.68, 8.77–8.78, 8.81
  see also **Immigration (European Economic Area) Regulations 2006**
exclusion measures, 10.16, 10.21, 10.97, 10.100–10.115
  see also **Exclusion**
public health, 8.32–8.33, 9.35–9.36,
public policy, 8.32–8.33, 9.35–9.36, 10.102–10.105, 10.107, 10.112, 10.115
public security, 8.32–8.33, 9.35–9.36, 10.103, 10.105, 10.107, 10.112, 10.115
removal provisions, 9.24, 9.35–9.37, 9.87, 9.95–9.96

Evidence
deprivation of citizenship, 12.46
fair trial, 5.89–5.90
obtained by torture, 5.89
Exclusion
aliens
  deportation, 8.3
  ECHR protection, 5.6
  exclusion measures, 2.45, 10.1
  right of expulsion, 2.53
  respect for private and family life, 5.6
  state responsibility, 2.40, 2.42
  torture, inhuman or degrading treatment, 5.6
CATHB protection, 10.14
children, 6.63–6.64
Citizens' Directive, 6.31, 6.35, 6.37, 6.39, 6.48–6.49, 6.57, 10.97
Council of Europe instruments, 10.12–10.15
CRPD protection, 10.9
CSR protection, 10.10
CSSP protection, 10.10
deportation orders, 10.21
  see also **Deportation orders**
discrimination, 5.218
domestic law
  prerogative powers, 10.17, 10.72
  statute law, 10.18–10.20
ECHR protection, 5.5–5.6, 10.12–10.13
EEA nationals, 10.16, 10.21
EEA regime
  breach of exclusion order, 10.113
  Citizens' Directive, 10.97
  CJEU jurisprudence, 10.100
  ECHR protection, 10.109
  EEA decisions, 10.114
  EEA identity document, 10.114
  exclusion pending appeal, 10.115
  existence of threat, 10.105
  freedom of expression, 10.109
  human rights violations, 10.109
  interests of society, 10.108
  lifting of exclusion order, 10.112
  proportionality, 10.101, 10.109, 10.111
  public policy considerations, 10.102–10.105, 10.107, 10.112, 10.115
  public security considerations, 10.103, 10.105, 10.107, 10.112, 10.115
  right of residence, 10.106, 10.110–10.111
EU citizenship, 6.22, 6.31, 6.35, 6.37, 6.39, 6.48–6.49, 6.51, 6.57
EU law, 6.1, 6.3, 6.28–6.32, 6.35, 6.37–6.58, 6.65–6.68, 6.72, 10.16
  see also **EU law**
exclusion decision
  absence of appeal, 10.82
  absence of notice requirement, 10.81
  challenges, 10.73, 10.89
  convicted offenders, 10.76, 10.92–10.93
  criminality, 10.77
  deportees, 10.76
  ECHR protection, 10.85–10.88, 10.92
  exclusionary powers, 10.71–10.73, 10.78

507

Facilitated Return Scheme, 10.75
fairness, 10.81
freedom of expression, 10.87
government policies, 10.78
Immigration Rules, 10.73–10.74, 10.76
judicial deference, 10.88
judicial review, 10.82, 10.91
margin of appreciation, 10.88
national security grounds, 10.88
public good, 10.74, 10.88
public order grounds, 10.88
respect for private and family life, 10.85
revocation of decision, 10.91–10.96, 10.114
revocation of entry clearance, 10.74
Secretary of State, 10.71, 10.73, 10.83–10.84, 10.88
statutory basis, 10.72
termination of prison sentence, 10.75
terrorist groups, 10.79
family members, 10.16, 10.21
freedom of expression, 5.193–5.195
guidance, 10.29
hybrid instruments, 10.10–10.11
Immigration Act (1971), 10.18–10.20
  see also **Immigration Act (1971)**
Immigration (European Economic Area) Regulations (2006), 10.21
  see also **Immigration (European Economic Area) Regulations (2006)**
Immigration Rules, 10.22–10.62, 10.73–10.74, 10.76
  see also **Immigration Rules**
international human rights law
  CAT provisions, 10.7
  CEDAW provisions, 10.9
  CERD provisions, 10.9
  ICCPR protection, 10.6, 10.8
  UDHR protection, 10.5
international law
  admission of aliens, 10.3–10.4
  admission of nationals, 10.2
  arbitrary action, 10.4
  general international law, 10.2–10.4
  international human rights law, 10.5–10.9
  state powers, 10.4
migrants, 10.15
peace, order and good governance, 10.1
proportionality assessment
  duration of exclusion, 5.166–5.173
  EU law, 6.48, 6.58–6.59, 6.65
  family reunion, 5.178–5.183
  pending family proceedings, 5.176–5.177
  relevant health issues, 5.174–5.175
public health, 10.16, 10.21
public policy, 10.16, 10.21
public security, 10.16, 10.21
racially-based exclusion, 11.4
refugees, 10.10, 10.15
refusal of entry clearance, 10.1
refusal of leave to enter, 10.1
right of abode, 10.1
social and economic interests, 10.1

state sovereignty, 10.1
Turkish nationals, 6.71
Expulsion
aliens
  see **Expulsion of aliens**
case review, 5.232, 5.237
children, 6.63–6.64
Citizens' Directive, 6.31, 6.35, 6.37, 6.39, 6.48–6.49, 6.57
discrimination, 5.218
ECHR protection, 5.225, 5.226–5.233
EU citizenship, 6.22, 6.31, 6.35, 6.37, 6.39, 6.48–6.49, 6.51, 6.57
EU law, 6.1, 6.3, 6.28–6.32, 6.35, 6.37–6.58, 6.65–6.68, 6.72
  see also **EU law**
fair trial, 5.90, 5.92–5.93
lawfulness requirement, 5.233–5.234
liberty and security of the person, 5.84
meaning, 5.236
national security, 5.232
nationals, 5.225–5.227
proportionality assessment
  applicant's age, 5.133–5.134
  applicant's family situation, 5.131, 5.151, 5.153
  best interests of the child, 5.131, 5.159–5.162
  children of the marriage, 5.131, 5.156
  EU law, 6.48, 6.58–6.59, 6.65
  frequency of behaviour, 5.140
  legitimate aim, 5.131
  length of applicants stay, 5.131, 5.143–5.148
  minors/young adults, 5.132
  mitigating factors, 5.141
  nationalities of those concerned, 5.131, 5.150
  nature of the offence, 5.131, 5.133–5.134, 5.136–5.142
  social, cultural and family ties, 5.131, 5.133–5.134, 5.163–5.165
  spouse's knowledge of offence, 5.131, 5.154–5.155
  spouse's likely difficulties, 5.131, 5.157–5.158
  time since offence committed, 5.131, 5.140–5.141, 5.149
punishment without law, 5.97
refoulement protection, 4.77, 4.80–4.82, 4.89
  see also **Refoulement**
refugees
  danger to the community, 4.82
  threat to life, 4.77, 4.80–4.81
  threat to security, 4.82
respect for private and family life, 5.128–5.129, 5.131
right to effective remedy, 5.204, 5.206
  see also **Right to effective remedy**
right to life, 5.33
stateless persons, 4.90
torture, inhuman and degrading treatment, 5.36–5.38, 5.40, 5.63, 5.66, 5.73–5.74
Turkish nationals, 6.71
Expulsion of aliens
arbitrariness, 2.43, 2.48–2.51
collective expulsions, 5.225, 5.228–5.231

customary international law, 2.43
ECHR protection, 5.6, 5.225, 5.228–5.233
exercise of power, 2.46
expulsion measures, 2.45
extreme instances, 2.46
human rights standards, 2.44, 2.50
humane practice, 2.41–2.42
international law, 2.45, 2.51
just cause, 2.43
lawfully present aliens, 2.46
margin of appreciation, 2.44
peacetime, 2.43
reasons for expulsion, 2.46
respect for private and family life, 5.6
right of expulsion, 2.45–2.47
state discretion, 2.43–2.44
state powers, 1.4, 8.3
state responsibility, 2.39–2.44
torture, inhuman or degrading treatment, 5.6
wartime, 2.43, 2.50

Extradition
fair trial, 5.92–5.94
right to effective remedy, 5.204–5.205
see also **Right to effective remedy**

Facilitated Return Scheme
exclusion decisions, 10.75

Fair trial
access to lawyer, 5.90
conviction in absentia, 5.90
denial of justice, 5.85
deportation, 8.14
detention, 5.90
diplomatic assurances, 5.94
ECHR protection, 4.49, 5.85–5.94, 8.14, 10.12, 14.14
EU fundamental rights, 6.19
entitlement, 5.88
evidence
  absence of evidence, 5.90
  obtained by torture, 5.89
exclusion measures, 10.12
expulsion cases, 5.90, 5.92–5.93
extradition cases, 5.92–5.94
extraterritorial context, 5.88, 5.92
flagrant breach, 5.88–5.91, 5.93–5.94
removals, 9.14
right to effective remedy, 5.204
  see also **Right to effective remedy**
right to liberty, 5.85
summary trial, 5.90

Family life
see **Respect for private and family life**

First-Tier Tribunal
appeals from outside UK, 16.12
error of law, 16.22, 16.24
fees, 16.15
immigration decisions, 16.13
in-country appeals, 16.11
jurisdiction, 16.6–16.7
legal aid, 16.15
notice of appeal, 16.11–16.12, 16.14

onward appeals, 16.8, 16.16, 16.23
procedure, 16.10–16.12
reduction in appeals, 16.54
review of own decision, 16.22

Foundations of the system
aliens and subjects distinguished, 1.2, 1.6
expulsion of aliens, 1.4
immigration control, 1.4, 1.6–1.9, 1.24
  see also **Immigration control**
introduction, 1.1
naturalisation, 1.3
  see also **Naturalisation**
personal liberties, 1.4
personal status, 1.2–1.3
right of entrance, 1.3
right of residence, 1.3, 1.8
subjecthood, 1.3
wartime restrictions, 1.7–1.12

Free movement provisions (EU)
Citizens' Directive, 6.30, 10.99
  see also **Citizens' Directive**
CJEU jurisprudence, 10.100
cross-border services, 6.20
EEA nationals, 6.21
EU citizens, 6.20, 6.28, 6.30
family members, 6.31–6.32, 6.35, 6.37
free movement of workers, 6.20
freedom of establishment, 6.20
fundamental economic freedom, 6.20
immigration control distinguished, 6.21
public health, 10.98–10.99
public policy, 10.98–10.99, 10.102–10.104
public security, 10.98–10.99
third country nationals, 6.33–6.34
UK incorporation, 1.23

Freedom of assembly and association
deportation cases, 8.14
ECHR protection, 5.188, 10.12
exclusion measures, 10.12
flagrant breach, 8.14
removals, 9.14

Freedom of expression
deportation cases, 5.193, 5.196, 8.14
derogation, 5.5
exclusion measures, 5.193–5.195, 10.12, 10.87, 10.109
ECHR protection, 5.5, 5.188, 5.193, 10.12, 10.109
flagrant breach, 8.14
influence of speaker, 5.194
interference, 5.194–5.195
national security, 5.196
removals, 9.14

Freedom of speech
derogation, 5.5
ECHR protection, 5.194

Freedom of thought, conscience and religion
conscientious objectors, 5.192
deportation cases, 5.189–5.190, 8.14
ECHR protection, 5.188, 10.12
exclusion measures, 10.12
extraterritorial violation, 5.191–5.192
flagrant denial, 5.191

national security, 5.190
removals, 9.14
residence permits, 5.190
Fundamental rights (UK)
access to legal advice, 7.6
access to judicial remedy, 7.6
common law rights, 7.6–7.9, 7.17
constitutional rights, 7.5–7.6, 7.10
constitutional statutes, 7.5–7.7, 8.117
fair hearing, 7.6
freedom of movement, 7.6
parliamentary sovereignty, 7.10, 7.14, 7.17
personal liberty, 7.6
principle of legality, 7.10
protection, 7.9–7.10
right of abode, 7.9, 7.25
right of return, 7.6
right to life, 7.6
rule of law, 7.10, 7.14

Group of Experts on Action against Trafficking in Human Beings (GRETA)
independence, 15.72
individual cases, 15.74
information requests, 15.72
membership, 15.71
monitoring mechanism, 15.71–15.72
recommendations, 15.73
reports, 15.72, 15.74
responsibility, 15.72
UK compliance, 15.74

Human rights
see also **European Convention on Human Rights (ECHR)**; **Human Rights Act 1998**
deprivation of nationality, 2.60, 2.68
disabled persons, 3.86
enforced disappearances, 3.88
erga omnes obligations, 2.60
fundamental rights
  see **EU fundamental rights**; **Fundamental rights (UK)**
international human rights law, 2.28, 3.1–3.14, 3.58
  see also **International human rights law (IHRL)**
international remedies, 13.2–13.4
racial discrimination, 2.60–2.61
refugees, 4.17, 4.20, 4.28–4.29, 4.44, 4.72, 4.74–4.75
right of abode, 12.51
right to nationality, 2.60
Human Rights Act 1998
damages awards, 16.126–16.127
declarations of incompatibility, 7.20, 14.14
ECHR violations, 16.120, 16.125–16.126
ECtHR referrrals, 15.6
  see also **European Court of Human Rights applications**
incorporation of Convention rights, 2.21, 5.7, 7.5, 8.76, 8.84, 8.96, 8.107, 15.6, 16.120
interpretative provision, 7.20
parliamentary sovereignty, 7.20

public authority activity, 16.126
right to effective remedy, 5.203
Human trafficking
see **International Law of Human Trafficking (ILHT)**; **Trafficking**

Immigration Act (1971)
Commonwealth citizens, 11.16
deportation orders, 8.22, 8.41, 8.47, 8.56–8.57, 8.61, 8.121–8.122, 8.124–8.130, 12.35
deportation provisions, 8.20–8.23, 16.31
deprivation of citizenship, 12.1–12.2
deprivation of nationality, 12.36
detention provisions, 8.23
discretionary judgment, 8.50
entry rules, 7.22
exclusion measures
  exclusion from entry, 10.19
  immigration control, 10.19–10.20
  leave to enter, 10.18, 10.20
  leave to remain, 10.18–10.19
  public good, 10.20
  right of abode, 10.19
  statutory discretion, 10.20
illegal entrants
  disembarkation, 9.42
  evading immigration control, 9.44
  forged passports, 9.46
  meaning, 9.41
  notice of illegal entry, 9.45
  unlawful entry, 9.43
immigration control, 7.25, 9.44
judicial review, 8.50, 8.55–8.56, 8.80
liability to deportation
  absence of policy, 8.80
  appeals, 8.120
  British Citizens, 8.38, 8.44
  children, 8.69, 8.81
  civil partners, 8.69
  consistency principle, 8.73, 8.79
  criminal conduct, 8.81
  discretionary power, 8.40, 8.50, 8.70–8.71, 8.79–8.80, 8.109–8.111, 8.117, 12.37
  duration of liability, 8.43–8.45
  ECHR obligations, 8.71–8.72, 8.80–8.81, 8.83–8.84
  EEA nationals, 8.68, 8.76–8.78, 8.81
  eligible persons, 12.35, 12.37
  exemptions, 8.42, 8.68
  exercise of powers, 8.63–8.67, 8.71, 8.75, 8.81
  fairness, 8.73, 8.79
  family members, 8.22, 8.39, 8.68–8.69
  foreign criminals, 8.46, 8.48, 8.57, 8.81
  group members, 8.37
  immunity, 8.38
  improper considerations, 8.80
  lawfulness requirement, 8.72–8.75
  legitimate expectations, 8.73
  limits, 8.39
  migrants, 16.31
  necessary deportation, 8.41
  non-automatic deportation, 8.50–8.55

notification requirement, 8.118–8.119
over-rigidity, 8.73
policy considerations, 8.73
previous positive adjudication, 8.74
proportionality principle, 8.77
public good, 8.81, 16.31
public health, 8.77
public interest, 8.71, 8.80–8.81
public law, 12.37
public policy, 8.77
public security, 8.77
recommendation case, 8.70
relevant factors, 8.73, 8.80–8.81
respect for private and family life, 8.71–8.72, 8.80–8.81, 8.83–8.86
right of abode, 7.25, 8.38
serious harm, 8.100
spouses, 8.69
non-automatic deportation
  appeals procedure, 8.53
  criminal association liability, 8.53–8.54
  criminal convictions, 8.52–8.55
  lawfulness requirement, 8.50
  marriages of convenience, 8.54
  public good requirement, 8.50–8.52, 8.54–8.55
  public interest, 8.52
  security-related cases, 8.51
public good requirement, 8.50–8.52, 8.54–8.55, 8.81, 10.20, 13.36, 12.49, 16.31
removal
  aircrew, 9.25, 9.28, 9.39
  alteration of documents, 9.49
  breach of conditions, 9.65
  breach of deportation order, 9.53
  categories of persons, 9.25–9.26
  Channel Tunnel, 9.27
  entry by deception, 9.47–9.48, 9.50
  entry through Common Travel Area, 9.54–9.55
  family members, 9.25, 9.39
  illegal entrants, 9.25, 9.39–9.46
  knowingly entering without leave, 9.50
  over-stayers, 9.70
  refusal of leave to enter, 9.25, 9.39–9.40
  removal after entry, 9.22
  removal directions, 9.26
  removal on entry, 9.22
  removal powers, 9.1, 9.21–9.22, 9.25
  ship's crew, 9.25, 9.28, 9.39
right of abode, 11.16, 12.1–12.2, 12.20, 12.49
subsidiary removal provisions, 8.23
Immigration Act (2014)
  administrative review, 16.58
  see also **Administrative review**
  appeals system
    appeal rights, 16.5, 16.29, 16.45, 16.49
    grounds of appeal, 16.53–16.54
    location of appeal, 16.56
    migration appeals, 16.4
    post-decision matters, 16.55
  deprivation of citizenship
    acquisition of foreign citizenship, 12.62–12.63, 12.65

CRS compliance, 12.66
CSR compliance, 12.66
exercise of power, 12.63
international obligations, 12.64, 12.66
naturalisation, 12.21
protecting vital interests, 12.61, 12.64
public good requirement, 12.61
reasonable grounds of belief, 12.61–12.63, 12.65
reasonable link test, 12.63, 12.65
Secretary of State's decision, 12.21
statelessness, 12.63
deprivation of nationality, 12.61–12.64
removal
  appeals regime, 9.96
  asylum claims, 9.82
  detention powers, 9.81
  directions for removal, 9.81
  family members, 9.81, 9.90–9.91, 9.93–9.94
  human rights claims, 9.82
  leave to remain, 9.80
  notice of removal, 9.81–9.82
  removal powers, 9.1
Immigration and Asylum Act (1999)
  removal
    adult children, 9.87
    appeal provisions, 9.31
    breach of conditions, 9.65–9.70, 9.75, 9.83, 9.99
    curtailment of leave, 9.74–9.79
    dependent children, 9.31
    entry clearance granted from abroad, 9.60
    family members, 9.83, 9.87, 9.89
    illegal entrants, 9.59
    notice of removal, 9.83
    removal after entry, 9.23
    removal directions, 9.30
    removal powers, 9.23, 9.29, 9.59
    leave to remain, 9.30–9.31, 9.59, 9.83, 9.73
    out-of-time applications, 9.31
    over-stayers, 9.61–9.64, 9.80
Immigration, Asylum and Nationality Act (2006)
  appeals procedure, 12.69
  deprivation of citizenship, 12.50, 12.55, 12.69
  removal
    appeals, 9.86
    combined decisions, 9.33–9.34, 9.79
    curtailment of leave to remain, 9.84
    enforcement action, 9.65
    extended leave, 9.32
    leave to remain, 9.33, 9.79, 9.71–9.72, 9.89
    pre-removal decision, 9.34
    refusal of leave to remain, 9.84–9.85
    removal after entry, 9.23
    removal decisions, 9.84–9.86
    use of deception, 9.79, 9.71–9.72, 9.89
Immigration (European Economic Area) Regulations (2006)
  deportation
    detention pending deportation, 8.33
    EEA nationals, 8.33
    entitlement to be admitted, 8.32

exclusion from UK, 8.32–8.33
public health considerations, 8.32–8.33
public policy considerations, 8.32–8.33
public security considerations, 8.32–8.33
right to reside, 8.32–8.33
exclusion measures, 10.21
removal
basis for removal, 9.37
human rights considerations, 9.37
public health, 9.35–9.36
public policy, 9.35–9.36
public security, 9.35–9.36
removal powers, 9.24, 9.35
urgent cases, 9.37

Immigration control
appeals system, 16.3, 16.13
British citizenship, 7.41
see also **British citizenship**
Caribbean migration, 1.13
clandestine arrivals, 1.16–1.17
decolonisation, 1.13
evasion, 9.44
exclusion measures, 10.19–10.20
executive power, 1.4, 1.6
human rights protection, 3.8–3.9
immigration policy, 6.75
Immigration Rules, 7.26
see also **Immigration Rules**
increased flow of immigrants, 1.6
limiting overseas access, 1.13
Nationality, Immigration and Asylum Act (2002), 8.105–8.106
persons with citizenship status, 7.41
post-WWII developments, 1.13–1.22
proportionality, 5.130
refugee law, 4.5
respect for private and family life, 5.117–5.119, 5.122, 5.128, 5.130
right of abode, 1.17–1.20
right of entry, 1.13, 1.15, 1.18
statutory development, 1.6–1.9, 1.24, 7.25

Immigration law
dependents, 7.22
guidance, 7.35–7.36
Immigration Act (1971)
see **Immigration Act (1971)**
persons seeking employment, 7.22
prerogative powers, 7.22–7.23
see also **Prerogative powers**
sources, 7.25–7.34
statement of rules, 7.22, 7.26–7.34
see also **Immigration Rules**
students, 7.22
visitors, 7.22

Immigration Rules
amendments, 7.27
appeals, 8.34
children, 8.34
complexity, 7.27–7.28, 7.34
deportation cases, 8.96–8.104
deportation orders, 8.34, 10.33–10.34
detention, 8.34

ECHR protection, 8.34
exceptionality test, 8.103–8.104
executive discretion, 7.37–7.38
exclusion measures
aggravating circumstances, 10.58
amendment, 10.22
breach of condition, 10.25
breaches of Immigration Rules, 10.56–10.60
Channel Tunnel, 10.25
children, 10.25
compassionate considerations, 10.25
conditional caution, 10.52–10.53
convicted offenders, 10.25, 10.35–10.36, 10.38, 10.63–10.67
curtailment of leave to remain, 10.25
deception, 10.25, 10.42–10.43, 10.48–10.49
discretionary grounds, 10.24
discretionary refusal, 10.54, 10.56
dishonesty, 10.46
entry clearance not previously obtained, 10.25
entry for purpose not covered by rules, 10.25, 10.31–10.32
exclusion decisions, 10.73–10.74, 10.76
exclusion powers, 10.23
failure to disclose, 10.47
failure to pay health charges, 10.25
failure to produce documents, 10.25, 10.55
failure to produce passport, 10.25, 10.39–10.40
false representations, 10.25, 10.42, 10.45
family members, 10.26
general grounds for refusal, 10.30
humanitarian protection, 10.26
mandatory entry bans, 10.35, 10.37, 10.45, 10.49
mandatory grounds, 10.24
medical grounds, 10.41
over-staying, 10.25, 10.49
persistent offenders, 10.25
possession of entry clearance, 10.25
previous breaches of immigration laws, 10.48–10.49
public good, 10.25, 10.28, 10.68–10.70
public interest, 10.25–10.26
re-entry bans, 10.48
refugees, 10.26
refusal of entry, 10.23, 10.25, 10.31, 10.33, 10.74
refusal to remain, 10.25
revocation of entry clearance, 10.74
sponsorship undertakings, 10.61–10.62
suitability grounds, 10.26–10.27, 10.40, 10.50
family members, 8.34
foreign criminals, 8.34
immigration control, 7.26
interpretation, 7.32–7.33
lawful residence, 8.34
legal status, 7.29–7.30
liability to deportation, 8.34
negative resolution procedure, 7.29
parental relationship, 8.34
public interest considerations, 8.34
returned deportees, 8.34

revocation of deportation, 8.127, 8.130
spouses and civil partners, 8.34
statements of the rules, 7.26
transitional provisions, 7.34
waiver, 7.31, 7.37
International Court of Justice (ICJ)
decisions, 2.7, 2.9
establishment, 2.7
international remedies, 13.5
jurisdiction, 2.7
International Covenant on Civil and Political Rights (ICCPR)
anti-discrimination provision, 3.30, 12.10
arbitrary or unlawful interference, 11.7
arrest or detention, 3.29, 8.6
children's rights, 3.14, 3.54–3.57
citizenship
  acquisition, 11.24
  denial, 11.6–11.8
  deprivation, 12.9–12.10
death penalty, 3.17
denial of private life, 11.7
deportation, 3.14, 3.20–3.32, 8.6, 8.8–8.9
deprivation of life, 3.14, 3.17, 8.6
derogation, 3.15
exclusion measures, 10.6, 10.8
expulsion, 3.14, 3.18, 3.33–3.35, 3.36–3.41, 3.45
extradition, 3.14
family and home protection, 3.14, 3.29, 3.46–3.48, 3.51
gender discrimination, 8.8
genocide, 3.17
immigration and nationality rights, 3.14, 3.54–3.56
individual's own country, 3.19–3.20, 3.22–3.24, 3.26, 3.28
lawful presence, 3.21, 3.33–3.35, 3.44
prohibition of slavery, 8.6
removals, 9.5, 9.7–9.8
right to enter and remain, 12.9
right to enter one's own country, 3.14, 3.18–3.32
right to life, 3.14, 3.17
right to nationality, 12.9
scope, 3.16
torture, cruel, inhuman or degrading treatment, 3.14, 3.17, 8.6
International Human Rights Law (IHRL)
acquisition of citizenship, 11.24
claim-right, 3.4
denial of citizenship, 11.5–11.9
deportation, 3.20–3.32, 8.2, 8.5–8.9
deprivation of citizenship, 12.8–12.11, 12.15
development, 3.3
exclusion, 10.5–10.9
International Covenant on Civil and Political Rights (ICCPR)
  see **International Covenant on Civil and Political Rights (ICCPR)**
origins, 3.1
removals, 9.5–9.8
specific rights protected, 3.58
United Nations Charter, 3.1–3.2

Universal Declaration of Human Rights (UDHR), 3.5–3.14, 8.84
International Law of Human Trafficking (ILHT)
see also **Convention on Action against Trafficking in Human Beings (CATHB); Group of Experts on Action against Trafficking in Human Beings (GRETA); Protocol to Prevent, Suppress and Punishment Trafficking in Persons (PPSTP)**
children, 4.98
EU law, 6.90–6.93
historical background, 4.94–4.95
international cooperation, 4.97
PPSTP provisions, 4.96–4.100
prostitution, 4.95
repatriation, 4.95, 4.100
UK position, 6.90
victims, 4.98–4.99, 6.91–6.93
International law
application, 2.15–2.16
classical international law, 2.1, 2.5, 2.41
customary international law, 2.4, 2.8, 2.18, 2.22, 2.43
dualist states, 2.17
hybrid regimes, 4.1–4.4
international arbitration, 2.8, 2.10
International Court of Justice (ICJ), 2.7, 2.9
international law of human trafficking, 4.3–4.4, 4.94–4.100, 6.90–6.93
  see also **International Law of Human Trafficking (ILHT); Trafficking**
international refugee law, 4.3–4.4
  see also **International refugee law**
international statelessness law, 4.3–4.4
  see also **International statelessness law (ISL)**
ius cogens, 2.4
judicial decisions, 2.8
monist states, 2.17
nationality, 2.6, 2.29–2.30
origins, 2.3
nationality
  attribution, 2.31–2.37
  bond of attachment, 2.35–2.37
  deprivation, 1.9–1.10, 1.14, 1.22, 2.58–2.69, 3.10
  domestic law, 2.31–2.34
  domestic sovereignty, 2.32
  international recognition, 2.32, 3.34
  significance, 2.6, 2.29–2.30
protection
  aliens, 2.23–2.25
  diplomatic protection, 2.26, 2.37
  economic interests, 2.27
  erges omnes norms, 2.24–2.25, 11.4
  human rights, 2.28
  international minimum standard, 2.27
  state nationals, 2.23, 2.38
relations between states, 2.1
scope, 2.1–2.2, 2.7
soft law, 2.10
sources, 2.7–2.10
state responsibility, 2.14, 2.23, 2.38–2.43, 2.52–2.56, 2.63

see also **State responsibility**
sub-regimes distinguished, 2.5
treatment of individuals, 2.28–2.30
treaty law, 2.4, 2.7–2.8, 2.11, 2.18–2.19, 2.21–2.22
United Kingdom position
  compliance, 2.15–2.16, 2.22
  customary international law, 2.18, 2.22
  direct effect, 2.17
  EU law, 2.20
  incorporation, 2.17–2.21
  judicial competence, 2.21
  mirror principle, 2.21
  prerogative, 2.17
  treaty law, 2.17–2.19, 2.21–2.22

International Refugee Law (IRL)
alienage, 4.13–4.14
asylum-seekers, 4.5
CSR protection, 8.10–8.11
  see also **Convention Relating to the Status of Refugees (CSR)**
economic survival, 4.44
development, 4.7
fear
  current fear, 4.15
  elimination of risk, 4.38
  internal relocation, 4.40–4.43, 4.45–4.47
  non-state agents, 4.38
  persecution, 4.16–4.36
  return to own country, 4.37
  subjective fear, 4.14
  unwillingness to return, 4.65–4.67
  well-founded fear, 4.15, 4.32, 4.37–4.47, 4.65
human rights protection, 4.17, 4.20, 4.28–4.29, 4.44, 4.72, 4.74–4.75
immigration controls, 4.5
internal protection, 4.44
Nazi Germany, 4.8
persecution 4.16–4.36
  see also **Persecution**
refoulement, 4.77, 4.80–4.82, 4.89, 8.11
refugee status
  cessation, 4.68–4.70
  CSR protection, 4.77–4.78, 4.83–4.84
  deprivation of nationality, 4.69
  exclusion, 4.71–4.76
  expulsion, 4.77–4.82
  fundamental changes, 4.70
  human rights protection, 4.72, 4.74–4.75
  lawful presence, 4.79
  naturalisation, 4.83–4.84
  re-acquisition of nationality, 4.69
  territorial asylum, 4.77
  UNRWA protection, 4.71
scope of protection, 4.10
state protection, 4.38–4.39
stateless persons, 4.6, 4.9, 8.12
UNHCR protection, 4.9

International remedies
effectiveness, 13.1
expulsion and exclusion cases, 13.1–13.2, 13.4
host state action, 13.2
human rights protection, 13.2–13.4
nationality cases, 13.1, 13.4
parallel with domestic remedies, 13.1
Special Rapporteurs, 13.4, 13.20–13.31
  see also **Special Rapporteurs**
UN Charter-based bodies, 13.4–13.32
  see also **United Nations**
UN Treaty-based bodies. 13.4, 13.33–13.50
  see also **United Nations**
wrongdoing by country of origin, 13.2

International Statelessness Law (ISL)
see also **Convention on the Reduction of Statelessness (CRS); Convention Relating to the Status of Stateless Persons (CSSP)**
citizenship
  denial, 11.10–11.11
  deprivation, 12.6–12.7, 12.12–12.14
exclusion measures, 10.10
expulsion, 4.90
foundlings, 4.93
fundamental rights and freedoms, 4.86
nationality, 4.93
naturalisation, 4.91–4.92
refoulement protection, 4.89–4.90
scope, 4.85–4.87
stateless persons defined, 4.87

Judicial review
acquisition of citizenship, 11.36–11.37
Administrative Court, 16.113, 16.128–16.139
  see also **Administrative Court**
amenability to review, 16.114
constitutional issues, 7.4
control of administrative action, 16.2, 16.5, 16.113
discretionary power, 16.119
ECHR breaches, 16.120, 16.125–16.126
EU law remedies, 14.11, 14.17–14.18
exclusion decisions, 10.82, 10.91
grounds
  illegality, 16.1, 16.119
  irrationality, 16.1, 16.119
  procedural impropriety, 16.119
  unfairness, 16.1
heads of review, 16.119–16.121
immigration decisions
  Home Office decisions, 16.115
  policies and procedures, 16.115
  transfer to Upper Tribunal, 16.143–16.150
importance, 7.44
injunctive relief, 16.161, 16.168
interim orders, 16.124
non-suspensive appeals, 16.162–16.167
proportionality, 16.121
remedies, 16.122–16.123
removal directions, 16.168–16.175
service of claims, 16.118
standing (*locus standi*), 16.116–16.117
stay of removal, 16.173
sufficient interest test, 16.116–16.117
Upper Tribunal, 16.113, 16.143–16.150, 16.155
urgent cases, 16.173–16.175

Index

Lawfulness requirement
  administrative decisions, 16.1
  deportation, 8.50, 8.72–8.75, 8.88, 5.115, 5.124–5.126
  ECHR provisions, 5.233–5.234
  expulsions, 5.233–5.234
  public authority intervention, 5.115, 5.124–5.126
  statutory provisions, 8.72–8.75, 8.113–8.114
Legitimate aim
  discrimination, 5.217
  proportionality, 5.115, 5.131, 5.194
  public authority interference, 5.115, 5.127–5.128, 5.131
Liberty and security of the person
  arbitrary detention, 5.85, 5.87
  denial of justice, 5.85
  deportation, 8.14
  deprivation of liberty, 5.85, 5.87
  exceptions, 5.84
  exclusion measures, 10.12
  expulsion cases, 5.84
  extraterritorial application, 5.84–5.85
  length of prison sentence, 5.86
  removals, 9.14

Margin of appreciation
  ECHR protection, 5.129, 5.197, 5.210, 15.8
  exclusion and expulsion decisions, 2.44, 10.88
  proportionality, 5.129
  public authority interference, 5.129
  respect for private and family life, 5.129
  right to effective remedy, 5.210
  right to marry and found a family, 5.197
Marriage
  see also **Right to marry and found a family**
  capacity, 5.197
  children of the marriage, 5.131, 5.156
  marriages of convenience, 5.200, 8.54, 14.20
  minimum age, 5.197
  prohibited degrees, 5.197
  same-sex couples, 5.198
Migrants
  see also **Convention on the Protection of Migrant Workers (MWC)**
  appeals system, 16.3–16.4, 16.30–16.32
  deportation, 16.31
  diplomatic protection, 3.85
  economic migrants, 16.54
  exclusion measures, 10.15
  increased flow, 1.6
  meaning of migrant worker, 3.85
  prohibition on expulsion, 3.85
  respect for private and family life, 5.111
  states of origin, 3.85

National security
  appeal rights, 16.32
  certified decisions, 16.80–16.82
  closed material, 16.90–16.92, 16.95–16.97, 16.100, 16.102, 16.108, 16.111
  deportation cases, 16.104–16.106, 16.108–16.111
  expulsions, 5.232
  freedom of expression, 5.196
  freedom of thought, conscience and religion, 5.190
  in-country deportation cases, 16.85
  respect for private and family life, 5.100, 5.115, 5.125, 5.127–5.128
  Special Immigration Appeals Commission (SIAC), 16.5, 16.7, 16.75–16.79, 16.83
    see also **Special Immigration Appeals Commission (SIAC)**
  torture, inhuman and degrading treatment, 5.36
  trafficking, 6.93
Nationality
  see also **European Convention on Nationality (ECN); Nationality law**
  admission of nationals, 2.38, 2.52–2.56, 2.63
  British Nationality Act (1981), 7.39–7.40
  British citizenship
    see **British citizenship**
  children, 3.83
  deprivation of nationality, 1.9–1.10, 1.14, 1.22, 2.58–2.69, 3.10, 4.22, 4.69, 5.184–5.186, 5.240, 6.25, 6.27, 8.4, 12.19, 12.36, 12.40, 14.1
    see also **Deprivation of nationality**
  determination of nationality, 11.2, 12.4
  domestic law, 2.6
  dual nationals 2.54
  ECHR protection, 5.5, 5.226
  function, 2.38
  international law
    attribution, 2.31–2.37
    bond of attachment, 2.35–2.37
    domestic law, 2.31–2.34
    domestic sovereignty, 2.32
    international recognition, 2.32, 3.34
    significance, 2.6, 2.29–2.30
  judicial review, 5.241
  loss of nationality
    proportionality principle, 6.25, 6.27
    terrorist offences, 6.27
  meaning, 2.6, 11.2
  multiple nationality, 5.239, 5.241
  nationality rules, 5.241
  nationality status, 11.2
  procedural standards, 5.241
  protection of nationals, 2.23, 2.38
  revocation, 5.226
  right to nationality, 3.10–3.11, 3.14, 5.240, 12.9
  spouses, 5.240
  stateless persons, 4.93, 5.240
  status, 2.6
Nationality, Immigration and Asylum Act (2002)
  administrative review, 16.58
    see also **Administrative review**
  appeals
    appeal rights, 16.5, 16.29–16.31, 16.33–16.40, 16.46–16.50
    appealable decisions, 16.35–16.40, 16.46–16.50, 16.52
    appeals outside UK, 16.32
    appeals procedure, 12.67, 12.69
    appeals scheme, 8.96, 8.112, 8.120, 8.131

515

EEA nationals, 16.41, 16.50
expulsion suspended, 16.32
grounds of appeal, 16.43–16.44, 16.51–16.53
human rights claims, 16.47
immigration appeals, 16.3, 16.13, 16.43, 16.46
in-country appeals, 16.32
location of appeal, 16.56
migration appeals, 16.3, 16.32
one-step procedure, 16.72–16.74
protection claims, 16.47–16.48, 16.52
revocation of protected status, 16.47
SIAC appeals, 16.42
asylum claims, 8.107
deeming provision, 4.76, 4.83
deprivation of citizenship, 12.50, 12.67, 12.69, 16.33
economic well-being, 8.105
foreign criminals, 8.105–8.106
human rights claims, 8.107
humanitarian protection, 16.52
immigration controls, 8.105–8.106
judicial response, 8.107
parental relationship, 8.105
public interest, 8.105–8.107
removal
  curtailment of leave to remain, 9.79
  respect for private and family life, 9.100–9.102
  revocation of leave to remain, 9.73
respect for private and family life, 8.105

Nationality law
British citizenship
  see **British citizenship**
denial of citizenship, 11.1, 11.27
development, 1.6–1.9, 1.24
naturalisation, 1.8
right of residence, 2.52
wartime restrictions, 1.8–1.12

Naturalisation
accessibility, 1.9
citizenship of acquisition, 1.21, 7.40, 7.42–7.43, 11.17–11.18, 11.20, 11.28–11.29, 11.38, 11.42
deprivation of citizenship, 12.21
Borders, Citizenship and Immigration Act 2009, 11.20
British Nationality Act (1981), 12.19, 12.40
certificate of naturalisation, 1.9, 1.11
denial of citizenship, 11.17–11.18, 11.20
fraud, 1.9–1.10, 1.22
grant of naturalisation, 12.27, 12.29, 12.31–12.32
nationality law, 1.8
  see also **Nationality law**
refugees, 4.83–4.84
stateless persons, 4.90–4.91

Parliamentary sovereignty
constitutional doctrine, 7.11, 7.13, 7.15
delegation, 7.20
ECHR provisions, 7.20
effect, 7.11
EU law, 7.18–7.19

EU membership, 7.14
fundamental rights, 7.10, 7.14, 7.17
judicial views, 7.14
qualification of sovereignty, 7.16
restriction, 7.20
rule of law, 7.16
Scotland, 7.12
statutory interpretation, 7.16–7.17, 7.20
statutory supremacy, 7.11

Passports
failure to produce, 10.25, 10.39–10.40
forged passports, 9.46

Persecution
breach of duty, 4.21
civil conflict, 4.32
definition, 4.16–4.17
deprivation of nationality, 4.22
detention, 4.30
discrimination in socio-economic rights, 4.35
ECHR protection, 4.29
enforced military service, 4.33–4.34
fear of persecution, 4.16–4.36
human rights approach, 4.17, 4.20, 4.28–4.29
human trafficking, 4.23
ICCPR protection, 4.17–4.19
inciting persecution, 4.26
indirect persecution, 4.25
interpretation, 4.20–4.21
likelihood of persecution, 4.37
nationality, 4.48, 4.52
non-state agents, 4.36, 4.38, 5.59–5.60
political opinion, 4.48, 4.64
prosecution amounting to persecution, 4.27–4.28
racial persecution, 4.48, 4.51
religious persecution, 4.31, 4.48, 4.52
sexual orientation, 4.60
social group, 4.48, 4.54–4.63
state persecution, 4.45
threats of serious harm, 4.24
unwillingness to return, 4.65–4.67
violence against women, 4.23
well-founded fear, 4.32, 4.37–4.47, 4.65

Preliminary reference procedure
asylum cases, 14.39
CJEU clarification, 14.36, 14.41
CJEU jurisdiction, 14.37, 14.41
delays, 14.50
directly enforceable rulings, 14.36
discretionary references, 14.37, 14.42–14.43
immigration cases, 14.39
legal basis, 14.37–14.38
mandatory references, 14.44–14.45
national court discretion, 14.40
reference procedure, 14.46–14.50
Treaty provisions, 14.37–14.42

Prerogative powers
citizenship
  denial, 11.15
  deprivation, 12.18
definition, 7.21
deportation, 8.19, 8.36

exclusion measures, 10.17, 10.72
immigration law, 7.22–7.23
nationality law, 7.24
removals, 9.20
Proportionality
balancing of rights, 5.129
deportation measures, 5.114
discrimination, 5.217
EU law, 6.12–6.13, 6.28, 6.37
exclusion cases, 5.166–5.183, 6.28, 6.37, 6.48, 6.58–6.59
see also **Exclusion**
expulsion cases, 5.130–5.165, 6.28, 6.37, 6.48, 6.58–6.59
see also **Expulsion**
immigration control, 5.130
legitimate aim, 5.115, 5.131, 5.194
loss of nationality, 6.25, 6.27
margin of appreciation, 5.129
public authority interference, 5.115, 5.120, 5.129–5.135
removals, 9.15
respect for private and family life, 5.115, 5.120, 5.129
Protocol to Prevent, Suppress and Punishment Trafficking in Persons (PPSTP)
see also **Convention on Action against Trafficking in Human Beings (CATHB); International Law of Human Trafficking (ILHT); Trafficking**
deportations, 8.13
international trafficking, 4.96–4.100
removals, 9.12
Public authority interference
arbitrariness, 5.124
balancing of rights, 5.129
consequences, 5.115
economic well-being, 5.100, 5.115, 5.127
ex-post facto developments, 5.122
expulsion cases, 5.128–5.129, 5.131
immigration control, 5.117–5.119, 5.122, 5.128
lawfulness requirement, 5.115, 5.124–5.126
legal foreseeability and accessibility, 5.124–5.125
legitimate aim, 5.115, 5.127–5.128, 5.131
margin of appreciation, 5.129
national security, 5.100, 5.115, 5.125, 5.127–5.128
necessary interference, 5.115
prevention of disorder 5.100, 5.115, 5.127–5.128
proportionality, 5.115, 5.120
protection of health and morals, 5.100, 5.115, 5.127–5.128
protection of other's rights, 5.100, 5.115, 5.127
public authority, 5.100, 5.115–5.116, 5.120
public safety, 5.100, 5.115, 5.127
residence issues, 5.123, 5.125
Public health
Citizens' Directive, 14.16–14.17
deportation, 8.77
European Economic Community (EEA), 8.32–8.33, 9.35–9.36
exclusion and expulsion issues, 6.28, 6.37–6.40, 6.43, 6.58–6.59, 6.62, 6.64, 6.70, 10.16, 10.21

free movement provisions, 10.98–10.99
Immigration Act (1971), 8.77
limitation of rights, 6.70
Public international law
see **International law**
Public policy
Citizens' Directive, 14.16–14.17
deportation, 8.77
European Economic Community (EEA), 8.32–8.33, 9.35–9.36, 10.103, 10.105, 10.107, 10.112, 10.115
exclusion and expulsion issues, 6.28, 6.37–6.41, 6.44, 6.46, 6.51, 6.58–6.59, 6.62, 6.64, 6.70, 10.16, 10.21
free movement provisions, 10.98–10.99, 10.102–10.104
Immigration Act (1971), 8.77
limitation of rights, 6.70
Public security
Citizens' Directive, 14.16–14.17
deportation, 8.77
European Economic Community (EEA), 8.32–8.33, 9.35–9.36, 10.103, 10.105, 10.107, 10.112, 10.115
exclusion and expulsion issues, 6.28, 6.37–6.42, 6.44, 6.46, 6.51, 6.58–6.59, 6.62, 6.64, 6.70, 10.16, 10.21
free movement provisions, 10.98–10.99
Immigration Act (1971), 8.77
limitation of rights, 6.70
Punishment without law
crimes against humanity, 5.99
criminal acts exception, 5.95, 5.99
deportation, 5.97, 8.14
exclusion measures, 10.12
expulsion measures, 5.97
extraterritorial context, 5.98
interpretation, 5.96
non-derogable guarantee, 5.95–5.96
rule of law, 5.95–5.96
war crimes, 5.99

Qualification Directive
armed conflicts, 6.78
death penalty, 6.78
exclusion from protection, 6.79–6.86
indiscriminate violence, 6.78
purpose, 6.77
serious criminal offence, 6.84
serious harm defined, 6.78
serious threat to life, 6.78
subsidiary protection, 6.78, 6.80, 6.82, 6.86

Refoulement
CAT protection, 3.70–3.75, 3.81
ECHR protection, 5.20, 5.23, 5.35, 5.37, 5.47, 5.63, 5.73
exclusion, 6.82
fear of ill-treatment, 5.208
non-refoulement obligation, 5.63, 5.73
refugees
  danger to the community, 4.82

protection, 8.11
threat to life, 4.77, 4.80–4.81
threat to security, 4.82
risk of refoulement, 6.88
stateless persons, 4.89–4.90

Refugee law
see also **Convention Relating to the Status of Refugees (CSR); Refugees**
denial of citizenship, 11.10
development, 3.9
international refugee law, 4.3–4.4, 8.10–8.11
see also **International refugee law**
refoulement, 8.11

Refugees
see also **United Nations Commissioner for Refugees (UNHCR)**
citizenship
 denial 11.10
 deprivation, 12.12, 12.66
definition, 4.7, 4.11–4.15
medical services, 5.207
refugee status
 cessation, 4.68–4.70
 CSR protection, 4.77–4.78, 4.83–4.84
 deprivation of citizenship, 12.29
 deprivation of nationality, 4.69
 Dublin III Regulation, 6.87
 exclusion, 4.71–4.76
 expulsion, 4.77–4.82
 fundamental changes, 4.70
 human rights protection, 4.72, 4.74–4.75
 lawful presence, 4.79
 naturalisation, 4.83–4.84
 re-acquisition of nationality, 4.69
 territorial asylum, 4.77
 UNRWA protection, 4.71
right to effective remedy, 5.207
see also **Right to effective remedy**
right to work, 5.207

Remedies
administrative review, 16.54, 16.58–16.68
see also **Administrative review**
appeals
 see **Appeals**
Council of Europe
 see **Council of Europe**
domestic remedies
 expulsion and exclusion cases, 16.1
 lawfulness of administrative decisions, 16.1
 public law challenges, 16.1
EU law remedies
 see **EU law remedies**
international remedies
 see **International remedies**
judicial review, 16.1–16.2, 16.5, 16.113–16.126
 see also **Judicial review**
right to effective remedy, 5.202–5.214
 see also **Right to effective remedy**

Removal
administrative review, 16.64
appeals, 9.96–9.99
breach of conditions, 9.65–9.70, 9.75, 9.83, 9.99

children, 9.87–9.88
claiming public funds, 9.69, 9.76
Council of Europe instruments, 9.14–9.17
CSR provisions, 9.9–9.10
CSSP provisions, 9.11
definition, 9.91
domestic law
 guidance, 9.38
 prerogative powers, 9.20
 statutory instrument, 9.35–9.37
 statute law, 9.21–9.34
EEA nationals, 9.24, 9.35–9.37, 9.87, 9.95–9.96
EU law, 9.18–9.19
family members, 9.83, 9.87–9.91, 9.93–9.94
hybrid instruments, 9.9–9.13
illegal entrants
 disembarkation, 9.42
 evading immigration control, 9.44
 forged passports, 9.46
 meaning, 9.41
 notice of illegal entry, 9.45
 unlawful entry, 9.43
illegal immigrants, 9.56–9.58
Immigration Act (1971), 9.1, 9.21–9.22, 9.25–9.26, 9.28, 9.39–9.50, 9.53–9.55, 9.65, 9.70
 see also **Immigration Act (1971)**
Immigration Act (2014), 9.80–9.82, 9.90–9.91, 9.93–9.94, 9.96
 see also **Immigration Act (2014)**
Immigration and Asylum Act (1999), 9.23, 9.29–9.31, 9.59–9.70, 9.73–9.80, 9.83, 9.87, 9.89
 see also **Immigration and Asylum Act (1999)**
Immigration, Asylum and Nationality Act (2006), 9.23, 9.32–9.34, 9.65, 9.79, 9.84–9.86
 see also **Immigration, Asylum and Nationality Act (2006)**
Immigration (European Economic Area) Regulations (2006), 9.24, 9.35–9.37
 see also **Immigration (European Economic Area) Regulations (2006)**
immigration status, 9.92
international human rights law
 basic standards, 9.7
 CAT provisions, 9.6
 CEDAW protection, 9.8
 CERD provisions, 9.8
 CRPD protection, 9.8
 ICCPR protection, 9.5, 9.7–9.8
 removal provisions, 9.4
international law
 arbitrary decisions, 9.3
 directly applicable, 9.2
 CATHB protection, 9.16–9.17
 ECHR protection, 9.14–9.15
 expulsion of aliens, 9.3
 international human rights law, 9.4–9.8
judicial review, 9.96, 16.168–16.175
Nationality, Immigration and Asylum Act (2002), 9.73, 9.79, 9.100–9.102

see also **Nationality, Immigration and Asylum Act (2002)**
  no evidence of lawful entry (NELE), 9.51–9.52
  notice requirement, 9.81–9.83, 9.89–9.90
  PPSPTP provisions, 9.12
  removal directions, 16.168–16.175
  statutory powers, 9.1, 9.95
  spouses, 9.87–9.88
  stay of removal, 16.173
  students, 9.67
  suspension, 16.64
  work permits, 9.68
Residence
  denial of residence, 5.184–5.186
  EU law, 6.75
  lawful residence, 5.235
  nationality law, 2.52
  public authority interference, 5.123, 5.125
  residence conditions, 6.75
  residence permits, 5.190, 5.247
  right of residence, 1.3, 1.8, 2.52, 6.31–6.33, 6.35, 6.51, 6.60, 6.63, 6.66, 6.69, 6.71, 6.93
  Turkish nationals, 6.69, 6.71
Respect for private and family life
  appeal rights, 16.53–16.54
  artificial insemination, 5.201
  assessment, 5.121
  case decisions
    immigration control, 5.117–5.119
    proportionality, 5.120
    public authority interference, 5.115–5.116, 5.120
  citizenship
    acquisition, 11.24, 11.38
    denial, 5.187, 11.7, 11.12
    deprivation, 12.9, 12.15, 12.45, 12.47
  classification of relationships, 5.114
  denial of residence, 5.184–5.186
  deportation
    best interests of the child, 8.94
    deportation orders, 8.114, 8.116
    disproportionate breach, 8.116, 8.130
    ECHR protection, 8.14, 8.85
    ECtHR decisions, 8.87–8.88
    extradition distinguished, 8.86
    family members, 8.129
    gravity of interference, 8.88
    Immigration Rules, 8.76, 8.81, 8.96–8.104, 8.108
    impact or removal, 8.91
    lawfulness of interference, 8.88
    length of exclusion, 8.130
    liability to deportation, 8.114, 8.116–8.117
    margin of discretion, 8.116
    necessary interference, 8.88
    proportionality, 5.114, 8.87–8.88, 8.90, 8.92–8.93, 8.95
    public authority interference, 8.88
    public interest considerations, 8.104–8.108
    statutory protection, 8.71–8.72, 8.80–8.81, 8.83–8.84
    threshold of engagement, 8.88–8.89, 8.92
  deprivation of nationality, 5.184–5.186

  ECHR protection, 3.49–3.50, 5.6, 5.24–5.25, 5.100–5.201, 8.14, 8.85, 10.12
  EU fundamental rights, 6.19
  exclusion/expulsion of aliens, 5.6
  exclusion measures, 10.12
  family life
    child continuing to live with parents, 5.103
    civil partnerships, 5.105
    cohabitation, 5.105
    de facto relationships, 5.101–5.104
    dependency, 5.108
    formal legal relations, 5.101
    intended family life, 5.107
    near relatives, 5.106
    parent/child relationship, 5.101–5.102
    relationships between adults, 5.108
    same-sex couples, 5.104
    unmarried couples, 5.104
  Immigration Rules, 8.76, 8.81, 8.96–8.104, 8.108
  importance, 5.100
  interference
    arbitrariness, 5.124
    balancing of rights, 5.129
    consequences, 5.115
    disproportionate interference, 9.15
    economic well-being, 5.100, 5.115, 5.127
    ex-post facto developments, 5.122
    expulsion cases, 5.128–5.129, 5.131
    immigration control, 5.117–5.119, 5.122, 5.128
    lawfulness requirement, 5.115, 5.124–5.126
    legal foreseeability and accessibility, 5.124–5.125
    legitimate aim, 5.115, 5.127–5.128, 5.131
    margin of appreciation, 5.129
    national security, 5.100, 5.115, 5.125, 5.127–5.128
    necessary interference, 5.115
    prevention of disorder 5.100, 5.115, 5.127–5.128
    proportionality, 5.115, 5.120
    protection of health and morals, 5.100, 5.115, 5.127–5.128
    protection of other's rights, 5.100, 5.115, 5.127
    public authority, 5.100, 5.115–5.116, 5.120
    public interest, 9.15
    public safety, 5.100, 5.115, 5.127
    residence issues, 5.123, 5.125
  judicial independence, 8.84
  Nationality, Immigration and Asylum Act 2002, 8.105–8.107
  personal correspondence, 5.100
  positive obligations, 5.24–5.25
  private life
    close relationships, 5.108
    decision to have children, 5.110
    evictions, 5.112
    exclusion cases, 5.111
    expulsion cases, 5.111
    gender issues, 5.110
    identity, 5.110
    meaning, 5.109–5.110
    mental health, 5.113
    migrants, 5.111
    physical and moral integrity, 5.113

physical health, 5.113
self-determination, 5.110
sexual orientation, 5.110
proportionality assessment
exclusion cases, 5.166–5.183
expulsion cases, 5.131–5.165
proportionality principle, 5.114–5.115, 5.129–5.135
see also **Proportionality**
public authority interference, 5.100, 5.115–5.116, 5.120
public interest considerations, 9.100–9.102
qualified protection, 8.83
removals, 9.14–9.15
right to develop relationships, 5.113
right to identity, 5.113
right to personal development, 5.113
right to UK presence, 5.113
Right of abode
British citizens, 1.19–1.21, 1.19–1.21, 7.40–7.41, 8.38
denial, 7.41, 11.16
deportation, 7.25, 8.38
deprivation, 12.51, 12.55
exclusion, 10.1, 10.19
fundamental rights, 7.9, 7.25
human rights protection, 12.51
Immigration Act (1971), 12.1–12.2, 12.20, 12.49
immigration control, 1.17–1.20, 7.25
loss of right, 12.1
statutory provisions, 11.16
subjects, 1.8, 1.17, 1.19–1.20
Right to effective remedy
accessory nature, 5.208
appropriate relief, 5.209
asylum cases, 5.207, 5.210–5.213
domestic courts, 5.203
expulsion cases, 5.204, 5.206
extent of protection, 5.214
extradition cases, 5.204–5.205
fair trial, 5.204
margin of appreciation, 5.210
procedural requirements, 5.209
refugees, 5.207
substance of complaint, 5.209
violation of Convention rights, 5.202, 5.208
Right to life
death penalty, 5.21. 5.28–5.31, 5.33
ECHR protection, 3.17, 5.21, 5.26, 5.32, 8.14, 10.12
exclusion measures, 10.12
expulsion cases, 5.33
extraterritorial protection, 5.21
ICCPR protection, 3.14, 3.17
immediate risk to life, 5.32
positive action, 5.27
removals, 9.14
sentence of the court, 5.26
torture, inhuman and degrading treatment, 5.33
use of force, 5.26
Right to marry and found a family
adoption, 5.201

capacity, 5.197
consent, 5.197
deportation cases, 8.14
ECHR protection, 5.197
founding a family, 5.201
fundamental right, 5.197
immigration measures, 5.199
margin of appreciation, 5.197
marriages of convenience, 5.200
minimum marriageable age, 5.197
national laws, 5.197, 5.201
prohibited degrees, 5.197
removals, 9.14
same-sex couples, 5.198
transsexuals, 5.198

Same-sex couples
respect for private and family life, 5.104
right to marry, 5.198
Sexual orientation
respect for private and family life, 5.110
Slavery, servitude and forced or compulsory labour
deportation, 8.14
ECHR protection, 5.22, 5.79–5.83, 8.14, 10.12
exclusion measures, 10.12
forced or compulsory labour, 5.77, 5.79
interpretation, 5.79
removals, 9.14
servitude, 5.78
trafficking, 5.80–5.83
Special Advocate
appointment, 16.93
closed material, 16.96–16.97, 16.100, 16.102
communication with client, 16.96
communication with SIAC, 16.97
responsibility, 16.95
role, 16.94, 16.102
submissions, 16.94
written replies, 16.100
Special Immigration Appeals Commission (SIAC)
chairman, 16.88–16.89
closed material, 16.90–16.92, 16.95–16.97, 16.100, 16.102, 16.108, 16.111
deportation, 16.42, 16.79, 16.104–16.111
disclosure rules, 16.101–16.103
ECHR protection, 16.99
establishment, 16.75, 16.77
exculpatory review, 16.99
exercise of powers, 16.89
function, 16.75–16.76
governing statute (SIACA (1997)), 16.78, 16.83, 16.85, 16.90–16.91
jurisdiction, 16.86
national security, 16.5, 16.7, 16.109
panels, 16.87
procedural rules, 16.100, 16.104–16.106
responsibility, 16.79
safety on return, 16.109–16.110
terrorist suspects, 16.79
SIAC appeals
appealable decisions, 16.83

closed judgment, 16.111
continuation of leave, 16.84
Court of Appeal, 16.89, 16.112
deprivation of citizenship, 12.56–12.60, 12.63,
    12.65, 12.67
directions hearings, 16.106
disclosure rules, 16.84, 16.98, 16.100
evidence, 16.84
ground of appeal, 16.83
notice of appeal, 16.105
onward appeal, 16.112
open judgment, 16.111
statutory provisions, 16.42, 16.83
summons, 16.107
written decisions, 16.111
torture, inhuman and degrading treatment, 16.99

Special Rapporteurs
communications, 13.23–13.26, 13.29–13.31
function, 13.4, 13.20
human rights protection, 13.21–13.23, 13.27,
    13.29
in-country visits, 13.23, 13.27, 13.32
mandates, 13.20–13.21
objectives, 13.23–13.24
reports, 13.23
rights of migrants, 13.21–13.22, 13.27, 13.29
torture, cruel, inhuman and degrading treatment,
    13.21, 13.28–13.29, 13.32
urgent appeals, 13.23–13.24, 13.28

Spouses
deportation measures, 8.34, 8.69
Immigration Rules, 8.34
nationality, 5.240
removal provisions, 9.87–9.88

State liability
breaches of EU law, 14.28–14.29, 14.31, 14.35
CJEU jurisprudence, 14.29
claims procedure, 14.34
damages claims, 14.2, 14.28–14.29, 14.33
direct causal link, 14.29, 14.32
directly effective rights, 14.30
duty of sincere cooperation, 14.28
judicial error, 14.33
limitation period, 14.34
reparation, 14.28
rights conferred on individuals, 14.29–14.30
state discretion, 14.29

State responsibility
admission of nationals, 2.38, 2.52–2.56, 2.63
aliens
    control of aliens, 2.38
    exclusion of aliens, 2.40, 2.42
    expulsion, 2.39–2.44
asylum-seekers, 2.41
children, 3.82
dual nationals 2.54
humane practice, 2.41–2.42
international law, 2.14
protection of state nationals, 2.23, 2.38

Statelessness
see also **International Statelessness Law (ISL)**
avoidance, 5.240

citizenship
    denial, 11.10–11.11
    deprivation, 12.6–12.7, 12.12–12.14,
        12.57–12.58, 12.57–12.58, 12.63, 12.66
deprivation of nationality, 2.59–2.60, 2.62–2.63,
    2.66–2.67, 5.240
exclusion measures, 10.10
removals, 9.11

Subjects
aliens and subjects distinguished, 1.2, 1.6
British patrials, 1.17, 1.19
Citizens of UK and Commonwealth (CUKC),
    1.13, 1.15, 1.19
freedom of movement, 1.12, 1.16
natural-born subjects, 1.3, 1.8
right of abode, 1.8, 1.17, 1.19–1.20
status, 1.13
subjecthood, 1.3

Subsidiarity principle
ECHR interpretation, 15.8
EU law, 15.8

Terrorist suspects
deprivation of citizenship, 12.50, 12.52, 12.56
detention, 5.224
exclusion and expulsion, 6.50, 10.79
loss of nationality, 6.27
removal, 13.37
Special Immigration Appeal
    Commission (SIAC), 16.79
torture, 5.49

Torture, inhuman or degrading treatment
aggravating factor, 5.41
balancing of interests, 5.37
definition of torture, 5.41
deportation, 8.14
detention
    abuse of detainees, 5.41, 5.50, 5.72
    prior to execution, 5.35
diplomatic assurances against ill treatment,
    5.63–5.64
disproportionate sentences, 5.51
Dublin Regulation returnees, 5.75–5.76
ECHR protection, 3.17, 5.6, 5.33–5.34, 8.14, 10.12
EU fundamental rights, 6.19
evidence, 5.47–5.48
evidence obtained by torture, 5.89
exclusion measures, 10.12
exclusion/expulsion of aliens, 5.6
expulsion, 5.36–5.38, 5.40, 5.63, 5.66, 5.73–5.74
extraterritorial context, 5.40
flexible standard, 5.42–5.46
group members, 5.53–5.55
health-related cases, 5.66–5.67, 5.69, 5.71–5.72
HIV patients, 5.72
ICCPR protection, 3.14, 3.17
internal relocation alternative, 5.61–5.62
interpretation, 5.39
interrogations, 5.39
lack of medical care, 5.50
lack of resources, 5.69, 5.71
living conditions, 5.68

mental illness, 5.50, 5.67, 5.70
mental violence, 5.41
national security, 5.36
non-state persecution, 5.59–5.60
prison conditions, 5.49
Qualification Directive, 6.78
race discrimination, 5.41
rape, 5.41
refoulement, 5.35, 5.37, 5.63, 5.73
removals, 9.14
right to life, 5.33
risk of ill-treatment, 5.74
sensory deprivation, 5.39
severity of treatment, 5.39–5.40
situations of violence, 5.56–5.58
Special Immigration Appeals Commission (SIAC), 16.99
Special Rapporteurs, 13.21, 13.28–13.29, 13.32
sufficient protection, 5.59
sur place activities, 5.52
systematic torture, 5.63, 5.65
terrorist suspects, 5.49
UN Committee against Torture, 13.34, 13.38
Trafficking
see also **Group of Experts on Action against Trafficking in Human Beings (GRETA); Convention on Action against Trafficking in Human Beings (CATHB); International Law of Human Trafficking (ILHT); Protocol to Prevent, Suppress and Punishment Trafficking in Persons (PPSTP)**
CEDAW protection, 3.65
children, 4.98, 5.242, 5.244
definition, 4.98
deportations, 8.16
ECHR protection, 5.80–5.82
elements, 5.244
EU law, 6.75, 6.90–6.93
exclusion measures, 10.14
international cooperation, 4.97
national security considerations, 6.93
non-discrimination, 5.242
penalties, 6.92
people smuggling distinguished, 5.243
persecution, 4.23
PPSTP provisions, 4.96–4.100
prostitution, 4.95
remedies, 15.2
removals, 9.12
repatriation, 4.95, 4.100
re-trafficking, 5.81–5.83
right of residence, 6.93
sanctions, 6.91
victims
  consent, 4.98, 5.242
  expulsion, 5.245–5.246
  identification, 5.245
  protection, 6.91–6.93
  residence permit, 5.247
  status, 4.99
Treaties
international law, 2.7–2.8, 2.11, 2.18–2.19

interpretation, 2.11–2.14
UK compliance, 2.17–2.19, 2.21–2.22
Vienna Convention, 2.11–2.13
Turkish nationals
deportation measures, 8.68
employment, 6.69
exclusion and expulsion, 6.71
family members, 6.69–6.70
legal rights, 6.69–6.70
legal status, 6.70
limitation of rights
  public health, 6.70
  public policy, 6.70
  public security, 6.70
procedural guarantees, 6.70
right of residence, 6.69, 6.71
self-employed workers, 6.69, 6.71

UK Borders Act (2007)
automatic deportation, 8.24, 8.35, 8.39–8.40, 8.100
convicted persons, 8.29, 8.31, 8.53, 8.100
deeming provision, 8.40, 8.46–8.49, 8.58, 8.113–8.114, 8.117
deportation orders, 8.24–8.27, 8.47, 8.59–8.62, 8.109–8.111, 8.114, 8.117, 8.122, 16.31
discretionary decisions, 8.117
discretionary powers, 12.35
disproportionate breach, 8.116
foreign criminals, 8.46–8.48, 8.57–8.58
interpretative provisions, 8.28–8.30
foreign criminals, 8.21, 8.24, 8.31, 8.40
lawfulness requirement, 8.113–8.114
legal challenge, 8.112–8.114
liability to deportation, 8.43, 8.53, 8.57–8.61, 8.112–8.117, 12.35
mandatory deportation, 8.21, 8.57
margin of discretion, 8.116
proportionality, 8.117
public good, 8.47
public interest, 8.114–8.117
representations, 8.111
respect for private and family life, 8.114, 8.116–8.117
UK Domestic law
see **Domestic law**
United Nations
UN Charter-based bodies (remedies)
  complaints procedure, 13.15–13.19
  function, 13.4
  Human Rights Council Advisory Committee, 13.14
  International Court of Justice (ICJ), 13.5
  special procedures, 13.20–13.32
  UN Commission on Human Rights, 13.6
  UN Human Rights Council, 13.6–13.8, 13.15
  universal periodic review, 13.8–13.13
UN Treaty-based bodies (remedies)
  Committee against Torture, 13.34, 13.38
  Committee on Economic, Social and Cultural Rights, 13.34
  Committee on Enforced Disappearances, 13.38

Committee on the Elimination of
    Discrimination against Women, 13.34, 13.38
Committee on the Elimination of Racial
    Discrimination, 13.34, 13.38
Committee on the Rights of the Child, 13.34
Committee on the Rights of Persons with
    Disabilities, 13.34, 13.38
complaints procedure, 13.39–13.41,
    13.43–13.44
establishment, 13.33
exclusion and expulsion cases, 13.35–13.37
function, 13.4, 13.33
Human Rights Committee (UNHRC), 13.34,
    13.37–13.38, 13.44
interim measures, 13.42
monitoring compliance, 13.36
reporting procedure, 13.36–13.37
terrorist suspects, 13.37
UK position, 13.44–13.50

United Nations Charter
international human rights law, 3.1–3.2
UN Charter-based bodies, 13.4–13.32

United Nations Commission on Human Rights
international remedies, 13.6

United Nations Commissioner for Refugees (UNHCR)
asylum-seekers, 3.42–3.43
establishment, 4.9
immigration bail applications, 3.42

United Nations Human Rights Committee (UNHRC)
arbitrary behaviour, 3.29, 3.31, 3.47
children's rights, 3.56–3.57
deportation cases, 3.25–3.28, 3.32–3.41, 3.52
family life and home, 3.48, 3.51–3.53
ICCPR protection, 3.16
immigration controls, 3.52–3.53
international remedies, 13.34, 13.37–13.38,
    13.44
right to enter one's own country, 3.18,
    3.20–3.26
right to return, 3.18
unlawful interference, 3.46–3.47

United Nations Human Rights Council
international remedies, 13.6–13.8, 13.15

United Nations Relief and Works Agency
protection of refugees, 4.71

Universal Declaration of Human Rights (UDHR)
asylum, 3.9
citizenship
    denial, 11.5
    deprivation, 12.8
enforceability, 3.13
exclusion measures, 10.5
general rights, 3.6
immigration control, 3.8–3.9
importance, 3.5
limitations on rights, 3.12
nationality, 3.10–3.11, 3.14
privacy rights, 8.84
prohibition of discrimination, 3.7

Universal periodic review
Draft Reports, 13.11
frequency of review, 13.10
human rights obligations, 13.9
UK-related issues, 13.12
UPR Working Group, 13.10–13.13

Upper Tribunal
acknowledgment of service, 16.158
applications issued, 16.152
applications without merit, 16.157
claim forms, 16.151
establishment, 16.128
extension of time, 16.158–16.159
fees, 16.153
judicial review. 16.113, 16.155
jurisdiction, 16.6
limited permission, 16.157
onward appeals, 16.8, 16.16, 16.21, 16.23–16.24
permission refused, 16.157
procedure, 16.10, 16.151–16.160
terminology, 16.154
time limits, 16.155
transfer of cases, 16.143–16.150
urgent cases, 16.160
written responses, 16.156